Database and Applications Security

Database and Applications Security

Integrating Information Security and Data Management

Bhavani Thuraisingham

CRC Press
Taylor & Francis Group
Boca Raton London New York

CRC Press is an imprint of the
Taylor & Francis Group, an **informa** business
AN AUERBACH BOOK

CRC Press
Taylor & Francis Group
6000 Broken Sound Parkway NW, Suite 300
Boca Raton, FL 33487-2742

First issued in hardback 2019

© 2005 by Taylor & Francis Group, LLC
CRC Press is an imprint of Taylor & Francis Group, an Informa business

No claim to original U.S. Government works

ISBN-13: 978-0-8493-2224-2 (hbk)

Library of Congress Card Number 2005043625

Library of Congress Cataloging-in-Publication Data

Thuraisingham, Bhavani M.
    Database and applications security : integrating information security and data management / Bhavani M. Thuraisingham.
        p. cm.
    Includes bibliographical references and index.
    ISBN 0-8493-2224-3 (alk. paper)
    1. Database security. 2. Database management. 3. Computer security. I. Title.

QA76.9.D314T47 2005
005.8--dc22   2005043625

Visit the Taylor & Francis Web site at
http://www.taylorandfrancis.com

and the CRC Press Web site at
http://www.crcpress.com

Dedication

To my friend and colleague, Dr. Maria Zemankova,
for her encouragement and support
during important stages of my career.

Table of Contents

PART VII: SECURE OBJECT AND MULTIMEDIA SYSTEMS

PART X: EMERGING SECURE DATA MANAGEMENT TECHNOLOGIES AND APPLICATIONS

Appendices

Foreword

Not too long ago, we collected data to understand what had happened in the past. We kept records on births and deaths, we kept records of inventory and sales, and we built databases of other bits of knowledge that seemed important for understanding the past.

Computing and data have changed the way we live and do business. Now, we keep databases to make decisions and drive business. We use data mining to help us optimize marketing. We use online data to track stocks and perform automated trades. We use dynamic inventory projections to do "just in time" ordering. We are organizing huge collections of data on the genome to find new pharmaceuticals and understand disease. The data we collect is growing in magnitude, and we are finding newer and more intricate ways to use the data. Instead of keeping databases to record the past, we are using them to shape the future.

Of course, if we use the data to drive the future, knowing what that future might be can pose an advantage. Thus, having access to the data used to drive those decisions becomes a strategic issue. Those who make the decisions would like to ensure that their databases are complete, accurate, and unread by the competition. Meanwhile, the competition — whether economic, political, ideological, or otherwise — may wish to read or corrupt the data for their own ends. The value of the database increases with the amount of data it contains, so long as that data remains intact and available.

It is thus that we see increasing adoption of database systems as key data management and decision technologies, and we also see that the security of the data managed by those systems becomes crucial. The recent rapid proliferation of Web-based applications and information systems adds another dimension to the problem of data protection because some accesses need to be allowed, but those accesses may be from anywhere in the world. New concerns regarding privacy make data security a question of interest not only to industries and commercial enterprises, but also to individuals. Add in various governmental regulations for storage, disclosure, update, and dissemination, and the problems grow even more significant. Now layer in different data models, heterogeneous systems, and representation, and the situation really becomes complicated.

Luckily, there are experts who understand complex database systems and how to make them manageable. Bhavani Thuraisingham is one such expert who has spent many years studying the complexities of database security and the security of the applications that access them. She has put together this book as a means of sharing that expertise with others — in effect, sharing her own extensive database of knowledge.

This book is the first authoritative source covering many important aspects related to the security of data and the applications that use it. Not only does this book cover conventional relational database systems, but it also describes security approaches and solutions for the semantic Web, sensor information systems, data warehousing systems, and a number of other data handling systems. The book provides accounts of the most relevant access control policies, including both discretionary and mandatory access control policies, and role-based access control (RBAC). The book also provides a comprehensive account of the inference problem and solutions to it.

What is also notable in Dr. Thuraisingham's treatise is the discussion about dependable data management, including a description of issues related to data quality — an increasingly important characteristic requiring comprehensive solutions related to data security. Many discussions throughout the book are illustrated by the description of several systems, each showing how solutions have been applied in practice. The book also provides insight into newer security problems and issues that are becoming important topics of research, such as comprehensive privacy, digital identity, and forensics.

Whether you are in academia, government, or industry, there is a wealth of useful material in this book for you to consider and use. Whether you are interested in learning about how a certain set of data security measures work or in finding some new ideas for research, you will find it here. As such, this is sure to occupy an important place in your own database of valued books.

Eugene H. Spafford
April 2005

Preface

Background

Recent developments in information systems technologies have resulted in computerizing many applications in various business areas. Data has become a critical resource in many organizations, and therefore, efficient access to data, sharing the data, extracting information from the data, and making use of the information has become an urgent need. As a result, there have been many efforts on not only integrating the various data sources scattered across several sites, but extracting information from these databases in the form of patterns and trends has also become important. These data sources may be databases managed by database management systems, or they could be data warehoused in a repository from multiple data sources.

The advent of the World Wide Web (WWW) in the mid-1990s has resulted in even greater demand for managing data, information, and knowledge effectively. There is now so much data on the Web that managing it with conventional tools is becoming almost impossible. New tools and techniques are needed to effectively manage this data. Therefore, to provide interoperability as well as warehousing between the multiple data sources and systems, and to extract information from the databases and warehouses on the Web, various tools are being developed.

As the demand for data and information management increases, there is also a critical need for maintaining the security of the databases, applications, and information systems. Data and information have to be protected from unauthorized access as well as from malicious corruption. With the advent of the Web it is even more important to protect the data and information as numerous individuals now have access to this data and information. Therefore, we need effective mechanisms for securing access to data and applications.

This book reviews the developments in data and applications security with a special emphasis on database security. Then it provides directions for data and applications security. These directions include securing emerging applications such as E-commerce, sensor information processing, and knowledge management.

We have written a series of book for CRC Press on data management and data mining. Book 1 (*Data Management Systems Evolution and Interoperation*) focused on general aspects of data management and also addressed interoperability and migration. Book 2 (*Data Mining: Technologies, Techniques, Tools, and Trends*) discussed data mining. It essentially elaborated on Chapter 9 of Book 1. Book 3 (*Web Data Management and E-Commerce*) discussed Web database technologies and discussed E-commerce as an application area. It essentially elaborated on Chapter 10 of Book 1. Book 4 (*Managing and Mining Multimedia Databases*) addressed both multimedia database management and multimedia data mining. It elaborated on both Chapter 6 of Book 1 (for multimedia database management) and Chapter 11 of Book 2 (for multimedia data mining). Book 5 (*XML, Databases, and the Semantic Web*) described XML technologies related to data management. It elaborated on Chapter 11 of Book 3. Book 6 (*Web Data Mining Technologies and Their Applications in Business Intelligence and Counter-Terrorism*) elaborated on Chapter 9 of Book 3.

Our current book (Book 7) examines security for technologies discussed in each of our previous books. It focuses on the technological developments in database and applications security. It is essentially the integration of information security and database technologies.

Developments in Database and Applications Security

Initial developments in database security began in the 1970s. For example, as part of the research on System R at the IBM Almaden Research Center, there was a lot of work on access control for relational database systems. At about the same time, some early work on MultiLevel Secure DataBase Management Systems (MLS/DBMS) was reported.

However, it was only after the Air Force Summer Study in 1982 that many of the developments on secure database systems began. There were the early prototypes based on the integrity lock mechanisms developed at the MITRE Corporation. Later in the mid-1980s pioneering research was carried out at SRI International and Honeywell Inc. on systems such as SeaView and LOCK Data Views. Some of the technologies developed by these research efforts were transferred to commercial products by corporations such as Oracle, Sybase, and Informix.

The research in the mid-1980s also resulted in exploring some new areas such as the inference problem, secure object database systems, and secure distributed database systems. In fact, Dr. John Campbell of the National Security Agency stated in 1990 that one of the important developments in database security was the work of Thuraisingham on the unsolvability of the inference problem. This research then led the way to examine various classes of the inference problem. Throughout the early 1990s, there were many efforts reported on these new types of secure database systems by researchers at organizations such as the MITRE Corporation, Naval Research Laboratory, University of Milano, and George Mason University. In addition, much work was also carried out on secure transaction processing.

In the mid-1990s, with the advent of the Web, there were many new directions for secure data management and applications research. These included secure workflow systems, secure digital libraries, Web security, and secure data warehouses. New technologies such as data mining exacerbate the inference problem as even naïve users could use data-mining tools and infer sensitive information. Closely related to the inference problem is the privacy problem where users associate pieces of public data and deduce private information. Data mining also exacerbates the privacy problem. However, data mining is also a very important technique for solving many security problems such as intrusion detection and auditing. Therefore the challenge is to carry out data mining but at the same time to ensure that the inference problem is limited. Developments in distributed object systems and E-commerce applications resulted in developments in secure distributed object systems and secure E-commerce applications. In addition, access control also has received a lot of attention especially in the area of Role-Based Access Control (RBAC). Many of the publications in secure data management have appeared in the proceedings of the IFIP 11.3 Working Conferences on Data and Applications Security as well as in the proceedings of various security and database conferences.

Directions for Database and Applications Security

Although there have been many developments in database security, there is still a lot of work to be done. Every day we are seeing developments in Web data management. For example, standards such as XML (eXtensible Markup Language) and RDF (Resource Description Framework) are emerging. Security for these Web standards has to be examined. Also, Web services are becoming extremely popular and therefore we need to examine secure Web services. The semantic Web is a concept that will soon become a reality. We need to examine security issues for the semantic Web.

Security needs to be examined for new application areas such as knowledge management, peer-to-peer computing, and sensor data management. For example, in the case of knowledge management applications, it is important to protect the intellectual property of an organization. Privacy should be an important consideration when managing surveillance data emanating from sensors. Peer-to-peer computing has received a lot of attention recently. There are numerous security issues for such systems including secure information sharing and collaboration. Furthermore, data is no longer only in structured databases. Data could be streams emanating from sensors and other sources as well as text, images, and video. Security for such data has not received much attention. Finally, one has to make trade-offs among security, data quality, and real-time processing. In other words, we need research on quality of service for information processing.

In summary, as new technologies emerge, there are many security issues that need to be examined. We have made much progress in data and applications security in the last three decades, however, there are many more security issues that need to be examined in the next several decades. To address these issues, there are now various research programs being funded mainly in the United States and in Europe.

Organization of This Book

This book is divided into ten parts. Part I provides some background information for database security. Database security essentially integrates two fields: information security and database management. Therefore we provide an overview of both computer security and database management. We also provide an overview of information management technologies as this book also discusses applications security. Part II discusses discretionary access control. The early models were based on discretionary access control. We discuss access-control models and policies including authorization policies. Part III describes multilevel secure databases. Many of the developments in the 1980s were on multilevel secure databases. We discuss historical developments as well as design principles. Part IV describes models, functions, prototypes, and products of multilevel secure relational database systems.

Part V discusses the inference problem. Inference is the process of posing queries and deducing unauthorized information from the legitimate responses. We focus on two aspects: one is security-constraint processing and the other is the use of conceptual models. Part VI addresses secure distributed databases including both multilevel security and discretionary security. A discussion of heterogeneous and federated database security is also given. Part VII discusses secure object systems including database systems and distributed object management systems. We also include a discussion of secure multimedia systems as many multimedia databases utilize object-oriented data models. Part VIII addresses security aspects of data warehousing and data mining. We also discuss the threats to privacy due to data mining and discuss privacy-preserving data mining. Part IX discusses secure Web database technologies including secure knowledge management and E-commerce. Finally Part X describes some emerging technologies such as secure dependable data management, secure sensor databases, and various aspects related to digital identity and digital forensics.

Data, Information, and Knowledge

In general, data management includes managing the databases, interoperability, migration, warehousing, and mining. For example, the data on the Web has to be managed and mined to extract information and patterns and trends. Data could be in files, relational databases, or other types of databases such as multimedia databases. Data may be structured or unstructured. We repeatedly use the terms data, data management, database systems, and database management systems in this book. We elaborate on these terms in the appendix. We define data management systems to be systems that manage the data, extract meaningful information from the data, and make use of the information extracted. Therefore, data management systems include database systems, data warehouses, and data-mining systems. Data could be structured data such as that found in relational databases, or it could be unstructured such as text, voice, imagery, and video.

There have been numerous discussions in the past to distinguish among data, information, and knowledge. In some of our previous books on data management and mining we did not attempt to clarify these terms. We simply stated that data could be just bits and bytes or it could convey some meaningful information to the user. However, with the Web and also with increasing interest in data, information, and knowledge management as separate areas, in this book we take a different approach to data, information, and knowledge by differentiating among these terms as much as possible. For us, data is usually some value such as numbers, integers, and strings. Information is obtained when some meaning or semantics is associated with the data such as John's salary is $20K. Knowledge is something that you acquire through reading and learning. That is, data and information can be transferred into knowledge when uncertainty about the data and information is removed from someone's mind. It should be noted that it is rather difficult to give strict definitions of data, information, and knowledge. Sometimes we use these terms interchangeably also. Our framework for data management discussed in the appendix helps clarify some of the differences. To be consistent with the terminology in our previous books, we also distinguish between database systems and database management systems. A database management system is that component which manages the database containing persistent data. A database system consists of both the database and the database management system.

Final Thoughts

This book provides a fairly comprehensive overview of database and applications security. It focuses on several aspects of the technology including secure relational databases, the inference problem, secure object databases, secure distributed databases, and emerging applications. It is written for technical managers and executives as well as for technologists interested in learning about the subject. This book is also intended for those who wish to pursue research in this area. Although it is written at a high level, it also discusses many of the technical details.

Various people have approached me and asked questions about database security. Although I began my research in this area back in 1985, I waited a long time to write this book as I felt the field was expanding very rapidly in the 1980s and 1990s. I wanted this book to cover several aspects of secure databases and be a reference guide for anyone wanting to work in the field. Furthermore, I have noticed that there are many newcomers to the field and often much of the useful work carried out in the 1980s and 1990s is overlooked. I believe strongly in taking as much advantage as possible of the knowledge that is out there rather than reinventing the wheel. It was for these reasons that I decided to write this book now instead of ten years ago.

Acknowledgments

I thank the administration at the Erik Jonsson School of Engineering and Computer Science at the University of Texas at Dallas for giving me the opportunity to direct the Cyber Security Research Center. I thank my management at MITRE and the National Science Foundation for giving me numerous opportunities to continue working in data management, information security, privacy, and data mining. I am especially grateful to the National Science Foundation for enabling me to start a new program in data and applications security. This renewed my extensive research on this subject.

I started my initial research in database security back in 1985 and was involved in the design of LOCK Data Views at Honeywell Inc. I continued with my research in the field, especially on the inference problem at MITRE between 1989 and 1995 and it was for this work I received the IEEE Computer Society's 1997 Technical Achievement Award and more recently IEEE's 2003 Fellow Award and AAAS (American Association of Advancement of Science) Fellow Award. I then focused on research in data management, data mining, and real-time objects and at the same time continued carrying out research in Web data management security. My interest in privacy began around 1996 when I started working in data mining. I began to realize the close relationships between the inference problem and the privacy problem around that time. My interest in national security began around the end of 2001, especially after September 11, 2001. Since then I have given several presentations on applying data mining to counter-terrorism as well as privacy including talks at the White House, the United Nations, conferences, and various universities. This resulted in my previous book, *Web Data Mining Technologies and their Applications in Business Intelligence and Counter-Terrorism*. It was also at this time that I began the new program at the National Science Foundation in data and applications security. This program enabled me to provide leadership and directions to the field.

I would like to thank many people who have supported my work including the following:

- My husband Thevendra for his continued support for my work and my son Breman for being such a wonderful person and for motivating me
- The Administration at the Erik Jonsson School of Engineering and Computer Science at the University of Texas at Dallas, including Dr. Doug Harris, Dr. D.T. Huynh, and Dr. Bob Helms for giving me the opportunity to direct the Cyber Security Research Center
- My Ph.D. advisors Dr. John Cleave at the University of Bristol and Dr. Roger Hindley at the University of Wales of the United Kingdom for their continued encouragement
- Professor C.V. Ramamoorthy at the University of California Berkeley for his constant encouragement
- Henry Bayard at MITRE for his mentoring and encouragement
- My managers and colleagues at NSF, especially Dr. Maria Zeman-kova, Dr. Michael Pazzani, Dr. Carl Landwehr, and Dr. William Bainbridge for their encouragement for my work in database security
- Patricia Dwyer, formerly at Honeywell Inc., for introducing me to Database Security as well as Dr. Tom Haigh, Dr. Paul Stachor, and Emmanuel Onuegbe all formerly at Honeywell Inc. for collaboration on the Lock Data Views project
- Dr. Dorothy Denning, formerly at SRI International, for building this field and providing us the leadership
- Dr. Dale Johnson for introducing me to MITRE
- Dr. Harvey Rubinovitz, John Maurer, and Dr. Chris Clifton at MITRE for their strong support and encouragement
- Reid Gerhart and Peter Tasker at MITRE for giving opportunities to work in the field during my early years at MITRE
- My managers at MITRE including Dr. Tom Gannon, John Wilson, Tom Backman, Ed Palo, Ed Green, Dr. Mark Maybury, and Ed Lafferty for their support
- My project leaders at MITRE including Al Grasso, Ed Bensley, Dan Grosshans, Beth Lavender, Maureen Cheheyl, Margie Zuk, Dr. Marion Michaud, Lou Montella, Gary Gagnon, Harriet Goldman, and Ann Cady for supporting my work
- My colleagues at MITRE including Tom Wheeler, William Ford, Dr. Jon Millen, Marie Collins, Jay Scarano, Dr. Scott Renner, Dr. Barbara Blaustein, Dr. Josh Guttman, Rich Graubart, Dr. Arnie Rosenthal, Joe Wood, Dr. Len Seligman, and many others who have collaborated with me over the years

- Dr. Rick Steinheiser of the Central Intelligence Agency, Dr. John Campbell and Mike Ware of the National Security Agency, Joe Giordano of the U.S. Air Force, Phil Andrews of the U.S. Navy, John Preusse of the U.S. Army, Steve Funk of the U.S. Treasury, and many others who have funded my work
- My colleagues around the world including Dr. Marion Ceruti of the U.S. Navy, Dr. Elisa Bertino of Purdue University, Dr. Gio Wiederhold of Stanford University, Dr. Wei-Tek Tsai of Arizona State University, Dr. Elena Ferrari and Dr. Barbara Carminati of the University of Como, Italy, Dr. Helene Bestougeff of the University Paris, Dr. Tom Keefe of Oracle Corporation, and many others for their encouragement of my work in database security
- My colleagues and students at the University of Texas at Dallas
- My colleagues at the IFIP 11.3 Working Group in Data and Applications Security for many discussions in database security
- My colleagues at WORDS, ISORC, COMPSAC, ISADS, and other groups for encouraging me to work in dependable secure systems
- My colleagues for inviting me to serve on editorial boards, advisory boards, and conference boards as well as nominating me for awards
- My late parents who encouraged me in my studies during my early years

I hope that we can continue to make progress in database and applications security and address the security of our nation.

About the Author

Bhavani Thuraisingham, Ph.D., recipient of IEEE Computer Society's prestigious 1997 Technical Achievement Award for "outstanding and innovative contributions to secure distributed data management," and the recipient of IEEE's 2003 Fellow Award for "pioneering research in secure systems including database systems, distributed systems and the Web," is a professor of computer science and the director of the Cyber Security Research Center in the Erik Jonsson School of Engineering and Computer Science at the University of Texas at Dallas. She also works for the MITRE Corporation part-time in data management and data security in Bedford, Massachusetts and McLean, Virginia. Prior to joining the University of Texas, Thuraisingham worked for the MITRE Corporation full-time for sixteen years, the last three of which she spent at the National Science Foundation (NSF) as an IPA (Interpersonnel Government Activity). At NSF she was first the director of the information and data management program and later the director of the data and applications security (DAS) program and was a co-founder of the CyberTrust Theme. She also managed the information management focus area for NSF's information technology research and was a team member of the Sensor Networks initiative. She was part of a team at NSF setting directions for cyber-security and data mining for counter-terrorism. She was elected a 2003 Fellow of the American Association of Advancement of Science (AAAS) for outstanding and innovative contributions to secure database systems and secure Web information systems, and a 2005 Fellow of the British Computer Society. Her current research interests are in security for the semantic Web, sensor information security, and privacy.

Prior to joining NSF in October 2001, Thuraisingham held various positions at the MITRE Corporation beginning in January 1989. Between May 1999 and September 2001, she was a chief scientist in data management at MITRE Corporation's Information Technology Directorate in Bedford,

Massachusetts. In this position she provided technology directions in data, information, and knowledge management for the Information Technology Directorate of MITRE's Air Force Center. In addition, she was also an expert consultant in computer software to MITRE's work for the Internal Revenue Service. In this position she evaluated the commercial research conducted at various Fortune 500 corporations in information technology including the financial, telecommunications, and data processing industries. Her recent research focused on data mining as it relates to multimedia databases and database security, distributed object management with emphasis on real-time data management, and Web data management applications in electronic commerce. She also served as adjunct professor of computer science at Boston University for two years and taught a course in advanced data management and data mining.

Between June 1995 and May 1999 she was the department head in data and information management in MITRE's information technology division in the Intelligence Center. In this position she was responsible for the management of about thirty technical staff in four key areas: distributed databases, multimedia data management, data mining and knowledge management, and distributed objects and quality of service. Prior to that, she had held various technical positions including lead, principal, and senior principal engineer, and was head of MITRE's research in evolvable interoperable information systems as well as data management, and co-director of MITRE's Database Specialty Group. Between 1993 and 1999 she managed fifteen research projects under the massive digital data systems effort for the intelligence community and was also a team member of the AWACS modernization research project for the Air Force. Before that she led team efforts on the design and prototypes of various secure database systems including secure distributed database systems, secure object systems and the inference problem for government sponsors including the Air Force, Navy, Army, and the National Security Agency between 1989 and 1996.

Prior to joining MITRE in January 1989, Dr. Thuraisingham worked in the computer industry between 1983 and 1989. She was first a senior programmer/analyst with Control Data Corporation for over two years working on the design and development of the CDCNET product and later she was a principal research scientist with Honeywell Inc. for over three years conducting research, development, and technology transfer activities. She was also an adjunct professor of computer science and a member of the graduate faculty at the University of Minnesota between 1984 and 1988. Prior to starting her industrial experience and after completing her Ph.D., she was a visiting faculty member first in the department of computer science at the New Mexico Institute of Technology, and then at the department of mathematics at the University of Minnesota between

1980 and 1983. Dr. Thuraisingham has a B.Sc., M.Sc., M.S., and also received her Ph.D. degree from the United Kingdom at the age of 24. In addition to being an IEEE Fellow, she is a distinguished lecturer for IEEE and a member of the ACM and AFCEA. She has a certification in Java programming and has also completed a Management Development Program. She is the recipient of the 2001 National Woman of Color Technology Research Leadership Award and was named one of Silicon India's top seven technology innovators in the United States of South Asian origin in 2002.

Dr. Thuraisingham has published over 60 journal articles and more than 200 conference papers. She has also delivered over 25 keynote presentations and over 50 panel presentations. She is the inventor of three U.S. patents for MITRE on database inference control. She serves (or has served) on the editorial boards of various journals, including the *IEEE Transactions on Knowledge and Data Engineering*, the *Journal of Computer Security, Computer Standards and Interfaces Journal, ACM Transactions on Information and Systems Security*, and *IEEE Transactions on Dependable and Secure Computing*. She currently serves on the technical advisory board for *IASTED, Journal of Computer Security, Journal of Privacy Technologies*, and the *Journal of Semantic Web and Information Systems*, and served on the conferences and tutorials board for IEEE. She gives tutorials in data management, data security, and data mining and has taught courses at both the MITRE Institute and the AFCEA Educational Foundation for several years. She has chaired or co-chaired several conferences and workshops including IFIP's 1992 Database Security Conference, ACM's 1993 Object Security Workshop, ACM's 1994 Objects in Healthcare Information Systems Workshop, IEEE's 1995 Multimedia Database Systems Workshop, IEEE's 1996 Metadata Conference, AFCEA's 1997 Federal Data Mining Symposium, IEEE's 1998 COMPSAC Conference, IEEE's 1999 WORDS Workshop, IFIP's 2000 Database Security Conference, IEEE's 2001 ISADS Conference, and IEEE's 2002 COMPSAC Web Security Workshop. She founded OMG's C4I special interest group, has been a member of various industry and government standards groups, and has served on panels in data management, data mining, and security. She has edited several books as well as special journal issues and was the consulting editor of the *Data Management Handbook* series by CRC's Auerbach Publications for 1996 and 1997. She is the author of the books *Data Management Systems Evolution and Interoperation; Data Mining: Technologies, Techniques, Tools, and Trends; Web Data Management and Electronic Commerce; Managing and Mining Multimedia Databases; XML, Databases and the Semantic Web;* and *Web Data Mining Technologies and Applications in Business Intelligence and Counter-Terrorism;* all published by CRC Press.

Dr. Thuraisingham has given invited presentations at conferences including keynote addresses at the IFIP Database Security Conference '96, the Second Pacific Asia Data Mining Conference '98, SAS Institute's Data Mining Technology Conference '99, IEEE Artificial Neural Networks Conference '99, IFIP Integrity and Control Conference '01, IEEE ICTAI Conference '02, IASTED Applied Informatics '03, and EDBT '04. She has also delivered the featured addresses at AFCEA's Federal Database Colloquium from 1994 through 2001. She has been a featured speaker at several object world conferences by Software Comdex as well as the client/server world and data warehousing conferences by DCI and also recently gave a featured talk on federated databases for bioinformatics at the Fourth Annual Bioinformatics Conference in Boston. Her presentations are worldwide and she also gives seminars and lectures at various universities around the world including the Universities of Oxford and Cambridge in England, as well as at Stanford University and the Massachusetts Institute of Technology, and participates in panels at the National Academy of Sciences and the Air Force Scientific Advisory Board. She was an expert information technology consultant to the Department of Health and Human Services states bioterrorism efforts, and has given several presentations on data mining for counter-terrorism including recent keynote addresses at the White House in Washington, DC and the United Nations in New York City.

Chapter 1

Introduction

1.1 Trends

Recent developments in information system technologies have resulted in computerizing many applications in various business areas. Data has become a critical resource in many organizations, and, therefore, efficient access to data, sharing the data, extracting information from the data, and making use of the information has become an urgent need. As a result, there have been many efforts on not only integrating the various data sources scattered across several sites, but extracting information from these databases in the form of patterns and trends has also become important. These data sources may be databases managed by database management systems, or they could be data warehoused in a repository from multiple data sources.

The advent of the World Wide Web (WWW) in the mid-1990s has resulted in even greater demand for managing data, information, and knowledge effectively. There is now so much data on the Web that managing it with conventional tools is becoming almost impossible. New tools and techniques are needed to effectively manage this data. Therefore, to provide interoperability as well as warehousing between the multiple data sources and systems, and to extract information from the databases and warehouses on the Web, various tools are being developed.

As the demand for data and information management increases, there is also a critical need for maintaining the security of the databases, applications, and information systems. Data and information have to be

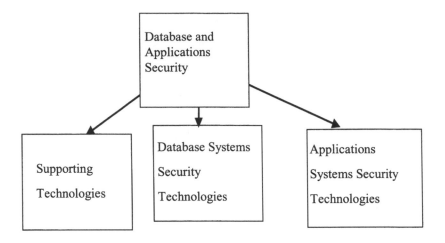

Figure 1.1 Components of database and applications security

protected from unauthorized access as well as from malicious corruption. With the advent of the Web it is even more important to protect the data and information as numerous individuals now have access to this data and information. Therefore, we need effective mechanisms for securing data and applications.

This book reviews the developments in data and applications security with a special emphasis on database security. Then it provides directions for data and applications security. These directions include securing semantic Webs as well as emerging applications such as E-commerce, knowledge management, and sensor information processing. Figure 1.1 illustrates the various technologies discussed in this book.

The organization of this chapter is as follows. In each of Sections 1.2 through 1.11 we elaborate on the various parts addressed in this book. For example, supporting technologies for database security are discussed in Section 1.2. Access control and discretionary security issues are the subject of Section 1.3. Multilevel secure databases are addressed in Section 1.4. Aspects of multilevel secure relational data models and systems are discussed in Section 1.5. The inference problem is the subject of Section 1.6. Secure distributed databases are discussed in Section 1.7. Secure object and multimedia systems are discussed in Section 1.8. Data warehousing, data mining, security, and privacy are discussed in Section 1.9. Secure Web information systems are the subject of Section 1.10. Some emerging data security technologies such as secure sensor information management and digital identities are discussed in Section 1.11. Finally in Section 1.12 we discuss a framework for database and applications security and discuss the organization of this book. Some final thoughts are given in Section 1.13.

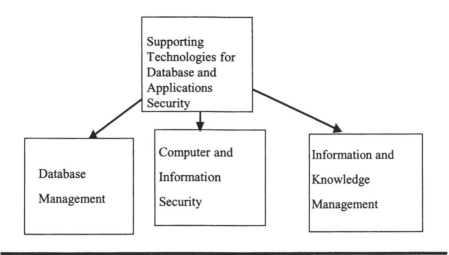

Figure 1.2   Supporting technologies for database and applications security

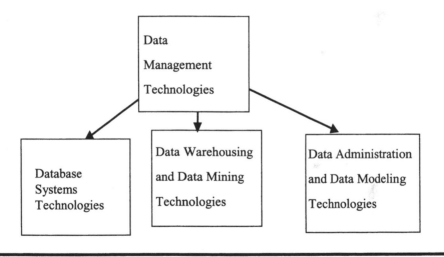

Figure 1.3   Data management technologies

1.2 Supporting Technologies for Database and Applications Security

As illustrated in Figure 1.2, database and applications security have evolved from database technologies, computer security technologies, and many other technologies including objects, distributed systems, infomation management, and applications such as medical informatics. Database technologies are

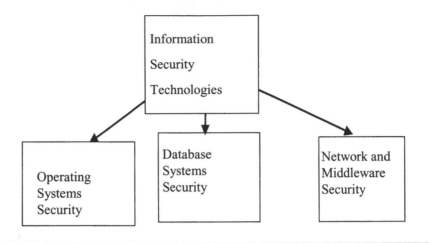

Figure 1.4   Information security technologies

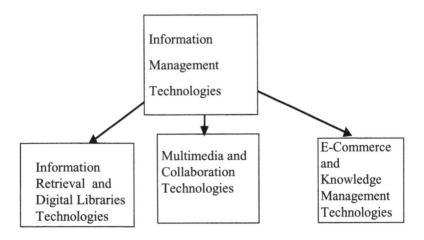

Figure 1.5   Information management technologies

illustrated in Figure 1.3. These include database systems, data modeling, data warehousing, and data mining. Information security technologies include operating systems security, network security, database security, middleware security, and Web security and are illustrated in Figure 1.4. Other technologies include almost every information management technology such as multimedia, knowledge management, and many more, and are illustrated Figure 1.5.

Part I of this book discusses in more detail database system technologies, information security technologies, and some of the other information management technologies. Because we are dealing with many

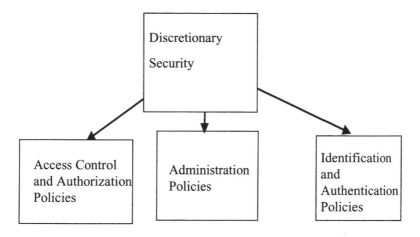

Figure 1.6   Discretionary security

"other technologies" we also discuss these other technologies as needed throughout the book. Note that data management is much broader than database systems. That is, data management includes database systems as well as data administration aspects. An evolution of database systems technologies is discussed in Appendix A.

1.3 Discretionary Security in Database Systems

Discretionary security deals with granting access to the data depending on the users, user groups, and other factors such as roles of users. Discretionary security was initially investigated for secure operating systems where access was granted to files depending on the kinds of processes. The types of access included read and write operations. Then the concept was extended to databases where access was granted, say, to relations, attributes, and elements. Now discretionary security also includes handling complex security policies, granting access to data based on roles and functions, and also both positive and negative authorization policies. Figure 1.6 illustrates various types of discretionary access control mechanisms.

Articles on discretionary security for database systems have consistently appeared since the mid-1970s. The field is still evolving as new models and paradigms are discovered. Furthermore as new kinds of systems emerge including multimedia systems, medical information systems, and E-commerce systems, discretionary security policies have been expanded and adapted.

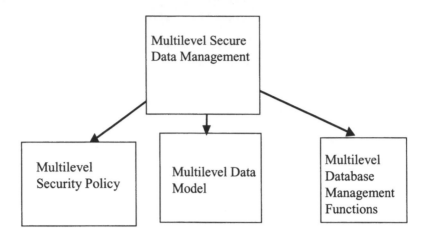

Figure 1.7 Multilevel secure data management

1.4 Multilevel Secure Data Management

Numerous developments on multilevel secure database systems were reported throughout the 1980s and during the early 1990s. These systems evolved from multilevel secure operating systems. The idea is for users to be granted access to the data depending on the user's clearance level and the sensitivity level of the data. For example, data is assigned sensitivity levels such as Unclassified, Confidential, Secret, and Top-Secret. Users are also cleared, say, at Confidential, Secret, and Top-Secret levels. In addition, there may also be compartments both for data and the users.

The early developments focused on multilevel secure relational database systems. Then the focus was on multilevel object database systems and multilevel distributed database systems. In Part III we focus mainly on historical developments and design principles. Specific multilevel secure database systems as well as the inference problem in such systems are discussed in Parts IV through VII. Figure 1.7 illustrates various aspects of multilevel secure data management.

1.5 Multilevel Secure Relational Data Models and Systems

Many of the early developments especially throughout the 1980s and early 1990s were in multilevel secure relational data models and systems. For example, after the Air Force Summer Study, various prototypes based on the integrity lock approach for relational models were developed at the

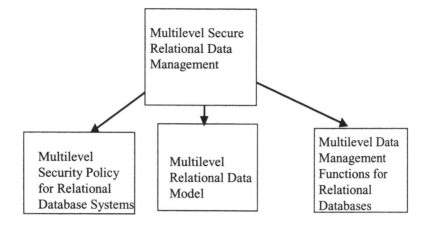

Figure 1.8   Multilevel secure relational data management

MITRE Corporation. Then there were the prominent multilevel secure relational database systems such as SeaView at SRI and LOCK Data Views at Honeywell Inc. In the early 1990s there was work at George Mason University on multilevel relational data models. At the same time, multilevel secure relational database systems based on a distributed systems approach were being designed at the Naval Research Laboratory.

In Part IV we discuss multilevel relational data models and the functions of a multilevel secure relational database system, as well as prototype developments and commercial products. Note that there are many commercial products, and some corporations are still maintaining their multilevel database system products. Figure 1.8 illustrates multilevel secure relational database technologies.

1.6 Inference Problem

Inference is the process of posing queries and deducing unauthorized information from the legitimate responses received. The inference problem exists for all types of database systems and has been studied extensively within the context of multilevel databases. Early developments on the inference problem focused on statistical database security. Then the focus was on security constraint processing to handle the inference problem. Researchers also used conceptual structures to design the database application and detect security violations via inferences during the design time. There are many technical challenges for the inference problem including the unsolvability and the complexity of the problem. The developments on the inference problem are illustrated in Figure 1.9. We discuss the inference problem in Part V.

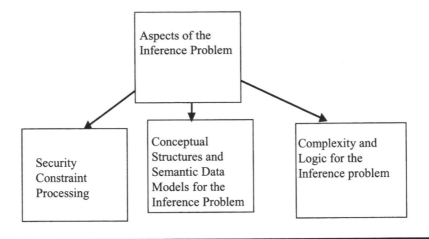

Figure 1.9 Aspects of the inference problem

Recently the inference problem is receiving much attention within the context of privacy. Technologies such as data mining are being used extensively for national security. This is causing privacy concerns. The privacy problem is a form of the inference problem where one deduces highly private information from public information. The privacy problem is discussed in Part VIII.

1.7 Secure Distributed Database Systems

Distributed database technology has advanced a great deal. The early systems were developed in the mid-1970s and we now have commercial products. Essentially the database is distributed and the goal is to provide seamless access to the user. Another type of distributed database technology is heterogeneous database technology where different databases are connected and interoperate with one another. Databases may also form federations. Such a collection of database systems is called a federated database system.

Security for distributed, heterogeneous, and federated database systems is critical for many operational environments. An organization needs to maintain security regardless of whether the databases are centralized or distributed. There are many challenges in securing distributed, heterogeneous, and federated databases. In Part VI we discuss the developments and challenges both for discretionary security as well as for multilevel security. We also focus on security for heterogeneous and federated databases. Figure 1.10 illustrates various aspects of secure distributed database systems.

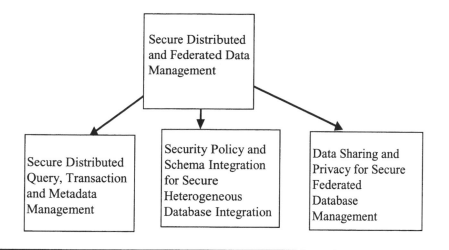

Figure 1.10 Secure distributed and federated data management

1.8 Secure Object and Multimedia Data Systems

Object technology is important for many applications including programming languages, design and analysis for applications and systems, interconnection, and databases. For example, programming languages such as Java are based on objects. Distributed object management systems connect heterogeneous databases and applications. Databases and applications are modeled using objects. Large systems are created using object components. Finally object technology is very popular for modeling and design. It is critical that objects be secure. That is, we need secure object programming languages, secure object databases, secure distributed object systems, secure object components, and the use of objects to model secure applications.

In Part VII of this book we discuss various types of secure object technologies relevant to databases and applications. Because we are not discussing programming languages we do not address Java security. One of the first efforts to introduce security for objects is the work of Keefe, Tsai, and Thuraisingam back in 1988. Since then, numerous developments have been reported not only on secure object databases but also on secure object operating systems and secure distributed object systems. Furthermore, objects have been used to model secure applications. Figure 1.11 illustrates the developments in secure object systems. It should be noted that multimedia databases often utilize variations of the object model for data representation. Therefore, we discuss secure multimedia databases in Part VI.

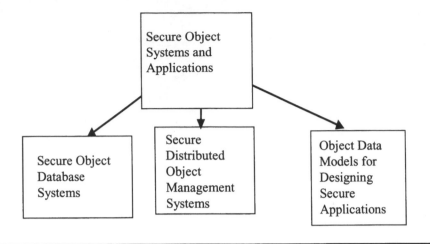

Figure 1.11 Secure object systems and applications

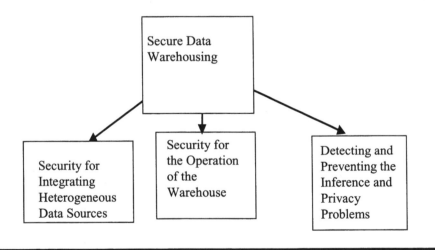

Figure 1.12 Secure data warehousing

1.9 Data Warehousing, Data Mining, Security, and Privacy

Many organizations are now developing data warehouses. Warehouses essentially provide different views of the data to different users. For example, a president of a company may want to see quarterly sales figures whereas a manager of a department may want to see the daily sales numbers. These data warehouses have to be secure. Figure 1.12 illustrates

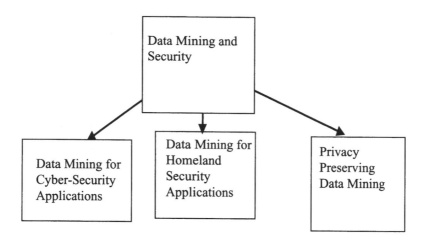

Figure 1.13   Data mining and security

security aspects of data warehouses and the issues are elaborated on in Part VIII.

Part VIII also discusses the relationship between data mining and security. For example, data mining could be used to handle security problems such as intrusion detection and auditing. On the other hand, data mining also exacerbates the inference and privacy problems. This is because a user can use the various data-mining tools and combine different pieces of information and deduce new information that may be sensitive and private. This is illustrated in Figure 1.13. Recently there has been much discussion on privacy violations that result due to data mining. We discuss privacy issues as well as the notion of privacy-preserving data mining in Part VIII.

1.10 Secure Web Information Management Technologies

The World Wide Web (WWW) was conceived in the 1990s and the developments since then have been tremendous. We are now able to get almost any information within a short space of time. There is so much data everywhere that managing the data and making sense out of the data have become a major challenge. Databases are being accessed through the Web. These databases are also being integrated. Standards such as XML (eXtensible Markup Language) have emerged. The Web is being made more intelligent so that ultimately it results in the semantic Web.

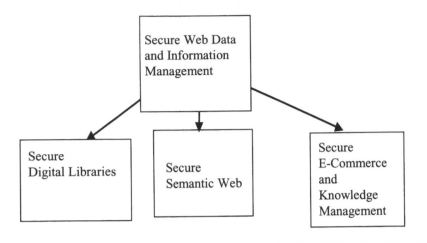

Figure 1.14   Secure Web data and information management

Because there are so many activities on the Web, it is critical that the Web be secure. Various secure E-commerce protocols are being developed. Security for XML and the semantic Web is being examined. Finally, knowledge management technologies have resulted in the need for protecting a corporation's assets and intellectual property. In Part IX we elaborate on various secure Web technologies that relate to secure Web data management. Several other Web technologies such as secure middleware, secure clients, and secure programming languages are beyond the scope of this book. It should be noted that secure Web information management will continue to evolve as progress is made on Web technologies. For example, we now have digital libraries, Web services, collaboration on the Web, and E-commerce. Security has to be incorporated into all of these important Web technologies. Figure 1.14 illustrates secure Web information management technologies.

1.11 Emerging Secure Information Management Technologies

Some emerging secure data and information management technologies are illustrated in Figure 1.15. These emerging technologies include secure dependable systems as well as secure sensor and wireless information systems. These technologies are discussed in Part X. Part X also discusses data quality issues as well as topics such as digital identity management and digital forensics. We also discuss various aspects of security such as risk assessment in Part X.

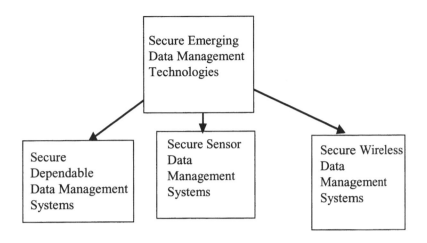

Figure 1.15   Secure emerging data management technologies

Note that emerging security technologies will continue to evolve as new technologies are discovered. Therefore, we encourage the reader to keep up with developments in the technologies and ensure that security is considered at the beginning of the design of a system and not as an afterthought.

1.12 Organization of This Book

This book covers the essential topics in database and applications security focusing on secure database systems, secure Web information management, and emerging applications such as secure knowledge management. To explain our ideas more clearly, we illustrate a database and applications security framework consisting of three layers as shown in Figure 1.16. Layer 1 is the Supporting Technologies Layer. It describes the various supporting technologies that contribute to database and applications security. Layer 2 is the Secure Database Systems Layer. This layer describes the various concepts in secure databases including secure relational databases, secure distributed databases, and secure object database systems. Layer 3 is the Applications Security layer and includes secure knowledge management and collaboration.

This book is divided into ten parts. Part I, consisting of three chapters, provides some background information for database security. Database security essentially integrates two fields: computer security and database management. Chapter 2 discusses data management technologies and Chapter 3 discusses information security technologies. Chapter 4 provides

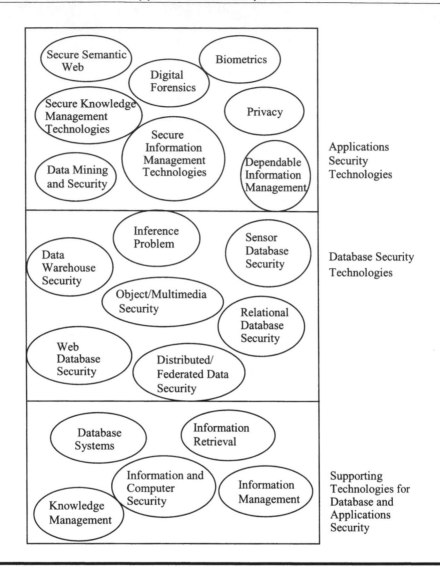

Figure 1.16 Framework for database and applications security technologies

an overview of some of the developments of other information management technologies including knowledge management and collaboration.

Part II, consisting of two chapters, discusses discretionary security in database systems. Chapter 5 discusses access-control models including authorization models and provides a general overview of discretionary security. Policy enforcement issues are discussed in Chapter 6.

Part III, consisting of two chapters, describes multilevel secure databases. Chapter 7 describes historical developments of multilevel secure data management and Chapter 8 describes design principles. Although the design principles are influenced by the relational data model, they can also be applied to other types of multilevel secure database systems such as object systems and distributed systems.

Part IV, consisting of three chapters, discusses multilevel secure relational data management. Multilevel relational data models including a discussion of polyinstantiation are discussed in Chapter 9. Functions of multilevel secure relational data management including transaction processing are the subject of Chapter 10. Secure database system prototypes and products are discussed in Chapter 11.

Part V, consisting of three chapters, discusses the inference problem. A perspective of the problem as well as statistical database security is discussed in Chapter 12. Security constraint processing is the subject of Chapter 13. Use of conceptual structures for designing secure databases is discussed in Chapter 14.

Part VI, consisting of three chapters, addresses secure distributed databases including both multilevel security and discretionary security. Chapter 15 discusses discretionary security in distributed databases. Multilevel security is discussed in Chapter 16. A discussion of secure federated database systems as well as secure heterogeneous databases is covered in Chapter 17.

Part VII, consisting of three chapters, discusses secure object systems including database systems and distributed object management systems. Chapter 18 discusses discretionary and multilevel security for object databases. Secure distributed object systems as well as the use of object models for secure database applications are the subject of Chapter 19. Because many of the multimedia databases utilize variations of the object models, securing multimedia databases is the subject of Chapter 20.

Part VIII, consisting of three chapters, discusses data warehousing, data mining, security, and privacy. Secure data warehousing is discussed in Chapter 21. Data mining and security are the subjects of Chapter 22, which also includes a discussion of data mining for intrusion detection. Privacy concerns are discussed in Chapter 23.

Part IX, consisting of three chapters, addresses secure Web technologies including secure knowledge management. Chapter 24 discusses secure Web data management as well as secure digital libraries technologies. Chapter 25 discusses security for XML, RDF, and the semantic Web. Chapter 26 discusses secure E-commerce applications as well as secure knowledge management and collaboration.

Finally Part X, consisting of three chapters, discusses various emerging secure data management and applications technologies. Chapter 27 discusses secure dependable data management including integrating security, real-time, and fault-tolerant data management. Secure sensor and wireless data management is the subject of Chapter 28. Topics such as digital

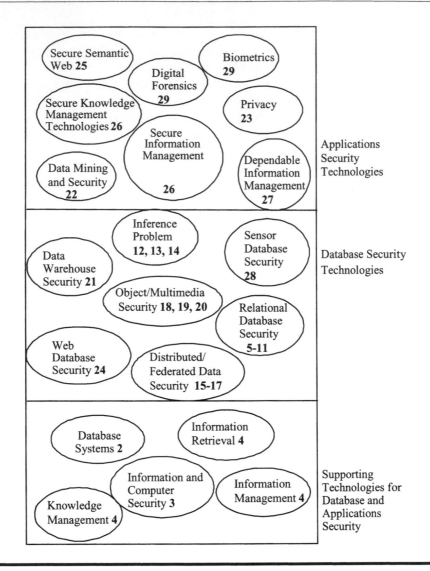

Figure 1.17 Components addressed in this book

identity and digital forensics as well as various emerging topics are discussed in Chapter 29.

Figure 1.17 illustrates the chapters in which the components of the framework in Figure 1.16 are addressed in this book. We summarize the book and provide a discussion of challenges and directions in Chapter 30. Each of the chapters in Parts I through X, that is, Chapters 2 through 29, starts with an overview of the chapter and ends with a summary of the chapter. Each of the chapters 2 through 29 also has its own references and a set of exercises intended for students who wish to pursue research in database and applications security. Each part also begins with an introduction and ends with a conclusion. Finally, we have an appendix that provides some background on the evolution of data management systems technology and provides a summary of our books and how they relate to one another.

Note that we have mixed secure databases with secure applications. In certain cases we have also discussed secure middleware as it is closely related to secure databases as some are proposing the integration of databases with middleware. In fact, integrating database systems with middleware was the main topic of the plenary closing panel at the IEEE 2002 Data Engineering Conference in San Jose, California. An example of mixing database and applications appears in Part VII when we discuss secure object database systems in Chapter 18 and secure distributed object systems as well as object models for designing secure applications in Chapter 19. Another example is in Part IX when we discuss secure Web data management, which deals with database security in Chapter 24 and secure knowledge management and E-commerce in Chapter 26. Many of the discussions in Parts II through VII deal with secure database management and those in Parts VIII through X deal with secure applications.

We also provide some additional references in the bibliography section at the end of this book. As stated earlier, each chapter (i.e., 2 through 29) as well as the appendix has its own set of references that are directly relevant to the contents of the chapter or to the appendix. We end this book with an index.

Note that database and applications security is mature in many respects. Therefore, there are numerous references on this subject and it is impossible for us to list all of the references. Furthermore, we need a good understanding of databases, information security, and information management technologies to understand the concepts in database and applications security. Therefore, we have provided a list of major conferences as well as articles in database management in Chapter 2. A list of major references on information security is provided in Chapter 3. Similarly, a list of major references on information management is provided in Chapter 4.

1.13 Next Steps

This chapter has provided an introduction to the book. We first provided a brief overview of the supporting technologies for database security. Then we discussed various topics addressed in this book including multilevel secure databases and secure object systems. Parts I through X of this book were elaborated on in Sections 1.2 through 1.11, respectively. The organization of this book was detailed in Section 1.12, which also included a framework for organization purposes. Our framework is a three-layer framework and each layer is addressed in one or more parts of this book.

This book provides the information for a reader to get familiar with database and applications security. We discuss some topics such as secure databases in more depth as much has been written on this topic. Furthermore we have conducted extensive research on topics such as the inference problem and therefore we have devoted a considerable amount of discussion to such topics. Some other topics are less concrete and we try our best to provide as much information as possible on these topics. Essentially we provide a tutorial on database and applications security and discuss some of the designs as well as theoretical concepts. For an in-depth understanding of the topics covered in this book, we recommend the reader to the references we have given. Various papers and articles have appeared on database security and related areas. We reference many of these throughout this book. Our main goal is to document many of the developments over the past three decades. However, due to the depth and breadth of this field, we were unable to cover all of the topics including benchmarking, performance analysis, and all of the products as well as designs.

There is so much to write about secure databases that we could be writing this book forever. That is, although we have tried to provide as much information as possible in this book, there is still so much more. Daily we hear about databases being compromised. It should, however, be noted that it is not our intention to educate the reader on all of the details of database security. Instead we provide the big picture and explain where database and applications security stand in the larger scheme of things. That is, to be consistent with our previous books, our purpose is to explain, especially to technical managers, what database security is all about. However, because of our fairly extensive research in this area, we have also tried to include a lot of technical details that would help the technologists, researchers, and developers. This is one of the few books that puts everything into context and provides a broad picture. One of the main contributions of this book is raising the awareness of the importance of database security. We have also given a set of exercises at the end of Chapters 2 through 29 intended for those who wish to pursue research in database and applications security.

We do provide several references that can help the reader in understanding the details of data security. My advice to the reader is to keep up with the developments in data and applications security. Various data and applications security- as well as information security-related conferences and workshops are being held. Most notable is the IFIP11.3 Data and Applications security conference series. Other security conferences include the IEEE Symposium on Security and Privacy, ACM Conference on Computers and Communications Security, and the Computer Security Applications Conference. Journals include the *Journal of Computer Security, Computers and Security Journal, ACM Transactions on Information and Systems Security, IEEE Magazine on Security and Privacy, IEEE Transactions on Dependable and Secure Computing*, and the *Journal of Privacy Technologies*. Papers on this topic have also appeared in database conferences including the Very Large Database Conference, ACM SIGMOD Conference, and IEEE Data Engineering Conference. We list the references to these conference series and some useful texts in database and applications security as well as in general database systems and information security-related topics in Chapters 2 through 4.

SUPPORTING TECHNOLOGIES FOR DATABASE AND APPLICATIONS SECURITY

I

To understand the concepts in database security we need to understand database management and information security. That is, database management and information security are key supporting technologies for database security. This book is also about applications security, which includes secure knowledge management, secure multimedia systems, and secure collaboration. Therefore, we also need an understanding of various information management technologies. That is, in Part I we discuss the supporting technologies for database and applications security and they are database management, information security, and information management.

Part I consists of three chapters. In Chapter 2 we discuss various database technologies including query processing, transaction management, and data warehousing. We also include a discussion of distributed databases and object technologies. Chapter 3 describes various information security technologies including database security and network security. Chapter 4 describes various information management technologies including multimedia, knowledge management, and collaboration.

Chapter 2

Data Management Technologies

2.1 Overview

As we have stated, database security has evolved from database management and information security technologies. Therefore, in Part I we give a brief introduction to database management and information security technologies. Furthermore, many of the data security technologies discussed in this book have evolved from various information management technologies. Therefore we also provide an overview of information management technologies. We focus on data management technologies in this chapter, and in Chapter 3 we discuss information security technologies. Information management technologies are discussed in Chapter 4. Much of our discussion on data management technologies focuses on database systems technologies. In Appendix A, we give a brief overview of the evolution of data management technologies. More details can be found in [THUR97].

Database systems technology has advanced a great deal during the past four decades from the legacy systems based on network and hierarchical models to relational and object-oriented database systems based on client/server architectures. We consider a database system to include both the Database Management System (DBMS) and the database (see also the discussion in [DATE90]). The DBMS component of the database system manages the database. The database contains persistent data. That is, the data is permanent even if the application programs go away.

The organization of this chapter is as follows. In Section 2.2, relational data models, as well as entity-relationship models are discussed. In Section 2.3 various types of architectures for database systems are described. These include architecture for a centralized database system and schema architecture, as well as functional architecture. Database design issues are discussed in Section 2.4. Database administration issues are discussed in Section 2.5. Database system functions are discussed in Section 2.6. These functions include query processing, transaction management, metadata management, storage management, maintaining integrity and security, and fault tolerance. Distributed database systems are the subject of Section 2.7. Heterogeneous database integration aspects are summarized in Section 2.8. Managing federated databases is the subject of Section 2.9. Client/server database management is the subject of Section 2.10. Migrating legacy databases is discussed in Section 2.11. Data warehousing is discussed in Section 2.12 and data mining is the subject of Section 2.13. The impact of the Web is discussed in Section 2.14. A brief overview of object technologies is discussed in Section 2.15. Some other database systems are discussed in Section 2.16. The chapter is summarized in Section 2.17.

2.2 Relational and Entity-Relationship Data Models

2.2.1 Overview

In general, the purpose of a data model is to capture the universe that it is representing as accurately, completely, and naturally as possible [TSIC82]. In this section we discuss the essential points of the relational data model, as it is the most widely used model today. In addition, we also discuss the entity-relationship data model, as some of the ideas have been used in object models and, furthermore, entity-relationship models are being used extensively in database design.

There do exist many other models such as logic-based, hypersemantic, and functional models. Discussion of all of these models is beyond the scope of this book. We do provide an overview of an object model in Section 2.15, as object technology is useful for data modeling as well as for database integration.

2.2.2 Relational Data Model

With the relational model [CODD70], the database is viewed as a collection of relations. Each relation has attributes and rows. For example, Figure 2.1 illustrates a database with two relations EMP and DEPT. EMP has four attributes: SS#, Ename, Salary, and D#. DEPT has three attributes: D#,

EMP

SS#	Ename	Salary	D#
1	John	20K	10
2	Paul	30K	20
3	Mary	40K	20

DEPT

D#	Dname	Mgr
10	Math	Smith
20	Physics	Jones

Figure 2.1   Relational database

Dname, and Mgr. EMP has three rows, also called tuples, and DEPT has two rows. Each row is uniquely identified by its primary key. For example, SS# could be the primary key for EMP and D# for DEPT. Another key feature of the relational model is that each element in the relation is an atomic value such as an integer or a string. That is, complex values such as lists are not supported.

Various operations are performed on relations. The SELECT operation selects a subset of rows satisfying certain conditions. For example, in the relation EMP, one may select tuples where the salary is more than 20K. The PROJECT operation projects the relation onto some attributes. For example, in the relation EMP one may project onto the attributes Ename and Salary. The JOIN operation joins two relations over some common attributes. A detailed discussion of these operations is given in [DATE90] and [ULLM88].

Various languages to manipulate the relations have been proposed. Notable among these languages is the ANSI Standard SQL (Structured Query Language). This language is used to access and manipulate data in relational databases [SQL3]. There is wide acceptance of this standard among database management system vendors and users. It supports schema definition, retrieval, data manipulation, schema manipulation, transaction management, integrity, and security. Other languages include the relational calculus first proposed in the INGRES project at the University of California at Berkeley [DATE90]. Another important concept in relational databases is the notion of a view. A view is essentially a virtual relation and is formed from the relations in the database. Further details are given in Chapter 5.

2.2.3 Entity-Relationship Data Model

One of the major drawbacks of the relational data model is its lack of support for capturing the semantics of an application. This resulted in the

Figure 2.2 Entity-relationship representation

development of semantic data models. The Entity-Relationship (ER) data model developed by Chen [CHEN76] can be regarded as the earliest semantic data model. In this model, the world is viewed as a collection of entities and relationships between entities. Figure 2.2 illustrates two entities, EMP and DEPT. The relationship between them is WORKS.

Relationships can be either one–one, many–one, or many–many. If it is assumed that each employee works in one department and each department has one employee, then WORKS is a one–one relationship. If it is assumed that an employee works in one department and each department can have many employees, then WORKS is a many–one relationship. If it is assumed that an employee works in many departments, and each department has many employees, then WORKS is a many–many relationship.

Several extensions to the entity-relationship model have been proposed. One is the entity-relationship-attribute model where attributes are associated with entities as well as relationships, and, in another, the notion of categories has been introduced into the model (see, for example, the discussion in [ELMA85]). It should be noted that ER models are used mainly to design databases. That is, many database CASE (Computer-Aided Software Engineering) tools are based on the ER model, where the application is represented using such a model and subsequently the database (possibly relational) is generated. Current database management systems are not based on the ER model. That is, unlike the relational model, ER models did not take off in the development of database management systems.

2.3 Architectural Issues

This section describes various types of architectures for a database system. First we illustrate a centralized architecture for a database system. Then we describe a functional architecture for a database system. In particular, the functions of the DBMS component of the database system are illustrated in this architecture. Then we discuss the ANSI/SPARC's (American National Standard Institute) three-schema architecture, which has been more or less accepted by the database community [DATE90]. Finally, we describe extensible architectures.

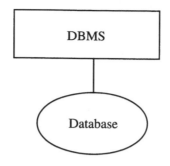

Figure 2.3   Centralized architecture

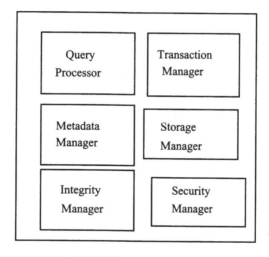

Figure 2.4   Functional architecture for a DBMS

Figure 2.3 is an example of a centralized architecture. Here, the DBMS is a monolithic entity and manages a database, which is centralized. Functional architecture illustrates the functional modules of a DBMS. The major modules of a DBMS include the query processor, transaction manager, metadata manager, storage manager, integrity manager, and security manager. The functional architecture of the DBMS component of the centralized database system architecture (of Figure 2.3) is illustrated in Figure 2.4.

A schema describes the data in the database. It has also been referred to as the data dictionary or contents of the metadatabase. The three-schema architecture was proposed for a centralized database system in the 1960s. This is illustrated in Figure 2.5. The levels are the external schema, which provides an external view, the conceptual schema, which

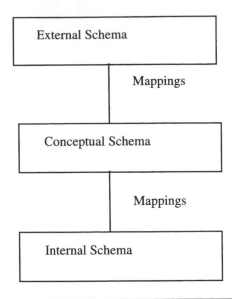

Figure 2.5 Three-schema architecture

provides a conceptual view, and the internal schema, which provides an internal view. Mappings between the different schemas must be provided to transform one representation into another. For example, at the external level, one could use ER representation. At the logical or conceptual level, one could use relational representation. At the physical level, one could use a representation based on B-trees.

There is also another aspect to architectures, and that is extensible database architectures. For example, for many applications, a DBMS may have to be extended with a layer to support objects or to process rules or to handle multimedia data types or even to do mining. Such an extensible architecture is illustrated in Figure 2.6.

2.4 Database Design

Designing a database is a complex process. Much of the work has been on designing relational databases. There are three steps, which are illustrated in Figure 2.7. The first step is to capture the entities of the application and the relationships among the entities. One could use a model such as the entity-relationship model for this purpose. More recently, object-oriented data models, which are part of object-oriented design and analysis methodologies, are becoming popular to represent the application.

The second step is to generate the relations from the representations. For example, from the entity-relationship diagram of Figure 2.2, one could

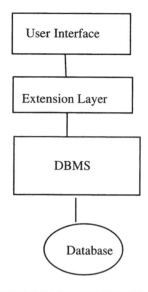

Figure 2.6 Extensible DBMS

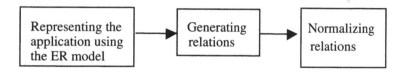

Figure 2.7 Database design process

generate the relations EMP, DEPT, and WORKS. The relation WORKS will capture the relationship between employees and departments.

The third step is to design good relations. This is the normalization process. Various normal forms have been defined in the literature (see, for example, [MAIE83] and [DATE90]). For many applications, relations in third normal form would suffice. With this normal form, redundancies, complex values, and other situations that could cause potential anomalies are eliminated.

2.5 Database Administration

A database has a DataBase Administrator (DBA). It is the responsibility of the DBA to define the various schemas and mappings. In addition, the functions of the administrator include auditing the database as well as implementing appropriate backup and recovery procedures.

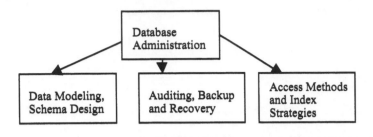

Figure 2.8 Some database administration issues

The DBA could also be responsible for maintaining the security of the system. In some cases, the System Security Officer (SSO) maintains security. The administrator should determine the granularity of the data for auditing. For example, in some cases there is tuple- (or row-) level auditing whereas in other cases there is table- (or relation-) level auditing. It is also the administrator's responsibility to analyze the audit data.

Note that there is a difference between database administration and data administration. Database administration assumes there is an installed database system. The DBA manages this system. Data administration functions include conducting data analysis, determining how a corporation handles its data, and enforcing appropriate policies and procedures for managing the data of a corporation. Data administration functions are carried out by the data administrator. For a discussion of data administration, we refer to [DMH96] and [DMH98]. Figure 2.8 illustrates various database administration issues.

2.6 Database Management System Functions

2.6.1 Overview

The functional architecture of a DBMS was illustrated in Figure 2.4 (see also [ULLM88]). The functions of a DBMS carry out its operations. A DBMS essentially manages a database, and it provides support to the user by enabling him to query and update the database. Therefore, the basic functions of a DBMS are query processing and update processing. In some applications such as banking, queries and updates are issued as part of transactions. Therefore transaction management is also another function of a DBMS. To carry out these functions, information about the data in the database has to be maintained. This information is called the metadata. The function that is associated with managing the metadata is metadata. management. Special techniques are needed to manage the data stores that actually store the data. The function that is associated with managing these techniques is storage management. To ensure that the above functions are carried out properly and that the user gets accurate data, there are some additional functions. These include security management, integrity management, and fault management (i.e., fault tolerance).

This section focuses on some of the key functions of a DBMS. These are query processing, transaction management, metadata management, storage management, maintaining integrity, and fault tolerance. We discuss each of these functions in Sections 2.6.2 to 2.6.7. In Section 2.6.8 we discuss some other functions.

2.6.2 Query Processing

Query operation is the most commonly used function in a DBMS. It should be possible for users to query the database and obtain answers to their queries. There are several aspects to query processing. First of all, a good query language is needed. Languages such as SQL are popular for relational databases. Such languages are being extended to other types of databases. The second aspect is techniques for query processing. Numerous algorithms have been proposed for query processing in general and for the JOIN operation in particular. Also, different strategies are possible to execute a particular query. The costs for the various strategies are computed, and the one with the least cost is usually selected for processing. This process is called query optimization. Cost is generally determined by the disk access. The goal is to minimize disk access in processing a query.

Users pose a query using a language. The constructs of the language have to be transformed into the constructs understood by the database system. This process is called query transformation. Query transformation is carried out in stages based on the various schemas. For example, a query based on the external schema is transformed into a query on the conceptual schema. This is then transformed into a query on the physical schema. In general, rules used in the transformation process include the factoring of common subexpressions and pushing selections and projections down in the query tree as much as possible. If selections and projections are performed before the joins, then the cost of the joins can be reduced by a considerable amount.

Figure 2.9 illustrates the modules in query processing. The user interface manager accepts queries, parses the queries, and then gives them to the query transformer. The query transformer and query optimizer communicate with each other to produce an execution strategy. The database is accessed through the storage manager. The response manager gives responses to the user.

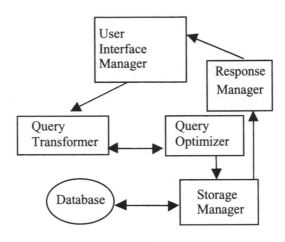

Figure 2.9   Query processor

2.6.3 Transaction Management

A transaction is a program unit that must be executed in its entirety or not executed at all. If transactions are executed serially, then there is a performance bottleneck. Therefore, transactions are executed concurrently. Appropriate techniques must ensure that the database is consistent when multiple transactions update the database. That is, transactions must satisfy the ACID (Atomicity, Consistency, Isolation, and Durability) properties. Major aspects of transaction management are serializability, concurrency control, and recovery. We discuss them briefly in this section. For a detailed discussion of transaction management, we refer the reader to [KORT86] and [BERN87].

Serializability: A schedule is a sequence of operations performed by multiple transactions. Two schedules are equivalent if their outcomes are the same. A serial schedule is a schedule where no two transactions execute concurrently. An objective in transaction management is to ensure that any schedule is equivalent to a serial schedule. Such a schedule is called a serializable schedule. Various conditions for testing the serializability of a schedule have been formulated for a DBMS.

Concurrency Control: Concurrency control techniques ensure that the database is in a consistent state when multiple transactions update the database. Three popular concurrency control techniques that ensure the serializability of schedules are locking, time-stamping, and validation (which is also called optimistic concurrency control).

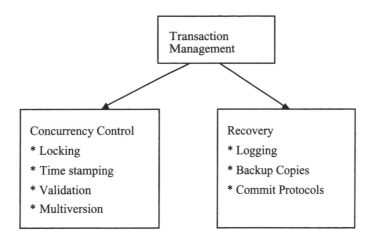

Figure 2.10 Some aspects of transaction management

Recovery: If a transaction aborts due to some failure, then the database must be brought to a consistent state. This is transaction recovery. Onc solution to handling transaction failure is to maintain log files. The transaction's actions are recorded in the log file. So, if a transaction aborts, then the database is brought back to a consistent state by undoing the actions of the transaction. The information for the undo operation is found in the log file. Another solution is to record the actions of a transaction but not make any changes to the database. Only if a transaction commits should the database be updated. This means that the log files have to be kept in stable storage. Various modifications to the above techniques have been proposed to handle the different situations.

When transactions are executed at multiple data sources, then a protocol called two-phase commit is used to ensure that the multiple data sources are consistent. Figure 2.10 illustrates the various aspects of transaction management.

2.6.4 Storage Management

The storage manager is responsible for accessing the database. To improve the efficiency of query and update algorithms, appropriate access methods and index strategies have to be enforced. That is, in generating strategies for executing query and update requests, the access methods and index strategies that are used need to be taken into consideration. The access methods used to access the database depend on the indexing methods.

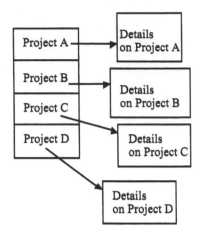

Figure 2.11   An example index of projects

Therefore, creating and maintaining an appropriate index file is a major issue in database management systems. By using an appropriate indexing mechanism, the query processing algorithms may not have to search the entire database. Instead, the data to be retrieved could be accessed directly. Consequently, the retrieval algorithms are more efficient. Figure 2.11 illustrates an example of an indexing strategy where the database is indexed by projects.

Much research has been carried out on developing appropriate access methods and index strategies for relational database systems. Some examples of index strategies are B-trees and hashing [DATE90]. Current research is focusing on developing such mechanisms for object-oriented database systems with support for multimedia data as well as for Web database systems, among others.

2.6.5 Metadata Management

Metadata describes the data in the database. For example, in the case of the relational database illustrated in Figure 2.1, metadata would include the following information: the database has two relations, EMP and DEPT; EMP has four attributes and DEPT has three attributes; and so on. One of the main issues is developing a data model for metadata. In our example, one could use a relational model to model the metadata also. The metadata relation REL shown in Figure 2.12 consists of information about relations and attributes.

In addition to information about the data in the database, metadata also includes information on access methods, index strategies, security

Relation REL

Relation	Attribute
EMP	SS#
EMP	Ename
EMP	Salary
EMP	D#
DEPT	D#
DEPT	Dname
DEPT	Mgr

Figure 2.12   Metadata relation

constraints, and integrity constraints. One could also include policies and procedures as part of the metadata. In other words, there is no standard definition for metadata. There are, however, efforts to standardize metadata (see, for example, the IEEE Mass Storage Committee efforts as well as IEEE Conferences on Metadata [MASS]). Metadata continues to evolve as database systems evolve into multimedia database systems and Web database systems.

Once the metadata is defined, the issues include managing the metadata. What are the techniques for querying and updating the metadata? Because all of the other DBMS components need to access the metadata for processing, what are the interfaces between the metadata manager and the other components? Metadata management is fairly well understood for relational database systems. The current challenge is in managing the metadata for more complex systems such as digital libraries and Web database systems.

2.6.6 Database Integrity

Concurrency control and recovery techniques maintain the integrity of the database. In addition, there is another type of database integrity and that is enforcing integrity constraints. There are two types of integrity constraints enforced in database systems. These are application-independent integrity constraints and application-specific integrity constraints. Integrity mechanisms also include techniques for determining the quality of the data. For example, what is the accuracy of the data and that of the source? What are the mechanisms for maintaining the quality of the data? How

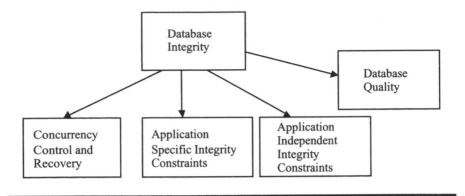

Figure 2.13   Some aspects of database integrity

accurate is the data on output? For a discussion of integrity based on data quality, we refer the reader to [DQ]. Note that data quality is very important for mining and warehousing. If the data that is mined is not good, then one cannot rely on the results. We discuss data quality in Parts VIII and IX.

Application-independent integrity constraints include the primary key constraint, the entity integrity rule, referential integrity constraint, and the various functional dependencies involved in the normalization process (see the discussion in [DATE90]). Application-specific integrity constraints are those constraints that are specific to an application. Examples include "an employee's salary cannot decrease" and "no manager can manage more than two departments." Various techniques have been proposed to enforce application-specific integrity constraints. For example, when the database is updated, these constraints are checked and the data is validated. Aspects of database integrity are illustrated in Figure 2.13.

2.6.7 Fault Tolerance

The previous two sections discussed database integrity and security. A closely related feature is fault tolerance. It is almost impossible to guarantee that the database will function as planned. In reality, various faults could occur. These could be hardware faults or software faults. As mentioned earlier, one of the major issues in transaction management is to ensure that the database is brought back to a consistent state in the presence of faults. The solutions proposed include maintaining appropriate log files to record the actions of a transaction in case its actions have to be retraced.

Another approach to handling faults is checkpointing. Various checkpoints are placed during the course of database processing. At each checkpoint it is ensured that the database is in a consistent state. Therefore, if a fault occurs during processing, then the database must be brought

```
Checkpoint A
Start Processing
*

*

Acceptance Test
If OK, then go to Checkpoint  B
Else Roll Back to Checkpoint A


Checkpoint B
Start Processing
*

*
```

Figure 2.14   Some aspects of fault tolerance

back to the last checkpoint. This way it can be guaranteed that the database is consistent. Closely associated with checkpointing are acceptance tests. After various processing steps, the acceptance tests are checked. If the techniques pass the tests, then they can proceed further. Some aspects of fault tolerance are illustrated in Figure 2.14.

2.6.8 Other Functions

In this section we briefly discuss some of the other functions of a database system: security, real-time processing, managing heterogeneous data types, view management, and backup and recovery.

- *Security:* Note that security is a critical function. This book focuses on database and applications security. Therefore, both discretionary security and mandatory security are discussed throughout this book.
- *Real-Time Processing:* In some situations, the database system may have to meet real-time constraints. That is, the transactions will have to meet deadlines. We discuss real-time data management and security in Part X.
- *Heterogeneous Data Types:* The database system may have to manage multimedia data types such as voice, video, text, and images. We discuss multimedia data management and security in Part VII.

- *Auditing:* The databases may have to be audited so that unauthorized access can be monitored. We discuss auditing in more detail in Part II.
- *View Management:* As stated earlier, views are virtual relations created from base relations. There are many challenges related to view management. We discuss views for security in Part II.
- *Backup and Recovery:* The DBA has to back up the databases and ensure that the database is not corrupted. Some aspects were discussed under fault tolerance. More details are given in [DATE90].

2.7 Distributed Databases

Although many definitions of a distributed database system have been given, there is no standard definition. Our discussion of distributed database system concepts and issues has been influenced by the discussion in [CERI84]. A distributed database system includes a Distributed DataBase Management System (DDBMS), a distributed database, and a network for interconnection. The DDBMS manages the distributed database. A distributed database is data that is distributed across multiple databases. Our choice architecture for a distributed database system is a multidatabase architecture, which is tightly coupled. This architecture is illustrated in Figure 2.15. We have chosen such an architecture because we can explain the concepts for both homogeneous and heterogeneous systems based on this approach. In this architecture, the nodes are connected via a communication subsystem and local applications are handled by the local DBMS. In addition, each node is also involved in at least one global

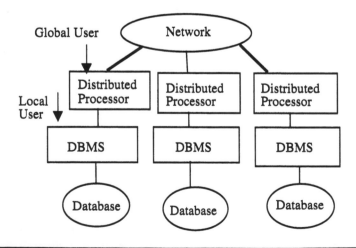

Figure 2.15   An architecture for a DDBMS

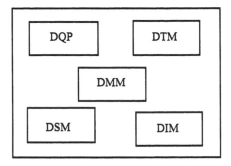

Figure 2.16   Modules of the DP

application, so there is no centralized control in this architecture. The DBMSs are connected through a component called the Distributed Processor (DP). In a homogeneous environment, the local DBMSs are homogeneous whereas in a heterogeneous environment, the local DBMSs may be heterogeneous.

Distributed database system functions include distributed query processing, distributed transaction management, distributed metadata management, and enforcing security and integrity across the multiple nodes. The DP is an essential component of the DDBMS. It is this module that connects the different local DBMSs. That is, each local DBMS is augmented by a DP. The modules of the DP are illustrated in Figure 2.16. The components are the Distributed Metadata Manager (DMM), the Distributed Processor (DQP), the Distributed Transaction Manager (DTM), the Distributed Security Manager (DSP), and the Distributed Integrity Manager (DIM). The DMM manages the global metadata. The global metadata includes information on the schemas, which describe the relations in the distributed database, the way the relations are fragmented, the locations of the fragments, and the constraints enforced. The DQP is responsible for distributed query processing; the DTM is responsible for distributed transaction management; the DSM is responsible for enforcing global security constraints; and the DIM is responsible for maintaining integrity at the global level. Note that the modules of the DP communicate with their peers at the remote nodes. For example, the DQP at node 1 communicates with the DQP at node 2 for handling distributed queries.

2.8 Heterogeneous Database Integration

Figure 2.17 illustrates an example of interoperability between heterogeneous database systems. The goal is to provide transparent access, both for users and application programs, for querying and executing transactions (see, for

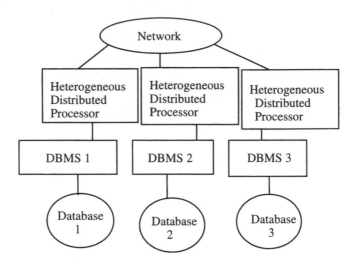

Figure 2.17 Interoperability of heterogeneous database systems

example, [IEEE91] and [WIED92]). Note that in a heterogeneous environment, the local DBMSs may be heterogeneous. Furthermore, the modules of the DP have both local DBMS specific processing as well as local DBMS independent processing. We call such a DP a Heterogeneous Distributed Processor (HDP).

There are several technical issues that need to be resolved for the successful interoperation among these diverse database systems. Note that heterogeneity could exist with respect to different data models, schemas, query-processing techniques, query languages, transaction management techniques, semantics, integrity, and security. There are two approaches to interoperability. One is the federated database management approach where a collection of cooperating, autonomous, and possibly heterogeneous component database systems, each belonging to one or more federations, communicates with one another. The other is the client/server approach where the goal is for multiple clients to communicate with multiple servers in a transparent manner. We discuss both federated and client/server approaches in Sections 2.9 and 2.10.

2.9 Federated Databases

As stated by Sheth and Larson [SHET90], a federated database system is a collection of cooperating but autonomous database systems belonging to a federation. That is, the goal is for the database management systems, which belong to a federation, to cooperate with one another and yet maintain some

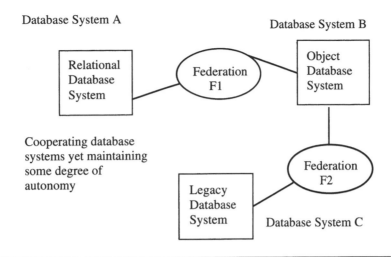

Figure 2.18   Federated database management

degree of autonomy. Note that to be consistent with the terminology, we distinguish between a federated database management system and a federated database system. A federated database system includes both a federated database management system, the local DBMSs, and the databases. The federated database management system is that component which manages the different databases in a federated environment.

Figure 2.18 illustrates a federated database system. Database systems A and B belong to federation F1 and database systems B and C belong to federation F2. We can use the architecture illustrated in Figure 2.18 for a federated database system. In addition to handling heterogeneity, the HDP also has to handle the federated environment. That is, techniques have to be adapted to handle cooperation and autonomy. We have called such an HDP an FDP (Federated Distributed Processor). An architecture for an FDS is illustrated in Figure 2.19.

Figure 2.20 illustrates an example of an autonomous environment. There is communication between components A and B and between B and C. Due to autonomy, it is assumed that components A and C do not wish to communicate with each other. Now, component A may get requests from its own user or from component B. In this case, it has to decide which request to honor first. Also, there is a possibility for component C to get information from component A through component B. In such a situation, component A may have to negotiate with component B before it gives a reply to component B. The developments to deal with autonomy are still in the research stages. The challenge is to handle transactions in an autonomous environment. Transitioning the research into commercial products is also a challenge.

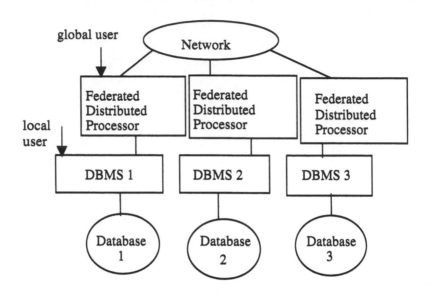

Figure 2.19 Architecture for a federated database system

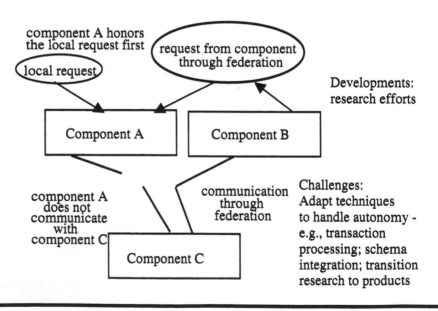

Figure 2.20 Autonomy

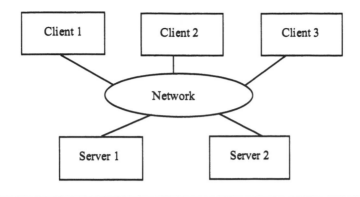

Figure 2.21   Client/server architecture-based interoperability

2.10 Client/Server Databases

Earlier sections described interoperability between heterogeneous data-base systems and focused on the federated database systems approach. In this approach, different database systems cooperatively interoperate with each other. This section describes another aspect of interoperability which is based on the client/server paradigm. Major database system vendors have migrated to an architecture called the client/server architec-ture. With this approach, multiple clients access the various database servers through some network. A high-level view of client/server com-munication is illustrated in Figure 2.21. The ultimate goal is for multivendor clients to communicate with multivendor servers in a transparent manner as illustrated in Figure 2.22.

One of the major challenges in client/server technology is to determine the modules of the distributed database system that need to be placed at the client and server sides. In one approach all the modules of the distributed processor may be placed at the client side, and the modules of the local DBMS placed at the server side. Note that with this approach the client does a lot of processing and this is called the "fat client" approach. There are other options also. For example, some of the modules of the distributed processor could be part of the server in which case the client would be "thinner".

In order to facilitate the communication between multiple clients and servers, various standards are being proposed. One example is the Inter-national Standards Organization's (ISO) Remote Database Access (RDA) standard. This standard provides a generic interface for communication between a client and a server. Microsoft Corporation's Open Database Connectivity (ODBC) is also becoming increasingly popular for clients to

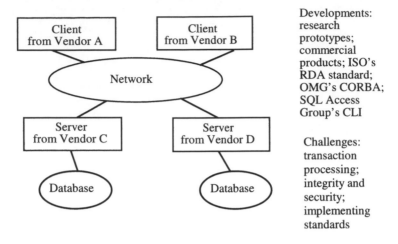

Developments:
research
prototypes;
commercial
products; ISO's
RDA standard;
OMG's CORBA;
SQL Access
Group's CLI

Challenges:
transaction
processing;
integrity and
security;
implementing
standards

Figure 2.22 Multivendor client/server interoperability

communicate with the servers. OMG's Common Object Request Broker
Architecture (CORBA) provides specifications for client/server communication based on object technology (see [OMG95]). Here, one possibility
is to encapsulate the database servers as objects and the clients to issue
appropriate requests and access the servers through an Object Request
Broker. Other standards include IBM's DRDA (Distributed Relational Database Access) and the SQL Access Group's Call Level Interface (CLI).

In our previous book [THUR97] we described various aspects of
client/server interoperability. In particular, technical issues for client/server
interoperability, architectural approaches, and the standards proposed for
communication between clients and servers were discussed. A useful
reference on client/server data management is [ORFA94]. It should be
noted that client/server data management technology is advancing rapidly,
and, for up-to-date information, we encourage the reader to keep up with
the developments obtained from the Web.

2.11 Migrating Legacy Databases and Applications

Many database systems developed some twenty to thirty years ago are
becoming obsolete. These systems use older hardware and software.
Between now and the next few decades, many of today's information
systems and applications may become obsolete. Due to resource and, in
certain cases, budgetary constraints, new developments of next-generation
systems may not be possible in many areas. Therefore, current systems
need to become easier, faster, and less costly to upgrade and less difficult
to support. Legacy database system and application migration is a complex

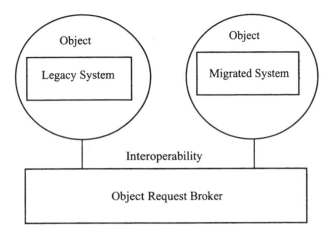

Figure 2.23 Migrating legacy databases

problem, and many of the efforts underway are still not mature. A good book has been published on this subject [BROD95], however, there is no uniform approach for migration. Because migrating legacy databases and applications is becoming a necessity for most organizations, both government and commercial, one could expect a considerable amount of resources to be expended in this area in the near future. The research issues are also not well understood.

Migrating legacy applications and databases also has an impact on heterogeneous database integration. Typically a heterogeneous database environment may include legacy databases as well as some of the next-generation databases. In many cases, an organization may want to migrate the legacy database system to an architecture such as the client/server architecture and still want the migrated system to be part of the hetero-geneous environment. This means that the functions of the heterogeneous database system may be affected due to this migration process.

Two candidate approaches have been proposed for migrating legacy systems. One is to do all of the migration at once. The other is incremental migration. That is, as the legacy system gets migrated, the new parts have to interoperate with the old parts. Various issues and challenges to migration are discussed in [THUR97]. Figure 2.23 illustrates an incremental approach to migrating legacy databases through the use of object request brokers.

2.12 Data Warehousing

Data warehousing is one of the key data management technologies to support data mining and data analysis. Several organizations are building their own warehouses. Commercial database system vendors are marketing

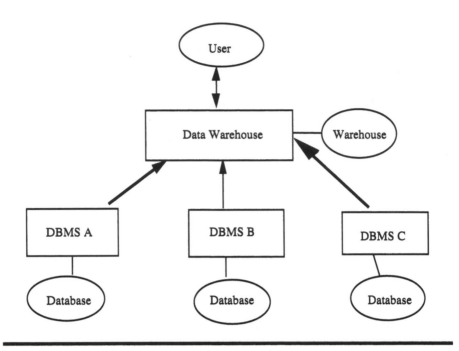

Figure 2.24 Data warehouse example

warehousing products. What then is a data warehouse? The idea behind this is that it is often cumbersome to access data from the heterogeneous databases. Several processing modules need to cooperate with one another to process a query in a heterogeneous environment. Therefore, a data warehouse will bring together the essential data from the heterogeneous databases. This way the users need to query only the warehouse.

As stated by Inmon [INMO93], data warehouses are subject-oriented. Their design depends to a great extent on the application utilizing them. They integrate diverse and possibly heterogeneous data sources. They are persistent. That is, the warehouses are very much like databases. They vary with time. This is because as the data sources from which the warehouse is built get updated, the changes have to be reflected in the warehouse. Essentially data warehouses provide support for decision support functions of an enterprise or an organization. For example, although the data sources may have the raw data, the data warehouse may have correlated data, summary reports, and aggregate functions applied to the raw data.

Figure 2.24 illustrates a data warehouse. The data sources are managed by database systems A, B, and C. The information in these databases is merged and put into a warehouse. The question is how do you merge the data sources and build the warehouse. One way is to determine the types of queries that users would pose, then analyze the data and store only the data that is required by the user. This is called OnLine Analytical Processing (OLAP) as opposed to OnLine Transaction Processing (OLTP).

Note that it is not always the case that the warehouse has all the information for a query. In this case, the warehouse may have to get the data from the heterogeneous data sources to complete the execution of the query. Another challenge is what happens to the warehouse when the individual databases are updated. How are the updates propagated to the warehouse? How can security be maintained? These are some of the issues that are being investigated.

With a data warehouse, data may often be viewed differently by different applications. That is, the data is multidimensional. For example, the payroll department may want data to be in a certain format and the project department may want data to be in a different format. The warehouse must provide support for such multidimensional data.

2.13 Data Mining

Data mining is the process of posing various queries and extracting useful information, patterns, and trends often previously unknown from large quantities of data possibly stored in databases. Essentially, for many organizations, the goals of data mining include improving marketing capabilities, detecting abnormal patterns, and predicting the future based on past experiences and current trends. There is clearly a need for this technology. There are large amounts of current and historical data being stored. Therefore, as databases become larger, it becomes increasingly difficult to support decision making. In addition, the data could be from multiple sources and multiple domains. There is a clear need to analyze the data to support planning and other functions of an enterprise.

Various terms have been used to refer to data mining. These include knowledge/data/information discovery and knowledge/data/information extraction. Note that some define data mining to be the process of extracting previously unknown information whereas knowledge discovery is defined as the process of making sense out of the extracted information.

Some of the data-mining techniques include those based on statistical reasoning techniques, inductive logic programming, machine learning, fuzzy sets, and neural networks, among others. The data-mining outcomes include classification (finding rules to partition data into groups), association (finding rules to make associations between data), and sequencing (finding rules to order data). Essentially one arrives at some hypothesis, which is the information extracted, from examples and patterns observed. These patterns are observed by posing a series of queries; each query may depend on the responses obtained to the previous queries posed. There have been several developments in data mining. A discussion of the various tools is given in [KDN]. A good discussion of the outcomes and techniques is given in [AGRA93] and [BERR97].

Data mining is an integration of multiple technologies. These include data management such as database management, data warehousing, statistics, machine learning, decision support, and others such as visualization and parallel computing. There is a series of steps involved in data mining. These include getting the data organized for mining, determining the desired outcomes to mining, selecting tools for mining, carrying out the mining, pruning the results so that only the useful ones are considered further, taking actions from the mining, and evaluating the actions to determine benefits.

Although several developments have occurred, there are also many challenges. For example, due to the large volumes of data, how can the algorithms determine which technique to select and what type of data mining to do? Furthermore, the data may be incomplete or inaccurate. At times there may be redundant information, and other times there may not be sufficient information. It is also desirable to have data-mining tools that can switch to multiple techniques and support multiple outcomes. Some of the current trends in data mining include mining Web data, mining distributed and heterogeneous databases, and privacy-preserving data mining where one ensures that one can get useful results from mining and at the same time maintain the privacy of the individuals. We have discussed many of these trends in [THUR98], [THUR01], and [THUR03]. We address privacy-preserving data mining in Part VIII. Figure 2.25 illustrates the various aspects of data mining.

2.14 Impact of the Web

The explosion of users on the Internet and the increasing number of World Wide Web servers with large quantities of data are rapidly advancing database management on the Web. For example, the heterogeneous information sources have to be integrated so that users access the servers in a transparent and timely manner. Security and privacy are becoming a major concern. So are other issues such as copyright protection and ownership of the data. Policies and procedures have to be set up to address these issues.

Database management functions for the Web include those such as query processing, metadata management, storage management, transaction management, security, and integrity. In [THUR00] we have examined various database management system functions and discussed the impact of Internet database access on these functions. Figure 2.26 illustrates

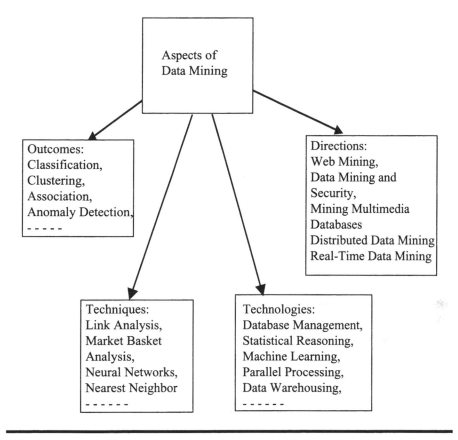

Figure 2.25   Aspects of data mining

applications accessing various database systems on the Web. For more details on Web data management we refer the reader to [THUR00] and [THUR02]. We provide an overview in Chapter 4.

2.15   Object Technology

2.15.1   Overview

Object Technology, also referred to as OT or OOT (Object-Oriented Technology), encompasses different technologies. These include object-oriented programming languages, object database management systems, object-oriented design and analysis, distributed object management, and components and frameworks. The underlying theme for all these types of object technologies is the object model. That is, the object model is the very essence of object technology. Any object system is based on some object model, whether it is a programming language or a database

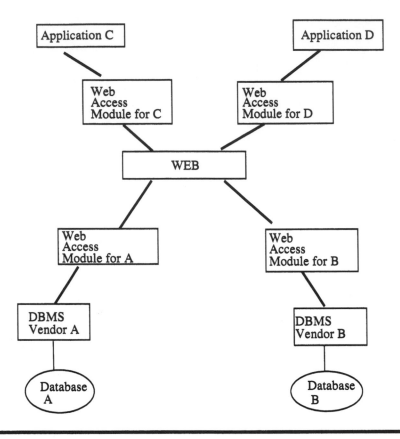

Figure 2.26 Database access through the Web

system. The interesting aspect of an object model is that everything in the real world can be modeled as an object.

The organization of this section is as follows. In Section 2.15.2 we describe the essential properties of object models (OODM). All of the other object technologies are summarized in Section 2.15.2. These include Object-Oriented Programming Languages (OOPL), Object-Oriented DataBase Systems (OODB), Object-Oriented Design and Analysis (OODA), Distributed Object Management (DOM), and Components and Frameworks (C&F). An overview of the various object technologies is illustrated in Figure 2.27.

2.15.2 Object Data Model

Several object data models were proposed in the 1980s. Initially these models were to support programming languages such as Smalltalk. Later these models were enhanced to support database systems as well as other complex systems. This section provides an overview of the essential

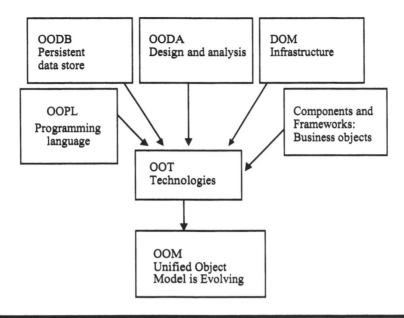

Figure 2.27 Object technologies

features of object models. Although there are no standard object models, the Unified Modeling Language (UML) proposed by prominent object technologists (Rumbaugh, Booch, and Jacobson) has gained increasing popularity and has almost become the standard object model in recent years. Our discussion of the object model has been influenced by much of our work in object database systems as well as the one proposed by Won Kim et al. [BANE87]. We call it an object-oriented data model.

The key points in an object-oriented model are encapsulation, inheritance, and polymorphism. With an object-oriented data model, the database is viewed as a collection of objects [BANE87]. Each object has a unique identifier called the object-ID. Objects with similar properties are grouped into a class. For example, employee objects are grouped into EMP class and department objects are grouped into DEPT class as shown in Figure 2.28. A class has instance variables describing the properties. Instance variables of EMP are SS#, Ename, Salary, and D#, and the instance variables of DEPT are D#, Dname, and Mgr. The objects in a class are its instances. As illustrated in the figure, EMP has three instances and DEPT has two instances.

A key concept in object-oriented data modeling is encapsulation. That is, an object has well-defined interfaces. The state of an object can only be accessed through interface procedures called methods. For example, EMP may have a method called Increase-Salary. The code for Increase-Salary is illustrated in Figure 2.29. A message, say Increase-Salary(1, 10K),

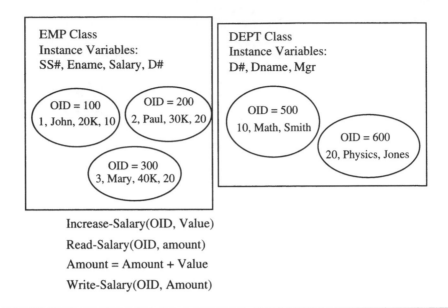

Increase-Salary(OID, Value)

Read-Salary(OID, amount)

Amount = Amount + Value

Write-Salary(OID, Amount)

Figure 2.28 Objects and classes

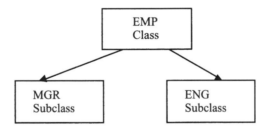

Figure 2.29   Class–subclass hierarchy

may be sent to the object with object ID of 1. The object's current salary is read and updated by 10K.

A second key concept in an object model is inheritance where a subclass inherits properties from its parent class. This feature is illustrated in Figure 2.29, where the EMP class has MGR (manager) and ENG (engineer) as its subclasses. Other key concepts in an object model include polymorphism and aggregation. These features are discussed in [BANE87]. Note that a second type of inheritance is when the instances of a class inherit the properties of the class.

A third concept is polymorphism. This is the situation where one can pass different types of arguments for the same function. For example, to calculate the area, one can pass a sphere or a cylinder object. Operators

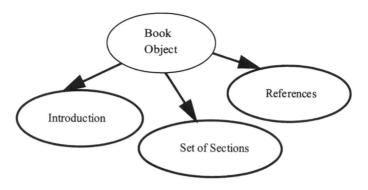

Figure 2.30   Aggregate object

can be overloaded also. That is, the add operation can be used to add two integers or real numbers.

Another concept is the aggregate hierarchy also called the composite object or the is-part-of hierarchy. In this case an object has component objects. For example, a book object has component section objects. A section object has component paragraph objects. Aggregate hierarchy is illustrated in Figure 2.30.

Objects also have relationships between them. For example, an employee object has an association with the department object, which is the department in which he is working. Also, the instance variables of an object could take integers, lists, arrays, or even other objects as values. Many of these concepts are discussed in the book by Cattell [CATT91]. The Object Data Management Group has also proposed standards for object data models [ODMG93].

Relational database vendors are extending their system with support for objects. In one approach the relational model is extended with an object layer. The object layer manages objects and the relational database system manages the relations. Such systems are called extended relational database systems. In another approach, the relational model has objects as its elements. Such a model is called an object-relational data model and is illustrated in Figure 2.31. A system based on the object-relational data model is called an object-relational database system.

2.15.3 Other Object Technologies

- *Programming Languages:* Object-oriented programming languages essentially go back to Simula in the 1960s. However, they really became popular with the advent of Smalltalk by the Xerox Palo Alto Research Center in the late 1970s. Smalltalk is a pure object-oriented

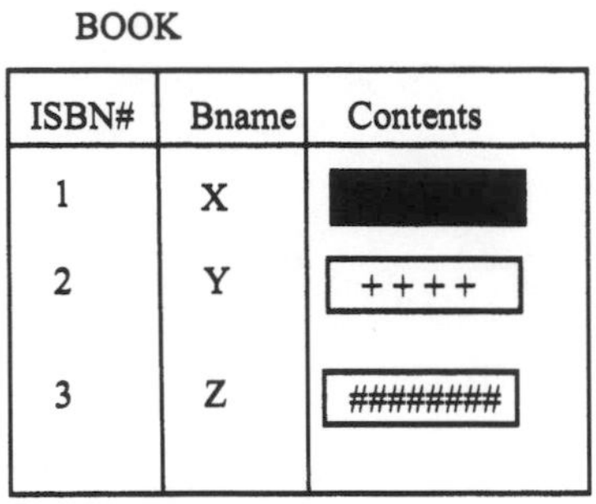

BOOK

ISBN#	Bname	Contents
1	X	███████
2	Y	+ + + +
3	Z	########

Figure 2.31   Object-relational data model

programming language where everything is considered to be an object. Around the mid-1980s, languages such as LISP and C were being made object-oriented by extending them to support objects. One such popular extension is the language C++. Around the 1990s Sun Microsystems wanted to develop a language for its embedded computing and appliance business that would not have all of the problems associated with C++ such as pointers. The result was the popular language Java.

■ *Database Systems:* We have discussed three types of object database systems: one is the object-oriented database system and such a system makes object-oriented programming languages persistent; the second is the extended-relational system and such a system extends relational database systems with object layers; and the third system is the object-relational database system where objects are nested within relations.

■ *Design and Analysis:* In the 1980s there was a lot of interest in using object technology to design and analyze applications. Various design and analysis methodologies were being proposed. Notable among them were the method of Booch, Usecases by Jacobson, and OMT (Object Modeling Technique) by Rumbaugh et al. Then the various groups merged and produced a unified methodology called UML (Unified Modeling Language) [FOWL97]. UML has essential features from the three approaches and is now more or less a standard for object modeling and analysis.

■ *Distributed Object Management:* Distributed object management technology is used to interconnect heterogeneous databases, systems, and applications. With this approach, the various systems and applications are encapsulated as objects and the objects communicate with each other through exchanging messages. An example of a DOM system that is being used as middleware to connect

```
Types of Database Systems:
Network and Hierarchical Databases;
Relational Databases;
Object and Object Relational Databases;
Distributed and Heterogeneous Databases
Functional Databases;
Real-time and Fault Tolerant Databases
Multimedia Databases;
Spatiotemporal and Scientific Databases;
High Performance and Parallel Database;
- - - - - - - - -
```

Figure 2.32 Types of database systems

heterogeneous database systems is a system based on OMG's CORBA. CORBA is a specification that enables heterogeneous applications, systems, and databases to interoperate (see [OMG95]).

■ *Components and Frameworks:* This is one of the more recent object technologies and has really taken off since the mid-1990s. A framework can be considered to be a skeleton with classes and interconnections. One then instantiates this skeleton for various applications. Frameworks are being developed for different application domains including financial and medical. Components, on the other hand, are classes, objects, and relationships between them that can be reused. Components can be built for different applications. A survey of the field was provided in the *Communications of the ACM* journal in October, 1997 by Fayad and Schmidt [ACM97].

2.16 Other Database Systems

This section briefly discusses various other database systems as illustrated in Figure 2.32. We examine security for some of these systems in Part IV.

■ *Real-Time Database Systems:* These are systems where the queries and transactions will have to meet timing constraints. Details are given in [RAMA93].

■ *Deductive Database Systems:* These are systems that use logic as a data model. These are essentially logic programming systems that manage data. More details can be found in [FROS86] and [LLOY87].

- *Multimedia Database Systems:* These are database systems that manage multimedia data such as text, audio, video, and images. Details can be found in [PRAB97].
- *Functional Database Systems:* These systems were developed in the early 1980s. The database is viewed as a collection of functions and query evaluation amounts to function execution. Details can be found in [BUNE82].
- *Parallel Database Systems:* These systems use parallel processing techniques for executing queries and transactions so that the speed can be improved. More details can be found in [DEWI90].
- *Spatiotemporal Database Systems:* For applications such as geospatial information systems and motion data management, one needs to model objects with spatial and temporal properties. Therefore managing spatiotemporal data structures is important for such applications.
- *Other Systems:* Many other systems such as scientific database systems and engineering information systems have been developed. An overview of some of these systems is given in [ACM90].

2.17 Summary and Directions

This chapter has discussed various aspects of database systems and provided some background information to understand the various chapters in this book. We began with a discussion of various data models. We chose relational and entity-relationship models as they are more relevant to what we have addressed in this book. Then we provided an overview of various types of architectures for database systems. These included functional and schema architectures. Next we discussed database design aspects and database administration issues. We also provided an overview of the various functions of database systems. These included query processing, transaction management, storage management, metadata management, integrity, and fault tolerance. Next we briefly discussed distributed databases and interoperability. This was followed by a discussion of data warehousing, data mining, and the impact of the Web. We also provided a brief overview of object technology as well as discussed various other database systems.

Many of the chapters in this book discuss secure data management technologies. These include secure query processing, secure transaction management, secure storage management, secure metadata management, and secure data distribution and interoperability. In particular, secure relational data management is discussed in Chapters 9 through 11. Secure distributed, heterogeneous, and federated databases as well as secure migration issues are discussed in Chapters 15 through 17. Secure object databases are discussed in Chapter 18. Secure distributed objects as well as object models for secure applications are discussed in Chapter 19. Secure multimedia database systems are discussed in Chapter 20. Secure data warehousing is discussed in Chapter 21. Data mining and security are covered in Chapter 22. Secure digital libraries and Web databases are discussed in Chapter 24. That is, security for the various data management technologies is examined in Parts II through X.

Various texts and articles have been published on database systems and we have referenced them throughout the book. There are also some major conferences on database systems and these include the ACM SIG-MOD Conference series [SIGM], Very Large Database Conference series [VLDB], IEEE Data Engineering Conference series [DE], and the European Extended Database Technology Conference series [EDBT].

References

[ACM90] Special issue on heterogeneous database systems. *ACM Computing Surveys* 22: 3, 1990.

[ACM97] Special issue on components and frameworks. *Communications of the ACM* 40: 10, 1997.

[AGRA93] Agrawal, A. et al. Database mining a performance perspective. *IEEE Transactions on Knowledge and Data Engineering* 5: 6, 1993.

[BANE87] Banerjee, J. et al. A data model for object-oriented applications. *ACM Transactions on Office Information Systems* 5: 1, 1987.

[BERN87] Bernstein, P. et al. *Concurrency Control and Recovery in Database Systems*. Addison-Wesley: Reading, MA, 1987.

[BERR97] Berry, M. and Linoff, G. *Data Mining Techniques for Marketing, Sales, and Customer Support*. Wiley: New York, 1997.

[BROD95] Brodie M. and Stonebraker, M. *Migrating Legacy Databases*. Morgan Kaufmann: San Francisco, 1995.

[BUNE82] Buneman, P. et al. An implementation technique for database query languages. *ACM Transactions on Database Systems* 7: 2, 1982.

[CATT91] Cattel, R. *Object Data Management Systems*. Addison-Wesley: Reading, MA, 1991.

[CERI84] Ceri, S. and Pelagatti, G. *Distributed Databases, Principles and Systems*. McGraw-Hill: New York, 1984.

[CHEN76] Chen, P. The entity relationship model—Toward a unified view of data. *ACM Transactions on Database Systems* 1: 1, 1976.

[CODD70] Codd, E.F. A relational model of data for large shared data banks. *Communications of the ACM* 13: 6, 1970.

[DATE90] Date, C. *An Introduction to Database Systems*. Addison-Wesley: Reading, MA, 1990

[DE] *Proceedings of the IEEE Data Engineering Conference Series*. IEEE Computer Society Press: Los Alamitos, CA.

[DEWI90] Dewitt, D.J. et al. The gamma database machine project. *IEEE Transactions on Knowledge and Data Engineering* (March) 1990.

[DMH96] *Data Management Handbook Supplement*. Ed. B. Thuraisingham. Auerbach: New York, 1996.

[DMH98] *Data Management Handbook*. ed. B. Thuraisingham. Auerbach: New York, 1997.

[DQ] MIT Total Data Quality Management Program. Available at http://web.mit.edu/tdqm/www/index.shtml.

[EDBT] *Proceedings of the Extended Database Technology Conference Series*. Springer Verlag: Heidelberg.

[ELMA85] Elmasri, R. et al. The category concept: An extension to the entity relationship model. *Data and Knowledge Engineering Journal* 1: 2, 1985.

[FOWL97] Fowler, M. et al. *UML Distilled: Applying the Standard Object Modeling Language*. Addison Wesley: Reading, MA, 1997.

[FROS86] Frost, R. *On Knowledge Base Management Systems*. Collins: London, UK, 1986.

[IEEE91] Special issue: Heterogeneous database systems, *IEEE Computer,* 24: 12, December 1999.

[IEEE98] *IEEE Data Engineering Bulletin*. 21: 2, 1998.

[INMO93] Inmon, W. *Building the Data Warehouse*. Wiley: New York, 1993.

[KDN] Kdnuggets. Available at www.kdn.com.

[KORT86] Korth, H. and Silberschatz, A. *Database System Concepts*. McGraw-Hill: New York, 1986.

[LLOY87] Lloyd, J. *Foundations of Logic Programming*. Springer-Verlag: Heidelberg, 1987.

[MAIE83] Maier, D. *Theory of Relational Databases*. Computer Science: Rockville, MD, 1983.

[MASS] IEEE Mass Storage Systems Technical Committee. Available at http://www.msstc.org/.

[ODMG93] *Object Database Standard: ODMB 93*. Object Database Management Group, Morgan Kaufmann: San Mateo, CA, 1993.

[OMG95] *Common Object Request Broker Architecture and Specification*. OMG Publications, Wiley: New York, 1995.

[ORFA94] Orfali, R. et al. *Essential, Client Server Survival Guide*. Wiley: New York, 1994.

[PRAB97] Prabhakaran, B. *Multimedia Database Systems*. Kluwer: Hingham, MA, 1997.

[RAMA93] Ramaritham, K. Real-time databases. *Journal of Distributed and Parallel Systems* 1: 2, 1993.

[SHET90] Sheth A. and Larson, J. Federated database systems. *ACM Computing Surveys* 22: 3, 1990.

[SIGM] *Proceedings of the ACM Special Interest Group on Management of Data Conference Series*. ACM: New York.

[SQL3] SQL3. American National Standards Institute, Draft, 1992.

[THUR97] Thuraisingham, B. *Data Management Systems Evolution and Interoperation*. CRC Press: Boca Raton, FL, 1997.

[THUR98] Thuraisingham, B. *Data Mining: Technologies, Techniques, Tools and Trends.* CRC Press: Boca Raton, FL, 1998.

[THUR00] Thuraisingham, B. *Web Data Management and Electronic Commerce.* CRC Press: Boca Raton, FL, 2000.

[THUR01] Thuraisingham, B. *Managing and Mining Multimedia Databases for the Electronic Enterprise.* CRC Press: Boca Raton, FL, 2001.

[THUR02] Thuraisingham, B. *XML, Databases and the Semantic Web.* CRC Press: Boca Raton, FL, 2002.

[THUR03] Thuraisingham, B. *Web Data Mining Technologies and Their Applications in Business Intelligence and Counter-Terrorism.* CRC Press: Boca Raton, FL, 2003.

[TSIC82] Tsichritzis, D. and Lochovsky, F. *Data Models.* Prentice-Hall: Englewood Cliffs, NJ, 1982.

[ULLM88] Ullman, J.D. *Principles of Database and Knowledge Base Management Systems,* Vol. I and II. Computer Science Press: Rockville, MD, 1988.

[VLDB] *Proceedings of the Very Large Database Conference Series.* Morgan Kaufmann: San Francisco.

[WIED92] Wiederhold, G. Mediators in the architecture of future information systems. *IEEE Computer.* 25: 3, (March) 1992.

Exercises

1. Describe query optimization and concurrency control techniques with examples.
2. Select three data warehousing and three data mining products and describe their key features.
3. Describe schema integration for federated databases.
4. Describe the object-relational data model.

Chapter 3

Information Security

3.1 Overview

As we have stated in the previous chapters, database security has evolved from database management and information security. Chapter 2 discussed various concepts in database management. In this chapter we provide a brief overview of information security. These two chapters provide the foundation for various topics in database and applications security which is the focus of this book.

As stated earlier, the number of computerized databases has been increasing rapidly over the past three decades. The advent of the Web as well as networking capabilities has made access to data and information much easier. For example, users can now access large quantities of information in a short space of time. As more and more tools and technologies are being developed to access and use the data, there is also now an urgent need to protect the data. Many government and industrial organizations have sensitive and classified data that has to be protected. Various other organizations such as academic institutions also have sensitive data about their students and employees. As a result, techniques for protecting the data stored in databases and managed by DBMSs have become an urgent need.

Over the past three decades various developments have been made on securing the databases. Much of the early work was on statistical database security. Then, in the 1970s, as research in relational databases began, attention was directed toward access-control issues. In particular, research was carried out on discretionary access-control models. Although some work on mandatory security started in the late 1970s, it was not until the Air Force Summer Study in 1982 that many of the efforts in multilevel secure database management systems were initiated [AFSB83]. This resulted in the development of various secure database system prototypes and products. In the 1990s, with the advent of new technologies such as digital libraries, the World Wide Web, and collaborative computing systems, there was much interest in security not only with government organizations, but also with the commercial industry.

This chapter provides an overview of the various developments in information security with special emphasis on database security. In Section 3.2 we discuss basic concepts such as access control for information systems. Section 3.3 provides an overview of secure systems. Secure operating systems are discussed in Section 3.4. Secure database systems are discussed in Section 3.5. Note that much of this book is about secure database systems. Network security is discussed in Section 3.6. Emerging trends are the subject of Section 3.7. The impact of the Web is given in Section 3.8. An overview of the steps to building secure systems is provided in Section 3.9. The chapter is summarized in Section 3.10.

3.2 Access Control and Other Security Concepts

Access-control models include those for discretionary security and mandatory security. In this section we discuss both aspects of access control and also consider other issues. In discretionary access-control models, users or groups of users are granted access to data objects. These data objects could be files, relations, objects, or even data items. Access-control policies include rules such as User U has read access to Relation R1 and write access to Relation R2. Access control could also include negative access control where user U does not have read access to Relation R.

In mandatory access control, subjects that act on behalf of users are granted access to objects based on some policy. A well-known policy is the Bell and LaPadula policy [BELL73] where subjects are granted clearance levels and objects have sensitivity levels. The set of security levels forms a partially ordered lattice where Unclassified < Confidential < Secret < TopSecret. The policy has two properties: a subject has read access to an object if its clearance level dominates that of the object, and a subject has write access to an object if its level is dominated by that of the object.

Other types of access control include role-based access control. Here access is granted to users depending on their roles and the functions they perform. For example, personnel managers have access to salary data whereas project mangers have access to project data. The idea here is generally to give access on a need-to-know basis.

Early access-control policies were formulated for operating systems, however, these policies have been extended to include other systems such

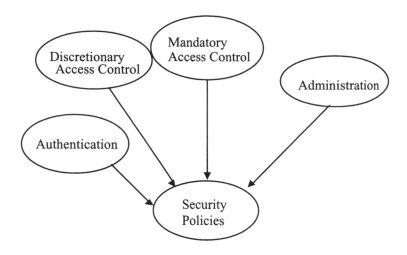

Figure 3.1   Security policies

as database systems, networks, and distributed systems. For example, a policy for networks includes policies for not only reading and writing but also for sending and receiving messages.

Other security policies include administration policies. These policies include those for ownership of data as well as how to manage and distribute the data. Database administrators as well as system security officers are involved in formulating the administration policies.

Security policies also include policies for identification and authentication. Each user or subject acting on behalf of a user has to be identified and authenticated, possibly using some password mechanisms. Identification and authentication become more complex for distributed systems. For example, how can a user be authenticated at a global level?

The steps to developing secure systems include developing a security policy, developing a model of the system, designing the system, and verifying and validating the system. The methods used for verification depend on the level of assurance that is expected. Testing and risk analysis are also part of the process. These activities will determine the vulnerabilities as well as assess the risks involved. Figure 3.1 illustrates various types of security policies.

3.3 Secure Systems

In the previous section we discussed various policies for building secure systems. In this section we elaborate on various types of secure systems. Much of the early research in the 1960s and 1970s was on securing operating systems. Early security policies such as the Bell and LaPadula policy were formulated for operating systems. Subsequently, secure operating systems such as Honeywell's SCOMP and MULTICS were developed (see [IEEE83]). Other policies such as those based on noninterference also emerged in the early 1980s.

Early research on secure database systems was reported in the 1970s, but it was not until the early 1980s that active research began in this area. Much of the focus was on multilevel secure database systems. The security policy for operating systems was modified slightly. For example, the write policy for secure database systems was modified to state that a subject has write access to an object if the subject's level is that of the object. Because database systems enforced relationships between data and focused on semantics, there were additional security concerns. For example, data could be classified based on content, context, and time. The problem of posing multiple queries and inferring sensitive information from the legitimate responses became a concern. This problem is now known as the inference problem. Also, research was carried out not only on securing relational systems but also object systems as well as distributed systems, among others.

Research on computer networks began in the late 1970s and throughout the 1980s and beyond. The networking protocols were extended to incorporate security features. The result was secure network protocols. The policies include those for reading, writing, sending, and receiving messages. Research on encryption and cryptography has received much prominence due to networks and the Web. Security for stand-alone systems was extended to include distributed systems. These systems included distributed databases and distributed operating systems. Much of the research on distributed systems now focuses on securing the Web, known as Web security, as well as securing systems such as distributed object management systems.

As new systems emerge, such as data warehouses, collaborative computing systems, multimedia systems, and agent systems, security for such systems has to be investigated. With the advent of the World Wide Web, security is being given serious consideration not only by the government organizations but also commercial organizations. With E-commerce it is important to protect the company's intellectual property. Figure 3.2 illustrates various types of secure systems.

3.4 Secure Operating Systems

Work on security for operating systems was carried out extensively in the 1960s and 1970s. The research still continues as new kinds of operating systems such as Windows, Linux, and other products emerge. The early ideas included access-control lists and capability-based systems. Access-control lists are lists that specify the types of access that processes, which

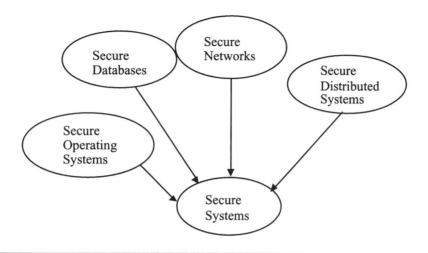

Figure 3.2   Secure systems

are called subjects, have on files, which are objects. The access is usually read or write access. Capability lists are capabilities that a process must possess to access certain resources in the system. For example, a process with a particular capability can write into certain parts of the memory.

Work on mandatory security for operating systems started with the Bell and LaPadula security model, which has two properties. The simple security property states that a subject has read access to an object if the subject's security level dominates the level of the object. The *-property (pronounced "star property") states that a subject has write access to an object if the subject's security level is dominated by that of the object. Since then variations of this model as well as a popular model called the noninterference model (see [GOGU82]) have been proposed. The noninterference model is essentially about higher-level processes not interfering with lower-level processes.

As stated earlier, security is becoming critical for operating systems. Corporations such as Microsoft are putting in many resources to ensure that their products are secure. Often we hear of vulnerabilities in various operating systems and about hackers trying to break into operating systems especially with networking capabilities. Therefore, this is an area that will continue to receive much attention for the next several years. Figure 3.3 illustrates some key aspects of operating systems security.

3.5 Secure Database Systems

Work on discretionary security for databases began in the 1970s when security aspects were investigated for System R at the IBM Almaden

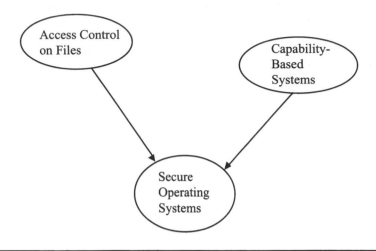

Figure 3.3   Secure operating systems

Research Center. Essentially the security properties specified the read and write access that a user may have to relations, attributes, and data elements. In the 1980s and 1990s security issues were investigated for object systems. Here the security properties specified the access that users had to objects, instance variables, and classes. In addition to read and write access, method execution access was also specified.

Since the early 1980s much of the focus has been on multilevel secure database management systems. These systems essentially enforce the mandatory policy discussed in Section 3.2 with the modification described in Section 3.3 (i.e., read at or below your level and write at your level policy). Since the 1980s various designs, prototypes, and commercial products of multilevel database systems have been developed. Ferrari and Thuraisingham give a detailed survey of some of the developments [FERR00] . Example efforts include the SeaView effort by SRI International and the LOCK Data Views effort by Honeywell. These efforts extended relational models with security properties. One challenge was to design a model where a user sees different values at different security levels. For example, at the Unclassified level an employee's salary may be 20K and at the secret level it may be 50K. In the standard relational model such ambiguous values cannot be represented due to integrity properties.

Note that several other significant developments have been made on multilevel security for other types of database systems. These include security for object database systems [THUR89]. In this effort, security properties specify read, write, and method execution policies. Much work was also carried out on secure concurrency control and recovery. The idea here is to enforce security properties and still meet consistency

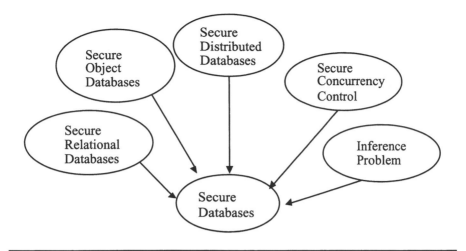

Figure 3.4 Secure database systems

without having covert channels. Research was also carried out on multi-level security for distributed, heterogeneous, and federated database systems. Another area that received a lot of attention was the inference problem. For details on the inference problem we refer the reader to [THUR93]. For secure concurrency control we refer the reader to the numerous algorithms by Atluri, Bertino, and Jajodia et al. (see, for example, [JAJO97]). For information on secure distributed and heterogeneous databases as well as secure federated databases we refer the reader to [THUR91] and [THUR94].

As database systems become more sophisticated, securing these systems will become more and more difficult. Some of the current work focuses on securing data warehouses, multimedia databases, and Web databases (see, for example, *Proceedings of the IFIP Database Security Conference Series*). Figure 3.4 illustrates various types of secure database systems.

3.6 Secure Networks

With the advent of the Web and the interconnection of different systems and applications, networks have proliferated over the past decade. There are public networks, private networks, classified networks, and unclassified networks. We continually hear about networks being infected with viruses and worms. Furthermore, networks are being intruded upon by malicious code and unauthorized individuals. Therefore, network security is emerging as one of the major areas in information security.

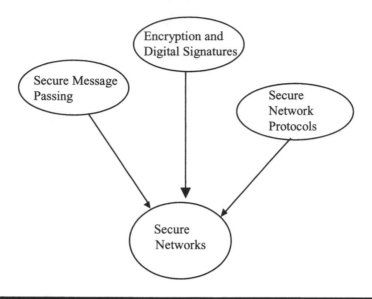

Figure 3.5 Secure networks

Various techniques have been proposed for network security. Encryption and cryptography are still dominating much of the research. For a discussion of various encryption techniques we refer the reader to [HESS00]. Data-mining techniques are being applied extensively for intrusion detection (see [NING04]). There has also been a lot of work on network protocol security where security is incorporated into the various layers, say, of the protocol stack such as the network layer, transport layer, and session layer (see [TANN90]). Verification and validation techniques are also being investigated for securing networks. Trusted Network Interpretation (also called the Red Book) was developed back in the 1980s to evaluate secure networks. Various books on the topic have also been published (see [KAUF02]). Figure 3.5 illustrates network security techniques.

3.7 Emerging Trends

In the mid-1990s research in secure systems expanded to include emerging systems. These included securing collaborative computing systems, multimedia computing, and data warehouses. Data mining has resulted in new security concerns. Because users now have access to various data-mining tools and they can make sensitive associations, it could exacerbate the inference problem. On the other hand, data mining could also help with security problems such as intrusion detection and auditing.

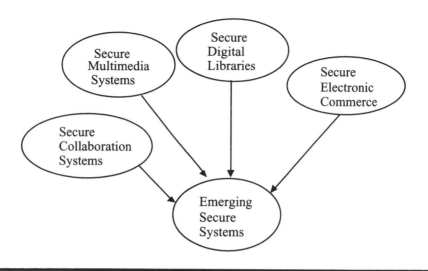

Figure 3.6 Emerging secure systems

The advent of the Web resulted in extensive investigations of security for digital libraries and electronic commerce. In addition to developing sophisticated encryption techniques, security research also focused on securing the Web clients as well as servers. Programming languages such as Java were designed with security in mind. Much research was also carried out on securing agents.

Secure distributed system research focused on security for distributed object management systems. Organizations such as OMG started working groups to investigate security properties (see [OMG]). As a result we now have secure distributed object management systems commercially available. Current focus is on securing Web services as well as on enterprise application integration. Figure 3.6 illustrates the various emerging secure systems and concepts.

3.8 Impact of the Web

The advent of the Web has had a great impact on security. Security is now part of mainstream computing. Government organizations as well as commercial organizations are concerned about security. For example, in a financial transaction, millions of dollars could be lost if security is not maintained. With the Web, all sorts of information are available about individuals and therefore privacy may be compromised.

Various security solutions are being proposed to secure the Web. In addition to encryption, the focus is on securing clients as well as servers. That is, end-to-end security has to be maintained. Web security also has an

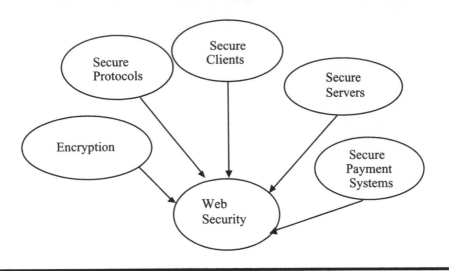

Figure 3.7   Aspects of Web security

impact on electronic commerce. That is, when one carries out transactions on the Web it is critical that security be maintained. Information such as credit card numbers and social security numbers have to be protected.

All of the security issues discussed in the previous sections have to be considered for the Web. For example, appropriate security policies have to be formulated. This is a challenge, as no one person owns the Web. The various secure systems including secure operating systems, secure database systems, secure networks, and secure distributed systems may be integrated in a Web environment. Therefore, this integrated system has to be secure. Problems such as the inference and privacy problems may be exacerbated due to the various data-mining tools (this aspect is detailed in Chapter 23). The various agents on the Web have to be secure. In certain cases trade-offs need to be made between security and other features. That is, quality of service is an important consideration. In addition to technological solutions, legal aspects also have to be examined. That is, lawyers and engineers have to work together. Although much progress has been made on Web security, there is still a lot to be done as progress is made on Web technologies. Figure 3.7 illustrates aspects of Web security. For a discussion of Web security we refer the reader to [GHOS98].

3.9 Steps to Building Secure Systems

In this section we outline the steps to building secure systems. Note that our discussion is general and applicable to any secure system. However we may need to adapt the steps for individual systems. For example, to build secure distributed database systems we need secure database systems as well as secure networks. Therefore the multiple systems have to be composed.

The first step to building a secure system is developing a security policy. The policy can be stated in an informal language and then formalized. The policy essentially specifies the rules that the system must satisfy. Then the security architecture has to be developed. The architecture will include the security-critical components. These are the components that enforce the security policy and therefore should be trusted. The next step is to design the system. For example, if the system is a database system, the query processor, transaction manager, storage manager, and metadata manager modules are designed. The design of the system has to be analyzed for vulnerabilities. The next phase is the development phase. Once the system is implemented, it has to undergo security testing. This will include designing test cases and making sure that the security policy is not violated. Furthermore, depending on the level of assurance expected of the system, formal verification techniques may be used to verify and validate the system. Finally the system will be ready for evaluation. Note that initially systems were being evaluated using the Trusted Computer Systems Evaluation Criteria [TCSE85]. There are interpretations of these criteria for networks [TNI87] and for databases [TDI91]. There are also several companion documents for various concepts such as auditing and inference control. Note that more recently some other criteria have been developed including the Common Criteria and the Federal Criteria.

Note that before the system is installed in an operational environment, one needs to develop a concept of operation of the environment. Risk assessment has to be carried out. Once the system is installed, it has to be monitored so that security violations including unauthorized intrusions are detected. Figure 3.8 illustrates the steps. An overview of building secure systems can be found in [GASS88].

3.10 Summary and Directions

This chapter has provided a brief overview of the developments in secure systems. We first discussed basic concepts in access control as well as discretionary and mandatory policies. Then we provided an overview of secure systems. In particular, secure operating systems, secure databases, secure networks, and emerging technologies were discussed. Next we discussed the impact of the Web. Finally we discussed the steps to building secure systems.

Directions in secure database systems will be driven by the developments on the World Wide Web. Database systems are no longer stand-alone

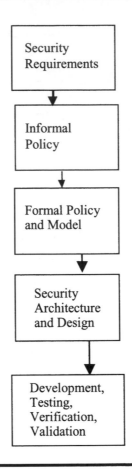

Figure 3.8 Building secure systems

systems. They are being integrated into various applications such as multimedia, electronic commerce, mobile computing systems, digital libraries, and collaboration systems. Therefore, security issues for all these new-generation systems will be very important. Furthermore, there are many developments on various object technologies such as distributed object systems, components, and frameworks. Security for such systems is being investigated. Eventually the security policies of the various subsystems and components have to be integrated to form policies for the entire system. There will be many challenges in formulating policies for such systems. New technologies such as data mining will help provide security solutions such as intrusion detection and auditing. However, these technologies could also violate the privacy of individuals. This is because adversaries can now use the mining tools and extract unauthorized information about various individuals. Finally, migrating legacy databases and applications will be a challenge. Security issues for such emerging systems and technologies cannot be overlooked.

To our knowledge this is the first book that provides a comprehensive and broad overview of the field of database and applications security. Some good books have been published in the past on database security that are focused on some specific topics. Notable among these are the books by Fernandez et al. [FERN81], Denning [DENN82], and Castano et al. [CAST95]. Notable books on information security in general include those by Gasser [GASS88], Anderson [ANDE00], and Bishop [BISH02]. As we have stated in Chapter 1, there are several conference series that have published interesting articles in database and applications security. These include IFIP Database Security Conferences [IFIP], IEEE Symposia on Security and Privacy [IEEE], Computer Security Applications Conferences [CSAC], National Computer Security Conference Series [NCSC], ACM Conference on Computer and Communications Systems [ACM], Symposia on Access Control Models and Technologies [SACM], and the European Symposia on Research in Computer Security [ESOR].

References

[ACM] *Proceedings of the ACM Conference Series on Computer and Communications Security.* ACM: New York.

[AFSB83] Air Force Studies Board, Committee on Multilevel Data Management Security, *Multilevel Data Management Security.* National Academy Press: Washington, DC, 1983.

[ANDE01] Anderson, R. *Security Engineering: A Guide to Building Dependable Distributed Systems.* Wiley: New York, 2001.

[BELL73] Bell, D. and LaPadula, L. Secure computer systems: Mathematical foundations and model. Technical Report M74-244. MITRE Corporation: Bedford, MA, 1973.

[BISH02] Bishop, M. *Computer Security: Art and Science.* Addison-Wesley: Reading, MA, 2002.

[CAST95] Castano, S. et al. *Database Security.* Addison-Wesley: Reading, MA, 1995.

[CSAC] *Proceedings of the Computer Security Applications Conference Series.* IEEE Computer Society Press: Los Alamitos, CA.

[DENN82] Denning, D. *Cryptography and Data Security.* Addison-Wesley: Reading, MA, 1982.

[ESOR] *Proceedings of the European Symposia Series on Research in Security and Privacy.* Springer-Verlag: Heidelberg.

[FERN81] Fernandez, E. et al. *Database Security and Integrity.* Addison-Wesley: Reading, MA, 1981.

[FERR00] Ferrari, E. and Thuraisingham, B. Secure database systems. In *Advances in Database Systems,* eds. M. Piatini and O. Diaz, Artech, London, UK, 2000.

[GASS88] Gasser, M. *Building a Secure Computer System.* Van Nostrand Reinhold: New York, 1988.

[GHOS98] Ghosh, A. *E-commerce Security, Weak Links and Strong Defenses.* Wiley: New York, 1998.

[GOGU82] Goguen, J. and Meseguer, J. Security policies and security models. In *Proceedings of the IEEE Symposium on Security and Privacy,* Oakland, CA, April 1982.

[HASS00] Hassler, V. *Security Fundamentals for E-Commerce.* Artech: London, UK, 2000.

[IEEE] *Proceedings of the IEEE Symposium on Research in Security and Privacy,* Oakland, CA. IEEE Computer Society Press, Los Alamitos, CA.

[IEEE83] *IEEE Computer.* Special issue on computer security 16: 7, 1983.

[IFIP] *Proceedings of the IFIP 11.3 Database Security Conference Series.* North Holland: Amsterdam; Chapman & Hall: London; Kluwer: Hingham, MA.

[JAJO90] Jajodia, S. and Kogan, B. Transaction processing in multilevel-secure databases using replicated architecture. In *Proceedings of the IEEE Symposium on Security and Privacy,* Oakland, CA, 1990.

[KAUF02] Kaufmann, C. et al. *Network Security: Private Communication in a Public World.* Pearson, 2002.

[NCSC] *Proceedings of the National Computer Security Conference Series.* National Computer Security Center and National Institute of Standards and Technology Publication, MD.

[NING04] Ning, P. et al. Techniques and tools for analyzing intrusion alerts. *ACM Transactions on Information and Systems Security* 7: 2, 2004.

[OMG] The Object Management Group. Available at www.omg.org.

[SACM] *Proceedings of the ACM Symposia Series on Access Control Models and Technologies.* ACM: New York.

[TCSE85] *Trusted Computer Systems Evaluation Criteria.* National Computer Security Center, Linthicum, MD, 1985.

[TDI91] *Trusted Database Interpretation.* National Computer Security Center, Linthicum, MD, 1991.

[TNI87] *Trusted Network Interpretation.* National Computer Security center, Linthicum, MD, 1987.

[TANN90] Tannenbaum, A. *Computer Networks.* Prentice-Hall: Upper Saddle River, NJ, 1990.

[THUR89] Thuraisingham, B. Mandatory security for object-oriented database systems. In *Proceedings of the ACM OOPOSLA Conference,* New Orleans, LA, October, 1989.

[THUR91] Thuraisingham, B. Multilevel security in distributed database systems. *Computers and Security* 10: 6, 1991.

[THUR93] Thuraisingham, B., Ford, W., and Collins, M. Design and implementation of a database inference controller. *Data and Knowledge Engineering Journal* 11: 3, 1993.

[THUR94] Thuraisingham, B. Multilevel security in federated database systems. *Computers and Security* 13: 6, 1994.

Exercises

1. Elaborate on the steps to designing a secure system for a secure database system.
2. Conduct a survey of network security technologies.
3. Select three secure operating system products and examine their features.
4. What are the important developments in database and applications security?
5. Select a topic in database and applications security and write a survey of this topic.
6. Compile a bibliography of the important papers in database and applications security.

Chapter 4

Information Management Technologies

4.1 Overview

The previous two chapters discussed the two key supporting technologies for database security: database management and information security. Because this book goes beyond database security and includes a discussion of applications security based on information management technologies, we consider information management to be a supporting technology for data and applications security. Therefore, in this chapter we provide a broad overview of various information management technologies.

Note that we have tried to separate data management and information management. That is, data management focuses on database systems technologies such as query processing, transaction management, and storage management. Information management is much broader than data management and we have included many topics in this category such as knowledge management and information retrieval. The organization of this chapter is as follows. Information retrieval is discussed in Section 4.2. Multimedia information management is the subject of Section 4.3. Digital libraries are discussed in Section 4.4. Knowledge management is discussed in Section 4.5. Collaboration is the subject of Section 4.6. E-commerce technologies are discussed in Section 4.7. The semantic Web and related technologies are discussed in Section 4.8. Wireless and sensor information management is the subject of Section 4.9. Real-time information management as well as quality-of-service issues are the subjects of Section 4.10.

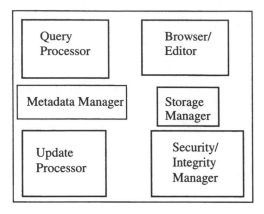

Figure 4.1 General-purpose information retrieval system architecture

High-performance computing technologies are the subject of Section 4.11. Some other information management technologies such as agents, visualization, and decision support systems are discussed in Section 4.12. The chapter is summarized in Section 4.13.

4.2 Information Retrieval Systems

In this section we discuss information retrieval systems. Information retrieval systems essentially provide support for managing documents. The functions include document retrieval, document update, and document storage management among others. These systems are essentially database management systems for managing documents. There are various types of information retrieval systems and they include text retrieval systems, image retrieval systems, and audio and video retrieval systems. Figure 4.1 illustrates a general-purpose information retrieval system that may be utilized for text retrieval, image retrieval, audio retrieval, and video retrieval. Such an architecture can also be utilized for a multimedia data management system. We discuss the special features of each type of information retrieval system (see also [THUR01]).

4.2.1 Text Retrieval

A text retrieval system is essentially a database management system for handling text data. Text data could be documents such as books, journals, magazines, and the like. One needs a good data model for document representation. A considerable amount of work has gone into developing semantic data models and object models for document management. For

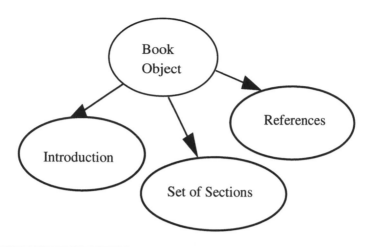

Figure 4.2   Data model for text

example, a document could have paragraphs and a paragraph could have sections, and so on, as shown in Figure 4.2.

Querying documents could be based on many factors. One could specify keywords and request the documents with the keywords to be retrieved. One could also retrieve documents that have some relationships with one another. Recent research on information retrieval is focusing on querying documents based on semantics. For example, "retrieve documents that describe scenic views" or "retrieve documents that are useful to children under ten years" are types of such queries.

Much of the information is now in textual form. This could be data on the Web, or library data, or electronic books, among others. One of the problems with text data is that it is not structured as relational data. In many cases it is unstructured and in some cases it is semistructured. Semistructured data, for example, is an article that has a title, author, abstract, and paragraphs. The paragraphs are not structured, whereas the format is structured.

Information retrieval systems and text-processing systems have been developed over the past few decades. Some of these systems are quite sophisticated and can retrieve documents by specifying attributes or key words. There are also text-processing systems that can retrieve associations between documents.

4.2.2 *Image Retrieval*

An image retrieval system is essentially a database management system for handling image data. Image data could be X-rays, pictures, satellite images, and photographs. One needs a good data model for image

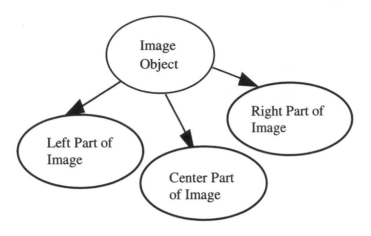

Figure 4.3 Data model for images

representation. Some work has gone into developing semantic data models and object models for image management. For example, image could consist of a right image and a left as shown in Figure 4.3 (an example is an X-ray of the lungs).

Querying images could be based on many factors. One could extract text from images and then query the text. One could tag images and then query the tags. One could also retrieve images from patterns. For example, an image could contain several squares. With a picture of a square, one could query the image and retrieve all the squares in the image. We can also query images depending on content. For example, "retrieve images that illustrate sunset" or "retrieve images that illustrate Victorian buildings" are types of queries.

Image processing has been around for quite a while. We have image-processing applications in various domains including medical imaging for cancer detection, processing satellite images for space and intelligence applications, and also handling hyperspectral images. Images include maps, geological structures, biological structures, and many other entities. Image processing has dealt with areas such as detecting abnormal patterns that deviate from the norm, retrieving images by content, and pattern matching.

4.2.3 Video Retrieval

A video retrieval system is essentially a database management system for handling video data. Video data could be documents such as books, journals, magazines, and the like. There are various issues that need to be considered. One needs a good data model for video representation.

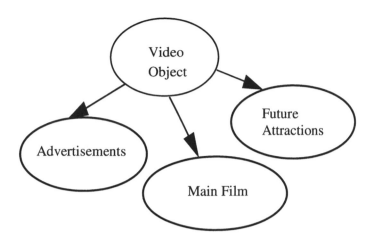

Figure 4.4 Data model for video

Some work has gone into developing semantic data models and object models for video data management (see [WOEL86]). For example, a video object could have advertisements, main film, and future attractions as shown in Figure 4.4.

Querying documents could be based on many factors. One could extract text from the video and query the text. One could also extract images from the video and query the images. One could store short video scripts and carry out pattern matching: that is, "find the video that contains the following script". Examples of queries include, "find films where the hero is John Wayne" or "find video scripts that show two presidents shaking hands". Recently there have been some efforts on mining video data.

4.2.4 Audio Retrieval

An audio retrieval system is essentially a database management system for handling audio data. Audio data could be documents such as books, journals, magazines, and the like. One needs a good data model for audio representation. Some work has gone into developing semantic data models and object models for audio data management (see [WOEL86]). For example, an audio object could have introductory remarks, speech, applause, and music as shown in Figure 4.5.

Querying documents could be based on many factors. One could extract text from the audio and query the text. One could store short audio scripts and carry out pattern matching: that is, "find the audio that contains the following script". Examples include, "find audio tapes containing the speeches of President John" or "find audio tapes of poems

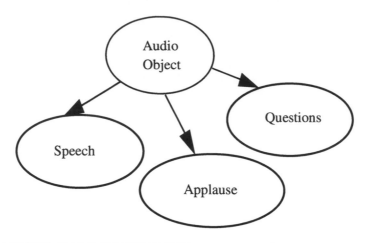

Figure 4.5 Data model for audio

recited by female narrators". Recently there have been some efforts on audio mining [IEEE03].

4.3 Multimedia Data and Information Management

In Section 4.2 we discussed retrieval for individual data types such as text, images, video, and audio. These are what we call information retrieval systems. However, we need to manage combinations of data types and the systems that manage them are multimedia database systems (see also [PRAB97] and [WOEL86]).

A MultiMedia DataBase Management System (MM/DBMS) provides support for storing, manipulating, and retrieving multimedia data from a multimedia database. In a sense, a multimedia database system is a type of heterogeneous database system, as it manages heterogeneous data types. Heterogeneity is due to the medium of the data such as text, video, and audio.

An MM/DBMS must provide support for typical database management system functions. These include query processing, update processing, transaction management, storage management, metadata management, security, and integrity. In addition, in many cases, the various types of data such as voice and video have to be synchronized for display and, therefore, real-time processing is also a major issue in an MM/DBMS. The functional architecture of a MM/DBMS is similar to the architecture illustrated in Figure 4.1 with the information retrieval manager being replaced by the multimedia data manager.

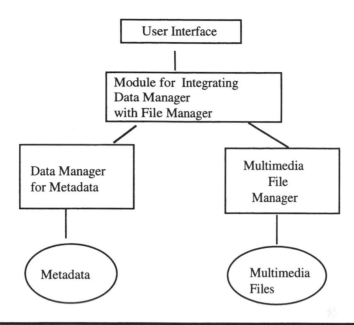

Figure 4.6   Loose coupling architecture

Various architectures are being examined to design and develop an MM/DBMS. In one approach, the DBMS is used just to manage the metadata, and a multimedia file manager is used to manage the multimedia data. There is a module for integrating the DBMS and the multimedia file manager. In this case, the MM/DBMS consists of three modules: (1) the DBMS managing the metadata, (2) the multimedia file manager, and (3) the module for integrating the two. The loose coupling architecture is illustrated in Figure 4.6.

The second architecture is the tight coupling approach illustrated in Figure 4.7. In this architecture, the DBMS manages both the multimedia database as well as the metadata. That is, the DBMS is an MM/DBMS. The tight coupling architecture has an advantage because all of the DBMS functions could be applied on the multimedia database. This includes query processing, transaction management, metadata management, storage management, and security and integrity management. Note that with the loose coupling approach, unless the file manager performs the DBMS functions, the DBMS only manages the metadata for the multimedia data.

There are also other aspects to architectures as discussed in [THUR97]. For example, a multimedia database system could use a commercial database system such as an object-oriented database system to manage multimedia objects. However, relationships between objects and the representation of temporal relationships may involve extensions to the database

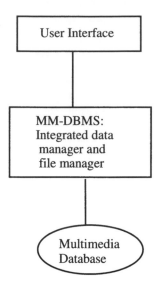

Figure 4.7 Tight coupling architecture

management system. That is, a DBMS together with an extension layer provides complete support to manage multimedia data. In the alternative case, both the extensions and the database management functions are integrated so that there is one database management system to manage multimedia objects as well as the relationships between the objects. Further details of these architectures as well as managing multimedia databases are discussed in [THUR01]. Note that a discussion of extensible database systems was given in Chapter 2. Multimedia databases could also be distributed. In this case, we assume that each MM/DBMS is augmented with a Multimedia Distributed Processor (MDP). The distributed architecture is illustrated in Figure 4.8.

4.4 Digital Libraries

4.4.1 Overview

Digital libraries gained prominence with the initial effort by the National Science Foundation (NSF), Defense Advanced Research Projects Agency (DARPA), and National Aeronautical and Space Administration (NASA). NSF continued to fund special projects in this area and, as a result, the field has grown very rapidly. The idea behind digital libraries is to digitize all types of documents and provide efficient access to these digitized documents.

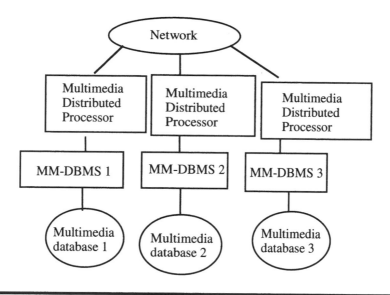

Figure 4.8   Distributed MM/DBMS

Several technologies have to work together to make digital libraries a reality. These include Web data management, markup languages, search engines, and question-answering systems. In addition, multimedia information management as well as information retrieval systems play an important role. This section reviews the various developments in some of the digital library technologies.

The organization of this section is as follows. We discuss Web data management in Section 4.4.2. Markup languages are discussed in Section 4.4.3. Search engines are discussed in Section 4.4.4. A note on question-answering systems is discussed in Section 4.4.5.

4.4.2 *Web Database Management*

This section discusses the core concepts in Web data management. A major challenge for Web data management researchers and practitioners is coming up with an appropriate data representation scheme. The question is whether there is a need for a standard data model for Web database systems. Is it at all possible to develop such a standard? If so, what are the relationships between the standard model and the individual models used by the databases on the Web?

Database management functions for the Web include those such as query processing, metadata management, security, and integrity. In [THUR00] we have examined various database management system functions and

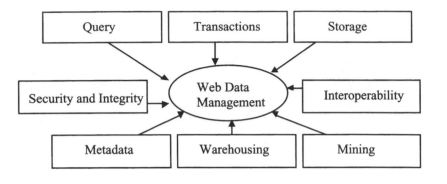

Figure 4.9   Web database management

discussed the impact of Web database access on these functions. Some of the issues are discussed here. Figure 4.9 illustrates the functions. Querying and browsing are two of the key functions. First of all, an appropriate query language is needed. Inasmuch as SQL is a popular language, appropriate extensions to SQL may be desired. XML-QL, which has evolved from XML (eXtensible Markup Language, discussed later) and SQL, is moving in this direction. Query processing involves developing a cost model. Are there special cost models for Internet database management? With respect to the browsing operation, the query-processing techniques have to be integrated with techniques for following links. That is, hypermedia technology has to be integrated with database management technology.

Updating Web databases could mean different things. One could create a new Web site, place servers at that site, and update the data managed by the servers. The question is can a user of the library send information to update the data at a Web site. An issue here is with security privileges. If the user has write privileges, then he could update the databases that he is authorized to modify. Agents and mediators could be used to locate the databases as well as to process the update.

Transaction management is essential for many applications. There may be new kinds of transactions on the Web. For example, various items may be sold through the Internet. In this case, the item should not be locked immediately when a potential buyer makes a bid. It has to be left open until several bids are received and the item is sold. That is, special transaction models are needed. Appropriate concurrency control and recovery techniques have to be developed for the transaction models.

Metadata management is a major concern for Web data management. The question is what is metadata. Metadata describes all of the information pertaining to the library. This could include the various Web sites, the types of users, access-control issues, and policies enforced. Where should the metadata be located? Should each participating site maintain its own metadata? Should the metadata be replicated or should there be a centralized metadata repository? Metadata in such an environment could be very dynamic especially because the users and the Web sites may be changing continuously.

Storage management for Web database access is a complex function. Appropriate index strategies and access methods for handling multimedia data are needed. In addition, due to the large volumes of data, techniques for integrating database management technology with mass storage technology are also needed. Other data management functions include integrating heterogeneous databases, managing multimedia data, and mining. We discussed them in [THUR02a].

4.4.3 Markup Languages

In general, markup languages provide the support to tag an entity of interest. These entities could be a person, place, or some object. Markup languages can provide structure to unstructured data such as text. One of the earliest markup languages is SGML (Standard Generalized Markup Language). Details of this language can be found in numerous texts including [SGML]. We briefly discuss some of the essential points in this section.

SGML is a descriptive language as opposed to being a procedural language. Essentially it uses markup codes to mark up the document. Note that procedural languages specify the processing to be carried out. In SGML, instructions to process the document are separated from the descriptive markup, which is the set of markup codes. With descriptive markup, the document can be independent of the system, which processes it. One can mark up the names, the places, or entities, and the processing program can handle various parts of the document.

Document type and Document Type Definitions (DTDs) are introduced in SGML and are now used in XML also. Documents have types. The type is defined by the structure of the document. For example, a book document type may contain title, front matter, introduction, set of chapters, references, appendices, and index. A document parser can check to see if the document conforms to its specified type.

The design goal of SGML was to ensure that a document written in one system could be transported to another without any loss of information. This means that there has to be a way of representing strings, numbers, and so on in a machine-independent way. SGML provokes support for such representations. Essentially there has to be a way to consistently represent various strings, letters, and characters.

It is impossible to give an overview of SGML in a few paragraphs. Nevertheless we have discussed some of the key points. One of the major

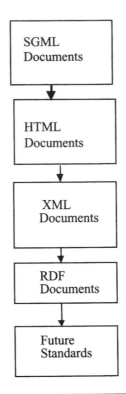

Figure 4.10 Markup languages

success stories of SGML is the development of XML. XML has been influenced by the developments with SGML and is the product of W3C (the World Wide Web Consortium). XML evolved from HTML and SGML. Furthermore, XML was primarily developed to tag text. However, XML is now being used to tag all kinds of documents including images, video, audio, and multimedia documents. XML is also being used for music and math as well as E-business documents. Essentially XML has become key to the exchange of not only text documents but also other types of documents, including relations and tables on the Web. More details on XML can be found in [LAUR00]. Also the next step to markup languages is RDF (Resource Description Framework). RDF uses the syntax of XML and also specifies semantics. It is the product of W3C. Some details are given in [THUR02a]. The evolution of markup languages is illustrated in Figure 4.10.

4.4.4 Search Engines

Since the early 1990s, numerous search engines have been developed. They have origins in the information retrieval systems developed in the

1960s and beyond. Typically when we invoke a browser such as Netscape or Microsoft's Explorer, we have access to several search engines. Some of the early search engines were Altavista, Yahoo, Infoseek, and Lycos. These systems were around in 1995 and were fairly effective for their times. They are much improved now. Since around 1999, one of the popular search engines has been Google. It started off as a Stanford University research project funded by organizations such as the National Science Foundation and the Central Intelligence Agency as well as the industry, and was later commercialized. Systems such as Google as well as some of the other search engines provide intelligent searches. However, they still have a long way to go before users can get exact answers to their queries.

Search engines are accessed via browsers. When you click on the search engines, you will get a window requesting what you want to search for. Then you list the keywords that you are searching for. The question is how does a search engine find the Web pages. It essentially uses information retrieval on the Web.

The rating of a search engine is determined by the speed with which it produces results and, more important, the accuracy with which it produces the results. That is, does the search engine list the relevant Web pages for the query? For example, when you type a query called "lung cancer", does it provide the relevant information you are looking for with respect to lung cancer? It can, for example, list resources about lung cancer or list information about who has had lung cancer. Usually people want to get resources about lung cancer. If they want to find out who has lung cancer then they could type in "people with lung cancer".

The problem with many searches, although extremely useful, is that they often provide a lot of irrelevant information. To get accurate results, they have to build sophisticated indexing techniques. They also may cache information from Web servers for frequently posed queries. Some typical modules of a search engine are illustrated in Figure 4.11. The search engines have a directory of the various Web servers they have to search. This directory is updated as new servers enter. Then the search engines build indices for the various keywords. When a user poses a query, the search engine will consult its knowledge base, which consists of information about the Web servers and various indices. It also examines the caches if it has any, and will then search the Web servers for the information. All this has to be carried out in real-time.

Web mining enables one to mine the user log and build profiles for the various users so that search can be made more efficient. Note that there are millions of users and building profiles is not straightforward. We need to mine the Web logs and find out what the preferences of the users are. Then we list those Web pages for the user. Furthermore, if a user is

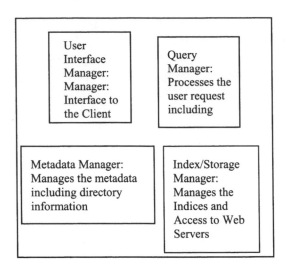

Figure 4.11 Modules of the search engines

searching for certain information, from time to time, the search engines can list Web pages that could be relevant to the user's request. That is, search engines will have to dynamically carry out searches depending on what the user wants.

4.4.5 Question-Answering Systems

Question-answering systems are a sort of the early information retrieval systems that were developed in the late 1960s. They would typically give yes or no answers. Since then there have been many advances in information retrieval systems including text, image, and video systems. However, with the advent of the Web, the question-answering systems have received much prominence. They are not just limited to a yes or no answer. They give answers to various complex queries such as, "What is the weather forecast today in Chicago?" or "Retrieve the flight schedules from London to Tokyo that make at most one stop".

The various search engines such as Google are capable of doing complex searches. But they are yet to answer complex queries. The research on question-answering systems is just beginning and we can expect search engines to have this capability. Question-answering systems integrate many technologies including natural language processing, information retrieval, search engines, and data management. This is illustrated in Figure 4.12.

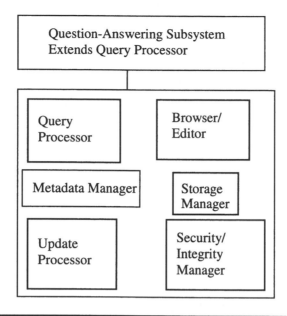

Figure 4.12   Question-answering and text retrieval

4.5 Knowledge Management

Knowledge management is the process of using knowledge as a resource to manage an organization. It could mean sharing expertise, developing a learning organization, teaching the staff, and learning from experiences, as well as collaboration. Essentially knowledge management will include data management and information management. However, this is not a view shared by everyone. Various definitions of knowledge management have been proposed. Knowledge management is a discipline invented mainly by business schools. The concepts have been around for a long time. But the term "knowledge management" was coined as a result of information technology and the Web.

In the collection of papers on knowledge management by Morey et al. [MORE01], knowledge management is divided into three areas. These are strategies such as building a knowledge company and making the staff knowledge workers, processes (such as techniques) for knowledge management including developing a method to share documents and tools, and metrics that measure the effectiveness of knowledge management. In the *Harvard Business Review* there is an excellent collection of articles on knowledge management describing a knowledge-creating company, building a learning organization, and teaching people how to learn

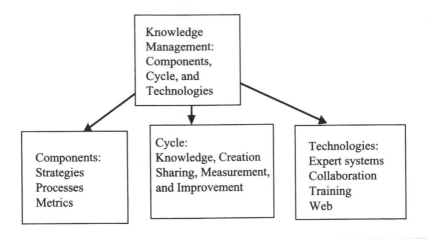

Figure 4.13 Knowledge management components and technologies

[HARV96]. Organizational behavior and team dynamics play major roles in knowledge management.

Knowledge management technologies include several information management technologies including knowledge representation and knowledge-base management systems. Other knowledge management technologies include collaboration tools and tools for organizing information on the Web, as well as tools for measuring the effectiveness of the knowledge gained such as collecting various metrics. Knowledge management technologies essentially include data management and information management technologies as well as decision support technologies. Figure 4.13 illustrates some of the knowledge management components and technologies. It also lists aspects of the knowledge management cycle. Web technologies play a major role in knowledge management. Knowledge management and the Web are closely related. Although knowledge management practices have existed for many years, it is the Web that has promoted knowledge management.

Many corporations now have intranets and an intranet is the single most powerful knowledge management tool. Thousands of employees are connected through the Web in an organization. Large corporations have sites all over the world and the employees are becoming well connected with one another. E-mail can be regarded as one of the early knowledge management tools. Now there are many tools such as search engines and E-commerce tools.

With the proliferation of Web data management and E-commerce tools, knowledge management will become an essential part of the Web and E-commerce. A collection of papers on knowledge management experiences including strategies, processes, and metrics is given in [MORE01]. Collaborative knowledge management is discussed in [THUR02b].

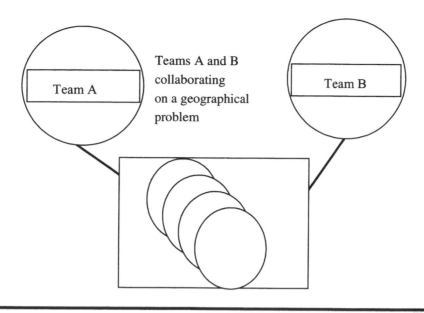

Figure 4.14   Collaboration example

4.6 Collaboration and Data Management

Although the notion of Computer-Supported Cooperative Work (CSCW) was first proposed in the early 1980s, it was only in the 1990s that much interest was shown on this topic. Collaborative computing enables people, groups of individuals, and organizations to work together to accomplish a task or a collection of tasks. These tasks could vary from participating in conferences, solving a specific problem, or working on the design of a system (see [ACM91]).

One aspect of collaborative computing of particular interest to the database community is workflow computing. Workflow is defined as the automation of a series of functions that comprise a business process such as data entry, data review, and monitoring performed by one or more people. An example of a process that is well suited for workflow automation is the purchasing process. Some early commercial workflow system products targeted for office environments were based on a messaging architecture. This architecture supports the distributed nature of current workteams. However, the messaging architecture is usually file-based and lacks many of the features supported by database management systems such as data representation, consistency management, tracking, and monitoring. The emerging workflow systems utilize data management capabilities.

Figure 4.14 illustrates an example where teams A and B are working on a meterological problem such as analyzing and predicting the weather

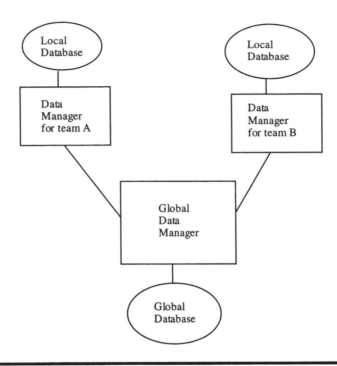

Figure 4.15 Data management support for collaboration

in North America. The two teams must have a global picture of the map as well as any notes that go with it. Any changes made by one team should be instantly visible to the other team, with both teams communicating as if they were in the same room.

To enable such transparent communication, data management support is needed. One could utilize a database management system to manage the data or some type of data manager that provides some of the essential features such as data integrity, concurrent access, and retrieval capabilities. In the above example, the database may consist of information describing the problem the teams are working on, the data that is involved, and history data, as well as the metadata information. The data manager must provide appropriate concurrency control features so that when both teams simultaneously access the common picture and make changes, these changes are coordinated.

One possible scenario for the data manager is illustrated in Figure 4.15 where each team has its own local data manager and there is a global data manager to maintain any global information, including the data and the metadata. The local data managers communicate with the global data manager. The global data manager illustrated in this figure is at the logical level. At the physical level the global data manager may also be distributed.

The data managers coordinate their activities to provide features such as concurrency control, integrity, and retrieval.

The Web has increased the need for collaboration even further. Users now share documents on the Web and work on papers and designs on the Web. Corporate information infrastructure promotes collaboration and sharing of information and documents. Therefore, the collaborative tools have to work effectively on the Web. More details are given in [IEEE99].

4.7 E-Commerce Technologies

Various models, architectures, and technologies are being developed. Business-to-business E-commerce is all about two businesses conducting transactions on the Web. For example, suppose corporation A is an automobile manufacturer and needs microprocessors to be installed in its automobiles. It will then purchase the microprocessors from corporation B who manufactures the microprocessors. Another example is when an individual purchases some goods such as toys from a toy manufacturer. This manufacturer then contacts a packaging company via the Web to deliver the toys to the individual. The transaction between the manufacturer and the packaging company is a business-to-business transaction. Business-to-business E-commerce also involves one business purchasing a unit of another business or two businesses merging. The main point is that such transactions have to be carried out on the Web. Business-to-consumer E-commerce is when a consumer such as a member of the mass population makes purchases on the Web. In the toy manufacturer example, the purchase between the individual and the toy manufacturer is a business-to-consumer transaction.

The modules of the E-commerce server may include modules for managing the data and Web pages, mining customer information, and security enforcement, as well as transaction management. E-commerce client functions may include presentation management and the user interface as well as caching data and hosting browsers. There could also be a middle tier, which may implement the business objects to carry out the business functions of E-commerce. These business functions may include brokering, mediation, negotiations, purchasing, sales, marketing, and other E-commerce functions. The E-commerce server functions are affected by the information management technologies for the Web. In addition to the data management functions and the business functions, the E-commerce functions also include those for managing distribution, heterogeneity, and federations.

E-commerce also includes nontechnological aspects such as policies, laws, social impacts, and psychological impacts. We are now doing business in an entirely different way and therefore we need a paradigm shift.

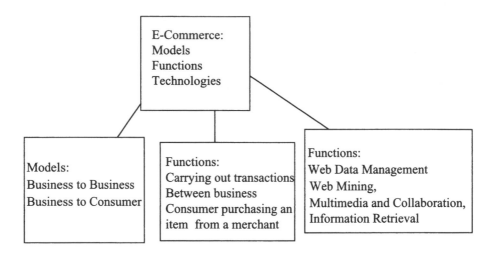

Figure 4.16   E-commerce models, functions, and technologies

We cannot do successful E-commerce if we still want the traditional way of buying and selling products. We have to be more efficient and rely on the technologies a lot more to gain a competitive edge. Some key points for E-commerce are illustrated in Figure 4.16.

4.8 Semantic Web Technologies

The semantic Web essentially is about machine-understandable Web pages. Tim Berners Lee has specified various layers for the semantic Web (see Figure 4.17). At the lowest level one has the protocols for communication including TCP/IP (Transmission Control Protocol/Internet Protocol), HTTP (HyperText Transfer Protocol), and SSL (Secure Socket Layer). The next level is the XML layer that also includes XML schemas. The next level is the RDF layer. Next comes the Ontologies and Interoperability layer. This is followed by the Query and Rules layer. Finally at the highest level one has the Trust Management layer. Each of the layers is discussed below.

TCP/IP, SSL, and HTTP are the protocols for data transmission. They are built on top of more basic communication layers. With these protocols one can transmit the Web pages over the Internet. At this level one does not deal with syntax or the semantics of the documents. Then comes the XML and XML Schemas layer. XML is the standard representation language for document exchange. For example, if a document is not marked up, then each machine may display the document in its own way. This makes document exchange extremely difficult. XML is a markup language that follows certain rules and if all documents are marked up using XML then

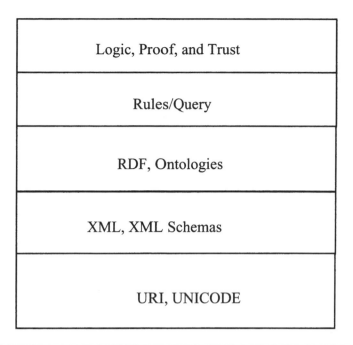

Logic, Proof, and Trust
Rules/Query
RDF, Ontologies
XML, XML Schemas
URI, UNICODE

Figure 4.17   Layers for the semantic Web

there is uniform representation and presentation of documents. This is one of the significant developments of the WWW. Without some form of common representation of documents, it is impossible to have any sort of meaningful communication on the Web. XML schemas essentially describe the structure of the XML documents. Both XML and XML schemas are the invention of Tim Berners Lee and the W3C (see [LAUR00]).

Now XML focuses only on the syntax of the document. A document could have different interpretations at different sites. This is a major issue for integrating information seamlessly across the Web. In order to overcome this significant limitation, W3C started discussions on a language called RDF in the late 1990s. RDF essentially uses XML syntax but has support to express semantics. One needs to use RDF for integrating and exchanging information in a meaningful way on the Web. Although XML has received widespread acceptance, RDF is only now beginning to get acceptance. XML documents are exchanged over protocols such as TCP/IP, HTTP, and SSL and RDF documents are built using XML.

The next layer is the Ontologies and Interoperability layer. Now RDF is only a specification language for expressing syntax and semantics. The question is what entities do we need to specify. How can the community accept common definitions? To solve this issue, various communities such as the medical community, financial community, defense community, and even the entertainment community have come up with what are called ontologies. One could use ontologies to describe the various wines of the world or the different types of aircraft used by the United States Air Force. Ontologies can also be used to specify various diseases or financial entities. Once a community has developed ontologies, the community has to publish these ontologies on the Web. The idea is that for anyone interested in the ontologies developed by a community to use those ontologies. Now, within a community there could be different factions and each faction could come up with its own ontologies. For example, the American Medical Association could come up with its onotologies for diseases and the British Medical Association could come up with its own ontologies. This poses a challenge as the system and in this case the semantic Web has to examine the ontologies and decide how to develop some common ontologies. Although the goal is for the British and American communities to agree and come up with common ontologies, in the real world differences do exist. The next question is what do ontologies do for the Web. Now, using these ontologies, different groups can communicate information. That is, ontologies facilitate information exchange and integration. Ontologies are used by Web services so that the Web can provide semantic Web services to the humans. Ontologies may be specified using RDF syntax.

The Query and Rules layer is responsible for querying the Web resources as well as using the Web rules language to support various policies. The final layer is logic, proof, and trust. The idea here is how do you trust the information on the Web. Obviously it depends on from whom it comes. How do you carry out trust negotiation? That is, interested parties have to communicate with each other and determine how to trust each other and how to trust the information obtained on the Web. Closely related to trust issues is security, which is discussed later. Logic-based approaches and proof theories are being examined for enforcing trust on the semantic Web.

4.9 Wireless and Sensor Information Management

During the past decade we have heard a lot about mobile information management or wireless information management. Mobile agents are an important aspect of wireless information management, however, there are many other issues that have to be taken into consideration.

In today's world, we are becoming more and more wireless with handheld devices, personal digital assistants, and even laptop personal computers. Managing the information and representing the information displayed on wireless devices is becoming critical. Various standards are

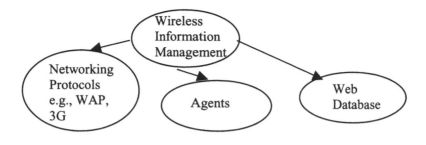

Figure 4.18 Wireless information technologies

being proposed for wireless technology. These include networking standards as well as information management standards. For example, WAP (Wireless Access Protocol) enables information on disks to be displayed on wireless devices such as mobile phones. More recently there are the 3G (third generation) wireless protocols. Finally XML extensions have also been proposed for wireless technologies.

The database community has been examining data management issues for mobile computing for the past decade [IMIE92]. These include query-processing techniques as well as indexing strategies. In addition, data modeling and display technologies have been examined for wireless technologies. We also need to investigate information retrieval for wireless information systems. Figure 4.18 illustrates wireless information management technologies.

Pervasive computing in a way encompasses wireless technologies. We assume here that there are computers everywhere embedded or otherwise. Closely related to wireless information management and pervasive computing is sensor information management. There are sensors all over the place and information sometimes in the form of streams is gathered and managed. For example, transportation services use sensors. Various government agencies use sensors to track individuals, vehicles, and other entities. A lot of data emanates from sensors. This data is in the form of streams and is continuous.

There is a lot of research now on managing sensor data. Various efforts have been reported on developing sensor database management systems. Query processing and optimization for sensor data processing has also received lot of attention (see, for example, [SIGM01]). All of these data streams have to be mined. That is, sensor data and information mining are becoming an important area. Figure 4.19 illustrates the notion of what is known as the sensor Web. Security and privacy are becoming critical for sensor information management and are discussed in Part X.

Note that wireless technologies emerged from the developments in telecommunications technologies. Telecommunications is all about transmitting

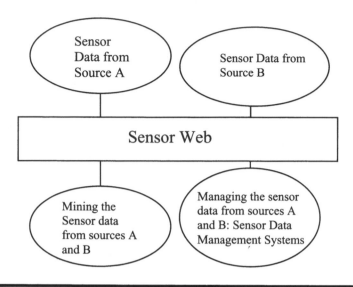

Figure 4.19   Sensor information management

information from one place to another. The technologies include wireless technologies and telegraph and telephone technologies, as well as fiber optic technologies. We briefly discuss secure information management for telecommunications in Part X.

4.10 Real-Time Processing and Quality-of-Service Aspects

There are so many Web data management technologies such as database management, security, multimedia, and integrity that it will be a challenge to make all of them work together effectively. For example, how can we guarantee that the stock information meets the timing constraints for delivery to the trader and yet maintain one hundred percent security? This will be very difficult. If we add the task of ensuring integrity of the data and techniques for recovering from faults, and presenting multimedia data in a timely manner, the problem becomes nearly impossible to solve. So the question is what do we do. This is when quality of service, popularly known as QoS comes in. It is almost impossible to satisfy all of the requirements all of the time. So, QoS specifies policies for trade-offs. For example, if security and real-time are both constraints that have to be met, then perhaps in some instances it is not absolutely necessary to meet all the timing constraints and we need to focus on security. In other instances, meeting timing constraints may be crucial. As another example,

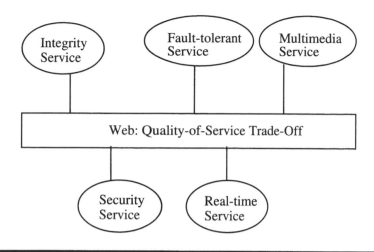

Figure 4.20   Quality-of-service trade-offs

consider multimedia presentation. In some instances we can live with low resolution whereas at other times we may need perfect pictures.

Recently there has been a lot of work on QoS. But we have yet to find a model that takes into consideration all factors for quality of service. This is a difficult problem and with so many research efforts under way we can expect to see progress. Essentially the user specifies what she wants and the user requirements get mapped down to the database system, operating system, and the networking requirements. Figure 4.20 illustrates an approach to QoS on the Web. The ideas are rather preliminary and a lot needs to be done.

4.11 High-Performance Computing Technologies

High-performance computing technologies include parallel processing technologies and more recently grid computing technologies. Parallel processing is a subject that has been around for a while. The area has developed significantly from single processor systems to multiprocessor systems. Multiprocessor systems could be distributed systems or they could be centralized systems with shared memory multiprocessors or with shared-nothing multiprocessors. There has been a lot of work on using parallel architectures for database processing (see, for example, [IEEE89]). Although considerable work was carried out, these systems did not take off commercially until the development of data warehousing. Many of the data warehouses employ parallel processors to speed up query processing.

In a parallel database system, the various operations and functions are executed in parallel. Research on parallel database systems began in the 1970s, but it is only recently that we are seeing these systems being used for commercial applications. This is partly due to the explosion of data warehousing and data-mining technologies where the performance of query algorithms is critical.

Let us consider a query operation that involves a join operation between two relations. If these relations are to be sorted first before the join, then the sorting can be done in parallel. We can take it a step further and execute a single join operation with multiple processors. Note that multiple tuples are involved in a join operation from both relations. Join operations between the tuples may be executed in parallel.

Many of the commercial database system vendors are now marketing parallel database management technology. This is an area we can expect to grow significantly over the next decade. One of the major challenges here is the scalability of various algorithms for functions such as data warehousing and data mining. Many of the data-mining techniques are computationally intensive. Appropriate hardware and software are needed to scale the data-mining techniques. Database vendors are using parallel processing machines to carry out data mining.

More recently grid computing is making a major impact on high-performance computing. The idea is to use clusters of computing systems including database systems to carry out various functions in parallel. The challenge is to allocate resources to various tasks so that high-performance computing applications can be executed efficiently. Figure 4.21 illustrates various high-performance computing technologies.

4.12 Some Other Information Management Technologies

4.12.1 Overview

This chapter has discussed various technologies and services for the Web. Much of our discussion was focused on collaboration, knowledge management, wireless information management, and E-commerce. Technologies for accessing the resources on the Web as well as processing these resources are critical for effective data management on the Web. Figure 4.22 illustrates how a distributed object management system can integrate the various technologies and services to provide effective Web data and information management.

There are several other technologies we have not mentioned and we briefly discuss them in this section. For example, visualization technologies

High Performance Computing
Technologies:

Parallel Processing
Real-time Computing
Grid Computing
Cluster Computing
Embedded System Technologies
Dependable Computing

Figure 4.21   High-performance computing technologies

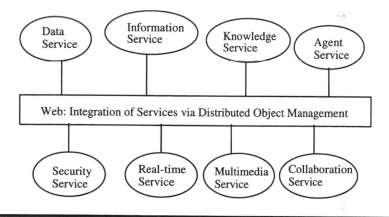

Figure 4.22   Integration of services on the Web

are useful to better understand the data in the database. Many of the technologies such as data, information, and knowledge management are being used ultimately for managers, policy makers, and other people in authority to make effective decisions. Therefore, decision support is an important technology area for the Web as in the future we can expect these managers and policy makers to access the Web and, based on the information they get, make effective decisions. Agent technology is essential for technologies such as the semantic Web. There are different types of agents. Some agents locate resources, some carry out mediation, and some are mobile and execute in different environments. A Java applet can be regarded as a simple agent. Peer-to-peer data management is an emerging technology for peers to share resources and solve problems.

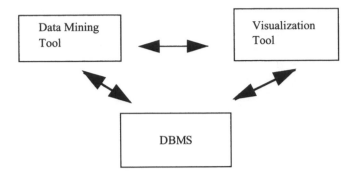

Figure 4.23 Visualization

The organization of this section is as follows. In Section 4.12.2 we discuss visualization technologies. Decision support is discussed in Section 4.12.3. Agents are discussed in Section 4.12.4. Peer-to-peer data management is discussed in Section 4.12.5.

4.12.2 Visualization

Visualization technologies graphically display the data in the databases. Much research has been conducted on visualization and the field has advanced a great deal especially with the advent of multimedia computing. For example, the data in the databases could be several rows of numerical values. Visualization tools take the data and plot them in some form of a graph. The visualization models could be two-dimensional, three-dimensional, or even higher. Recently, several visualization tools have been developed to integrate with databases, and workshops are devoted to this topic [VIS95]. An example illustration of integration of a visualization package with a database system is shown in Figure 4.23.

More recently there has been a lot of discussion on using visualization for data mining. There has also been some discussion on using data mining to help the visualization process (see [GRIN95]). As data-mining techniques mature, it will be important to integrate them with visualization techniques (see also [THUR96]).

4.12.3 Decision Support

Although data mining deals with discovering patterns from the data and machine-learning deals with learning from experiences to do predictions as well as analysis, decision support systems are tools that managers use to make effective decisions. They are based on decision theory. One can

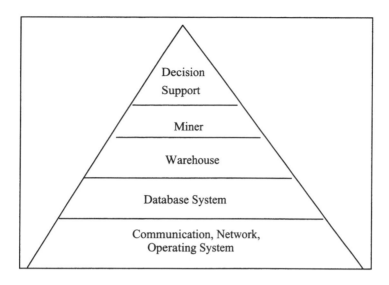

Figure 4.24   Decision support

consider data-mining tools to be special kinds of decision support tools. So are tools based on machine-learning, as well as tools for extracting data from data warehouses. Decision support tools belong to a broad category (see [TURB00]).

In general, decision support tools could also be tools that remove unnecessary and irrelevant results obtained from data mining. These pruning tools could also be decision support tools. They could also be tools such as spreadsheets, expert systems, hypertext systems, Web information management systems, and any other system that helps analysts and managers to effectively manage the large quantities of data and information.

In summary, we believe that decision support is a technology that overlaps data mining, data warehousing, knowledge management, machine learning, statistics, and other technologies that help to manage an organization's knowledge and data. We illustrate related decision support technologies in Figure 4.24.

4.12.4 Agents

Agents are essentially processes that carry out various tasks. Agents communicate with each other using various agent protocols. KQML (Knowledge Query Manipulation Language) is an example of an agent communication language. Various types of agents have been defined. These include locator agents that typically locate resources on the Web,

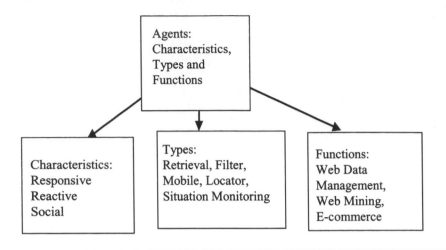

Figure 4.25 Agents

query agents that query the databases, intelligent agents that read and understand Web pages, and mobile agents that execute programs at different nodes. An agent could be as simple as a program that executes, say, a Java applet, or it could be a complex process that coordinates activities and schedules appointments.

Agents are a key supporting technology for the semantic Web. That is, agents are the processes that collaboratively work together to solve problems, understand Web pages, and coordinate events. DARPA's DAML (DARPA Agent Markup Language) program has developed agent technologies for the semantic Web. Various standards have also been proposed for agent communication. In addition, researchers have examined security for agents as well as examined agents that function in real-time (see [MILO99] and [DIPP99]). Figure 4.25 provides an overview of agents. More details can be found in [THUR00].

4.12.5 Peer-to-Peer Data Management

In Chapter 2 we discussed federated data management and in Section 4.4 we discussed collaborative data management. Federated data management is about organizations forming federations and working together and sharing data. Collaborative data management is about individuals working together collaboratively on projects and sharing data and resources. A closely related concept is peer-to-peer data management. Here the nodes act as peers and work together to carry out a task. If a node does not have the resources, then it communicates with its peers. All peers are treated the same way.

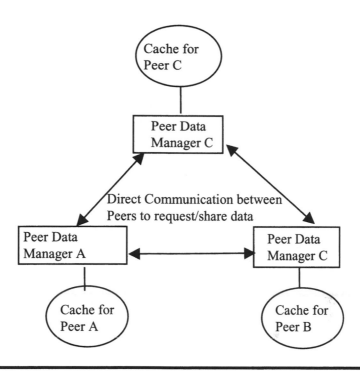

Figure 4.26   Peer-to-peer data management

There has been much research recently on peer-to-peer computing, peer-to-peer networking, and peer-to-peer data management. No one peer can have all the resources. Therefore, the resources are managed by different peers and shared so that the peers can carry out the tasks. There has been much discussion recently as to the similarities and differences between the various terms such as federated data management, collaborative data management, grid data management, and peer-to-peer data management. We have tried to discuss the key points of the various systems. More details on peer-to-peer data management can be found in [TATA03]. We discuss security issues in Chapter 26. Figure 4.26 illustrates peer-to-peer data management.

4.13 Summary and Directions

This chapter has provided an overview of a number of information management technologies. These include information retrieval, multimedia, collaboration, and knowledge management, as well as technologies such as sensor information management and E-commerce. There is still a lot to be done in information management especially with respect to managing large quantities of data and information on the Web.

This chapter essentially provides the background for an exploration of applications security in this book. In particular, visualization of security policies is part of Chapter 6. Chapter 20 discusses secure multimedia data and information management. Chapter 21 includes a discussion of secure decision support when we discuss secure data warehousing. Chapter 24 discusses security for Web databases as well as secure information retrieval and digital libraries. Chapter 25 discusses security for the semantic Web. Some aspects of secure agents are also discussed in Chapter 25 inasmuch as agents are a supporting technology for the semantic Web. Chapter 26 discusses secure knowledge management, and collaboration as well as E-commerce. In addition, Chapter 26 also discusses some other emerging aspects such as secure peer-to-peer data management as well as security for virtual databases. Secure dependable data management, which includes a discussion of quality-of-service and real-time processing issues, is discussed in Chapter 27. Secure sensor and wireless information management is discussed in Chapter 28. Secure high-performance computing technologies are discussed in multiple chapters. For example, security and parallel data management are discussed in Chapter 5. Secure grid computing is discussed in Chapter 25. The above discussion shows that every information management technology discussed here is examined for security in Parts II through X.

Note that there are also many other information management technologies that have security considerations. These include multilingual translations, text summarization, robotics and vision, e-mail filtering, and electronic voting systems. It is impossible for us to list all of the information management technologies in this chapter. However, some of the security considerations are briefly discussed in Chapter 29.

Various conferences are now devoted to specific information management technologies. For example, the annual ACM SIGIR Conference Series focuses on information retrieval [SIGI] and the ACM Multimedia Conference Series focuses on all aspects of multimedia technologies [MULT]. Conferences on knowledge management, E-commerce, sensors, and real-time processing also take place frequently. We list them as needed throughout this book.

References

[ACM91] Special issue on computer-supported cooperative work. *Communications of the ACM*, 34: 12, December 1991.

[DIPP99] DiPippo, L., Hodys, E., and Thuraisingham, B. Towards a real-time agent architecture: A white paper. In *Proceedings of IEEE WORDS*, Monterey, CA, 1999.

[GRIN95] Grinstein, G. and Thuraisingham, B. Data mining and visualization: A position paper. In *Proceedings of the Workshop on Databases in Visualization*, Atlanta, GA, October 1995.

[HARV96] *Harvard Business School Articles on Knowledge Management*. Harvard University Press: Cambridge, MA, 1996.

[IEEE89] *Parallel Architectures for Databases, IEEE Tutorial*. ed. A. Hurson et al. IEEE Computer Society Press: Los Alamitos, CA, 1989.

[IEEE99] Special issue in collaborative computing. *IEEE Computer* 32: 9, 1999.

[IEEE03] Special issue in audio mining. *IEEE Computer* 36: 2, 2003.

[IMIE92] Imielinski, T., Imielinski, T., and Badrinath, B. Querying in highly mobile distributed environments. In *Proceedings of the VLDB Conference*, Vancouver, BC, August 1992.

[LAUR00] St. Laurent, S. *XML: A Primer*. Power: London, UK, 2000.

[MILO99] Milojicic, D. et al. *Mobility: Processes, Computers, and Agents*. ACM: New York, 1999.

[MORE01] Morey, D., Maybury, M., and Thuraisingham, B. (eds.) *Knowledge Management*. MIT Press: Cambridge, MA, 2001.

[MULT] *ACM Multimedia Conference Series*. ACM: New York.

[PRAB97] Prabhakaran, B. *Multimedia Database Management Systems*, Kluwer: Hingham, MA, 1997.

[SGML] Available at http://www.w3.org/MarkUp/SGML/.

[SIGI] *ACM Special Interest Group on Information Retrieval Conference Series*. ACM: New York.

[SIGM01] *ACM SIGMOD Record* 30: 3, 2001.

[TATA03] Tatarinov, I. et al. Piazza peer-to-peer data management. *ACM SIGMOD Record* 32: 3, 2003.

[THUR96] Thuraisingham, B. Interactive data mining and the World Wide Web. In *Proceedings of Compugraphics Conference*, Paris, December 1996.

[THUR97] Thuraisingham, B. *Data Management Systems Evolution and Interoperation*. CRC Press: Boca Raton, FL, 1997.

[THUR00] Thuraisingham, B. *Web Data Management and Electronic Commerce*. CRC Press: Boca Raton, FL, 2000.

[THUR01] Thuraisingham, B. *Managing and Mining Multimedia Databases for the Electronic Enterprise*. CRC Press: Boca Raton, FL, 2001.

[THUR02a] Thuraisingham, B. *XML, Databases and the Semantic Web*. CRC Press: Boca Raton, FL, 2002.

[THUR02b] Thuraisingham, B. et al. Knowledge management and collaborative commerce. *Journal of Knowledge and Process Management*, 9: 1, 2002.

[TURB00] Turban E. and Aronson, J. *Decision Support Systems and Intelligent Systems*, Prentice-Hall: Upper Saddle River, NJ, 2000.

[VIS95] *Proceedings of the 1995 IEEE Conference Workshop on Databases in Visualization*, Atlanta, GA, October 1995. Springer Verlag: Heidelberg, Germany, 1996.

[WOEL86] Woelk, D. et al. An object-oriented approach to multimedia databases. In *Proceedings of the ACM SIGMOD Conference*, Washington, DC, June 1986.

Exercises

1. Select three information management technologies and write a survey of these technologies.
2. Design a multimedia database management system.
3. Discuss issues on integrating heterogeneous data sources on the Web.
4. Describe peer-to-peer data management.

Conclusion to Part I

In Part I we have provided an overview of the various supporting technologies for database and applications security. Note that the supporting technologies include database management, information security, and information management. Chapter 2 described various database technologies including query-processing transaction management and data warehousing. We also included a discussion of distributed databases and object technologies. Chapter 3 described various information security technologies including database security and network security. Chapter 4 described various information management technologies including multimedia, knowledge management, and collaboration.

Now that we have provided an overview of the various supporting technologies we are ready to embark on a very important topic in information security and that is database and applications security. Parts II through X discuss database and applications security. In particular, discretionary security, mandatory security, the inference problem, secure distributed databases, secure object databases, secure data warehousing, privacy, secure knowledge management, secure Web databases, secure sensor information management, and secure dependable data management are discussed.

DISCRETIONARY SECURITY FOR DATABASE SYSTEMS

II

Now that we have discussed the supporting technologies for database and applications security, we can begin to explore various aspects of database and applications security. Much of the earlier work in the 1970s was on discretionary database security. Many of the commercial database systems products enforce this type of security. Therefore, in Part II we explore discretionary security.

Part II consists of two chapters: 5 and 6. In Chapter 5 we introduce discretionary security including access control and authorization models for database systems. We also discuss role-based access-control systems. In Chapter 6 we discuss ways of enforcing discretionary security including a discussion of query modification. We also provide an overview of the various commercial products. The discussion in the two chapters provides an overview of the basics of discretionary security focusing primarily on relational database systems. In future chapters we explore the techniques for other types of systems such as distributed databases, object databases, and Web databases.

Chapter 5

Security Policies

5.1 Overview

Before one designs a secure system, the first question that must be answered is what security policy is to be enforced by the system. Security policy is essentially a set of rules that enforce security. Security policies include mandatory security policies and discretionary security policies. Mandatory security policies are the policies that are "mandatory" in nature and are application independent. Discretionary security policies are policies that are specified by the administrator or anyone who is responsible for the environment in which the system will operate. We discuss mandatory security policies such as the Bell and LaPadula policy for database systems in Chapter 8. In this chapter we focus on discretionary security policies. In particular we discuss various types of policies. Enforcing such policies is the subject of Chapter 6.

The most popular discretionary security policy is the access-control policy. Access-control policies were studied for operating systems back in the 1960s and then for database systems in the 1970s. The two prominent database systems, System R and INGRES, were among the first to investigate access control for database systems (see [GRIFF76] and [STON74]). Since then several variations of access-control policies have been reported. Other discretionary policies include administration policies. We also discuss identification and authentication under discretionary policies. Note that much of the discussion in this chapter and in the next focuses on discretionary security in relational database systems. Many of the principles are applicable to other systems such as object database systems and

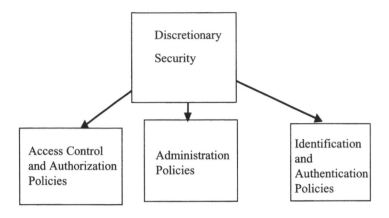

Figure 5.1 Discretionary security policies

distributed database systems. Discretionary security in distributed database systems is discussed in Chapter 15. Discretionary security in object database systems is discussed in Chapter 18. We also discuss various aspects of discretionary security for emerging data management systems such as data warehouses, sensor systems, and knowledge management systems in Parts VIII through X.

The organization of this chapter is as follows. In Section 5.2 we provide an overview of access-control policies. Administration policies are discussed in Section 5.3. Issues on identification and authentication are discussed in Section 5.4. Auditing a database management system is discussed in Section 5.5. Views as security objects are discussed in Section 5.6. The chapter is concluded in Section 5.7. Figure 5.1 illustrates various components of discretionary security policies. For more details we refer the reader to [FERR00].

5.2 Access-Control Policies

5.2.1 Overview

As stated in the previous section, access-control policies were first examined for operating systems. The essential point here is whether a process can be granted access to a file. Access could be read access or write access. Write access could include access to modify, append, or delete. These principles were transferred to database systems such as Ingres and System R. Since then various forms of access-control policies have been studied. Notable among those are the role-based access-control policies now implemented in several commercial systems. Note that access-control

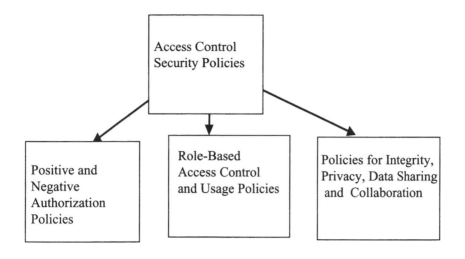

Figure 5.2 Access-control security policies

policies also include mandatory policies. Such policies are discussed in Part III. In this section we discuss only discretionary access-control policies.

The organization of this section is as follows. In Section 5.2.2 we provide an overview of authorization-based access-control policies. These are the most common form of policies studied. Then in Section 5.2.3 we discuss role-based access-control policies. Many commercial products are now implementing role-based access control. Such policies are also being enforced for a variety of applications including for knowledge management and collaboration. Figure 5.2 illustrates the various access-control policies.

5.2.2 Authorization Policies

Many of the access-control policies are based on authorization policies. Essentially what this means is that users are granted access to data based on authorization rules. In this section we discuss various types of authorities' rules. Note that a detailed discussion of authorization policies can be found in the book chapter by Ferrari and Thuraisingham [FERR00].

- *Positive Authorizations:* Early systems focused on what are now called positive authorization rules. Here user John is granted access to relation EMP or user Jane is granted access to relation DEPT. These are access-control rules on relations. One can also grant access to other entities such as attributes and tuples. For example, John has read access to attribute Salary and write access to attribute

Name in relation EMP. Write access could include append, modify, or delete access.

- *Negative Authorization:* If John's access to an object is not specified, does this mean John does not have access to that object? In some systems any authorization rule that is not specified is implicitly taken to be a negative authorization whereas in other systems negative authorizations are explicitly specified. For example, we could enforce rules such as John does not have access to relation EMP or Jane does not have access to relation DEPT.

- *Conflict Resolutions:* When we have rules that are conflicting, then how do we resolve the conflicts? For example, we could have a rule that grants John read access to relation EMP. However, we can also have a rule that does not grant John read access to the salary attribute in EMP. This is a conflict. Usually a system enforces the least privilege rule in which case John has access to EMP except for the salary values.

- *Strong and Weak Authorization:* Systems also enforce strong and weak authorizations. In the case of strong authorization the rule holds regardless of conflicts. In the case of weak authorizations, the rule does not hold in case of conflict. For example, if John is granted access to EMP and it is a strong authorization rule and the rule where John is not granted access to salary attribute is a weak authorization, there is a conflict. This means the strong authorization will hold.

- *Propagation of Authorization Rules:* The question here is how do the rules get propagated. For example, if John has read access to relation EMP, then does it automatically mean that John has read access to every element in EMP? Usually this is the case unless we have a rule that prohibits automatic propagation of an authorization rule. If we have a rule prohibiting the automatic propagation of a rule then we must explicitly enforce authorization rules that specify the objects to which John has access.

- *Special Rules:* In our work on mandatory policy extensions, we have explored extensively the enforcement of content- and context-based constraints. Note that security constraints are essentially the security rules. Content- and context-based rules are rules where access is granted depending on the content of the data or the context in which the data is displayed. Such rules also can be enforced for discretionary security. For example, in the case of content-based constraints, John has read access to tuples only in DEPT D100. In the case of context- or association-based constraints, John does not have read access to names and salaries taken together, however, he can have access to individual names and

Authorization Rules:

* John has read access to employee
relation
* John does not have write access to
department relation
* Jane has read access to name values
in employee relation
* Jane does not have read access to
department relation

Figure 5.3   Authorization rules

salaries. In the case of event-based constraints, after the election, John has access to all elements in relation EMP.

■ *Consistency and Completeness of Rules:* One of the challenges here is ensuring the consistency and completeness of constraints. That is, if the constraints or rules are inconsistent then do we have conflict resolution rules that will resolve the conflicts? How can we ensure that all of the entities (such as attributes, relations, elements, etc.) are specified in access-control rules for a user? Essentially what this means is, are the rules complete? If not, what assumptions do we make about entities that do not have either positive or negative authorizations specified on them for a particular user or a class of users?

We have discussed some essential points with respect to authorization rules. Some examples are given in Figure 5.3. In the next section we discuss a very popular access-control policy and that is role-based access control, which is now implemented in commercial systems.

5.2.3 Role-Based Access Control

Role-Based Access Control (RBAC) has become one of more popular access-control methods (see [SAND96]). This method has been implemented in commercial systems including Trusted Oracle. The idea here is to grant access to users depending on their roles and functions.

The essential idea behind role-based access control is as follows. Users need access to data depending on their roles. For example, a president may have access to information about her vice presidents and the members

Figure 5.4 Role hierarchy

of the board, and the chief financial officer may have access to the financial information and information on those who report to him. A director may have access to information about those working in his division and the human resources director may have information on personal data about the employees of the corporation. Essentially role-based access control is a type of authorization policy that depends on the user role and the activities that go with the role.

Various research efforts on role hierarchies have been discussed in the literature. There is also a conference series called SACMAT (Symposium on Access Control Models and Technologies) that evolved from role-based access-control research efforts. For example, how does access get propagated? Can one role subsume another? Consider the role hierarchy illustrated in Figure 5.4. This means if we grant access to a node in the hierarchy, does the access propagate upwards? That is, if a department manager has access to certain project information, does that access get propagated to the parent node, which is a director node? If a section leader has access to employee information in her section, does the access propagate to the department manager who is the parent in the role hierarchy? What happens to the child nodes? That is, does access propagate downwards? For example, if a department manager has access to certain

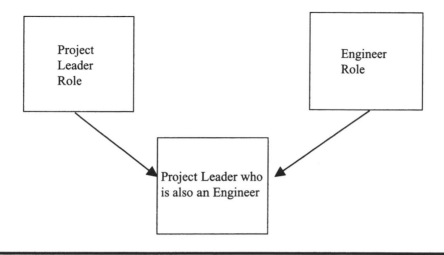

Figure 5.5   Multiple parents

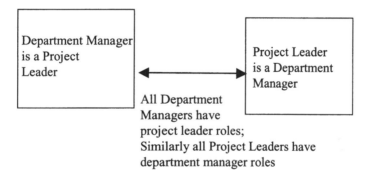

Figure 5.6   Cyclic graph

information, then do his subordinates have access to that information? Are there cases where the subordinates have access to data that the department manager does not have? What happens if an employee has to report to two supervisors, one his department manager and the other his project manager? What happens when the department manager is working on a project and has to report to his project leader who also works for him? Multiple parents are illustrated in Figure 5.5 and a cycle is represented in Figure 5.6.

Role-based access control has been examined for relational systems, object systems, distributed systems, and now some of the emerging technologies such as data warehouses, knowledge management systems, semantic Web, E-commerce systems, and digital libraries. Furthermore, object models have been used to represent roles and activities (see, for example, *Proceedings of the IFIP Database Security Conference Series*). This is an area that will continue to be discussed and the ACM SACMAT (*Symposium on Access Control Models and Technologies*) is a venue for publishing high-quality papers on this topic.

More recently Sandhu et al. have developed yet another access-control-like model, the Usage Control Model, which is referred to as UCON (see, for example, the work reported in [PARK04]). The UCON model attempts to integrate three policies: (1) trust management, (2) access control, and (3) rights management. The idea is to provide control on the usage of objects. Although the ideas are somewhat preliminary, this model shows a lot of promise.

5.3 Administration Policies

Access-control policies specify access that specific users have to the data, whereas administration policies specify who is to administer the data. Administration duties include keeping the data current, making sure the metadata is updated whenever the data is updated, and ensuring recovery from failures and related activities.

Typically the DataBase Administrator (DBA) is responsible for updating, say, the metadata, the index, and access methods and also ensuring that the access-control rules are properly enforced. The System Security Officer (SSO) may also have a role. That is, the DBA and SSO may share the duties between them. The security-related issues might be the responsibility of the SSO and the data-related issues might be the responsibility of the DBA. Some other administration policies being considered include assigning caretakers. Usually owners have control of the data that they create and may manage the data for its duration. In some cases owners may not be available to manage the data in which case they may assign caretakers.

Administration policies get more complicated in distributed environments, especially in a Web environment. For example, in Web environments, there may be multiple parties involved in distributing documents including the owner, the publisher, and the users requesting the data. Who owns the data? Is it the owner or the publisher? Once the data has left the owner and arrived at the publisher, does the publisher take control of the data?

There are many interesting questions that need to be answered as we migrate from a relational database environment to a distributed and perhaps a Web environment. These also include managing copyright issues, data quality, data provenance, and governance. Many interesting

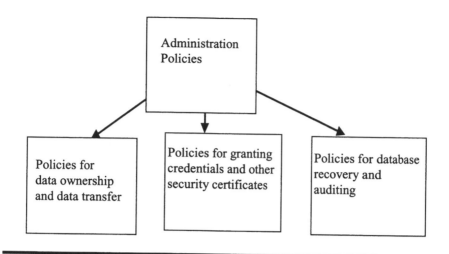

Figure 5.7   Administration policies

papers have appeared in recent conferences on administration policies. Figure 5.7 illustrates various administration policies.

5.4 Identification and Authentication

For the sake of completeness we discuss identification and authentication as part of our discussion of discretionary security. By identification we mean users must identify themselves with their user ID and password. Authentication means the system must then match the user ID with the password to ensure that this is indeed the person he is purporting to be. A user may also have multiple identities depending on his roles. Identity management is receiving a lot of attention lately (see [BERT04]). We discuss identity management in Chapter 29.

Numerous problems have been reported with the password-based scheme. One is that hackers can break into the system and get the passwords of users and then masquerade as the users. In a centralized system, the problems are not as complicated as in a distributed environment. Now, with the World Wide Web and E-commerce applications, financial organizations are losing billions of dollars when hackers masquerade as legitimate users.

More recently biometrics techniques are being applied. These include face and voice recognition techniques to authenticate the user. These techniques are showing lot of promise and are already being used. We can expect widespread use of biometric techniques as face recognition technologies advance. We discuss biometrics in Chapter 29.

5.5 Auditing a Database System

Databases are audited for multiple purposes. For example, they may be audited to keep track of the number of queries posed, the number of updates made, the number of transactions executed, and the number of times the secondary storage is accessed so that the system can be designed more efficiently. Databases can also be audited for security purposes. For example, have any of the access-control rules been bypassed by releasing information to the users? Has the inference problem occurred? Has privacy been violated? Have there been unauthorized intrusions?

Audits create a trail and the audit data may be stored in a database. This database may be mined to detect any abnormal patterns or behaviors. There has been a lot of work in using data mining for auditing and intrusion detection and we discuss this in Chapter 22. Audit trail analysis is especially important these days with E-commerce transactions on the Web. An organization should have the capability to conduct an analysis and determine problems such as credit card fraud and identity theft. We address these topics in Chapter 29.

5.6 Views for Security

Views as a mechanism for security have been studied a great deal both for discretionary security and mandatory security. For example, one may not want to grant access to an entire relation especially if it has, say, 25 attributes such as healthcare records, salary, travel information, personal data, and the like. Therefore, the DBA could form views and grant access to the views. Similarly in the case of mandatory security, views could be assigned security levels; we discuss this in Part IV.

Views have problems associated with them including the view update problem (see [DATE90]). That is, if the view is updated then we need to ensure that the base relations are updated. Therefore, if a view is updated by John and John does not have access to the base relation, then can the base relation still be updated? That is, do we create different views for different users and then the DBA merges the updates on views as updates on base relations? Figure 5.8 illustrates views for security.

5.7 Summary and Directions

In this chapter we have provided an overview of discretionary security policies in database systems. We started with a discussion of access-control policies including authorization policies and role-based access control. Then we discussed administration policies. We briefly discussed identification and

V1: VIEW EMP (D# = 20)

SS#	Ename	Salary
2	Paul	30K
3	Mary	40K
4	Jane	20K
1	Michelle	30K

EMP

SS#	Ename	Salary	D#
1	John	20K	10
2	Paul	30K	20
3	Mary	40K	20
4	Jane	20K	20
5	Bill	20K	10
6	Larry	20K	10
1	Michelle	30K	20

V2: VIEW EMP (D# = 10)

SS#	Ename	Salary
1	John	20K
5	Bill	20K
6	Larry	20K

Rules:
John has Read access to V1
John has Write access to V2

Figure 5.8   Views for security

authentication. Finally we discussed auditing issues as well as views for security. Note that access control also includes mandatory access control and this aspect is discussed in Chapter 8.

There is still a lot of work to be done, for example, on role-based access control for emerging technologies such as digital libraries and the semantic Web. We need administration policies to mange multiparty transactions in a Web environment. Finally we need biometric technologies for authenticating users. Digital identity is becoming an important research area especially with wireless communication and mobile devices. We discuss some of the aspects in later chapters.

Note that in this chapter and the next we focus mainly on relational database systems. Discretionary security for distributed database systems and object database systems is discussed in Parts VI and VII. In the next chapter we discuss various aspects of enforcing the security policies discussed in this chapter.

References

[BERT06] Bertino, E. et al. Identity management, In *Proceedings of the CERIAS Symposium,* Lafayette, IN, March, 2004.

[DATE90] Date, C. *An Introduction to Database Systems.* Addison-Wesley: Reading, MA, 1990.

[FERR00] Ferrari E. and Thuraisingham, B. Secure database systems. In *Advances in Database Management,* ed. M. Piatini and O. Diaz, Artech: London, UK, 2000.

[GRIFF76] Griffiths P. and Wade, B. An authorization mechanism for a relational database system. *ACM Transactions on Database Systems* 1: 3, 1976.

[PARK04] Park, J. and Sandhu, R. The UCON usage control model. *ACM Transactions on Information and Systems Security* 7: 1, 2004.

[SAND96] Sandhu, R. et al. Role-based access control models. *IEEE Computer* 29: 2, 1996.

[STON74] Stonebraker, M. and Wong, E. Access control in a relational data base management system by query modification. In *Proceedings of the ACM Annual Conference,* ACM: New York, 1974.

Exercises

1. Conduct a survey of the various access-control policies in databases.
2. Describe in detail role-based access-control policies.
3. Examine techniques for audit trail analysis.

Chapter 6

Policy Enforcement and Related Issues

6.1 Overview

In Chapter 5 we discussed security policies for database systems. We focused mainly on discretionary security policies including access control, authorization, and administration policies. We also discussed role-based access-control policies. In Part III, we discuss mandatory access-control policies such as policies for multilevel security. In this chapter we discuss policy enforcement issues. In particular, we focus on discretionary security policy enforcement issues. Many of the arguments apply to mandatory security. Policy enforcement for mandatory security is discussed in various chapters in Parts III through V.

By policy enforcement, we mean the mechanisms to enforce the policies. For example, back in the 1970s, the relational database system products such as System R and INGRES developed techniques such as the query modification mechanisms for policy enforcement (see, for example, [GRIFF76] and [STON74]). The query language SQL (Structured Query Language) has been extended to specify security policies and access-control rules. More recently languages such as XML (eXtensible Markup Language) and RDF (Resource Description Framework) have been extended to specify security policies (see, for example, [BERT02] and [CARM04]).

The organization of this chapter is as follows. SQL extensions for security are discussed in Section 6.2. In Section 6.3 we discuss query

```
┌─────────────────────────────────────────┐
│                                           │
│   Policy Enforcement Mechanisms:          │
│                                           │
│   Query Modification Algorithm            │
│                                           │
│   Rule processing to enforce the access   │
│   control rules                           │
│                                           │
│   Theorem proving techniques to determine │
│   if policies are violated                │
│                                           │
│   Consistency and completeness checking of│
│   policies                                │
└─────────────────────────────────────────┘
```

Figure 6.1   Policy enforcement

modification. The impact of discretionary security on other database functions is discussed in Section 6.4. Visualization of security policies is discussed in Section 6.5. Discussion of prototypes and products that implement discretionary security policies is given in Section 6.6. Note that we focus on relational database systems. Policies in other systems such as object systems are discussed in Part VII. The chapter is summarized in Section 6.7. Figure 6.1 illustrates the various aspects involved on enforcing security policies. These include specification, implementation, and visualization.

6.2 SQL Extensions for Security

This section discusses policy specification. Although much of the focus is on SQL extensions for security policy specification, we also briefly discuss some of the emerging languages. Note that SQL was developed for data definition and data manipulation for relational systems. Various versions of SQL have been developed including SQL for objects, SQL for multimedia, and SQL for the Web. That is, SQL has influenced data manipulation and data definition a great deal over the past 20 years (see [SQL3]).

As we have stated, SQL is a data definition and data manipulation language. Security policies could be specified during data definition. SQL has GRANT and REVOKE constructs for specifying grant and revoke access to users. That is, if a user John has read access to relation EMP, then one could use SQL and specify something like "GRANT JOHN EMP READ" and if the access is to be revoked, then we need something like "REVOKE JOHN EMP READ". SQL has also been extended with more complex constraints such as granting John read access to a tuple in a relation and granting Jane write access to an element in a relation.

In [THUR89] we specified SQL extensions for security assertions. These assertions were for multilevel security. We could use similar reasoning for specifying discretionary security policies. For example, consider the situation where John does not have read access to names and salaries in EMP taken together, but he can read names and salaries separately. One could specify this in SQL-like language as follows.

```
GRANT JOHN READ
EMP.SALARY
GRANT JOHN READ
EMP.NAME
NOT GRANT JOHN READ
Together (EMP.NAME, EMP.SALARY).
```

If we are to grant John read access to the employees who earn less than 30K, then this assertion is specified as follows.

```
GRANT JOHN READ
EMP
Where EMP.SALARY < 30K
```

Note that the assertions we have specified are not standard assertions. These are some of our ideas. We need to explore ways of incorporating these assertions into the standards. SQL extensions have also been proposed for role-based access control. In fact, products such as Oracle's Trusted database product enforce role-based access control. The access-control rules are specified in an SQL-like language.

There are many other specification languages that have been developed. These include XML, RDF, and related languages for the Web and the semantic Web. The semantic Web is essentially an intelligent Web and we address security issues for the semantic Web in Part IX. We also discuss XML and RDF security in Part IX. Figure 6.2 illustrates specification aspects for security policies.

6.3 Query Modification

Query modification was first proposed in the INGRES project at the University of California at Berkeley (see [STON74]). The idea is to modify the query based on the constraints. We have successfully designed and implemented query modification for mandatory security (see [DWYE87], [THUR87], and [THUR93]). However, much of the discussion in this section

```
Policy Specification:

SQL extensions to specify security policies

Rule-based languages to specify policies

Logic programming languages such as
Prolog to specify policies
```

Figure 6.2   Policy specification

is on query modification based on discretionary security constraints. We illustrate the essential points with some examples.

Consider a query by John to retrieve all tuples from EMP. Suppose that John only has read access to all the tuples where the salary is less than 30K and the employee is not in the Security department. Then the query

```
Select * from EMP
Will be modified to
Select * from EMP
Where salary < 30K
And Dept is not Security
```

where we assume that the attributes of EMP are, say, Name, Salary, Age, and Department.

Essentially what happens is that the "where" clause of the query has all the constraints associated with the relation. We can also have constraints that span across multiple relations. For example, we could have two relations EMP and DEPT joined by Dept #. Then the query is modified as follows.

```
Select * from EMP
Where EMP.Salary < 30K
And EMP.D# = DEPT.D#
And DEPT.Name is not Security
```

We have used some simple examples for query modification. The detailed algorithms can be found in [DWYE87] and [STON74]. The high-level algorithm is illustrated in Figure 6.3.

Query Modification Algorithm:

Input: Query, Security Constraints
Output: Modified Query

For constraints that are relevant to the
Query, modify the where clause of
the query via a Negation

For example: If salary should not be released to
Jane and if Jane requests information from employee,
then modify the query to retrieve information from
employee where attribute is not salary

Repeat the process until all relevant constraints
are processed

The end result is the modified query

Figure 6.3   Query modification algorithm

6.4 Discretionary Security and Database Functions

In Section 6.3 we discussed query modification which is essentially processing security constraints during the query operation. Query optimization will also be affected by security constraints. That is, once the query is modified, then the query tree has to be built. The idea is to push selections and projection down in the query tree and carry out the join operation later.

Other functions are also affected by security constraints. Let us consider transaction management. Bertino et al. have developed algorithms for integrity constraint processing for transactions management (see [BERT89]). We have examined their techniques for mandatory security-constraint processing during transaction management. The techniques may be adapted for discretionary security constraints. The idea is to ensure that the constraints are not violated during transaction execution.

Constraints may be enforced on the metadata. For example, one could grant and revoke access to users to the metadata relations. Discretionary security constraints for metadata could be handled in the same way they are handled for data.

Secure Database Functions:

Query processing: Enforce access control rules during query processing; inference control; consider security constraints for query optimization

Transaction management: Check whether security constraints are satisfied during transaction execution

Storage management: Develop special access methods and index strategies that take into consideration the security constraints

Metadata management: Enforce access control on metadata; ensure that data is not released to unauthorized individuals by releasing the metadata

Integrity management: Ensure that integrity of the data is maintained while enforcing security

---

Figure 6.4 Security impact on database functions

Other database functions include storage management. The issues in storage management include developing appropriate access methods and index strategies. One needs to examine the impact of the security constraints on the storage management functions. That is, can one partition the relations based on the constraints and store them in such a way that the relations can be accessed efficiently? We need to develop secure indexing technologies for database systems. Some work on secure indexing for geospatial information systems is reported in [ATLU04].

In Chapter 5 we discussed auditing and views for security. That is, databases are audited to determine whether any security violation has occurred. Furthermore, views have been used to grant access to individuals for security purposes. We need efficient techniques for auditing as well as for view management.

In this section we have examined the impact of security on some of the major database functions including query management, transaction processing, metadata management, and storage management. We also need to investigate the impact of security on other functions such as integrity-constraint processing and fault-tolerant computing. Figure 6.4 illustrates the impact of security on the database functions.

Visualization of Policies

Semantic data models to represent the application, security constraints, and detect security violations via inference

Apply visualization tools to check for the consistency of policies

Example: Jane has access to salary values in relation EMP and at the same time Jane does not have read access to EMP. Use colors to represent data to which Jane does and does not have access. If a data element has two colors associated with it then there is a conflict.

Use hyper media systems to browse security policies

Figure 6.5   Visualization for policy integration

6.5 Visualization of Policies

As we have mentioned there are three aspects to policy enforcement: (1) policy specification, (2) policy implementation, and (3) policy visualization. Policy visualization is especially useful for complex security policies.

Visualization tools are needed for many applications including geospatial applications as well as Web-based applications so that the users can better understand the data in the databases. Visualization is also useful for integrating security policies. For example, if multiple systems from multiple organizations are to be merged then their policies have to be visualized and merged so that the administrator can have some idea of the integrated policy. Figure 6.5 illustrates visualization for policy integration. There are now tools available for policy visualization (see, for example, [SMAR]).

Policy visualization is also helpful for dynamic policies. That is, when policies change often, visualizing the effects would be quite useful in designing secure systems. In some of our work we have used graph structures to specify constraints instead of simple rules. This is because graphs enable us to visualize what the rules look like. Furthermore, policies may be linked to one another and with graph structures one can analyze the various links to obtain the relationships among the policies.

The area of policy visualization is a relatively new research area. There are some research programs at DARPA (Defense Advanced Research Projects Agency) on policy visualization. This is an area that needs work especially in a Web environment where organizations collaborate with

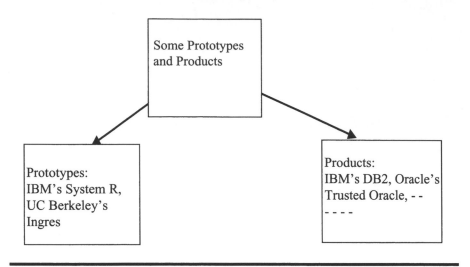

Figure 6.6   Prototypes and products

each other and carry out E-business. Policy visualization is also important for homeland security applications where various agencies have to work together and share information and yet maintain their autonomy.

6.6 Prototypes and Products

We now discuss discretionary security as implemented in System R and Oracle. Note that System R is a prototype and Oracle is a product. Both are based on the relational model. Secure object systems and secure distributed database systems are discussed in later chapters. Several prototypes and products have implemented discretionary access control and some of them are listed in Figure 6.6.

Note that information on prototypes and products will be changing continually as technology progresses. Therefore, in many cases information about the prototypes and products may be soon outdated. Our purpose in discussing prototypes and products is to explain the concepts. Up-to-date information on prototypes and products can be obtained from the vendor and possibly from the Web.

System R was one of the first systems to introduce various discretionary security concepts (see [GRIFF76]). In this system objects to be protected are represented by tables and views. Subjects can enforce several privileges on the security objects. Privileges supported by the model include select (select tuples), update (modify tuples), insert (add tuples), delete (delete tuples), and drop (delete table). The model also supports decentralized administration facilities. A subject can grant privileges it has to other subjects. The model also enforces recursive revocation. That is, when a subject A revokes an authorization on a table to subject B, then B in turn revokes authorization of the table to C to which it had previously granted access.

The System R model has been extended in many directions. These include group management where access is granted and revoked to groups of users, distributed database management where authorization is extended for System R*, which is the distributed version of System R, and negative authorizations. Note that much of the research carried out for System R on security has been transferred to the DB2 commercial product. A detailed discussion of the System R authorization model and its extensions can be found in [FERR00].

In the Oracle Databases server, privileges can be granted to either users or roles. Roles are hierarchically organized. A role acquires all the privileges that are in lower positions of the hierarchy. A user can be authorized to take on several roles, but there is a limit. A role can be enabled or disabled at a given time. With each role, a password may be assigned to ensure only authorized use of privileges are granted to the role.

The privileges can be divided into two categories: (1) system privileges and (2) object privileges. System privileges allow subjects to perform systemwide action on a particular type of object. Examples of system privileges are the privileges to delete the tuples of any table in a database or create a cluster. Object privileges allow subjects to perform a particular action on a particular object. Examples include insert or delete tuples from a particular table. Other issues such as cascading privileges and revocation of privileges are discussed in detail in [FERR00].

6.7 Summary and Directions

In this chapter we have discussed policy enforcement issues with respect to the various policies we discussed in Chapter 5. The major issues in policy enforcement are policy specification, policy implementation, and policy visualization. We discussed SQL extensions for specifying policies as well as provided an overview of query modification. We also briefly discussed how policy visualization might be used to integrate multiple policies. Finally we discussed some prototypes and products that implement discretionary security. We focused mainly on relational database systems.

Security policy enforcement is a topic that will continue to evolve as new technologies emerge. We have advanced from relational to object to multimedia to Web-based data management systems. Each system has some unique features that are incorporated into the security policies. Enforcing policies for the various systems will continue to be a major research focus. We also need to carry out research on the consistency and completeness of policies. Policy visualization may help toward this. There is still a lot to be done.

References

[ATLU04] Atluri, V. and Guo, Q. STAR-tree: An index structure for efficient evaluation of spatiotemporal authorization, In *Proceedings of the IFIP Database Security Conference,* Sitges, Spain, July, 2004.

[BERT89] Bertino, E. and Musto, D. Integrity constraint processing during transaction processing. *Acta Informatica,* 26: 1, 1989.

[BERT02] Bertino, E. et al. Access control for XML documents. *Data and Knowledge Engineering* 34: 3, 2002.

[CARM04] Carminati, B. et al. Security for RDF. In *Proceedings of the DEXA Conference Workshop on Web Semantics,* Zaragoza, Spain, August, 2004.

[DWYE87] Dwyer, P. et al. Multilevel security for relational database systems. *Computers and Security* 6: 3, 1987.

[FERR00] Ferrari E. and Thuraisingham, B. Secure database systems. In *Advances in Database Management,* ed. M. Piatini and O. Diaz, Artech: London, UK, 2000

[GRIFF76] Griffiths P. and Wade, B. An authorization mechanism for a relational database system. *ACM Transactions on Database Systems* 1: 3, 1976.

[KEEF89] Keefe, T. et al. Secure query processing strategies. *IEEE Computer* 22: 3, 1989.

[SMAR] Smart Center Management. Available at http://www.unipalm.co.uk/products/e-security/check-point/$smartcenter-management.cfm.

[SQL3] *SQL3*.Draft. American National Standards Institute, 1992.

[STON74] Stonebraker, M. and Wong, E. Access control in a relational data base management system by query modification. In *Proceedings of the ACM Annual Conference,* ACM: New York, 1974.

[THUR87] Thuraisingham, B. Security checking in relational database management systems augmented with inference engines. *Computers and Security* 6: 6, 1987.

[THUR89] Thuraisingham, B. and Stachour, P. SQL extensions for security assertions. *Computer Standards and Interface Journal* 11: 1, 1989.

[THUR93] Thuraisingham, B., Ford, W., and Collins, M. Design and implementation of a database inference controller. *Data and Knowledge Engineering Journal* 11: 3, 1993.

Exercises

1. Describe the query modification algorithm in detail.
2. Examine SQL for specifying access-control rules.
3. Examine discretionary security for three commercial relational database system products.
4. Examine the use of visualization for security policies.

Conclusion to Part II

In this part we introduced discretionary security for databases. In particular access-control and authorization models including role-based access-control models were discussed. We also addressed the implementation of the policies. For example, in Chapter 5 we introduced discretionary security including access-control and authorization models for database systems. We also discussed role-based access-control systems. In Chapter 6 we discussed ways of enforcing discretionary security including a discussion of query modification. We also provided an overview of some commercial products.

The discussion in the two chapters has provided an overview of essentially the basics of discretionary security focusing primarily on relational database systems. The ideas are extended to distributed databases, object databases, and other types of applications such as knowledge management in later chapters.

Now that we have introduced discretionary security, we are ready to introduce mandatory security for database systems. Many of the developments throughout the 1980s were in mandatory security and in particular in multilevel secure relational database systems. Part III introduces mandatory security.

Mandatory Security for Database Systems

In Part I we discussed supporting technologies for database and applications security and in Part II we discussed discretionary security for database systems. We introduced various concepts such as access-control models and administration policies. As we have stated, there are two aspects to security in database systems. One is discretionary security and the other is mandatory security. Part III discusses mandatory security.

Part III consists of two chapters. Chapter 7 provides a historical perspective of mandatory security for database systems. The main focus is on a specific type of mandatory security, which is multilevel security. We discuss the various types of MultiLevel Secure DataBase Systems (MLS/DBMS) designed since the 1970s. Chapter 8 discusses a taxonomy for designing such MLS/DBMSs. This taxonomy results in security architectures for DBMSs.

Part III essentially provides the foundations for various types of MLS/DBMSs including relational database systems, distributed database systems, and object database systems. Such systems are described in Parts IV, VI, and VII.

Chapter 7

Historical Developments

7.1 Overview

Many of the developments in the 1980s and 1990s in database security were on MultiLevel Secure Database Management Systems (MLS/DBMS). These systems were also called Trusted DataBase Management Systems (TDBMS). In a MLS/DBMS, users are cleared at different clearance levels such as Unclassified, Confidential, Secret, and TopSecret. Data is assigned different sensitivity levels such as Unclassified, Confidential, Secret, and TopSecret. It is generally assumed that these security levels form a partially ordered lattice. For example, Unclassified < Confidential < Secret < TopSecret. Partial ordering comes from having different compartments. For example, Secret Compartment A may be incomparable to Secret Compartment B. This is illustrated in Figure 7.1.

MLS/DBMSs have evolved from the developments in multilevel secure operating systems such as MULTICS and SCOMP (see, for example, [IEEE83]) and the developments in database systems (see Chapter 2). Few developments were reported in the late 1970s on MLS/DBMSs. However, during this time there were many developments in discretionary security such as access control for System R and INGRES as well as many efforts on statistical database security. Then there was a major initiative by the Air Force and a Summer Study was convened. This Summer Study marks a significant milestone in the development of MLS/DBMSs.

Since the Summer Study, several efforts were reported throughout the 1980s. Many of the efforts were based on the relational data model. At

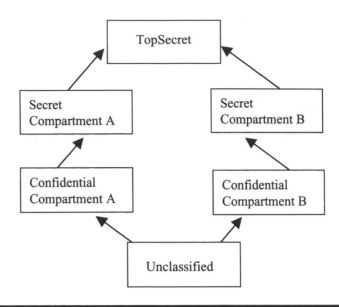

Figure 7.1 Security levels

the end of that decade, the National Computer Security Center started a major effort to interpret the Trusted Computer Systems Evaluation Criteria for database systems [TCSE85]. This interpretation was called the Trusted Database Interpretation [TDI91].

In the 1990s research focused on nonrelational systems including MLS object database systems and deductive database systems. Work was also carried out on multilevel secure distributed database systems. Challenging research problems such as multilevel data models, the inference problem, and secure transaction processing were being investigated. Several commercial products began to emerge. Since the late 1990s, although interest in MLS/DBMSs has begun to decline a little, efforts are still under way to examine multilevel security for emerging data management technologies [IFIP00].

This chapter provides a historical overview of the developments in MLS/DBMSs. The organization of this chapter is as follows. In Section 7.2 we describe the efforts in the late 1970s. In Section 7.3 we provide a summary of the Air Force Summer Study [AFSB83]. In Section 7.4 we discuss some key developments throughout the 1980s. In Section 7.5 we briefly discuss the TDI. In Section 7.6 we describe the various secure database systems that emerged in the 1980s and 1990s. More details of some of these systems are discussed in Chapters 9 through 11 and 16 through 18. In Section 7.7 we discuss some hard problems such as the inference problem, transaction processing, and polyinstantiation. More

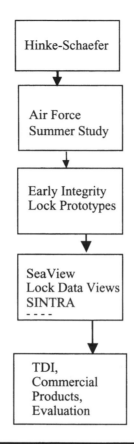

Figure 7.2   Evolution of MLS/DBMS

details of these problems are given in Chapters 9, 10, and 12 through 14. Multilevel security for some of the emerging technologies such as warehousing and E-commerce systems is discussed in Section 7.7. Summary and directions are given in Section 7.8. Figure 7.2 illustrates the evolution of MLS/DBMSs.

7.2 Early Efforts

The early developments in MLS/DBMSs influenced the Air Force Summer Study a great deal. Notable among these efforts are the Hinke–Schaefer approach to operating systems providing mandatory security, the PhD thesis of Deborah Downs at UCLA (University of California at Los Angeles), the IP Sharp Model developed in Canada, and the Naval Surveillance Model developed at the MITRE Corporation.

```
┌─────────────────────────────────────┐
│                                     │
│   Early Efforts:                    │
│   Hinke-Schaefer Architecture       │
│   using MULTICS operating           │
│   System, 1975                      │
│   I.P, Sharp Model, 1976            │
│   Deborah Downs PhD Thesis, 1980    │
│                                     │
│                                     │
└─────────────────────────────────────┘
```

Figure 7.3   Early efforts

The Hinke–Schaefer approach (see [HINK75]) essentially developed a way to host MLS/DBMSs on top of the MULTICS MLS operating system. The system was based on the relational system and the idea was to partition the relation based on attributes and store the attributes in different files at different levels. The operating system would then control access to the files. This approach is elaborated on in Chapter 8 when we discuss design principles.

The PhD thesis of Deborah Downs examined several issues for designing a MLS/DBMS (see [DOWN77]). The IP Sharp model essentially developed a secure relational data model (see [GROH76]). The Naval Surveillance Model of Graubart and Woodward developed a relational model based on the notion of containers [GRAU82]. For example, what is the relationship between the security levels of the elements and the security level of the container of the elements?

These early efforts showed a lot of promise in designing and developing MLS/DBMSs. As a result, the Air Force started a major initiative, which resulted in the Summer Study of 1982 (see [AFSB83]). A summary of this study is given in Section 7.3. The early efforts are illustrated in Figure 7.3.

7.3 Air Force Summer Study

As we have stated earlier, the Air Force Summer Study was a major milestone in the development of MLS/DBMSs. Top experts in the field including Dorothy Denning, Carl Landwehr, and others participated in the Summer Study. The goal was to examine the issues and come up with viable approaches to designing MLS/DBMSs. The study was influenced by the early efforts discussed in Section 7.2.

The study group was divided into three. The first group focused on near-term approaches to designing MLS/DBMSs. These approaches

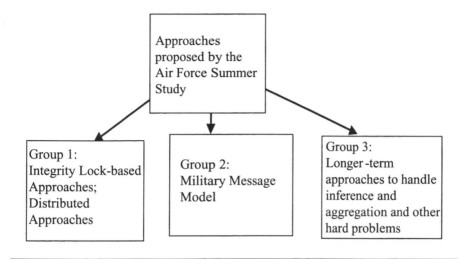

Figure 7.4   Approaches proposed by the Air Force Summer Study

included the integrity lock approach and the distributed architecture approach. Both approaches are discussed under the design principles in Chapter 9. The second group focused on the military message system model for an MLS/DBMS. The military message system model was being developed at that time and the goal of this group was to examine the applicability of this model for MLS/DBMSs. The third group focused on long-term approaches and examined issues such as content- and context-based classification of data, multilevel relational data models, and the inference problem.

Many of the key developments of MLS/DBMSs in the 1980s were based on the reports produced by the first and third groups. These efforts are discussed in Section 7.4. The Air Force Summer Study Report was published in 1983 (see [AFSB83]). Figure 7.4 illustrates the approaches examined by the three groups.

7.4 Major Research and Development Efforts

Numerous developments on the designs and developments were reported throughout the 1980s especially since the Air Force Summer Study. The initial developments were based on the integrity lock approach developed at the MITRE Corporation (see, for example, [GRAU84], [GRAU85], and [BURN86]). Two prototypes were designed and developed. One used the MISTRESS relational database system [GRAU85] and the other used the INGRES relational database system [BURN86]. These prototypes are discussed in more detail in Chapter 11.

Around 1985 TRW designed and developed a MLS/DBMS called ASD and this system was designed to be hosted on the ASOS (the Army Secure Operating System). The approaches were based on the trusted subject-based architecture. Later on, TRW developed some extensions to ASD and the system was called ASD Views where access was granted on views. Both ASD and ASD Views are discussed in Chapter 11. The trusted subject architecture is discussed in Chapter 8 (see also [GARV88]).

Two of the notable systems designed in the late 1980s were the SeaView system by SRI International and LOCK Data Views system by Honeywell (see [DENN87] and [STAC90]). These two efforts were funded by the then Rome Air Development Center and the goal was to focus on the longer-term approaches proposed by the Summer Study. Both efforts influenced the commercial developments a great deal. Details of these efforts can be found in Chapter 11. Some of the research issues addressed by these efforts including inference, aggregation, and multilevel data models can be found in Chapters 9 and 12.

Three other efforts worth mentioning are the SINTRA system developed by the Naval Research Laboratory, the SWORD system developed by the then Defense Research Agency and funded by the Ministry of Defense in the United Kingdom, and the SDDBMS effort by Unisys. The SINTRA system was based on the distributed architecture proposed by the Air Force Summer Study (see [FROS88]). The SWORD system proposed some alternatives to the SeaView and LOCK Data Views data models (see [WISE92]). Although the initial planning for these systems began in the late 1980s the designs were actually developed in the early 1990s. The SDDBMS effort was funded by the Air Force Rome Laboratory and investigated both the partitioned and replicated approaches to designing an MLS/DBMS. All three efforts are discussed in Chapter 11. Figure 7.5 illustrates the developments in the 1980s.

```
Major Research Efforts:
Integrity Lock Prototypes, MITRE
SeaView, SRI
Lock Data Views, Honeywell
ASD Views, TRW
SDDBMS, Unisys
SINTRA, NRL
SWORD, DRA
```

Figure 7.5 Major research and development efforts

7.5 Trusted Database Interpretation

Because there was much progress throughout the 1980s in designing and developing MLS/DBMS prototypes, the National Computer Security Center (NCSC) correctly assumed that commercial products would then follow. This was around 1988 and at that time there were already many commercial operating system products such as MULTICS and SCOMP. These systems were being evaluated by the NCSC using what is now called the *Orange Book* [TCSE85], which is the Trusted Computer Systems Evaluation Criteria. The criteria consist of rules that a system has to satisfy to be certified at a given level. The highest level was A and beyond, and the lowest level was C1. In between there were multiple levels such as C2, B1, B2, and B3.

Now, to evaluate the MLS/DBMSs, the TCSEC was not sufficient. One needed the interpretation of the TCSEC for database systems. Such an interpretation was called the Trusted Database Interpretation (TDI). A TDI draft was published in early 1989. The TDI focused on an approach called TCB (Trusted Computing Base) subsetting. Note that TCB is that part of the system which enforces the security policies. The TDI proposed multiple TCBs to carry out different functions. After many discussions and iterations, the TDI was published in 1991. Around this time quite a few commercial products were ready to be evaluated. These commercial products included those by Oracle, Sybase, Informix, Digital Equipment Corporation, and Ingres. These products are discussed in Chapter 11. Many of the products were based on the relational model. However, one commercial effort by the Ontos Corporation was based on the object model and was also reported in the early 1990s.

7.6 Types of Multilevel Secure Database Systems

7.6.1 Overview

As we have stated in the previous sections, since the Air Force Summer Study report, numerous MLS/DBMSs were designed and developed. Many of them were based on the relational model. However, there were also efforts based on other models such as object models and functional models. In this section we provide an overview of various MLS/DBMSs. Note that we discuss relational, distributed, and object-based systems in more detail in Chapters 9 through 11 and 16 through 18. We give references to various papers on other systems such as those based on logic, functions, entity relationships, and parallel processing.

The organization of this section is as follows. Relational systems are discussed in Section 7.6.2. Entity-relationship systems are discussed in Section 7.6.3. Object systems are discussed in Section 7.6.4. Distributed

```
Types of MLS/DBMSs:

MLS Relational Databases
MLS Object Databases
MLS Distributed Databases
MLS Parallel Databases
MLS Real-time Databases
MLS Functional Databases
MLS Logic Databases
```

Figure 7.6   Types of MLS/DBMSs

database systems are discussed in Section 7.6.5. Logic-based systems are discussed in Section 7.6.6. Functional systems are discussed in Section 7.6.7. MLS/DBMSs based on parallel architectures are discussed in Section 7.6.8. MLSs for real-time database systems are discussed in Section 7.6.9. Figure 7.6 illustrates the various types of MLS/DBMSs.

7.6.2 Relational Database Systems

As we have discussed in the previous sections, many of the developments are based on the relational data model. The early efforts such as the Hinke–Schaefer approach as well as the Air Force Summer Study focused mainly on the relational approach.

Systems such as SeaView, LOCK Data Views, and ASD Views focused on designing multilevel relational data models as well as providing access based on views. These efforts also formulated the notion of polyinstantiation where users are given different views of an element based on their clearance levels.

Other research issues examined in MLS/DBMSs based on the relational data model included secure transaction processing and the inference problem. Security-constraint processing was also explored a great deal. Some of these issues are discussed in Chapters 9 through 14.

7.6.3 Entity-Relationship Systems

Around 1987, the then Rome Air Development Center (now known as Air Force Research Laboratory in Rome) funded an effort to design an MLS/DBMS based on the Entity-Relationship (ER) model. The ER model was initially developed in 1976 by Peter Chen and since then it has been used extensively to model applications [CHEN76]. The goal of the security effort was to explore security properties for the ER model as well as to explore the use of secure ER models to design DBMSs (see [GAJN88]).

The effort produced MLS ER models that have since been used to model secure applications by various research efforts such as [SMIT88]. Furthermore, variations of this model have been used to explore the inference problem (see [THUR91a]). However, to our knowledge there have been no efforts on designing MLS/DBMSs based on the ER model. In summary, the ER approach has contributed extensively toward designing MLS applications.

7.6.4 Object Database Systems

During the late 1980s efforts began on designing MLS/DBMSs based on object models. Notable among these efforts is the one by Keefe, Tsai, and Thuraisingham who designed the SODA model (see [KEEF88] and [KEEF89]). Later Thuraisingham designed the SORION and SO2 models (see [THUR89a] and [THUR89b]. These models extended models such as ORION and O2 with security properties. Around 1990 Millen and Lunt produced an object model for secure knowledge base systems [MILL92]. Jajodia and Kogan developed a message-passing model in 1990 [JAJO90c]. Finally MITRE designed a model called UFOS [ROSE94].

Designs of MLS/DBMSs were also produced based on the various models. The designs essentially followed the designs proposed for MLS/DBMSs based on the relational model. However, with the object model, one had to secure complex objects as well as handle secure method execution. Secure object systems are elaborated on in Chapter 18.

While research progressed on designing MLS/DBMSs based on objects, there were also efforts on using object models for designing secure applications. Notable efforts were those by Sell and Thuraisingham (see [SELL93]). Today with the development of UML (Unified Modeling Language) there are efforts to design secure applications based on UML (see [RAY03]). We discuss object models for designing secure applications in Chapter 19. Object models have also been used to represent secure multimedia databases. This work is elaborated on in Chapter 20 (see also [THUR90a]).

7.6.5 Distributed and Heterogeneous Database Systems

Although the Air Force Summer Study discussed the designs of MLS/DBMSs based on distributed architectures, they essentially partitioned the data depending on the security levels. That is, the goal was to develop centralized database systems. However, around 1989 work began at MITRE on the design and development of multilevel secure distributed database systems (MLS/DDBMS). The efforts focused on architectures, models, query, and transactions for MLS/DDBMSs. These efforts are discussed in Chapter 16. Prototypes connecting MLS/DBMSs at different sites were also developed (see, for example, [THUR91b] and [RUBI93]).

Work was then directed toward designing and developing MLS heterogeneous distributed database systems. These efforts focused on connecting multiple MLS/DBMSs, which are heterogeneous in nature. Research was also carried out on MLS federated databases (see, for example, [THUR94]). MLS heterogeneous database systems are discussed in Chapter 17.

7.6.6 Deductive Database Systems

In the late 1970s and throughout the 1980s there were many efforts on designing and developing logic-based database systems. These systems were called deductive databases (see [GALL78] and [ULLM88]). While investigating the inference problem, we designed multilevel secure deductive database systems. These systems were based on a logic called NTML (Nonmonotonic Typed Multilevel Logic) that we designed [THUR91c].

NTML essentially provides reasoning capability across security levels, which are nonmonotonic in nature. It incorporates constructs to reason about the applications at different security levels. We also designed a Prolog language based on NTML, which is called NTML-Prolog. We investigated both reasoning with the Closed World Assumption as well as with the Open World Assumption. Details of NTML and MLS deductive database systems can be found in [THUR91c].

Due to the fact that there was limited success with logic programming and the Japanese Fifth Generation Project, deductive systems are being used only for a few applications. If such applications are to be multilevel secure, then systems such as those based on NTML will be needed. Nevertheless there is use for NTML on handling problems such as the inference problem. The inference problem is discussed in Chapters 12 through 14. Note that we are at present exploring the integration of NTML-like logic with descriptive logics for secure semantic Webs. A discussion of descriptive logics can be found in [MCGU02].

7.6.7 Functional Database Systems

In the early 1980s there was much interest in functional data models for database systems. Essentially, these models are based on functions and query evaluation that amounts to function execution (see [BUNE82]). There was also hope that functional database systems would take over the relational database systems.

MLS for functional database systems was briefly examined in [THUR89c]. We introduced the notion of multilevel functions and the execution of multilevel functions. Unfortunately this work did not take off mainly due to the fact that functional database systems did not really progress beyond the research prototype stage. Nevertheless we got some useful insights on applying the techniques for secure object systems.

7.6.8 Parallel Database Systems

In the 1980s there were efforts on designing parallel database systems. Examples include the systems developed at the University of Wisconsin (see [DEWI90]) and the commercial Teradata system.

Multilevel security for parallel database systems received some attention in the late 1980s. Teradata Corporation designed a MLS/DBMS product, which was evaluated by NCSC. Furthermore, we carried out an investigation on using parallel processing technology for MLS/DBMSs. This effort was reported in [THUR93a]. We designed a parallel MLS/DBMS as well as explored the use of parallel processing techniques for enhancing the performance of secure join operations. Some of this technology shows promise now for secure warehousing and secure data mining as discussed in Part VIII.

7.6.9 Real-Time Database Systems

Real-time database systems have been examined for numerous applications including command and control and process control. In our work we designed and developed real-time concurrency-control algorithms for the AWACS (Airborne Warning and Control System) as well as designed and developed a real-time main memory data manager (see, for example, [BENS96]).

One of the challenges here is to incorporate security into real-time processing. Now security and real-time processing are conflicting goals. For example, if we are to make all the access control checks, the transactions may miss deadlines. There is also the potential for covert channels when integrating security and real-time processing. We have investigated secure real-time concurrency-control algorithms (see, for example, [SON95]). We have also discussed issues on incorporating security, real-time processing, and fault tolerance (see [THUR99]). There is still much to be done in this area. This is also becoming critical for many applications including embedded systems.

7.7 Hard Problems

The previous section provided a brief overview of various types of MLS/DBMSs. Some of the systems are elaborated on in the following chapters. In this section we discuss some hard problems in MLS/DBMSs. The most notable hard problem is the inference problem. The inference problem is the process of posing queries and deducing sensitive information from the legitimate responses received. Many efforts have been discussed in the literature to handle the inference problem. First of all we proved that the general inference problem was unsolvable (see [THUR90b]). Then we explored the use of security constraints and conceptual structures to handle various types of inferences (see [THUR91a]). We elaborate on the inference problem in Chapters 12 through 14. Note that the aggregation problem is a special case of the inference problem where collections of data elements are sensitive but the individual data elements are unclassified.

Another hard problem is secure transaction processing. Many efforts have been reported on reducing covert channels when processing transactions in MLS/DBMSs (see, for example, [JAJO90a] and [ATLU95]). A survey of various secure concurrency-control efforts in MLS/DBMSs is reported in [THUR93b]. As stated in the previous section, the challenge is to design MLS/DBMSs that function in a real-time environment. That is, not only do the transactions have to be secure they also have to meet timing constraints. We discuss secure transaction processing in Chapter 10.

A third challenging problem is developing a multilevel secure relational data model. Various proposals have been developed including those by Jajodia and Sandhu [JAJO90b], the Sea View model [DENN87], and the LOCK Data Views model [STAC90]. SWORD also proposed its own model (see [WISE92]). Thuraisingham has proposed an approach to unify the various models [THUR93c]. The problem is due to the fact that different users have different views of the same element. If we use multiple values to represent the same entity then we are violating the integrity of databases. However, if we do not enforce what is called polyinstantiation, then there is a potential for signaling channels. This is still an open problem. Potential solutions are discussed in Chapter 9.

This section has discussed only some of the challenges. Many other challenges are discussed as we describe various types of MLS/DBMSs including relational systems, object systems, and distributed systems. Figure 7.7 illustrates the research challenges.

7.8 Emerging Technologies

As technologies emerge, one can examine multilevel security issues for these emerging technologies. For example, as object database systems emerged in the 1980s we started examining multilevel security for object

Hard Problems:
Inference and Aggregation,
Secure Concurrency Control,
Polyinstantiation: Multiple
views at different levels,
Auditing

Figure 7.7   Hard problems and research challenges

Emerging Technologies:

Secure data warehousing
Secure data mining
Secure digital libraries
Secure semantic Web
Secure collaboration
Secure knowledge management
Secure E-commerce

Figure 7.8   Emerging technologies

databases. Today we have many new technologies including data ware-housing, E-commerce systems, multimedia systems, and the Web and digital libraries. Only a limited number of efforts have been reported on investigating multilevel security for the emerging data management systems. This is partly due to the fact that even for relational systems there are hard problems to solve with respect to multilevel security. As the system becomes more complex, developing high-assurance multilevel systems becomes an enormous challenge.

For example, how can one develop usable multilevel secure systems, say, for digital libraries and E-commerce systems? How can we get accept-able performance? How do we verify huge systems such as the World Wide Web? At present we still have a lot to do with respect to discretionary security for such emerging systems. We believe that as we make progress with assurance technologies and if there is a need for multilevel security for such emerging technologies, then research initiatives will commence for these areas. Figure 7.8 illustrates some of the emerging technologies.

7.9 Summary and Directions

This chapter has provided a broad overview of the historical developments of MLD/DBMSs. We defined MLS/DBMSs and discussed the early efforts. Then we focused on the developments with the Air Force Summer Study as well as provided a summary of the major efforts in the 1980s. Then we provided an overview of the TDI and discussed several types of MLS/DBMSs. Finally, we discussed some hard problems as well as issues on examining multilevel security for emerging systems.

Although MLS/DBMSs are not getting the attention they received in the 1980s and in the 1990s, we believe that there will always be a use for such systems, especially for military environments. We need to focus on building high-performance MLS/DBMSs that are user friendly. There are still many hard and unsolved problems. We should continue with research in these areas as new technologies emerge.

References

[AFSB83] Air Force Studies Board, Committee on Multilevel Data Management Security. *Multilevel Data Management Security.* National Academy Press: Washington, DC, 1983.

[ATLU95] Atluri, V. et al. Providing different degrees of recency options to transactions in multilevel secure databases. In *Proceedings of the IFIP Database Security Conference*, Rensselaerville, New York, August 1995. North Holland: Amsterdam, 1996.

[BENS96] Bensley E. et al. Object-oriented approach to developing real-time infrastructure and data manager. In *Proceedings of the IEEE Workshop on Object-Oriented Real-Time Systems*, Laguna Beach, CA, February 1996.

[BUNE82] Buneman, P. et al. An implementation technique for database query languages. *ACM Transactions on Database Systems* 7: 2, 1982.

[BURN86] Burns, R. Integrity lock DBMS. In *Proceedings of the National Computer Security Conference*, Gaithersburg, MD, September 1986.

[CHEN76] Chen, P. The entity-relationship model—Toward a unified view of data. *ACM Transactions on Database Systems* 1: 1, 1976.

[COST94] Costich, O. et al. The SINTRA data model: Structure and operations. In *Proceedings of the IFIP Database Security Conference*, Huntsville AL, 1993. North Holland: Amsterdam, 1994.

[DENN87] Denning, D. et al. A multilevel rational data model, In *Proceedings of the IEEE Symposium on Security and Privacy,* Oakland, CA, April 1987.

[DEWI90] Dewitt, D.J. et al. The gamma database machine project. *IEEE Transactions on Knowledge and Data Engineering* 2: 1, 1990.

[DOWN77] Downs, D. and Popek, G. A kernel design for a secure data base management system. In *Proceedings of Very Large Database Systems*, Tokyo, Japan, 1977.

[FROS88] Froscher J. and Meadows, C. Achieving a trusted database management system using parallelism. In *Proceedings of the IFIP Database Security Conference*, Kingston, Ontario, Canada, 1988.

[GAJN88] Gajnak, G. Some results from the entity/relationship multilevel secure DBMS project. In *Proceedings of the Fourth Aerospace Computer Security Applications Conference*, Orlando, FL, December 1988.

[GALL78] Gallaire, H. and Minker, J. *Logic and Databases*, Plenum Press: New York, 1978.

[GARV88] Garvey, C. and Wu, A. Views as the security objects in a multilevel secure relational database management system. In *Proceedings of the IEEE Symposium on Security and Privacy,* Oakland, CA, April 1988.

[GRAU82] Graubart, R. and Woodward, J. A preliminary naval surveillance DBMS security model. In *Proceedings of the IEEE Symposium on Security and Privacy,* Oakland, CA, April 1982.

[GRAU84] Graubart, R. The integrity-lock approach to secure database management. In *Proceedings of the IEEE Symposium on Security and Privacy,* Oakland, CA, April 1984.

[GRAU85] Graubart, R. and Duffy, K. Design overview for retrofitting integrity-lock architecture onto a commercial DBMS. In *Proceedings of the IEEE Symposium on Security and Privacy,* Oakland, CA, April 1985.

[GROH76] Grohn, M. A model of a protected data management system. Technical Report ESD-TR-76-289, I. P. Sharp Associates: Bedford, MA, June 1976.

[HINK75] Hinke T. and Schaefer, M. Secure data management system. Technical Report RADC-TR-75-266, System Development Corp. Santa Monica, CA, November 1975.

[IEEE83] *IEEE Computer* 16: 7, 1983.

[IFIP00] *Proceedings of the IFIP Database Security Conference,* Amsterdam, The Netherlands. Kluwer: Hingham, MA, 2001.

[JAJO90a] Jajodia, S. and Sandhu, R. Polyinstantiation integrity in multilevel relations. In *Proceedings of the IEEE Symposium on Security and Privacy,* Oakland, CA, April 1990.

[JAJO90b] Jajodia, S. and Kogan, B. Transaction processing in multilevel-secure databases using replicated architecture. In *Proceedings of the IEEE Symposium on Security and Privacy,* Oakland, CA, April 1990.

[JAJO90c] Jajodia, S. and Kogan, B. Interpreting an object-oriented data model with multilevel security, *Proceedings of the IEEE Symposium on Security and Privacy,* Oakland, CA, May 1990.

[KEEF88] Keefe, T. et al. Security for object-oriented database systems. In *Proceedings of the National Computer Security Conference,* Baltimore, MD, October 1988.

[KEEF89] Keefe, T. et al. Secure query processing strategies. *IEEE Computer* 22: 3, March 1989.

[LUNT90] Lunt, T. et al. The SeaView security model. *IEEE Transactions on Software Engineering* 16: 6, 1990.

[MCGU02] McGuinness, D. et al. (eds.) *The Description Logic Handbook: Theory, Implementation, and Applications.* Cambridge University Press: New York, 2002.

[MILL92] Millen, J. and Lunt, T. Security for object-oriented database systems. In *Proceedings of the IEEE Symposium on Security and Privacy,* Oakland, CA, April 1992.

[RAY03] Ray, I. et al. Using parameterized UML to specify and compose access control models. In *Proceedings of the IFIP Conference on Integrity and Control,* Lausanne, Switzerland, 2003. Kluwer: Hingham, MA, 2004.

[ROSE94] Rosenthal, A. et al. A fine grained access control model for object-oriented DBMSs. In *Proceedings IFIP Database Security Conference*, Hildesheim, Germany, August 1994.

[RUBI93] Rubinovitz, H. and Thuraisingham, B. Design and implementation of a secure distributed query processor. *Journal of Systems and Software*, 21: 1, 1993.

[SELL93] Sell, P. and Thuraisingham, B. Applying OMT for designing multilevel database applications. In *Proceedings of the IFIP Database Security Conference*, Huntsville, AL, September 1993. North Holland: Amsterdam, 1994.

[SON95] Son, S. et al. An adaptive policy for improved timeliness in secure database systems. In *Proceedings of the IFIP Databases Security Conference*, Rensselaerville, New York, August 1995. Chapman & Hall: London, 1996.

[STAC90] Stachour, P. and Thuraisingham, B. Design of LDV: A multilevel secure relational database management system. *IEEE Transactions on Knowledge and Data Engineering* 2: 2, June 1990.

[TCSE85] Trusted Computer Systems Evaluation Criteria, National Computer Security Center, MD, 1985.

[TDI91] *Trusted Database Interpretation*. National Computer Security Center, Linthicum, MD, 1991.

[THUR87] Thuraisingham, B. Security checking in relational database management systems augmented with inference engines. *Computers and Security* 6: 6, 1987.

[THUR89] Thuraisingham, B. Secure query processing in intelligent database systems. In *Proceedings of the Computer Security Applications Conference*, Tucson, AZ, December 1989.

[THUR89a] Thuraisingham, B. Mandatory security for object-oriented database systems. In *Proceedings of the ACM OOPOSLA Conference*, October 1989. ACM: New York, 1989.

[THUR89b] Thuraisingham, B. Multilevel security for object-oriented database systems. In *Proceedings of the National Computer Security Conference*, Baltimore, MD, October, 1989.

[THUR89c] Thuraisingham, B. Multilevel security for functional database systems. *Computers and Security*, 9: 6, 1989.

[THUR90a] Thuraisingham, B. Multilevel security for multimedia database systems. In *Proceedings of the IFIP Database Security Conference*, Halifax, England, September 1990. North Holland: Amsterdam, 1991.

[THUR90b] Thuraisingham, B. Recursion theoretic properties of the inference problem. Presented at the *IEEE Computer Security Foundations Workshop*, Franconia, NH, June 1990 (also available as MITRE Technical Paper MTP291 June 1990).

[THUR91a] Thuraisingham, B. The use of conceptual structures to handle the inference problem. In *Proceedings of the IFIP Database Security Conference*, Shepherdstown, WV. North Holland: Amsterdam, 1992)

[THUR91b] Thuraisingham, B. Multilevel security for distributed database systems. *Computers and Security*, 11: 6, 1991.

[THUR91c] Thuraisingham, B. A nonmonotmic typed multilevel logic for secure data and knowledge base management systems. In *Proceedings of the Computer Security Foundations Workshop*, 1991.

[THUR93a] Thuraisingham, B. Trusted database systems and parallel processing. In *Proceedings of the ACM Computer Science Conference*. ACM: New York, 1993.

[THUR93b] Thuraisingham, B. and Ko, H. Concurrency control in trusted database management systems: A survey, *ACM SIGMOD Record*, 22: 4, 1993.

[THUR93c] Thuraisingham, B. Towards the design of a standard multilevel relational data model, *Computer Standards and Interface Journal*, 15: 1, 1993.

[THUR94] Thuraisingham, B. Multilevel security for federated database system. *Computers and Security*, 14: 6, 1994.

[THUR99] Thuraisingham, B. and Maurer, J. Information survivability of command and control systems. *IEEE Transactions on Knowledge and Data Engineering*, 11: 1, January 1999.

[ULLM88] Ullmann, J. *Principles of Database Systems*, Computer Science Press: Rockville, MD, 1988.

[WISE92] Wiseman, S. Using SWORD for the military aircraft command example database. In *Proceedings of the IFIP Database Security Conference*, Vancouver, British Columbia. North Holland: Amsterdam, 1993.

Exercises

1. Describe in detail the major aspects of the TDI.
2. Give a summary of the Air Force Summer Study Report.
3. Conduct a survey of MLS/DBMSs.

Chapter 8

Design Principles

8.1 Overview

This chapter describes design principles for MLS/DBMSs. These are the principles based upon which the various MLS/DBMSs have been designed. In particular, we provide a taxonomy for the various designs for a MLS/DBMS. Note that these DBMSs may be based on relational models or they may be based on object models, logic-based models, or any of the other models discussed in Chapter 7.

Before we discuss the taxonomy, we provide some information on mandatory access control for DBMSs. This type of access control is the one that is utilized by MLS/DBMSs. We discuss the Bell and LaPadula security policy and its interpretation for MLS/DBMSs. Then we describe the taxonomy for MLS/DBMSs. Note that the taxonomy essentially gives us various security architectures to design MLS/DBMSs.

The organization of this chapter is as follows. Mandatory access control including a discussion of security policies is provided in Section 8.2. Various security architectures are discussed in Section 8.3. The chapter is summarized in Section 8.4.

8.2 Mandatory Access Control

8.2.1 Overview

This section describes mandatory access-control models that have been developed for DBMSs. Although DBMSs must deal with many of the same security concerns as trusted operating systems (identification and authentication, access control, auditing), there are characteristics of DBMSs that introduce additional security challenges. For example, objects in DBMSs tend to be of varying sizes and can be of fine granularity such as relations, attributes, and elements. This contrasts with operating systems where the granularity tends to be coarse such as files or segments. Because of the fine granularity in MLS/DBMSs, also often called Trusted DataBase Systems (TDBMS), the objects on which MAC (Mandatory Access Control) and DAC (Discretionary Access Control) are performed may differ. In MLS operating systems, also called Trusted Operating Systems, MAC and DAC are usually performed on the same object such as a file.

There are also some functional differences between operating systems and DBMSs. Operating systems tend to deal with subjects attempting to access some object. DBMSs are employed for sharing data between users and to provide users with a means to relate different data objects. Also, DBMSs are generally dependent upon operating systems to provide resources such as interprocess communication and memory management. Therefore, trusted DBMS designs often must take into account how the operating systems deal with security.

The differences between DBMSs and operating systems discussed above mean that the traditional approaches utilized to developing secure systems need to be adapted for trusted DBMSs. Currently there is no standard architectural approach in the development of MLS/DBMSs. A variety of approaches to designing and building MLS/DBMSs has been proposed. Taxonomies for mandatory access control have been proposed by Hinke and Graubart among others (see [HINK89] and [GRAU89]).

In this chapter we describe various approaches for designing a MLS/DBMS. This is also referred to as a taxonomy for MLS/DBMSs (see [HINK89] and [GRAU89]). Some information on these architectures is also given in [THUR89]. Essentially, MLS/DBMSs have been designed based on one of the several architectures discussed in Section 8.3. Figure 8.1 illustrates the essential differences between access control in operating systems and access control in DBMSs.

8.2.2 Mandatory Access-Control Policies

Mandatory access-control policies specify access that subjects have to objects. Many of the commercial DBMSs are based on the Bell and LaPadula policy [BELL73] specified for operating systems. Therefore, we first state this policy and then discuss how this policy has been adapted for DBMSs. Note that other mandatory policies include the noninterference policy by Goguen and Messeguer [GOGU82]. However, these policies are

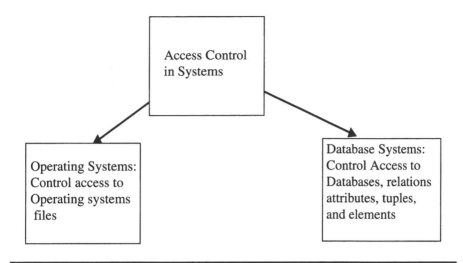

Figure 8.1   Access control in operating systems and database systems

yet to be investigated fully for DBMSs, although the LOCK Data Views project did some preliminary investigation (see [STAC90]).

In the Bell and LaPadula policy, subjects are assigned clearance levels and they can operate a level up to and including their clearance levels. Objects are assigned sensitivity levels. The clearance levels as well as the sensitivity levels are called security levels. The set of security levels forms a partially ordered lattice with Unclassified < Confidential < Secret < TopSecret. The following are the two rules of the policy.

1. *Simple Security Property:* A subject has read access to an object if its security level dominates the level of the object.
2. **-Property (read star property):* A subject has write access to an object if the subject's security level is dominated by that of an object.

These properties apply to database systems also. However, for database systems, the *-property is usually modified to read as follows.

A subject has write access to an object if the subject's level is that of the object.

This means a subject can modify relations at its level.

An important aspect now considered to be part of the security policy for database systems is polyinstantiation [DENN87]. That is, the same object can have different interpretation and values at different levels. For example,

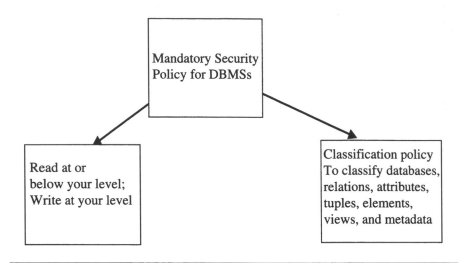

Figure 8.2   Mandatory policy for DBMSs

at the Unclassified level an employee's salary may be 30,000 and at the Secret level the salary may be 70,000. With multilevel relational models one can have both entries but with their security levels as an additional attribute. One of the main motivations toward handling polyinstantiation is to avoid what are called covert channels. For example, if there is an entry at the Secret level that John's salary is 70K and if an Unclassified subject wants to enter that John's salary is 30K, and if the update is not permitted, there could be a signaling channel from a higher level to a lower level. Over time this could become a covert channel. Many discussions and debates have taken place on polyinstantiation in the early 1990s (for example, the panel at the Computer Security Foundations Workshop in Franconia, NH in 1991). No consensus has been reached. Various systems have implemented multilevel relational data models in different ways. We discuss polyinstantiation in more detail when we discuss multilevel relational data models in Chapter 9. Figure 8.2 illustrates a mandatory policy for DBMSs.

8.3   Security Architectures

8.3.1   Overview

Various security architectures have been proposed for secure database systems (see [FERR00]). Security architectures are essentially system architectures that have been designed with security in mind. In this section we examine five architectures for MLS/DBMSs. As stated in Section 8.1, these architectures provide a taxonomy for MLS/DBMSs.

```
Taxonomy/Security
Architectures for MLS/DBMSs:

Integrity Lock
Trusted Subject
Operating System Providing
Mandatory Access Control
Distributed: Partitioned and Replicated
Kernel Extensions
```

Figure 8.3   Security architectures and taxonomy

Figure 8.3 illustrates the various security architectures. These architectures are: integrity lock architecture, operating system enforcing mandatory security architecture, kernel extensions architecture, trusted subject architecture, and the distributed architecture. Note that the distributed architecture is divided further based on the partitioned approach and the replication approach. Sections 8.3.2 to 8.3.6 describe the five architectures. A comparison of the various architectures is discussed in [GRAU89].

8.3.2 Integrity Lock

This approach utilizes an untrusted back-end DBMS with access to the data in the database, an untrusted front end that communicates with the user, and a trusted front end that makes use of encryption technology (see Figure 8.4). The untrusted components are isolated from each other so that there is no communication between the two without the mediation of the trusted filter (also called the trusted front end). The back-end DBMS is maintained at system-high. Note that system-high is the highest level supported by the system and system-low is the lowest level. Multiple instantiations of the front end are maintained. There is one instantiation for each user level. The trusted filter is also maintained at system-high.

Under this approach every tuple that is inserted into the database has associated with it a security label (also called a sensitivity label) and a cryptographic checksum. The security label is encrypted and the data is unencrypted. The checksums are computed by the trusted filter on insertion and recomputed during retrieval. For insertions, the trusted filter computes the checksum and the untrusted back-end DBMS takes the data (i.e., the tuple) and associated label and checksum and stores them in the database. On retrieval, the back end retrieves the data tuples and

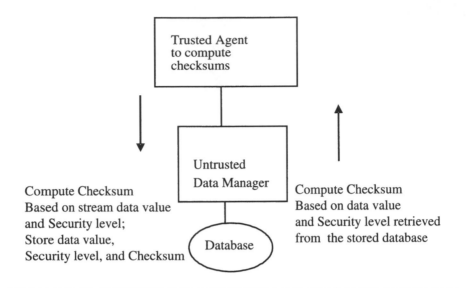

Compute Checksum
Based on stream data value
and Security level;
Store data value,
Security level, and Checksum

Compute Checksum
Based on data value
and Security level retrieved
from the stored database

Figure 8.4 Integrity lock architectures

passes them to the trusted filter which recomputes the checksum based on the tuple and label retrieved. If the trusted filter determines that the data has not been tampered with, it passes the data to the user via the untrusted front end.

The advantage of this approach is that a small amount of additional trusted code is required for the MLS/DBMS, and performance is independent of the number of security levels involved. The disadvantage is that this approach is subject to an inference threat. This threat occurs because the untrusted back end is able to view classified data, encode it as a series of unclassified data tuples, and pass the encoded data tuples to the trusted front end. Because the data tuples are unclassified, the trusted filter will not be able to detect the covert operations of the untrusted back-end DBMS.

8.3.3 Operating System Providing Access Control

This approach (see Figure 8.5), also known as the Hinke–Schaefer approach, utilizes the underlying trusted operating system to perform the access-control mediation. No access-control mediation is performed by the DBMS. The DBMS objects (e.g., tuples) are aligned with the underlying operating system objects (e.g., files). Thus, Secret tuples are stored in Secret files and Top Secret tuples are stored in Top Secret files.

With this approach there is no single DBMS that has access to the data in the database. There is an instantiation of the DBMS for each security level. The advantage of this approach is that it is simple and secure. The

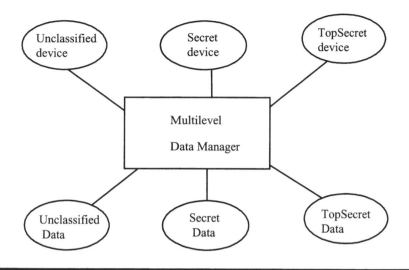

Figure 8.5   Operating systems providing mandatory access control

disadvantage is that performance will increase with the number of security levels (see [GRAU89] and [HINK89]). Note that this approach is also called the single kernel approach.

8.3.4 Kernel Extensions Architecture

This approach (Figure 8.6) is an extension of the single kernel approach. The underlying operating system is utilized to provide the basic MAC and DAC mediation. However, the MLS/DBMS will supplement this access mediation by providing some additional access-control mediation. For example, the MLS/DBMS might provide context-dependent DAC on views. This approach differs from the trusted subject approach because the policies enforced by the MLS/DBMS do not depend on those of the operating system. An example of this architecture is that of LOCK Data Views system described in Chapter 11.

This approach has the same performance problems associated with the single kernel approach. However, because it provides more sophisticated access-control mechanisms, it could address some real-world access-control needs.

8.3.5 Trusted Subject Architecture

This approach (Figure 8.7), also sometimes called dual kernel-based architecture, does not rely on the underlying operating system to perform

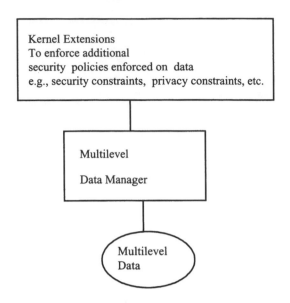

Figure 8.6 Kernel extensions architecture

access-control mediation. The DBMS performs its own access mediation for objects under its control. Thus, access to DBMS records is mediated by the trusted DBMS. The architecture is referred to as a trusted subject approach because the DBMS is usually a trusted subject (or process) hosted on top of the operating system. Essentially, the DBMS has access to the data in the database.

The advantage of this architecture is that it can provide good security, and its performance is independent of the number of security levels involved. The disadvantage is that the DBMS code that performs access mediation must be trusted. This means that a large amount of trusted code may be needed for this approach.

8.3.6 Distributed Architecture

In this approach, there are multiple untrusted back-end DBMSs and a single trusted front-end DBMS. Communication between the back-end DBMSs occurs through the front-end DBMS. There are two main approaches to this architecture. In one approach each back-end DBMS has data at a particular level and operates at that level (Figure 8.8). That is, the back-end DBMS at the Secret level will manage the Secret data and the back-end DBMS at the TopSecret level will manage the TopSecret data. We refer to this as the partitioned approach. With the second approach (Figure 8.9), lower-level data is replicated at the higher levels.

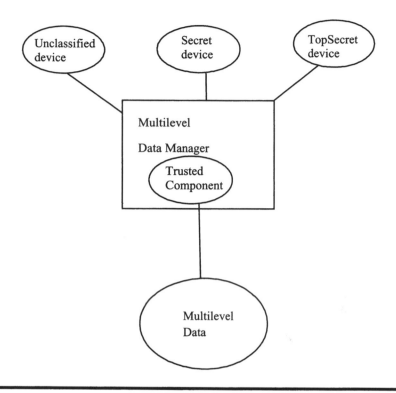

Figure 8.7 Trusted subject architecture

Thus, the Secret DBMS will manage the Secret data, the Confidential data, and the Unclassified data.The Confidential DBMS will manage the Confidential data and the Unclassified data. We refer to this second approach as the replicated approach.

With the partitioned approach the trusted front end is responsible for ensuring that the query is directed to the correct back-end DBMS as well as for performing joins on the data sent from the back-end DBMSs. Because the query itself could contain information classified higher than the back-end DBMSs (such as the values in the where clause of the query), this approach suffers from a potentially high signaling channel. This is because queries are sent to the DBMSs that are operating at levels lower than the user.

For the replicated approach the trusted front end ensures that the query is directed to a single DBMS. Because only the DBMSs operating at the same level as the user are queried, this approach does not suffer from the signaling channel of the first approach. Furthermore, this approach does not require front-end DBMSs to perform the join operations. However, because the data is replicated, the trusted front end must ensure consistency of the data maintained by the different DBMSs.

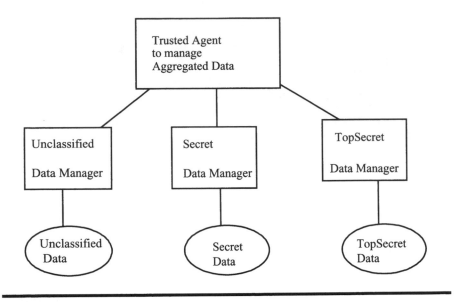

Figure 8.8 Distributed architecture: partitioned approach

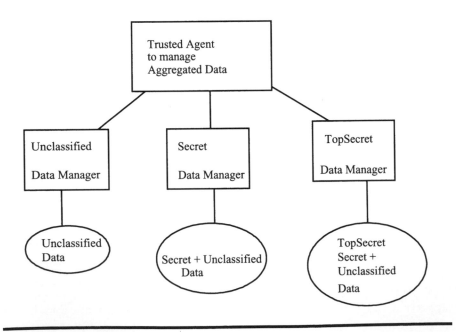

Figure 8.9 Distributed architecture: replicated approach

8.4 Summary and Directions

This chapter has provided an overview of mandatory access control and policies for MLS/DBMSs as well as described a taxonomy for the designs of MLS/DBMSs. We first described the differences between access control in operating systems and access control in DBMSs. Then we provided an overview of the Bell and LaPadula security policy and its adaptation for MLS/DBMSs. Finally we provided a detailed overview of various security architectures for MLDS/DBMSs. These include integrity lock, operating system providing access control, kernel extensions, trusted subject, and distributed architectures. We discussed the advantages and disadvantages of each architecture. For more details we refer the reader to [HINK89] and [GRAU89].

Several research prototypes and commercial products have been developed based on these architectures. We discuss the systems based on relational models in Chapter 11. Some information on MLS/DBMSs based on object models is discussed in Chapter 18.

Although interest in MLS/DBMSs is not as high as it was in the 1980s and 1990s, these systems are still being used for various applications. Therefore, we need to focus on the evaluation of various architectures especially based on features such as performance, usability, and extensibility. That is, we want the systems to be efficient, usable, and also extensible as new technologies are developed. In summary, there is still a lot to be done on the designs of MLS/DBMSs.

References

[BELL73] Bell, D. and LaPadula, L. Secure computer systems: Mathematical foundations and model. Technical Report M74-244, MITRE Corporation: Bedford, MA, 1973.

[DENN87] Denning, D. et al. A multilevel relational data model. In *Proceedings of the IEEE Symposium on Security and Privacy,* Oakland, CA, April 1987.

[FERR00] Ferrari E. and Thuraisingham, B. Secure database systems. In *Advances in Database Management,* eds. M. Piatini and O. Diaz, Artech: London, UK, 2000.

[GOGU82] Goguen, J. and Meseguer, J. Security policies and security models. In *Proceedings of the IEEE Symposium on Security and Privacy,* Oakland, CA, April 1982.

[GRAU89] Graubart, R. A comparison of three secure DBMS architectures. In *Proceedings of the IFIP Database Security Conference,* Monterey, CA, 1989. North Holland: Amsterdam, 1989.

[HINK89] Hinke, T. DBMS trusted computing base taxonomy. In *Proceedings of the IFIP Database Security Conference,* Monterey, CA, 1989. North Holland: Amsterdam, 1989.

[STAC90] Stachour, P. and Thuraisingham, B. Design of LDV: A multilevel secure relational database management system. *IEEE Transactions on Knowledge and Data Engineering* 2: 2, 1990.

[TDI91] *Trusted Database Interpretation*. National Computer Security Center. Linthicum, MD, 1991.

[THUR89] Thuraisingham, B. Recent developments in database security. In *Proceedings of the 1989 IEEE COMPSAC Conference Tutorial Proceedings*, Orlando, FL, September 1989. Also available as MITRE Paper, 1989 (publicly released).

Exercises

1. Compare the security architectures described in this chapter and discuss the advantages and disadvantages of each architecture.
2. Can you think of other security architectures to design an MLS/DBMS?

Conclusion to Part III

In this part we introduced mandatory security for databases. In particular we provided a historical perspective of MLS/DBMSs and then discussed designs for MLS/DBMSs. For example, in Chapter 7 we discussed the Bell and LaPadula policy for database systems and then provided an overview of various types of MLS/DBMSs. In Chapter 8 we described various designs for MLS/DBMSs including the integrity lock architecture, operating system providing mandatory access architecture, trusted subject architecture, extended kernel architecture, and the distributed architecture.

In Parts IV through VII we discuss MLS/DBMSs based on the relational model, data distribution, and the object model. We also discuss the inference problem. Essentially Part III has provided the foundation for a more detailed discussion of MLS/DBMSs.

Multilevel Secure Relational Database Systems

IV

In Part I we discussed supporting technologies for database and applications security and in Part II we discussed discretionary security for database systems. We introduced mandatory security in Part III. In Part IV we discuss systems that enforce mandatory security based on the relational data model. Such a system is called a MultiLevel Secure Relational DataBase Management System (MLS/RDBMS). Much of the early work in MLS/DBMSs focused on the relational data model.

Part IV consists of three chapters. In Chapter 9 we describe various aspects of multilevel secure relational data models. Functions of a MLS/RDBMS are discussed in Chapter 10. Prototypes and products for MLS/RDBMSs are discussed in Chapter 11. Many of the issues addressed in Part IV are applicable to other types of MLS/DBMSs such as MLS distributed database systems and MLS object database systems. Such systems are discussed in Parts VI and VII. Part V discusses the inference problem that arises mainly in MLS/RDBMSs.

Chapter 9

Multilevel Relational Data Models

9.1 Overview

Part III discussed the principles of multilevel secure database systems. In particular, we provided a historical perspective including a discussion of the Air Force Summer Study report as well as the TDI. We also provided an overview of the various architectures for MLS/DBMSs. As we have stated, many of the developments in MLS/DBMSs have focused on the relational model. Therefore, in Part IV we discuss various aspects of MLS/DBMSs based on the relational data model.

The first step toward developing an MLS/RDBMS is developing a multilevel secure relational data model. In the late 1980s and early 1990s there were several efforts on multilevel relational data models. Notable among these efforts are those of SeaView [DENN87], LOCK Data Views [STAC90], SWORD [WISE92], and the work of Jajodia and Sandhu [JAJO90]. Furthermore, ASD-Views also developed a multilevel relational data model where the granularity of classification is based on views [GARV88]. Figure 9.1 illustrates the various multilevel relational data models discussed in the literature. There were also efforts on developing a standard multilevel relational data model [THUR93]. In this chapter we discuss some of the essential points regarding multilevel relational data models.

The organization of this chapter is as follows. In Section 9.2 we discuss issues on the granularity of classification. Note that although in a file system we assign classification levels to the entire files, in the relational

Multilevel Relational Data Model:

Classifying Databases, Relations, Attributes, Tuples, Elements, Metadata, and Views

Polyinstantiation

Security Constraints

Normal forms and theory for Multilevel Relations

Figure 9.1   Multilevel relational data models

model we could classify attributes, relations, tuples, and elements. In Section 9.3 we discuss the notion of polyinstantiation and also provide an overview of the advantages and disadvantages. In Section 9.4 we discuss some of the ideas on standards for multilevel relational data models. The chapter is summarized in Section 9.5.

Note that we do not discuss each multilevel relational data model. We have given many references so that the interested reader can follow up on the various efforts. Our goal is to explain the major issues and constructs. It should be noted that various commercial products have been developed based on the research prototypes such as SeaView and LOCK Data Views. These products are discussed in Chapter 11. Chapter 11 also discusses the various prototypes. Chapter 10, which is also one of the chapters of Part IV, discusses the various functions such as query processing, transaction processing, and metadata management based on the relational data model for MLS/DBMSs.

9.2 Granularity of Classification

As mentioned in Section 9.1, the granularity of classification in a relational database system could be at the database level, the attribute level, tuple level, or even at the element level. Furthermore, one could also assign security levels to views as well as to collections of attributes. Essentially, security levels are assigned based on what we have called security constraints and these constraints classify data based on content, context, association, and events. We discuss security constraints in more detail

DATABASE D: Level = Secret

EMP

SS#	Ename	Salary	D#
1	John	20K	10
2	Paul	30K	20
3	Mary	40K	20

DEPT

D#	Dname	Mgr
10	Math	Smith
20	Physics	Jones

Figure 9.2 Classifying databases

EMP: Level = Secret

SS#	Ename	Salary	D#
1	John	20K	10
2	Paul	30K	20
3	Mary	40K	20

DEPT: Level = Unclassified

D#	Dname	Mgr
10	Math	Smith
20	Physics	Jones

Figure 9.3 Classifying relations

when we discuss the inference problem in Part V. In this chapter we discuss classifying databases, relations, tuples, attributes, and elements, which are the components of the relational data model.

Figure 9.2 illustrates how a database D consisting of relations EMP and DEPT is classified at the Secret level. This means that all of the contents of the relations EMP and DEPT are assigned the level Secret. It does not mean that the existence of the relations is classified. We discuss metadata classification later on in this section.

The next level of classification is classifying relations. Figure 9.3 shows how relation EMP is classified at the level Secret and the relation DEPT

EMP

SS#: S	Ename: U	Salary: S	D#: U
1	John	20K	10
2	Paul	30K	20
3	Mary	40K	20

DEPT

D#: U	Dname: U	Mgr: S
10	Math	Smith
20	Physics	Jones

U = Unclassified
S = Secret

Figure 9.4 Classifying attributes

EMP

SS#	Ename	Salary	D#	Level
1	John	20K	10	U
2	Paul	30K	20	S
3	Mary	40K	20	TS

DEPT

D#	Dname	Mgr	Level
10	Math	Smith	U
20	Physics	Jones	C

U = Unclassified
C = Confidential
S = Secret
TS = TopSecret

Figure 9.5 Classifying tuples

is assigned the level Unclassified. This means the contents of EMP are Secret and the contents of DEPT are Unclassified. Note that here again we are not classifying the existence of the relations.

Figure 9.4 illustrates the classification of attributes. Here the attributes Ename and D# in EMP are Unclassified whereas the attributes SS# and Salary in EMP are Secret. This means all the names and department numbers in EMP are Unclassified and the salaries and social security numbers are Secret. Note that we have also classified some of the attributes in DEPT. We can apply security constraints to classify collections of attributes. We discuss such classification policies when we discuss the inference problem in Part V.

Figure 9.5 illustrates the classification of tuples. Here the tuples relating to John are Unclassified and the tuples relating to Paul are Secret. Furthermore the tuples relating to Mary are TopSecret. Note that we have also assigned tuple-level labeling to the relation DEPT. Here again we can classify collections of tuples taken together at, say, the TopSecret level. We discuss such aggregation-based classification policies in Part V.

EMP

SS#:	Ename:	Salary	D#:
1, S	John, U	20K, C	10, U
2, S	Paul, U	30K, S	20, U
3, S	Mary, U	40K, S	20, U

DEPT

D#: U	Dname: U	Mgr: S
10, U	Math, U	Smith, C
20, U	Physics, U	Jones, S

U = Unclassified

C = Confidential

S = Secret

Figure 9.6   Classifying elements

Figure 9.6 illustrates element-level classification. This is the finest level of granularity. For example, we classify the salary of John at the Confidential level and the salaries of Paul and Mary are Secret. Note that each element in EMP and DEPT is assigned a label which is its security level. Here again we may use constraints to assign the classification levels. Such constraints are discussed in Part V.

In Figure 9.7 we illustrate the classification of views. Here we have formed two views from relation EMP. One view consists of all those who work in department number 20 and this view is classified at the Secret level. The other view is all those who work in department number 10 and this view is classified at the Unclassified level. Here again we may use constraints to classify the views and these constraints are discussed in Part V. Note also when we classify views there are some issues to be considered. That is, if we classify the view that consists of all those who work in department number 20 at the Secret level, then do we still classify all those who work in department number 20 in the base relation EMP at the Secret level? If we are to ensure consistency as well as not leak classified information from the base relations, we have to assign the Secret level to all those work in department number 20 in the relation EMP.

Finally we discuss the classification of the existence of relations, attributes, and tuples. This is essentially classifying the metadata. For example, the relation EMP could be Secret, but its existence could be Confidential. This means that although all the contents of EMP are Secret, the fact that there is a relation called EMP is Confidential. Figure 9.8 illustrates the classification of metadata. Here we have a relation called REL, which is Unclassified, but the existence of certain attributes such as Salary in EMP and Mgr in DEPT are Confidential and the existence of SS# in EMP is Secret. Note that one cannot have the existence of the relation be Secret while its contents are Unclassified. That is, one cannot classify

SECRET VIEW EMP (D# = 20)

SS#	Ename	Salary
2	Paul	30K
3	Mary	40K
4	Jane	20K
1	Michelle	30K

EMP

SS#	Ename	Salary	D#
1	John	20K	10
2	Paul	30K	20
3	Mary	40K	20
4	Jane	20K	20
5	Bill	20K	10
6	Larry	20K	10
1	Michelle	30K	20

UNCLASSIFIED VIEW EMP (D# = 10)

SS#	Ename	Salary
1	John	20K
5	Bill	20K
6	Larry	20K

Figure 9.7 Classifying views

Relation REL

Relation	Attribute	Level
EMP	SS#	Secret
EMP	Ename	Unclassified
EMP	Salary	Confidential
EMP	D#	Unclassified
DEPT	D#	Unclassified
DEPT	Dname	Unclassified
DEPT	Mgr	Confidential

Figure 9.8 Classifying metada

the existence of relation EMP at Secret while the contents of EMP are Unclassified. This means the security level of the existence of EMP must be dominated by the security levels of the contents of EMP. Various multilevel relational data models such as SeaView and LOCK Data Views have studied security properties for metadata (see [STAC90]).

The discussion in this section has illustrated how classification levels, which we also refer to as security levels, may be assigned to the data in a relational database. As we have stated, more complex classification policies are discussed in Part V when we discuss the inference problem. In the next section we discuss a concept that has been discussed at length in the definition of multilevel relational data models. This concept is called polyinstantiation. This is the situation where users cleared at different levels have different views of the same data. This causes inconsistencies in a database. However, if we do not have polyinstantiation, then there is a potential for signaling channels. We discuss different viewpoints in Section 9.3.

9.3 Polyinstantiation

As discussed earlier, polyinstantiation is the technique used in relational databases to represent the fact that users at different levels have different views of the same entity. For example, at the TopSecret level John's salary would be 70K but at the Secret level it would be 60K, at the Confidential level it would be 50K, and at the Unclassified level it would be 40K. In the case of Jane's salary at the Unclassified and Confidential levels it would be 80K but at the Secret and TopSecret levels it would be 90K. Polyinstantiation is illustrated in Figure 9.9. Note that in this figure we have multiple entries for Mary and Paul. For Mary we have four entries as her salary is different at different levels. For Paul we have two entries as the users cleared at the Secret level will read the Secret and the Unclassified value and those cleared at the Unclassified level will read only the Unclassified value.

Now there have been numerous discussions and debates about polyinstantiation as it violates the properties of the relational data model. In the relational model, every entity is represented uniquely. But in the polyinstantiated model, an entity has multiple representations. The question is why do we need polyinstantiation. The main answer is to avoid signaling and covert channels. For example, if we are to have only one answer for John and Jane's salaries and if they are to be the actual values, then John's salary will be 70K and Jane's salary will be 90K. If a user at the Unclassified, Confidential, or Secret level queries for John's salary, then he will not get any answer. Similarly if a user at the Unclassified and

EMP

SS#	Ename	Salary	D#	Level
1	John	20K	10	U
2	Paul	30K	20	S
3	Mary	40K	20	TS
3	Mary	10K	20	U
3	Mary	30K	20	S
3	Mary	20K	20	C
2	Paul	15K	20	U

U = Unclassified
C = Confidential
S = Secret
TS = TopSecret

Figure 9.9   Polyinstantiated relation

EMP

SS#	Ename	Salary	D#	Level
1	John	20K	10	U
2	Paul	15K	20	U
3	Mary	10K	20	U

U = Unclassified

Figure 9.10   Unpolyinstantiated relation

Confidential levels asks for Jane's salary, he will not get an answer. By not giving an answer we have caused a signaling channel. That is, some information at the higher level has interfered with the lower-level world. If there are malicious processes that collude, they could insert or delete values at the higher level and exploit the signaling channel so that it becomes more of a covert channel over time. For example, an Unclassified user may want to insert a salary value for John. Suppose at the Secret level there is already a salary value for John. If the Unclassified user's insertion is not permitted then there is a potential for the signaling channel as the actions of the Secret user have interfered with those of the Unclassified user. An unpolyinstantiated relation is shown in Figure 9.10.

Polyinstantiation was introduced by Dorothy Denning and others in the SeaView model (see [DENN87]). It was adapted in the LOCK Data Views model (see [STAC90]). Normalization of polyinstantiated relations was studied extensively by Jajodia and Sandhu (see [JAJO90]). Each of these efforts supported polyinstantiation but had different views of handling polyinstantiation. Wiseman has argued that polyinstantiation could be quite dangerous (see [WISE89]) and has developed a model that does not support polyinstantiation. There are essentially two debates: one is whether to have polyinstantiation and the other is the correct way to carry out polyinstantiation. Over the years, the preferred approach has been to develop flexible systems. As Thuraisingham argues in her standardization paper in 1993, the model must accurately reflect the real world. That is, if in the real world there are multiple representations and, say, versions of an entity, then we cannot expect the database to hide this fact (see [THUR93]). We discuss standardization aspects in Section 9.4.

9.4 Toward Developing a Standard Multilevel Relational Data Model

The various efforts on multilevel relational data models led to the discussion toward standardizing these models. However, because of the disparate views and the flexible approaches preferred by many, such efforts were abandoned. We discuss some of our ideas on this topic as published in [THUR93]. Note that around that time the Department of the Navy had a standardization effort called NGCR (Next Generation Computing Resources) under which database interface standards were being explored. We presented our views on multilevel relational data models at the NGCR meetings. Although there was much interest, there was insufficient support for converging toward a standard model.

Our thesis toward standardization is that we need to represent the real world as naturally and completely as possible. That is, if the real world is multilevel, then we cannot force the database to be single-level. If the real world is single-level, then we cannot force the database to be multilevel. That is, polyinstantiation is needed only if the real world is multilevel. We also found an issue with Wiseman's arguments against polyinstantiation and we argued that if one would properly represent the real world, then we would not have inconsistencies.

Figure 9.11 illustrates a single-level universe and Figure 9.12 illustrates a multilevel universe. It should be noted that although there have been many discussions on multilevel data models since the mid-1990s, the arguments are now applicable with respect to privacy. That is, there are multiple privacy levels such as public, semi-public, semi-private, and

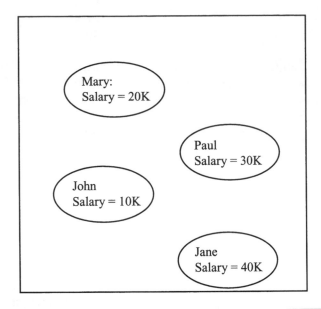

Figure 9.11 Single-level universe

Figure 9.12 Multilevel universe

private. We can apply the arguments for the multilevel secure relational data model for developing, say, a multilevel privacy model. Some aspects are given in [THUR04]. It should also be noted that much of the discussion on relational data models applies to other models such as objects. We have carried out extensive investigations for multilevel object models. We address this topic in Part VII.

9.5 Summary and Directions

In this chapter we have discussed multilevel relational data models. We started with a discussion of granularity of classification and provided an overview of classifying various entities such as relations, tuples, and attributes. Then we discussed the concept of polyinstantiation and also provided an overview of standards for multilevel relational data models.

Note that even though there are now major efforts on developing multilevel relational data models, as long as the multilevel systems are in use, we have to pay attention to the various aspects of multilevel relations. Furthermore, there is much interest now in adapting the concepts to handle privacy. Finally we need to examine the concepts for new kinds of models such as multidimensional data models. Such models are needed for secure data warehousing as well as for data mining of secure databases.

References

[DENN87] Denning, D. et al. A multilevel relational data model. In *Proceedings of the IEEE Symposium on Security and Privacy*, Oakland, CA, April 1987.

[GARV88] Garvey, C. et al. The advanced secure DBMS: Making secure DBMSs usable. In *Proceedings of the IFIP Database Security Conference*, Kingston, Canada, October 1988. North Holland: Amsterdam, 1989.

[JAJO90] Jajodia, S. and Sandhu, R. Polyinstantiation, integrity in multilevel relations. In *Proceedings of the IEEE Symposium on Security and Privacy*, Oakland, CA, May 1990.

[STAC90] Stachour, P. and Thuraisingham, B. Design of LDV: A multilevel secure relational database management system. *IEEE Transactions on Knowledge and Data Engineering* 2: 2, 1990.

[THUR93] Thuraisingham, B. et al. Design and implementation of a database inference controller. *Data and Knowledge Engineering Journal* 11: 3, 1993.

[THUR04] Thuraisingham, B. Privacy constraint processing in a privacy enhanced database system. *Data and Knowledge Engineering Journal*, 2005 (to appear).

[WISE89] Simon, W. On the problem of security in data bases. In *Proceedings of the IFIP Database Security Conference*, Monterey, CA, 1989. North Holland: Amsterdam, 1990.

[WISE92] Wiseman, S. Using SWORD for the military aircraft command example database. In *Proceedings of the IFIP Database Security Conference*, Vancouver, British Columbia, August 1992. North Holland: Amsterdam, 1993.

Exercises

1. Survey the multilevel relational data models for SeaView, LOCK Data Views, SWORD, and ASD-Views and discuss the advantages and disadvantages of each model.
2. Develop a theory of multilevel relational data models.

Chapter 10

Security Impact on Database Functions

10.1 Overview

The previous chapter discussed multilevel data modeling issues. Note that two of the important aspects of database management are data modeling and database functions. In this chapter we discuss the security impact on the various database functions. Our focus is on MLS/DBMSs. Furthermore, in our discussions we mainly focus on the relational data model discussed in Chapter 9. However, many of the arguments apply to nonrelational database systems also.

In Chapter 2 we discussed various functions for a DBMS. These functions include query processing, transaction management, storage management, metadata management, and others such as integrity and security management. Note that in this chapter we examine the security impact on these functions. Other functions include some special operations such as real-time processing, fault-tolerant computing, and multimedia data management. Security impact on such functions is discussed in later chapters.

The organization of this chapter is as follows. In Section 10.2 we discuss secure query processing. In Section 10.3 we discuss secure transaction management which also includes a discussion of concurrency control. In Section 10.4 we discuss secure storage management. Secure metadata management is the subject of Section 10.5. In Section 10.6 we discuss the security impact on other functions such as integrity management. The chapter is summarized in Section 10.7. Figure 10.1 illustrates the functions of a MLS/DBMS.

Multilevel Secure Database Functions:

Query Processing: Enforce mandatory access control rules during query processing; inference control; consider security constraints for query optimization

Transaction management: Check whether security constraints are satisfied during transaction execution; Concurrency control algorithms that prevent covert challenges; Ensure actions of higher-level processes do not affect those of lower-level processes

Metadata management: Classify metadata in such a way that information is not leaked to lower levels

Storage management: Ensure that security levels are assigned to storage structures so that information is not leaked to lower levels

Integrity management: Example: payload problem. Ensure that integrity constraints enforced at lower level do not take into consideration high-level data

---

Figure 10.1   Functions of a MLS/DBMS

10.2 Query Processing

Query processing is one of the major functions of a DBMS. In an MLS/DBMS, the trust placed on the query processor depends on the architecture used to design the system. If the system is based on the operating system providing mandatory access control, then the DBMS is essentially untrusted and the operating system controls access to the files. The data will be partitioned according to the security level. For example, Secret tuples will be stored in Secret files and Unclassified tuples will be stored in Unclassified files.

If additional security constraints are to be enforced, then part of the DBMS that enforces the constraints has to be trusted. For example, consider the query modification operation where a query is modified according to the constraints. Parts of the query modifier have to be trusted to ensure that the query is modified correctly. In this case we assume that the extended kernel architecture is used to design the DBMS. We discuss query modification as well as constraint processing in more detail in Chapter 13.

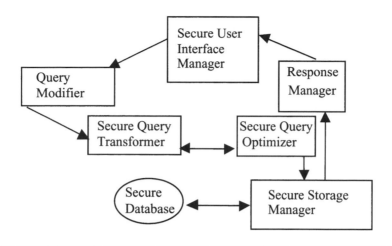

Figure 10.2   Secure query processing

In the case of the trusted subject architecture, the DBMS provides access control. That is, the multilevel relations are stored in multilevel files. The portion of the DBMS that enforces access control must be trusted. For the integrity lock architecture, the trusted front end performs operations such as checksum computation upon storage and checksum comparison upon retrieval. In the case of the distributed architecture, the front end is trusted both for the partitioned approach and for the replicated approach. In the case of the replicated architecture, the query is sent to the database at the level of the user. In the case of the partitioned approach, the trusted front end must ensure that the query sent to the back-end DBMS does not have where clauses because untrusted subjects could send sensitive information embedded in the where clauses such as "salary > 50K".

Another issue that must be considered in secure query processing is the impact of security on query optimization. That is, how can the query be optimized so that the data at different levels is accessed efficiently and securely? Thuraisingham et al. have carried out extensive investigations on secure processing (see, for example, [DWYE87], [THUR87], and [KEEF89]). The approaches are essentially based on constraint processing. The LOCK Data Views project has also carried out investigations on secure query processing (see [STAC90]). Other projects such as SeaView assume that the operating system provides mandatory access control. Therefore the DBMS is untrusted with respect to query processing. Figure 10.2 illustrates secure query processing.

10.3 Transaction Processing

The most widely studied security function is transaction processing. This is because traditional algorithms for transaction processing cause covert

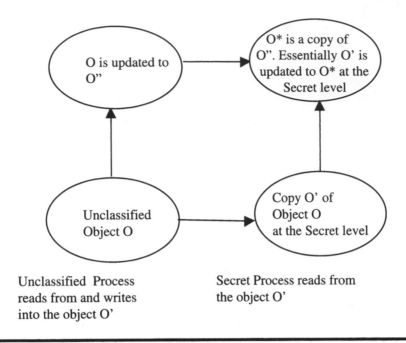

Figure 10.3 Secure concurrency control

channels. As mentioned in Chapter 2, the challenges in transaction processing are concurrency control and recovery. Traditional concurrency-control algorithms such as locking cause covert channels. This subject has been studied extensively by Jajodia, Keefe, and Bertino among others (see [JAJO90], [COST92], [KEEF90], and [ATLU97]). An overview of secure concurrency control was provided by Ko and Thuraisingham (see [KO93]). In this section we discuss the problem and then provide a solution given by Rubinovitz and Thuraisingham (see [RUBI92] and [THUR91]).

Consider the case where there are two transactions operating at the Secret and Unclassified levels (see Figure 10.3). Suppose the Secret transaction reads an Unclassified object while the Unclassified transaction attempts to update the object. Then the Unclassified transaction will not be able to update the object. This will be a signaling channel as the actions of a Secret process have interfered with those of an Unclassified process. Now over time, if the processes are malicious, the Secret process could acquire and release read locks for the Unclassified objects and the Unclassified process could observe the pattern, say a "1" for object available for update and "0" for object not available for update and over time get a sensitive string such as 1000111000011.

Rubinovitz and Thuraisingham have proposed a simple scheme (see [RUBI92]). In this scheme for every Unclassified object O, there is a Secret object which is a duplicate of O, say, O' and a Secret object, say, O" that is only updated by the Secret process or transaction. Therefore, when an Unclassified transaction updates O, the duplicate O' gets updated. The Secret transaction reads from O' and writes into O". This way the actions of the Secret transaction do not interfere with those of the Unclassified transaction.

Jajodia and others have also studied the impact of multilevel security for recovery, the other major aspect of transaction processing (see, for example, [JAJO93]). The idea here is for transactions at different levels to recover from failures while at the same time to ensure that the actions of higher-level transactions do not interfere with lower-level ones. Much of the work has focused on transactions that operate at single levels. Multilevel transactions where transactions operate at multiple levels have been studied by Keefe and Jajodia among others (see, for example, [KEEF90] and [BLAU93]). The idea here is for the portion of the transaction that operates at, say, the Secret level not to interfere with the portion of the transaction that operates at the Unclassified level. Trust issues must also be considered in the case of multilevel transactions.

Although many efforts have been reported on secure transaction processing, benchmarking studies as well as performance studies have not yet been carried out extensively. It should be noted, however, that research in this area has slowed down somewhat during the past five years or so. Nevertheless it is an important area especially for applications such as E-commerce where transactions at different levels will have to operate together to carry out some business operation.

10.4 Storage Management

Storage management in a DBMS includes two major aspects and they are designing efficient access methods and indexing strategies. In an MLS/DBMS, storage management is about securely storing the multilevel data. Here again the trust placed on the DBMS depends on the architecture upon which the system is designed. If the operating system provides access control, then the DBMS is untrusted and therefore the access methods and indexing algorithms are also untrusted. If the system is based on trusted subject architecture, then we need to determine the trust placed on the access-control and indexing algorithms.

There have been many efforts on secure query processing and secure transaction management but not much work has been carried out on secure storage, access methods, and indexing strategies. Some research on these topics has been carried out as part of the research on multilevel data models, polyinstantiation, and normalization (see, for example,

---

Multilevel Secure Storage Management

Assign security levels to storage data

Mappings between storage data and database data

Secure access methods and index strategies for storage data

Example: Index file say on medical records cannot be
Unclassified while the medical records are Secret

Secure query processing and update management on storage
files

Figure 10.4   Secure storage management

[JAJO90]). For example, if a multilevel relation consists of tuples that are
of multiple security levels, then how do you efficiently access, say, the
Secret, Confidential, and Unclassified tuples when a Secret user poses
queries? What are the index strategies for multilevel relations? How can
we normalize multilevel relations for efficient access? These are some of
the research questions and there is little work reported.

As we have stated earlier, although MLS/DBMSs are not receiving as
much attention as they did back in the 1990s, as long as we need such
systems we need to investigate efficient access methods, indexing algorithms, and storage management. Figure 10.4 illustrates the issues in secure
storage management.

10.5 Metadata Management

In Chapter 9 we discussed issues on classifying metadata. That is, like the
data, metadata could also be assigned security levels. When we say that
the metadata of the relation EMP is classified at the Secret level, essentially
it means that the existence of the data itself is assigned the Secret level.
Like the data, metadata has to be managed securely. In this section we
briefly examine secure metadata management.

Metadata management issues are similar to data management. That is,
metadata management functions include query processing, transaction
management, storage management, and integrity management. Like the
data, metadata may be classified. Therefore, it must be ensured that the
metadata is queried securely. Furthermore, if transactions update the

---

Multilevel Secure Metadata Management

Existence of relation EMP is Secret

All the elements in relation EMP are Unclassified

Security problem: By reading the values in relation EMP, the existence of EMP is inferred

Solution: The level of the existence of EMP should dominate the levels of all the information relating to EMP

Metadata management functions are similar to data management functions

---

Figure 10.5   Secure metadata management

metadata, it must be ensured that higher-level transactions do not interfere with lower-level ones.

Metadata has to be stored and accessed securely. That is, we need to examine the access methods and index strategies and determine the applicability of the techniques for metadata management. Storage management issues also include whether the metadata is stored in single-level or multilevel files. If the operating system is to provide access control to metadata, then metadata management functions may be untrusted. If the DBMS controls access then metadata management may be trusted.

In Chapter 9 we examined the relationship between the classification of data and the classification of metadata. That is, if the existence of EMP is classified at the Secret level, then all the information in EMP must be at least Secret. Essentially metadata includes such security rules. Metadata also includes integrity and security constraints. Constraint enforcement is discussed in Chapter 13. The impact of security on integrity in databases is discussed in Section 10.6. Figure 10.5 illustrates secure metadata management.

10.6 Other Functions

Other DBMS functions include integrity management, data distribution, real-time processing, data quality, fault tolerance, and multimedia information processing. We address data distribution issues when we discuss

---

Integrity Management:

TopSecret Constraint: Maximum weight of an aircraft is 1000 lbs

Unclassified level: Weights are added but the TopSecret constraint is not visible;
Unclassified level: there is no constraint

Problem: If TopSecret constraint is checked at the Unclassified level it is a security violation; if not it could cause serious integrity problems

Challenge: Enforce constraints in such a away that high-level constraints do not affect lower-level operations

Polyinstantiation also introduces integrity problems

Figure 10.6   Integrity management with security

secure distributed data management in Part VI. Data quality, real-time processing, and fault-tolerant computing with respect to security are discussed in Part X. Secure multimedia data management is discussed in Part VII. In this section we examine the security impact on integrity.

In Chapter 9 we discussed the need for polyinstantiation and the integrity problem that it causes. That is, due to polyinstantiation, we cannot represent an entity uniquely in the relational database. However, we have argued that if the real world is multilevel, then we cannot force unique representations in the database. That is, an entity may have multiple representations at different levels.

Other aspects of integrity include concurrency control. In Section 10.3 we discussed the covert channels that could result with traditional concurrency-control algorithms and discussed an approach that would avoid covert channels. By keeping multiple copies of the objects at multiple levels, we can ensure that the integrity of the data is maintained and, at the same time, transactions execute securely. Figure 10.6 illustrates integrity management with security.

Note that integrity constraints may be assigned security levels. Only those constraints classified at or below the user's level are taken into consideration during query and transaction management. Essentially the constraints are considered part of the metadata. Note that classifying the integrity constraints may cause a problem. For example, suppose we have a Top-Secret constraint that states that the maximum cargo of a plane cannot exceed 10 tons. This constraint will not be invoked at the Secret level. Therefore at the Secret level one could keep adding weights and the weight of the cargo could well exceed 10 tons. This could cause serious problems. Also, if the cargo is distributed, then we need to carry out computations across the sites.

Other functions include auditing and fault tolerance. We discussed auditing for DBMSs in Chapter 5. In the case of MLS/DBMSs, we need to ensure that auditing the actions of higher-level processes does not interfere with those of the lower-level processes. Similarly when the MLS/DBMS has to be recovered from failures, we need to ensure that there are no covert or signaling challenges.

10.7 Summary and Directions

In this chapter we have examined the functions of a DBMS and discussed the security impact. In particular, we discussed query processing, transaction management, storage management, metadata management, and integrity management for an MLS/DBMS.

Much progress has been made on some functions such as secure query processing and secure transaction management. However, functions such as secure storage management which includes algorithms for access methods and indexing need more work with respect to security. We also need to examine the security impact on functions for next-generation data management systems such as data warehousing, Web databases, and knowledge management systems. We discuss some of the developments in later chapters.

Finally we need benchmarking studies for secure databases. Some preliminary work on this topic was conducted and reported in [DOSH94]. However, not much has been done on benchmarking important functions such as secure transaction management. More work also needs to be carried out on performance evaluation. Some performance as well as simulation studies were carried out for secure query processing and secure transaction management. This work is reported in [RUBI91] and [RUBI92].

References

[ATLU97] Atluri, V. Transaction processing in multilevel secure databases with kernelized architectures: Challenges and solutions. *IEEE Transactions on Knowledge and Data Engineering* 9: 5, 1997.

[BLAU93] Blaustein, B. A model of atomicity for multilevel transactions. In *Proceedings of the IEEE Symposium on Security and Privacy*, Oakland, CA, May 1993.

[COST92] Costich, O. and Jajodia, S. Maintaining multilevel transaction atomicity in MLS database systems with kernelized architecture. In *Proceedings of the IFIP Database Security Conference*, Vancouver, Canada 1992. North Holland: Amsterdam, 1993.

[DOSH94] Doshi, V. et al. Benchmarking multilevel secure database systems using the MITRE Benchmark. In *Proceedings of the Tenth Annual Computer Security Applications Conference*, Orlando, FL, December 1994.

[DWYE87] Dwyer, P. et al. Multilevel security for relational database systems. *Computers and Security* 6: 3, 1987.

[JAJO90] Jajodia, S. and Kogan, B. Transaction processing in multilevel secure databases using replicated architecture. In *Proceedings of the IEEE Symposium on Security and Privacy*, Oakland, CA, May 1990.

[JAJO93] Jajodia, S. Integrating concurrency control and commit algorithms in distributed multilevel secure databases. In *Proceedings of the IFIP Database Security*, Huntsville, AL, 1993. North Holland: Amsterdam, 1994.

[KEEF89] Keefe, T. et al. Secure query processing strategies. *IEEE Computer* 22: 3, 1989.

[KEEF90] Keefe, T. and Tsai, W. Multiversion concurrency control for multilevel secure database systems. In *Proceedings of the IEEE Symposium on Security and Privacy*, Oakland, CA, May 1990.

[KO93] Ko, H. and Thuraisingham, B. A survey of concurrency control in trusted database management systems. *ACM SIGMOD Record* 22: 4, 1993.

[RUBI91] Rubinovitz, H. and Thuraisingham, B. Implementation and simulation of secure distributed query processing algorithms. In *Proceedings of the Computer Simulation Conference*, Baltimore, 1991.

[RUBI92] Rubinovitz, H. and Thuraisingham, B. Design and simulation of secure distributed concurrency control algorithms. In *Proceedings of the 1992 Computer Simulation Conference*, Reno, NV, July 1992.

[THUR87] Thuraisingham, B. Security checking for relational database systems augmented with inference engines. *Computers and Security* 6: 6, 1987.

[THUR91] Thuraisingham, B. Multilevel security in distributed database systems. *Computers and Security* 10: 6, 1991.

Exercises

1. Describe algorithms for secure query processing.
2. Survey secure concurrency-control algorithms and discuss the advantages and disadvantages of the various approaches.
3. Investigate techniques for access methods and indexing for MLS/DBMSs.

Chapter 11

Prototypes and Products

11.1 Overview

The previous chapter provided a discussion of MLS/DBMSs for the relational data model. In particular we discussed data modeling as well as functional issues for MLS/DBMSs. As we have stated in Chapter 7, several MLS/DBMS products emerged in the late 1980s and early 1990s. Many of these products have also been evaluated using the TCSEC and TDI. These products have been influenced by the various design and prototype developments of the 1980s such as Sea View and LOCK Data Views. In this chapter we provide an overview of MLS/DBMS prototypes and products.

The organization of this chapter is as follows. MLS/DBMS prototypes such as SeaView, LOCK Data Views, and ASD/ASD Views are discussed in Section 11.2. Commercial products are discussed in Section 11.3. Note that we use the original information about these products when they appeared in the marketplace. Some of these products have been discontinued and some others have evolved over the years. Furthermore, some corporations have been purchased by others and therefore the products have also evolved. For example, Digital Equipment Corporation's database business was purchased by Oracle and Informix was purchased by IBM. Therefore, we urge the reader to keep up with the developments with the various products. Our purpose in discussing the products is to illustrate the technical concepts and the technology transfer of the research to products as well as to give a historical perspective. We are not endorsing any of the products or prototypes.

Discretionary security with respect to products and prototypes was discussed in Chapter 6. In this chapter we briefly discuss discretionary security for the products and prototypes if relevant to mandatory security. Discretionary and mandatory security for distributed database systems is discussed in Chapters 15 and 16. Furthermore, discretionary and mandatory security including a discussion of the designs and prototypes for object systems is discussed in Chapter 18.

11.2 Prototypes

11.2.1 Overview

Since 1975 various designs and prototypes of MLS/DBMSs have been developed. The earliest was the Hinke–Schaefer architecture which has come to be called the "operating system providing mandatory access control" architecture. In their design, the relations were partitioned vertically (i.e., by attributes) and each partition was stored at a single security level. The operating system provided access to the partitions. This is the approach that influenced a prominent MLS/DBMS design and that is SeaView.

Since the Air Force Summer Study several designs and prototypes were developed. Notable among these are the integrity lock prototypes by MITRE, SeaView by SRI International, LOCK Data Views by Honeywell, ASD and ASD-Views by TRW, SDDBMS by Unisys, SINTRA by the Naval Research Laboratory, and SWORD by the Defense Research Agency in the United Kingdom. Note that an MLS/DBMS based on the trusted subject-based architecture was developed at MITRE in the 1980s using the MIS-TRESS relational database system by Graubart and others. However, to our knowledge there is no publicly available information discussing the design of this prototype.

In Section 11.2.2 we briefly discuss each of the designs and prototypes. Note that the commercial products were influenced heavily by these early designs. Commercial products are discussed in Section 11.3. Figure 11.1 illustrates the designs and prototypes. Note that we have only discussed information about products and prototypes that are publicly available.

11.2.2 Discussion of Prototypes

11.2.2.1 Hinke–Schaefer

As stated earlier, this is one of the earliest MLS/DBMSs to be designed (see [HINK75]). It is a single-kernel approach where operating systems provide all of the mandatory access control. It is hosted on the MULTICS operating system whose storage objects are segments. Columns (or

MLS/DBMS Prototypes:

SeaView (SRI)
LOCK Data Views (Honeywell)
SINTRA (NRL)
SDDBMS (Unisys)
ASD-Views (TRW)
Naval Surveillance Model (MITRE)
Integrity Lock: Mistress and
Ingres (MITRE)
SWORD (DRA)

Figure 11.1   MLS/DBMS designs and prototypes

attributes) of a relation are labeled. Relations are vertically fragmented according to security levels and stored in segments. A segment at level L is stored at level L.

The vertical alignment has a problem inasmuch as a user may have to log in at different security levels to insert a tuple. Another solution is to have a trusted mechanism to insert tuples. This means a portion of the DBMS would have to be trusted and this contradicts the assumption that the DBMS is untrusted. Some recent architectures based on the single-kernel approach assume a row- (or tuple-) level labeling. This avoids the insertion problem. Such an approach has also come to be called the Hinke–Schaefer approach.

11.2.2.2 Naval Surveillance Model

The Naval Surveillance Model was designed by Graubart and Woodward (see [GRAU82]). The subjects of the model are users such as analysts, remote users, the SSO, and the DBA. The user has a clearance level (maximum level at which she can process data) and access level (which is her current level). Each user has an operator authorization list (the operators that the user can and cannot use). Objects include devices, databases, relations, data fields, and data elements. All objects except devices are data objects. Databases, relations, records, and fields are called containers. That is, the database contains relations; relations contain columns, fields, and records; and fields contain elements.

Each object may have a default security level (DSL); if it does not, then it takes the level of its container. An object's level may be less than, equal to, or greater than the level of its container. In case of conflicts, the user specifies precedence rules. Each container has an ISL (Implicit

Security Level) which is the highest level of any data that it contains. Access-control lists specify various types of access to noncontainers, containers, and special rules for relations and databases. Operators are grouped into different operator classes. Policies are specified for operator authorization, nondiscretionary and discretionary security, data access, and data definition. The model is applied to different types of users.

11.2.2.3 Integrity Lock Prototypes

Two integrity lock prototypes were developed in the mid-1980s; one by Graubart and Duffy using the MISTRESS relational database system [GRAU85] and the other by Burns using the INGRES relational database system [BURN86]. We discuss both prototypes. Note that it has been pointed out that the integrity lock approach has inference threats because the DBMS is untrusted and may contain Trojan horses [GRAU89]. Nevertheless the advantage of this approach is that only the filter needs to be trusted.

The MISTRESS prototype consists of four components: (1) parser, (2) Untrusted Front End (UTFE), (3) Trusted Front End (TFE), and (4) Untrusted Back End (UBE). The MISTRESS database is a UNIX directory, which is at database-low (lowest level supported by the database). Relations are maintained at database-high (highest level supported by the database) and dominates the level of the directory. The data dictionary is maintained at the level of the directory.

The TFE runs at system-high and the UBE also runs at system-high. Only the UBE has access to the database. The parser is instantiated at the user's level. The UTFE is also at the user's level. The TFE creates the other three components and ensures that they are created at the appropriate security levels. For a given query, the parser parses the query and gives it to the TFE. The TFE gives it to the UTFE and UBE; the UBE does selects and joins and gives the result to the TFE. The TFE does the filtering by computing the checksum and comparing it with what is stored in the database. The TFE gives the result to the UTFE, and the UTFE performs projects and aggregate operations.

The INGRES prototype utilizes the UC Berkeley version of the system. The approach is similar to the MISTRESS prototype approach except that tuples are retrieved first and the filter checks are performed by the TFE before selections and joins. Burns argues that this limits the Trojan horse problem but adds to the performance problem.

11.2.2.4 SeaView

SeaView is perhaps the most prominent MLS/DBMS to be designed. It is a joint effort by SRI, Gemini, and Oracle funded by the Air Force Research

Laboratory in Rome, New York. It is targeted at the A1 level. The operating system provides mandatory access control and it is based on the TDI approach called TCB subsetting. That is, the TCB is layered. At each layer the TCB performs different types of access mediation. The operating system TCB provides MAC and is at the lowest layer. The DBMS TCB performs DAC and it is at the next layer. The MAC model enforces the following policy: read at or below your level and write at your level. The TCB model defines discretionary security supporting policies for multilevel relations, views, and constraints (see also [DENN87] and [LUNT90]).

The project proposed MSQL (Multilevel SQL) and handles element-level classification. It introduced polyinstantiation. Multilevel (virtual) relations are decomposed into single-level relations. A relation at level L is stored in a file at level L. Algorithms have been designed to decompose multilevel relations into single-level relations and later recombine the single-level relations to form a multilevel relation. There is a DBMS instance per security level. Each database operation is carried out by a single-level subject.

11.2.2.5 Lock Data Views

While Sea View was being designed at SRI, the Air Force Research Laboratory funded another effort by Honeywell to design and develop an A1 level MLS/DBMS. This system came to be known as LOCK Data Views, also called LDV, as it ran on the LOCK operating system which is targeted at the A1 assurance level. The idea is for the operating system to provide the basic mandatory access control. However, policy extensions for inference and aggregation as well as for content- and context-dependent access control are to be enforced by kernel extensions. Multilevel relations are decomposed into single-level relations. Single-level relations are recombined to form a multilevel relation during the query. The level relation at level L is stored in a file at level L.

The initial design supported element-level labeling and polyinstantiation. Later designs supported tuple-level labeling and polyinstantiation. LOCK's type enforcement mechanism is key to the design of LDV. It allows for the encapsulation of applications such as LDV in a protected subsystem. LOCK's mandatory, discretionary, and type enforcement mechanism is utilized by LDV. Security policy extensions are proposed for response and update processing. In addition, SQL extensions are defined for security assertions also called security constraints (see [STAC90] and [THUR89a]).

11.2.2.6 ASD and ASD-Views

ASD and ASD-Views are two systems developed by TRW. ASD was built on the ASOS operating system. It is targeted at the A1 level. It is based on the trusted subject-based architecture. It enforces content-independent MAC on tuples. Only the DBMS kernel has modify access to the tuples. The DBMS kernel performs filtering based on security labels.

TRW then built ASD-Views on top of ASD. The idea here was to provide MAC on views where views are the security objects. The project used a restricted definition of views where views are formed from a single relation. Only simple operators such as projects and selections are permitted to define views (see [GARV88]).

11.2.2.7 SINTRA and SDDBMS

SINTRA and SDDBMS are two efforts based on the distributed approach. SINTRA was designed and developed at the Naval Research Laboratory in the 1990s and SDDBMS was designed and developed at Unisys in the late 1980s. We discuss each of these efforts briefly.

SINTRA's design is based on the replicated distributed approach where the data is replicated at the higher levels. That is, the Unclassified database is replicated in the Secret and TopSecret databases and the Secret database is replicated in the TopSecret database. It is targeted at the B3 level of assurance. It proposes to use the XTS-200 system developed by Honeywell for the front-end and the Oracle DBMS for the back-end systems. The goal is to develop a high-performance, high-assurance system that also utilizes parallel processing. The project also designed and developed concurrency-control algorithms for handling replication and minimizing signaling challenges (see [FROS88] and [COST94]).

The SDDBMS effort was funded by the Air Force Research Laboratory at Rome and is also based on the distributed approach. It is also targeted at the B3 level. Each untrusted machine operates at a single level and data is replicated at the option of the DBA. The trusted front end is connected to untrusted back-end machines. The project studied three configurations: the fully replicated, partially replicated, and no replication. The advantages and disadvantages of each approach were documented. A prototype system was also developed utilizing Unisys' Mermaid distributed database system and reported in [JENS89].

11.2.2.8 SWORD

Although the other prototypes were developed in the United States, SWORD was developed by the Defense Research Agency in the United Kingdom. It is driven by the concerns due to polyinstantiation (see [WISE89] and [WISE92]). The whole idea behind SWORD is the insert-low approach. The prototype builds a front end to a nonsecure relational database system. It is similar to the integrity lock approach but no encryption is used. It relies on the correct operation of the DBMS. The project had planned to use formal software development techniques.

In the insert-low approach, the client may only insert or delete from a table if no client with a lower or incomparable clearance can access the table. Different "bottom-classification" is given to each table. Only clients whose levels dominate the level of the table level may access the table. The project extended SQL to SSQL (Secure SQL). Field contents and existence are also classified. Multilevel rows are entered via placeholders.

Much of the debate on polyinstantiation is due to the views taken by the researchers who designed SWORD. Their view is that databases should not be polyinstantiated. Therefore the insert-low approach avoided poly-instantiation and also the signaling channel. However, it does not support the situation where users at multiple levels have different views of the same entity.

11.3 Products

11.3.1 Overview

Since 1988, several commercial MLS/RDBMS products have been developed. However, some of these products are no longer being marketed. Furthermore, some of the corporations have merged with other corporations and so the ownership of these products has also changed. In this section we give an overview of the commercial products that emerged between 1988 and 1993. Note that because of all the changes the information may not be current and the best way to obtain up-to-date information about products is through the vendor. Nevertheless the information here gives the reader some idea of the issues involved and the various access-control models that were utilized when the systems were being designed.

Because the MLS/DBMS commercial marketplace has been dominated by relational systems, we only discuss relational databases. Note that there has been some work on a multilevel secure object system by Ontos Corporation in the early 1990s. However, little work has been reported on that effort. The products to be discussed include Trudata, Sybase Secure SQL Server, Trusted Oracle, Trusted Rubix, Secure RDB, and Secure Teradata. Our emphasis is on the technical aspects of the products. We briefly mention the platforms they were intended to run on initially. Furthermore, we discuss the features of the initial designs of the products, which were released in the late 1980s and early 1990s. All of the information about the products has been obtained from published material or

```
┌─────────────────────────────────────────┐
│                                         │
│   MLS/DBMS Products:                     │
│                                         │
│   Trusted Oracle (Oracle)               │
│   Secure SQL Server (Sybase)            │
│   SeRdb (DEC)                           │
│   Trudata (Infosys)                     │
│    Secure Informix (Informix)           │
│    Secure Teradata (Teradata)           │
│                                         │
│   Ingres Intelligent Database (Ingres)  │
│                                         │
└─────────────────────────────────────────┘
```

Figure 11.2   MLS/DBMS products

from user manuals published by the vendor when the products were first developed. Some information was also given in [THUR89b]. Figure 11.2 illustrates the various products.

11.3.2 Discussion of Products

11.3.2.1 TRUDATA

The TRUDATA system is based on the integrity lock approach whose underlying security model is derived from the Naval Surveillance Model [GRAU82]. The architecture of the system is based on the MISTRESS integrity lock architecture [GRAU85].

The initial version of TRUDATA utilized an untrusted Britton Lee database machine as a back end and an AT&T 3B2 system V/MLS System as a front end. The back-end database machine is untrusted and has access to the data in the database. The back-end machine performs DBMS selections, joins, and projections, and is also responsible for data storage and retrieval. The trusted front end computes the checksum based on the labels and the data. The trusted filter also performs access control for MAC and DAC.

The objects of classification in TRUDATA are view instances called pviews and mviews. Pviews are projections from a given relation. The pviews are defined before the data is inserted into the database. Mviews are the joins between two or more pviews. Views are labeled mainly to limit the inference threat inherent with the integrity lock approach (see the discussion in Chapter 8). TRUDATA provides two versions of its MAC policy. One is the "restricted" version, which is the write at your level policy, and the other is the "unrestricted" version, which is the write at or above your level policy.

Objects in TRUDATA may be labeled with one of three types of labels: (1) an ASL, (2) a DSL, or (3) a CCR label. An ASL (Actual Security Label) may be associated with a pview instance. A DSL (Default Security Label) is attached to every container. Pview instances that do not have an ASL associated with them inherit the security label (DSL) of their container. The inheritance mechanism allows users to avoid having to explicitly label all pview instances. The CCR (Container Clearance Requirement) label is associated with containers. The CCR label is a pair of labels: one is the top and the other is the bottom of the labels that may be associated with objects within the container. All labels may be changed through the use of the change command by an authorized user.

In addition to providing MAC, TRUDATA also provides DAC. DAC is handled in TRUDATA via a combination of Access Control Lists (ACLs), exclusionary access control lists (XACLs), and operator authorization lists (OALs). OALs are associated with subjects and specify which operators the subjects may apply to the objects. The operators supported by TRU-DATA are read, write, delete, create, change-level, and change-access.

ACLs and XACLs are associated with objects. ACLs indicate which subjects may access the object (from a discretionary point of view) and in what manner the objects may be accessed (e.g., read, write, etc.). XACLs essentially specify negative access-control policies. When an ACL is associated with a container the access permission of the ACL applies to all of the objects within the container unless excluded by an XACL. If an ACL associated with a database provides a user with read and write permission, that permission applies to all of the relations and pviews in the database, unless there is an XACL associated with a particular object (i.e., relation or pview). However, once an XACL excludes a subject from accessing an object, subsequent ACLs will not restore that permission. That is, in case of conflict XACL permissions dominate those of ACLs. Note that permissions granted to DBAs and SSOs cannot be denied by ordinary users.

11.3.2.2 Sybase Secure SQL Server

Sybase's Secure SQL Server was the first MLS/DBMS to be developed. It is a trusted subject-based DBMS and is based on the client/server architecture. For the initial release the client portion of the architecture ran on Ultrix, SE/VMS, and SUN MLS. The initial release of the server ran only on Ultrix. Because Ultrix is not a trusted product it may not provide the trusted operating system support environment that a trusted DBMS requires. However, Sybase had discussed porting the server to DEC RISC CMW, the SUN CMW, and SeVMS. (Note that RISC stands for Reduced Instruction Set Architecture and CMW stands for Compartmented Mode Workstation.)

Secure Sybase provides a security label on each tuple of the system, and performs MAC based on these labels. There are 16 hierarchical security labels, and 64 nonhierarchical security labels. Sybase stores its metadata in relations. Therefore, Sybase is capable of labeling each row of the metadata relation.

Secure Sybase provided DAC on tables (i.e., relation) for the create, select, delete, update, and insert operators. It does not support DAC on views. The identification and authentication functions are handled by the DBMS and not by the underlying operating system. In particular, identification and authentication are handled by the client. Secure Sybase supports auditing including auditing on log-ons, log-outs, all requests, and integrity violations. The Secure Sybase Server also provides a trusted facility management by supporting security officer and system administrator roles.

Secure Sybase supports polyinstantiation for insertion, updates, and deletion. Polyinstatiation may be turned off for deletions and updates; it may not be turned off for insertions. Secure Sybase allows for downgrading of the entire content of a relation. Users create empty relations at the lower level, and then the contents of the original relation are copied into the new relation. Concurrency control is handled in the system via locking, and is supported at the table and page level.

11.3.2.3 Trusted Oracle

Oracle's product has developed two approaches to designing a MLS/DBMS: (1) the Hinke–Schaefer approach and (2) the trusted subject approach. The Hinke–Schaefer approach utilizes the Seaview model described in the previous section. The early releases of trusted Oracle were targeted to run on the SE/VMS operating systems and the HP/UX operating system.

The system enforces tuple-level MAC. In the Hinke–Schaefer version this is done by storing the tuples in the underlying trusted operating system storage object. Under both approaches, the number of security levels is the same as that enforced by the underlying operating system. Trusted Oracle provides polyinstantiation on insertions. The polyinstantiation is on a relation basis and can be turned on and off as needed. The system enforces a write at your level policy for updates and deletes. Users who have the appropriate privilege may change the security labels associated with tuples.

DAC is enforced on views. Trusted Oracle does not employ locking to enforce concurrency control. Instead it employs a single-level multiversioning mechanism. A series of single-level schedulers is used and the transactions are marked with time stamps. Because there is no locking and no writing down under this approach, there is no possibility of a covert signaling channel occurring.

The system metadata is stored in relations. For the Hinke–Schaefer version of the product this means that the metadata is partitioned into operating system objects of the appropriate security level. Thus, the Secret metadata is in Secret operating system files and the Top Secret metadata is in Top Secret operating system files. For the trusted subject version of the product each tuple of the metadata relation is labeled. The system supports trusted facility management.

It should be noted that Trusted Oracle is one of the few MLS/DBMSs that is still being maintained. With each release several enhancements have been made including the implementation of role-based access control in their recent releases (such as Oracle 11i). We urge the reader to visit www.oracle.com to get up-to-date information about their products.

11.3.2.4 Trusted Informix

Trusted Informix utilizes a trusted subject-based architecture and was intended to run on both the HP UX operating system, and the ATT System V MLS system. Security labels are assigned to tuples. To enforce MAC, the system calls the underlying trusted operating system, which in turn calls the operating system. Trusted Informix supports the ability to change the labels of tuples. This is accomplished by copying the data into a new tuple at a different level and then deleting the original tuple.

Content-independent DAC is enforced on databases, relations, tuples, and attributes. Polyinstantiation is supported on insert. The metadata is stored at system-high. Concurrency control is achieved via locking as follows. If a higher-level subject locks an object, a lower-level subject is still allowed to write into the object. By permitting this write operation the product ensures that the higher-level subject cannot signal to the lower-level subject via the locking mechanism. However, with this approach there is a potential for the data integrity problem because the locked objects can be written into by lower-level subjects. This integrity problem is addressed by alerting the higher-level subjects when a locked object has been written into. This gives the higher-level subject the option of either backing out of the transaction or continuing. The system supports trusted facility management by providing for the System Security Officer and Database System Administrator roles.

11.3.2.5 Trusted Rubix

Trusted Rubix is a product of Infosystems Technology Incorporated. The effort was funded by what used to be the Rome Laboratory (and now the Air Force Research Laboratory at Rome). The product is based on a trusted subject architecture. The system was developed to run on top of the AT&T 3B2/600 UNIX version V operating system.

The product enforces tuple-level MAC, with the number of security levels the same as that of the operating system. The MAC policy ensures that inserts, updates, and deletes all occur at the same security level as the requesting user (subject). That is, the system supports write at your level policy. Trusted Rubix enforces polyinstantiation on insert, and allows the user a choice between two types of polyinstantiation. In one case, polyinstantiation is only enforced on insertions when identical data exists at a level that dominates the level of the insertion. In the other case, polyinstantiation is enforced for all insertions regardless of the level of the requesting user. In addition to these two options, the user has the option of turning off polyinstantiation.

DAC is enforced on relations, views, and databases. The mechanism for enforcing DAC is through access control lists. The system metadata is stored in a relation. Therefore, tuple-level labeling of metadata is permitted. This supports the labeling of relation names and attribute names.

11.3.2.6 SERdb

Secure RDB (SERdb) is a trusted DBMS product from what used to be Digital Equipment Corporation (DEC), now part of Oracle Corporation. The product utilizes a trusted subject architecture and runs on the operating system SEVMS. The product enforces tuple-level MAC. The number of security levels supported by SERdb is the same as that for SEVMS (256 hierarchical levels, 128 nonhierarchical levels). Security labels are maintained in a separate attribute of a relation. However, only authorized users are allowed to modify the label attribute. DAC is enforced by ACLs and is supported on databases, relations, views, and attributes.

SERdb supports polyinstantiation on insertions of specified databases. Authorized users can turn off polyinstantiation. All updates and deletions must be at the same security level as the user. The system metadata is stored in a relation. Therefore tuple-level labeling of metadata is permitted. However, polyinstantiation is not allowed for the metadata relations.

11.3.2.7 Secure Teradata Machine

Teradata has developed a trusted database machine prototype funded by the National Security Agency and had plans to incorporate the features into the commercial version. The Teradata product is a database machine integrated with the underlying operating system. It essentially utilizes a trusted subject architecture, without an underlying operating system. The system is a parallel processor-based architecture with 1024 processors each responsible for some DBMS function. Each processor is part of the system TCB.

The system supports 16 hierarchical and 64 nonhierarchical security levels. The Teradata architecture allows relations to be either single-level or multilevel. For multilevel relations the labels are associated with each tuple in the relation. For single-level relations the relation's security level is maintained as part of the table definition in the metadata. The metadata itself is maintained in relations. This means that multilevel metadata can be supported.

The system supports DAC on the database, relation, or view. The system does not explicitly support polyinstantiation, but the user can effectively provide polyinstantiation for insertion by defining a unique key which is the concatenation of the existing key attribute and the security attribute of a relation.

11.3.2.8 INGRES

The INGRES Intelligent Database is a product of the INGRES Corporation and is based on the trusted subject-based architecture. It was intended to run on DEC SeVMS as well as AT&T System V MLS. Note that unlike the other products, INGRES evolved from UC Berkeley's INGRES research prototype. Therefore, the system is a fully fledged relational database system and supports many of the theoretical concepts.

The MLS INGRES enforces mandatory access control on tuples and discretionary access control on tables and views. The part of the DBMS that controls the access to the tuples must be trusted. It supports essentially tuple-level labeling.

The goal of the project was to evaluate it using both the TCSEC/TDI as well as the ITSEC, which is the European criterion. The system was also very popular in Europe, and, at one time, it was reported that the Ministry of Defense in the United Kingdom was examining this system for its use. Note also that one of the integrity lock prototypes developed at MITRE used the UC Berkeley version of the INGRES prototype.

11.4 Summary and Directions

In this chapter we have provided an overview of the prominent MLS/DBMS prototypes and products. Many of the developments began after the Air Force Summer Study in 1982 and were funded by federal agencies such as the Air Force Research Laboratory in Rome, the Naval Research Laboratory, the National Security Agency, United States Army CECOM, and the Department of the Navy SPAWAR. Our purpose was to discuss the technical concepts and not promote any particular prototype or product. Furthermore, as we have stressed, information on prototypes and products gets outdated as developments are made. Up-to-date information can be obtained from the vendors and possibly from the Web.

The prototypes and products discussed are all based on the relational data model. As mentioned, there is very little information on products for nonrelational systems. In Parts V through VII we discuss additional prototypes that describe inference controllers, secure distributed database systems, and secure object database systems mainly for mandatory security. However, there are products that implement discretionary security for nonrelational database systems and we discuss these products in Part VII.

The early prototypes and products discussed in this chapter have influenced the development of MLS/DBMSs a great deal. Furthermore, the experiences that have been gained by these efforts are having an impact on emerging secure data management technologies. Emerging secure data management technologies are discussed in Parts XIII through X.

References

[BURN86] Burns, R. Integrity lock DBMS. In *Proceedings of the National Computer Security Conference*, Gaithersburg, MD, September 1986.

[COST94] Costich, O. et al. The SINTRA data model: Structure and operations. In *Proceedings of the IFIP Database Security Conference*, Huntsville, AL, 1993. North Holland: Amsterdam, 1994.

[DENN87] Denning, D. et al. A multilevel relational data model. In *Proceedings of the IEEE Symposium on Security and Privacy* 1987.

[FROS88] Froscher, J. and Meadows, C. A trusted database management system using parallelism. In *Proceedings of the IFIP Database Security Conference*, Kingston, Ontario, Canada, October 1988.

[GARV88] Garvey, C. et al. The advanced secure DBMS: Making secure DBMSs usable. In *Proceedings of the IFIP Database Security Conference*, Kingston, Ontario, Canada, 1988. North Holland: Amsterdam, 1989.

[GRAU82] Graubart, R. and Woodward, J. A preliminary naval surveillance DBMS' security model. In *Proceedings of the IEEE Symposium on Security and Privacy,* Oakland, CA, April 1982.

[GRAU84] Graubart, R. The integrity-lock approach to secure database management. In *Proceedings of the IEEE Symposium on Security and Privacy,* Oakland, CA, 1984.

[GRAU85] Graubart, R. and Duffy, K. Design overview for retrofitting integrity-lock architecture onto a commercial DBMS. In *Proceedings of the IEEE Symposium on Security and Privacy,* Oakland, CA, 1985.

[GRAU89] Graubart, R. A comparison of three secure DBMS architectures. In *Proceedings of the IFIP Database Security Conference*, Monterey, CA, 1989. North Holland: Amsterdam, 1990.

[HINK75] Hinke,T. and Schaefer, M. Secure data management. Technical Report, Systems Development Corporation, 1975.

[JENS89] Jensen, C. SDDM—A prototype of a distributed architecture for database security. In *Proceedings of the IEEE Data Engineering Conference*, Los Angeles, February 1989.

[LUNT90] Lunt, T. et al. The SeaView security model. *IEEE Transactions on Software Engineering* 16: 6, 1990.

[STAC90] Stachour, P. and Thuraisingham, B. Design of LDV: A multilevel secure relational database management system. *IEEE Transactions on Knowledge and Data Engineering* 2: 2, 1990.

[THUR89a] Thuraisingham, B. and Stachour, P. SQL extensions for security assertions. *Computer Standards and Interface Journal* 11: 1, 1989.

[THUR89b] Thuraisingham, B. Recent developments in database security. In *Proceedings of the 1989 IEEE COMPSAC Conference Tutorial*. Also available as MITRE Paper, 1989 (publicly released).

[WISE89] Simon, W. On the problem of security in data bases. In *Proceedings of the IFIP Database Security Conference*, Monterey, CA, 1989.

[WISE92] Wiseman, S. Using SWORD for the military aircraft command example database. In *Proceedings of the IFIP Database Security Conference*, Vancouver, BC, North Holland: Amsterdam, 1993.

Exercises

1. Select a prototype based on each of the architectures discussed in Chapter 8 and describe the features.
2. Conduct a survey of the security features for three commercial products.
3. Design a MLS/DBMS based on the relational data model.

Conclusion to Part IV

Part IV described MLS/RDBMSs. In Chapter 9 we described a multilevel secure relational data model including a discussion of polyinstantiation. We also discussed aspects of developing a standard multilevel relational data model. Functions of a MLS/RDBMS were discussed in Chapter 10. In particular, query processing, transaction management, metadata management, and storage management were discussed. Prototypes and products for MLS/RDBMSs were discussed in Chapter 11. The prototypes included discussions of the prominent Sea View and LOCK Data Views Systems and products included those by Oracle, Sybase, and others.

As stated earlier, many of the issues addressed in Part IV are applicable to other types of MLS/DBMSs such as MLS distributed database systems and MLS object database systems. Such systems are discussed in Parts VI and VII. Part V discusses the inference problem that arises in MLS/RDBMSs. The inference problem in such systems was studied extensively in the early 1990s. This work is having a significant impact on current directions on handling the privacy problem. Therefore, it is important to understand the issues involved in handling the inference problem if we are to make progress on the privacy problem.

THE INFERENCE PROBLEM

V

In Part I we discussed supporting technologies for database and applications security and in Part II we discussed discretionary security for database systems. We introduced mandatory security in Part III and in Part IV we discussed MLS/DBMSs based on the relational data model. In Part V we focus on an important topic in database security and that is the inference problem. Inference is the process of posing queries and deducing new information from the responses received. If the information deduced is something that the user is not authorized to know, then it becomes a problem. Our focus is mainly on the inference problem that occurs in MLS/RDBMSs.

Part V consists of three chapters. In Chapter 12 we provide a perspective of the inference problem and include a discussion of statistical database security. In Chapters 13 and 14 we discuss our research on the inference problem. In Chapter 13 we discuss security-constraint processing as well as the designs of MLS/DBMSs that handle the inference problem. In Chapter 14 we discuss the use of conceptual structures such as semantic nets to detect security violations via inference. Although the focus is on MLS/DBMSs based on the relational data model, our approaches can be used for other types of database systems.

Chapter 12

A Perspective of the Inference Problem

12.1 Overview

Parts III and IV focused on MLS/DBMSs; Part V discusses the inference problem. Note that although much of the discussion is influenced by the developments with MLS/DBMSs, we also address some other aspects of the inference problem such as statistical database inference. It should be noted that much of the work carried out on the inference problem is having a major impact on the developments of the privacy problem. We discuss the privacy problem in a later chapter.

The inference problem was studied extensively in statistical databases for several years before it became a very popular topic for MLS/DBMSs. Inference is the process of posing queries and deducing information from the legitimate response received. It becomes a problem if the information deduced is something that a user is not authorized to know. For example, if one deduces, say, Secret information from Unclassified pieces of data, then the inference problem has occurred.

In the case of statistical databases, Dorothy Denning and others were the first to study the problem extensively (see [IEEE83]). Here the idea is to give out, say, averages and sums while protecting the individual pieces of data. The census bureau also studied the inference problem in collecting and maintaining census data. However, it was not until the late 1980s

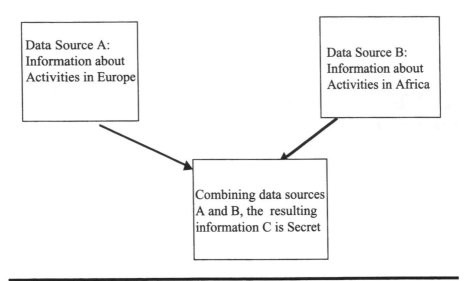

Data Source A:
Information about
Activities in Europe

Data Source B:
Information about
Activities in Africa

Combining data sources
A and B, the resulting
information C is Secret

Figure 12.1   Inference problem

when there were many activities on MLS/DBMSs that the inference problem was investigated extensively. Morgenstern at SRI International
[MORG87], Thuraisingham at Honeywell [THUR87], and Hinke at TRW
[HINK88] developed the early solutions. Later Thuraisingham at MITRE
carried out extensive work on the problem together with Ford, Rubinovitz,
and Collins (see [THUR89], [THUR93], and [THUR95]). Since then many
efforts have been reported, say, by Marks and Farkas among others (see
[MARK96] and [FARK01]). Today the inference problem is resurfacing due
to technologies such as data warehousing and data mining. This is because
data warehousing and data mining exacerbate the inference problem and
they also contribute toward privacy violations via inference. We discuss
data warehousing, data mining, and privacy in Part VIII.

In this chapter we give a perspective of the inference problem. In
Section 12.2 we discuss statistical databases briefly. In Section 12.3 we
discuss the various approaches proposed for the inference problem.
Complexity of the inference problem which was examined by Thuraisingham in 1990 is discussed in Section 12.4. Summary and directions are
provided in Section 12.5. Figure 12.1 illustrates the process whereby users
infer unauthorized information from the legitimate responses. Figure 12.2
illustrates the early approaches to handling the inference problem by
Morgenstern, Thuraisingham, and Hinke. Figure 12.3 illustrates the various
types of the inference problem such as inference by deduction, induction,
and other inference strategies. Figure 12.4 illustrates the inference problem
in various information systems.

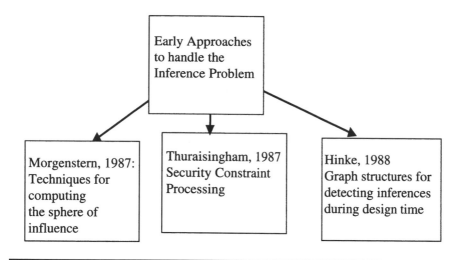

Figure 12.2   Early approaches

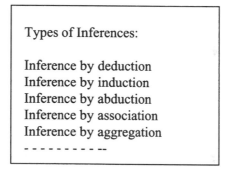

Figure 12.3   Types of inference problem

12.2 Statistical Database Inference

As we have stated, the inference problem was studied in statistical databases especially by the census bureau. Statistical databases are used by various organizations starting from the census bureau to marketing organizations that want to study the behavior patterns of population. Statistical databases essentially give out values such as sums, averages, mean, deviation, and the like, that are useful in studying the population in terms of their numbers or their behavior patterns. More recently with applications such as E-commerce, organizations carry out targeted marketing based on salaries, property owned, purchase patterns, and other somewhat personal information. With such information, organizations can then focus on the

```
┌─────────────────────────────────────────────┐
│                                             │
│   Inference Problem in different            │
│   Information Systems:                       │
│                                             │
│   Inference problem in relational databases  │
│   Inference problem in object databases      │
│   Inference problem in distributed databases │
│   Inference problem in heterogeneous databases │
│   Inference problem in multimedia databases  │
│                                             │
│   - - - - - - - - - - - - - - - -           │
│                                             │
│                                             │
└─────────────────────────────────────────────┘
```

Figure 12.4　Inference problem in different information systems

population that would be most suitable to which to market a product. For example, expensive jewelry could be marketed to wealthy women earning more than, say, 200K whereas clothes such as blue jeans could be marketed to teen-aged girls.

Dorothy Denning and others have studied various types of statistical databases and the inference problem that arises in such databases. This problem is called the statistical inference problem. For example, one could give out average salaries while protecting the individual salaries. Another example would be that one could give out healthcare information about a particular county while protecting the individual healthcare records of the people in the county. The question is can an adversary infer the individual salaries by posing queries to obtain the average salary of ten people and then nine people and then eight people and so on.

Another practice with statistical databases is not to use all of the values in the databases, but work with sample values. That is, averages and mean are computed from a representative sample. From the sample values, it probably would be more difficult to divulge the individual sensitive information. Here again the challenge is that of inferring sensitive data from the averages and sums computed from the sample records. Figure 12.5 illustrates the approaches to handling the statistical inference problem.

Although statistical inference has been explored extensively for the past several decades, more recently it has gained a lot of prominence especially with emerging technologies such as data warehousing and data mining. For example, data warehouses have been developed to give out specific information for decision makers including sums and averages. Therefore, the warehouse data may be Unclassified, but there could be sensitive information residing in the back-end databases. That is, based on the information the warehouse gives out, can one determine the

```
┌─────────────────────────────────────┐
│                                      │
│   Statistical Inference Techniques:  │
│                                      │
│   Computing Averages, Mean,          │
│   Mode, Standard Deviation;          │
│   Sampling;                          │
│   Estimation;                        │
│   Hypothesis testing;                │
│                                      │
│   ----------                         │
│                                      │
└─────────────────────────────────────┘
```

Figure 12.5   Statistical inference

sensitive data in the back-end databases? We address this again in Part VIII when we discuss data warehouses. Note also that statistical inference has emerged as a machine-learning method and is being used extensively for machine-learning and data mining in order to extract information previously unknown from large collections of data (see [MITC98]).

Data mining has also resulted in much interest in statistical databases. Data mining gives out information not previously known using various reasoning techniques such as statistical inference. Therefore, the challenge is one of uncovering sensitive or private information by mining. Essentially the inference problem is exacerbated by data mining. More recently there is also much concern about the privacy problem. Clifton et al. (see [CLIF00]) and many others are now working on what is called privacy-preserving data mining. The idea is to maintain privacy and at the same time give out information perhaps slightly perturbed. The same techniques can be used to handle the inference problem also. We discuss privacy-preserving data mining in a later section.

In summary, statistical databases and statistical inference will continue to be studied as new technologies emerge. That is, not only is the census bureau interested in statistical databases and statistical inference, various organizations including marketing, sales, healthcare, finance, manufacturing, and the like are now interested in using statistical reasoning techniques to get as much information as possible through mining. This causes major concern for both the inference and privacy problems.

12.3 Discussion of Approaches for Handling Inference in a MLS/DBMS

In the previous section we discussed statistical inference. In this section we discuss the approaches that have been developed to handle the inference problem. The approaches can essentially be divided into two groups: one is based on security constraints and the other based on conceptual structures. We discuss both approaches briefly in this section. In Chapters 13 and 14 we elaborate on these two sets of approaches.

Security constraints are essentially rules that assign security levels to the data. The approach was first introduced by Thurasingham et al. in 1987 as a result of the LOCK Data Views effort (see [THUR87] and [STAC90]). In this approach some security constraints are handled during query processing. That is, during the query operation, the constraints are examined and the query is modified. Furthermore, before the release operation the constraints are examined to determine which information can be released. The approach also allows for some constraints to be processed during database updates. That is, the constraints are examined during the update operation and the data is assigned appropriate security levels. Finally some constraints are handled during database design where the metadata or schemas are assigned security levels. In Chapter 13 we give many more details on security-constraint processing including a discussion of architectures and algorithms. Note that more recently Wiederhold [WIED00] and Jajodia [JAJO03] have developed an approach where constraints are examined only after the data is released. This approach is called release control. Figure 12.6 illustrates aspects of constraint processing.

In the second set of approaches, conceptual structures are used to represent the application and reason about the application. If there are potential security violations via inference then they are detected during application design time. Hinke was the first to examine graphs for representing and reasoning about applications [HINK88]. Later a more extensive investigation was carried out by Thuraisingham using conceptual structures such as semantic nets and conceptual graphs (see [THUR91a]). Following this, Hinke and Delugach carried out an extensive investigation on the use of conceptual graphs (see [DELU92]). Around the mid to late 1990s, Thuraisingham, Binns, Marks, and Collins explored various other conceptual structures such as hypersemantic data models (see [MARK94]) and Deductive Object Models (see [COLL96]). More recently Thuraisingham is examining the use of conceptual structures to handle the privacy problem. Figure 12.7 briefly illustrates the use of conceptual structures.

Another direction worth mentioning is Thuraisingham's work on multilevel deductive databases and the logic called NTML (Nonmonotnic Typed Multilevel Logic). The idea here is to develop a MLS/DBMS based on logic so that the resulting deductive MLS/DBMSs could also handle the inference problem while carrying out other functions (see [THUR91b] and [THUR92]). This approach shows a lot of promise and should be examined now for the privacy problem. However, it should be noted that deductive databases have not resulted in much commercial interest. Therefore, there have been some questions as to whether we need to invest

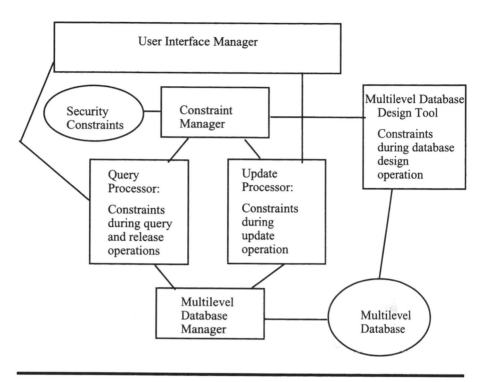

Figure 12.6 Security constraint processing

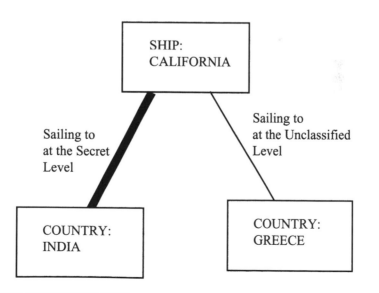

Figure 12.7 Conceptual structures

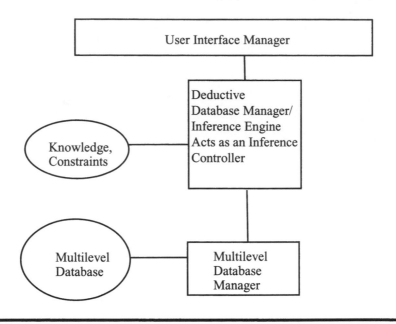

Figure 12.8   Deductive databases for inference problem

in deductive MLS/DBMSs. We have provided a brief overview of such systems in Chapter 7. Figure 12.8 illustrates a logic database system for handing the inference problem.

In addition to the work of Morgenstern, Hinke, and Thuraisingham, other notable efforts have been reported on the inference problem. Meadows showed how the Chinese Wall Policy Model of Brewer and Nash (see [BREW89]) could be applied to the inference problem (see [MEAD90]). Lin refuted some of the concepts of applying the Chinese Wall Policy Model in [LIN02]. Lin also pursued some early work on the inference problem and applied fuzzy logic (see [LIN92]). Lunt published an interesting paper discussing the facts and fallacies of the inference problem (see [LUNT89]). In addition to the inference problem, researchers also examined the aggregation problem where collections of elements taken together are Classified and the individual pieces are Unclassified (see also [LUNT89]).

This section has briefly examined the approaches to handle the inference problem. We examine conceptual structures in more detail in Chapter 14. Security-constraint processing is the subject of Chapter 13. In the next section we discuss the complexity of the inference problem.

12.4   Complexity of the Inference Problem

Although many of the efforts have focused on approaches to handle the inference problem, Thuraisingham examined the complexity of the inference problem in [THUR90]. This work was quoted by Dr. John Campbell as one of the major developments in secure databases in 1990 in the *Proceedings of the 1990 National Computer Systems Security Conference* [CAMP90].

In [THUR90] we examined the recursion-theoretic complexity of the inference problem. Our ultimate goal is to obtain a complete characterization of the inference problem and investigate measures of complexity. Such an investigation could usefully begin with aspects of recursive-function theory. This is because recursive-function theory from which the notion of computability is derived (see [ROGE67]) has provided the basis from which other abstract theories such as computational complexity (see [BLUM67]) and Kolmograv complexity theory (see [KOLM65]) have evolved. Moreover the work of Rosza Peters (see [PETE81]) has shown the practical significance of recursive-function theory in computer science and provided the basis for possible exploitation of such results. Therefore the study of the foundations of the inference problem could usefully begin with aspects of recursive-function theory. We have investigated the recursion-theoretic properties of the inference problem associated with database design. We gave a formulation of the inference problem as a database design problem and investigated the recursion-theoretic properties of this problem. Our research is influenced by our work on security constraints.

The essence of our work is as follows. We defined a set X(L) corresponding to each security level L. This set consists of all databases D that are not secure with respect to security level L. The inference problem with respect to level L would then be the membership problem for the set X(L). That is, given a database D, if it can be effectively decided whether D belongs to X(L), then one can decide whether the design of the database D is secure with respect to level L. By a secure database at a level L we mean that all information that should be labeled at security level L is correctly labeled at level L. We proved properties of the set X(L). For more details of this work we refer the reader to [THUR90] and [THUR91c]. It should be noted that more recently we are applying the techniques explored for the inference problem to the privacy problem. Furthermore, there is a lot of research that needs to be done on the computational complexity of both the inference and the privacy problems. Figure 12.9 illustrates our view of the complexity of the inference problem.

12.5 Summary and Directions

In this chapter we defined the inference problem and examined the approaches to handle the problem. In particular we discussed statistical inference, security-constraint processing, and the use of conceptual structures. We also briefly discussed deductive MLS/DBMSs for inference as well as the complexity of the inference problem.

```
Complexity of the Inference Problem:

Unsolvability of the Inference Problem:
Analyzing the recursion theoretic properties
of the inference problem

Complexity of the Inference Problem:
Computational complexity theories for the
inference problem


Logic: Special logics for MLS/DBMSs
 (example: NTML, Nonmonotonic Typed
 Multilevel Logic)
```

Figure 12.9 Complexity of the inference problem

As new technologies emerge, the inference problem continues to receive attention. This is especially the case for data warehousing, data mining, and Web data management. Furthermore applications such as medical informatics are also examining the inference problem. Finally, research on the privacy problem is following along the lines of inference problem research. In summary, although much progress has been made, there is still a lot of research to carry out on the inference problem not only for MLS/DBMSs, but also for DBMSs that enforce discretionary security. The inference problem also needs to be examined for the emerging database systems and applications.

References

[BLUM67] Blum, M. A machine independent theory of the complexity of recursive functions. *Journal of the Association for Computing Machinery* 2: 14, 1967.
[BREW89] Brewer, D. and Nash, M. The Chinese wall security policy. In *Proceedings of the IEEE Symposium on Security and Privacy*, Oakland, CA, April 1989.
[CAMP90] Campbell, J. Progress in database security. In *Proceedings of the National Computer Security Conference*, Washington, DC, October 1990.
[CLIF00] Clifton, C. Using sample size to limit exposure to data mining. *Journal of Computer Security* 8: 4, 2000

[COLL96] Collins, M. et al. Deductive object-oriented data model for handling the inference problem. In *Proceedings of the AFCEA Database Colloquium*, San Diego, CA, August 1996.

[DELU92] Delugach, H.S. and Hinke, T. AERIE: Database inference modeling and detection using conceptual graphs. In *Proceedings of the Workshop on Conceptual Graphs*, Seattle, WA, 1992.

[DENN79] Denning, D. The tracker: A threat to statistical database security. *ACM Transactions in Database Systems* 4: 2, 1979.

[FARK01] Farkas, C. et al. The inference problem and updates in relational databases. In *Proceedings of the IFIP Database Security Conference*, Lake Niagara, Canada, 2001. Kluwer: Hingham, MA, 2002.

[HINK88] Hinke, T. Inference aggregation detection in database management systems. In *Proceedings of the IEEE Symposium on Security and Privacy*, Oakland, CA, April 1988.

[IEEE83] Special issue on computer security. *IEEE Computer* 16: 7, 1983.

[JAJO03] Jajodia, S. Release control for XML documents. In *Proceedings of the IFIP Conference on Integrity and Control*, Lausanne, Switzerland, November 2003. Kluwer: Hingham, MA, 2004.

[KOLM65] Kolmogorov, A. Three approaches for defining the concept of information quantity. *Problemv Peredaci Informacii*, 1965.

[LIN92] Lin, T.Y. Inference secure multilevel databases. In *Proceedings of the IFIP Database Security Conference*, Vancouver, British Columbia, 1992. North Holland: Amsterdam, 1993.

[LIN02] Lin, T.Y. Placing the Chinese walls on the boundary of conflicts analysis of symmetric binary relations. In *Proceedings of the IEEE COMPSAC Conference*, Oxford, UK, August 2002.

[LUNT89] Lunt, T. Inference and aggregation, facts and fallacies. In *Proceedings of the IEEE Symposium on Security and Privacy*, Oakland, CA, April 1989.

[MARK94] Marks, D. et al. Hypersemantic data modeling for inference analysis. In *Proceedings of the IFIP Database Security Conference*, Hildesheim, Germany, 1994. North Holland: Amsterdam, 1995.

[MARK96] Marks, D. Inference in MLS database systems. *IEEE Transactions on Knowledge and Data Engineering* 8: 1, 1996.

[MEAD90] Meadows C. Extending the Brewer-Nash model to a multilevel context. In *Proceedings of the IEEE Symposium on Security and Privacy*, Oakland, CA, May 1990.

[MITC97] Mitchell, T. *Machine Learning*. McGraw-Hill: New York, 1997.

[MORG87] Morgenstern, M. Security and inference in multilevel database and knowledge base systems. In *Proceedings of the ACM SIGM CD Conference*, San Francisco, May 1987.

[PETE8I] Peter, R. *Recursive Functions in Computer Theory*. Ellis Horwood: Chichester, UK, 1981.

[ROGE67] Rogers, H., Jr. *Theory of Recursive Functions and Effective Computability*. McGraw-Hill: New York, 1967.

[STAC90] Stachour, P. and Thuraisingham, B. Design of LDV: A multilevel secure relational database management system. *IEEE Transactions on Knowledge and Data Engineering* 2: 2 (June), 1990.

[THUR87] Thuraisingham, B. Security checking in relational database management systems augmented with inference engines. *Computers and Security* 6: 6, 1987.

[THUR89] Thuraisingham, B. Secure query processing in intelligent database systems. In *Proceedings of the Computer Security Applications Conference*, Tucson, AZ, December 1989.

[THUR90] Thuraisingham, B. Recursion theoretic properties of the inference problem. Presented at the *IEEE Computer Security Foundations Workshop*, Franconia, NH, June 1990 (also available as MITRE Technical Paper MTP291, June 1990).

[THUR91a] Thuraisingham, B. The use of conceptual structures to handle the inference problem. In *Proceedings of the IFIP Database Security Conference*, Shepherdstown, WV, North Holland: Amsterdam, 1992.

[THUR 91b] Thuraisingham, B. A nonmonotonic typed multilevel logic for multilevel secure database and knowledge base management systems. In *Proceedings of the IEEE Computer Security Foundations Workshop*, Franconia, NH, June 1991.

[THUR91c] Thuraisingham, B. Recursion theoretic properties of the inference problem. *IEEE CIPHER* (winter) 1991.

[THUR92] Thuraisingham, B. A nonmontonic typed multilevel logic for multilevel secure database and knowledge base management systems II. In *Proceedings of the IEEE Computer Security Foundations Workshop*, Franconia, NH, June 1992.

[THUR93] Thuraisingham, B., Ford, W., and Collins, M. Design and implementation of a database inference controller. *Data and Knowledge Engineering Journal* 11: 3, 1993.

[THUR95] Thuraisingham B. and Ford, W. Security constraint processing in a multilevel distributed database management system. *IEEE Transactions on Knowledge and Data Engineering* 7: 2, 1995.

[WIED00] Wiederhold, G. Release control in database systems. In *Proceedings of the IFIP Database Security Conference*, Amsterdam, August 2000. North Holland: Amsterdam, 2001.

Exercises

1. Conduct a survey of statistical database inference techniques.
2. Conduct a survey of the inference problem in MLS/DBMSs.

Chapter 13

Security-Constraint Processing for Inference Control

13.1 Overview

In this chapter we discuss approaches to processing security constraints to handle the inference problem. Back in 1987 we introduced the notion of security constraints, which are rules that assign security levels to the data (see [DWYE87]). We also designed and developed an architecture for a database management system augmented with inference engines to handle the inference problem by processing the security constraints. Our initial work on the inference problem was published in [THUR87] and elaborated on in [THUR90]. This work spawned several activities on the inference problem and security-constraint processing (see also [THUR93] and [THUR95]). This chapter essentially summarizes our work on security constraint processing.

The organization of this chapter is as follows. In Section 13.2 we provide some background on security constraints. In Section 13.3 we describe the various types of security constraints that we have considered. In Section 13.4 we provide a high-level overview of our approach to handling the security constraints. Constraint generation aspects are discussed in Section 13.5. In Section 13.6 we discuss the design of the query processor. In our design, a MLS/DBMS is augmented with an inference

229

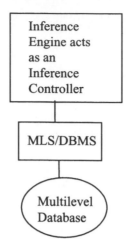

Figure 13.1 Inference engine approach

engine (which we also call a security engine). The inference engine has the capability of processing all of the security constraints in such a way that certain security violations via inference cannot occur. In Section 13.7 we describe the design of a database update processor, which is responsible for processing certain constraints during database updates. That is, appropriate security levels to the data are assigned based on the constraints during the update operation. In Section 13.8 we describe algorithms that could be utilized by the Systems Security Officer (SSO) in order to design the schema of the database. These algorithms handle certain security constraints. Handling release information is briefly discussed in Section 13.9. Section 13.10 gives a summary and directions. Figure 13.1 illustrates the inference engine approach.

13.2 Background

The security constraints that we have identified include those that classify data based on content, context, aggregation, and time. The work reported in [THUR87] and [KEEF89] suggests ways of handling security constraints during query processing in such a way that certain security violations via inference do not occur. The work reported in [MORG87] and [HINK88] focuses on handling constraints during database design where suggestions for database design tools are given. They expect security constraints during database design to be handled in such a way that security violations cannot occur. We describe the design techniques for processing security constraints. We believe that appropriate handling of security constraints is essential for developing a useful MLS/DBMS.

From an analysis of the various types of security constraints, we believe that they are a form of integrity constraint enforced in a MLS/DBMS. This is because in a multilevel database one can regard the security level of an entity to be part of the value of that entity. Therefore, security constraints specify permissible values that an entity can take. Because a security constraint can be regarded as a form of integrity constraint, many of the techniques developed for handling integrity constraints in non-MLS relational database systems by the logic programming researchers could be used for handling security constraints in a MLS/DBMS. In these techniques, some integrity constraints (which are called derivation rules) are handled during query processing, some integrity constraints (known as integrity rules) are handled during database updates, and some integrity constraints (known as schema rules) are handled during database design (see [GALL78]). Our approach to handling security constraints has been influenced by the approach taken to process integrity constraints by the logic programming researchers [LLOY87].

Before designing a constraint processor, a question that must be answered is whether a constraint should be processed during query processing, during database updates, or during database design. When constraints are handled during query processing, they are treated as a form of derivation rule. That is, they are used to assign security levels to the data already in the database before it is released. In other words, new information (e.g., the security labels) is deduced from information already in the database. When the security constraints are handled during update processing, they are treated as a form of integrity rule. That is, they are constraints that must be satisfied by the data in the multilevel database. When the constraints are handled during database design, then they must be satisfied by the database schema in the same way functional and multivalued dependency constraints must be satisfied by the schema of a relational database.

We believe that it is essential for the query processor to have the capability of processing the security constraints. This is because most users usually build their reservoir of knowledge from responses that they receive by querying the database. It is from this reservoir of knowledge that they infer secret information. Moreover, no matter how well the database has been designed with respect to security, or the data in the database is accurately labeled with security labels, users could eventually violate security by inference because they are continuously updating their reservoir of knowledge as the world evolves. It is not feasible to have to redesign the database or to reclassify the data continuously. It should, however, be noted that processing a large number of security constraints could have an impact on the performance of the query-processing algorithms. Therefore, it is desirable to process as many constraints as possible during database updates and during database design. This is because, in general, the database design and the update operation are performed less frequently than the query operation. Therefore, when the database is designed initially, the security constraints should be examined and the schema should be generated. Whenever the data is updated, the constraints are examined and the security levels are assigned or reassigned to the affected data. Periodically the System Security Officer (SSO) should examine the security constraints and redesign the database and reclassify the data. If the application is static and if the data in the database is consistent with the security constraints, the query processor need not examine the constraints handled by the update processor and the database designer. If there is some change that has occurred in the real world, which makes the database or the schema inconsistent, then the query processor should be triggered so that it can process the relevant constraints during its operation. This way, much of the burden placed on the query processor is alleviated.

13.3 Security Constraints

We have defined various types of security constraints. They include the following.

1. Constraints that classify a database, relation, or an attribute. These constraints are called simple constraints.
2. Constraints that classify any part of the database depending on the value of some data. These constraints are called content-based constraints.
3. Constraints that classify any part of the database depending on the occurrence of some real-world event. These constraints are called event-based constraints.
4. Constraints that classify associations between data (such as tuples, attributes, elements, etc.). These constraints are called association-based constraints.
5. Constraints that classify any part of the database depending on the information that has been previously released. These constraints are called release-based constraints. We have identified two types of release-based constraints. One is the general release constraint which classifies an entire attribute depending on whether any value of another attribute has been released. The other is the individual release constraint which classifies a value of an attribute depending on whether a value of another attribute has been released.
6. Constraints that classify collections of data. These constraints are called aggregate constraints.

7. Constraints that specify implications. These are called logical constraints.
8. Constraints that have conditions attached to them. These are called constraints with conditions.
9. Constraints that classify any part of the database depending on the security level of some data. These constraints are called level-based constraints.
10. Constraints that assign fuzzy values to their classifications. These are called fuzzy constraints.

We give examples of constraints belonging to each category. In our examples, we assume that the database consists of two relations SHIP and MISSION where SHIP has attributes S#, SNAME, CAPTAIN, and M# (with S# as the key), and MISSION has attributes M#, MNAME, and LOCATION (with M# as the key). Note that M# in SHIP and M# in MISSION take values from the same domain. The constraints may be expressed as some form of logical rule. We have chosen Horn clauses to represent the constraints. This way we could eventually take advantage of the techniques that have been developed for logic programs.

13.3.1 Simple Constraints

```
R(A1, A2,...An)  —>  Level(Ail, Ai2,...Ait) = Secret
{Each attribute Ail, Ai2,...Ait of relation R is Secret}
Example: SHIP(S#, SNAME, CAPTAIN, M#) —>
Level(CAPTAIN) = Secret.
```

13.3.2 Content-Based Constraints

```
R(Al, A2,...An) AND COND(Value(Bl, B2,...Bm)) —>
   Level(Ail, Ai2,...Ait) = Secret {Each attribute Ail,
   Ai2,...Ait of relation R is Secret if some specific
   condition is enforced on the values of some data
   specified by Bl, B2,...Bm)
Example: SHIP(S#, SNAME, CAPTAIN, M#) AND (Value(SNAME)
   = Washington) —> Level(CAPTAIN) = Secret.
```

13.3.3 Association-Based Constraints
(also Called Context or Together Constraints)

```
R(A1, A2,...An)  —>  Level(Together(Ail, Ai2,...Ait)) =
   Secret
```

```
(The attributes Ail, Ai2,...Ait of relation R taken
   together is Secret)
Example: SHIP (S#, SNAME, CAPTAIN, M#) —>
Level(Together(SNAME, CAPTAIN)) = Secret.
```

13.3.4 Event-Based Constraints

```
R(Al, A2,...An) AND Event(E) —> Level(Ail, Ai2,...Ait) =
   Secret
(Each attribute Ail, Ai2,...Ait of relation R is Secret
   if event E has occurred)
Example: SHIP(S#, SNAME, CAPTAIN, M#) AND Event(Change
   of President) —> Level(CAPTAIN, M#) = Secret.
```

13.3.5 General Release-Based Constraints

```
R(Al, A2,...An) AND Release(Ai, Unclassified) —>
   Level(Aj) = Secret
(The attribute Aj of relation R is Secret if the attribute
   Ai has been released at the Unclassified level)
Example: SHIP(S#, SNAME, CAPTAIN, M#) AND Release(SNAME,
   Unclassified) —> Level(CAPTAIN) = Secret.
```

13.3.6 Individual Release-Based Constraints

```
R(Al, A2,...An) AND Individual-Release(Ai, Unclassified)
   —> Level(Aj) = Secret.
```

The individual release-based constraints classify elements of an attribute at a particular level after the corresponding elements of another attribute have been released. They are more difficult to implement than the general release-based constraints. In our design, the individual release-based constraints are handled after the response is assembled and all of the other constraints are handled before the response is generated.

13.3.7 Aggregate Constraints

Aggregate constraints classify collections of tuples taken together at a level higher than the individual levels of the tuples in the collection. There could be some semantic association between the tuples. We specify these tuples in the following form.

```
R(A1, A2,...An) AND Set(S, R) AND Satisfy(S, P) ->
  Level(S) = Secret
```

This means that if R is a relation and S is a set containing tuples of R and S satisfies some property P, then S is classified at the Secret level. Note that P could be any property such as "number of elements is greater than 10".

13.3.8 Logical Constraints

Logical constraints are rules that are used to derive new data from the data in the database. The derived data could be classified using one of the other constraints. Logical constraints are of the form: Ai => Aj; where Ai and Aj are attributes of either a database relation or a real-world relation. Note that logical constraints are not really security constraints. That is, they do not assign security levels to the data. They are, in fact, integrity constraints. In particular, they can be regarded as integrity constraints which are treated as derivation rules.

13.3.9 Constraints with Conditions

An example of a constraint with a condition is a condition-based constraint. Other constraints such as association-based constraints and logical constraints can also be specified with conditions.

Consider the following example.

```
Ai => Aj if condition C holds.
```

This constraint can be instantiated as follows.

- The LOCATION of a MISSION implies its MNAME if the
- LOCATION = Atlantic Ocean

13.3.10 Other Constraints

There are several other types of constraints that could be incorporated into our design fairly easily. These include level-based constraints and fuzzy constraints. We describe them below.

13.3.11 Level-Based Constraints

```
R(A1, A2,...An) AND Level(Ai) = Unclassified -> Level(Aj)
  = Secret
```

```
(The attribute Aj of relation R is Secret if the attribute
   Ai is Unclassified)
Example: SHIP(S#, SNAME, CAPTAIN, M#) AND Level(SNAME)
   = Unclassified --> Level(CAPTAIN) = Secret.
```

13.3.12 Fuzzy Constraints

Fuzzy constraints are constraints that use fuzzy values. They can be associated with any of the other types of constraints. An example of a fuzzy constraint that is associated with a content-based constraint is given below.

```
R(A1, A2,...An) AND COND(Value(B1, B2,...Bm)) -->
   Level(Ai1, Ai2,...Ait) = Secret and Fuzzyvalue = r
(Each attribute Ai1, Ai2,...Ait of relation R is Secret
   with a fuzzy value of r if some specific condition
   is enforced on the values of some data specified by
   B 1, B2,...Bm)
Example: SHIP(S#, SNAME, CAPTAIN, M#) AND (Value(SNAME)
   = Washington) --> Level(CAPTAIN) = Secret and Fuzzyvalue
   = 0.8.
```

13.3.13 Complex Constraints

The examples of constraints that we have given above are enforced on a single relation only. Note that constraints can also be enforced across relations. We call such constraints complex constraints. An example is given below.

```
R1(A1,A2 An)&R2(B1,B2 Bm)&R1.Ai=R2.Bj -->
Level(Together(Ak, Bp)) = Secret.
```

This constraint states that a pair of values involving the kth attribute of R1 and the pth attribute of R2 are Secret provided the corresponding values (i.e., in the same row) of the ith attribute of R1 and the jth attribute of R2 are equal.

This constraint may be instantiated as follows.

```
SHIP(S#, SNAME, CAPTAIN, M#) & MISSION(M#, MNAME LOCA-
   TION) & SHIP.M# = MISSION.M# --> Level(Together(SNAME,
   MNAME) = Secret.
```

13.4 Approach to Security Constraint Processing

As stated in Section 13.1, security constraints enforce a security policy. Therefore, it is essential that constraints be manipulated only by an authorized

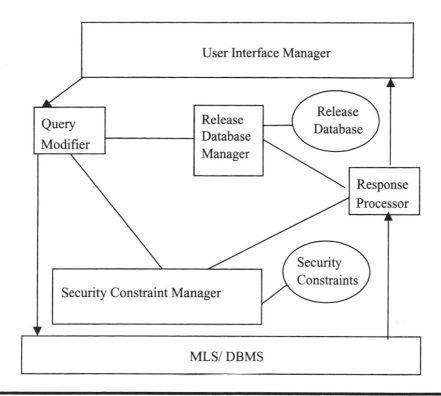

Figure 13.2   Query processor

individual. In our approach constraints are maintained by the SSO. That is, constraints are protected from ordinary users. We assume that constraints themselves could be classified at multiple security levels. However, they are stored at system-high. The constraint manager, which is trusted, will ensure that a user can read the constraints classified only at or below her level. Our approach to security constraint processing is to handle certain constraints during query processing, certain constraints during database updates, and certain constraints during database design.

Below we briefly illustrate the architectures for processing constraints during the query, update, and database design operations. The architecture for query processing is shown in Figure 13.2. This architecture can be regarded as a loose coupling between a MLS/DBMS and a deductive manager. The deductive manager is what we have called the query processor. It has to operate online. The architecture for update processing is shown in Figure 13.3. This architecture can also be regarded as a loose coupling between a MLS/RDBMS and a deductive manager. The deductive manager is what we have called the update processor. It could be used online where the security levels of the data are determined during database inserts and updates, or it could be used offline as a tool that ensures that data entered via bulk data

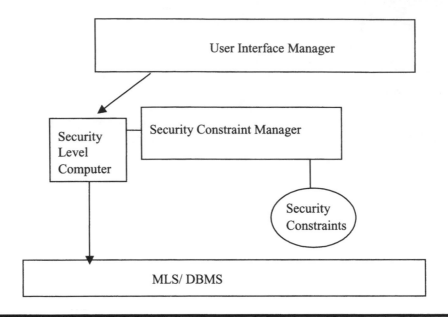

Figure 13.3 Update processor

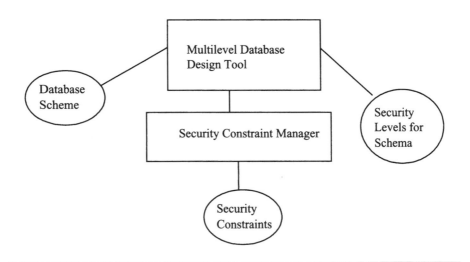

Figure 13.4 Database design tool

loads and bulk data updates is accurately labeled; if the tool is used offline, however, it may be difficult to recompute the levels of the data already in the database if these levels are affected by the new data that is being inserted. The tool, which handles security constraints during database design, illustrated in Figure 13.4, can be used by the SSO to design the schema. The

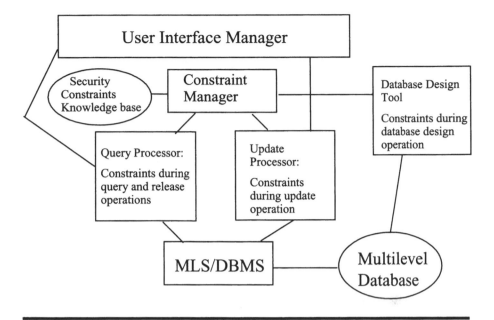

Figure 13.5 Integrated architecture

input to the tool is the set of security constraints that should be handled during database design and the schema. The output of the tool is the modified schema and the constraints.

Although the query processor, the update processor, and the database design tool are separate modules, they all constitute the solution to constraint processing in multilevel relational databases. That is, they provide an integrated solution to security constraint processing in a multilevel environment.

Figure 13.5 illustrates the integrated architecture. In this architecture, the constraints and schema produced by the constraint generator are processed further by the database design tool. The modified constraints are given to the Constraint Updater in order to update the constraint database. The schema is given to the Constraint Generator. The constraints in the constraint database are used by the query and update processors. We assume that there is a trusted constraint manager process, which manages the constraints. In a dynamic environment where the data and the constraints are changing, then the query processor will examine all the relevant constraints and ensure that users do not obtain unauthorized data.

13.5 Consistency and Completeness of the Constraints

In Section 13.2 we described the two tasks involved in constraint handling. They are constraint generation and constraint enforcement. Although our

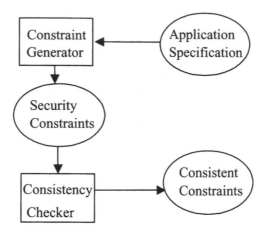

Figure 13.6   Constraint generation

main focus is on constraint enforcement, the relationship between the two tasks is illustrated in Figure 13.6. That is, the constraint generator takes the specification of the multilevel application and outputs the initial schema and the constraints that must be enforced. The database design tool takes this output as its input and designs the database. The update processor and the query processor use the constraints and schema produced by the database design tool. Generating the initial set of constraints remains a challenge. We need to examine the use of conceptual structures and semantic data models to see if we can specify the application and subsequently generate the security constraints. Algorithm A checks for the consistency and completeness of the security constraints.

13.5.1 Algorithm A: Consistency and Completeness Checker

Input: Set of Security Constraints
Output: Set of consistent and complete security constraints

- Step 1: For each relation and attribute compute the security level of the relation and attribute.
- Step 2: If there are constraints that assign multiple security levels to a relation or attribute, then delete or modify the constraint that assigns the lower security level; the constraint is modified if that constraint assigns security levels to other attributes and relations.
- Step 3: If there is some relation or attribute that is not assigned a security level by the constraints, then create a constraint that will assign the lowest security level to the relation or attribute.

■ Step 4: The resulting set of constraints is the output.

13.6 Design of the Query Processor

We first describe a security policy for handling inferences during query processing and then discuss our design approach.

13.6.1 Security Policy

A security policy for query processing that we propose extends the simple security property in [BELL73] to handle inference violations. This policy is stated below.

Given a security level L, E(L) is the knowledge base associated with L. That is, E(L) will consist of all responses that have been released at security level L over a certain time period and the real-world information at security level L.

```
Let a user U at security level L pose a query. Then the
    response R to the query will be released to this user
    if the following condition is satisfied.
For all security levels L* where L* dominates L, if
    (E(L*) UNION R) ==> X (for any X) then L* dominates
    Level(X).
Where A ==> B means B can be inferred from A using any
    of the inference strategies and Level(X) is the
    security level of X.
```

We assume that any response that is released into a knowledge base at level L is also released into the knowledge base at level L* >= L. The policy states that whenever a response is released to a user at level L, it must be ensured that any user at level L* >= L cannot infer information classified at a level L+ >= L from the response together with the knowledge that he has already acquired. Note that although we consider only hierarchical levels in specifying the policy, it can be extended to include nonhierarchical levels also.

13.6.2 Functionality of the Query Processor

The strength of the query processor depends on the type of inference strategies that it can handle. In our design we consider only a limited set of inference strategies such as inference through association and deduction. In this section, we discuss the techniques that we have used to implement the security policy: query modification and response processing.

Each technique is described below. Note that much of the code of the query-modification module and the response-processing module has to be trusted because they perform security-critical functions. Detailed discussion of the trusted modules is given in [THUR93].

13.6.2.1 Query Modification

The query-modification technique has been used in the past to handle discretionary security and views [STON74]. This technique has been extended to include mandatory security in [DWYE87]. In our design of the query processor, this technique is used by the inference engine to modify the query depending on the security constraints, the previous responses released, and real-world information. When the modified query is posed, the response generated will not violate security.

Consider the architecture for query processing illustrated in Figure 13.2. The inference engine has access to the knowledge base which includes security constraints, previously released responses, and real-world information. Conceptually one can think of the database as part of the knowledge base. We illustrate the query-modification technique with examples. The actual implementation of this technique could adapt any of the proposals given in [GALL78] for deductive query processing.

Consider a database that consists of relations SHIP and MISSION where the attributes of SHIP are S#, SNAME, CAPTAIN, and M# with S# as the key; and the attributes of MISSION are Mt#, MNAME, and LOCATION with M# as the key. Suppose the knowledge base consists of the following rules.

1. SHIP(X,Y,Z,A) and Z = Smith —> Level(Y,Secret)
2. SHIP(X,Y,Z,A) and A = 10—> Level(Y,TopSecret)
3. SHIP(X,Y,Z,A) —> Level(Together(Y,Z), Secret)
4. SHIP(X,Y,Z,A) and Release(Z,Unclassified) —> Level(Y,Secret)
5. SHIP(X,Y,Z,A) and Release(Y,Unclassified) —> Level(Z,Secret)
6. NOT(Level(X,Secret) or Level(X,TopSecret)) —> Level(X,Unclassified)

The first rule is a content-based constraint, which classifies a ship name whose captain is Smith at the Secret level. Similarly, the second rule is also a content-based constraint which classifies a ship name whose M# number is 10 at the TopSecret level. The third rule is an association-based constraint, which classifies ship names and captains taken together at the Secret level. The fourth and fifth rules are additional restrictions that are enforced as a result of the context-based constraint specified in Rule 3. The sixth rule states that the default classification level of a data item is Unclassified.

Suppose an Unclassified user requests the ship names in SHIP. This query is represented as follows.

```
SHIP (X,Y,Z,D).
```

Because a ship name is classified at the Secret level if either the captain is "Smith" or the captain name is already released at the Unclassified level, and it is classified at the TopSecret level if the M# is "10", assuming that the captain names are not yet released to an Unclassified user, the query is modified to the following.

```
SHIP(X,Y,Z,D) and NOT (Z = Smith and D = 10).
```

Note that because query modification is performed in real-time, it will have some impact on the performance of the query-processing algorithm. However, several techniques for semantic query optimization have been proposed for intelligent query processing (see, for example, [MINK88]). These techniques could be adapted for query processing in a multilevel environment in order to improve the performance.

13.6.2.2 Response Processing

For many applications, in addition to query modification, some further processing of the response such as response sanitization may need to be performed. We illustrate this point with examples.

Example

Consider the following release constraints.

> All ship names whose corresponding captain names are already released to Unclassified users are Secret.
> All captain names whose corresponding ship names are already released to Unclassified users are Secret.

Suppose an Unclassified user requests the ship names first. Depending on the other constraints imposed, let us assume that only certain names are released to the user. Then the ship names released have to be recorded into the knowledge base. Later, suppose an Unclassified user (does not necessarily have to be the same one) asks for captain names. The captain name values (some or all) are then assembled in the response. Before the response is released, the ship names that are already released to the Unclassified user need to be examined. Then the captain name value that corresponds to a ship name value that is already released is suppressed from the response. Note that there has to be a way of correlating the ship names with the captains. This means the primary key values (which is the S#) should also be retrieved with the captain names as well as stored with the ship names in the release database.

Example

Consider the following aggregate constraint.

A collection of ten or more tuples in the relation SHIP is Secret.

Suppose an Unclassified user requests the tuples in SHIP. The response is assembled and then examined to see if it has more then ten tuples. If so, it is suppressed.

There are some problems associated with maintaining the release information. As more and more relevant release information gets inserted, the knowledge base could grow at a rapid rate. Therefore, efficient techniques for processing the knowledge base need to be developed. This would also have an impact on the performance of the query-processing algorithms. One solution would be to include only certain crucial release information in the knowledge base. The rest of the information can be stored with the audit data, which can then be used by the SSO for analysis.

13.7 Design of the Update Processor

We first discuss the security policy for database updates and then describe the design approach.

13.7.1 Security Policy

MLS/DBMSs ensure the assignment of a security level to data as data is inserted or modified. The security level assigned to the data, however, is generally assumed to be the log-in security level of the user entering the data. A more powerful and dynamic approach to assigning security levels to data is through the utilization of security constraints during update operations.

The security policy of the update processor is formulated from the simple security property in [BELL73] and from a security policy provided by the underlying MLS/DBMS. This policy is as follows.

1. All users are granted a maximum clearance level with respect to security levels. A user may log in at any level that is dominated by his maximum clearance level. Subjects act on behalf of users at the user's log-in security level.

2. Objects are the rows, tables, and databases, and every object is assigned a security level upon creation.
3. A subject has read access to an object if the security level of the subject dominates the security level of the object.
4. A subject has write access to an object if the security level of the object dominates the security level of the subject.

Statements 3 and 4 of the policy presented above are the simple * - property of the Bell and LaPadula policy.

13.7.2 Functionality of the Update Processor

The update processor utilizes simple and content-dependent security constraints as guidance in determining the security level of the data being updated. The use of security constraints can thereby protect against users incorrectly labeling data as a result of logging in at the wrong level, against data being incorrectly labeled when it is imported from systems of different modes of operation such as a system-high, and against database inconsistencies as a consequence of the security label of data in the database being affected by data being entered into the database.

The security level of an update request is determined by the update processor as follows. The simple and content-dependent security constraints associated with the relation being updated and with a security label greater than the user log-in security level are retrieved and examined for applicability. If multiple constraints apply, the security level is determined by the constraint that specifies the highest classification level; if no constraints apply, the update level is the log-in security level of the user. The update processor, therefore, does not determine the security level of the data solely from the security constraints, but utilizes the constraints as guidance in determining the level of the input data. The following examples illustrate the functionality of the update processor.

Consider a database that consists of a relation SHIP whose attributes are ship number, name, class, date, and MISSION, with mission number as its primary key. The content-based constraint that classifies all SHIP values with the name Josephine as secret is expressed as

```
SHIP.sname = "Josephine" --> Secret.
```

A user at log-in security level, say, Confidential enters the following data to insert a tuple into the SHIP relation.

```
Insert SHIP values ("SSN 729", "James",
  "Thomsen","MR1800").
```

That is, the ship number for James is SSN729, his captain is Thomsen, and his mission record number is MR1800.

The update processor will receive this insert and retrieve the constraints associated with the SHIP relation that specify a level greater than the user level, which is Confidential, and whose level is less than or equal to the user level. The content-based constraint stated above is retrieved. Because the data entered for the name field is not "Josephine", the security constraint associated with the SHIP relation will not affect the classification level of the insert, and the update processor will determine the insert level to be the user level, which is Confidential.

Suppose a user at the log-in security level Confidential then enters the following.

```
Insert SHIP values ("SSN 730", "Josephine", "Jane",
    "MR2100").
```

The update processor will again retrieve the content-based constraint associated with the SHIP relation, which specifies a level greater than the user level and whose level is less than or equal to the user level. Because the data for the name field is "Josephine", the update processor will determine the insert level to be Secret. If, however, the user entered this insert at log-in security level TopSecret, the update processor would perform the insert at the user level because the user level is higher than the level specified by the security constraint.

The update operation of the update processor functions similarly to the insert operation. As an example, suppose a user at the Confidential level enters the following.

```
Update SHIP set Sname = "Josephine" where captain =
    "Thomsen".
```

The update processor will retrieve the security constraints associated with the SHIP relation that specify a level greater than the user level and whose level is less than or equal to the user level. The content-dependent constraint stated above will be retrieved, and the update processor will determine the update level to be secret because the name field is being modified to "Josephine". The tuple with a primary key of "SSN 729" as defined above will then be updated at the Secret level, and the original tuple will be deleted.

In addition to describing the functionality of the update processor, the examples above illustrate the potential signaling channels that exist when operating with the update processor. A signaling channel is a form of covert channel that occurs when the actions of a high-security-level user or subject interfere with a low-security-level user or subject in a visible manner. Potential signaling channels occur when data is entered at a level higher than the user level and the user attempts to retrieve the data that he has entered, or when the update processor attempts to enter data at a higher level, but cannot because a tuple with the same primary key already exists at this level. More details on the design of the update processor and the trusted components are discussed in [THUR93].

13.8 Handling Security Constraints During Database Design

13.8.1 Overview

The main focus of this section is a discussion on how security constraints could be handled during database design. We then briefly discuss how simple constraints as well as logical constraints could be handled.

An association-based constraint classifies a collection of attributes taken together at a particular security level. What is interesting about the association-based constraint is that it can generate several relationships among the various attributes. For example, if there is a relation SHIP whose attributes are S#, SNAME, and CAPTAIN, and if an association-based constraint classifies the SNAME and CAPTAIN taken together at the Secret level, then one of the pairs (S#, SNAME), (S#, CAPTAIN) should also be classified at the Secret level. Otherwise, an Unclassified user can obtain the (S#, SNAME) and the (S#, CAPTAIN) pairs and infer the Secret association (SNAME, CAPTAIN).

We have designed an algorithm that processes a given set of association-based constraints and outputs the schema for the multilevel database (see [THUR93] and [THUR95]). Given a set of association-based constraints and an initial schema, the algorithm will output clusters of attributes and the security level of each cluster. We then prove that the attributes within a cluster can be stored securely at the corresponding level. A tool based on this algorithm can help the systems security officer design the multilevel database. The algorithm that we have designed does not necessarily have to be executed during database design only. It can also be executed during query processing. That is, the query processor can examine the attributes in the various clusters generated by the algorithm and then determine which information has to be released to the users. For example, if the algorithm places the attributes Al, A2 in cluster 1 at level L, and the attributes A3, A4 in cluster 2 at level L, then, after an attribute in cluster 1 has been released to a user at level L, none of the attributes in cluster 2 can be released to users at level L.

Because simple constraints can be regarded as a special form of association-based constraints, where only one attribute is classified, we feel that such constraints could also be handled during database design.

Another constraint that could be handled during database design is the logical constraint. For example, if attribute A implies an attribute B, and if attribute B is classified at the Secret level, then attribute A must be classified at least at the Secret level. It should be noted that if any of the constraints have conditions attached to them, then handling them during database design time would be difficult. For example, consider the constraint: "SNAME and LOCATION taken together are Secret if LOCATION is from company X". Such a constraint depends on data values. Therefore, it is best handled during either query or update processing.

We first elaborate on the processing of association-based constraints. The input to this algorithm is a set of association-based constraints and a set of attributes. The output of this algorithm is a set of clusters for each security level. Each cluster for a security level L will have a collection of attributes that can be safely classified at the level L. That is, if Al, A2, and A3 are attributes in a cluster C at level Secret, then the attributes Al, A2, and A3 can be classified together safely at the security level Secret without violating security. The clusters are formed depending on the association-based constraints, which are input to the program. Once the clusters are formed, then the database can be defined according to the functional and multivalued dependencies that are enforced.

Next let us consider the simple constraints. Because simple constraints classify individual attributes at a certain security level, they could also be handled during database design. Note that when an attribute A in relation R is classified at level L, then all elements that belong to A are also classified at level L. Therefore, we can store A itself at level L.

The algorithm that handles simple constraints is straightforward. Each attribute that is classified by a simple constraint is stored at the level specified in the constraint. Once the algorithm for processing simple constraints is applied and the corresponding schema is obtained, then this schema is given as input to the algorithm handling association-based constraints. The association-based constraints are then applied and the final schema is obtained.

Logical constraints are rules that can be used to deduce new data from existing data. If a security constraint classifies the new data at a level higher than that of the existing data, then the existing data must be reclassified. Logical constraints could be straightforward such as $Ai => Aj$ or they could be more complex such as $Al \& A2 \& A3 \& An => Am$. If Aj is classified at the Secret level then Ai must be classified at least at the Secret level. If Am is classified at the Secret level, then at least one of Al, $A2, \ldots, An$ must be classified at least at the Secret level. Further details of the algorithms on processing constraints during database design are given in [THUR93] and [THUR95].

13.9 Security Control Processing and Release Control

Until now we have discussed an integrated architecture mainly for a centralized environment where constraints are examined during query, database update, and database design time. That is, in the case of the query operation much of the work is carried out before the query is sent to the MLS/DBMS. Once the query is executed, then we examine certain release constraints to see what has been released before.

Recently there has been some work on processing constraints only after the response is released by the DBMS but before the response is given to the user. These approaches can be found in [WIED00] and [JAJO03]. The idea behind this approach is that it may not be feasible to modify the query especially if there are many constraints. Therefore, rather than doing the work before the query is executed, why not do all of the processing after the response is released by the DBMS?

This approach does have some disadvantages. That is, after the response is released, one has to examine all of the security constraints and determine what information to release to the user. Essentially many of the operations carried out by the DBMS will now have to be carried out by the Release Control Manager (RCM). That is, the release control manager will have to carry out selections, projects, joins, and the like to obtain the final result. However, the advantage with this approach is that if there are many constraints the complex query-modification process is avoided.

Note that the DBMS will produce the result at the user's security level. The RCM will then examine the result and the constraints and determine whether all of the data could be released. Suppose there is a constraint that states that LOCATION values in MISSION are Secret and the user's level is Unclassified. The release data will have all of the information in the relation MISSION. RCM will apply the constraint and only give out the mission names and not the location values. Figure 13.7 illustrates the RCM.

13.10 Summary and Directions

In this chapter we first defined various types of security constraints. Security constraints are rules that assign security levels to the data. Then we described an integrated approach to constraint processing. That is, some constraints are handled during query processing, some during database updates, and some during database design. We then described the design of a system that processes constraints during query and update operations. We also described the design of a database design tool. Finally,

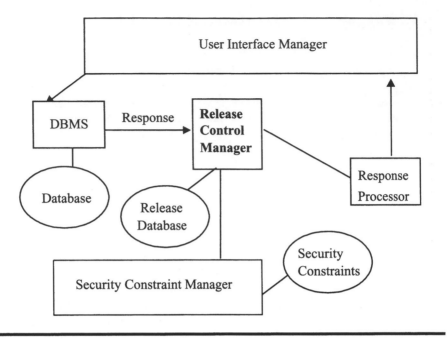

Figure 13.7   Release control manager

we discussed an alternative approach to security constraint processing called release processing.

Future work includes examining the release control approach further. In addition we need to conduct research on security control algorithms for distributed and federated environments. Some initial directions for distributed environments are given in Part VI. We also need to develop techniques for generating constraints. For example, we may need to examine the use of semantic models and conceptual structures to specify the application and reason about the application and detect security violations during design time. We also need to examine the enforcement of more complex constraints. In other words, there is lot of research to be done on security constraint processing.

References

[BELL73] Bell, D. and LaPadula, L. Secure computer systems: Mathematical foundations and model. Technical Report M74-244, MITRE Corporation, Bedford, MA, 1973.

[DWYE87] Dwyer, P. et al. Multilevel security for relational database systems. *Computers and Security* 6: 3, 1987.

[GALL78] Gallaire, H. and Minker, J. *Logic and Databases*. Plenum: New York, 1978.

[HINK88] Hinke T. Inference and aggregation detection in database management systems. In *Proceedings of the 1988 Conference on Security and Privacy*, Oakland, CA, April 1988.

[JAJO03] Jajodia, S. Release control for XML documents. In *Proceedings of the IFIP Conference in Integrity and Control*, Lausanne, Switzerland, November 2003. Kluwer: Hingham, MA, 2004.

[KEEF89] Keefe, T. et al. Secure query processing strategies. *IEEE Computer* 22: 3, 1989.

[LLOY87] Lloyd, J. *Foundations of Logic Programming*. Springer-Verlag: Heidelberg, 1987.

[MINK88] Minker, J. *Foundation of Deductive Databases and Logic Programming*, Morgan Kaufmann: San Francisco, CA, 1988.

[MORG87] Morgenstern, M. Security and inference in multilevel database and knowledge base systems. In *Proceedings of the ACM SIGM CD Conference*, San Francisco, May 1987.

[STON74] Stonebraker, M. and Wong, E. Access control in a relational data base management system by query modification. In *Proceedings of the ACM Annual Conference*. ACM: New York, 1974.

[THUR87] Thuraisingham, B. Security checking in relational database management systems augmented with inference engines. *Computers and Security* 6: 6, 1987.

[THUR90] Thuraisingham, B. Towards the design of secure database and knowledge base management system. *Data and Knowledge Engineering Journal* 5: 1, 1990.

[THUR93] Thuraisingham, B., Ford, W., and Collins, M. Design and implementation of a database inference controller. *Data and Knowledge Engineering Journal* 11: 3, 1993.

[THUR95] Thuraisingham B. and Ford, W. Security constraint processing in a multilevel distributed database management system. *IEEE Transactions on Knowledge and Data Engineering* 7: 2, 1995.

[WIED00] Wiederhold, G. Release control in database systems. In *Proceedings of the IFIP Database Security Conference*, Amsterdam, August 2000. Kluwer: Hingham, MA, 2001.

Exercises

1. Can you think of alternative approaches to security-constraint processing in a MLS/RDBMS?
2. Design an efficient inference engine to process security constraints.
3. Investigate the idea of release control.

Chapter 14

Conceptual Structures for Inference Control

14.1 Overview

Due to the complexity of the inference problem we need several approaches to handle the problem. In Chapter 13 we discussed security-constraint processing. In particular, we described the design of a MLS/DBMS that manages various types of security constraints. We stated the need to process security constraints during database design, database updates, and query operations. However, before the database is designed, we need to examine the application and see if there are potential violations to security. Essentially we need semantic data models such as semantic nets and conceptual graphs to model an application and reason about the application. This chapter attempts to examine the use of conceptual structures for inference control.

Some types of semantic data models, such as Sowa's conceptual graphs [SOWA84], have been shown to be as powerful as first-order logic. It has also been argued that conceptual graphs can be naturally extended to cope with modality and time. The primary motivation for using semantic data models is as follows.

1. The use of semantic data models for representing applications is consistent with the way humans view the world.
2. It is more convenient to analyze the application manually when it is represented as a graph rather than, say, a table or in some language.

253

3. A representation of the application using semantic data models can be used as a front-end subsystem to a logic-programming system.
4. Reasoning strategies for representations based on semantic data models are well developed.

To our knowledge, the use of semantic data models to handle the inference problem was first proposed by Hinke [HINK88], Smith [SMIT90], and Thuraisingham [THUR91]. Hinke's work was on the use of graphs for representing the application. He showed how inferences might be detected by traversing alternate paths between two nodes in the graph. Although this technique enables simple inferences to be detected via the transitivity property, it does not enable the detection of more complex inferences. Further work on the use of semantic data models for inference handling was proposed by Smith [SMIT90]. Smith suggests extensions to the semantic data model discussed in [URBA89] to represent multilevel applications. He has developed a fairly substantial model to represent some complex situations. However, reasoning techniques have not yet been developed for this model. Smith states that eventually the representation should be translated into statements of a logic-programming system. The techniques developed for such logic-programming systems could then be used to detect inferences. Thuraisingham proposes the use of semantic nets and conceptual graphs for handling the inference problem (see [THUR91]).

To successfully handle inferences that result in security violations, it is not only important to be able to represent the application semantics, but it is also essential that appropriate reasoning strategies be applied. Therefore, we have investigated semantic data models which are not only powerful representation schemes, but also a complete set of reasoning strategies has been developed for them. Our main focus is on the use of semantic nets. This is because semantic nets have been used extensively for a variety of data modeling, artificial intelligence, and natural language processing applications. However, because we are dealing with a multilevel environment, we have developed the concept of multilevel semantic nets and show how multilevel information can be captured by such a representation. We then make use of the complete set of reasoning strategies that have been developed for semantic nets to detect security violations via inference. The System Security Officer (SSO) could use the techniques we have developed to analyze the application manually. On the other hand, automated tools based on our approach can also be developed which could be used by the SSO.

Although semantic nets are powerful for representing and reasoning about a variety of applications, it has been shown that that they do not have the capabilities of first-order logic. As a result, several extensions to semantic nets have been proposed. One particular extension which is theoretically complete is the conceptual graph of Sowa [SOWA84]. We have also briefly investigated the use of conceptual graphs in handling inferences. In particular, we have investigated issues on developing multilevel conceptual graphs and shown how the reasoning techniques such as restriction, joining, and simplifying could be applied to handle our problem. In this chapter we focus only on the use of semantic nets to handle the inference problem. Details on the use of conceptual graphs are given in [THUR91].

The organization of this chapter is as follows. In Section 14.2 we discuss the use of semantic nets in detail. In particular we define the notion of a multilevel semantic net and describe reasoning strategies that can be pursued to detect security violations via inference. The chapter is concluded in Section 14.3. An excellent introduction to semantic nets is given in [RICH89] and [RING88]. Much of the information in this chapter is taken from [THUR91].

14.2 Semantic Nets and the Inference Problem

14.2.1 Overview

Quillian was the first to use semantic networks in problem solving [QUIL66]. In his work, Quillian's aim was to find a representation format for storing words so that a humanlike interpretation of the words would be possible. Basically, a semantic net can be regarded as a collection of nodes connected via links. The nodes represent entities, events, and concepts and the links represent relationships between the nodes. Since Quillian's work on semantic networks, numerous variations of the semantic networks have been proposed. These include the conceptual dependencies of Schank [SCHA72], Brachman's KL-ONE [BRAC85], conceptual graphs of Sowa [SOWA84], and Wood's work on the foundations [WOOD75]. Such representational schemes are called semantic data models. What is useful about these semantic data models is that they can represent and reason about the real world like humans. Therefore, they are increasingly used for a variety of artificial intelligence and natural language processing applications.

We are interested in semantic data models because they can be used to represent a multilevel application. Such a representation can be used by the SSO to manually analyze the application to ensure that users cannot draw unauthorized inferences. On the other hand, we can build a system that processes the knowledge using strategies that have been developed for semantic data models and performs automatic security analysis of the applications. Our initial focus is on semantic nets, due to their simplicity and humanlike reasoning power.

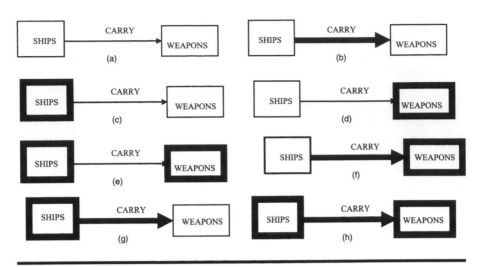

Figure 14.1 Multilevel semantic nets

Inasmuch as the application under consideration is multilevel, standard semantic nets cannot represent it. In other words, extensions to these semantic nets are needed to support multilevel. In Section 14.2.2, we introduce the notion of multilevel semantic nets. Reasoning in a multilevel semantic net is the subject of Section 14.2.3. Enforcing security constraints, which are rules that assign security levels to the various concepts and relationships, are discussed in Section 14.2.4. Universal and existential conditionals are treated in Section 14.2.5. Interpretations of multilevel semantic nets are discussed in Section 14.2.6. A refutation procedure for multilevel semantic nets is given in Section 14.2.7. We consider a semantic net to be a collection of nodes connected via links. The nodes represent concepts, entities, and so on, and the links represent relationships among them. Our treatment of semantic nets is influenced by the work reported in [RICH89].

14.2.2 Multilevel Semantic Nets

A Multilevel Semantic Net (MSN) is a semantic net with nodes and links classified at different security levels. Figure 14.1 shows some simple multilevel semantic nets. We assume that there are only two security levels, Unclassified and Secret, although our ideas can be extended to include multiple security levels such as Confidential and TopSecret. Note that the darkened shapes and lines are assumed to be Secret.

Consider Figure 14.1(a). It states that Ships carry Weapons and this information is Unclassified. In Figure 14.1(a), both the node and link are Unclassified (we use dark lines to represent Secret information). That is,

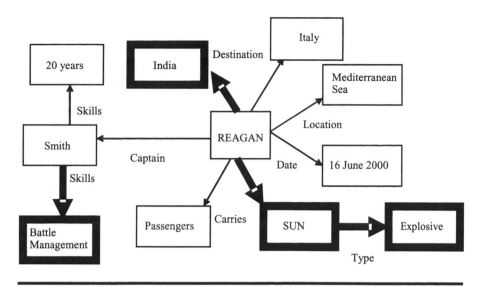

Figure 14.2   Complex multilevel semantic net

the fact that Ships carry Weapons can be seen by all. In Figure 14.1(b), Ships and Weapons are Unclassified, but the fact that Ships carry Weapons is Secret. In Figure 14.1(c), the Unclassified users know that something carries weapons, but they do not know that Ships carry weapons. In Figure 14.1(d), the Unclassified users know that Ships are carrying something, but they do not know that they are Weapons. In Figure 14.1(e), the Unclassified users know that someone is carrying something but do not know that the carrier is Ships and the Objects are weapons. In Figure 14.1(f), Unclassified users know only about Ships and nothing about Weapons. In Figure 14.1(g), Unclassified users know only about Weapons and nothing about Ships. In Figure 14.1(h), nothing is visible to the Unclassified users.

It needs to be determined whether all the links described in Figure 14.1 should be permitted. For example, it may make sense to classify a link at a level that dominates the levels of the nodes associated with the link. That is, the level of the "carries" relationship must dominate the levels of Ships and Weapons.

Figure 14.2 shows a more elaborate multilevel semantic net. The Unclassified interpretation of this figure is as follows. REAGAN carries passengers. Its captain is Smith who has 20 years experience. The ship is located in the Mediterranean Sea on 16 June 2000. Its destination is Italy. The Secret interpretation is as follows. REAGAN carries SUN which is an explosive. Its captain is Smith who has battle management experience. The ship is located in the Mediterranean on 16 June 2000. Its destination is India.

Figure 14.3 ISA, AKO links

We can see that certain information is polyinstantiated. Note that polyinstantiation occurs when users at different security levels have different views of the same "thing" in the real world. By "thing" we mean concept, entity, event, or any relationship. That is, polyinstantiation is the mechanism used to represent cover stories. Figure 14.2 illustrates how cover stories may be represented.

The links we have defined in the semantic nets, considered so far, illustrate special relationships. In addition to such links, a semantic net also has two standard links: ISA links and AKO links. An ISA link is used to specify that a particular individual belongs to a particular group. Figure 14.3(a) shows an ISA link where REAGAN is defined to be a particular ship such as a battle ship. An AKO link defines a subset of a collection of vehicles. Figure 14.3(b) defines the collection of vehicles to be a subset of a collection of Water Vehicles. Note that in this example, the AKO relationship is assigned to be Secret.

It does not make sense to classify REAGAN at the Unclassified level and Ship at the Secret level. This is because REAGAN is an instantiation of Ship. By classifying Ship at the Secret level we are implicitly assuming that any Ship must be classified at least at the Secret level. It should also be noted that it does not make sense to classify Ship at the Unclassified level and Water Vehicle at the Secret level. This is because classifying Ship at the Unclassified level implicitly assumes that Water Vehicle should be classified at least at the Unclassified level. Classifying Ship at the Secret level implicitly assumes that any vehicle (Water Vehicle) should be classified at least at the Secret level. This results in a conflict. Therefore, we enforce the following rules for consistency.

> **Rule Al:** If X ISA Y, then Level(X) $>=$ Level(Y).
>
> **Rule A2:** If X AKO Y, then Level(X) $>=$ Level(Y).

14.2.3 Reasoning with Multilevel Semantic Nets

In order to reason with multilevel semantic nets, we first need rules, which can be used to reason. In this section, we describe some rules that can be used for reasoning purposes.

14.2.3.1 Implicit Information

Most real-world applications deal with very large quantities of information. Therefore, capturing all of the information in a semantic net would make the net extremely complex. What we need is a minimal semantic net with a powerful set of reasoning strategies so that other information can be deduced. The information that is deduced is implicit information. For a multilevel application it should be ensured that the level of the implicit information that can be deduced by a user at level L should be dominated by L.

Some rules for deducing implicit information are the following.

> **Rule A3:** If X AKO Y and Y AKO Z then X AKO Z. The level of the AKO link from X to Z is the least upper bound of the levels of AKO links from X to Y and Y to Z.

Figure 14.4(a) illustrates an example. The semantic net has Ship AKO Water Vehicle and Water Vehicle AKO Vehicle. The AKO link from Ship to Water Vehicle is Secret. Then, at the Secret level, one can conclude that Ship AKO Vehicle.

> **Rule A4**: If X AKO Y and Y has relationship R with Z, then X has relationship R with Z. The level of the relationship R that X has with Z is the least upper bound of the levels of the AKO link from X to Y and the relationship R from Y to Z.

Figure 14.4(b) illustrates an example. The semantic net has Ship AKO Water Vehicle and Water Vehicle has captain Person. Then Ship has captain Person.

> **Rule A5**: If X ISA Y and Y AKO Z, then X ISA Z. The level of the ISA link from X to Z is the least upper bound of the levels of the AKO link from Y to Z and the ISA link from X to Y.

Figure 14.4(c) illustrates an example: REAGAN ISA Ship. This link is Secret. Ship AKO Water Vehicle. Therefore, there is a Secret ISA link from REAGAN to Water Vehicle.

> **Rule A6**: If X ISA Y and Y has relationship R with Z, then X has relationship R with Z. The level of the relationship R that X has with Z is the least upper bound of the levels of the AKO link from X to Y and the relationship R from Y to Z.

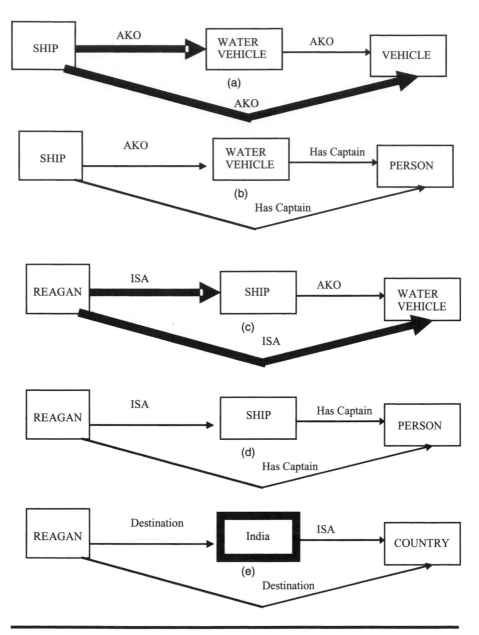

Figure 14.4   Sample rules

Figure 14.4(d) illustrates an example. The semantic net has REAGAN ISA Ship. Ship has captain Person. Therefore REAGAN has captain Person.

Rule A7: If X ISA Y and Z has relationship R with X, then Z has relationship R with Y. The level of the relationship R that

Z has with Y is the least upper bound of the levels of the ISA link from X to Y and the relationship R from Z to X.

Figure 14.4(e) illustrates an example. The semantic net has India ISA Country. REAGAN's destination is India. Therefore, the destination of REAGAN is a Country.

14.2.4 Conditional Statements and Auxiliary Nets

Conditional statements are of the form:

A if B 1 and B2 and B3 and . . ., Bn where Bi, B2, . . ., Bn are the antecedents and A is the consequent.

Note that conditional statements are clauses of a logic program [KOWA79]. Such a conditional statement can be represented by auxiliary semantic sets. We illustrate the essential points with an example. Consider the following conditional statement.

REAGAN's destination is India if it is located in the Mediterranean and it carries SUN, which is an explosive.

The conditional statement is represented by the auxiliary net shown in Figure 14.5(a). That is, the conditions are represented by dotted lines, and the conclusion is represented by solid lines. The transfer rule is applied in order to process conditional statements. The following is the transfer rule. (The dotted lines in the figure are darkened if they represent Secret relationships.)

Rule A8 (Transfer Rule): If all the dotted lines in the auxiliary net are shown as solid lines in a main multilevel semantic net, and the level of each solid line of the main net dominates the level of the corresponding dotted line in the auxiliary net, then the solid line in the auxiliary net is drawn as a solid line in the main net. The security level of the line drawn is the least upper bound of the levels of all the lines in the auxiliary net and the levels of all the corresponding solid lines already in the main net.

Figure 14.5(b) shows that the dotted lines in the auxiliary net occur as solid lines in the multilevel semantic net. Figure 14.5(c) shows that the solid line in the auxiliary net is added to the multilevel semantic net at the appropriate security level.

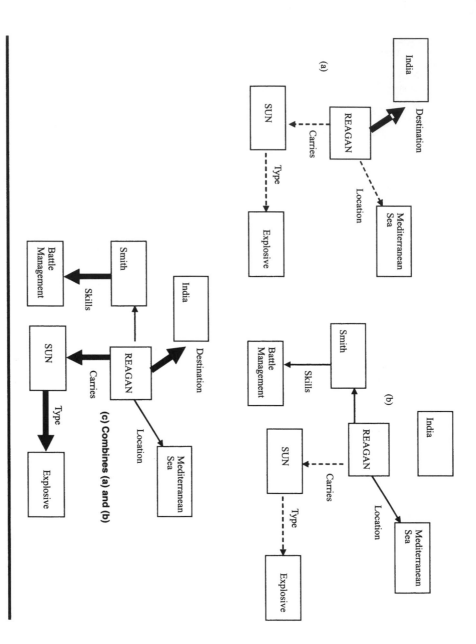

Figure 14.5   Application of transfer rule

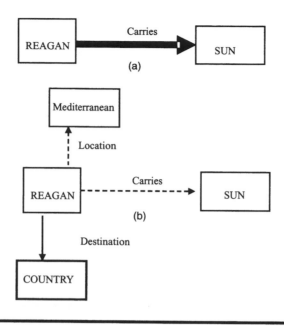

Figure 14.6   Representing security constraints

14.2.5 Enforcing Security Constraints

As stated in Chapter 13, security constraints are rules that assign security levels to the data. We represent security constraints by what we call "constraint nets". A constraint net is a semantic net or an auxiliary semantic net that specifies only constraints. However, although semantic nets are used in general to represent application information, constraint semantic nets are used to represent the security constraints so that any security violation in the application can be detected. Similarly, auxiliary semantic nets are used to derive implicit information, and security constraints (which are represented as auxiliary semantic nets) are used to detect security violations. Therefore, we differentiate between ordinary auxiliary nets and constraint auxiliary nets. Figure 14.6(a) classifies the fact that REAGAN carries anything at the Secret level. Figure 14.6(b) shows a constraint, which classifies the destination country of REAGAN at the Secret level, if REAGAN is located in the Mediterranean and it carries SUN.

Security violations occur (either directly or indirectly) if the constraint net contradicts the multilevel semantic net that represents the application (either directly or indirectly). The semantic net of Figure 14.7(a) violates both constraints of Figure 14.6 directly. That is, in Figure 14.7(a), the fact that REAGAN carries something is not Secret. This directly violates the constraint of Figure 14.6(a). Also, in Figure 14.7(a), REAGAN is located

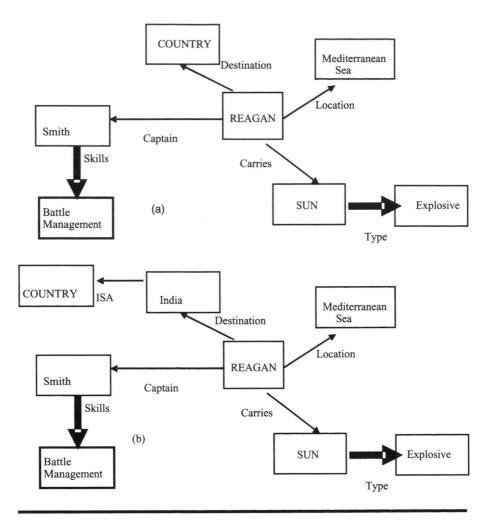

Figure 14.7 Security-constraint violation

in the Mediterranean and it carries SUN. However, its destination country is Unclassified. This directly violates the constraint of Figure 14.6(b).

Constraints can also be violated indirectly. This occurs when the implicit information that can be inferred contradicts the security constraints. Figure 14.7(b) shows how the security constraint of Figure 14.6(b) is violated indirectly. Here, REAGAN carries SUN and it is located in the Mediterranean. Its destination country, India, is Unclassified. Because India is a country, by Rule A7, the destination of REAGAN must be Secret. Therefore, the constraint of Figure 14.6(b) is violated indirectly.

Another example of indirect constraint violation is shown in Figure 14.8. Consider the constraint of Figure 14.8(a). This constraint classifies at the Secret level the fact that REAGAN carries explosive weapons.

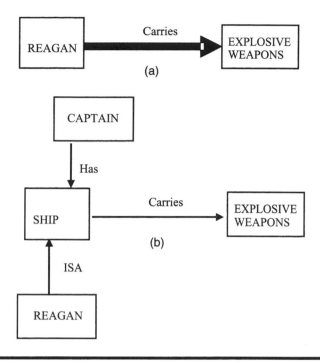

Figure 14.8 Security-constraint violation

Consider the semantic net of Figure 14.8(b). In this net, SHIP carries explosive weapons. This means that all ships carry explosive weapons. It is also specified that REAGAN ISA SHIP. Then, applying Rule A4, one can infer that REAGAN carries explosive weapons. But the "Carries" relationship between REAGAN and explosive weapons is Unclassified. This violates the constraint of Figure 14.8(a). Note that, in this example, implicit information that can be inferred from the information in the multilevel semantic net violates the security constraints.

14.2.6 Universal and Existential Conditionals

Consider the security constraint illustrated in Figure 14.6(b). This constraint specifies that whenever REAGAN is in the Mediterranean and it carries SUN, then the destination country is Secret. Suppose we want the same constraint for any ship. This means that for a ship in the list of the U.S. Navy, we must have an explicit constraint. It is not practical to have a constraint for each ship. What we need is a way to specify that for every ship X, if X is in the Mediterranean and it carries SUN, then X's destination is secret. One way to specify this is to use the type of a ship, which is SHIP instead of the name of a particular ship. Suppose, instead, we want to classify the fact that whenever SHIP carries one or more weapons then its destination must be kept Secret. In this case, if we use the type of weapons, which is WEAPONS, then there is ambiguity as to whether we mean all weapons or at least one weapon. In order to unambiguously represent information such as "all ships" and "some weapons," we need to introduce the notion of universal and existential conditionals.

A conditional is an auxiliary semantic net. A universal conditional is a conditional with only universally quantified variables. An existential conditional is one with only existentially quantified variables. A mixed conditional is one with both types of variables. Universal and existential conditionals are powerful, as they can handle vast quantities of information. In order to treat universal and existential conditionals, we need to handle variables. The constraint semantic net for specifying a constraint using universal and existential conditionals is shown in Figure 14.9(a). By "SHIP: ALL X" and "COUNTRY: SOME Y" we mean "all ships X" and "some country Y", respectively. This constraint states that for all X, if X is in the Mediterranean and it carries SUN, then its destination country is Secret.

Conditionals are useful for not only specifying the constraints, but also for stating information in any auxiliary net. For example, suppose any ship carrying explosive weapons located in the Mediterranean is going to India. In addition, we assume that the destination is Secret. The auxiliary net for specifying the universal conditional is shown in Figure 14.9(b). Note that this net uses universal as well as existential conditionals. This net states that for all ships X, if X is in the Mediterranean and it carries explosive weapons, then its destination is India. Furthermore, the destination is Secret.

The proof theory for variables is pattern matching and binding. We formally define pattern matching and binding as follows.

> **Rule A9 (Pattern-Matching Rule)**: Let A and B be subnets of two multilevel semantic nets. Note that a subnet is any subset (nodes and links) of a semantic net. Subnets are also called vectors. A matches B if the following are satisfied.
>
> 1.   The links are labeled the same and have the same security levels.
> 2.   If a node in A is labeled with a constraint, then the corresponding node in B is labeled with the same term, and the two nodes have the same security levels.
> 3.   If two nodes in A are labeled with the same variable, then the corresponding two nodes in B are labeled with the same constant. Furthermore, the security levels of the corresponding nodes in the two nets are the same.

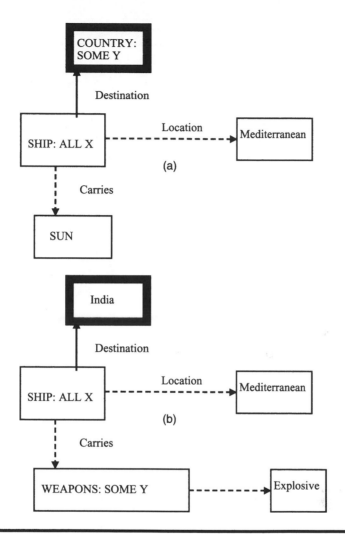

Figure 14.9 Universal and existential conditionals

Figure 14.10 shows two vectors, A and B, where A matches B.

Rule A10 (Binding Rule): If a vector A matches with vector B, then for any variable X in A, the corresponding node in B that matches with X is called the binding of X.

In Figure 14.10, the binding for the variable X in A is the constant REAGAN in B. We now illustrate the pattern-matching and binding processes with an example. Consider the auxiliary net of Figure 14.11(a). Also, consider the semantic net shown in Figure 14.11(b). We can bind REAGAN and FLORIDA with the variable X and SUN and MOON with

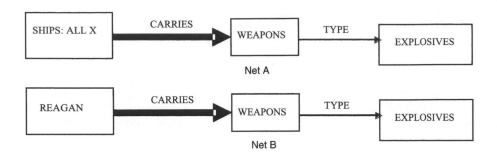

Figure 14.10   Matching vectors

the variable Y. The constant Explosive and the links Location, Carries, and Type are matched in both nets. Therefore, applying the transfer rule, we can add Secret links from REAGAN to India and FLORIDA to India. This is shown in Figure 14.11(c).

14.2.7 Semantics

In the previous sections, we discussed representational issues as well as proof-theoretic issues for multilevel semantic nets. In this section, we discuss the semantics of multilevel semantic nets. We first define the notion of a multilevel world and then discuss interpretations. Truth and satisfaction in interpretations are also discussed.

14.2.7.1 Multilevel Worlds

A multilevel world is the portion of the real world under consideration. It is multilevel because we assume that not all entities, concepts, events, relationships, and the like are assigned the same security level. The following is a description of an example multilevel world.

There is a ship called REAGAN. Its captain is Smith. It is in the Mediterranean on June 16, 2000. At the Secret level, its destination is India and carries SUN, which is an explosive weapon, and its captain has battle management experience. At the Unclassified level, it carries passengers and its destination is Italy and its captain has 20 years experience.

Note that a multilevel world can be decomposed into single-level worlds. That is, there is a world corresponding to each security level. Information in the Unclassified world is accessible to the Secret world. But the converse is not true. Also, it is possible for conflicting information to be present in different worlds. For example, in the Secret world REAGAN's destination is India whereas in the Unclassified world it is Italy.

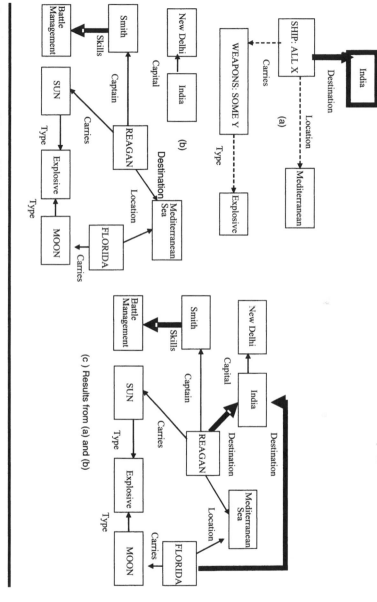

Figure 14.11 Matching and binding process

Therefore, in the Secret world there is conflicting information about the destination. Whenever there is conflicting information present about some event or concept at security level L, we take the information associated with that event or concept at level L*, where L* is the highest security level dominated by L and no information about that event or concept is specified at any security level L+ where L* < L+ L.

The set of objects associated with a world is a domain of discourse of that world. If level L+ dominates the level L*, we assume that D(L*) is a subset of D(L+), where for each L we assume that D(L) is the domain of discourse of the world associated with L. Note that this is a form of polyinstantiation where users at different levels have different views of the entity or the relationships.

14.2.7.2 Interpretations

We first associate (or relate) multilevel semantic nets with multilevel worlds. The rules for relating the world and the net are as follows.

1. For each constant at level L in the net, there is an object associated with the domain of discourse of the world at level L. The object is called the assignment of the constant.
2. For each predicate at level L in the net, there is a relationship in the world at level L. The relationship is called the assignment of the predicate.

The multilevel world, together with its denotations, is called the interpretation of the corresponding semantic net. This view of interpretation can be regarded as the proof-theoretic view. That is, the world is an interpretation of a theory, which is the logic of semantic nets. Note that the multilevel semantic net of Figure 14.2 relates to the multilevel world described in this section. That is, the multilevel world described in this section is an interpretation of the multilevel semantic net of Figure 14.2. For a detailed discussion on the various views, we refer to [GALL78].

Once we have defined interpretations, we need to define the notion of truth in an interpretation. We define truth of ground vectors (which are vectors with no variables), ground conditionals, universal conditionals, and existential conditionals.

14.2.7.3 Ground Vectors

Let A and B be two nodes of a net with relationship R between them. Then the ground vector, which consists of the two nodes and link, is true in an interpretation I with respect to security level L, if the security levels of A, B, and R are all dominated by L, and if A*, B*, and R* are the assignments of A, B, and R, respectively, then A* is in relationship R* with B* in the world at level L.

Example

Consider the ground vector of Figure 14.1(a). Let us assume that ships in the real world is the assignment of the node SHIPS and weapons in the real world is the assignment of the node WEAPONS. Let us also assume that act of carrying is the assignment of the predicate CARRY. Suppose, in the Unclassified as well as in the Secret world, it is true that each ship carries a weapon. Then the ground vector of Figure 14.1(a) is true with respect to Unclassified and Secret levels.

14.2.7.4 Ground Conditionals

A ground conditional is false in interpretation I with respect to security level L, if all of its antecedents are true in I with respect to L, and its consequent is false in I with respect to L. Otherwise, the ground conditional is true in I with respect to L.

Example

Consider the ground conditional of Figure 14.5(a). Let the assignments of REAGAN, LOCATION, India, CARRIES, Mediterranean Sea, Explosive, SUN, and TYPE be a particular ship, its location, act of carrying, the Mediterranean Sea, an explosive weapon, a particular weapon, and belonging to a specific kind, respectively. Suppose in the Secret world it is true that the particular ship is located in the Mediterranean and is carrying a particular weapon, which is an explosive. Then the ground conditional of Figure 14.5(a) is true if in the Secret world it is also true that the particular ship is going to India.

14.2.7.5 Universal Conditionals

We first define satisfaction of a universal conditional. In order to do this, we need to define the notion of a valuation.

A valuation for a universal conditional is an assignment of objects for all its variables. Let C be a universal conditional. An interpretation I satisfies C with respect to level L and valuation V if the ground conditional that results from replacing the variables in C by the objects associated with V is true in I with respect to L.

A universal conditional C is true in I with respect to L if I satisfies C with respect to L and all possible valuations.

14.2.7.6 Existential Conditionals

We first define satisfaction of an existential conditional. In order to do this, we need to define the notion of a valuation. A valuation for an existential conditional is an assignment of objects for all its variables. Let C be an existential conditional. An interpretation I satisfies C with respect to level L and valuation V if the ground conditional that results from replacing the variables in C by the objects associated with V is true in I with respect to L. We discuss negative statements in Section 14.2.7.

An existential conditional C is true in I with respect to L if I satisfies C with respect to L for at least one valuation.

Example

Consider the conditional of Figure 14.9(b). Consider the following two possible valuations for the universal variable X of this conditional: (i) REAGAN and (ii) FLORIDA. Consider the following two possible valuations for the existential variable Y of this conditional: (i) SUN and (ii) MOON. The conditional is satisfied with respect to the Secret level for the valuation REAGAN of X if in the Secret world it is true that REAGAN either carries SUN or MOON and is located in the Mediterranean, then it is also true that REAGAN's destination is India. The conditional is satisfied with respect to the Secret world for the second valuation FLORIDA for X if in the Secret world it is true that FLORIDA carries either SUN or MOON and is located in the Mediterranean, then it is also true that FLORIDA's destination is India. The conditional is true with respect to the Secret world, if it is satisfied with respect to the Secret level for both valuations of X.

14.2.8 Refutations

The proof theory that we have described can be used by an SSO in order to analyze the application. However, if we want to automate the analysis process, then a theory based on the refutation procedure would be more efficient. Refutation procedures have been developed for semantic nets. We describe how such a procedure could be adapted for multilevel semantic nets.

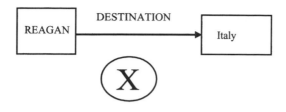

Figure 14.12   Negative statement

In order to develop a refutation procedure for multilevel semantic nets, we need to first introduce the notion of negation. That is, there has to be a way of specifying negative information (or statements).

Negative statements can be assumed by default. This is the closed-world assumption where anything that is not specified in the semantic net is assumed to be false. On the other hand, negative statements can also be explicitly specified. When proofs are automated, negative statements have to be explicitly specified. For example, a concept, event, or relationship can have different values at different security levels. We assumed that if in the Unclassified world a ship's destination is Italy then in the Secret world it is assumed that the ship's destination is India. That is, the SSO could make such inferences when given conflicting statements. However, if the proofs are automated, then the negation of the fact that the ship's destination is Italy has to be specified. Figure 14.12 shows how such a negative statement can be specified by an auxiliary net.

We now illustrate the refutation procedure with an example. Consider the auxiliary net, main net, and the auxiliary net for the negative statement shown in Figures 14.13(a), 14.13(b), and 14.13(c), respectively. The auxiliary net of Figure 14.13(a) states that if REAGAN is located in the Pacific, then at the Secret level one can conclude that its destination is Australia. The main net shown in Figure 4.13(b) states that the destination of FLORIDA is Australia. It does not give any information on REAGAN except its name. The negative statement shown in Figure 4.13(c) states that, at the Secret level, the destination of REAGAN is not Australia. Suppose at the Secret level we want to show that REAGAN is not in the Pacific. Then, we must add its negation (which is "REAGAN is in the Pacific") to the main net. This is shown in Figure 14.13(d). Then applying the transfer rule, we can conclude that REAGAN is going to Australia. This is shown in Figure 14.13(e). This is a contradiction because of the negative statement of Figure 14.13(c). Therefore, the assumption that REAGAN is in the Pacific is false. Note that we cannot arrive at this contradiction at the Unclassified level. This is because, at the Unclassified level, we cannot apply the transfer rule, nor can we assume that the negative statement is true.

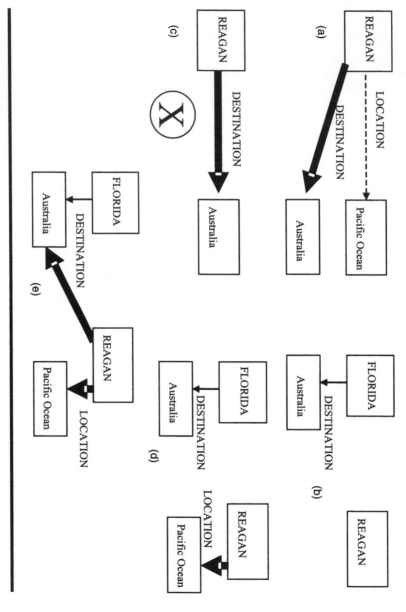

Figure 14.13 Refutation process

14.3 Summary and Directions

Semantic data models have been used extensively in the past for artificial intelligence and natural language processing applications. This is because structures such as these make possible the capture of certain semantics of applications as well as languages. In this chapter we have extended semantic data models to multilevel semantic data models in order to capture the semantics of multilevel applications. This is necessary because, in a multilevel application, not all of the concepts and relationships are assigned the same security level. We have also used various reasoning strategies in order to reason about the multilevel application represented by multilevel semantic data models. The SSO could use the techniques that we have developed to manually analyze the multilevel application and detect possible security violations that could occur. On the other hand, a tool based on our approach could also be developed that could be used by the SSO to design the multilevel database.

There is much to be done in this area. We need to design a complete system based on multilevel semantic nets. We also need to explore other semantic models such as conceptual graphs and hypersemantic data models to represent and reason about the application. The ideas discussed in [THUR91] are just the beginning. Delugah and Hinke have extended this work in [DELU96]. More recently we are exploring the ideas to handle the privacy problem in databases.

References

[BRAC85] Brachmann, R. and Schmalze, J. An overview of the KL-ONE knowledge representation system, *Cognitive Science,* 9: 2, 1985.

[DELU96] Delugach, H. and Hinke, T. Wizard: A database inference analysis and detection system. *IEEE Transactions on Knowledge and Data Engineering* 8:1, 1996.

[GALL78] Gallaire, H. and Minker, J. *Logic and Databases,* Plenum Press: New York, 1978.

[HINK88] Hinke, T. Inference aggregation detection in database management systems. In *Proceedings of the IEEE Symposium on Security and Privacy,* Oakland, CA, April 1988.

[QUIL66] Quillian R. Semantic memory. PhD Thesis, Carnegie Institute of Technology, 1966.

[RICH89] Richards, T. *Clausal Form Logic: An Introduction to the Logic of Computer Reasoning.* Addison-Wesley: Reading, MA, 1989.

[RING88] Ringland, G. and Duda, D. *Approaches to Knowledge Representation: An Introduction.* Research Studies: Letchworth, UK; Wiley: New York, 1988.

[SCHA72] Schank, R. Conceptual dependency: A theory of natural language understanding, *Cognitive Science,* 3: 4, 1972.

[SMIT90] Smith, G. Modeling security-relevant data semantics. In *Proceedings of the IEEE Symposium on Security and Privacy*, Oakland, CA, May 1990.

[SOWA84] Sowa, J. *Conceptual Structures: Information Processing in Minds and Machines*. Addison-Wesley: Reading, MA, 1984.

[THUR91] Thuraisingham, B. The use of conceptual structures to handle the inference problem. In *Proceedings of the IFIP Database Security Conference*, Shepherdstown, WV. North Holland: Amsterdam, 1992.

[URBA89] Urban, S. and Delcambre, L. Constraint analysis for specifying perspectives of class objects. In *Proceedings of the IEEE Data Engineering Conference*, Los Angeles, February 1990.

[WOOD75] Woods, W. *What's in a Link: Foundations for Semantic Networks in Representation and Understanding Studies in Cognitive Science*, Bobrow, D. and Collins, A., Eds., Academic Press: New York.

Exercises

1. Examine the various conceptual structures proposed for handling the inference problem and design your own approach.
2. Design a tool that can handle multiple inference strategies and detect security violations.

Conclusion to Part V

Part V described the inference problem in MLS/RDBMSs. In Chapter 12 we provided a perspective of the inference problem. We also discussed statistical database inference as well as the complexity of the inference problem. In addition we discussed the use of logic databases for handling the inference problem. In Chapters 13 and 14 we discussed our research on the inference problem. In Chapter 13 we discussed security-constraint processing and in Chapter 14 we discussed the use of conceptual structures.

As stated earlier, many of the issues addressed in Part V are applicable to other types of MLS/DBMSs such as MLS distributed database systems. The inference problem in MLS distributed database systems, as well as heterogeneous database systems is discussed in Part VI. The inference problem in various systems was studied extensively in the early 1990s. This work is having a significant impact on current directions in handling the privacy problem. Therefore, it is important to understand the issues involved in handling the inference problem if we are to make progress on the privacy problem. Privacy is discussed in Part VIII.

SECURE DISTRIBUTED AND HETEROGENEOUS DATABASE SYSTEMS

VI

In Part I we discussed supporting technologies for database and applications security and in Part II we discussed discretionary security for database systems. We introduced mandatory security in Part III and in Part IV we discussed MLS/DBMSs based on the relational data model. In Part V we discussed the inference problem. In Part VI we continue with our discussion on security for various types of database systems and focus on distributed and heterogeneous database systems. This is an important topic as more and more databases are getting distributed. Furthermore, there is also a need to integrate heterogeneous database systems.

Part VI consists of three chapters. In Chapter 15 we discuss discretionary security for distributed database systems. Essentially, we examine the security mechanisms discussed in Chapters 5 and 6 and extend them to a distributed environment. In Chapter 16 we discuss multilevel security for distributed database systems. Much of the discussion in this chapter is based on our own research on this topic. In Chapter 17 we discuss security for heterogeneous and federated database systems. We discuss architectures as well as challenges in integrating multiple security policies.

Chapter 15

Discretionary Security for Distributed Database Systems

15.1 Overview

The developments in computer networking technology and database systems technology resulted in the development of distributed databases in the mid-1970s. It was felt that many applications would be distributed in the future and therefore the databases had to be distributed also. Although many definitions of a distributed database system have been given, there is no standard definition. Our discussion of distributed database system concepts and issues has been influenced by the discussion in [CERI84]. A distributed database system includes a Distributed DataBase Management System (DDBMS), a distributed database, and a network for interconnection. The DDBMS manages the distributed database. A distributed database is a database that is distributed across multiple sites.

Distributed database system functions include distributed query management, distributed transaction processing, distributed metadata management, and enforcing security and integrity across the multiple nodes. This chapter describes discretionary security aspects for distributed database systems. Note that secure distributed database systems have evolved from distributed database systems as well as secure database systems. Therefore, the background information on distributed database systems provided in Chapter 2 and discretionary security mechanisms provided in Chapter 5

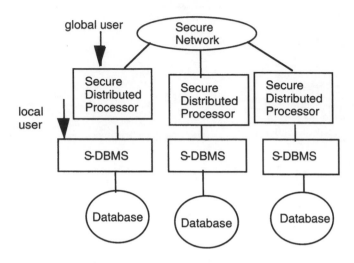

Figure 15.1 Distributed database security

are needed to understand security for distributed database systems. We provide an overview of various discretionary security concepts in Section 15.2. Security impact on distributed database functions is discussed in Section 15.3. Security for some emerging distributed databases is discussed briefly in Section 15.4. The chapter is summarized in Section 15.4. Note that although we are focusing on discretionary security in this chapter, in Chapter 16 we focus on multilevel security and in Chapter 17 we discuss security for heterogeneous and federated database systems. The topics addressed in this chapter are illustrated in Figure 15.1.

15.2 Discretionary Security

15.2.1 Overview

Discretionary security mechanisms enforce rules, which specify the types of access that users or groups of users have to the data. In a distributed environment, users need to be authenticated with respect to the local system as well as the global environment. An issue here is whether the authentication mechanism should be centralized or distributed. If it is centralized, then the authenticator needs to have information about all of the users of the system. If the authenticator is distributed, then the various components of the authenticator need to communicate with each other to authenticate a user.

The access-control rules enforced in a distributed environment may be distributed, centralized, or replicated. If the rules are centralized, then the central server needs to check all accesses to the database. If the rules are

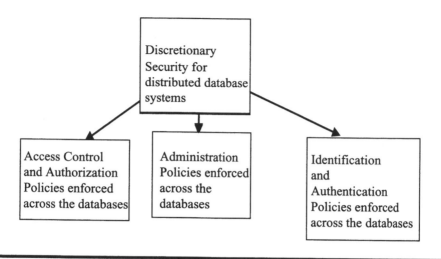

Figure 15.2 Discretionary security

distributed, then appropriate rules need to be located and enforced for a particular access. Often the rules associated with a particular database may also be stored at the same site. If the rules are replicated, then each node can carry out the access-control checks for the data that it manages.

Some work has been reported on discretionary security for distributed databases. Notable among these works are those by Oliva et al., Olivier et al., and Jajodia et al. (see, for example, [OLIV00], [OLIV96], and [JAJO93]). All of these efforts have focused on secure federated database systems. In particular, they examine various access-control policies including role-based access control, integrating the various policies to form a secure federated policy, as well as authorization rules for federated databases. A summary of the various developments can be found in [FERR00]. Discretionary security for federated databases is revisited in Chapter 17.

The organization of this section is as follows. In Section 15.2.2 we discuss access-control policies. Identification and authentication are discussed in Section 15.2.3. In Section 15.2.4 we discuss auditing a distributed database system. Security policy integration issues are discussed in Section 15.2.5. Query modification is the subject of Section 15.2.6. Views are discussed in Section 15.2.7. Finally, SQL extensions are discussed in Section 15.2.8. Figure 15.2 illustrates discretionary security mechanisms.

15.2.2 Access-Control Policies

15.2.2.1 Distributed Access Control

In Chapter 5 we discussed access control and authentication in a centralized environment. The concepts can be extended for a distributed environment.

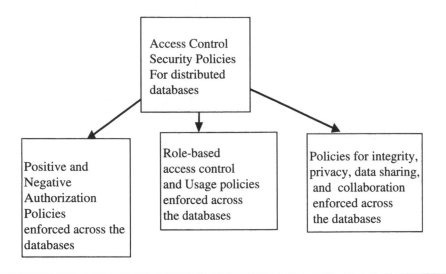

Figure 15.3   Access control

First consider access-control rules. These rules are enforced on data across the different nodes. Enforcing such rules may be quite complex especially if the rules depend on the content of the fragmented relations.

Let us consider some examples. Suppose we have a rule that states that John has access only to the employee salaries if the employees are in the math department. Suppose the database has two relations EMP and DEPT where EMP is stored in site A and has attributes E#, Ename, Salary, and D#. DEPT is stored in site B and has attributes D#, Dname, and Mgr. Now to access the salary values in EMP, one needs to do a join between EMP and DEPT at different sites and make the connection between Salary and Dname. If the Dname is MATH, then John has access to the salary values of the employees in the math department. This is illustrated in Figure 15.3.

Consider another example, where John has access to the Employee relation only if the total salaries of employees are less then one million dollars. Also suppose that the employee relation is fragmented and stored at sites A and B. In this case, one has to compute the total salaries of all the employees across the sites and then determine whether John has access to the relation.

The access-control rules could be centralized or they could be replicated at every site. Another approach is to distribute the rules. If they are centralized, then each time a query is posed the request is sent to the database that stores the rules. If the rules are replicated, then it makes query processing efficient. However, we need to ensure that the rules are consistent at all sites and, when a rule is updated, that update has to be propagated. If the rules are distributed, then we need to come up with a scheme as to how to distribute the rules. For example, it may make sense to store the rules near the relations on which the rules are enforced.

Access control in a distributed database system has been studied a great deal (see [CERI84]). The techniques have been implemented on systems such as R* and Distributed INGRES. Many research prototypes have also been developed. Many of the commercial products implement access-control rules for distributed environments. However, many of the rules enforced are rather simple rules and we still need efficient algorithms to enforce rules across multiple databases.

15.2.2.2 Role-Based Access Control

As we have stated in Chapter 5, role-based access control is being implemented in various commercial database system products. The idea is for users, depending on their roles, to access data as well as to carry out activities. Role-based access control is also being investigated for distributed and collaborative environments. For example, Bertino et al. have developed a model for controlling access in workflow systems (see [BERT99]).

In a distributed database environment users may have different roles at different nodes and may try to access the distributed database to carry out their functions. The ideas developed for a centralized system would be extended for a distributed environment. In the simple case, the user's role is verified in a distributed environment by contacting, say, the local authority, and access is then granted.

In a multiorganizational environment, there may be some additional concerns. A user may have one role in one organization and another role in another organization. For example, in department A he may be a manager and in department B he may be a project leader. Therefore, he may have access to certain data in department A and certain other data in department B. His roles in different departments will have to be verified before granting his access. In a way this is a problem with a heterogeneous environment, as in a homogeneous environment we assume that the environment is the same everywhere. Nevertheless, even if the distributed database functions in a homogeneous environment, some may argue that the roles of individuals may be different at different organizations.

As new technologies emerge including knowledge management, E-commerce, and collaboration, there are additional challenges for role-based access control. Many developments have been reported recently in the *ACM SACMAT (Symposium on Access Control Management and Technologies) Conference Series.*

15.2.3 Identification and Authentication

With respect to identification and authentication, the question is do we have a centralized authority or do we have a distributed authority. That is, when a user types in her user ID and password, should the information be sent to a single site so that the user is authenticated or should the site where the user logs in have the capability to authenticate the user? Having a single site to authenticate the user means that if that site fails then the user cannot be authenticated. If we give every site the capability to authenticate the users, as users can log in from anywhere, then we need to ensure that the password information is protected at all sites.

Note that with emerging technologies such as biometrics, sophisticated identification and authentication techniques are being developed. For example, each node could install a biometric device that could do some local identification and authentication of a person. In addition there could be some central node that performs some additional identification and authentication. We revisit access control, identification, and authentication in a Web environment especially for E-commerce applications in Part IX. We also briefly discuss digital identity and related issues in Part X.

15.2.4 Auditing a Distributed Database System

In Chapter 5 we discussed auditing in a centralized database system. Usually the DBA audits the queries posed, the updates made, and other activities that may be performed. Data-mining techniques are also being explored to analyze the audit data and determine whether any intruders have accessed the system and whether access-control rules have been bypassed.

The techniques developed for centralized systems could be extended to audit a distributed database. One could have a central audit manager auditing the distributed database or have an audit manager at each site. The advantage of having a central audit manager is that all the information is gathered centrally and managed centrally. However, this means that if the central site crashes, there is essentially no audit mechanism. Alternatively one could have audit managers at the different sites communicating with each other to form a big picture. The advantage of this approach is that it does not depend on a central audit mechanism. However, the individual audit managers will have to communicate with each other and share the audit data to determine if there is any problem.

As new technologies emerge there are new challenges for auditing. For example, some work has been done on auditing a data warehouse and we discuss this in Part VIII. Auditing in a Web environment is also

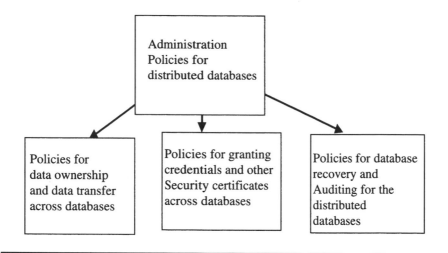

Figure 15.4 Aspects of administration policies

becoming very important especially with E-commerce transactions. We briefly discuss auditing Web databases in Part IX. Figure 15.4 illustrates aspects of administration policies.

15.2.5 Security Policy Integration

In Chapter 2 we discussed schema integration issues for distributed database management system. The idea is to form a global schema from the individual database schemas. The concepts have been extended for heterogeneous and federated databases. When integrating the schemas to form a global schema, the security policy enforced on the individual databases has to be enforced at the global level. Essentially the security policies of the components databases have to be integrated to form a global security policy.

Figure 15.5 illustrates security policy integration. Because we are assuming that the environment is homogeneous, the policies expressed at each site are also homogeneous. That is, we can expect the same language to be used to specify the policies. However, the individual policies have to be integrated. For example, at node A one could enforce a policy where the salary values of the relation EMP cannot be accessed by John. At node B one could enforce a policy where the healthcare record of the relation MEDICAL cannot be accessed by John. Therefore, at the global level one enforces a policy where John does not have access to salaries in EMP or healthcare records in MEDICAL. We discuss policy integration for heterogeneous and federated environments in Chapters 16 and 17.

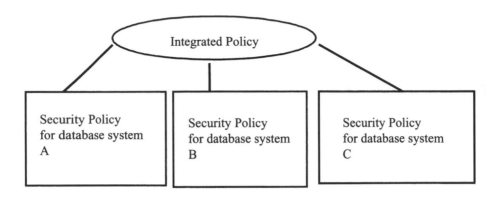

Figure 15.5 Security policy integration

15.2.6 Query Modification

In Chapter 6 we discussed query modification for a central database system. With query modification, the query is modified based on the access-control rules (also called security constraints). The modified query is optimized and executed. Query modification has been examined for distributed systems such as Distributed INGRES. That is, the query is modified according to the access-control rules enforced by a distributed database system. The modified query is executed.

If the access-control rules are replicated, the query modification can be performed at the site where the query is posed. The modified query is optimized using techniques for distributed query optimization and the optimized query is executed. The query may be executed at multiple sites and the results are combined and the response is given to the user. If the access-control rules are distributed, then the query is modified at each site according to the rules enforced at that site and then the pieces are combined to form the final modified query. In combining the pieces it must be ensured that all the AND, OR, and NOT operators in the where clause are correctly selected. Another option is to combine all the rules relevant to the query and use the combined rules to modify the query at the query site.

15.2.7 View Mechanism

Views are essentially virtual relations and are computed from the base relations. Views have been used to provide discretionary as well as mandatory access control in databases. Systems such as SeaView and LOCK Data Views started off with providing mandatory access control on views. However, because the DBMS should then be trusted and both projects relied on the underlying operating system to provide mandatory access control, they abandoned the idea and focused on tuple- and element-level classification. However, SeaView enforced discretionary access control on views. Furthermore, as discussed in Chapter 11, TRW's ASD-Views provided mandatory access control on views.

In Chapter 5 we discussed the use of views for providing access control in relational databases. The idea is to define views and then grant access depending on, say, the user's role and the contents of the view. That is, views are the objects of access control. Now, in a distributed database environment, views may be computed from relations and fragments stored at multiple sites. Users are then granted access to the resulting views. For example, EMP could be stored at site A and DEPT at site B and a view may be formed consisting of employee names and their managers. Access may be granted on this view and access denied on the base relations. The challenges include computing the views as well as applying access-control rules on the views themselves. That is, access may be granted on the views or granted on a subset of the views. Figure 15.6 illustrates views as security objects.

15.2.8 SQL for Distributed Database Security

In Chapter 6 we discussed SQL extensions for specifying security constraints or access-control rules. For example, GRANT and REVOKE statements provide a way to grant and revoke access to users. We also gave some examples of specifying access based on content and context. For example, John has access to retrieve salary values only for those employees working for him or John does not have access to Names and Salaries taken together. In this section we briefly examine SQL for specifying access control in a distributed environment.

Now, the access-control rules usually remain the same whether they are stored in site A or site B. That is, for such rules, the SQL specifications for a central system are sufficient for a distributed environment. However, in some cases there may be site-specific access-control rules. For example, John does not have access to any databases in Europe but he has access to databases in the United States. Usually such rules are not desirable as the whole idea in a distributed database system is location transparency. However, if we need to enforce site-specific rules, then SQL has to be extended to enforce such rules.

SITE 1

EMP1

SS#	Name	Salary	D#
1	John	20	10
2	Paul	30	20
3	James	40	20
4	Jill	50	20
5	Mary	60	10
6	Jane	70	20

DEPT1

D#	Dname	MGR
10	C. Sci.	Jane
30	English	David
40	French	Peter

SITE 2

EMP2

SS#	Name	Salary	D#
9	Mathew	70	50
7	David	80	30
8	Peter	90	40

DEPT2

D#	Dname	MGR
50	Math	John
20	Physics	Paul

EMP-DEPT View
(all those who work in the
Physics Department)

Ename
Paul
James
Jill
Jane

Figure 15.6 Views as security objects

15.3 Security Impact on Distributed Database Functions

In this section we examine the functions of a distributed database management system discussed in Chapter 2 and describe the security impact. Note that in Chapter 6 we examined the security impact on the functions of a centralized database system. This chapter essentially integrates the techniques discussed in Chapters 2 and 6.

Note that in Section 15.2 we discussed query modification and views as security objects. This is part of query management. The challenge is to develop efficient techniques for query modification and query optimization in a distributed environment. Furthermore, forming global views as well as enforcing access control on these views remains a challenge.

Secure Distributed Database Functions:

Distributed Query Processing: Enforce access control rules during query processing across databases; distributed inference control; consider security constraints during distributed query optimization

Distributed Transaction Management: Ensure security constraints are satisfied during transaction processing.

Metadata Management: Enforce access control on distributed metadata

Integrity Management: Ensure that integrity of the data is maintained while enforcing security across the databases

Figure 15.7   Secure distributed database management functions

Other functions of distributed database management include transaction processing and metadata management. In the case of transaction management, all of the subtransactions must be executed in order to commit the global transaction. Therefore, if any of the subtransactions cannot meet the security constraints, then the transaction has to be aborted. Therefore, the challenge is to enforce constraints during transaction processing and to integrate this mechanism with the commit protocols.

Metadata management issues include distributing as well as replicating the metadata. Note that access-control rules can be considered as part of the metadata. Therefore, consistency of the constraints enforced across the sites is an issue. Furthermore, access-control rules may be enforced on the metadata. We need techniques to manage such rules.

Functions such as storage management are the responsibility of the central database manager. However, fragmenting and distributing the relations is a function of the DBA. The DBA may need to take into consideration the access-control rules when distributing the database. Figure 15.7 illustrates secure distributed database management functions.

15.4 Security for Emerging Distributed System Technologies

This section briefly examines various emerging technologies that have evolved in some way or another from distributed databases and discusses the security impact. These include data warehouses and data-mining systems, collaborative computing systems, distributed object systems, and the Web. We address security for such systems in more detail in Parts VII through X.

First let us consider data-warehousing systems. We introduced security for data warehouses in [THUR97]. The major issues here are ensuring that security is maintained in building a data warehouse from the back-end database systems and also enforcing appropriate access-control techniques when retrieving the data from the warehouse. For example, security policies of the different data sources that form the warehouse have to be integrated to form a policy for the warehouse. This is not a straightforward task, as one has to maintain security rules during the transformations. For example, one cannot give access to an entity in the warehouse, whereas the same person cannot have access to that entity in the data source. Next, the warehouse security policy has to be enforced. In addition, the warehouse has to be audited. Finally, the inference problem also becomes an issue here. For example, the warehouse may store average salaries. A user can access average salaries and then deduce the individual salaries in the data sources that may be sensitive and, therefore, the inference problem could become an issue for the warehouse. To date, little work has been reported on security for data warehouses as well as the inference problem for the warehouse. This is an area that needs much research.

Data mining causes serious security problems. For example, consider a user who has the ability to apply data-mining tools. This user can pose various queries and infer sensitive hypotheses. That is, the inference problem occurs via data mining. There are various ways to handle this problem. Given a database and a particular data-mining tool, one can apply the tool to see if sensitive information can be deduced from the legitimately obtained unclassified information. If so, then there is an inference problem. There are some issues with this approach. One is that we are applying only one tool. In reality, the user may have several tools available to her. Furthermore, it is impossible to cover all ways that the inference problem could occur. Another solution to the inference problem is to build an inference controller that can detect the motives of the user and prevent the inference problem from occurring. Such an inference controller lies between the data-mining tool and the data source or database, possibly managed by a DBMS. Data-mining systems are being extended to function in a distributed environment. These systems are called distributed data-mining systems. Security problems may be exacerbated in distributed data-mining systems. This area has received little attention.

Other emerging technologies that have evolved in some way from distributed databases are collaborative computing systems, distributed

```
┌─────────────────────────────────────────────────┐
│                                                   │
│   Secure Emerging Distributed Systems             │
│                                                   │
│   Secure Distributed Object Management Systems    │
│                                                   │
│   Secure Data Warehousing and                     │
│   Distributed Data Mining Systems                 │
│                                                   │
│   Secure Web Information Systems                  │
│                                                   │
└─────────────────────────────────────────────────┘
```

Figure 15.8   Secure emerging distributed systems

object management systems, and the Web. Much of the work on securing distributed databases can be applied to securing collaborative computing systems. Some of the issues in workflow security systems have been examined by Bertino et al. [BERT99]. With respect to distributed object systems security, there is a lot of work by the Object Management Group's Security Special Interest Group (see, for example, [ORFA96]). There has been a lot of work on securing the Web (see, for example, [GHOS98]). The main issue here is ensuring that the databases, the operating systems, the applications, the Web servers, the clients, and the network are not only secure, but they are also securely integrated. As we have stated earlier, we discuss security for the emerging technologies related to distributed databases in Parts VII through X. Figure 15.8 illustrates security for emerging distributed system technologies.

15.5   Summary and Directions

This chapter has provided an overview of the developments in secure distributed database systems. We focused mainly on discretionary security. In particular, we discussed security policies, access control, and query modification. Various issues on integrating security policies as well as enforcing access-control rules were discussed. Finally we discussed the security impact on some of the emerging technologies such as data warehousing, data mining, collaboration, distributed objects, and the Web. A summary of secure distributed database management is given in [THUR01].

   Distributed database systems are a reality. Many organizations are now deploying distributed database systems. Therefore, we have no choice but to ensure that these systems operate in a secure environment. We believe that as more and more technologies emerge, the impact of secure distributed database systems on these technologies will be significant. Although some progress has been made, there are still many challenges in developing techniques for secure distributed query processing and secure distributed transaction management.

References

[BERT99] Bertino, E. et al. The specification and enforcement of authorization constraints in workflow management systems. *ACM Transactions on Information and Systems Security* 2: 1, 1999.

[CAST96] Castano, S. et al. An approach to deriving global authorizations in federated database systems. In *Proceedings of the IFIP Database Security Conference*, 1996. Chapman & Hall: London, 1997.

[CERI84] Ceri, S. and Pelagatti, G. *Distributed Databases, Principles and Systems.* McGraw-Hill: New York, 1984.

[FERR00] Ferrari, E. and Thuraisingham, B. Secure database systems. In *Advances in Database Management,* Piattin, M. and Diaz, O., Eds., Artech, London, UK, 2000.

[GHOS98] Ghosh, A. *E-Commerce Security, Weak Links and Strong Defenses.* Wiley: New York, 1998.

[JAJO93] Jajodia, S. et al. Integrating concurrency control and commit algorithms in distributed multilevel secure databases. In *Proceedings of the IFIP Database Security*, Huntsville, AL, 1993. North Holland: Amsterdam, 1994).

[OLIV00] Oliva, M. and Salter, F. Integrating security policies in federated database systems. In *Proceedings of the IFIP Database Security Conference*, 1996. Kluwer: Hingham, MA, 2001.

[OLIVI96] Olivier, M. Integrity constraints in federated databases. In *Proceedings of the IFIP Database Security Conference*, 1996. Chapman & Hall: London, 1997.

[ORFA96] Orfali, R. et al. *The Essential, Distributed Objects Survival Guide.* Wiley: New York, 1994.

[THUR97] Thuraisingham, B. Data warehousing, data mining and security. In *Proceedings of the IFIP Database Security Conference*, Como, Italy, 1996. Chapman & Hall: London, 1997.

[THUR01] Thuraisingham, B. Security for distributed database systems. *Information Security Journal*, 2001.

Exercises

1. Describe the design of an access-control module for a distributed database management system.
2. Develop a security policy for a distributed database management system.
3. Design secure query processing and secure transaction management algorithms.

Chapter 16

Multilevel Security for Distributed Database Systems

16.1 Overview

In Chapter 15 we discussed discretionary security for distributed database systems. Although many of the commercial distributed database systems enforce discretionary security, if these systems are to function in a multilevel environment, they have to enforce mandatory security. The type of mandatory security we are interested in is multilevel security. Multilevel security controls ensure that users cleared at different security levels access and share a distributed database in which the data is assigned different sensitivity levels without compromising security. In this section we describe both types of security.

During the early 1990s we conducted research on multilevel secure distributed database systems. In this chapter we provide an overview of the essential concepts. A MultiLevel Secure Distributed DataBase System (MLS/DDBMS) includes a multilevel distributed database. Each multilevel database is managed by a MLS/DBMS and connected through what we have called a Secure Distributed Processor (SDP). We describe the architecture in more detail in Section 16.3. In our investigation we have designed and implemented a MLS/DDBMS that connects multiple

MLS/DBMSs at different sites. We have investigated query processing as well as transaction management techniques. We have conducted simulation studies as well as prototype development. Our research is discussed in [THUR91], [THUR93], [RUBI91], [RUBI92a], [RUBI92b], [RUBI93a], and [RUBI93b].

The organization of this chapter is as follows. Some background information is given in Section 16.2. Architectural aspects are discussed in Section 16.3. In particular, architectures based on central control and distributed control are discussed. Data-modeling issues are discussed in Section 16.4. Note that we assume all the systems are relational systems. Security impact on the functions such as query processing, transaction management, and metadata management are discussed in Section 16.4. The inference problem in a distributed environment is discussed in Section 16.5. The chapter is summarized in Section 16.6. Note that in order to develop a multilevel secure distributed database system we also need multilevel secure networks. We provided a brief introduction to network security in Chapter 3. A detailed discussion of multilevel network security is beyond the scope of this book.

16.2 Background

Much of the work in secure distributed database systems has focused on multilevel security. Some of the early work in the field began with the Air Force Summer Study. Specifically, approaches based on distributed data and centralized control architectures were proposed. Prototypes based on these approaches were also developed during the late 1980s and early 1990s. Notable among these approaches are the efforts by Unisys Corporation and the Naval Research Laboratory (see, for example, [JENS89] and [FROS89]). Note that although the distributed architecture assumed that the data was distributed, it was developed mainly for a centralized MLS/DBMS. We discussed this architecture in Chapter 8 and revisit it for completeness in this chapter.

In the early to mid-1990s there were efforts at MITRE on secure distributed database systems based on the architecture proposed in [CERI84]. The project investigated secure query processing and secure transaction management techniques (see [THUR91]). Prototypes and simulation studies were also carried out (see [RUBI91], [RUBI92a], and [RUBI92b]). This work also included an investigation of secure heterogeneous databases as well as the inference problem (see, for example, [THUR92], [THUR93], [THUR94], and [THUR95]). Some parallel work on secure distributed transactions was carried out at MITRE and reported in

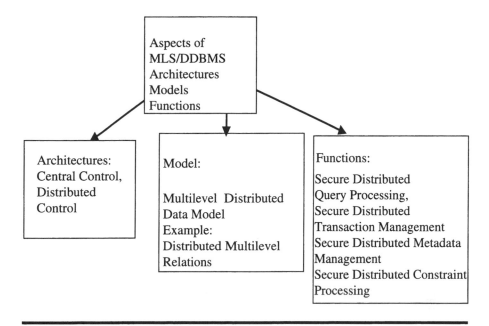

Figure 16.1 Aspects of MLS/DDBMS

various papers (see, for example, [BLAU93]). Much of the discussion on data modeling and functions for a secure distributed database system discussed in this chapter is based on the developments reported in [THUR91], [THUR93], and [THUR95].

Much of the work in the late 1990s focused on discretionary security for distributed and federated databases. In addition, work has also been reported on related technologies such as secure data warehouses, secure distributed objects, secure collaboration, and secure Web. These emerging developments are discussed in later parts. This chapter provides an overview of the various aspects of multilevel secure distributed database systems. We focus mainly on homogeneous secure distributed databases where we assume that all of the nodes are identical. Secure heterogeneous and federated database systems are discussed in Chapter 17.

We have defined a multilevel secure distributed database system as follows. In a MLS/DDBMS, users with different clearance levels access and share a multilevel distributed database with data at different sensitivity levels according to the security policy. The security policy enforced is essentially the one developed for MLS/DBMSs where users read at or below their level and write at their level. We discuss architectures, models, and functions in the remaining sections. Figure 16.1 illustrates the contents addressed in this chapter.

16.3 Architectures

16.3.1 Distributed Data and Centralized Control

As mentioned in Chapter 8, the Air Force Summer Study examined a distributed architecture for developing MLS/DBMSs. In this architecture the data is distributed and control is centralized. Two approaches were proposed at the Summer Study. In the first of these approaches, known as the partitioned approach, a trusted front-end database system is connected to untrusted back-end database systems. Each back-end database system operates at a single level and manages data at that level. For example, an Unclassified DBMS manages the Unclassified data whereas a Secret DBMS manages Secret data. All communication between the back-end database systems is through the front-end database system. A user's query is sent to the DBMS at or below the user's level. Update requests are sent only to the DBMS at the user's level. For example, a Secret user's query is sent to the Secret and Unclassified DBMSs and a Secret user's update request is sent only to the Secret DBMS.

It was found that there was the potential for covert channels with this approach as a Secret user's query could have sensitive information and be sent to an Unclassified DBMS. As a result, a second approach was examined where the data is replicated. In this approach, the Unclassified data is replicated at the Secret and TopSecret databases and the Secret data is replicated at the TopSecret database. This way, a user's query is sent only to the DBMS at the user's level. The update request is sent to the replicated databases. Although there is no covert channel for the query operation, because a user's update is propagated upward, there is a potential for covert channels during the update operation. Nevertheless, this issue has been studied extensively and shown that the bandwidth of the channel is fairly low. Therefore, the preferred approach is the replicated approach. As mentioned in Chapter 11, this approach has been studied extensively both by Unisys and by the Naval Research Laboratory (see [JENS89] and [FROS89]). Figures 16.2 and 16.3 illustrate the architecture discussed in this section.

16.3.2 Distributed Data and Distributed Control

A more realistic architecture for a MLS/DDBMS is one in which the data as well as control is distributed. As stated earlier, in a multilevel secure distributed database management system, users cleared at different security levels access and share a distributed database consisting of data at different security levels without violating security. A system architecture for a MLS/DDBMS was described in [THUR91]. This architecture has been

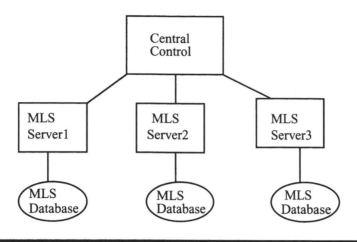

Figure 16.2 Distributed data and centralized control—1

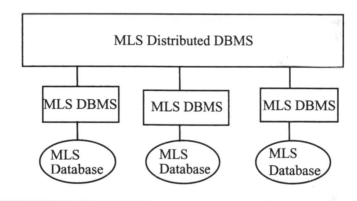

Figure 16.3 Distributed data and centralized control—2

derived from the architecture for a DDBMS in [CERI84] and is based on distributed data and distributed control. In this architecture, the MLS/DDBMS consists of several nodes that are interconnected by a multilevel secure network. In a homogeneous environment, all of the nodes are designed identically. Each node is capable of handling multilevel data. Each node has a MLS/DBMS, which manages the local multilevel database. Each node also has a distributed processing component called the secure distributed processor.

The modules of the SDP are similar to those of the DP for a DDBMS described in Chapter 2. These modules are the Secure Distributed Query Processor (SDQP), the Secure Distributed Transaction Manager (SDTM), the Secure Distributed Metadata Manager (SDMM), and the Secure Distributed

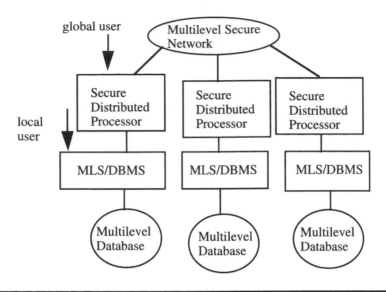

Figure 16.4   Multilevel secure distributed DBMS

Security and Integrity Manager (SDSIM). Multilevel security must be taken into consideration during all of the processing. First of all, an appropriate security policy has to be formulated. This policy will depend on the policies of the local DBMS, the network, and the distributed processor. The algorithms for query, update, and transaction processing in a DDBMS have to be extended to handle multilevel security. Locking techniques could cause covert channels. Therefore, algorithms for MLS/DBMSs have to be integrated with algorithms for DDBMSs to handle MLS/DDBMSs. These algorithms are implemented by the SDTM. Finally, security and integrity-processing techniques for MLS/DBMSs and DDBMSs have to be extended to MLS/DDBMSs. For example, in the case of the SDSM, it has to consider multilevel security in its functions such as identification, authentication, and enforcing discretionary security controls. Details on the design of a MLS/DDBMS can be found in [THUR91] and [THUR93]. Architectures for a MLS/DDBMS and a SDP are illustrated in Figures 16.4 and 16.5.

16.4 Data Modeling

In Chapter 9 we discussed the multilevel relational data model and described the notion of polyinstantiation. In Chapter 11 we provided an overview of some of the prototypes and commercial products. These prototypes and products utilized various versions of the multilevel relational

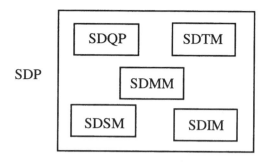

Figure 16.5   Modules of the Secure DP (SDP)

data model. Some provided support for classifying views and others provided tuple- and element-level classification.

A distributed database also utilizes a data model. Inasmuch as we are assuming that the environment is homogeneous and each DBMS is based on the relational data model, the data model for the distributed database may also be based on the relational data model. Because the environment is multilevel, the data model utilized by the MLS/DDBMS is a multilevel relational data model.

Note that one of the goals of a distributed database is to ensure transparency. Therefore, one needs to define a multilevel relational data model at the global level. If we are assuming a homogeneous environment, the local models and the global model may be the same. However, if we are connecting systems such as, say, ASD-Views, SeaView, and LOCK Data Views, then the global model may be different from the local models. For example, ASD-Views classifies views, SeaView provides element-level classification, and LOCK Data Views provides tuple-level classification. Therefore, if the global model provides, say, tuple-level classification then we need to provide mapping between the local models and the global models. More details of a heterogeneous environment are given in Chapter 17. Figure 16.6 illustrates a multilevel relational database that is distributed at different sites. Note that we also assume there is polyinstantiation and that classification is at the tuple level. The tuples may be polyinstantiated across the sites. In [RUBI91], we studied the performance of secure query-processing algorithms based on such a multilevel distributed data model. More details on the functions are given in the next section.

16.5   Functions

In Chapter 2 we discussed the functions of a DDBMS. These include query processing, transaction management, metadata management, and integrity

SITE 1

EMP1 = Secret

SS#	Name	Salary	D#
1	John	20	10
2	Paul	30	20
3	James	40	20
4	Jill	50	20
5	Mary	60	10
6	Jane	70	20

DEPT1 = Unclassified

D#	Dname	MGR
10	C. Sci.	Jane
30	English	David
40	French	Peter

SITE 2

EMP2 = Secret

SS#	Name	Salary	D#
9	Mathew	70	50
7	David	80	30
8	Peter	90	40

DEPT2 = Unclassified

D#	Dname	MGR
50	Math	John
20	Physics	Paul

Figure 16.6   Multilevel data model for a MLS/DDBMS

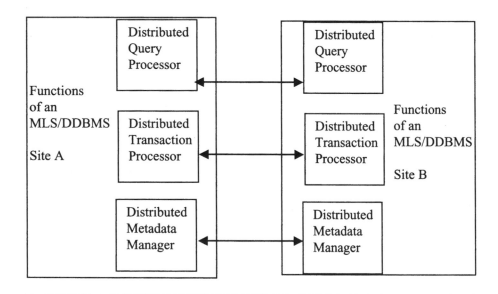

Figure 16.7   Functions of a MLS/DDBMS

management. In this section we examine the multilevel security impact on each of these functions. Figure 16.7 illustrates the functions.

First consider the query-processing operation. In the case of a MLS/DDBMS, users should query the multilevel distributed database and retrieve data at or below their level. We have carried out extensive prototyping and simulation studies on secure query processing. We carried out performance evaluation on the impact of polyinstantiation in a distributed environment. Essentially the DQPs at multiple sites communicate with each other and process the queries. We also used semijoin as a query-processing strategy for MLS/DDBMS. The query processor was augmented with a constraint processor to process the security constraints. Constraint processing is discussed when we describe the inference problem for a MLS/DDBMS.

Next consider transaction management. Here we assumed that each node implemented the concurrency-control algorithm that we described in Chapter 10. That is, multiple copies of an object are maintained, one for each security level for the algorithm. In addition, we also designed algorithms based on time-stamping and optimistic concurrency control for MLS/DDBMS (see [THUR91]). The third algorithm we designed was based on optimistic concurrency control. An overview of the algorithms is provided in [THUR91] and simulation studies are discussed in [RUBI92a] and [RUBI92b]. We evaluated the performance of the various concurrency-control algorithms and utilized the two-phase commit technique for committing a distributed transaction. We assumed that transactions were single-level and all of the operations for a transaction, including the commit operation, were carried out at the same level. The goal of the concurrency-control algorithms was to ensure that actions of a higher-level transaction did not interfere with those of a lower-level one.

In the case of distributed metadata management, the issues include distributing the metadata as well as replicating the metadata. In our experiments we found that it was less complex to replicate the metadata when it came to query processing. However, we had to ensure that the multiple copies of the metadata were kept consistent during the update operation. We assumed that the entire operation was carried out at the user's level and therefore only the metadata at or below the user's level was taken into consideration for query and transaction management.

Other functions include storage management and integrity management. In the case of storage management, each MLS/DBMS manages its own storage. The SDP manages multilevel data distribution and could use load balancing to distribute the multilevel data. Integrity constraints are rules that must be satisfied by the data in the database. For example, if we have a constraint that the total hours worked by an employee cannot exceed 40 hours and if the information is distributed across the nodes, the MLS/DDBMS needs to perform computations across the nodes. The constraints themselves may be assigned security levels. Only those constraints classified at or below the user's level are taken into consideration during query and transaction management. Essentially the constraints are considered part of the metadata. Note that as stated in Chapter 8, classifying the integrity constraints may cause a problem. For example, suppose we have a Top-Secret constraint which states that the maximum cargo of a plane cannot exceed 10 tons. This constraint will not be invoked at the Secret level. Therefore, at the Secret level one could keep adding weights and the weight of the cargo could well exceed 10 tons. This could cause serious problems. Also, if the cargo is distributed, then we need to carry out computations across the sites.

In this section we have briefly examined the security issues for a MLS/DDBMS. More details on secure query processing and transaction management are found in [THUR91]. Performance studies are discussed in [RUBI91], [RUBI92a], and [RUBI92b]. The inference problem and security-constraint processing are discussed in the next section.

16.6 Inference Problem for a MLS/DDBMS

As we have discussed in Part V, the inference problem has received a lot of attention for many years. There is still work being done on this problem especially with emerging technologies such as data warehousing, data mining, and the Web. Inference is the process of users posing queries and deducing unauthorized information from the legitimate responses that they receive. Much of the work has focused on the inference problem in a centralized environment. Data distribution exacerbates the problem as users from different sites can retrieve information and make associations. A summary of the various developments on the inference problem for centralized database systems was discussed in Part V.

An investigation of the inference problem for distributed database systems began around 1992. This approach was based on processing security constraints in a multilevel secure distributed database system. Essentially the secure distributed processor of the MLS/DDBMS described in Section 16.2 was augmented with constraint processors. Details of this work are reported in [THUR95].

Figure 16.8 illustrates a distributed inference controller. The distributed constraint processor examines the constraints at the global level, communicates with its peer distributed constraint processors and determines whether security violations via inference can occur. The techniques are similar to the ones we have discussed in Chapter 13 except that the constraints are now enforced across the nodes. We explain with an example. Suppose we have a constraint that classified a ship's mission at the Secret level after the location had been released at the Unclassified level. An Unclassified user can pose a query at site A to retrieve the location and pose a query at site B to retrieve the mission and this violates

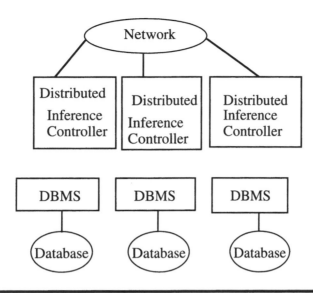

Figure 16.8   Distributed inference controller/constraint processor

security. Therefore, the fact that the location has been released at site A has to be recorded and available to all the distributed constraint processors. We have also designed techniques for handling security constraints during distributed update processing and during multilevel distributed database design. Modules of the distributed constraint processor are illustrated in Figure 16.9. Details of our algorithms can be found in [THUR95].

16.7 Summary and Directions

This chapter has provided an overview of the developments in multilevel secure distributed database systems. We started with a discussion of both the partitioned approach and the replication approach proposed by the Air Force Summer Study in 1982 and then discussed security for architectures based on distributed control and distributed data. Next we provided an overview of data modeling and secure distributed database functions. Finally we discussed the inference problem in distributed databases.

In our discussion we assumed that the MLS/DBMSs that constitute the MLS/DDBMS are homogeneous and are based on the relational data model. There is still work to be done on secure transaction processing. We assumed that transactions operate at a single level. In some cases the transactions may be multilevel. Some work on multilevel transactions is given in [BLAU93]. Furthermore, commit algorithms for a MLS/DDBMS are discussed in [JAJO93]. Many of the concepts need to be investigated for

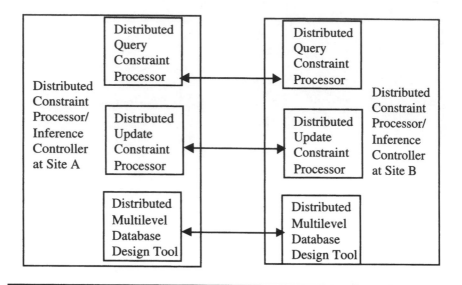

Figure 16.9   Modules of the distributed constraint processor

heterogeneous environments as well as for emerging technologies including E-commerce and the Web.

References

[BLAU93] Blaustein, B. A model of atomicity for multilevel transactions. In *Proceedings of the IEEE Symposium on Security and Privacy*, Oakland, CA, May 1993.

[CERI84] Ceri, S. and Petagetti, G. *Distributed Databases: Principles and Systems*, McGraw-Hill: New York, 1984.

[FROS89] Froscher J. and Meadows, C. Achieving a trusted database management system using parallelism. In *Proceedings of the IFIP Database Security Conference*, Kingston, Ontario, 1988. North Holland: Amsterdam, 1989.

[JAJO93] Jajodia, S. et al. Integrating concurrency control and commit algorithms in distributed multilevel secure databases. In *Proceedings of the IFIP Database Security*, Huntsville, AL, 1993. North Holland: Amsterdam, 1994.

[JENS89] Jensen, C. SDDM—A prototype of a distributed architecture for database security. In *Proceedings of the IEEE Data Engineering Conference*, Los Angeles, February 1989.

[RUBI91] Rubinovitz, H. and Thuraisingham, B. Implementation and simulation of secure distributed query processing algorithms. In *Proceedings of the Computer Simulation Conference*, Baltimore, 1991.

[RUBI92a] Rubinovitz, H. and Thuraisingham, B. Design and simulation of secure distributed concurrency control algorithms. In *Proceedings of the 1992 Computer Simulation Conference*, Reno, NV, July 1992.

[RUBI92b] Rubinovitz, H. and Thuraisingham, B. Simulation of query processing and concurrency control algorithms for a trusted distributed database management system. MITRE Technical Report approved for public release, June 1992.

[RUBI93a] Thuraisingham, B. and Rubinovitz, H. Design and implementation of a distributed query processor for a trusted distributed database management systems. *Journal of Systems and Software*, April 1993.

[RUBI93b] Rubinovitz H. and Thuraisingham, B. Simulation of secure distributed join query processing algorithms. *Information and Software Technology Journal*, 1993.

[THUR91] Thuraisingham, B. Multilevel security issues in distributed database management systems—II. *Computers and Security Journal* 10: 6, 1991.

[THUR92] Thuraisingham, B. and Rubinovitz, H. Multilevel security for distributed database management system—III, *Computers and Security*, 10: 5, 1992.

[THUR93] Thuraisingham, B. et al. Design and implementation of a distributed database inference controller. In *Proceedings of the IEEE COMPSAC Conference*, Phoenix, AZ, October 1993.

[THUR94] Thuraisingham, B. Security issues for federated database systems, *Computers and Security*, 13: 6, 1994.

[THUR95] Thuraisingham B. and Ford, W. Security constraint processing in a multilevel distributed database management system. *IEEE Transactions on Knowledge and Data Engineering* 7: 2,1995.

Exercises

1. Design query processing strategies for a MLS/DDBMS.
2. Design concurrency-control algorithms for a MLS/DDBMS.
3. Examine the inference problem for a MLS/DDBMS.

Chapter 17

Secure Heterogeneous and Federated Database Systems

17.1 Overview

In Chapter 15 we discussed discretionary security and in Chapter 16 we discussed multilevel security for distributed database systems. We assumed that the systems were homogeneous. That is, the database systems were designed identically. In the case of discretionary security, the major issue was enforcing security policies and access-control rules across the nodes. In the case of multilevel security, we assumed that the distributed processors operating at level L communicate with each other. Furthermore, we also assumed that all MLS/DBMSs were designed identically and were augmented by multilevel distributed processors.

In this chapter we examine heterogeneity. That is, we assume that the DBMSs are not identical. For example, the DBMS at site 1 could be designed based on the relational model and the DBMS at site 2 could be designed based on the object model. In Parts II and III we discussed discretionary and multilevel security for relational databases. In Part VII we discuss discretionary and multilevel security for object databases. The challenge is how do the different secure systems interoperate. In addition to data model heterogeneity, the system could enforce different security policies. How do you integrate the heterogeneous security policies? Heterogeneity could also be with respect to query processing and transaction management. What is the security impact? Note that we are seeing the need for the interoperation of heterogeneous databases because organizations want to collaborate with each other and yet maintain their autonomy. These organizations have already implemented their own database systems and applications. Therefore, the challenge is to integrate the systems and applications for collaboration and for other purposes.

Another challenge is managing secure federated databases. For example, the database systems may not only be heterogeneous but they may also form federations. How do you build secure federations when components join and leave the federations dynamically? Another issue is secure migration of legacy databases and applications. We hear a lot about migrating large databases and applications. How do you maintain security when the databases and applications are migrated?

This chapter examines secure heterogeneous and federated databases. We also examine the security impact on migration. The organization of this chapter is as follows. We focus both on discretionary security and multilevel security. In Section 17.2 we provide some background on secure heterogeneous and federated databases. In Section 17.3 we discuss architectural issues. Schema heterogeneity including data model heterogeneity is discussed in Section 17.4. Policy heterogeneity and integration are discussed in Section 17.5. Functions are discussed in Section 17.6. The inference problem is the subject of Section 17.7. Security for client/server databases is discussed in Section 17.8. Migrating legacy databases and applications are discussed in Section 17.9. Summary and directions are provided in Section 17.10.

17.2 Background

The earliest effort to investigate multilevel security for heterogeneous and federated database systems began around 1991 and was reported in [THUR92], [THUR94a], and [THUR94b]. In particular, various approaches to designing heterogeneous and federated database systems were examined and the security impact was investigated. The issues include security for integrating the federated schemas as well as handling different ranges of security levels. For example, one system could handle the range from Secret to TopSecret and another system could handle the range from Unclassified to Secret. The work also investigated the integration of multiple security policies where component systems export policies to the federations. Issues on integrating heterogeneous database schemas in a secure environment were also investigated. Much of the work here focused on query-processing issues. In addition, prototype systems were also developed (see also [THUR94b]).

Around 1992, the MITRE Corporation began an effort called the MUSET (MUltilevel SEcure Transactions) database system. This effort focused mainly on transaction management in a heterogeneous database system [BLAU93]. This effort also investigated concurrency control, recovery, and commit protocols for multilevel transactions (see, for example, [JAJO93]). A multilevel transaction is a transaction that can operate at multiple security levels. For example, a subtransaction at one site could operate at the Unclassified level, and another subtransaction at a different site could operate at the Secret level. The challenge here is to ensure consistency and at the same time minimize covert channels. This is more complex than the single-level transaction approach proposed in [THUR91].

Other work on secure distributed database systems includes various concurrency-control algorithms for transactions. Many of the papers on this topic were published by Bertino and Jajodia et al. at the various security conferences during the mid-1990s (see, for example, *Proceedings of the IEEE Symposia on Security and Privacy* and *Proceedings of the IFIP Database Security Conference Series*). Discretionary security for federated database systems has been investigated by Olivier et al. at the Rand Africaan University and presented at the IFIP conference series (see [OLIVI99]). We discuss some of the key issues in secure heterogeneous and federated database systems in the remaining sections. As we have stated in Section 17.1, we focus both on multilevel security and discretionary security. Some of the ideas are used in future chapters especially when we discuss secure data warehouses, secure information integration, and secure collaboration and E-commerce.

17.3 Architectures

In a heterogeneous database environment, we assume that the DBMSs are heterogeneous in nature. Heterogeneity could be with respect to data models or security policies, and functions such as query and transaction processing. Figure 17.1 illustrates an architecture for a Secure Heterogeneous Database Management System (SHDBMS). Here we assume that the various Secure Database Management Systems (SDBMS) are connected through the Secure Heterogeneous Distributed Processors (SHDP). These SHDPs are responsible for handling heterogeneity as well as for communication between the different nodes. The secure DBMSs at different nodes are designed differently. That is, one could be a secure object database system and the other could be a secure relational database system. Note also that these database systems could be multilevel as illustrated in Figure 17.2. In this case, the SHDPs are multilevel secure and are called Multilevel Secure Distributed Heterogeneous Processors (MLS/DHP).

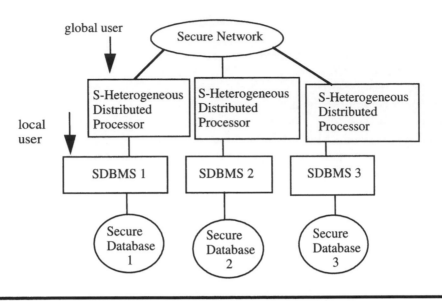

Figure 17.1 Secure heterogeneous database systems

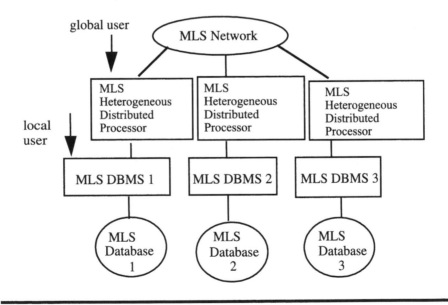

Figure 17.2 Multilevel secure heterogeneous database systems

As we have stated, some systems may form federations. These database systems could be SDBMSs or MLS/DBMSs. Figure 17.3 illustrates the case where multiple SDBMSs form two federations. That is, systems 1 and 2 form federation I and systems 2 and 3 form federation II. The question

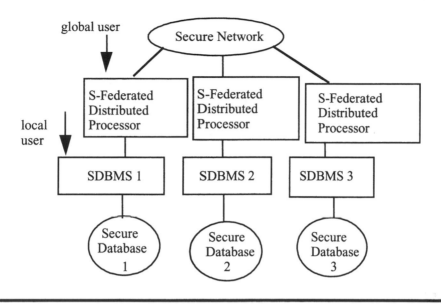

Figure 17.3   Secure federated database system

is what do 1 and 2 as well as 2 and 3 share with one another. For example, 1 may send information to 2 only if 2 does not give 3 access to that information. Therefore, 1 and 2 will have to make negotiations. There has been a lot of research on trust management and negotiation systems (see [BERT04] and [YU03]). The concepts are being examined for federated environments. Figure 17.3 illustrates secure federated database systems. Note that we can design a multilevel secure federated database system (MLS/FDBMS) if we assume that the component DBMSs are multilevel secure. This is illustrated in Figure 17.4.

In the remaining sections we include discussions of schema heterogeneity and policy integration. We also discuss the security impact on the heterogeneous database system functions.

17.4 Schema Integration

There are several aspects to heterogeneity. One is schema heterogeneity where system A is based on a relational system and system B is based on object systems. That is, when the two systems are based on different models we need to resolve the conflicts. One option is to have a common data model. This means that the constructs of both systems have to be transformed into the constructs of the common data model. When you consider security properties, we have to ensure that the policies enforced by the individual systems are maintained. Figure 17.5 illustrates the use

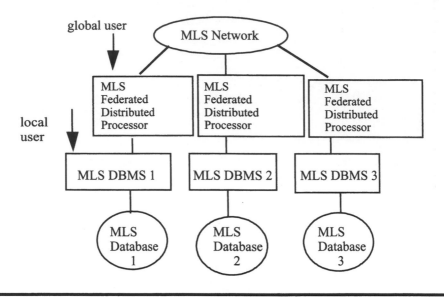

Figure 17.4 Multilevel secure federated database system

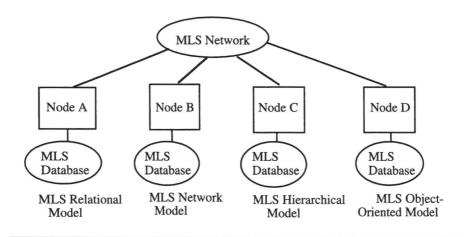

Figure 17.5 Secure data model heterogeneity

of a common secure data model to handle data model heterogeneity. In some cases we may need bidirectional transformation where the constructs of one data model have to be translated into those of another.

Figure 17.6 illustrates the situation where the multiple schemas are integrated to form, say, a federated schema for a secure federated database system. Essentially we have adopted Sheth and Larson's schema architecture for a secure federated environment. Some of the challenges in

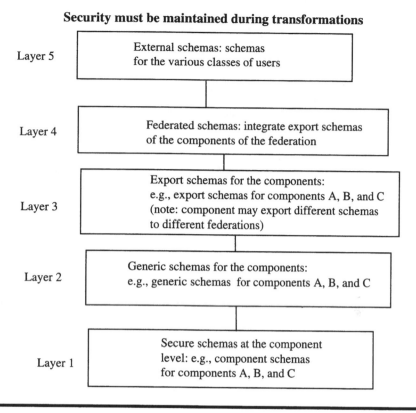

Security must be maintained during transformations

Layer 5 — External schemas: schemas for the various classes of users

Layer 4 — Federated schemas: integrate export schemas of the components of the federation

Layer 3 — Export schemas for the components: e.g., export schemas for components A, B, and C (note: component may export different schemas to different federations)

Layer 2 — Generic schemas for the components: e.g., generic schemas for components A, B, and C

Layer 1 — Secure schemas at the component level: e.g., component schemas for components A, B, and C

Figure 17.6 Secure schema integration

integrating heterogeneous schemas are discussed in [THUR94a]. We assume that each component exports certain schema to the federation. Then these schemas are integrated to form a federated policy. In a secure environment, we need to ensure that the security properties of the individual systems are maintained throughout the federation. In the next section we discuss security policy integration issues.

17.5 Policy Integration

In the previous section we discussed heterogeneity with respect to schemas and data models. In this section we discuss security policy integration. Initial investigation of security policy integration for federated databases was reported in [THUR94a]. Here we assumed that heterogeneous MLS/DBMSs had to be integrated to form a MLS/FDBMS. We illustrate the policy architecture in Figure 17.7. Our approach is very similar to the approach taken by Sheth and Larson for schema integration [SHET90]). In

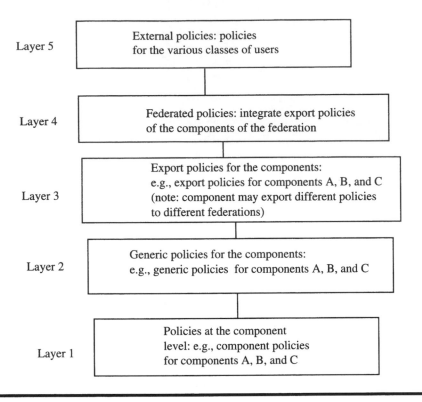

Layer 5 — External policies: policies for the various classes of users

Layer 4 — Federated policies: integrate export policies of the components of the federation

Layer 3 — Export policies for the components: e.g., export policies for components A, B, and C (note: component may export different policies to different federations)

Layer 2 — Generic policies for the components: e.g., generic policies for components A, B, and C

Layer 1 — Policies at the component level: e.g., component policies for components A, B, and C

Figure 17.7 Security policy integration

the case of policy integration, each system exports security policies to the federation. We assume that the component systems have more stringent access-control requirements for foreign users. That is, export policies may have access-control rules in addition to the rules enforced by the local system. The challenge is to ensure that there is no security violation at the federation level. A view of agencies sharing data and enforcing policies is illustrated in Figure 17.8.

Figure 17.9 illustrates the situation where the systems have incomparable security levels. That is, system A handles the range Unclassified to Confidential and system B handles the range Secret to TopSecret. In this case the two systems can communicate through some form of trusted guard as illustrated in Figure 17.9. However, if we have a third system that has overlapping security levels such as from Confidential to Secret, then A and B can communicate via C. This is illustrated in Figure 17.10. Note that integrating multiple policies for computing systems in general has been investigated by researchers including Hosmer (see [HOSM96]). Some of the research has been published in the *Proceedings of the New Computer Security Paradigm Workshop Series*.

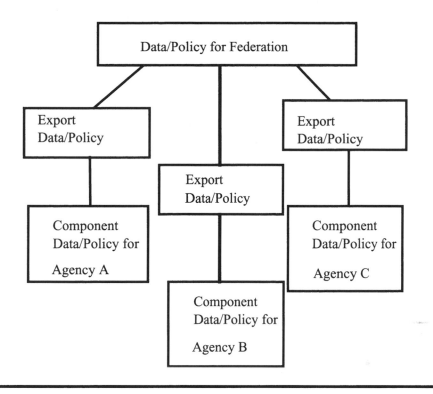

Figure 17.8   Integrated policy/data sharing

17.6 Functions

The previous sections discussed architectures, schema integration, and policy integration. In this section we examine the security impact on the functions of heterogeneous and federated database systems. In particular we discuss the security impact of functions such as query processing, transaction management, metadata management, storage management, and integrity management.

Consider the query operation. We need to ensure that secure query processing is maintained throughout the federation. Suppose a user queries the federated system. Then the query is sent to the different components by the secure federated system. The security policies and schemas are used at the global level to modify the query as illustrated in Figure 17.11. The modified queries are sent to the individual components and the results are combined at the federation level. If there is no tight integration between the systems, then the components have to communicate with each other and aggregate the results where the query site may act as the coordinator.

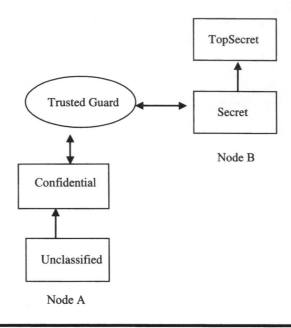

Figure 17.9 Incomparable security levels

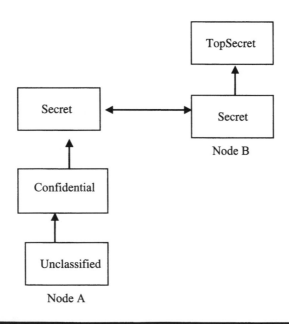

Figure 17.10 Overlapping security levels

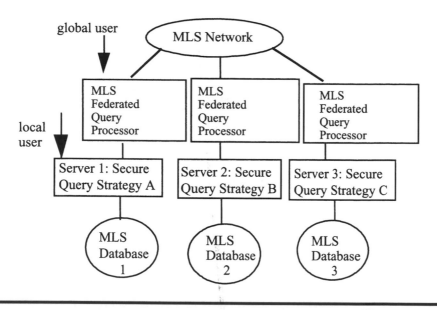

Figure 17.11 Secure query processing in a federated system

Consider secure transaction management. In a heterogeneous environment, we could assume that system A enforces locking for secure concurrency control and system B enforces time stamping for secure concurrency control. The challenge is to obtain consistency as well as security. Although we have studied secure concurrency control in centralized database systems as well as distributed database systems, secure concurrency control and transaction management in heterogeneous and federated environments remain a challenge. In addition we also have to ensure that the commit and recovery algorithms ensure security and consistency. Secure transaction management is illustrated in Figure 17.12.

Secure metadata management issues include handling data model and schema heterogeneity. Other challenges include querying and updating metadata. Furthermore, when changes are made to the component database system with respect to security policies as well as schemas, how do you propagate the changes to the federation? In addition, we have to ensure that the changes do not cause any security violations.

Storage management has very little impact on secure federated environments mainly because the component database system manages the storage. Furthermore, because we assume that integration and federations occur because organizations, say, within and across corporations, want to collaborate with one another and therefore want to connect existing database systems, these existing database systems manage the data stores. However, at the federation level the system has to manage global

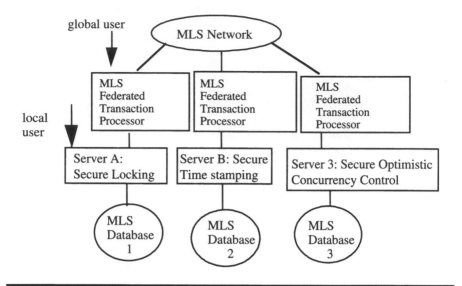

Figure 17.12 Secure transaction processing in a federated system

resources, the schemas, the policies, and the metadata. Security impact on such storage issues has to be investigated.

Finally we discuss the security impact on integrity. Like security policies, the various integrity constraints have to be managed across the federations. Furthermore, the challenge is to ensure that consistency is maintained and there is no security violation. Security constraints also may be inconsistent. That is, one system may enforce a policy where salaries are Confidential whereas another system may enforce a policy where salaries may be Unclassified. Such inconsistencies have to be resolved at the federation level. Essentially we need to integrate integrity policies with security policies. We could use the policy integration architecture illustrated earlier for integrity policy integration. Note also that the "weights" example we discussed in Chapters 10 and 16 is applicable for multilevel heterogeneous and federated database systems also. We need to develop techniques to enforce integrity constraints and at the same time minimize signaling channels.

17.7 Inference Problem

We carried out an extensive investigation of the inference problem for heterogeneous environments back in the mid-1990s (see [THUR94b]). Essentially we designed and developed security-constraint processing in a heterogeneous environment. We extended the distributed inference controller discussed in Chapter 16 to a heterogeneous environment. Figure

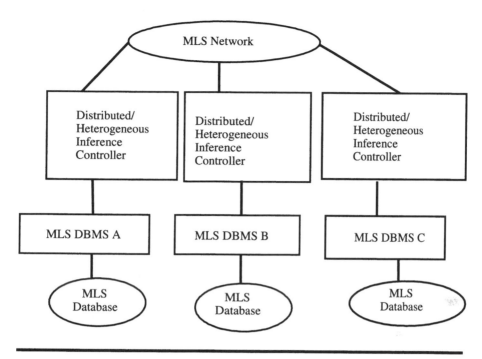

Figure 17.13   Constraint processing in a heterogeneous environment

17.13 illustrates a heterogeneous inference controller. Here the SHDP includes a component for security-constraint management.

Although there is little other work reported on inference control in federated environments, more recently this area is getting attention especially when agencies have to form federations and share information and at the same time enforce inference control and privacy control. We discuss privacy in federated environments in Part VIII when we discuss data mining and privacy control. Figure 17.14 illustrates inference control in a federated environment.

17.8 Secure Client/Server Database Management

As we have stated in Chapter 2, in a client/server data management environment, clients of multiple vendors access database servers of multiple servers. Note that the client as well as the servers may enforce their own security policies. That is, access to client resources is controlled by the client policy and the server enforces access to the server databases. Now, there may be policies that have to be enforced across servers. In such a situation, the client may enforce such policies, which makes the client a fat client, or the server may enforce such policies, which makes

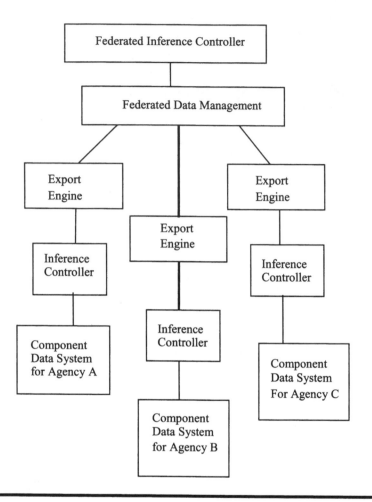

Figure 17.14 Federated inference controller

the client a thin client. On the other hand one could have a middle tier to enforce policies across servers.

The secure distributed database functions that we have described in the previous section such as query processing, transaction management, and metadata management have to be examined for the client/server data management environment. For example, in the case of secure transaction management does the client act as the coordinator or should the middle tier act as the coordinator and ensure that security as well as consistency is maintained? Although the commercial client/server products offer some degree of security, a detailed study of the security impact on the database functions needs to be carried out. Secure client/server data management is illustrated in Figure 17.15.

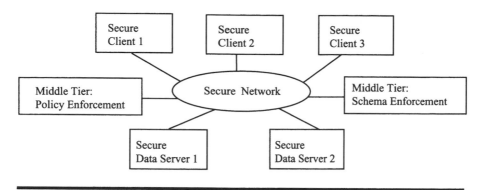

Figure 17.15   Secure client/server data management

17.9   Secure Migration of Legacy Databases and Applications

Many corporations such as banks as well as the government are migrating their databases and applications to take advantage of the new generation architectures. In [THUR97] we discussed some of the issues involved in migrating legacy databases and applications. We also discussed the use of object technology and object request brokers in migration (see also [BENS95]). Many strategies have been reported on migrating databases and applications, but little work has been reported on maintaining security.

One of the major challenges with migrating databases and applications is maintaining security. That is, the security policies enforced by the old system have to be migrated to the new system. Furthermore, data integrity has to be maintained. Database migration includes designing the schemas of the new system and then migrating the data to the new system. Therefore, data model and schema integration issues discussed in Section 17.4 are applicable to migration. Application migration includes migrating the applications of a system one by one to the new environment. Therefore, the application security policies have to be maintained during migration. Figure 17.16 illustrates the security impact on database and application migration. It should be noted that there is little research on secure migration and a lot needs to be done.

17.10   Summary and Directions

In this chapter we have discussed security for heterogeneous and federated databases. We started by providing some background and related work and then discussed architectures, schema integration, and security policy

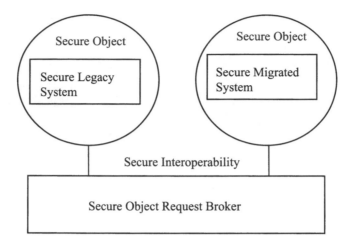

Capture the security policy of the legacy system and
enforce the policy on the migrated system

Figure 17.16   Secure databases and application migration

integration. We also discussed the security impact on the functions of a
secure federated system and provided an overview of the inference
problem in a federated environment. Next we discussed security for
client/server databases. Finally, we discussed the security impact on the
migration of databases and applications.

It should be noted that much of the work on security for heterogeneous
and federated databases is preliminary in nature. However, with information integration on the Web as well as the interest in the federated approach
for interagency data sharing, work is beginning on areas such as the
secure semantic Web, secure information integration, and privacy control
in federated environments. Furthermore, there is also much interest now
in trust and negotiation management systems. Therefore we can expect
to see much progress on security for heterogeneous and federated database systems.

References

[BENS95] Bensley, E. et al. Evolvable systems initiative for real-time command
and control systems. In *Proceedings of the First IEEE Complex Systems
Conference*, Orlando, FL, November 1995.

[BERT04] Bertino, E. et al. Secure third party publication of XML documents. *IEEE
Transactions on Knowledge and Data Engineering*, 16, 2004.

[BLAU93] Blaustein, B. A model of atomicity for multilevel transactions. In *Proceedings of the IEEE Symposium on Security and Privacy*, Oakland, CA, May 1993.

[HOSM96] Hosmer, H. Availability policies in an adversarial environment. In *Proceedings of the New Computer Security Paradigms Workshop*, Los Angeles, CA, 1996.

[JAJO93] Jajodia, S. et al. Integrating concurrency control and commit algorithms in distributed multilevel secure databases. In *Proceedings of the IFIP Database Security*, Huntsville, AL, 1993. North Holland: Amsterdam, 1994.

[OLIVI96] Olivier, M. Integrity constraints in federated databases. In *Proceedings of the IFIP Database Security Conference*, Como, Italy, 1996. Chapman & Hall: London, 1992.

[THUR91] Thuraisingham, B. Multilevel security issues in distributed database management systems—II. *Computers and Security Journal* 10: 6, 1991.

[THUR92] Thuraisingham, B. and Rubinovitz, H. Multilevel security issues for distributed database management systems—III. *Computers and Security* 11: 5, 1992.

[THUR94a] Thuraisingham, B. and Rubinovitz, H. Security constraint processing in a heterogeneous database system. In *Proceedings of the ACM Computer Conference*, Phoenix, AZ, March 1994.

[THUR94b] Thuraisingham, B. Security issues for federated database systems. *Computers and Security* 13: 6, 1994.

[THUR97] Thuraisingham, B., *Data Management Systems: Evolution and Interoperation,* CRC Press, Boca Raton, FL, 1997.

[YU03] Yu, T. and Winslett, M. A unified scheme for resource protection in automated trust negotiation. In *Proceedings of the IEEE Symposium on Security and Privacy*, Oakland, CA, 2003.

Exercises

1. Incorporate discretionary and multilevel security into a heterogeneous database management system.
2. Design security policy integration techniques for federated database systems.
3. Examine security when migrating legacy databases and applications.

Conclusion to Part VI

Part VI described security for distributed and heterogeneous database systems. In Chapter 15 we discussed discretionary security for distributed database systems. Essentially, we examined the security mechanisms discussed in Chapters 5 and 6 and extended them to a distributed environment. In Chapter 13 we discussed multilevel security for distributed database systems. Much of the discussion in this chapter is based on our own research on this topic in the 1990s. In Chapter 17 we discussed security for heterogeneous and federated database systems. We discussed architectures as well as challenges on integrating multiple security policies. We also discussed the inference problem both for distributed and heterogeneous database systems.

Research in secure distributed databases has resulted in new directions for security for the various emerging technologies. For example, since the late 1990s, there have been research and development efforts on secure distributed object systems, secure data warehousing, secure collaboration, secure Web information systems, and secure sensor information management. This work is discussed in Parts VII through X.

SECURE OBJECT AND MULTIMEDIA SYSTEMS

In Part I we discussed supporting technologies for database and applications security and in Part II we discussed discretionary security for database systems. We introduced mandatory security in Part III and in Part IV we discussed MLS/DBMSs based on the relational data model. In Part V we discussed the inference problem. In Part VI we discussed security for distributed and heterogeneous database systems. In Part VII we focus on secure object systems. Because object models are being used to represent multimedia data, we also discuss secure multimedia data management systems.

Part VII consists of three chapters. In Chapter 18 we discuss discretionary and mandatory security for object database systems. We discuss policy and design issues as well as provide an overview of specific systems. In Chapter 19 we focus on two important aspects of objects and security. First we discuss security for distributed object systems and then we discuss the use of object modeling to design secure applications. In Chapter 20 we discuss secure multimedia data management systems. In particular, models, architectures, and functions of a secure multimedia data management system are described.

Chapter 18

Discretionary and Multilevel Security for Object Database Systems

18.1 Overview

Parts II through VI discussed discretionary and mandatory security for databases and distributed databases mainly based on the relational data model. In particular, we discussed discretionary security mechanisms, mandatory security mechanisms, designs of MLS/DBMSs, secure data models, the inference problem, and secure distributed database management with the relational model in mind. However, many of the discussions and arguments can be extended to nonrelational database systems. Most popular among the nonrelational database systems are object-oriented database systems. At one time there was a belief that object databases would supersede relational databases. Although that has not happened, relational databases have become more powerful by incorporating support for objects. Such databases are called object-relational databases.

Whether we are dealing with object databases or object-relational databases, we need to examine security for object models. Furthermore, secure object models can also be used for secure distributed object systems as well as to design secure applications. Secure distributed object systems as well as designing secure applications are discussed in Chapter 19. In this chapter we discuss both discretionary security as well as mandatory security for object data models. We also give examples of secure object database systems. In particular, we discuss both research prototype efforts as well as commercial products whenever applicable.

The organization of this chapter is as follows. In Section 18.2 we discuss discretionary security for object database systems. In Section 18.3 we discuss multilevel security. Securing object models as well as designs of systems is described. Summary and directions are provided in Section 18.4. Note that many of the concepts discussed in this chapter are applied to object models discussed in Chapter 19. Note also that object databases have many applications in multimedia systems as well as in geospatial information systems. Therefore, in Chapter 20 we provide an overview of secure multimedia database systems.

18.2 Discretionary Security

18.2.1 Overview

Discretionary security mechanisms for object databases include access control and authorization for objects as well as controls for method execution. One can also enforce access control at the level of object classes, instance variables, instances, composite objects, and class hierarchies. One of the comprehensive models for discretionary security for object systems is the ORION model proposed by Rabbitti, Kim, Bertino et al. (see [RABB91]). This model had a major impact on commercial products. In this section we discuss some of the key issues.

The organization of this section is as follows. Discretionary security policies are discussed in Section 18.2.2. Policy enforcement issues are discussed in Section 18.2.3. Example systems including a discussion of ORION are given in Section 18.2.4.

18.2.2 Policy Issues

Discretionary security policy for object database systems includes access control for objects, classes, instances, instance variables, class hierarchy, and component hierarchy as well as access control for method execution. For example, some access-control rules would include User Group A has read access to Object Class EMP and write access to Object Class DEPT. This could mean that A can access everything in class EMP for reading and everything in class DEPT for writing. We can also have finer granularity and grant access to instances and instance variables, That is, unless a positive authorization is explicitly specified, we may not assume that A has read access to everything in EMP. As an example, A has read access to instance variables Name and Department # and does not have read

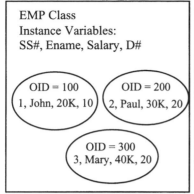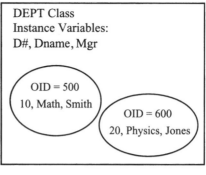

EMP Class
Instance Variables:
SS#, Ename, Salary, D#

OID = 100
1, John, 20K, 10

OID = 200
2, Paul, 30K, 20

OID = 300
3, Mary, 40K, 20

DEPT Class
Instance Variables:
D#, Dname, Mgr

OID = 500
10, Math, Smith

OID = 600
20, Physics, Jones

Increase-Salary(OID, Value)

Read-Salary(OID, amount)

Amount = Amount + Value

Write-Salary(OID, Amount)

Access Control Rules:
John has update access to EMP Class
Jane has read access to DEPT Class
Jane has update access to object with OID = 500
Mary has execute access to Increase Salary method

Figure 18.1 Access control on objects and methods

access to salary in EMP. Another example is for A to have read access to instance with ID = 10 and write access to instance with ID = 20.

One can also enforce access control on method execution. For example, method update-salary could be executed only by processes acting on behalf of user group B whereas the method update-age could be executed by user groups both A and B. Figure 18.1 illustrates access control on objects and methods.

We can also enforce access control on the class hierarchy. For example, we can have a rule that states that although John has read access to class EMP, he does not have read access to all subclasses of EMP. This is illustrated in Figure 18.2. We can enforce access control on component hierarchy as illustrated in Figure 18.3. Here John has read access to sections 1 and 3 and he does not have read access to sections 2 and 4. In the next section we discuss policy enforcement issues.

In the case of object-relational models, we need to integrate security both for object models as well as for the relational models. For example, one may grant or revoke access to the object, object instances, and so on, as well as to the relationships. This is illustrated in Figure 18.3.

18.2.3 Policy Enforcement

The security policy enforcement mechanism includes query modification. SQL has been developed for relational database systems, and variations

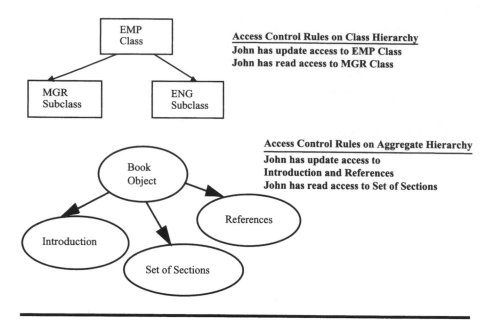

Figure 18.2 Access control on hierarchies

BOOK

ISBN#	Bname	Contents
1	X	██████
2	Y	+ + + +
3	Z	########

Access Control Rules

John has update access to Book object with ISBN #1

Jane has read access to Book object with ISBN #2

Figure 18.3 Secure object-relational model

of SQL, such as Object SQL, have been developed for object systems. The query may be expressed in Object SQL and modified according to the access-control rules. For example, consider a rule where John does not have access to employee instances with ID = 20 and he cannot read any

Policy Enforcement Mechanisms:

Query Modification Algorithm on objects
and instance variables

Rule processing integrated with method
execution for enforcing access control

Visualizing access control policies on objects
using UML and other specifications

Figure 18.4 Policy enforcement

salary values of Employees. Suppose the employee instance variables are
ID, Name, Salary, and Age. If John queries to

```
Retrieve information about all employees from the EMP
    class
```

Then the query is modified to

```
Retrieve all information from EMP.ID, EMP.Name, EMP.Age
    where EMP.ID <> 20
```

As mentioned in Section 18.2.2, access-control rules may be enforced
on method execution. Furthermore, credentials may be passed from one
method to another during method calls. For example, consider John having
some credentials. The process acting on his behalf could call method A
with his credentials. If A calls method B during execution, then B can get
the credentials with which A executes. One could also place some restriction on what credentials can be passed.

Other policy enforcement mechanisms include those discussed for
relational databases. These include visualization of security policies. Object
models with their power to represent complex data types are richer than
relational models. Therefore policies expressed on the object models may
be more complex especially when policies are enforced on class and
component hierarchies. For example, do the rules propagate down the
hierarchies? Visualization techniques may help to understand the policies
enforced. Figure 18.4 illustrates the policy enforcement mechanisms
including extensions to Object SQL to specify policies, query modification,
and visualization. Furthermore, security policies may be integrated for
different objects. Object models have been explored to specify role-based

```
┌─────────────────────────────────────────────┐
│                                               │
│   Example Systems:                            │
│   Security for                                │
│   Gemstone (originally Servio Logic)          │
│   Objectstore (originally Object Design)      │
│   Ontos (originally Ontos Inc.)               │
│   Starburst (IBM Almaden)                     │
│   O2 (Altair Group)                           │
│   ORION (MCC)                                 │
│   IRIS (HP Labs)                              │
│                                               │
└─────────────────────────────────────────────┘
```

Figure 18.5   Example systems

access controls (see, for example, the work reported in the *Proceedings of the IFIP Database Security Conference Series*). Policy integration is another issue that must be investigated for object systems. We discuss policy integration further in Chapter 19.

18.2.4 Example Systems

18.2.4.1 Overview

Since the late 1980s, we have seen at least a dozen commercial object databases emerge. Many of the designs have been influenced by research systems including MCC's ORION system and HP's IRIS system. These systems have been developed mainly for CAD/CAM (Computer-Aided Design/Computer-Aided Manufacturing) and similar applications that require the representation of complex data structures. Furthermore, relational systems such as System R have been extended to support rules. These systems are called active database systems.

In this section we provide a brief overview of some of the systems. These include research systems such as ORION and IRIS and commercial systems such as GEMSTONE. We also provide an overview of the Starburst authorization model and this system is really an extended relational database system, which extends a relational system with support for rules. Such systems are called active database systems. The various systems are illustrated in Figure 18.5. Note that we discuss only some of the systems shown in Figure 18.5. There have been many other research efforts on discretionary security including those by Demurjian et al. at the University of Connecticut, Olivier et al. at Raand Afrikaans University, and Osborn et al. at the University of Western Ontario. These efforts have been reported in the *IFIP Database Security Conference Proceedings* (see, for example, [OSBO00] and [DEMU00]).

18.2.4.2 ORION

The ORION system was one of the first to explore security. The ORION authorization model supports both positive and negative authorizations as well as weak and strong authorizations [RABB91]. Strong authorization always has higher priority than weak authorization. Authorizations are granted to roles instead of to single users and a user is authorized to exercise a privilege on an object if the user has a role that is authorized to access the object. Roles, objects, and privileges are organized into hierarchies. Rules apply to the propagation of the authorization policies as follows.

■ If a role has an authorization to access an object, all the roles that precede it in the role hierarchy have the same authorization.
■ If a role has a negative authorization to access an object, then all the roles that follow it in the role hierarchy have the same negative authorization.

Similar propagation rules are defined for privileges. Finally, propagation rules on objects allow authorization on an object to be derived from the authorizations on objects semantically related to it. For example, the authorization to read a class implies the authorization to read all its instances. ORION also specifies conflict rules so that the authorization rules are consistent. Extensions to the original ORION model have been proposed in various efforts (see [BERT98]).

18.2.4.3 IRIS

The IRIS model developed at HP supports attributes and methods represented as functions. Essentially it combines both concepts in object models and functional models. The only privilege supported by the model is the "call" privilege. A subject who owns the privileges to a function can call that function. An owner of the function automatically gets the privilege. The owner can grant the privilege to other subjects. Privileges can be granted or revoked on a user or group basis. A user can belong to multiple groups and groups can be nested. The model also protects derived functions, which are functions derived from other functions. In what is called static authorization, a subject requesting the execution of the derived function must have the call privilege on the derived function. In the dynamic authorization approach, the subject must have the privilege on the derive function as well as on all the functions executed by the derived function. When a function is created, the creator must specify which of the two authorizations must be used to check the execution request of the function.

The IRIS model also supports guard and proxy functions to control access. The guard function expresses preconditions on the call of a function. The function to which the guard function refers is the target function. A target function is executed only if the preconditions associated with the guard function are satisfied. Proxy functions provide different implementations of specific functions for different subjects. When a function is invoked, the appropriate proxy function is executed instead of the original one. More details on this model can be found in [FERR00].

18.2.4.4 STARBURST

We discuss the STARBURST authorization model, even though it is not strictly an object database system and is considered to be an extended relational system. Starburst is a prototype developed by IBM and is characterized by a rule language fully integrated with the system. The authorization model for Starburst provides a hierarchy of privileges that can be exercised on the database objects where higher types subsume lower types. Examples of privileges include control that subsumes all other privileges and write, alter, and attach. When a table is created, the owner receives control privilege on the table. The owner can grant or revoke all other privileges.

The creation and modification of rules are governed by various criteria including the following. A creator of a rule on a table must have both attach and the read privilege on the table. Subjects requesting the activation/deactivation of a rule must have the activation/deactivation privilege on the rule. Various other criteria have been defined and can be found in [WIDO91].

18.2.4.5 GEMSTONE

GEMSTONE was one of the first commercial systems to be developed. It provides a simple authorization model. Authorization can be granted to users or groups. The only type of authorization provided is the segment. A segment groups together a set of objects with the same level of protection. This implies that if a subject has the authorization to read a segment then it can read all the objects within the segment. Each segment has one owner who can grant or revoke access to the segment.

Privileges that can be granted on a segment are of two distinct types and they are the read privilege and the write privilege. The read privilege allows a subject to read all the objects in a segment and a write privilege allows a subject to modify all the objects in a segment. In some ways the Gemstone authorization model resembles the Hinke–Schafer approach where access is granted to segments and each segment is stored at a security level. However, the Hinke–Schafer approach is for multilevel security whereas GEMSTONE provides only discretionary security.

18.3 Multilevel Security

18.3.1 Overview

Section 18.2 focused on discretionary security; in this section we discuss multilevel security. Several efforts on multilevel security for object systems were reported in the late 1980s and early 1990s. The earliest effort was the SODA model of Keefe, Tsai, and Thuraisingham [KEEF89]. Later Thuraisingham extended ORION and O2 models for security ([THUR89a] and [THUR89b]). These models were called SORION and SO2. In the early 1990s, Jajodia and Kogan developed a system based on message passing [JAJO90]. Thuraisingham and Chase also explored the message-passing approach [THUR89c]. Around the same time Millen and Lunt developed a model similar to the one proposed by SORION (see [MILL92]). Around 1993 MITRE began an effort to secure object databases and developed the UFOS model (see [ROSE94]). Almost all of these efforts developed security properties for objects. Thuraisingham went further and described designs of secure object systems (see [THUR90a], [THUR91], and [THUR95]).

In this section we discuss multilevel security. The organization of this section is as follows. Policy issues are discussed in Section 18.3.2. System design issues are discussed in Section 18.3.3. Example systems including a discussion of systems such as SORION and SO2 are discussed in Section 18.3.4.

18.3.2 Policy Issues

Mandatory security policies for object systems are essentially a variation of the Bell and LaPadula policy enforced for relational systems. These are essentially read at or below your level and write at your level policies. Much of the work has focused on developing security properties between the levels of the various object constructs. The investigations have also focused on classifying metadata for objects as well as assigning levels for the methods themselves.

Some examples are the following.

■ Property 1: The security level of a class must be dominated by the security levels of the instances and the instance variables.

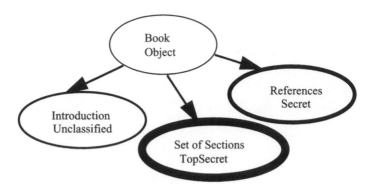

Figure 18.6 Multilevel security for objects

- Property 2: The security level of a subclass must dominate the security level of the superclass.
- Property 3: The security level of the components of an object must dominate the security level of the object.
- Property 4: This variation of the Bell and LaPadula policy, is a read at or above your level and write at your level policy and enforced for method execution.
- Property 5: The security level of the method is dominated by the level at which it executes.

Note that these properties are just some examples discussed in the SORION model. Variations of these properties have been examined by the different efforts. For example, the UFOS model does not classify the instance variables. It classifies the association between the instance variables and the values. Delegation-based models have also been explored. We discuss the examples further in Section 18.3.4. Figure 18.6 illustrates mandatory security for object systems. Note that security has to be enforced for object-relational systems also. Here we need to integrate concepts from relational systems as well as object systems. That is, in addition to securing the various components for objects, we may also assign, say, tuple-level classifications for the relations. An example is given in Figure 18.7.

18.3.3 System Design Issues

In [THUR95] designs of multilevel object databases were explored. For example, can we apply the architectures developed for relational systems? That is, can approaches such as operating systems providing access control, trusted subject, integrity lock, extended kernel, and distributed

BOOK

ISBN#	Bname	Contents	Level
1	X	████████	TopSecret
2	Y	++++	Secret
3	Z	########	Unclassified

Figure 18.7   Multilevel security for object-relational model

architectures be used to design secure object systems? We discuss some of the issues.

In the operating system providing access control, it is assumed that the object database is untrusted and access control is provided by the operating system. The challenge here is to store the multilevel objects in single-level files. In the trusted subject approach the database is trusted with respect to mandatory access control. The challenge here is to determine which portions of the database are trusted. In the integrity lock approach, the trusted front end computes checksums. The challenge here is to compute checksums for classes, instances, instance variables, class hierarchies, and component hierarchies. In the extended kernel approach additional constraints are enforced on objects. The challenge is to develop algorithms to enforce the constraints on objects. Finally in the distributed approach the challenge is to partition the objects according to the security levels. Here again the multilevel objects have to be decomposed into single-level objects. In the case of the replicated distributed approach, one would have to simply replictate the lower-level objects at the higher levels.

There has been some work reported on designing secure object systems (see [THUR95]). There is still much to be done. For example, we need to carry out an investigation as to which approach is suitable for secure object systems. Figure 18.8 illustrates the various approaches.

18.3.4 Example Systems

18.3.4.1 Overview

The first MLS/DBMS based on the object model was designed by Keefe, Tsai, and Thuraisingham and it was called the SODA model (see [KEEF88] and KEEF89]). Since then several efforts have been reported. The most

```
Design Approaches:
SORION (Thuraisingham, MITRE)
SO2 (Thuraisingham, MITRE)
Millen–Lunt(Millen and Lunt, SRI)
SODA (Keefe et al. U. of MN)
Morgenstern (Morgenstern, SRI)
UFOS (Rosenthal et al. MITRE)
Message Passing (Jajodia and Kogan, GMU)
```

Figure 18.8 Design approaches

popular is Thuraisingham's effort to secure the ORION model, called the SORION model (Secure ORION). This work was published in the *ACM OOPSLA Conference Proceedings* in 1989 and received a lot of prominence and influenced many of the other efforts. Thuraisingham also examined security for the O2 model and this model was called SO2. Later other efforts were reported including the approaches by Millen and Lunt, Jajodia and Kogan, Morgenstern, and Rosenthal et al. We describe each of these models in this section.

Note that in the early 1990s Ontos Corporation developed a MLS/DBMS funded by the Rome Laboratory and there is very little reported on this approach. Therefore, we do not discuss any commercial efforts. Although MLS/DBMSs based on the object model have had limited success, many of the ideas have been applied to designing secure applications as well as secure distributed object systems. These approaches are discussed in Chapter 19.

18.3.4.2 SODA System

Keefe, Tsai, and Thuraisingham were the first to incorporate multilevel security in object-oriented database systems. The system they subsequently developed called SODA (Secure Object-Oriented DAtabase system) has a number of unique properties, both in its security model and in its data model (see [KEEF88] and [KEEF89]).

The rules that govern operations within SODA are designed to enforce the Bell and LaPadula properties and are conceptually quite simple. First, any method activation can read a value within a labeled object or a labeled instance variable provided the classification of the object is dominated by the clearance level of the method. However, if the classification of the object dominates the current classification of the method, the method's classification is raised to the level of the object being read. Second, a method activation may modify or create a new object of a particular classification if the method's current classification equals that of the object in question, the method's current classification is dominated by the upper bound of the classification range (as specified by the constraint), and the lower bound of the classification range (as specified by the constraint) is dominated by the subject's clearance. If these rules are not satisfied then a write/create operation fails. Because method activations in SODA can have their classifications dynamically upgraded, the TCB must be involved to perform the level change. If the nature of methods can be determined in advance, then a level-change operation could be restricted to the message-passing mechanism. However, this situation is not generally the case and the TCB must be invoked when method activation attempts to read an object whose classification dominates the method's current classification. The TCB must then restart the method activation at the point where it invoked the TCB.

18.3.4.3 SORION Model

Thuraisingham investigated security issues for the ORION object-oriented data model (see [THUR89a]). The secure data model was called SORION. It extends MCC's ORION model with multilevel security properties. In SORION's security policy, subjects and objects are assigned security levels. The following rules constitute the policy.

1. A subject has read access to an object if the subject's security level dominates that of the object.
2. A subject has write access to an object if the subject's security level is equal to that of the object.
3. A subject can execute a method if the subject's security level dominates the security level of the method and that of the class with which the method is associated.
4. A method executes at the level of the subject that initiated the execution.
5. During the execution of a method m, if another method m2 has to be executed, m2 can execute only if the execution level of m1 dominates the levels of m2 and of the class with which m2 is associated.
6. Reading and writing of an object during method execution are governed by Rules 1 and 2.

Different architectures for implementing a system based on the SORION model have been examined, and an approach in which the TCB enforces all MAC has been general purpose. Basically the system runs as an untrusted application on a general-purpose TCB. The TCB controls all access to read, write, and method execution.

18.3.4.4 SO2 Model

Thuraisingham also developed the SO2 model [THUR89b]. This model extends Altair Group's O2 model with multilevel security properties. The O2 model is based on theoretical foundations and type theory. Thuraisingham subsequently developed a multilevel type theory (see also [THUR90b]).

The SO2 model specifies properties for read, write, and method execution. In addition, the interpretation of the model specifies the versions that users can read at different security levels. Thuraisingham also explores the algebra- and calculus-based approaches to multilevel secure object models.

18.3.4.5 Millen–Lunt Model

Millen and Lunt have proposed a secure object model for knowledge-based applications based on a layered architecture (see [MILL91]). At the lowest layer is the security kernel, which provides MAC. At the next layer is the object system, which implements object-oriented services, providing the abstraction of objects, methods, and messages. The object system layer is assumed to be layered with respect to mandatory security. Here are the security properties of the model.

- The hierarchy property states that the level of an object dominates that of its class.
- The subject-level property states that the level of a subject created to handle a message dominates the level of the subject that originated the message and the level of the object receiving the message.
- The object locality property states that a subject can execute a method or read variables only in the object where it is located or any superclass of that object. It can write variables only in that object.
- The *-property states that a subject may write into an object only if its security level is equal to that of the object.
- The return value property states that an involving subject can receive a return value from a message only if the message handler subject is at the same security level as the invoking subject.

■ The object-creation property states that the security level of a newly created object must dominate the level of the subject that requested its creation.

18.3.4.6 Jajodia–Kogan Model

Jajodia and Kogan describe a secure object model that is unique in that it relies almost on the message-passing mechanism for enforcing security [JAJO90]. Some preliminary work was carried out on the law-governed approach to secure object systems proposed by Thuraisingham and Chase [THUR89c]. However, Jajodia and Kogan have described a comprehensive model.

Two concepts are key to this model. One is that the methods must have two states: they are either restricted or unrestricted. If restricted, the method is prevented from modifying attributes or creating new objects. If unrestricted, the method can modify object attributes and create new objects. Under certain circumstances method activation can attain a restricted status, and once attained, any further method invocations will also be restricted. The second concept is an assumption that is made in the model with respect to the nature of the methods of the following types.

■ *Read:* a method that reads the value of an attribute
■ *Write:* a method that modifies the value of an attribute
■ *Invoke:* a method that invokes another method via sending of a message
■ *Create:* a method that creates a new object

The rules enforced by the message-filtering algorithms are separated into two sets. The first set restricts messages sent from one object to another. The second restricts messages sent from an object to itself. Because the message-passing mechanism contains the filtering algorithm and all information flows are determined at the time the message is sent, the TCB of this model could include the message passer and nothing more.

18.3.4.7 Morgenstern's Model

Morgenstern has proposed an object security model for multilevel objects with bidirectional relationships [MORG90]. He argues that the use of multilevel attributes in the relational model suggests the need for multilevel objects in the object model. The model also distinguishes between the security levels of binary and *n*-ary relationships. Security constraints are used to specify the types of operations to be executed. Some of the constraints are listed here.

- The method invocation constraint states that the level of a method invocation is the least upper bound of (i) the minimum level among the range of levels associated with the method; (ii) the level of the subject who requested the invocation; and (iii) the levels of the arguments provided for that invocation.
- The method output constraint states that the level of any output or insertion produced by the method execution must dominate the level of the method invocation.
- The property update constraint states that the modification of a property must not change its level.

Morgenstern's model does not address issues on TCB enforcement. Because multilevel objects are decomposed by access classes, one could envision that the operating system provides the MAC to the decomposed objects. However, the module that enforces the security constraints must be trusted.

18.3.4.8 UFOS Model

Rosenthal and Thuraisingham et al. developed a model called the UFOS model (Uniform Fine-grained Object Security) and this work is reported in [ROSE94]. This is in fact the last of the major models described in the literature. The team examined the various models such as SORION and found that there was a need for a model to be consistent with industry trends and be flexible. The team also felt that element-level access control was needed in addition to supporting collections of data. The key idea behind UFOS is to classify the associations between an instance variable and its value. For example, consider a ship on a mission called JANE. Now, mission as well as JANE may be Unclassified, but the fact that JANE is the mission may be Secret.

The UFOS model also supports polyinstantiation. That is, the association between mission and its name could be different at different levels. For example, at the Secret level it could be JANE and at the TopSecret level it could be FLOWER. The security policy enforced by UFOS is a read at or below your level and write at your level policy. UFOS focuses mainly on the model. Details of the TCB and the design are not discussed in [ROSE94].

18.4 Summary and Directions

We have provided an overview of discretionary security and mandatory security for object database systems. We started with a discussion of discretionary security policies and also provided an overview of prototypes and products including a discussion of the ORION and GEMSTONE systems. Then we discussed mandatory security policy as well as system design issues. This was followed by a discussion of the various efforts in developing multilevel secure object database systems.

Although not much has been done since on secure object databases, the work reported in this chapter has had a major impact on many of the developments on secure object systems including secure distributed object systems as well as the use of object modeling for secure applications and this is discussed in Chapter 19. Security for object databases has also had an impact on securing multimedia systems and this is discussed in Chapter 20. Finally, many of the concepts on secure object models are applicable to securing XML documents and this topic is discussed in Part IX. Progress has been made on secure object database systems, but we still have a lot to do on securing object-based programming languages, frameworks, and components.

References

[BERT98] Bertino, E. and Guerrini, G. Extending the ODMG object model with composite objects. *Proceedings of the ACM OOPSLA Conference*, Vancouver, British Columbia, Canada, 1998.

[DEMU00] Demurjian, S. et al. Role-based security in a distributed resource environment. In *Proceedings of the IFIP Database Security Conference*, Amsterdam, The Netherlands, August 2000.

[FERR00] Ferrari E. and Thuraisingham, B. Secure database systems. In *Advances in Database Management*, ed. M. Piatini and O. Diaz, Artech: London, UK, 2000.

[JAJO90] Jajodia, S. and Kogan, B. Integrating an object-oriented data model with multilevel security. In *IEEE Symposium on Security and Privacy*, Oakland, CA, May 1990:

[KEEF88] Keefe, T. et al. A multilevel security policy for object-oriented systems. In *Proceedings of the Eleventh National Computer Security Conference*, Baltimore, 1988.

[KEEF89] Keefe, T. et al. SODA—A secure object-oriented database system. *Computers and Security* 9: 5, 1989.

[MILL92] Millen, J. and Lunt, T. Security for object-oriented database systems. In *Proceedings of the IEEE Symposium on Security and Privacy*, Oakland, CA, May 1992.

[MORG90] Morgenstern, M. A security model for multilevel objects with bi-directional relationships. In *Proceedings of the IFIP Database Security Conference*, Halifax, UK, 1990. North Holland: Amsterdam, 1991.

[OSBO00] Osborne, S. Database security using role-based access control. In *Proceedings of the IFIP Database Database Security Conference*, Amsterdam, The Netherlands, August 2000.

[RABB91] Rabitti, F. et al. A model of authorization for next-generation database systems. *ACM Transactions on Database Systems* 16: 1, 1991.

[ROSE94] Rosenthal, A. et al. Security for object-oriented systems. In *Proceedings of the Database Security Conference*, Hildesheim, Germany 1994. North Holland: Amsterdam, 1995.

[THUR89a] Thuraisingham, B. Mandatory security in object-oriented database systems. In *Proceedings of the ACM Conference on Object-Oriented Programming, Systems, Languages and Applications (ACM OOPSLA) Conference*, New Orleans, October 1989.

[THUR89b] Thuraisingham, B. Multilevel security in object-oriented database systems. In *Proceedings of the Twelfth National Computer Security Conference*, Baltimore, October 1989.

[THUR89c] Thuraisingham, B. and Chase, F. An object-oriented approach for designing secure systems. *IEEE CIPHER*, 1989.

[THUR90a] Thuraisingham, B. Security in object-oriented database systems. *Journal of Object-Oriented Programming* 3: 2, 1990.

[THUR90b] Thuraisingham, B. Mathematical formalisms for multilevel object-oriented systems, June 1990, Technical Report, MTP-291 (also presented at the Object Systems Security Workshop, Karlsruhe, Germany, April 1990).

[THUR91] Thuraisingham, B. Multilevel secure object-oriented data model—Issues on noncomposite objects, composite objects, and versioning. *Journal of Object-Oriented Programming* 4: 6 1991.

[THUR95] Thuraisingham, B. Towards the design of a multilevel secure object-oriented database management system. *Journal of Object-Oriented Programming* 8: 3, 1995.

[WIDO91] Widom, J. et al. Implementing set-oriented production rules as an extension to Starburst. In *Proceedings of the Very Large Database Conference*, Barcelona, Spain, August 1991.

Exercises

1. Conduct a survey of discretionary security in object databases.
2. Describe a security policy and design for a MLS object database system.
3. Compare and contrast the various MLS/DBMS designs for object databases.

Chapter 19

Aspects of Objects and Security

19.1 Overview

In Chapter 18 we focused on security for object databases. We discussed both discretionary security and multilevel security. We also gave examples of secure data models and systems. As we have stated in Chapter 2, there are various other aspects of object technology and they include programming languages, distributed object systems, and object modeling. Security issues have been investigated for object technologies such as secure programming languages including secure Java, secure Object Request Brokers (ORBs), and object modeling for secure applications. Objects and security are illustrated in Figure 19.1.

In this chapter we explore aspects of objects and security. In particular we explore secure object request brokers and the use of object modeling for secure applications. Note that some argue that database systems have to be integrated with middleware to produce middleware data management systems (see, for example, the panel discussion at the 2002 IEEE Data Engineering Conference). Furthermore, object models such as OMT and UML (see [RUMB91] and [FOWL97]) are being examined to design secure database applications. Therefore distributed object systems as well as object modeling have close connections to data management.

There are also other object technologies that have been integrated with security and these include object programming languages as well as components and frameworks. A discussion of secure programming languages

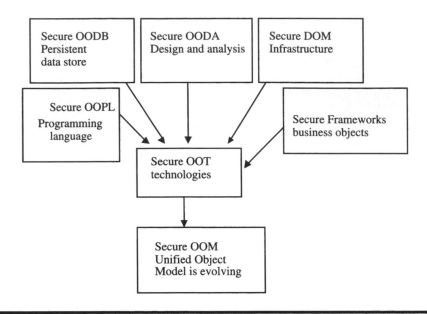

Figure 19.1   Objects and security

such as Secure Java is beyond the scope of this book. Various articles and books have appeared on this topic (see [GOSL96] and [JAVA]). The organization of this chapter is as follows. In Section 19.2 we discuss secure object request brokers and in Section 19.3 we provide an overview of object models for secure applications. The chapter is summarized in Section 19.4.

19.2 Security for Object Request Brokers

19.2.1 Overview

Work on security for object request brokers started around 1993. It was during that time that we had a workshop on secure objects at OOPSLA and also had a panel on this topic at the OOPSLA conference (see [THUR93] and [THUR94]). During that time there was much interest in exploring all aspects of secure objects including object databases, programming languages, and applications. Around the time of the workshop, the Object Management Group started the Security Special Interest Group (SIG). The SIG later evolved into a task force. This SIG focused on security for distributed objects. In this section we discuss some of the developments on this topic.

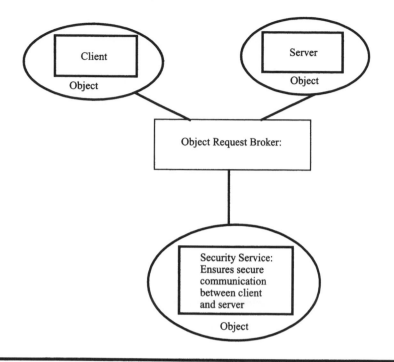

Figure 19.2   Secure object request brokers

Figure 19.2 provides a high-level illustration of secure object request brokers. The idea is essentially for clients and servers to communicate with each other securely. That is, essentially we have secure clients, secure servers, and secure ORBs. All of the secure object modeling properties and secure method execution issues we discussed in Chapter 18 are applicable to secure object brokers. The question is what are the additional challenges in securing the ORBs. In Section 19.2.2 we discuss some of the developments with OMG as given in [OMG]. In Section 19.2.3 we discuss some other aspects of secure objects such as secure components and frameworks.

19.2.2 OMG Security Services

Since 1994 OMG has developed various specifications for security. We discuss some of the recent developments including OMG security services as given in [OMG]. OMG has specifications both for secure infrastructure and security functionality at the API (Application Programming Interface) level. The infrastructure security services are CSlv2 (Common Secure Interoperability, Version 2) and CORBA security service. The API-level security specifications are ATLAS (Authorization Token Layer Acquisition Service) and RAD (Resource Access Decision Facility). We briefly discuss each of the specifications as given in [OMG].

ATLAS is a service that is needed to get authorization tokens to access a target system. The target system is accessed using the CSlv2 protocol. The client gets an authorization token with this service and uses CSLv2 to access a CORBA invocation on the target. Essentially with this service the client gets privileges that the target will understand.

CSlv2 is a Security Attribute Service (SAS) that supports interoperation, authentication, delegation, and privileges. Essentially SAS is a protocol that ensures secure interoperability and uses the transport layer security mechanism. The transport layer protects messages and also ensures client/target authentication. If the transport layer does not provide the protection service, the SAS will provide message protection and authentication service on top of the transport service. SAS also provides security contexts for the duration of the single request and reply combination. These security contexts may be reused according to certain rules specified by SAS.

Applications such as healthcare, finance, and telecommunications require access control at finer granularity. The infrastructure security service such as the CORBA security service supports coarser granularity. For example, access may be granted to entire objects. In order to provide access to the components of an object, OMG's RAD was developed. RAD is essentially a specification that supports an enterprise security policy. This policy can be used by various software components of an enterprise. RAD provides support for credentials supplied by various sources including public or private key infrastructure. RAD also supports flexible policies and access-control rules. Vendors who provide security solutions can also deliver RAD.

Finally, the CORBA security service provides basic security for the infrastructure. It provides a security architecture that can support various security policies. The functionality provided by this service includes identification and authentication, authorization and access control, auditing, secure communication between objects, and nonrepudiation. The security model developed by OMG is neutral to any particular technology. This way, if the policies change, the security model can still be used. Furthermore, the approach can also accommodate products from different vendors as long as the products conform to the interface specifications specified by OMG. The CORBA security service can also be ported to different environments. However, if an object requires application-level security, then some additional mechanisms are needed. These mechanisms are discussed in [OMG]. Figure 19.3 illustrates CORBA security features.

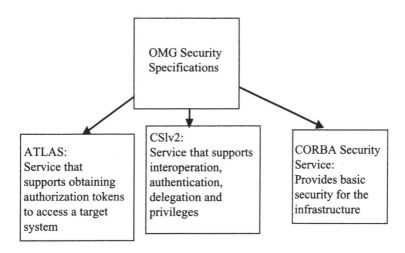

Figure 19.3   OMG security specifications

Note that as progress is made with the standards, the features will also evolve.

19.2.3 Secure Components and Frameworks

As stated in Chapter 2, the purpose of object components is to be able to reuse software. That is, a vendor can supply components that can be used for multiple applications. The components are put together to form frameworks. There has been work on security for components and frameworks. For example, enterprise security with components such as Sun Microsystem's EJB (Enterprise Java Beans) has been studied (see, for example, [EJB]). Security architecture as well as role-based access-control policies have been developed for EJB.

Now when components are put together to form a framework that can be used for various applications, it is critical that the composition of the components is secure. Note that each component may enforce its own security policies. The composition as well as the interfaces between the various components have to be secure. Furthermore, even within a component, integration of the secure objects that form the component has to enforce security.

EJBs rely on the container to invoke external objects. Therefore, they rely on the container to provide security when creating EJB instances as well as to invoke methods and connect to an EJB. The vendors of the EJB container and server must provide various security features including

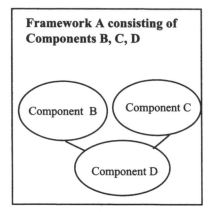
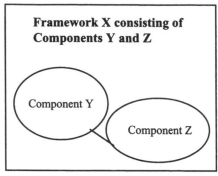

Access Control on Components and Frameworks:
John has update access to components B, C, and Y
Jane has update access to Framework A and
read access to Framework X

Figure 19.4 Secure component objects

authentication, identity delegation, identity propagation, and secure communication. A tutorial in EJB security is given in [EJB]. Figure 19.4 illustrates the composition of secure objects to form a secure framework.

19.3 Object Modeling for Secure Applications

19.3.1 Overview

In Chapter 14 we discussed the use of conceptual data structures for modeling secure applications. Structures such as semantic nets have reasoning power and therefore they can represent and reason about applications and detect security violations via inference. Although semantic nets are very useful, many real-world applications have been modeled using the entity-relationship models and more recently object models.

In the early 1990s we explored the use of object models for secure database applications. In fact, Sell and Thuraisingham were among the first to model secure applications using object models (see [SELL93]). They extended the Object Modeling Technique of Rumbaugh et al. (see [RUMB91]) and called the resulting model Multilevel OMT or MOMT (see also [MARK96]). Since then the Unified Modeling Language was conceived and extensions have been proposed to model secure applications (see [RAY03]). In this section we first explore the use of OMT and then discuss how UML may be used for modeling secure applications. MOMT is discussed in Section

> **Object Modeling Technique for**
> **Secure Database Applications:**
>
> Object Model: Models the static aspects
> of the application and security properties
> using objects
>
> Dynamic Model: Models the activities
> and the security properties of the activities
>
> Functional Model: Generates the data flow
> diagrams and the security levels of the methods

Figure 19.5   Object models for secure applications

19.3.2. Secure UML is discussed in Section 19.3.4. Figure 19.5 illustrates the use of object models for designing secure applications.

19.3.2 Multilevel OMT

OMT was developed by Rumbaugh et al. back in the late 1980s [RUMB91]. We have extended OMT to MOMT and used it to model secure applications (see [SELL93] and [MARK96]). MOMT consists of three phases: the object model, dynamic model, and functional model. We discuss each of the phases.

The object modeling phase consists of developing a secure data model to represent the entities of the applications. We have defined security properties for objects, classes, methods, links, associations, and inheritance. We essentially follow the model developed in the SORION project with some minor variations given in [MARK96]. Figure 19.6 illustrates the security model for object attributes and instances of class SHIP.

The dynamic modeling stage generates event diagrams. For example, Figure 19.7 illustrates an example where a Ship's Captain requests a mission to be carried out. Here we have four classes: Captain, Ship, Mission-Plan, and Mission. Figure 19.7 illustrates the communication among the different entities. There is a problem when communication flows from, say, Secret to the Unclassified level. The purpose of this phase is to eliminate activities that cause security violations.

The third phase is the function modeling phase. During this phase, the methods for the classes are generated. These methods are based on the activity diagrams that are generated during the dynamic modeling phase. The methods are generated by carrying out a data flow analysis. For example, suppose a Captain operating at the Confidential level reserves

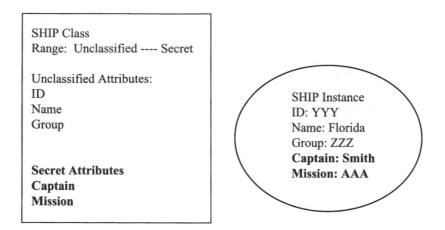

Figure 19.6 Object attributes and instances

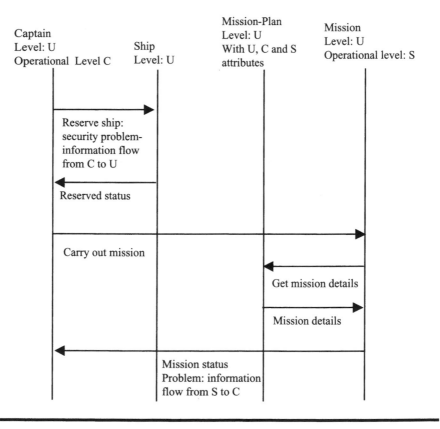

Figure 19.7 Event diagram

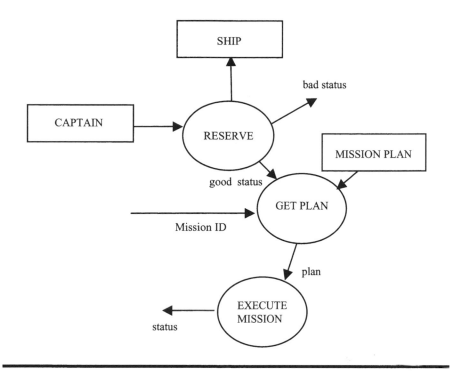

Figure 19.8   Data flow diagram

an Unclassified ship to carry out a mission operating at the Secret level. The object and dynamic models would have generated the classes, instances, attributes, and activity/event diagrams. The functional model would generate the data flow diagram illustrated in Figure 19.8. The methods are generated from the functional diagrams.

The above discussion shows some of the essential points of MOMT. It has the representational power of OMT and incorporates security properties for objects and activities. For further details on the MOMT we refer to [SELL93] and [MARK96]. As we have stated in Chapter 2, the various design and analysis methodologies have now merged and a language called UML has been developed. We examine UML and security in the next section.

19.3.3 UML and Security

Various efforts have been reported recently on using UML for designing secure applications. Let us call such a language SUML (Secure UML). An example of an effort is given by Wijesekera in a set of lecture notes (see [WIJE]). The author uses UML to specify role-based access-control rules. As we have stated in Chapter 5, with role-based access control, a user is

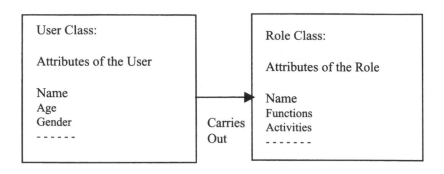

Figure 19.9 RABC policy in UML-like specification

given access to resources depending on his role. In [WIJE], the UML model is examined and the role-based access-control rules are incorporated into the model. Furthermore, application-specific RBAC constraints are specified in OCL (Object Constraints Language) and the object constraints language specified by UML. Figure 19.9 illustrates an example of specifying RBAC in UML.

Other efforts on using UML for security include the work by Ray [RAY03]. Here the author argues that there is a need to merge policies that are different. Examples of policies are RBAC and MAC. She goes on to argue that when the policies are merged security should still be maintained. She then shows how UML could be used to merge the policies specified in RBAC and MAC. Figure 19.10 illustrates policy merging.

MOMT is the first step toward using object technology for modeling secure applications. Because UML is the standard object language for modeling applications, a SUML-like language is also becoming the preferred approach to modeling security policies. We have discussed a few efforts. Various other efforts have been reported in the *IFIP Database Security Conference Series*.

19.4 Summary and Directions

In this chapter we have discussed the various aspects of objects and security. We note that security could be incorporated into object databases, object languages such as Java, and object-based middleware such as object request brokers. We also noted that object models could be used to represent and reason about secure applications. We first discussed security for object request brokers and described various standards being developed by the OMG. Then we discussed the use of object models for designing secure applications and described in particular the use of OMT and UML.

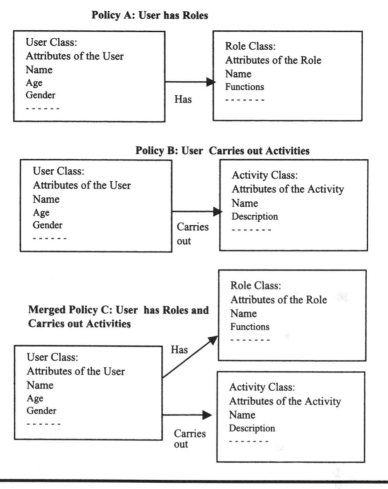

Figure 19.10   Merging security policies with UML-like specifications

As object models such as UML become common practice for designing applications, we will continue to explore the use of object models for designing secure applications. Although the work on the OMT was an excellent start, UML has become the standard language. Therefore as progress is made with UML, we need to explore the use of UML for secure applications. Much progress has been made but we still have lot to do in terms of designing and implementing secure applications with UML.

References

[EJB] Available at http://www.samspublishing.com/articles/article.asp?p=21643.
[FOWL97] Fowler, M. et al. *UML Distilled: Applying the Standard Object Modeling Language*. Addison Wesley: Reading, MA, 1997.

[GOSL96] Gosling, J. et al. *The Java™ Language Specification*. Addison-Wesley: Reading, MA, 1996.

[JAVA] Java security. Available at http://java.sun.com/security/.

[MARK96] Marks, D. et al. MOMT: A multilevel object modeling technique for designing secure database applications. *Journal of Object-Oriented Programming* 8: 3, 1996.

[OMG] Available at http://www.omg.org/technology/documents/formal/omg_security.htm.

[RAY03] Ray, I. et al. Using parameterized UML to specify and compose access control models. In *Proceedings of the IFIP Integrity and Control Conference*, Lausanne, Switzerland, November 2003. Kluwer: Hingham, MA, 2003.

[RUMB91] Rumbaugh, J. et al. *Object-Oriented Modeling and Design*, Prentice-Hall: Upper Saddle River, NJ, 1991.

[SELL93] Sell, P. and Thuraisingham, B. Applying OMT for designing multilevel database applications. In *Proceedings of the IFIP Database Security Conference*, Huntsville, AL, September 1993. North Holland: Amsterdam, 1994.

[THUR93] Thuraisingham, B. Security for object-oriented systems. In *Proceedings of the ACM OOPSLA Conference*, Washington, DC, October 1993.

[THUR94] Thuraisingham, B., et al. *Security for Object-Oriented Database Systems*, Springer-Verlag: London, UK, 1994.

[WIJE] Wijesekera, D. Available at http://www.isse.gmu.edu/dumindaclasses/spring02/umlSecurity3.ppt.

Exercises

1. Conduct a survey of security services for CORBA.
2. Investigate security for EJB.
3. Develop SUML and illustrate how it can be used to model security policies.

Chapter 20

Secure Multimedia Data Management Systems

20.1 Overview

Multimedia database management systems manage multimedia data including text, images, audio, and video. More and more multimedia data is now available on the Web and effective management of this data is becoming a critical need. We also need to ensure that the data is protected from unauthorized access as well as malicious corruption.

In Chapter 4 as well as in [THUR01] we provided an overview of the characteristics of multimedia database management systems. In particular, the use of object models to represent multimedia data management systems as well as discussions of functions and architectures were provided. In this chapter we review various security mechanisms and access-control policies and discuss the applicability of these mechanisms and policies for multimedia data. We discuss specific security challenges for text, imagery, audio, and video data. Various security architectures for multimedia information systems are examined.

The organization of this chapter is as follows. Security for multimedia database systems including a discussion of discretionary security and multilevel security is covered in Section 20.2. Security for special kinds of multimedia systems such as geospatial information systems is discussed in Section 20.3. Summary and directions are given in Section 20.4.

20.2 Security for Multimedia Data Management Systems

20.2.1 Overview

Many of the multimedia data management systems are based on the variation of the object model. That is, the data in the multimedia database is represented using objects. Some of the more recent versions of systems such as Oracle are based on the object-relational data model. We need to ensure that the multimedia data is protected. Therefore, many of the concepts and ideas discussed in Chapter 18 are applicable for securing multimedia database systems. In this section we explore various aspects of secure multimedia database systems.

The organization of this section is as follows. In Section 20.2.2 we discuss the elements that constitute a security policy for multimedia databases. We examine access-control models as well as multilevel security for multimedia databases. We also discuss security constraints. Security architectures for multimedia data are discussed in Section 20.2.3. Secure data models are the subject of Section 20.2.4. Then in Section 20.2.5 we examine various multimedia database functions and discuss the security impact on these functions. Managing multimedia data in a secure distributed environment is discussed in Section 20.2.6. The inference problem for multimedia data is discussed in Section 20.2.7.

In our discussion of security for multimedia database systems we make many assumptions. For example, we assume that the components supporting the data management systems are secure. These include the communication subsystem and operating system as well as the middleware. Note that to have a completely secure multimedia information system, we need secure multimedia database management systems, secure multimedia information management systems, secure networks, secure operating systems, secure middleware, and secure applications. That is, we need end-to-end security. We need to ensure that each component of the integrated system is secure. In this chapter we focus only on securing the multimedia data manager component of the integrated system.

20.2.2 Security Policy

Security policy essentially specifies the application-specific security rules and application-independent security rules. Application-independent security rules would be rules such as

- The combination of data from two video streams is sensitive, and

- A user operating at level L1 cannot read/view data from a text object, image object, audio object, or video object classified at level L2 if L2 is a more sensitive level than L1.

The second rule above is usually enforced for multilevel security (see Chapter 7). In a MultiLevel Secure MultiMedia DataBase Management System (MLS/MMDBMS), users cleared at different clearance levels access the multimedia data assigned different sensitivity levels so that the user only gets the data (e.g., video, audio, etc.) he or she can access. For example, a user at the Secret level can read all the text at the Secret level or below and a user at the Unclassified level can only read the Unclassified text.

Now the main question is how does the policy apply for multimedia data. We could have video cameras operating at different levels. Video cameras operating in the Middle East may be highly classified whereas video cameras in Europe may be less classified. Classified instruments will gather Classified data and Unclassified instruments will gather Unclassified data. Furthermore, video data may be in the form of streams. Therefore we need access control policies for data streams. Within each level, one could enforce application-specific rules.

Application-specific security rules include the following.

- Only law enforcement officials have authorization to examine video streams emanating from video camera A.
- Data from video streams A and B taken together are sensitive.
- All the data emanating from video cameras in Washington, DC federal buildings is sensitive but the data emanating from video cameras in North Dakota federal buildings is not sensitive.

Essentially, application-specific rules are specified using security constraints. Note that in addition to video streams, the discussion also applies to document sources, audiotapes, and image data. Another question is do the multimedia data collection instruments at different levels communicate with each other. Now, if the Bell and LaPadula policy is to be enforced, a classified instrument cannot send any data to an unclassified instrument. Data can move in the opposite direction. The multimedia network must ensure such communication.

A multimedia data collection instrument could also be multilevel. That is, an instrument could process data at different levels. Data could be text, video, audio, or imagery. The multilevel data collector can then give data to the users at the appropriate level. For example, a multilevel video camera may give Secret video streams to an Intelligence officer, but it may give out only Unclassified streams or images to a physician. One could also enforce role-based access control where users access data depending on their roles. A physician may have access to video/audio information about the spread of diseases, but he may not have access to video/audio data about potential terrorists.

Granularity of access control could be at different levels for multimedia data. In the case of text one could grant access at the chapter level or even at the paragraph level. One could also classify the existence of certain chapters or sections. In the case of images, one could grant access depending on the content or at the pixel level. In the case of audio and video, one could grant access at the frame level. For example, John can read frames 1000 to 2000 and he can update frames 3000 to 4000. He has no access to any of the other frames.

Security policy integration is a challenge. That is, each multimedia database may enforce its own security policy and have its own constraints. The challenge is to integrate the different policies, especially in distributed and federated environments. For example, in the case of a federation, each federation of multimedia databases may have its own policy, which is derived from the security policies of the individual databases. The policies of the federations will have to be combined to get an integrated policy (see also Chapter 17). Figure 20.1 illustrates access control for multimedia data management systems.

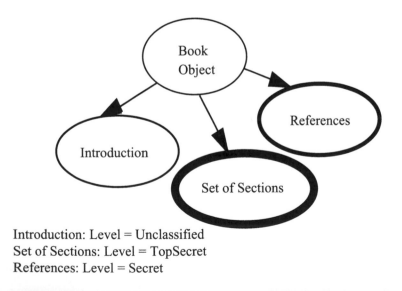

Introduction: Level = Unclassified
Set of Sections: Level = TopSecret
References: Level = Secret

Figure 20.1   Access control

20.2.3 Secure System Architectures for Multimedia Database Systems

Various security architectures have been proposed for secure database systems (see [FERR00]). We described these architectures in Chapter 8. We need to examine these architectures for MLS/MMDBMS. Consider architecture I, which is the integrity lock architecture. In this architecture, there is a trusted agent that resides between the multimedia data collector and the multimedia data manager. The trusted agent computes a cryptographic checksum for each multimedia object (e.g., paragraphs, images, audio frames, video frames, etc.) depending on the security level of the data collector and the value of the data. The data object, the level, and the checksum are stored in the multimedia database. When the data is retrieved, the trusted agent recomputes the checksum based on the data value and the level retrieved. If the newly computed checksum equals the checksum that is stored, then the trusted agent assumes that there has been no tampering with the data. The idea here is to make the multimedia data manager untrusted.

The next architecture is the distributed architecture. Here we partition the data depending on the level. Here again there is a trusted agent that receives multimedia data and sends the data to the appropriate multimedia data manager. Classified data such as Classified video is sent to the classified multimedia data manager and the Unclassified video is sent to the Unclassified multimedia data manager. These data managers could be managing text, images, audio, video, or a combination of the data types. If data has to be retrieved, say, by an intelligence officer to view the video, then the trusted agent retrieves the data from both the Classified and Unclassified data managers. If the data has to be retrieved by, say, a physician to read the images then the data is retrieved from only the Unclassified data manager. The issues discussed in Chapter 8 for this architecture apply to MLS/MMDBMSs also. Another option is to replicate all the Unclassified video data at the classified level. Note that this is the replicated architecture discussed in Chapter 8.

The third architecture is the operating system providing access-control architecture. Here, although each multimedia data manager can handle multiple levels, there is an instance of a multimedia data manager operating at each level. The multimedia data is partitioned and access to the data is managed by the operating system. That is, the Unclassified multimedia video objects are stored in an Unclassified file and the Secret multimedia video objects are stored in a Secret file. Then the video objects are recombined during query and managed by the multimedia data manager operating at the user's level. Note that with this architecture the multimedia data manager is untrusted.

The fourth architecture is the extended kernel architecture where the operating system provides mandatory access control. However, extensions to the kernel enforce other security policies such as the classification policies resulting from security constraints enforced on multimedia data.

The fifth architecture is the trusted subject architecture where we trust a portion of the multimedia data manager that is controlling access to the multimedia data. We need to conduct an architecture analysis study and experimentation to determine which architectures are suited for multimedia data management. Figure 20.2 illustrates the architectures for secure multimedia data management systems.

20.2.4 Secure Data Models for Multimedia Database Systems

Security has an impact on the data models for MM/DBMSs (see Figure 20.3). Note that relational, object, and object-relational data models have been examined for MM/DBMSs. We need to examine security properties for these models.

We have discussed secure object models in Chapter 18. Such secure models have been examined for multimedia data in [THUR90]. We have also applied the ideas to secure information retrieval systems based on objects (see [THUR93] and [THUR95]). For example, do we classify the entire video or do we classify certain frames? Can we classify the pixels in an image? How can we classify a composite multimedia object where the components are at different levels? How can we decompose the multilevel multimedia objects into single-level objects and then recombine the single-level objects? Can a malicious intruder send information by modifying parts of the pixels or frames? Can such malicious modifications be detected? These are some of the questions that need to be answered when developing a secure data model for multimedia databases.

20.2.5 Security Impact on Multimedia Data and Information Management Functions

Security has an impact on all of the functions of a multimedia data manager. Consider the query operation. The query processor has to examine the access-control rules and security constraints and modify the query accordingly. For example, if the existence of Operation X is classified, then this query cannot be sent to an Unclassified multimedia data collector such as a video camera to film the event. Similarly the update processor also examines the access-control rules and computes the level of the multimedia data to be inserted or modified. Security also has an impact on multimedia editing and browsing. When one is browsing multimedia data,

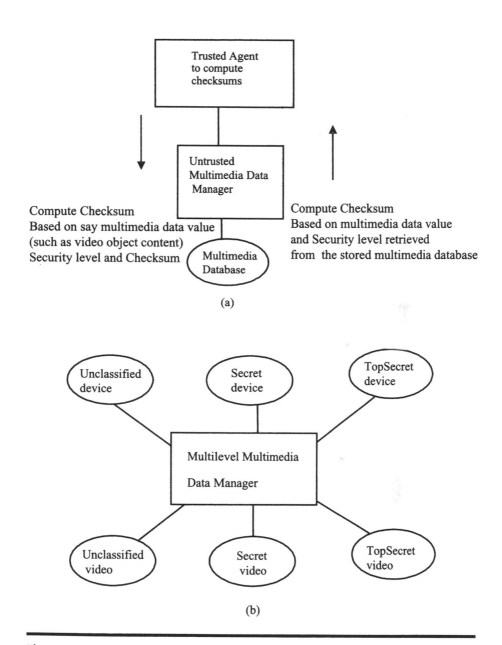

Figure 20.2 Security architectures: (a) integrity lock architecture for multimedia data management; (b) operating system provides mandatory security architecture for multimedia data management; (c) kernel extensions architecture for multimedia data management; (d) trusted subject architecture for multimedia data management; (e) partitioned distributed approach for multimedia data management; (f) replicated distributed multimedia data management

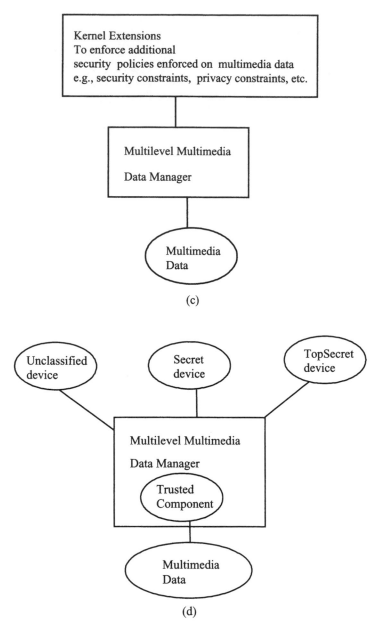

(c)

(d)

Figure 2.2 (continued)

the system must ensure that the user has the proper access to browse the link or access the data associated with the link. In the case of multimedia editing, when objects at different levels are combined to form a film, then the film object has to be classified accordingly. One may need to classify the various frames or assign the high-water mark associated with the levels

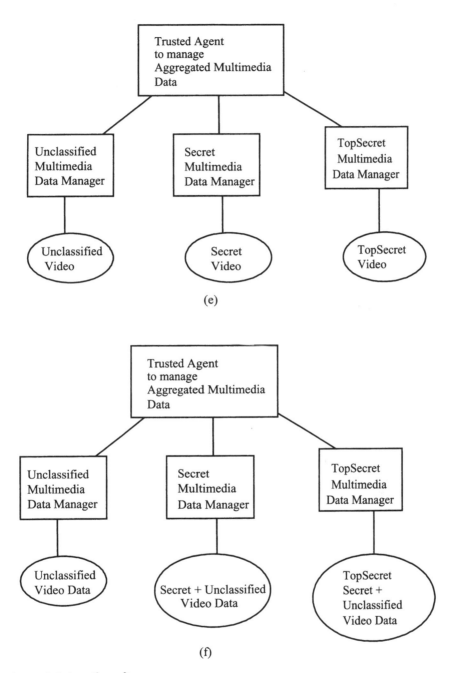

Figure 2.2 (continued)

of the individual objects that compose the film. Furthermore, when films are edited (such as deleting certain portions of the film), then one needs to recompute the level of the edited object.

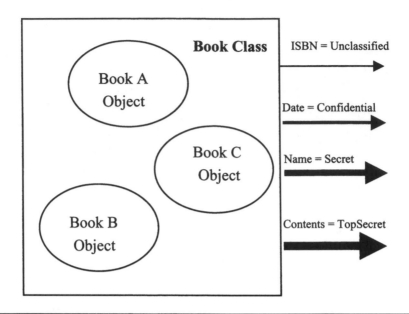

Figure 20.3 Example secure data model for a MLS/MMDBMS

Secure multimedia transaction processing is another issue. First, what does transaction processing mean? One could imagine data being gathered from two different locations (e.g., video streams) and simultaneous updates made to the multimedia database. Both updates have to be carried out as a transaction. This is conceivable if, say, an analyst needs both films to carry out the analysis. So assuming that the notion of a transaction is valid, what does it mean to process transactions securely?

Next consider the storage manager function. The storage manager has to ensure that access to the multimedia database is controlled. The storage manager may also be responsible for partitioning the data according to the security levels. The security impact of access methods and the indexing strategy for multimedia data are yet to be determined. Numerous indexing strategies have been developed for multimedia data including text, images, audio, and video. We need to examine the strategies and determine the security impact. Another issue is the synchronization between storage and presentation of multimedia data. For example, we need to ensure that the video is displayed smoothly and that there are no bursts in traffic. There could be malicious programs manipulating the storage and presentation managers so that information is covertly passed from higher-level to lower-level processes.

Metadata management is yet another issue. For example, we need to first determine the types of metadata for multimedia data. Metadata may include descriptions of the data and the source of the data, as well as the

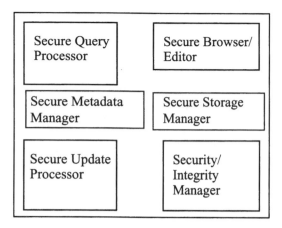

Figure 20.4 Secure multimedia data management functions

quality of the data. Metadata may also include information such as Frames 100 to 2000 are about the president's speech. Metadata may also be classified. In some cases the metadata may be classified at a higher level than the data itself. For example, the location of the data may be highly sensitive and the data could be unclassified. We should also ensure that one cannot obtain unauthorized information from the metadata. Figure 20.4 illustrates secure multimedia data management functions.

20.2.6 Secure Distributed Multimedia Data Management

There may be multiple multimedia databases connected throughout the network. Some of the databases may contain single media data such as text, images, video, or audio and some others may contain multimedia data. Some of them may be unstructured and others may be semistructured. There is also a need to connect multimedia data with relational and structured data. The collection of multimedia databases functions as does a distributed database management system. Therefore, ensuring security for such a network is in many ways like ensuring security for distributed database management systems.

Each multimedia node would have its own security policy. We need to form an integrated policy. The integrated policy has to be enforced across all the multimedia nodes. The aggregation problem is exacerbated as the multimedia data managers process data and the processed data may have to be aggregated across the data managers. The aggregated data may be highly sensitive. For example, one may have to merge two video objects to form a larger video object. The combined object may be highly sensitive. We discuss the inference problem in the next section. Figure 20.5 illustrates secure distributed multimedia data management.

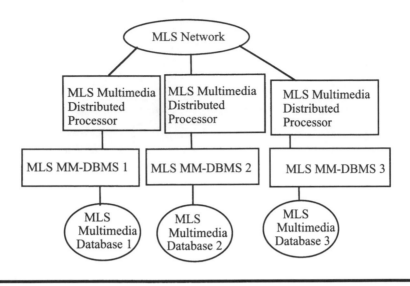

Figure 20.5 Secure distributed multimedia data management

20.2.7 Inference Problem

As stated in Part V, inference is the process of users deducing information from the legitimate responses received. If the deduced information is something that the user is not allowed to see, then it becomes a problem. This is known as the inference problem. In Part V we discussed various approaches to handling the inference problem for relational database systems. In the case of multimedia databases, because of the rich data content, handling the inference problem is even more challenging.

In a shared data-processing environment, because a lot of multimedia data has to be aggregated, there could be potential for inference problems. That is, the aggregated data from multimedia nodes A, B, and C could be highly sensitive. The aggregated data could be combined speeches or combined video. For example, one multimedia data manager could be managing video streams emanating from the situation in the Middle East and another multimedia data manager could be managing video streams emanating from the situation in Asia and the combined sensor information could be highly sensitive. The inference controller (Figure 20.6) has to examine the constraints and prevent such sensitive information from being released to individuals who are not authorized to acquire this information.

20.3 Secure Geospatial Information Systems

Security for multimedia data and information systems was discussed in Section 20.2. There are various kinds of multimedia systems including

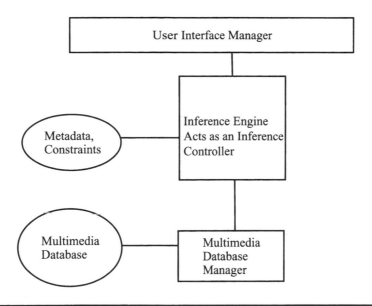

Figure 20.6   Multimedia inference controller

those for entertainment, broadcasting, and managing special structures for geoinformatics and bioinformatics. Geospatial information systems have many applications in weather forecasting, earthquake predictions, and in related areas. The idea here is to manage various types of data especially in the form of images.

There are many security challenges for geospatial databases. First of all, what is the granularity of classification? Do you classify the pixels of an image or do you classify the entire image? Information may be hidden in images; how do you detect such hidden information in images? This area is called steganalysis and is revisited in Chapter 29.

Geospatial data may be in the form of streams. What are the security policies for stream data? Closely related to geospatial information systems are motion databases where the data is not residing in one place. The data changes continually and this data must be captured and managed. Geospatial data may emanate from a variety of sources and therefore the data has to be integrated, possibly through the Web or by other means. Information integration has many security challenges. Some work in this area has been reported in [ATLU02] and [ATLU04].

We address various aspects in future chapters. For example, secure information integration is discussed in Chapter 25 when we discuss the secure semantic Web. Steganalysis is discussed in Chapter 29. Security for streams and sensor databases is discussed in Chapter 28. Secure dependable data management is discussed in Chapter 27.

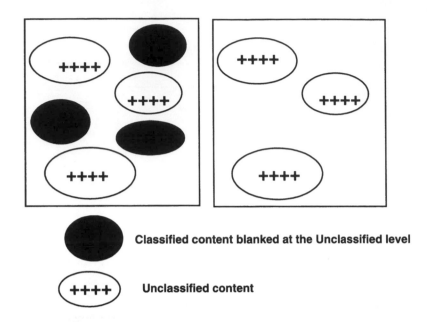

Classified content blanked at the Unclassified level

Unclassified content

Figure 20.7   Secure geospatial systems

Note that we have only raised the security concerns for geospatial information systems. These systems are a special kind of multimedia system. We need to integrate technologies for secure multimedia databases, secure semantic Web, secure information integration, and secure sensor/stream data management to provide solutions to secure geospatial information systems. Figure 20.7 illustrates secure geospatial information systems.

20.4   Summary and Directions

This chapter has provided some of the developments and directions in secure multimedia database management. We started with a discussion of security policy issues and then discussed secure multimedia data management functions. We also discussed some special secure multimedia systems such as secure geospatial information systems.

There is still a lot to be done. Security research for multimedia database management is just beginning. Although there have been some efforts over the past decade, there is still much to be done on developing security policies, architectures, and query strategies. As new kinds of multimedia systems such as geospatial information systems emerge, there are more security challenges. We also need to ensure privacy. For example, with video cameras all over the place, we need to ensure that the privacy of individuals is protected. We discuss privacy in Chapter 23. Privacy for surveillance data is discussed in Chapter 28.

References

[ATLU02] Atluri, V. and Mazzoleni, P. Uniform indexing for geospatial data and authorizations. In *Proceedings of the IFIP Database Security Conference*, July, Cambridge, UK, 2002. Kluwer: Hingham, MA, 2003.

[ATLU04] Atluri, V. and Guo, Q. Star-tree: An index structure for efficient evaluation of spatiotemporal authorizations. In *Proceedings of the IFIP Database Security Conference*, Sitges, Spain. Kluwer: Hingham, MA, July 2004.

[CHUN00] Chun, S. and Atluri, V. Protecting privacy from continuous high-resolution satellite surveillance. In *Proceedings of the IFIP Database Security Conference*, Amsterdam, The Netherlands, August 2000. Kluwer: Hingham, MA, 2001.

[FERR00] Ferrari, E. and Thuraisingham, B. Secure database systems. In *Advances in Database Management,* Piatinni, M. and Diaz, O., Eds. Artech: London, UK, 2000.

[THUR90] Thuraisingham, B. Multilevel security for multimedia systems. In *Proceedings of the Fourth IFIP WG 11.3 Conference on Database Security*, Halifax, England, September 1990 (also published as book chapter by North Holland, 1991).

[THUR93] Thuraisingham, B. Multilevel security in information retrieval systems. *Information and Management Journal* 24, 1993.

[THUR95] Thuraisingham, B. Multilevel security in information retrieval systems—II. *Information and Management Journal* 26, 1995.

[THUR01] Thuraisingham, B. *Managing and Mining Multimedia Databases for the Electronic Enterprise.* CRC Press: Boca Raton, FL, 2001.

Exercises

1. Develop a security policy for text, images, audio, video, and multimedia data.
2. Design a MLS/DDBMS.
3. Discuss security issues for geospatial information systems.

Conclusion to Part VII

Part VII described security for object and multimedia systems. In Chapter 18 we discussed discretionary and mandatory security for object database systems. We discussed policy and design issues as well as provided an overview of specific systems. In Chapter 19 we focused on two important aspects of objects and security. First we discussed security for distributed object systems. Then we discussed the use of object modeling to design secure applications. In Chapter 20 we discussed secure multimedia data management systems. In particular, models, architectures, and functions of a secure multimedia data management system were described.

The research in secure object databases and systems has resulted in new directions for emerging technologies such as E-commerce, knowledge management, and the semantic Web. Many of the emerging applications are built using objects and components. Therefore, securing objects is key to developing security for the emerging applications such as E-commerce, knowledge management, the semantic Web, agents, collaborative data management, and grid data management. We discuss these applications in Parts IX and X. In Part VIII we continue with our investigation of security for data management systems. In particular, we discuss security for data warehousing as well as explore the connection between data mining and security. Privacy is also addressed.

DATA WAREHOUSING, DATA MINING, SECURITY, AND PRIVACY

In Part I we discussed supporting technologies for database and applications security and in Part II we discussed discretionary security for database systems. We introduced mandatory security in Part III and in Part IV we discussed MLS/DBMSs based on the relational data model. In Part V we discussed the inference problem. In Parts VI and VII we discussed discretionary and multilevel security for object database systems as well as distributed and heterogeneous database systems. Essentially Parts II through VII discussed database security work that was carried out until around the end of the 1990s. In Part VIII we discuss security for some of the emerging technologies such as data warehousing.

Part VIII consists of three chapters. In Chapter 21 we discuss security for data warehouses. We discuss both aspects: forming the secure data warehouse from the secure heterogeneous data sources as well as managing the secure data warehouse. In Chapter 22 we discuss data-mining applications for security. We discuss both national security and cyber-security. We discuss various security threats and data-mining solutions.

Both data warehousing and data mining exacerbate the inference and privacy problems. We address privacy in Chapter 23. We discuss various aspects of privacy and provide an overview of privacy-preserving data mining. We also discuss the federated database approach to data sharing and at the same time ensuring privacy.

Chapter 21

Secure Data Warehousing

21.1 Overview

Data warehousing is one of the key data management technologies to support data mining and other decision support functions. Several organizations are building their own warehouses. Commercial database system vendors are marketing warehousing products. As stated in Chapter 2, the idea behind a data warehouse is that it is often cumbersome to access data from the heterogeneous databases. Several processing modules need to cooperate with each other to process a query in a heterogeneous environment. Therefore, a data warehouse will bring together the essential data from the heterogeneous databases. This way the users need to query only the warehouse. Essentially data warehouses provide support for decision support of an enterprise. For example, although the data sources may have the raw data, the data warehouse may have correlated data, summary reports, and aggregate functions applied to the raw data.

Now, in order for the data warehouse to be useful in many applications such as medical, financial, defense, and intelligence, it must be secure. In other words, the data warehouse must enforce the security policies enforced by the back-end data sources in addition to possibly enforcing additional security properties. Figure 21.1 illustrates a high-level view of a secure data warehouse. The data sources are managed by secure database systems A, B, and C. The information in these secure databases is merged and put into a secure warehouse.

In this chapter we discuss security for data warehousing. The organization of this chapter is as follows. Some background information on

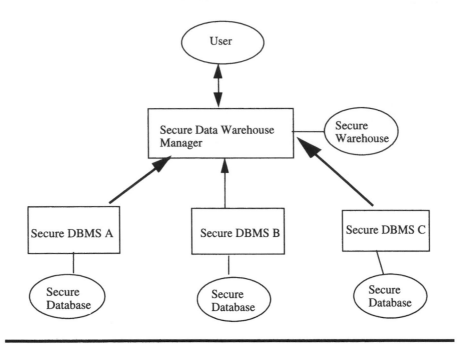

Figure 21.1   Secure data warehouse example

building a secure warehouse is discussed in Section 21.2. Secure information technologies for data warehousing are the subject of Section 21.3. Designing the secure data warehouse is discussed in Section 21.4. In particular, secure data modeling, secure data distribution, and secure integration of heterogeneous data sources are discussed. Data quality issues are discussed in Section 21.5. A note on multilevel security is given in Section 21.6. In Section 21.7, we describe secure data warehousing and its relationship to data mining and decision support. The chapter is summarized in Section 21.8.

21.2 Background

There are various ways to build a secure data warehouse. One is simply to replicate the secure databases and enforce an integrated security policy. This does not have any significant advantage over accessing the secure heterogeneous databases. The second approach is to replicate the information, but to remove any inconsistencies and redundancies. This has some advantage, as it is important to provide a consistent picture of the databases. The third approach is to select a subset of the information from the databases and place it in the warehouse and at the same time ensure that security is maintained by the warehouse. There are several issues here. How are the subsets selected? Are they selected at random or is some method used to select the data? For example, one could take every other row in a relation (assuming it is a relational database) and store these rows in the warehouse. The fourth approach, which is a slight variation of the third approach, is to determine the types of queries that users would pose, then analyze the data, examine security policies to be enforced, and store only the data that is required by the user. We call this Secure OnLine Analytical Processing (SOLAP) as opposed to Secure OnLine Transaction Processing (SOLTP) where the back-end secure database systems are queried.

With a data warehouse, data may often be viewed differently by different applications. That is, the data is multidimensional. For example, the payroll department may want data to be in a certain format and the project department may want data to be in a different format. The warehouse must provide support for such multidimensional data. Furthermore, different security policies may be enforced at different levels. For example, only managers can see the individual salaries whereas the project leaders see average salaries.

In integrating the data sources to form the warehouse, a challenge is to analyze the application and select appropriate data to be placed in the warehouse. At times, some computations may have to be performed so that only summaries and averages are stored in the data warehouse. Note that it is not always the case that the warehouse has all the information for a query. In this case, the warehouse may have to get the data from the heterogeneous data sources to complete the execution of the query. Another challenge is what happens to the warehouse when the individual databases are updated. How are the updates propagated to the warehouse? How can security be maintained when propagating the updates? These are some of the issues that are being investigated. Security cuts across all layers and operations of the warehouse. In [THUR97] we discussed security for data warehousing. Since then there have been some efforts on secure data warehouses (see, for example, [BEST02]). In this chapter we explore various issues including secure information technologies for data warehousing as well as security policy integration.

21.3 Secure Information Technologies for Data Warehousing

Figure 21.2 illustrates secure data warehousing technologies. As can be seen in this figure, several secure information technologies have to be integrated to develop a secure data warehouse. These include secure heterogeneous database integration, statistical databases, secure data modeling,

Secure Data Warehousing Technologies:

Secure data modeling
Secure heterogeneous database integration
Database security
Secure access methods and indexing
Secure query languages
Secure database administration
Secure high performance computing technologies
Secure metadata management

Figure 21.2 Some secure data warehousing technologies

secure metadata management, secure access methods and indexing, secure query processing, secure database administration, general database security, and secure high-performance database management. In this section we briefly examine these technologies within the context of secure data warehousing.

Secure heterogeneous database integration is an essential component of data warehousing. This is because data from multiple secure heterogeneous data stores may have to be integrated to build the warehouse. In the case of secure heterogeneous database integration discussed in Chapter 17, there is usually no single repository to store the data. However, in a secure warehouse there is usually a single repository for the warehouse data and this repository has to be managed and security policies enforced.

Statistical databases keep information such as sums, averages, and other aggregates. There are various issues for statistical databases. For example, how can summary data be maintained when the database gets updated? How can the individual data items be protected? For example, the average salary may be Unclassified and the individual salaries be Secret. Because warehouses keep summary information, techniques used to manage statistical databases need to be examined for warehouses.

Secure data modeling is an essential task for building a data warehouse. Is the secure data model influenced by the data models used by the back-end secure heterogeneous data sources? Should a data model be developed from scratch? Inmon has outlined several steps to developing a data model [INMO93]. He says that at the higher level there are three stages: developing (1) a corporate model, (2) an enterprise model, and (3) a warehouse model. At the middle level there may be a model possibly for each subject, and at the physical level it includes features such as keys. Some argue this is too lengthy a process and that one should get to the warehouse

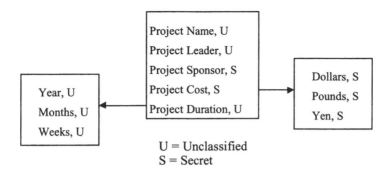

Figure 21.3   Multilevel multidimensional tables

model directly. As more experiences are reported on developing data warehouses, this issue may be resolved. New types of data models such as multidimensional data models and schemas such as star-schemas have been proposed for data warehousing. We need to integrate these models with secure data models as we have discussed in Chapter 9. Essential points of the star-schema (also called *-schema) with security are illustrated in Figure 21.3. For example, in a project database, there is a central table that has key information on projects such as project number, project leader, estimated time duration, cost, and other pertinent data. Each of the entries in this table could be elaborated on in other tables. For example, estimated time duration could be in days, months, and years. Cost could be dollars, pounds, yen, and other currency. Depending on who is using the data, different views of the data could be provided to the user.

Appropriate access methods and index strategies have to be developed for the warehouse. For example, the warehouse is structured in such a way as to facilitate query processing. An example query may be: how many red cars costing more than 50K were bought in 1995 by physicians? Many relations have to be joined to process this query. Instead of joining the actual data, one could get the result by combining the bit maps for the associated data. The warehouse may utilize an index strategy called a bit map index where essentially there is a one in the bit map if the answer is positive in the database. So, if the color of the car is red, then in the associated bit map, there will be a one. This is a simple example. Current research is focusing on developing more complex access methods and index strategies. We need to examine the security impact on query-processing strategies for the warehouse. For example, does query modification apply to secure warehousing? Suppose the user is not able to see the sales figures for those living in region X. Then the query has to be modified as follows. How many red cars costing more than 50K did physicians who do not live in region X buy in Detroit in 1995?

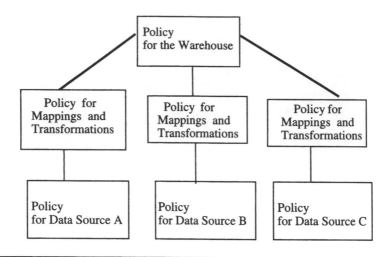

Figure 21.4 Security policy integration

Developing an appropriate query language for the warehouse is an issue. This would depend on the data model utilized. If the model is relational, then an SQL-based language may be appropriate. We then need to examine extending SQL to specify security constraints such as User Group A cannot see any information about the purchase of red cars by physicians from region X. One may also need to provide visual interfaces for the warehouse.

Secure database administration techniques may be utilized for administering the warehouse. Is there a warehouse administrator? What is the relationship between the warehouse administrator and the administrator of the data sources? How often should the warehouse be audited? Another administration issue is propagating updates to the database. In many cases, the administrators of the data sources may not want to enforce triggers on their data. If this is the case, it may be difficult to automatically propagate the updates. What is the security impact on update propagation? What are the functions of the Systems Security Officer (SSO) for the warehouse? Should there be a Warehouse Security Offer (WSO)?

Security solutions for integrating heterogeneous and federated database systems discussed in [THUR94] may be applied to secure data warehouses. For example, we need to examine the challenges for secure federated database management to integrate the security policies for data warehousing. Figure 21.4 illustrates security policy integration for data warehousing. We need to develop secure transformations as we move from one layer to the next in building a warehouse.

As stated earlier, statistical database security is one of the technologies for securing the data warehouse. Because the warehouse gives out sums

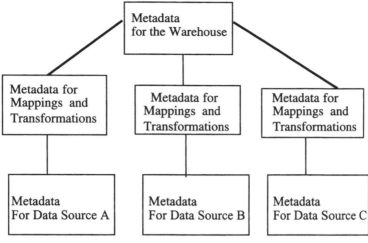

Security manager maintains security during transformations

Figure 21.5   Types of metadata

and averages, how can one protect the sensitive values from which the sums and averages are computed? Security controls also have to be enforced in maintaining the warehouse as well. This will have an impact on querying, managing the metadata, and updating the warehouse. In addition, if multilevel security is needed, then there are additional considerations. For example, what are the trusted components of the warehouse?

High-performance computing including parallel database management plays a major role in data warehousing. The goal is for users to get answers to complex queries rapidly. Therefore, parallel query-processing strategies are becoming popular for warehouses. Appropriate hardware and software are needed for efficient query processing. We need to integrate security into parallel database systems. Some preliminary work was reported in [THUR93]. We need to carry out further investigations.

Secure metadata management is another critical technology for data warehousing. The problem is defining the metadata. Metadata could come from the data sources. Metadata will include the mappings between the data sources and the warehouse. There is also metadata specific to the warehouse. We need to examine the security impact on metadata management. Figure 21.5 illustrates the various types of metadata that must be maintained in developing a secure data warehouse. There are three types of metadata: one is metadata for the individual data sources, the second is the metadata needed for mappings and transformations to build the warehouse, and the third is the metadata to maintain and operate the warehouse.

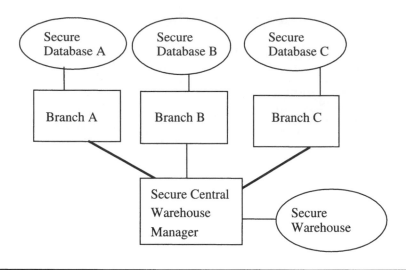

Figure 21.6 Secure nondistributed data warehouse

Secure distributed database technology, as discussed in Chapters 15 and 16, plays a role in data warehousing. Should the warehouse be centralized or distributed? If it is distributed, then much of the technology for secure distributed database management discussed in Chapters 15 and 16 is applicable for data warehousing. Figures 21.6 and 21.7 illustrate architectures for nondistributed and distributed secure data warehouses. In the nondistributed case, there is a central warehouse for the multiple branches, say, in a bank. In the distributed warehouse case, one may assume that each bank has its local warehouse and the warehouses communicate with each other.

21.4 Designing a Secure Data Warehouse

Designing and developing the secure data warehouse is a complex process and in many ways depends on the application. A good reference to data warehousing is the book by Inmon [INMO93]. It describes the details of the issues involved in building a data warehouse. In this section we outline some of the steps in designing the secure warehouse. Figure 21.8 illustrates some of these steps.

There are three phases in developing a secure warehouse. One phase focuses on structuring the secure warehouse so that secure query processing is facilitated. In other words, this phase focuses on getting the data out of the warehouse. Another phase focuses on bringing the data into the warehouse. For example, how can the secure heterogeneous data

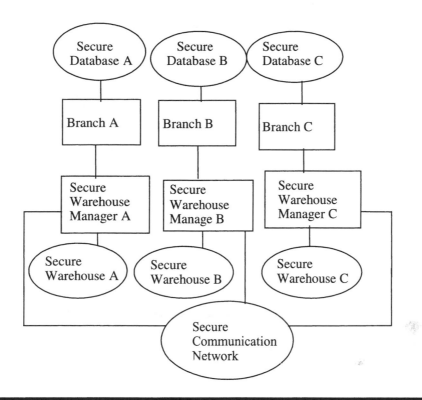

Figure 21.7   Secure distributed data warehouse

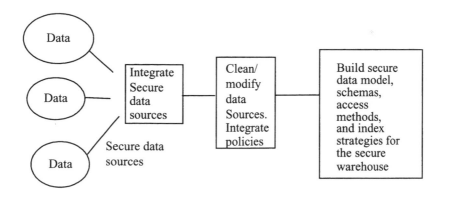

Figure 21.8   Developing a secure data warehouse

sources be integrated so that the data can be brought into the warehouse and yet security be maintained? The third phase maintains the warehouse once it is developed. This means the process does not end when the secure warehouse is developed. It has to be continually maintained. We first outline the steps in each of the phases.

One of the key steps in getting the data out of the warehouse is application analysis. For example, what types of queries will the users pose? How often are the queries posed? Will the responses be straight-forward? Will the users need information such as summary reports? A list consisting of such questions needs to be formulated. Furthermore, we need to examine the security constraints enforced by the warehouse and determine how these constraints may be enforced.

Another step is to determine what the user would expect from the warehouse. Would she want to deal with a multilevel relational model or a multilevel object-oriented model or both? Are multiple views needed? How can access to the views be controlled? Once this is determined, how do you go about developing a secure data model? Are there intermediate models?

A third step is to determine the metadata, index strategies, and access methods. Once the query patterns and data models have been determined, one needs to determine what kinds of metadata have to be maintained. What are the index strategies and access methods enforced? What are the security controls on the index strategies and access methods?

A closely related task is developing the various schemas and policies for the warehouse. Note that the individual databases will have their own schema and security policies. The complexity here is in integrating these schemas to develop a global schema for the warehouse. Although schema integration techniques for distributed and heterogeneous databases may be used, the warehouse is developed mainly to answer specific queries for various applications. Therefore, special types of schemas such as star schemas and constellation schemas have been proposed in the literature. Products based on these schemas have also been developed. However, we need to take a closer look at the schemas and examine the security impact. Furthermore, we need to explore techniques to integrate the security policies.

There are several technical issues in bringing the data into the ware-house from the different data sources. What information should be deleted from the individual databases when migrating the data to the warehouse? How should integrity be maintained? What is the security policy? How can inconsistencies be resolved? For example, we need to ensure that by querying the warehouse the sensitive information in the back-end data-bases is not revealed to the user who does not have proper access control to this information. This requires a lot of work. Various algorithms for integrating heterogeneous databases have to be examined. At the end of this stage, one would have some form of a secure warehouse. Multitier architecture is becoming popular for data warehousing (see, for example,

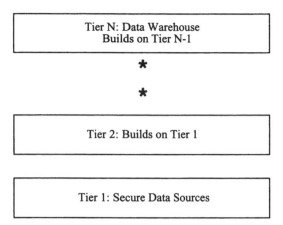

Figure 21.9   Multitier architecture

[ROSE00]). Essentially, data passes through multiple tiers before reaching the warehouse. We need to examine the security impact on multitier architecture. At the bottom tier are the data sources. At the top tier is the data warehouse. Between the top and bottom there may be multiple tiers. Each tier has its own schemas, metadata, and various administration details as well as policies, and each tier takes advantage of the work done at lower tiers. This is illustrated in Figure 21.9.

Once the secure warehouse is designed and developed, there are also some additional considerations for maintaining the warehouse. How is the security of the warehouse maintained? Should the warehouse be audited? How often is the warehouse updated? How are the changes to the local databases to be propagated to the warehouse? What happens if a user's query cannot be answered by the warehouse? Should the warehouse go to the individual databases to get the data if needed? How can data quality and integrity be maintained?

We have outlined a number of phases and steps to developing a secure data warehouse. The question is should these phases and steps be carried out one after the other or should they be done in parallel. As in most software systems, there is a planning phase, a development phase, and a maintenance phase. However, there are some additional complexities. The databases themselves may be migrating to new architectures or data models. This would have some impact on the warehouse. New databases may be added to the heterogeneous environment. The additional information should be migrated to the warehouse without causing inconsistencies. These are difficult problems and there are investigations on how to resolve them. Although there is much promise, there is a long way to go before viable commercial secure data warehouse products are developed.

In summary, a secure data warehouse enables different applications to view the data differently and at the same time enforce the security policies. That is, it supports multidimensional and multilevel data. Data warehouse technology is an integration of multiple technologies including heterogeneous database integration, statistical databases, and parallel processing. The challenges in data warehousing include developing appropriate data models, architectures (e.g., centralized or distributed), query languages, and access methods/index strategies, as well as developing techniques for query processing, metadata management, maintaining integrity and security, and integrating heterogeneous data sources. Integrating structured and unstructured databases, such as relational and multimedia databases, is also a challenge. Security cuts across all layers and all stages of the development.

The notion of data warehousing has been around for a while, however, it is only recently that we are seeing the emergence of commercial products. This is because many of the related technologies such as parallel processing, heterogeneous database integration, statistical databases, and data modeling have evolved a great deal and some of them are fairly mature technologies. Furthermore, secure database technology is also fairly mature. There are now viable technologies to build a secure data warehouse. We expect the demand for secure data warehousing to grow rapidly over the next few years.

It should be noted that many of the developments in data warehousing focus on integrating the data stored in structured databases such as relational databases. In the future we can expect to see secure multimedia data sources being integrated to form a warehouse.

21.5 Data Quality and Data Warehousing

In building a data warehouse, we need to ensure that data quality is maintained. We consider data quality to be an aspect of dependable computing. Dependable computing also includes security. We discuss secure dependable data management in Chapter 27. However, in this chapter we discuss data quality for data warehousing, which is essentially dependable data warehousing.

Note that data in the data warehouse may emanate from a variety of sources including the back-end databases. In many cases the data sources may be managed by multiple individuals and, furthermore, the warehouse administrator or the system security officer for the warehouse may not have any control of the individual data sources. This means that the warehouse administrator or the warehouse security officer must ensure the quality of the data.

For many applications including command and control as well as intelligence, decisions may have to be made based on information retrieved from the warehouse. That is, warehouses are used as decision support systems. If the data quality cannot be guaranteed then the decision made as a result could be disastrous. A potential solution here is to compute the quality of each piece of data depending on the trustworthiness of the sources from which the data was retrieved. Recently there was a panel at the IFIP Integrity Conference on the challenges for data quality (see [THUR04]). We need to address the challenges for many systems including data warehouses and Web database systems. Data quality is discussed further in Chapter 27.

21.6 A Note on Multilevel Security

Much of the discussion on secure data warehousing has focused on discretionary security. That is, what sort of access control do we enforce on the warehouse data? How can we integrate the security policies to build a policy for the warehouse? Now the challenge is what happens if the back-end data sources are multilevel data management systems. For example, one source may be TopSecret and another source may handle multiple security levels. In this case what is the security level of the warehouse data? What is the trusted computing base? That is, what are the components that must be trusted? Do we trust the transformations when we build the warehouse? Should the warehouse be trusted?

There is little work on multilevel secure data warehouses. This is a very challenging area especially if the data warehouses have to operate at different security levels. Nevertheless if we are to integrate data sources at multiple levels and build a warehouse, then we need to investigate multilevel security issues for the warehouse. Figure 21.10 illustrates a multilevel secure data warehouse. We can also build an inference controller for the data warehouse as shown in Figure 21.11. Note that a warehouse computes sums and averages and as a result a user may use statistical inferencing techniques and deduce information that may be sensitive or private. An inference controller should try to detect such security violations.

21.7 Secure Data Warehousing, Data Mining, and Decision Support

In Chapter 2 we discussed data warehousing and its relationship to data mining. It is difficult to state where data warehousing ends and data

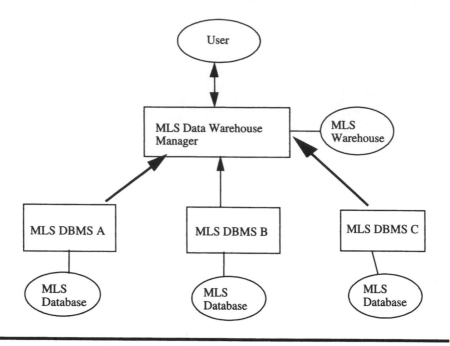

Figure 21.10 Multilevel data warehouse

mining begins. Data warehousing attempts to integrate the data sources so that complex queries can be answered efficiently to help decision support, and data mining is about extracting information previously unknown from large quantities of data. One of the main challenges in data mining with respect to security is that the information extracted could be highly sensitive and one has to make sure that unauthorized users do not get access to this information. On the other hand, data mining has many applications including solving security problems such as unauthorized intrusions.

In Chapters 22 and 23 we discuss data mining and security aspects. In particular we discuss the use of data mining to handle security problems. We also discuss the privacy problems that arise due to data mining. Although privacy problems are also exacerbated by data warehousing, the responses given by the data warehouse may be used to solve security problems. For example, answers to queries such as who was doing what, where, and when could help with cyber-security and national security problems.

Decision support technologies help managers and analysts make effective decisions. Data warehousing and data mining may be regarded as decision support technologies (see [TURB00]). The security issues include ensuring that the managers are authorized to receive the information from data warehouses or data miners. Furthermore, if the actions to be carried

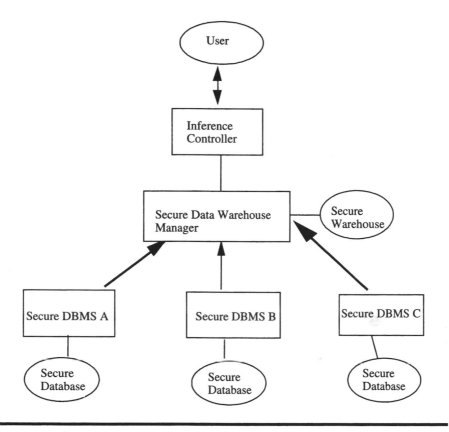

Figure 21.11   Warehouse inference controller

out involve security, then the managers need to ensure that security is maintained throughout the operation. For example, the data warehouse may give out security strategies or battle plans to the managers. The managers execute the strategies and plans securely. The relationships among security, data warehousing, data mining, and decision support are illustrated in Figure 21.12.

21.8 Summary and Directions

This chapter has discussed secure data warehousing. We started with a discussion of a definition for a secure data warehouse, the technologies for a secure data warehouse, functions of a secure data warehouse, and issues on developing a secure data warehouse. Key concepts in secure data warehousing include developing a secure data model, security architecture, and access methods and index strategies. We also discussed data quality

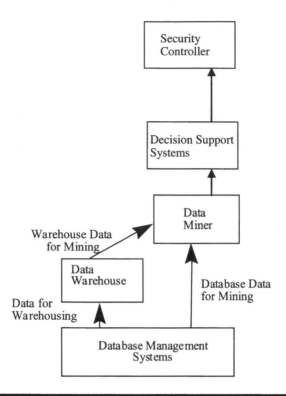

Figure 21.12   Data warehousing, data mining, decision support, and security

and multilevel security issues as well as the relationships among secure data warehousing, data mining, and decision support.

Some progress has been made on secure data warehousing and we are seeing commercial products incorporate some security features, but there is still a lot to do. We need to develop ways to integrate security policies in building a warehouse. We also need a thorough investigation of the security issues in both building a warehouse as well as extracting data from the warehouse. We need to examine the security impact on integrating data mining with data warehousing. Finally we need to examine the inference problem and privacy problem that arise due to data warehousing and data mining. Some discussions on data mining, security, the inference problem, and the privacy problem are given in the next two chapters.

References

[BEST02] Bestougeff, H. et al. (Eds.) *Heterogeneous Information Exchange and Organizational Hubs.* Kluwer: Hingham, MA, 2002.
[INMO93] Inmon, W. *Building the Data Warehouse.* Wiley: New York, 1993.

[ROSE00] Rosenthal, A. and Sciore, E. View security as the basis for data warehouse security. In *Proceedings of the Second International Workshop on Design and Management of Data Warehouses,* Stockholm, Sweden, 2000.

[THUR93] Thuraisingham, B. Parallel processing and trusted database management systems. In *Proceedings of the ACM Computer Science Conference,* Indianapolis, IN, February 1993.

[THUR94] Thuraisingham, B. Security issues for federated database systems. *Computers and Security* 13: 6, 1994.

[THUR97] Thuraisingham, B. Data warehousing, data mining and security. In *Proceedings of the IFIP Database Security Conference,* Como, Italy, 1996. Chapman & Hall, London, 1997.

[THUR04] Thuraisingham, B. Grand challenges in data integrity and quality: Panel discussion. In *Proceedings of the IFIP Database Integrity Conference,* Lausanne, Switzerland, 2003. Kluwer: Hingham, MA, 2004.

[TURB00] Turban, E. and Aronson, J. *Decision Support Systems and Intelligent Systems.* Prentice-Hall, Upper Saddle River, NJ, 2000.

Exercises

1. Discuss a methodology for building a secure data warehouse from heterogeneous data sources.
2. Design the secure operation of a warehouse.
3. Investigate data quality issues for data warehouses.

Chapter 22

Data Mining for Security Applications

22.1 Overview

Data mining has many applications in security including homeland security (also called national security) as well as for cyber-security. The threats to national security include attacking buildings and destroying critical infrastructure such as power grids and telecommunication systems (see [BOLZ01]). Data-mining techniques are being investigated to find out who the suspicious people are and who is capable of carrying out terrorist activities. Cyber-security is involved with protecting the computer and network systems against corruption due to Trojan horses and viruses. Data mining is also being applied to provide solutions such as intrusion detection and auditing. In this chapter we discuss data mining for national security as well as for cyber-security.

To understand the mechanisms to be applied to safeguard the nation and the computers and networks, we need to understand the types of threats. In [THUR03] we described real-time threats as well as non-real-time threats. A real-time threat is a threat that must be acted upon within a certain time to prevent some catastrophic situation. Note that a non-real-time threat could become a real-time threat over time. For example, one could suspect that a group of terrorists will eventually perform some act of terrorism. However, when we set time bounds such as a threat will likely occur, say, before July 1, 2004, then it becomes a real-time threat and we have to take action immediately. If the time bounds are tighter

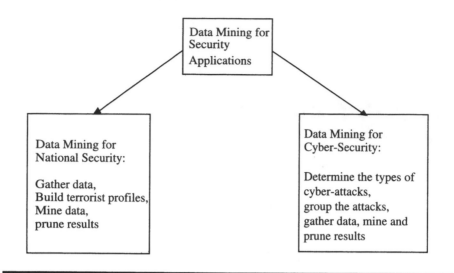

Figure 22.1   Data-mining applications in security

such as a threat will occur within two days then we cannot afford to make any mistakes in our response.

In Section 22.2 we discuss data mining for national security applications. We discuss both threats and countermeasures. In Section 22.3 we discuss data mining for cyber-security applications. In particular, we discuss the threats to the computers and networks and describe the applications of data mining to detect such threats and attacks. We examine the various data-mining outcomes and techniques and see how they can help toward counter-terrorism. The chapter is summarized in Section 22.4. Figure 22.1 illustrates data-mining applications in security.

22.2 Data Mining for National Security

22.2.1 Overview

We are now ready to embark on a critical application of data-mining technologies. This application is counter-terrorism. Counter-terrorism is mainly about developing countermeasures to threats occurring from terrorist activities. In this section we focus on the various types of threats that could occur. We discuss how data mining could help prevent and detect the threats.

Note that threats could be malicious threats due to terror attacks or non-malicious threats due to inadvertent errors. The types of terrorist threats we have discussed include non-information-related terrorism and information-related terrorism. By non-information-related terrorism we

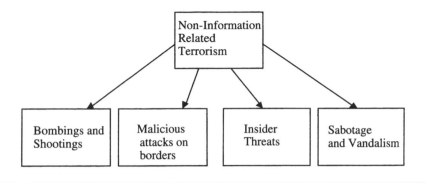

Figure 22.2   Non-information-related threats

mean people attacking others with, say, bombs and guns. For this we need to find out who these people are by analyzing their connections and then develop counter-terrorism solutions. By information-related threats we mean threats due to the existence of computer systems and networks. Such information-related attacks are discussed in Section 22.3.

The organization of this section is as follows. Non-information-related threats are discussed in Section 22.2.2. These include terrorist attacks, insider threats, and border and transportation threats. Data-mining techniques to combat terrorism are discussed in Section 22.2.3. Note that to carry out effective data mining to combat terrorism, we need good data. This means that we need data about terrorists as well as terrorist activities. This also means we will have to gather data about people, events, and entities. This could be a serious threat to privacy. We address privacy and civil liberties in Chapter 23. Topics such as bioterrorism and chemical and nuclear attacks are beyond the scope of this book. More details can be found in [THUR03]. Figure 22.2 illustrates non-information-related terrorist threats.

22.2.2 *Non-Information-Related Terrorism*

22.2.2.1 *Terrorist Attacks and External Threats*

When we hear the word terrorism it is the external threats that come to our mind. My earliest recollection of terrorism is "riots" where one ethnic group attacks another ethnic group by essentially killing, looting, setting fires to houses, and other acts of terrorism and vandalism. Then later on we heard of airplane hijackings where a group of terrorists hijacked airplanes and then made demands on governments such as releasing political prisoners who could possibly be terrorists. Then we heard of suicide bombings where terrorists carried bombs and blew themselves up as well as others nearby. Such attacks usually occur in crowded places. More recently we have heard of using airplanes to blow up buildings. Threats also include shootings and killings.

All of the threats we have discussed above are kinds of external threats. These are threats occurring from the outside. In general, the terrorists are usually neither friends nor acquaintances of the victims involved. But there are also other kinds of threats and they are insider threats. We discuss them in the next section.

22.2.2.2 Insider Threats

Insider threats are threats from people inside an organization attacking the others around them, through perhaps not bombs and airplanes, but using other sinister mechanisms. Examples of insider threats include someone from a corporation giving information of proprietary products to a competitor. Another example is an agent from an intelligence agency committing espionage. A third example is a threat coming from one's own family. For example, betrayal by a spouse who has insider information about assets and the betrayer giving the information to a competitor to his or her advantage. That is, insider threats can occur at all levels and all walks of life and can be quite dangerous and sinister because you never know who these terrorists are. They may be your so-called "best friends" or even your spouse or your siblings.

Note that people from the inside could also use guns to shoot people around them. We often hear about office shootings. But these shootings are not in general insider threats, as they are not happening in sinister ways. That is, these shootings are a kind of external threat although they are coming from people within an organization. We also hear often about domestic abuse and violence such as husbands shooting wives or vice versa. These are also external threats although they are occurring from the inside. Insider threats are threats where others around are totally unaware until perhaps something quite dangerous occurs. We have heard that espionage goes on for years before someone gets caught. Although both insider threats and external threats are very serious and could be devastating, insider threats can be even more dangerous because one never knows who these terrorists are.

22.2.2.3 Transportation and Border Security Violations

Let us examine border threats first and then discuss transportation threats. Safeguarding the borders is critical for the security of a nation. There could be threats at borders from illegal immigration to gun and drug trafficking as well as human trafficking to terrorists entering a country. We are not saying that illegal immigrants are dangerous or are terrorists. They may be very decent people. However, they have entered a country without the proper papers and that could be a major issue. For official immigration into, say, the United States, one needs to go through interviews at United States embassies, go through medical checkups and x-rays as well as checks for diseases such as tuberculosis, background checks, and many more things. It does not mean that people who have entered a country legally are always innocent. They could be terrorists also. At least there is some assurance that proper procedures have been followed. Illegal immigration can also cause problems to the economy of a society and violating human rights through cheap illegal labor.

As we have stated, drug trafficking has occurred a lot at borders. Drugs are a danger to society. Such trafficking could cripple a nation, corrupt its children, cause havoc in families, damage the education system, and cause extensive damage. It is therefore critical that we protect the borders from drug trafficking as well as other types of trafficking including firearms and human slaves. Other threats at borders include prostitution and child pornography, which are serious threats to decent living. It does not mean that everything is safe inside the country and these problems are only at the borders. Nevertheless we have to protect our borders so that there are no additional problems to the nation.

Transportation system security violations can also cause serious problems. Buses, trains, and airplanes are vehicles that can carry tens of hundreds of people at the same time and any security violation could cause serious damage and even deaths. A bomb exploding in an airplane or a train or a bus could be devastating. Transportation systems are also the means for terrorists to escape once they have committed crimes. Therefore, transportation systems have to be secure. A key aspect of transportation systems security is port security. These ports are responsible for the ships of the United States Navy. Because these ships are at sea throughout the world, terrorists may have opportunities to attack these ships and the cargo. Therefore, we need security measures to protect the ports, cargo, and our military bases.

22.2.3 Data Mining for National Security Applications

22.2.3.1 Non-Real-Time Threats

Non-real-time threats are threats that do not have to be handled in real-time. That is, there are no timing constraints for these threats. For example, we may need to collect data over months, analyze the data, and then detect and prevent some terrorist attack, which may or may not occur.

The question is how does data mining help toward such threats and attacks.

As we have stressed in [THUR03], we need good data to carry out data mining and obtain useful results. We also need to reason having only incomplete data. This is the big challenge, as organizations are often not prepared to share their data. Data-mining tools therefore have to make assumptions about the data belonging to other organizations. The other alternative is to carry out federated data mining under some federated administrator. For example, the homeland security department could serve as the federated administrator and ensure that the various agencies have autonomy but at the same time collaborate when needed.

Next, what data should we collect? We need to start gathering information about various people. The question is who. Everyone in the world? This is quite impossible. Nevertheless we need to gather information about as many people as possible because sometimes even those who seem most innocent may have ulterior motives. One possibility is to group the individuals depending on, say, where they come from, what they are doing, who their relatives are, and so on. Some people may have more suspicious backgrounds than others. If we know that someone has had a criminal record, then we need to be more vigilant about that person.

To have complete information about people, we need to gather all kinds of information about them. This information could include information about their behavior, where they have lived, their religion, ethnic origin, their relatives and associates, their travel records, and so on. Yes, gathering such information is a violation of one's privacy and civil liberties. The question is what alternative do we have. By omitting information we may not have the complete picture. From a technology point of view, we need complete data not only about individuals but also about various events and entities. For example, suppose I drive a particular vehicle and information is being gathered about me. This will also include information about my vehicle, how long I have driven, do I have other hobbies or interests such as flying airplanes, or have I enrolled in flight schools and told the instructor that I would like to learn to fly an airplane, but do not care to learn about take-offs or landings.

Once the data is collected, the data has to be formatted and organized. Essentially one may need to build a warehouse to analyze the data. Data may be structured or unstructured data. Also, there will be some data that is warehoused that may not be of much use. For example, the fact that I like ice cream may not help the analysis a great deal. Therefore, we can segment the data in terms of critical data and noncritical data.

Once the data is gathered and organized, the next step is to carry out mining. The question is what mining tools to use and what outcomes to find. Do we want to find associations or clusters? This will determine what our goal is. We may want to find anything that is suspicious. For example, the fact that I want to learn flying without caring about take-off or landing should raise a red flag as, in general, one would want to take a complete course on flying. Once we determine the outcomes we want, we determine the mining tools to use and start the mining process.

Then comes the hard part. How do we know that the mining results are useful? There could be false positives and false negatives. For example, the tool could incorrectly produce the result that John is planning to attack the Empire State Building on July 1, 2005. Then the law enforcement officials will be after John and the consequences could be disastrous. The tool could also incorrectly produce the result that James is innocent when he is in fact guilty. In this case the law enforcement officials may not pay much attention to James. The consequence here could be disastrous also. As we have stated we need intelligent mining tools. At present we need human specialists to work with the mining tools. If the tool states that John could be a terrorist, the specialist will have to do some more checking before arresting or detaining John. On the other hand, if the tool states that James is innocent, the specialist should do some more checking in this case also.

Essentially with non-real-time threats, we have time to gather data; build, say, profiles of terrorists; analyze the data; and take action. Now, a non-real-time threat could become a real-time threat. That is, the data-mining tool could state that there could be some potential terrorist attacks. But after a while, with some more information, the tool could state that the attacks will occur between September 10, 2001 and September 12, 2001. Then it becomes a real-time threat. The challenge is to find exactly what the attack will be. Will it be an attack on the World Trade Center or will it be an attack on the Tower of London or will it be an attack on the Eiffel Tower? We need data-mining tools that can continue with the reasoning as new information comes in. That is, as new information comes in, the warehouse needs to get updated and the mining tools should be dynamic and take the new data and information into consideration in the mining process.

22.2.3.2 Real-Time Threats

In the previous section we discussed non-real-time threats where we have time to handle the threats. In the case of real-time threats there are timing constraints. That is, such threats may occur within a certain time and therefore we need to respond immediately. Examples of such threats are the spread of smallpox virus, chemical attacks, nuclear attacks, network intrusions, and bombing of a building before 9 AM. The question is what type of data-mining techniques do we need for real-time threats.

By definition, data mining works on data that has been gathered over a period of time. The goal is to analyze the data and make deductions and predict future trends. Ideally it is used as a decision support tool. However, the real-time situation is entirely different. We need to rethink the way we do data mining so that the tools can give out results in real-time.

For data mining to work effectively, we need many examples and patterns. We use known patterns and historical data and then make predictions. Often for real-time data mining as well as terrorist attacks we have no prior knowledge. For example, the attack on the World Trade Center came as a surprise to many of us. As ordinary citizens, there was no way could we have imagined that the buildings would be attacked by airplanes. Another good example is the 2002 sniper attacks in the Washington, DC area. Here again many of us could never have imagined that the sniper would do the shootings from the trunk of a car. So the question is how do we train the data-mining tools such as neural networks without historical data. Here we need to use hypothetical data as well as simulated data. We need to work with counter-terrorism specialists and get as many examples as possible. Once we gather the examples and start training the neural networks and other data-mining tools, the question is what sort of models do we build. Often the models for data mining are built beforehand. These models are not dynamic. To handle real-time threats, we need the models to change dynamically. This is a big challenge.

Data gathering is also a challenge for real-time data mining. In the case of non-real-time data mining, we can collect data, clean data, format the data, build warehouses, and then carry out mining. All these tasks may not be possible for real-time data mining as there are time constraints. Therefore, the questions are what tasks are critical and what tasks are not. Do we have time to analyze the data? Which data do we discard? How do we build profiles of terrorists for real-time data mining? We need real-time data management capabilities for real-time data mining.

From the previous discussion it is clear that a lot has to be done before we can effectively carry out real-time data mining. Some have argued that there is no such thing as real-time data mining and it will be impossible to build models in real-time. Some others have argued that without real-world examples and historical data we cannot do effective data mining. These arguments may be true. However, our challenge is then perhaps to redefine data mining and figure out ways to handle real-time threats.

As we have stated, there are several situations that have to be managed in real-time. Examples are the spread of smallpox, network intrusions, and even analyzing data emanating from sensors. For example, there are surveillance cameras placed in various places such as shopping centers and in front of embassies and other public places. The data emanating from the sensors has to be analyzed in many cases in real-time to detect and prevent attacks. For example, by analyzing the data, we may find that there are some individuals at a mall carrying bombs. Then we have to alert the law enforcement officials so that they can take action. This also raises the questions of privacy and civil liberties. The question is what alternatives do we have. Should we sacrifice privacy to protect the lives of millions of people? As stated in [THUR98] we need technologists, policy makers, and lawyers to work together to come up with viable solutions.

22.2.3.3 *Analyzing the Techniques*

We have discussed data mining both for non-real-time threats as well as real-time threats. As we have mentioned, applying data mining for real-time threats is a major challenge. This is because the goal of data mining is to analyze data and make predictions and trends. Current tools are not capable of making the predictions and trends in real-time, although there are some real-time data-mining tools emerging and some of them have been listed in [KDN]. The challenge is to develop models in real-time as well as get patterns and trends based on real-world examples.

In this section we examine the various data-mining outcomes and discuss how they could be applied to counter-terrorism. Note that the outcomes include making associations, link analysis, forming clusters, classification, and anomaly detection. The techniques that result in these outcomes are techniques based on neural networks, decision trees, market-basket analysis techniques, inductive logic programming, rough sets, link analysis based on graph theory, and nearest-neighbor techniques. As we have stated in [THUR03], the methods used for data mining are top-down reasoning where we start with a hypothesis and then determine whether the hypothesis is true or bottom-up reasoning where we start with examples and then come up with a hypothesis.

Let us start with association-mining techniques. Examples of these techniques are market-basket analysis techniques. The goal is to find which items go together. For example, we may apply a data-mining tool to data that has been gathered and find that John comes from Country X and he has associated with James who has a criminal record. The tool also outputs the result that an unusually large percentage of people from Country X have performed some form of terrorist attacks. Because of the association between John and Country X, as well as between John and James, and James and criminal records, one may need to conclude that John has to be under observation. This is an example of an association.

Link analysis is closely associated with making associations. Although association-rule-based techniques are essentially intelligent search techniques, link analysis uses graph-theoretic methods for detecting patterns. With graphs (i.e., node and links), one can follow the chain and find links. For example, A is seen with B and B is friends with C and C and D travel a lot together and D has a criminal record. The question is what conclusions can we draw about A. Link analysis is becoming a very important technique for detecting abnormal behavior. Therefore, we discuss this technique in a little more detail in the next section.

Next let us consider clustering techniques. One could analyze the data and form various clusters. For example, people with origins from country X and who belong to a certain religion may be grouped into Cluster I. People with origins from country Y and who are less than 50 years old may form Cluster II. These clusters are formed based on their travel patterns or eating patterns or buying patterns or behavior patterns. Clustering divides the population not based on any prespecified condition, and classification divides the population based on some predefined condition. The condition is found based on examples. For example, we can form a profile of a terrorist. He could have the following characteristics: male less than 30 years of a certain religion and of a certain ethnic origin. This means all males under 30 years belonging to the same religion and the same ethnic origin will be classified into this group and could possibly be placed under observation.

Another data-mining outcome is anomaly detection. A good example here is learning to fly an airplane without wanting to learn to take off or land. The general pattern is that people want to get a complete training course in flying. However, there are now some individuals who want to learn flying but do not care about take-off or landing. This is an anomaly. Another example is John always goes to the grocery store on Saturdays. But on Saturday October 26, 2002 he goes to a firearms store and buys a rifle. This is an anomaly and may need some further analysis as to why he is going to a firearms store when he has never done so before. Is it because he is nervous after hearing about the sniper shootings or is it because he has some ulterior motive? If he is living, say, in the Washington, DC area, then one could understand why he wants to buy a firearm, possibly to protect himself. But if he is living in, say, Socorro, New Mexico, then his actions may have to be followed up further.

As we have stated, all of the discussions on data mining for counter-terrorism have consequences when it comes to privacy and civil liberties. As we have mentioned repeatedly, what are our alternatives? How can we carry out data mining and at the same time preserve privacy? We discuss privacy in Chapter 23. Figure 22.3 illustrates data-mining techniques for national security applications.

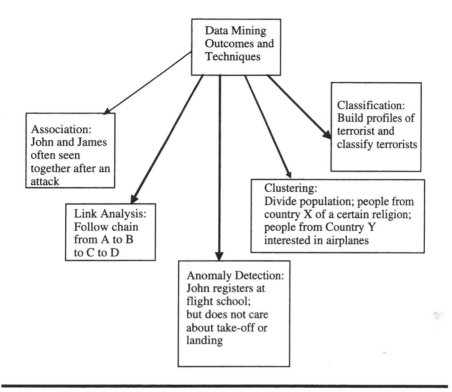

Figure 22.3   Data-mining techniques for national security

22.2.3.4 Link Analysis

In this section we discuss a particular data-mining technique that is especially useful for detecting abnormal patterns. This technique is link analysis. There have been many discussions in the literature on link analysis. In fact, one of the earlier books on data mining by Berry and Linoff [BERR97] discussed link analysis in some detail. Link analysis uses various graph-theoretic techniques. It is essentially about analyzing graphs. Note that link analysis is also used in Web data mining, especially for Web structure mining. With Web structure mining the idea is to mine the links and extract the patterns and structures about the Web. Search engines such as Google use some form of link analysis for displaying the results of a search.

As mentioned in [BERR97], the challenge in link analysis is to reduce the graphs to manageable chunks. As in the case of market-basket analysis, where one needs to carry out intelligent searching by pruning unwanted results, with link analysis one needs to reduce the graphs so that the analysis is manageable and not combinatorially explosive. Therefore, results in graph reduction need to be applied to the graphs that are obtained by representing the various associations. The challenge here is to find the interesting associations and then determine how to reduce the graphs. Various graph-theoreticians are working on graph-reduction problems. We need to determine how to apply the techniques to detect abnormal and suspicious behavior.

Another challenge of using link analysis for counter-terrorism is reasoning with partial information. For example, agency A may have a partial graph, agency B another partial graph, and agency C a third partial graph. The question is how do you find the associations among the graphs when no agency has the complete picture. One would argue that we need a data miner that would reason under uncertainty and be able to figure out the links among the three graphs. This would be the ideal solution and the research challenge is to develop such a data miner. The other approach is to have an organization above the three agencies that will have access to the three graphs and make the links. One can think of this organization as the Homeland Security Agency.

We need to conduct extensive research on link analysis as well as on other data and Web data-mining techniques to determine how they can be applied effectively to counter-terrorism. For example, by following the various links, one could perhaps trace, say, the financing of the terrorist operations to the president of, say, country X. Another challenge with link analysis as well as with other data-mining techniques is having good data. However, for the domain that we are considering, much of the data could be classified. If we are truly to get the benefits of the techniques we need to test with actual data. But not all of the researchers have the clearances to work on classified data. The challenge is to find unclassified data that is a representative sample of the classified data. It is not straightforward to do this, as one has to make sure that all classified information, even through implication, is removed. Another alternative is to find as good data as possible in an unclassified setting on which the researchers can work. However, the researchers have to work not only with counter-terrorism experts but also with data-mining specialists who have the clearances to work in classified environments. That is, the research carried out in an unclassified setting has to be transferred to a classified setting later to test the applicability of the data mining algorithms. Only then can we get the true benefits of data mining (see also [NGDM02] and [THUR04] for more information on next-generation data-mining techniques as well as on data mining for counter-terrorism).

22.3 Data Mining for Cyber-Security

22.3.1 Overview

This section discusses information-related terrorism. By information-related terrorism we mean cyber-terrorism as well as security violations through

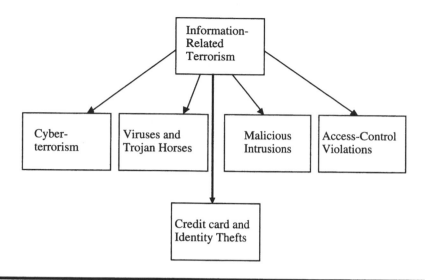

Figure 22.4 Cyber-security threats

access control and other means. Trojan horses as well as viruses are also information-related security violations, which we group into information-related terrorism activities.

In the next few subsections we discuss various information-related terrorist attacks. In Section 22.3.2 we give an overview of cyber-terrorism and then discuss insider threats and external attacks. Malicious intrusions are the subject of Section 22.3.3. Credit card and identity theft are discussed in Section 22.3.4. Attacks on critical infrastructure are discussed in Section 22.3.5 Data mining for cyber-security is discussed in Section 22.3.6. Figure 22.4 illustrates cyber-security threats.

22.3.2 Cyber-Terrorism, Insider Threats, and External Attacks

Cyber-terrorism is one of the major terrorist threats posed to our nation today. As we have mentioned earlier, there is now much information available electronically and on the Web. Attacks on our computers as well as networks, databases, and the Internet could be devastating to businesses. It is estimated that cyber-terrorism could cost businesses billions of dollars. For example, consider a banking information system. If terrorists attack such a system and deplete the accounts of funds, then the bank could lose millions and perhaps billions of dollars. By crippling the computer system, millions of hours of productivity could be lost and that equates to money in the end. Even a simple power outage at work through some accident could cause several hours of productivity loss and as a result a major financial loss. Therefore it is critical that our information systems be secure. We discuss various types of cyber-terrorist attacks. One is spreading viruses and Trojan horses that can wipe away files and other important documents; another is intruding on the computer networks. Information security violations such as access-control violations as well as a discussion of various other threats such as sabotage and denial of service are given in Chapter 24.

Note that threats can occur from outside or from inside an organization. Outside attacks are attacks on computers from someone outside the organization. We hear of hackers breaking into computer systems and causing havoc within an organization. There are hackers who start spreading viruses and these viruses cause great damage to the files in various computer systems. But a more sinister problem is the insider threat. Just as with non-information-related attacks, there is the insider threat with information-related attacks. There are people inside an organization who study the business practices and develop schemes to cripple the organization's information assets. These people could be regular employees or even those working at computer centers. The problem is quite serious as someone may be masquerading as someone else and causing all kinds of damage. In the next few sections we examine how data mining could detect and perhaps prevent such attacks.

22.3.3 Malicious Intrusions

We have discussed some aspects of malicious intrusions. These include intrusions on networks, the Web clients and servers, the databases, and operating systems. Many of the cyber-terrorism attacks that we have discussed are malicious intrusions. We revisit them in this section.

We hear much about network intrusions. What happens here is that intruders try to tap into the networks and get the information that is being transmitted. These intruders may be human intruders or Trojan horses set up by humans. Intrusions could also happen on files. For example, one can masquerade as someone else and log onto someone else's computer system and access the files. Intrusions can also occur on databases. Intruders posing as legitimate users can pose queries such as SQL queries and access the data that they are not authorized to know.

Essentially cyber-terrorism includes malicious intrusions as well as sabotage through malicious intrusions or otherwise. Cyber-security consists of security mechanisms that attempt to provide solutions to cyber-attacks or cyber-terrorism. When we discuss malicious intrusions or cyber attacks, we may need to think about the noncyber world, that is, non-information-related terrorism, and then translate those attacks to attacks on computers and networks. For example, a thief could enter a building through a trap door. In the same way, a computer intruder could enter the computer or network through some sort of a trap door that has been intentionally built by a malicious insider and left unattended through perhaps careless design. Another example is a thief entering a bank with a mask and stealing the money. The analogy here is an intruder masquerading as someone else, legitimately entering the system, and taking all the information assets. Money in the real world would translate to information assets in the cyber-world. That is, there are many parallels between non-information-related attacks and information-related attacks. We can proceed to develop countermeasures for both types of attacks.

22.3.4 Credit Card Fraud and Identity Theft

We are hearing a lot these days about credit card fraud and identity theft. In the case of credit card fraud, others get hold of a person's credit card and make all kinds of purchases. By the time the owner of the card finds out, it may be too late. The thief may have left the country by then. A similar problem occurs with telephone calling cards. In fact this type of attack happened to me once. Perhaps while I was making phone calls using my calling card at airports someone may have noticed, say, the dial tones and used my calling card. This was my company calling card. Fortunately our telephone company detected the problem and informed my company. The problem was dealt with immediately.

A more serious theft is identity theft. Here one assumes the identity of another person, say, by getting hold of the social security number and essentially carrying out transactions under the other person's name. This could even be selling houses and depositing the income in a fraudulent bank account. By the time, the owner finds out it is far too late. It is very likely that the owner may have lost millions of dollars due to the identity theft.

We need to explore the use of data mining both for credit card fraud detection as well as for identity theft. There have been some efforts on detecting credit card fraud (see [CHAN99]). We need to start working actively on detecting and preventing identity thefts.

22.3.5 Attacks on Critical Infrastructure

Attacks on critical infrastructure could cripple a nation and its economy. Infrastructure attacks include attacking the telecommunication lines, the electronic, power, gas, reservoirs and water supplies, food supplies, and other basic entities that are critical for the operation of a nation.

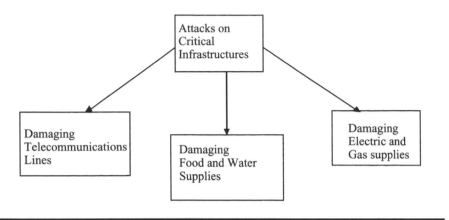

Figure 22.5 Attacks on critical infrastructure

Attacks on critical infrastructure could occur during any type of attack whether they are non-information-related, information-related, or bioterrorism attacks. For example, one could attack the software that runs the telecommunications industry and close down all the telecommunications lines. Similarly software that runs the power and gas supplies could be attacked. Attacks could also occur through bombs and explosives. That is, the telecommunication lines could be attacked through bombs. Attacking transportation lines such as highways and railway tracks are also attacks on infrastructure.

Infrastructure could also be attacked by natural disasters such as hurricanes and earthquakes. Our main interest here is the attacks on infrastructure through malicious attacks both information-related and non-information-related. Our goal is to examine data-mining and related data management technologies to detect and prevent such infrastructure attacks. Figure 22.5 illustrates attacks on critical infrastructure.

22.3.6 Data Mining for Cyber-Security

Data mining is being applied to cyber-security (also known as information security) problems (see [THUR05] for more information on this topic). These include problems such as intrusion detection and auditing. For example, anomaly detection techniques could be used to detect unusual patterns and behaviors. Link analysis may be used to trace viruses to their perpetrators. Classification may be used to group various cyber-attacks and then use the profiles to detect an attack when it occurs. Prediction may be used to determine potential future attacks depending in a way on information learned about terrorists through e-mail and phone conversations. Also, for some threats non-real-time data mining may suffice whereas for certain other threats such as network intrusions we may need real-time data mining. Many researchers are investigating the use of data mining for intrusion detection. Although we need some form of real-time data mining, that is, the results have to be generated in real-time, we also need to build models in real-time. For example, credit card fraud detection is a form of real-time processing. However, here models are usually built ahead of time. Building models in real-time remains a challenge. Data mining can also be used for analyzing Web logs as well as analyzing the audit trails. Based on the results of the data-mining tool, one can then determine whether any unauthorized intrusions have occurred or whether any unauthorized queries have been posed.

Other applications of data mining for cyber-security include analyzing the audit data. One could build a repository or a warehouse containing the audit data and then conduct an analysis using various data-mining tools to see if there are potential anomalies. For example, there could be a situation where a certain user group may access the database between 3 and 5 AM. It could be that this group is working the night shift in which case there may be a valid explanation. However, if this group is working between, say, 9 AM and 5 PM, then this may be an unusual occurrence. Another example is when a person always accesses the databases between 1 and 2 PM; but for the last two days he has been accessing the database between 1 and 2 AM. This could then be flagged as an unusual pattern that would need further investigation.

Insider threat analysis is also a problem both from a national security as well from a cyber-security perspective. That is, those working in a corporation who are considered to be trusted could commit espionage. Similarly those with proper access to the computer system could plant Trojan horses and viruses. Catching such terrorists is far more difficult than catching terrorists outside an organization. One may need to monitor the access patterns of all the individuals of a corporation even if they are system administrators to see whether they are carrying out cyber-terrorism activities. There is some research now on applying data mining for such applications by various groups including Kumar et al. at the University of Minnesota [LAZA03].

Data mining can be used to detect and prevent cyber-attacks, however, data mining also exacerbates some security problems such as the inference and privacy problems. With data-mining techniques one could infer sensitive associations from the legitimate responses. We address privacy concerns in the next chapter. Figure 22.6 illustrates data mining for cyber-security.

22.4 Summary and Directions

This chapter has discussed data mining for security applications. We first started with a discussion of data mining for national security and then

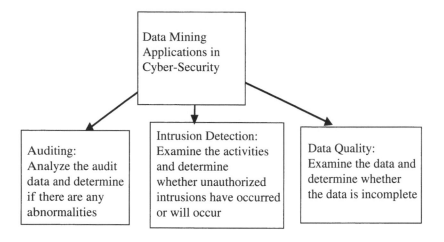

Figure 22.6 Data mining for cyber-security

provided an overview of data mining for cyber-security. In both cases we discussed the various threats and showed how data-mining techniques could help detect abnormal behavior patterns.

Data mining for national security as well as cyber-security has been a very active research area for the past three years or so. Various data-mining techniques including link analysis and association-rule mining are being explored to detect abnormal patterns. Because of data mining, users can now make all kinds of correlations. This also raises privacy concerns. Therefore, we address privacy in the next chapter.

References

[BERR97] Berry, M. and Linoff, G. *Data Mining Techniques for Marketing, Sales, and Customer Support.* Wiley: New York, 1997.

[BOLZ01] Bolz, F. et al. *The Counter-Terrorism Handbook: Tactics, Procedures, and Techniques.* CRC Press: Boca Raton, FL, 2001.

[CHAN99] Chan, P. et al. Distributed data mining in credit card fraud detection. *IEEE Intelligent Systems* 14: 6, 1999.

[KDN] Available at Kdnuggets, www.kdnuggets.com.

[LAZA03] Lazarevic, A. et al. Data mining for computer security applications, tutorial. In *Proceedings of the IEEE Data Mining Conference*, Melbourne, FL, 2003.

[NGDM02] *Proceedings of the NSF Workshop in Next Generation Data Mining*, Baltimore, November 2002.

[THUR98] Thuraisingham, B. *Data Mining: Technologies, Techniques, Tools and Trends.* CRC Press: Boca Raton, FL, 1998

[THUR03] Thuraisingham, B. *Web Data Mining Technologies and Their Applications in Business Intelligence and Counter-Terrorism.* CRC Press: Boca Raton, FL, 2003.

[THUR04] *Data Mining for Counter-Terrorism, Next Generation Data Mining.* Ed. H. Kargupta et al. AAAI Press: Cambridge, MA, 2004.

[THUR05] Thuraisingham, B. *Managing Threats to Web Databases and Cyber Systems, Issues, Solutions and Challenges.* Ed. V. Kumar et al. Kluwer: Hingham, MA, 2005.

Exercises

1. Describe the application of data-mining techniques for handling threats to national security.
2. Describe the application of data-mining techniques for cyber-security solutions such as intrusion detection and auditing.
3. Describe data mining for critical infrastructure protection.
4. Examine the use of link analysis for security applications.

Chapter 23

Privacy

23.1 Overview

In the previous chapter we discussed data mining for security applications. We addressed both homeland security (that is, national security) and cyber-security. As we have mentioned, there has been much interest recently on using data mining for counter-terrorism applications. For example, data mining can be used to detect unusual patterns, terrorist activities, and fraudulent behavior. All of these applications of data mining can benefit humans and save lives, however, there is also a negative side to this technology, inasmuch as it could be a threat to the privacy of individuals. This is because data-mining tools are available on the Web or otherwise, and even naïve users can apply these tools to extract information from the data stored in various databases and files and consequently violate the privacy of the individuals. As we have stressed in [THUR03a], to carry out effective data mining and extract useful information for counter-terrorism and national security, we need to gather all kinds of information about individuals. However, this information could be a threat to the individual's privacy and civil liberties.

Privacy is getting more attention partly because of counter-terrorism and national security. We started giving talks on privacy due to data mining back in 1996 [THUR96] and wrote about data mining and privacy in [THUR98]. Although this work received some attention, the topic did not get the widespread attention it is receiving today. Recently we have heard a lot about national security versus privacy in newspapers, magazines, and television talk shows. This is mainly due to the fact that people are now realizing that to handle terrorism, the government may need to collect information about individuals. This is causing a major concern with various civil liberties unions.

We are beginning to realize that many of the techniques that were developed for the past two decades or so on the inference problem can now be used to handle privacy. One of the challenges to securing databases is the inference problem. Inference is the process of users posing queries and deducing unauthorized information from the legitimate responses that they receive. This problem has been discussed quite a lot over the past two decades. However, data mining makes this problem worse. Users now have sophisticated tools that they can use to get data and deduce patterns that could be sensitive. Without these data-mining tools, users would have to be fairly sophisticated in their reasoning to be able to deduce information from posing queries to the databases. That is, data-mining tools make the inference problem quite dangerous. Although the inference problem mainly deals with secrecy and confidentiality, we are beginning to see many parallels between the inference problem and what we now call the privacy problem.

This chapter focuses on the privacy problem. In Section 23.2 we discuss privacy considerations. These privacy considerations also depend on the various policies and procedures enforced. That is, technical and political, as well as social issues play a role here. In Section 23.3 we discuss data warehousing, data mining, security, and privacy. Then in Section 23.4 we revisit the inference problem with respect to privacy. Note that the inference problem was discussed in Part V. We can take similar approaches to handle the privacy problem. Privacy-enhanced/sensitive/preserving data mining is discussed in Section 23.5. There has been much discussion about the relationship between confidentiality and privacy. We discuss this in Section 23.6. We provide an overview of civil liberties and national security in Section 23.7. A note on federated data management and data sharing is discussed in Section 23.8. The chapter is summarized in Section 23.9.

23.2 Privacy Considerations

At the IFIP (International Federation for Information Processing) Working Conference In Database Security in 1997 at Lake Tahoe, the group began discussions on privacy issues and the roles of the Web, data mining, and data warehousing. This discussion continued at the IFIP meeting in Greece in 1998 and it was felt that the IFIP group should monitor the developments made by the security working group of the World Wide Web consortium. The discussions included those based on technical, social, and political aspects. However, it was only at the IFIP Conference in July 2002 at the University of Cambridge, England that there was tremendous interest in privacy. In this section we examine all aspects (see also [THUR03b]).

First of all, with the World Wide Web, there is now an abundance of information about individuals that one can obtain within seconds. This information could be obtained through mining or just from information retrieval. Therefore, one needs to enforce controls on databases and data-mining tools. This is a very difficult problem especially with respect to data mining. In summary, one needs to develop techniques to prevent users from mining and extracting information from the data whether they are on the Web or on servers. Now this goes against all that we have said about data mining (see, for example, [THUR03a]). That is, we have portrayed data mining as a technology that is critical for, say, analysts and other users so that they can get the right information at the right time. Furthermore, they can also extract previously unknown patterns. This is all true. However, we do not want the information to be used in an incorrect manner. For example, based on information about a person, an insurance company could deny insurance or a loan agency could deny loans. In many cases these denials may not be legitimate. Therefore, information providers have to be very careful in what they release. Also, data-mining researchers have to ensure that privacy aspects are addressed.

Next, let us examine the social aspects. In most cultures, privacy of the individuals is important. However, there are certain cultures where it is impossible to ensure privacy. These could be related to political or technological issues, or the fact that people have been brought up believing that privacy is not critical. There are places where people divulge their salaries without thinking twice about it, but in many countries, salaries are very private and sensitive. It is not easy to change cultures overnight, and in many cases you do not want to change them, as preserving cultures is important. So what overall effect does this have on data mining and privacy? We do not have an answer to this yet as we are only beginning to look into it. We are, however, beginning to realize that perhaps we do have many of the technological solutions for handling privacy. That is, many of the technologies we have proposed for information security in general and secrecy and confidentiality in particular could be applied to privacy. However, we have to now focus on the social aspects. That is, we need the involvement of social scientists to work with computer scientists on privacy and data mining.

Next, let us examine the political and legal aspects. We include policies and procedures under this. What sort of secrecy/privacy controls should one enforce for the Web? Should these secrecy/privacy polices be mandated or should they be discretionary? What are the consequences of violating the secrecy/privacy polices? Who should be administering these

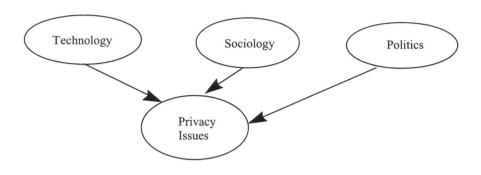

Figure 23.1 Aspects of privacy

policies as well as managing and implementing them? How is data mining on the Web affected? Can one control how data is mined on the Web? Once we have made technological advances on data mining, can we then enforce secrecy/privacy controls on the data-mining tools? How is information transferred between countries? Again we have no answers to these questions. We have, however, begun discussions. Note that some of the issues we have discussed are related to privacy and data mining, and some others are related to just privacy in general.

We have raised some interesting questions on privacy issues and data mining as well as privacy in general. As mentioned earlier, data mining is a threat to privacy. The challenge is one of protecting privacy but at the same time not losing all the great benefits of data mining. At the 1998 Knowledge Discovery In Database Conference in New York City, there was an interesting panel on the privacy issues for Web mining. Much of the focus at that panel was on legal issues. Since then there have been many more discussions on this topic. It appears that the data mining as well as the information security communities are now conducting research on privacy. Furthermore, social scientists are also now interested in privacy in the new information technology era (see, for example, the work by William Bainbridge [BAIN03]). For more details on policy issues for privacy we refer to the work of Latanya Sweeney (see, for example, [SWEE97] and [SWEE04]). Figure 23.1 illustrates the various aspects of privacy.

23.3 Data Warehousing, Data Mining, Security, and Privacy

We have provided an overview of data warehousing and data mining in Chapter 2. In Chapter 21 we discussed secure data warehousing. Data-mining applications in security were given in Chapter 22. With data

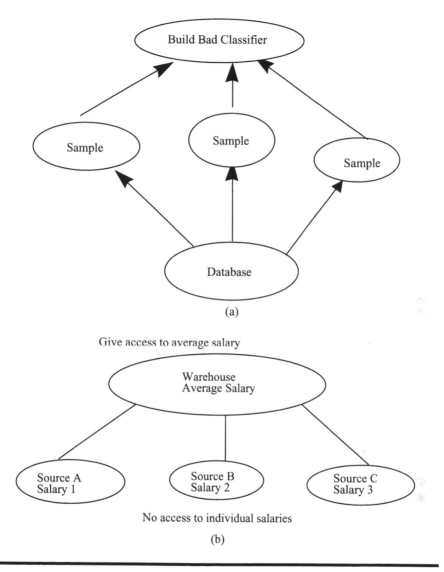

Figure 23.2   Data warehousing, data mining, and privacy

warehousing and data mining, users can make correlations between the data. For example, in the case of data warehouses, they can give out sums, averages, and statistical information. Using statistical inference techniques, users may be able to make sensitive and privacy associations from unclassified and public information. This means there is a potential for security and privacy violations via inference. Similarly with data mining users can extract information previously unknown from large quantities of data. The extracted information could be highly sensitive or highly private. That is, data warehousing and data mining exacerbate the inference and privacy problems.

The challenge for researchers is to come up with techniques that can make useful associations and correlations and yet ensure that security and privacy are maintained. Some of the techniques explored include privacy-constraint processing as well as privacy-preserving data mining. We have seen that the privacy problem is a variation of the inference problem. Therefore, solutions proposed for the inference problem can be applied to the privacy problem. We discuss this in Section 23.4. Privacy-sensitive/preserving data mining is the subject of Section 23.5. In summary, although data warehousing and data mining are very useful tools for decision support and data analysis, they also cause inference and privacy problems. Figure 23.2 illustrates data warehousing, data mining, and privacy.

23.4 Inference Problem and Privacy

In an earlier section we discussed the inference problem. In general when we think of the inference problem we have secrecy in mind. However, many of the concepts apply to privacy also. In our previous work (see, for example, [THUR93]) we defined various types of security constraints and subsequently designed and developed systems to process these security constraints. For example, ship locations and missions taken together are Classified, but individually they are Unclassified. Similarly we can define privacy constraints such as names and salaries taken together are Private and individually they are Public. Similarly names and healthcare records taken together are Private but individually they are Public.

When the inference problem is considered to be a privacy problem, then we can use the inference controller approach to address privacy. For example, we can develop privacy controllers similar to our approach to developing inference controllers [THUR93]. Furthermore, we can also have different degrees of privacy. For example, names and ages together could be less private whereas names and salaries together could be more private. Names and healthcare records together could be most private. One can then assign some probability or fuzzy value associated with the privacy of an attribute or a collection of attributes. We need to investigate further as to whether the privacy controllers could process the privacy constants during database design, update, and query operations.

Much work has been carried out on the inference problem in the past. We need to revisit this research and see whether it is applicable to the privacy problem. Some preliminary work is reported in [THUR05]. Figure 23.3 illustrates a privacy controller that we have adapted from the inference

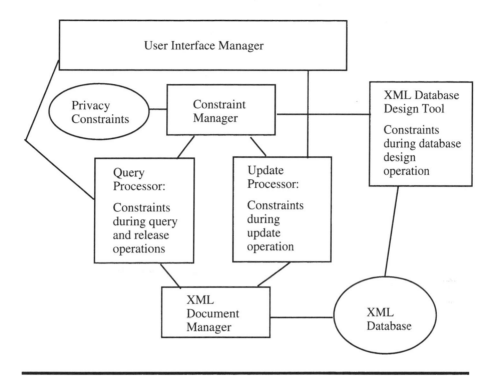

Figure 23.3 Privacy controller

controller discussed in Chapter 13. The privacy controller processes what we have defined as privacy constraints. An example of a privacy constraint is a rule that assigns the level Private to names and healthcare records taken together but individually the values are public.

23.5 Privacy-Enhanced/Sensitive/Preserving Data Mining

As we have mentioned, the challenge is to provide solutions to enhance national security but at the same time ensure privacy. Privacy-constraint processing (discussed in Section 23.4) is one approach. The type of data mining that it limits is when users deduce sensitive information from legitimate responses received to the queries. However, there are many aspects to data mining such as classification, association anomaly detection, and sequence analysis. We need to develop a comprehensive approach to carry out data mining, extract useful results, and still maintain some level of privacy. There is now research at various laboratories on privacy-enhanced/sensitive data mining (e.g., Agrawal at IBM Almaden, Gehrke at Cornell University, and Clifton at Purdue University; see, for example, [AGRA00], [CLIF00], and [GEHR02]). The idea here is to continue with mining but at the same time ensure privacy as much as possible. In this section we discuss the various efforts regarding privacy-sensitive data mining and discuss some directions. Much of the information has been taken from [THUR04b].

Clifton et al. have proposed various approaches to privacy-sensitive data mining. In one approach they propose the use of the multiparty security policy approach for carrying out privacy-sensitive data mining. In the multiparty approach, the idea is that each party does not know anything except its own inputs and the results. That is, a party does not know about another party's inputs. The solution is to carry out encryption on a randomly chosen key. Clifton has used this principle and developed privacy-preserving data-mining techniques. Essentially he has developed various computations based on the multiparty principle (see [CLIF02]).

Clifton et al. have also proposed a number of other approaches. In [CLIF03], they have used a number of tools including secure multipart computation to develop a distributed association-rule mining algorithm that preserves privacy of the individual sites. The idea behind this algorithm is that for three or more sites with each site having a private transaction database, the goal is to discover all associations satisfying some given thresholds. Furthermore, no site should be able to learn the contents of a transaction at any other site of specific value of support or confidence for any rule at any other site. In another approach by Clifton et al. (see [VAID03]), they develop a version of the K-means clustering algorithms over vertically partitioned data. The algorithms they have designed essentially follow the standard K-means algorithms. The approximations to the true means are iteratively refined until the improvement in one iteration is below a threshold. At each iteration, every point is assigned to the appropriate cluster with the minimum distance for each point. As stated in [VAID03], once their mappings are known the local components are computed locally. Then a termination test is carried out. That is, was the improvement to the mean approximation in that iteration below a threshold?

Clifton et al. have also proposed a number of other distributed data-mining algorithms. In one of their other approaches (see [LIN03]) they present a secure method for generating an Exception Maximation mixture model (EM) from distributed data sources, Essentially they show that EM cluster modeling can be done without revealing the data points and without revealing which portion of the model came from which site.

IBM Almaden was one of the first to develop algorithms for privacy-preserving data mining. In their seminal paper (see [AGRA00]) they establish this research as an area and discuss various aspects of privacy-preserving data mining and the need for this work. They introduce a quantitative measure to evaluate the amount of privacy offered by a method and evaluate proposed methods against the measure. The approach is essentially to let the users provide a modified value to the sensitive value. They also show a method to reconstruct the original distribution from the randomized data. In another paper (see [AGRA01]), the authors propose a variation of the results in [AGRA00]. For example, they develop optimal algorithms and models for the perturbation approach proposed in [AGRA00]. Since then several papers presenting some variation of the original work have been published by the IBM Almaden Research Center on privacy-preserving data mining.

In addition to Clifton at Purdue, and Agrawal at IBM, there are also efforts by Gehrke at Cornell, Kargupta at Baltimore County, and Lindell et al. in Israel. In Gehrke et al. (see [EVFI02]) the authors present a new formulation of privacy breaches together with an approach called "amplification" for limiting the breaches. They argue that amplification makes it possible to have limits on breaches without knowledge of the original data distribution. They use mining-association rules as an example to illustrate their approach. Lindell and Pinkas show how two parties having private databases can carry out data mining on the union without having to ever know the contents of the other party's database. They show how a decision tree based on their approach can be efficiently computed. Subsequently they demonstrate their approach on ID3, a well-known decision-tree data-mining algorithm (see [LIN03]). Kargupta et al. consider the problem of computing the correlation matrix from distributed data sets where the owner of the data does not trust the third party who developed the data-mining program. They develop a novel approach to compute the correlation matrix from privacy-sensitive data by using a random project-based approach (see [KARG03]).

Since around the year 2000, numerous papers have been published on privacy-sensitive data mining. We have listed some of the key approaches. Each approach essentially takes a data-mining algorithm and shows how it can be modified to take privacy into consideration. Some approaches are based on multiparty computation, some based on perturbation, and some based on matrix correlation. We feel that the field, although still not mature, is producing results that can be evaluated using some sort of testbed. We are now ready to develop a testbed with the appropriate data and give feedback to the researchers about their approaches. We need a government initiative to develop such a testbed. In the meantime we also need to continue with the research on privacy-preserving data mining. We have come a long way and we still have a lot to do. Classification of privacy-preserving data-mining techniques is given in Figure 23.4.

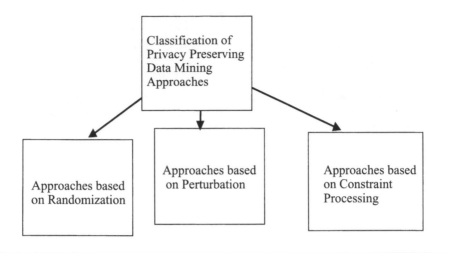

Figure 23.4   Classification of privacy-preserving data-mining techniques

23.6 Confidentiality and Privacy

There have been many debates on the relationship between confidentiality and privacy. Confidentiality deals with the authorized release of sensitive information, and privacy deals with the authorized release of private information. If this is the case, then privacy is an aspect of confidentiality. This means that the techniques developed for confidentiality such as access-control techniques can be applied to privacy. In fact, this is the approach we have taken in our work on the privacy controller (see [THUR05]).

However, some argue that this is not the correct view. That is, although confidentiality deals with the unauthorized release of sensitive information, privacy is all about what an individual wants to keep private about him- or herself. This means I as an individual can specify, say, to a Web server, what information can be released about me and to whom. When I fill out the documents, say, on the Web, I read the privacy policies specified by the Web and if I agree then I sign the document. If I do not then I could perhaps specify what information can and cannot be released. It is up to the Web server to satisfy my constraints. In fact W3C has adopted P3P (Platform for Privacy Preferences) as a starting point to enforce privacy on the Web. We discuss privacy and the semantic Web in Chapter 25.

Now, with this view of privacy we feel that only the interpretation is different. The techniques that must be enforced to ensure privacy are still those used to enforce confidentiality. That is, the Web server must ensure that the privacy constraints about me as an individual are enforced when

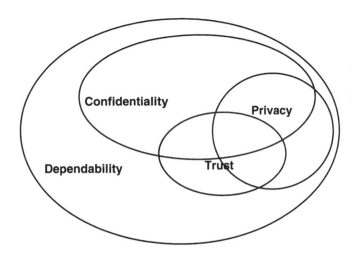

Figure 23.5 Confidentiality and privacy

information about me is released. That is, I specify the privacy policies about myself unlike, say, someone in authority in the case of confidentiality. The system must ensure that the privacy policies are enforced correctly. We can use the techniques developed for confidentiality for this purpose. Figure 23.5 illustrates our view of the relationship between confidentiality and privacy.

23.7 Civil Liberties and National Security

Civil liberties are about protecting the rights of the individual whether privacy rights, human rights, or civil rights. There are various civil liberties unions and laws protecting the rights of individuals (see, for example, http://www.aclu.org/).

There has been much debate recently among the counter-terrorism experts and civil liberties unions and human rights lawyers about the privacy of individuals. That is, gathering information about people, mining information about people, conducting surveillance activities, and examining, say, e-mail messages and phone conversations are all threats to privacy and civil liberties. However, what are the alternatives if we are to combat terrorism effectively? Today we do not have any effective solutions. Do we wait until privacy violations occur and then prosecute or do we wait until national security disasters occur and then gather information? What is more important? Protecting nations from terrorist attacks or protecting the privacy of individuals? This is one of the major challenges faced by technologists, sociologists, and lawyers. That is, how can we have privacy but at the same time ensure the safety of nations? What should we be sacrificing and to what extent?

I have served on panels on national security, database technologies, and privacy as well as given various keynote addresses including at the White House and at the United Nations. I have heard audiences say that if they can be guaranteed that there is national security, then they would not mind sacrificing privacy. However, they would not want to sacrifice privacy for a false sense of security. On the other hand, I have heard people say that some security is better than nothing. Therefore, even if one cannot guarantee national security, if some security is provided, then sacrificing privacy is not an issue. I have also heard from human rights lawyers about privacy violations by government under the pretext of national security. Some others are very nervous that all the information gathered about individuals may get into the wrong hands now or one day after we have, we hope, eliminated terrorism and then things could be disastrous. Yet some others say that under no condition will they sacrifice privacy.

Although we have no solutions today, we will certainly hear more about it in the coming months and years. The question is, if we assume that there will be no misuse of information, then should we sacrifice privacy for national security. Is it reasonable to make such an assumption? On the other hand, should national security be of utmost importance and we prosecute those who have violated privacy on a case-by-case basis? Do we have adequate laws? We have no answers, just questions. However, I have been raising the awareness since my first keynote address on this topic in 1996 at the IFIP Database Security Conference in Como, Italy. It is now that we are hearing much more about this. We still have a lot to do here. Figure 23.6 illustrates aspects of national security and privacy.

23.8 Federated Data Management, Data Sharing, and Privacy

In Chapter 17 we discussed security issues for federated database systems. A federated database system enables organizations to share data but at the same time maintain autonomy. We find that the federated database concept is very useful for federal organizations to form federations and share data.

Figure 23.7 illustrates an architecture for federated data management and privacy. In this architecture, each agency or organization has its own component data management system. Each component is augmented by a privacy controller, which controls privacy violations at the local level. An export engine further determines the data that can be exported to the

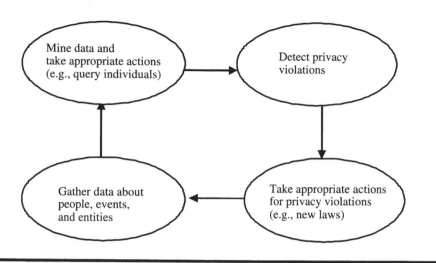

Figure 23.6   National security and privacy

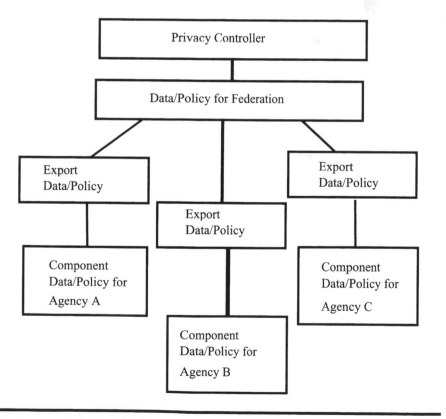

Figure 23.7   Federated data management and privacy—Approach I

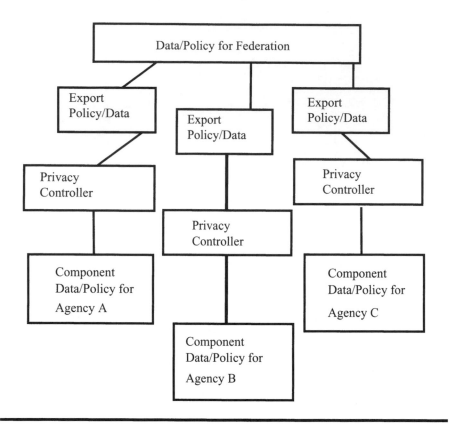

Figure 23.8   Federated data management and privacy—Approach II

federation. The federated data management system manages the federated data. It is also augmented by a privacy controller to ensure privacy at the global level.

An alternative approach is illustrated in Figure 23.8. The idea here is to integrate the data and schema and then enforce a privacy controller. That is, the privacy controller is enforced at the global level. We need to design the details on both architectures and carry out an analysis as to which approach is more feasible.

23.9 Summary and Directions

This chapter is devoted to the important area of privacy related to Web and data mining. There have been efforts on applying data mining for handling national security and information security problems such as intrusion detection, however, in this chapter we have focused on the negative effects of data mining. In particular, we discussed the inference problem that can result due to mining as well as ways of compromising privacy especially due to Web data access.

First, we gave an overview of the inference problem and then discussed approaches to handling this problem that results from mining. Warehousing and inference issues were also discussed. Then we provided an overview of the privacy issues. Next we discussed the inference controller approach for handling privacy and also examined privacy-sensitive data mining. Next we discussed civil liberties versus national security. Finally we examined federated architectures for data sharing and enforcing privacy.

Although little work has been reported on privacy issues for data mining, we are moving in the right direction. There is increased awareness of the problems, and groups such as the IFIP Working Group in Database Security are making this a priority. As research initiatives are started in this area, we can expect some progress to be made. Note that there are also social and political aspects to consider. That is, technologists, sociologists, policy experts, counter-terrorism experts, and legal experts have to work together to combat terrorism as well as to ensure privacy. Note that the number of Web security conferences is increasing including workshops on privacy (see [ACM02]). Recently the NSF-sponsored Workshop on Next Generation Data Mining focused on both counter-terrorism and privacy (see [NGDM02]). As the Web becomes more and more sophisticated, there is also the potential for more and more threats. Therefore, we have to be ever vigilant and continue to investigate, design, and implement various privacy measures for the Web, but at the same time we must ensure national security. This will be our major challenge.

References

[ACM02] *ACM Computer Security Conference Workshop on Privacy.* Washington, DC, November 2002.

[AGRA00] Agrawal, R. and Srikant, R. Privacy-preserving data mining. In *Proceedings of the ACM SIGMOD Conference*, Dallas, TX, May 2000.

[AGRA01] Agrawal, D. and Aggrawal, C. On the design and quantification of privacy preserving data mining algorithms. In *Proceedings of the ACM Principles of Database Systems Conference*, Santa Barbara, CA, May 2001.

[BAIN03] Bainbridge, W. Privacy. In *Encyclopedia of Community*, Sage Reference: Thousand Oaks, CA, 2003

[CLIF00] Clifton, C. Using sample size to limit exposure to data mining. *Journal of Computer Security* 8: 4, 2000.

[CLIF02] Clifton, C., Kantarcioglu, M., and Vaidya, J. Defining privacy for data mining. Technical Report, Purdue University, 2002.

[CLIF03] Clifton, C. et al. Tools for privacy preserving distributed data mining. *SIGKDD Explorations*, 4: 2, 2003.

[EVFI02] Evfimievski, A., Srikant, R., Agrawal, R., and Gehrke, J. Privacy preserving mining of association rules. In *Proceedings of the Eighth ACM SIGKDD International Conference on Knowledge Discovery and Data Mining*. Edmonton, Alberta, July 2002.

[GEHR02] Gehrke, J. Research problems in data stream processing and privacy-preserving data mining. In *Proceedings of the Next Generation Data Mining Workshop*, Baltimore, November 2002.

[KANT03] Kanmtarcioglu, M. and Clifton, C. Privacy preserving distributed mining association rules on horizontally partitioned data. Purdue University Report, 2003; *IEEE Transactions on Knowledge and Data Engineering* (to appear).

[KARG03] Kargupta, H. et al. Privacy sensitive distributed data mining from multi-party data. In *Proceedings of the Security Informatics Symposium*, Tucson, AZ, June 2003.

[LIN03] Lin, A. et al. Privacy preserving clustering with distributed EM mixture modeling. Purdue University Report, 2003 (submitted for publication).

[LIND00] Lindell Y. and Pinkas, B. Privacy preserving data mining. In *Proceedings of the Crypto Conference*, Santa Barbara, CA, 2000.

[NGDM02] *Proceedings of the Next Generation Data Mining Workshop*, Baltimore, November 2002.

[SWEE97] Sweeney, L. Datafly: A system for providing anonymity in medical data. In *Proceedings of the IFIP Database Security Conference*, Lake Tahoe, CA, August 1997. Chapman & Hall: London, 1998.

[SWEE04] Sweeney, L. Navigating computer science research through waves of privacy concerns: Discussions among computer scientists at Carnegie Mellon University. *ACM Computers and Society*, 2004

[THUR93] Thuraisingham, B., Ford, W., and Collins, M. Design and implementation of a database inference controller. *Data and Knowledge Engineering Journal* 11: 3, 1993.

[THUR96] Thuraisingham, B. Datawarehousing, data mining, and security. In *Proceedings of the IFIP Database Security Conference*, Como, Italy, July 1996.

[THUR98] Thuraisingham, B. *Data Mining: Technologies, Techniques, Tools, and Trends*. CRC Press: Boca Raton, FL, 1998.

[THUR03a] Thuraisingham, B. *Web Data Mining: Technologies and Their Applications to Business Intelligence and Counter-Terrorism*. CRC Press: Boca Raton, FL, 2003.

[THUR03b] Thuraisingham, B. Data mining, national security, privacy and civil liberties. *SIGKDD Explorations*, 4: 2, 2003.

[THUR04] Thuraisingham, B. Privacy preserving data mining: Developments and directions, *Journal of Database Management* 2004 (to appear).

[THUR05] Thuraisingham, B. Privacy constraint processing in a privacy enhanced database system. *Data and Knowledge Engineering Journal* 2005 (to appear).

[VAID03] Vaidya, J. and Clifton, C. Privacy-preserving K-means clustering over vertically partitioned data. In *Proceedings ACM SIGKDD*, Washington, DC, 2003.

Exercises

1. Conduct a survey of privacy-preserving data mining.
2. Can you design a new approach for privacy-preserving data mining?
3. Extend the inference controller approach discussed in Chapter 13 for privacy.
4. Discuss how technologists, social scientists, policy makers, and lawyers can work together to enforce privacy.
5. Examine the federated data management approach for data sharing and privacy.

Conclusion to Part VIII

Part VIII described security for emerging technologies such as data warehousing. It also addressed data mining for security applications as well as the privacy problem. In Chapter 21 we discussed security for data warehouses. We discussed both forming the secure data warehouse from the secure heterogeneous data sources as well as managing the secure data warehouse. In Chapter 22 we discussed data-mining applications for security. We discussed both national security and cyber-security. We discussed various security threats and data-mining solutions. Both data warehousing and data mining exacerbate the inference and privacy problems. We addressed privacy in Chapter 23. We discussed various aspects of privacy and provided an overview of privacy-preserving data mining. We also discussed the federated database approach to data sharing and at the same time ensuring privacy.

Work on secure data warehousing and data mining for security applications as well as on privacy is just beginning. We have made much progress during the last few years. Privacy will continue to receive a lot of attention especially due to technologies such as data mining and sensor information processing. We continue to explore security for emerging technologies in Parts IX and X.

SECURE WEB DATA AND INFORMATION MANAGEMENT TECHNOLOGIES

IX

In Part I we discussed supporting technologies for database and applications security and in Part II we discussed discretionary security for database systems. We introduced mandatory security in Part III and in Part IV we discussed MLS/DBMSs based on the relational data model. In Part V we discussed the inference problem. In Parts VI and VII we discussed discretionary and multilevel security for object database systems as well as for distributed and heterogeneous database systems. Essentially Parts II through VII discussed database security work that was carried out until around the late 1990s. In Part VIII we discussed security for some of the emerging technologies such as data warehousing. Part IX discusses security for Web data and information management technologies.

Part IX consists of three chapters. In Chapter 24 we discuss security for Web databases and digital libraries. We discuss threats to Web databases and provide security solutions. In Chapter 25 we discuss security for the semantic Web. We discuss XML and RDF security as well as address privacy for the semantic Web. In Chapter 26 we discuss security for various information management technologies. In particular, security for E-commerce, collaboration, and knowledge management systems, and applications are discussed.

Chapter 24

Secure Web Data Management and Digital Libraries

24.1 Overview

Part VIII discussed security and privacy for some of the emerging technologies such as data warehousing and data mining. As we have stated, the Web has had a major impact on developments in data management technologies. However, the Web also causes major security concerns. This is because Web users from all over the world can access the data and information on the Web as well as compromise the security of the data, information, systems, and applications. Therefore, protecting the information and applications on the Web is critical.

This chapter reviews the various threats to information systems on the Web with a special emphasis on threats to Web databases. Then it discusses some solutions to managing these threats. The threats include access-control violations, integrity violations, unauthorized intrusions, and sabotage. The solutions include data-mining techniques, cryptographical techniques, and fault-tolerance processing techniques. This chapter also discusses security for digital libraries including secure Web databases and information retrieval systems.

The organization of this chapter is as follows. In Section 24.2 we provide an overview of some of the cyber-threats (which are essentially threats to Web security). Much of our focus is on threats to the public and private databases on the Web. In Section 24.3 we discuss potential solutions. Secure digital libraries are discussed in Section 24.4. In particular, secure Web database functions, secure markup languages, secure information retrieval, secure search engines, and secure question-answering systems are discussed. Directions are given in Section 24.5. Note that some of the information presented here has been given in previous chapters in different contexts. For example, data mining for cyber-security was discussed in Chapter 22. However, we repeat some of the information in this chapter for completeness. We also introduce many other issues, concepts, solutions, and challenges in this chapter for various aspects of secure Web and digital libraries.

24.2 Threats to Web Security

24.2.1 Overview

In recent years we have heard a lot about viruses and Trojan horses that disrupt activities on the Web. These security threats and violations are costing businesses several million dollars. Identity thefts are quite rampant these days. Furthermore, unauthorized intrusions, the inference problem, and privacy violations are also occurring. In this section we provide an overview of some of these threats. A very good overview of these threats has been provided in [GHOS98]. We also discuss some additional threats such as those to Web databases and information systems. Some of the threats and solutions discussed here are also given in [THUR05a].

We have grouped the threats into two: one group consists of some general cyber-threats, which may include threats to Web databases and the second group consists of threats to Web databases. Note that we have only provided a subset of all possible threats. There are many more threats such as threats to networks, operating systems, middleware, and electronic payment systems including spoofing, eavesdropping, covert channels, and other malicious techniques. Section 24.2.2 focuses on some general cyber-threats and Section 24.2.3 discusses threats specific to Web databases. It should be noted that it is difficult to group the threats so that one threat is exclusive for Web databases and another is relevant only for operating systems. Threats such as access-control violations are applicable both for databases and operating systems. However, due to complex relationships in databases, access controls are much harder to enforce whereas for operating systems, access controls are granted or denied at the file level. Another example is natural disasters as well as attacks on infrastructure. These attacks and disasters could damage the networks, databases, and operating systems.

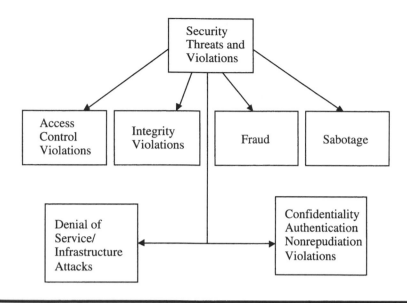

Figure 24.1   Attacks on Web security

24.2.2 General Cyber-Threats

In this section we discuss some general cyber-threats applicable to information systems including data management systems, operating systems, networks, and middleware. Figure 24.1 illustrates threats to Web security.

- *Authentication Violations*: Passwords could get stolen and this could result in authentication violations. One may need to have multiple passwords and additional information about the user to solve this problem. Biometrics and other techniques are also being examined to handle authentication violations.
- *Nonrepudiation*: The sender of a message could very well deny that he has sent the message. Nonrepudiation techniques will ensure that one can track the message to the sender. Today it is not difficult to track the owner of the message. However, it is not easy to track the person who has accessed the Web page. That is, although progress has been made to analyze Web logs, it is still difficult to determine the exact location of the user who has accessed a Web page.
- *Trojan Horses and Viruses*: Trojan horses and viruses are malicious programs that can cause all sorts of attacks. In fact, many of the threats discussed in this section could be caused by Trojan horses and viruses. Viruses could spread from machine to machine and

could erase files in various computers. Trojan horses could leak information from a higher level to a lower level. Various virus protection packages have been developed and are now commercially available.

▪ *Sabotage*: We hear of hackers breaking into systems and posting inappropriate messages. For example, some information on the sabotage of various government Web pages is reported in [GHOS98]. One only needs to corrupt one server, client, or network for the problem to cascade to several machines.

▪ *Fraud*: With so much of business and commerce being carried out on the Web without proper controls, Internet fraud could cause businesses to lose millions of dollars. An intruder could obtain the identity of legitimate users and through masquerading may empty bank accounts.

▪ *Denial-of-Service and Infrastructure Attacks*: We hear about infrastructure being brought down by hackers. Infrastructure could be the telecommunication system, power system, or the heating system. These systems are controlled by computers, often through the Web. Such attacks would cause denial of service.

▪ *Natural Disasters*: In addition to terrorism, computers and networks are also vulnerable to natural disasters such as hurricanes, earthquakes, fire, and other similar disasters. The data has to be protected and databases have to be recovered from disasters. In some cases the solutions to natural disasters are similar to those for threats due to terrorist attacks. For example, fault-tolerant processing techniques are used to recover the databases from damages. Risk analysis techniques may contain the damage. In Section 24.3 we discuss some of the solutions.

24.2.3 Threats to Web Databases

This section discusses some threats to Web databases. Note that although these threats are mainly applicable to data management systems, they are also relevant to general information systems. Figure 24.2 illustrates threats to Web databases.

▪ *Access-Control Violations*: The traditional access-control violations could be extended to the Web. Users may access unauthorized data across the Web. Note that with the Web there is so much data all over the place that controlling access to this data will be quite a challenge.

▪ *Integrity Violations*: Data on the Web may be subject to unauthorized modifications. Also, data could originate from anywhere and

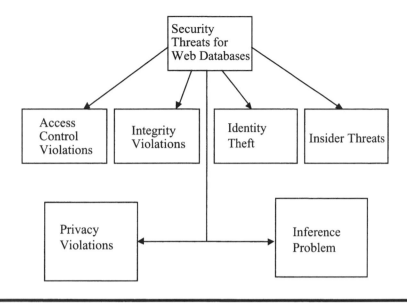

Figure 24.2   Attacks on Web databases

the producers of the data may not be trustworthy. This makes it easier to corrupt the data. Incorrect data could cause serious damage, such as incorrect bank accounts, which could result in incorrect transactions

■ *Confidentiality Violations*: Security includes confidentiality as well as integrity. That is, confidential data has to be protected from those who are not cleared. This book has discussed multilevel security a great deal, where users access only the information at or below their clearance levels. Statistical database techniques have also been developed to prevent confidentiality violations.

■ *Authenticity Violations*: This is a form of data integrity violation. For example, consider the case of a publisher, subscriber, and the owner. The subscriber subscribes to various magazines, the owner creates the magazines (in electronic form), and the publisher who is the third party publishes the magazines. If the publisher is not trusted, she could alter the contents of the magazine. This violates the authenticity of the document. Various solutions have been examined to determine the authenticity of documents (see, for example, [BERT04]). These include cryptography and digital signatures.

■ *Privacy Violations*: As stated in Chapter 23, with the Web one can obtain all kinds of information collected about individuals. Also, with data-mining tools and other analysis tools one can make all kinds of unauthorized associations about individuals

- *Inference Problem*: As stated in Part V, inference is the process of posing queries and deducing unauthorized information from the legitimate responses. In fact we consider the privacy problem to be a form of inference problem (see the discussion in Chapter 23). Various solutions have been proposed to handle the inference problem including constraint processing and the use of conceptual structures. We discuss some of them in the next section.
- *Identity Theft*: We are hearing a lot about identity theft these days. The thief gets hold of one's social security number and from there can wipe out the bank account of an individual. Here the thief is posing legitimately as the owner and he now has much of the critical information about the owner. This is a threat that is very difficult to handle and manage. Viable solutions are yet to be developed. Data mining offers some hope, but may not be sufficient.
- *Insider Threats*: Insider threats are considered to be quite common and quite dangerous. In this case one never knows who the terrorists are. They could be the database administrators or any person who may be considered to be trusted by the corporation. Background checks alone may not be sufficient to detect insider threats. Role-based access controls as well as data-mining techniques are being proposed. We examine these solutions in the next section.

All of the threats and attacks discussed here plus various other cyber-security threats and attacks collectively have come to be known as cyber-terrorism. Essentially cyber-terrorism is about corrupting the Web and all of its components so that the enemy or adversary's system collapses. Currently a lot of funds are being invested by the various governments in the United States and Europe to conduct research on protecting the Web and preventing cyber-terrorism. Note that terrorism includes cyber-terrorism, bioterrroism, and violations to physical security including bombing buildings and poisoning food supplies and water supplies. Chapter 22 provided an overview of data-mining solutions for national security and cyber-security. We revisit some of the discussion in this chapter.

24.3 Web Security Solutions

24.3.1 Overview

This section discusses various solutions to handle the threats mentioned in Section 24.2.2. The goals are to prevent as well as detect security violations and mitigate risks. Furthermore, damage has to be contained

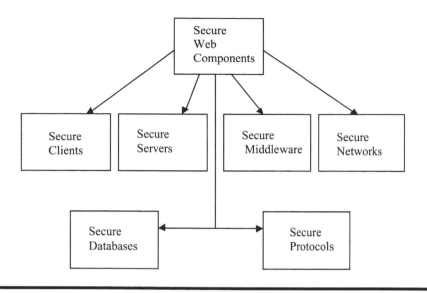

Figure 24.3   Solutions for Web security

and not allowed to spread further. Essentially we need effective damage control techniques. The solutions discussed include securing components, cryptography, data mining, constraint processing, role-based access control, risk analysis, and fault-tolerance processing (see also [THUR05a]).

The organization of this section is as follows. In Section 24.3.2 we discuss solutions for some generic threats. These solutions include firewalls and risk analysis. In Section 24.3.3 we discuss solutions for some of the threats to Web databases. Note that although the solutions for generic threats are applicable to threats to Web databases, the solutions for threats to Web databases are also applicable to generic threats. For example, risk analysis has to be carried out for Web databases as well as for general information systems. Furthermore, data mining is a solution for intrusion detection and auditing both for Web databases as well as for networks. We have included them in the section on solutions for Web databases, as data mining is part of data management. Figure 24.3 illustrates potential solutions.

24.3.2 Solutions for General Threats

24.3.2.1 Securing Components and Firewalls

Various components have to be made secure to get a secure Web. We need end-to-end security and therefore the components include secure clients, secure servers, secure databases, secure operating systems, secure infrastructure, secure networks, secure transactions, and secure protocols.

One needs good encryption mechanisms to ensure that the sender and receiver communicate securely. Ultimately whether it be exchanging messages or carrying out transactions, the communication between sender and receiver or the buyer and the seller has to be secure. Secure client solutions include securing the browser, securing the Java virtual machine, securing Java applets, and incorporating various security features into languages such as Java. Note that Java is not the only component that has to be secure. Microsoft has come up with a collection of products including ActiveX and these products have to be secure also. Securing the protocols include securing HTTP (HyperText Transfer Protocol) and the Secure Socket Layer (SSL). Securing the Web server means the server has to be installed securely as well as it has to be ensured that the server cannot be attacked. Various mechanisms that have been used to secure operating systems and databases may be applied here. Notable among them are access control lists, which specify which users have access to which Web pages and data. The Web servers may be connected to databases at the back end and these databases have to be secure. Finally various encryption algorithms are being implemented for the networks and groups such as OMG are investigating security for middleware such as ORBs.

One of the challenges faced by the Web managers is implementing security policies. One may have policies for clients, servers, networks, middleware, and databases. The question is how do you integrate these policies. That is, how do you make these policies work together? Who is responsible for implementing these policies? Is there a global administrator or are there several administrators who have to work together? Security policy integration is an area that is being examined by researchers.

Finally, one of the emerging technologies for ensuring that an organization's assets are protected is firewalls. Various organizations now have Web infrastructure for internal and external use. To access the external infrastructure one has to go through the firewall. These firewalls examine the information that comes into and out of an organization. This way, the internal assets are protected and inappropriate information may be prevented from coming into an organization. We can expect sophisticated firewalls to be developed in the future.

24.3.2.2 Cryptography

Numerous texts and articles have been published on cryptography (see, for example, [DENN82]). In addition, annual cryptology conferences also take place. Yet cryptography is one of the areas that needs continuous research as the codes are being broken with powerful machines and sophisticated techniques. There are also many discussions on export/import controls on encryption techniques. This section briefly provides an overview of some of the technical details of cryptography relevant to the Web and therefore to E-commerce. Cryptography is the solution to various threats including authenticity verification as well as ensuring data integrity. It is also useful for ensuring privacy.

The main issue with cryptology is ensuring that a message is sent properly. That is, the receiver gets the message the way it was intended for her to receive. This means that the message should not be intercepted or modified. The issue can be extended to transactions on the Web also. That is, transactions have to be carried out the way in which they were intended. Scientists have been working on cryptography for many decades. We hear about codes being broken during World War II. The study of codebreaking has come to be known as cryptanalysis. In cryptography, essentially the sender of the message encrypts the message with a key. For example, he could use the letter B for A, C for D, . . ., A for Z. If the receiver knows the key, then she can decode this message. So a message with the word COMPUTER would be DPNQVUFS. Now this code is simple and will be easy to break. The challenge in cryptography is to find a code that is difficult to break. Number theorists have been conducting extensive research in this area.

Essentially in cryptography, encryption is used by the sender to transform what is called a plaintext message into ciphertext. Decryption is used by the receiver to obtain the plaintext from the received ciphertext. Two types of cryptography are gaining prominence. One is public key cryptography where there are two keys involved for the sender and the receiver: the public key, visible to everyone, and the private key. The sender encrypts the message with the recipient's public key. Only the recipient can decode this message with his private key. The second method is private key cryptography. Here both users have a private key. There is also a key distribution center involved. This center generates a session key when the sender and receiver want to communicate. This key is sent to both users in an encrypted form using the respective private keys. The sender uses her private key to decrypt the session key. The session key is used to encrypt the message. The receiver can decrypt the session key with his private key and then use this decrypted session key to decrypt the message.

In the preceding paragraphs we have discussed some of the basic concepts in cryptography. The challenge is how to ensure that an intruder does not modify the message and that the desirable security properties such as confidentiality, integrity, authentication, and nonrepudiation are maintained. The answer is in message digests and digital signatures. Using hash functions on a message, a message digest is created. If appropriate functions are used, each message will have a unique message digest.

Therefore, even a small modification to the message will result in a completely different message digest. This way integrity is maintained. Message digests together with cryptographic receipts, which are digitally signed, ensure that the receiver knows the identity of the sender. That is, the sender may encrypt the message digests with the encryption techniques described in the previous paragraphs. In some techniques, the recipient may need the public key of the sender to decrypt the message. The recipient may obtain this key with what is called a certificate authority. The certificate authority should be a trusted entity and must make sure that the recipient can legitimately get the public key of the sender. Therefore, additional measures are taken by the certificate authority to make sure that this is the case.

24.3.2.3 Risk Analysis

Before developing any computer system for a particular operation, one needs to study the security risks involved. The goal is to mitigate the risks or at least limit and contain them if the threats cannot be eliminated. Several papers have been published on risk analysis especially in the *National Computer Security Conference Proceedings* in the 1990s. These risk analysis techniques need to be examined for cyber-threats.

The challenges include identifying all the threats that are inherent to a particular situation. For example, consider a banking operation. The bank has to employ security experts and risk analysis experts to conduct a study of all possible threats. Then they have to come up with ways of eliminating the threats. If that is not possible, they have to develop ways of containing the damage so that it is not spread further.

Risk analysis is especially useful for viruses. Once a virus starts spreading, the challenge is how do you stop it. If you cannot stop it, then how do you contain it and also limit the damage that is caused? Running various virus packages on one's system will perhaps limit the virus from affecting the system or causing serious damage. The adversary will always find ways to develop new viruses. Therefore, we have to be one step or many steps ahead of the enemy. We need to examine the current state of the practice in risk analysis and develop new solutions especially to handle the new kinds of threats present in the cyber-world.

24.3.2.4 Biometrics, Forensics, and Other Solutions

Some of the recent developments in computer security are tools for biometrics and forensic analysis. Biometrics tools include understanding handwriting and signatures as well as recognizing people from their

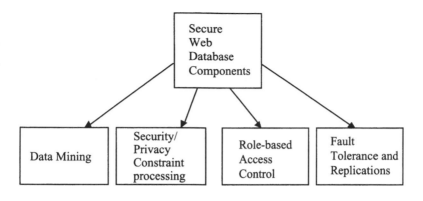

Figure 24.4   Solutions for Web database security

features and eyes including the pupils. Although this is a very challenging area, much progress has been made. Voice recognition tools to authenticate users are also being developed. In the future we can expect many of us to use these tools.

Forensic analysis essentially carries out postmortems just as they do in medicine. Once the attacks have occurred then how do you detect these attacks? Who are the enemies and perpetrators? Progress has been made, but there are still challenges. For example, if one accesses the Web pages and uses passwords that are stolen, then it will be difficult to determine from the Web logs who the culprit is. That is, we still need a lot of research in the area.

Biometrics and forensics are just some of the new developments. Other solutions being developed include smartcards and tools for detecting spoofing and jamming, as well as tools to carry out sniffing. We discuss some of these solutions in Chapter 29.

24.3.3 Solutions for Threats to Web Databases

Figure 24.4 illustrates solutions for Web database security. These include data mining, security-constraint processing, and role-based access control.

24.3.3.1 Data Mining

Data mining is the process of posing queries and extracting patterns, often previously unknown, from large quantities of data using pattern matching or other reasoning techniques (see [THUR98]). In [THUR03] we examine data mining for counter-terrorism. We discuss various types of terrorist attacks including information-related terrorism. As mentioned in [THUR03], by information-related terrorism we essentially mean cyber-terrorism. Cyber-security is the area that deals with cyber-terrorism. We listed various cyber-attacks including access-control violations, unauthorized intrusions, and denial of service in Chapter 22. We are hearing that cyber-attacks will cost corporations billions of dollars. For example, one could masquerade as a legitimate user and swindle, say, a bank of billions of dollars.

Data mining may be used to detect and possibly prevent cyber-attacks. For example, anomaly detection techniques could be used to detect unusual patterns and behaviors. Link analysis may be used to trace the viruses to the perpetrators. Classification may be used to group various cyber-attacks and then use the profiles to detect an attack when it occurs. Prediction may be used to determine potential future attacks depending in a way on information learned about terrorists through e-mail and phone conversations. Also, for some threats non-real-time data mining may suffice whereas for certain other threats such as for network intrusions we may need real-time data mining.

Many researchers are investigating the use of data mining for intrusion detection. Although we need some form of real-time data mining, that is, the results have to be generated in real-time, we also need to build models in real-time. For example, credit card fraud detection is a form of real-time processing. However, here models are built ahead of time. Building models in real-time remains a challenge.

Data mining can also be used for analyzing Web logs as well as analyzing the audit trails. Based on the results of the data-mining tool, one can then determine whether any unauthorized intrusions have occurred and whether any unauthorized queries have been posed. There has been much research on data mining for intrusion detection and reported at the IFIP Database Security Conferences (see also [NING04]). This is an area where we can expect to see much progress. Some interesting work on data mining for intrusion detection is given in [DOKA02]. More recently, data-mining techniques are being examined for insider cyber-threat detection. The main question is, are general-purpose data-mining techniques usable for such applications or do we need special-purpose data-mining techniques. We need a research agenda for data-mining applications in information security. Note that some directions were given in Chapter 22.

24.3.3.2 Constraint Processing

We introduced the idea of security-constraint processing for the inference problem. We discussed some details in Chapter 13. We revisit some of the points. We defined security constraints to assign security levels to the data and then developed a system to process the constraints (see

[THUR93]). We have now adapted these techniques for privacy (see Chapter 23). In a recent paper we elaborated on privacy-constraint processing [THUR05b]. Essentially privacy constraints are rules that are enforced on the data. These rules determine the level of privacy of the data (called privacy levels or privacy values). Our definition of privacy constraints follows along the lines of our work on security constraints discussed in [THUR93]. Privacy values of the data could take a range of values including public, semipublic, semiprivate, and private. Even within a privacy value we could have different levels of privacy including low-private, medium-private, and high-private.

We have defined various types of privacy constraints. We give examples using a medical informatics database. The constraints we have identified include simple constraints, content-based constraints, context- or association-based constraints, release constraints, and event constraints. Although we use a relational database to illustrate the concepts, constraints can be defined on object as well as on XML databases.

Simple constraints assign privacy values to attributes, relations, or even a database. For example, all medical records are private. Content-based constraints assign privacy values to data depending on content. For example, all financial records are private except for those who are in public office (e.g., the president of the United States). Association-based constraints assign privacy values to collections of attributes taken together. For example, names and medical records are private; individually they are public. That is, one can release names and medical records separately, but one cannot release them together. Furthermore, one has to be careful so that the public user cannot infer medical records for a particular person by posing multiple queries. Event constraints are constraints that change privacy values after an event has occurred. For example, after a patient has been released, some information about him or her could be made public, but while he is in the hospital, information about him or her is private. A good example was the sniper shootings that occurred in the Washington, DC area in the fall of 2002. After the victim died, information about him or her was released. Until then the identity of the person was not available to the public. Finally, release constraints assign privacy values to the data depending on what has already been released. For example, after the medical records have been released, one cannot release any information about the names or social security numbers that can form a link to the medical information.

One could define many more types of privacy constraints. As we explore various applications, we start defining various classes of constraints. Our main purpose in [THUR04b] is to show how privacy constraints can be processed in a database management system. We call such a system a privacy-enhanced database system. Our approach is to augment a DataBase Management System (DBMS) with a privacy controller. Such a DBMS is called a privacy-enhanced DBMS. The privacy controller will process the privacy constraints. The question is what are the components of the privacy controller and when do the constraints get processed. We take an approach similar to the approach proposed in [THUR93] for security-constraint processing. In our approach, some privacy constraints are processed during database design and the database is partitioned according to the privacy levels. Then some constraints are processed during database updates. Here, the data is entered at the appropriate privacy levels. Because the privacy values change dynamically, it is very difficult to change the privacy levels of the data in the database in real-time. Therefore, some constraints are processed during the query operation.

The modules of the privacy controller include the constraint manager, query manager, database design tool, and the update manager. The constraint manager manages the constraints. The database design tool processes constraints during database design and assigns levels to the schema. The query processor processes constraints during the query operation and determines what data is to be released. The update processor processes constraints and computes the level of the data (see also the discussion in Chapter 23).

24.3.3.3 Role-Based Access Control

One popular access-control technique is role-based access control. The idea here is that users, based on their roles, are given access to certain data. For example, the engineer has access to project data and the accountant has access to financial data. The challenges include handling multiple roles and conflicting roles. For example, if one is an engineer and he cannot have access to financial data and if he also happens to be an accountant, then how can the conflict be resolved? Maintaining the consistency of the access control rules is also a challenge.

Many papers have been published on role-based access control. There is also now a conference devoted entirely to role-based access control called SACMAT (ACM Symposium on Access Control Models and Technologies). Also papers relevant to role-based access control on databases have been presented at the IFIP database security conferences. It is also being examined for handling insider threats. That is, using a combination of data-mining techniques to find out information about employees and granting them roles depending on their trustworthiness, one could perhaps manage the insider threat analysis problem. More work needs to be done in this area (see also the discussion in Chapter 5).

24.3.3.4 Fault-Tolerant Processing, Recovery, and Replication

As stated earlier, the databases could be national databases that contain critical information about individuals, private corporate databases, or bank databases that contain financial information. They could also be agency databases that contain highly sensitive information. When such databases are attacked, it is then possible for the enemy to obtain classified information or wipe out bank accounts. Furthermore, even if the enemy does not do anything with the data, just by corrupting the databases the entire operation could be thwarted, Today computer systems control the operation of manufacturing plants, process control plants, and much critical infrastructure. Corrupting the data could be disastrous.

The fault-tolerance computing community has come up with several algorithms for recovering databases and systems from failures and other problems. These techniques include acceptance testing and checkpointing. Sometimes data is replicated so that there are backup copies. These techniques have to be examined for handling malicious attacks on the databases and corrupting the data. We also need to conduct research on dependable computing where we need security, integrity, fault tolerance, and real-time processing. That is, we need to develop quality-of-service metrics for dependable computing. We also need flexible security policies as the requirements such as security and real-time processing may be conflicting (see also the discussion in Chapter 27).

24.4 Secure Digital Libraries

24.4.1 Overview

In the previous section we discussed threats and solutions for general Web security as well as security for Web databases. We focused on various types of threats including insider threat analysis and sabotage as well as discussed techniques such as data mining and risk analysis. In this section we discuss various aspects of security for digital libraries.

In Chapter 4 we discussed various aspects of digital libraries including Web databases, information retrieval, question-answering, and search engines (see also [LESK97]). In this chapter we examine each of these techniques and discuss the security impact. Secure Web database functions are discussed in Section 24.4.2. Secure information retrieval systems are discussed in Section 24.4.3. Secure markup languages such as secure XML are discussed in Section 24.4.4. Secure search engines are discussed in Section 24.4.5. Finally, in Section 24.4.6 we discuss security for question-answering systems. Various aspects discussed in this chapter are illustrated in Figure 24.5 (see also [SAMA96]).

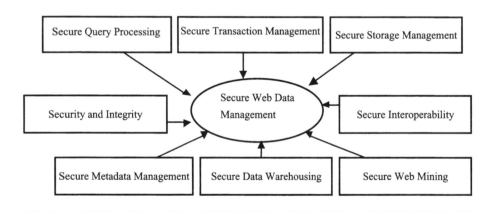

Figure 24.5 Secure digital libraries

Figure 24.6 Secure Web database functions

24.4.2 Secure Web Database Functions

Managing the databases on the Web is essential for the development of digital libraries. In Chapter 4 we discussed various aspects of Web database management. In this section we examine the security issues. Figure 24.6 illustrates secure Web database management.

A major challenge for Web data management researchers and practitioners is coming up with an appropriate data representation scheme. The question is whether there is a need for a standard data model for digital libraries and Web database access. Is it at all possible to develop such a standard? If so, what are the relationships between the standard model and the individual models used by the databases on the Web? Recently several models including secure models for XML and RDF have been developed. Security impact is also being examined. We discuss secure XML later on in this section as well as in Chapter 25 when we discuss the secure semantic Web. Languages such as SQL are also being examined to incorporate security as well as to use for Web databases.

Database management functions for the Web include those such as query processing, metadata management, security, and integrity. In [THUR00] we have examined various database management system functions and discussed the impact of Web database access on these functions. In this section we discuss the security impact. Querying and browsing are two of the key functions. First of all, an appropriate query language is needed. Because SQL is a popular language, appropriate extensions to SQL may be desired. XML-QL is moving in this direction. We need to incorporate security constructs to specify the security constraints and the assertions. For example, the Web rules language of the W3C community has to be extended to specify security policies.

Query processing involves developing a cost model. How do we take into consideration the access-control rules for these cost models? How do we perform, say, query modification in a Web environment? When data is updated in the Web databases, does the user have the authorization to do so? Transaction management is essential for many applications. As we have stated, there may be new kinds of transactions on the Web. For example, various items may be sold through the Web. In this case, the item should not be locked immediately when a potential buyer makes a bid. It has to be left open until several bids are received and the item is sold. How can access control and other security features be incorporated into concurrency-control and recovery schemes? In Chapter 10 we discussed multilevel database concurrency control. Are these schemes relevant for a Web environment?

Metadata management is a major concern for digital libraries. The question is what is metadata. Metadata describes all of the information pertaining to the digital library. This could include the various Web sites, the types of users, access-control issues, and policies enforced. What sorts of access-control methods are enforced on the metadata? Can security be violated by releasing metadata? Storage management for Web database access is a complex function. Appropriate index strategies and access methods for handling various types of data including semistructured data and multimedia data are needed. In addition, due to the large volume of data, techniques for integrating database management technology with mass storage technology are also needed. The challenge is to maintain security for storage management.

Maintaining the integrity of the data is critical. Because the data may originate from multiple sources around the world, it will be difficult to keep tabs on the accuracy of the data. Data quality maintenance techniques need to be developed for digital libraries and Web database access. For example, special tagging mechanisms may be needed to determine the quality of the data.

Other functions include integrating the databases on the Web as well as managing semistructured and multimedia data. In Chapter 20 we discussed some of the issues involved in securing multimedia databases. When integrating multiple databases, one also needs to integrate the various security policies. Security policy integration has been discussed in Chapters 15 through 17. We need to examine these techniques for Web databases.

As can be seen, security and privacy are major challenges for all of the functions. Once you put the data at a site, who owns the data? If a user copies the data from a site, can he distribute the data? Can he use the information in papers that he is writing? Who owns the copyright to the original data? What role do digital signatures play? Mechanisms for copyright protection and plagiarism detection are needed. In addition, some of the issues discussed in Chapter 17 on handling heterogeneous security policies are of concern.

24.4.3 Secure Information Retrieval

In Chapter 4 we discussed information retrieval systems. These systems include text retrieval systems, image retrieval systems, video retrieval systems, and audio retrieval systems. We also discussed multimedia data management systems. In Chapter 20 we discussed security for multimedia data management systems. In this section we briefly discuss security for information retrieval systems. Note that information retrieval is another major component of digital libraries. That is, much of the data on the Web is in the form of text. There are also image, video, and audio data. Therefore, secure information retrieval is critical if we are to ensure security for digital libraries.

In [THUR93] we provided some information on multilevel security for information retrieval systems. The challenges include securing the information retrieval system as well as securing browsers and search engines. Secure search engines are discussed in Section 24.4.4. In this section we identify the issues involved in securing text, images, audio, and video.

When securing text-processing systems, the challenge is to protect certain words, paragraphs, and sentences from unauthorized access. This is far more complex than protecting relational databases where the database is structured. Note that words and paragraphs could appear anywhere in the document. For example, how do you classify certain words and sentences? Do you blank them as we see in physical documents? What sort of metadata do we maintain? That is, do we have constraints such as "the fifth line in paragraph 3 of chapter 6 of document A is classified"? We may have hundreds of such access-control rules and therefore how do we manage these rules?

Similar challenges exist for images, audio, and video data. How do we classify pixels? That is, do we state that the pixel in this particular position is classified? In the case of video and audio do we classify frames? How can we enforce content-dependent access control? An example of a content-dependent rule is: User Group A does not have any access to scenes illustrating terrorist activities.

There have been debates in panels that techniques for securing information retrieval systems are almost identical to securing relational database systems. However, with information retrieval systems, the data to be managed is complex. Therefore, we may have more constraints and more challenges in terms of extracting semantics. Therefore, the challenge is to develop efficient techniques for controlling access to the data such as text, images, video, and audio. Some of the challenges were discussed in Chapter 20. In addition, we also need to ensure copyright protection of the documents on the Web as well as ensure data quality. Finally, privacy has to be maintained. Figure 24.7 illustrates secure information retrieval.

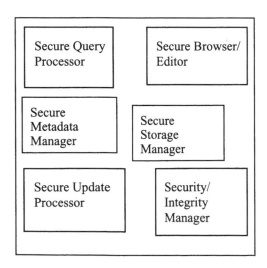

Figure 24.7   Secure information retrieval

24.4.4 Secure Search Engines

In Chapter 4 we provided an overview of search engines and gave some examples of using data mining within search engines so that one can carry out intelligent searching. There are many dependability issues that need to be addressed. These include security, privacy, and data quality. We want to make sure that the search engines list Web pages that can be accessed by the user. Furthermore, they have to ensure that the user's privacy is maintained. Finally, the search engines have to ensure that the information they provide is of high quality.

For example, a Web page may have incorrect information. Then the question is who is responsible for the information given to the user. There are legal issues involved here. Although there have been discussions on security, privacy, and data quality, there has been little work reported. That is, search engines in general do not enforce access-control rules. Essentially access control is maintained by those providing the services. The question is should the search engines also enforce security. For example, there have been some discussions on protecting children from inappropriate content on the Web (see, for example, the study at the National Academy of Sciences [NAS02]). How can search engines be improved so they can ensure that children do not get inappropriate material?

There are many questions that need answers and Web mining is one of the technologies that could help toward finding useful and relevant searches on the Web. Note that although data mining helps solve security problems such as intrusion detection and auditing, there are also privacy concerns. Many Web servers now specify privacy policies enforced by the server. If a user can agree with the policy then he or she can fill out the various forms. The W3C community is also starting with P3P (Platform for Privacy Preferences) to enforce privacy. We need an active research program on semantic Web security within which we need to examine security for search engines. In Figure 24.8 we illustrate some aspects of secure search engines.

24.4.5 Secure Markup Languages

Markup languages are an essential part of digital libraries and the semantic Web. We discussed markup languages in Chapter 4. In Chapter 25 we provide some details on security for languages such as XML. In this section we discuss some of the key points.

In securing the markup language, the first question is what is the granularity of classification. For example, in the case of XML we may give access to parts of the XML documents. If we give negative access to a

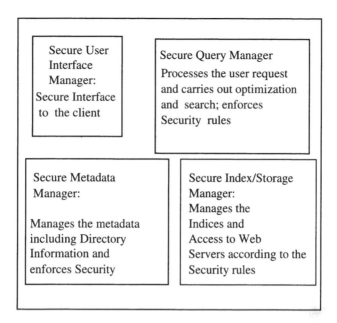

Figure 24.8   Secure search engines

node, then does it propagate to all the children? Another challenge is how do you securely publish documents written in XML and, say, HTML. That is, do we trust the entire Web or can we have untrusted publishers and use appropriate encryption techniques?

We have provided an overview on securing XML documents in [BERT04]. We discuss access control as well as maintaining authenticity and completeness of the documents. The challenge is to secure other types of documents such as RDF. Some issues on securing RDF documents are given in [CARM04]. There is still a lot to do in this area. Figure 24.9 illustrates some aspects of secure markup languages.

24.4.6 Secure Question-Answering Systems

As we have stated in Chapter 4, the early question-answering systems give just "Yes" or "No" answers. However, more recently question-answering systems have become quite sophisticated and can answer questions such as "Find the directions between New York and Boston where these is no traffic". With more sophisticated technologies there are more problems with respect to security. For example, A may be authorized to get one set of directions and B may be authorized to get another set of directions.

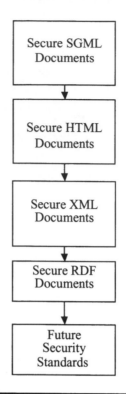

Figure 24.9 Secure markup languages

When the question-answering systems were simply Yes/No systems, then the system could analyze whether the Yes/No answers had to be given to certain users. Now, with more complex questions and more complex answers, the challenge is to determine what information is to be released to which users. Therefore, secure question-answering systems combine techniques for secure information retrieval, secure search engines, secure Web databases, and secure markup languages. Very little work has been reported on secure question-answering. Figure 24.10 illustrates some aspects.

24.5 Summary and Directions

This chapter has discussed various cyber-threats in general and threats to Web databases in particular. The threats include access-control violations, sabotage, infrastructure attacks, and insider threat analysis. Next we proposed various solutions including data-mining techniques and role-based access control. As we have stated, the cyber-threats are very real and we need to do everything we can to detect, prevent, and manage the threats.

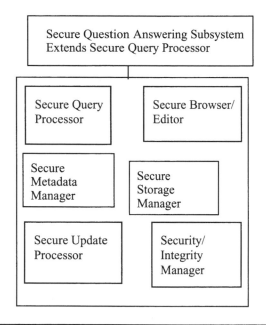

Figure 24.10 Secure question answering

The damages have to be contained. We have also provided an overview of secure digital libraries including secure Web databases and secure information retrieval systems.

Various research programs are now under way to develop solutions for cyber-attacks. The National Science Foundation has various programs including the Trusted Computing Program and the Data and Applications Security Program (see [NSF]). There is now an umbrella theme called Cyber Trust. Other organizations such as the Defense Advanced Research Projects Agency, Advanced Research and Development Activity, the National Security Agency, the National Institute of Standards and Technology, and the Department of Defense also have programs in cyber-security. Although several techniques have been developed, we need to ensure that these techniques scale for very large databases and large numbers of interconnected systems. We need end-to-end security. That is, the clients, the servers, and the infrastructure have to be secure.

References

[BERT04] Bertino, E. et al. Secure third party publication of XML documents. *IEEE Transactions on Knowledge and Data Engineering*, 16: 10, 2004.

[CARM04] Carminati, B. et al. Security for RDF. In *Proceedings of the DEXA Conference Workshop on Web Semantics*, Zaragoza, Spain, 2004.

[DENN82] Denning, D. *Cryptography and Data Security.* Addison-Wesley: Reading, MA, 1982.

[DOKA02] Dokas, P. et al. Data mining for intrusion detection. In *Proceedings of the NSF Workshop on Next Generation Data Mining,* Baltimore, November 2002.

[GHOS98] Ghosh, A. *E-Commerce Security, Weak Links and Strong Defenses.* Wiley: New York, 1998.

[LESK97] Lesk, M. *Practical Digital Libraries.* Morgan-Kaufmann: San Francisco, 1997.

[NAS02] National Academy of Sciences Study Report: Protecting Children from Inappropriate Content on the Internet. National Academy Press: Washington, DC, 2002.

[NSF] The National Science Foundation. Available at www.nsf.gov.

[SAMA96] Samarati, P. et al. An authorization model for a distributed hypertext system. *IEEE Transactions on Knowledge and Data Engineering* 8: 4, 1996.

[THUR93] Thuraisingham, B., Ford, W., and Collins, M. Design and implementation of a database inference controller. *Data and Knowledge Engineering Journal* 11: 3, 1993.

[THUR98] Thuraisingham, B. *Data Mining: Technologies, Techniques, Tools and Trends.* CRC Press: Boca Raton, FL, 1998.

[THUR00] Thuraisingham, B. *Web Data Management and Electronic Commerce.* CRC Press: Boca Raton, FL, 2000.

[THUR03] Thuraisingham, B. *Web Data Mining Technologies and Their Applications for Counter-Terrorism.* CRC Press: Boca Raton, FL, 2003.

[THUR05] Thuraisingham, B. Managing threats to Web databases and cyber systems: Issues, solutions and challenges. In *Cyber Security: Threats and Solutions,* Ed., V. Kumar et al. Kluwer: Hingham, MA, 2005.

[THUR05] Thuraisingham, B. Privacy constraint processing in a privacy enhanced database system. *Data and Knowledge Engineering Journal,* 2005 (to appear).

Exercises

1. Conduct a survey of Web security threats and solutions.
2. Design a secure digital library system.
3. Investigate security issues for search engines and question-answering systems.

Chapter 25

Security for XML, RDF, and the Semantic Web

25.1 Overview

As stated in Chapter 1, the advent of the World Wide Web (WWW) in the mid-1990s has resulted in even greater demand for managing data, information, and knowledge effectively. There is now so much data on the Web that managing it with conventional tools is becoming almost impossible. New tools and techniques are needed to effectively manage this data. Therefore, to provide interoperability as well as warehousing among the multiple data sources and systems, and to extract information from the databases and warehouses on the Web, various tools are being developed. Consequently the Web is evolving into what is now called the semantic Web.

In [THUR02a] we provided an overview of some directions in data and applications security research. In this chapter we focus on one of the topics: securing the semantic Web. Although current Web technologies facilitate the integration of information from a syntactic point of view, there is still a lot to be done to integrate the semantics of various systems and applications. That is, current Web technologies depend a lot on the "human-in-the-loop" for information integration. Tim Berners Lee, the father of WWW, realized the inadequacies of current Web technologies and subsequently strived to make the Web more intelligent. His goal was to have a Web that would essentially alleviate humans from the burden of having to integrate disparate information sources as well as to carry out extensive searches. He then came to the conclusion that one needs machine-understandable Web pages and the use of ontologies for information integration. This resulted in the notion of the semantic Web [LEE01].

A semantic Web can be thought of as a Web that is highly intelligent and sophisticated so that one needs little or no human intervention to carry out tasks such as scheduling appointments, coordinating activities, and searching for complex documents, as well as integrating disparate databases and information systems. Much progress has been made toward developing such an intelligent Web but there is still a lot to be done. For example, technologies such as ontology matching, intelligent agents, and markup languages are contributing toward developing the semantic Web. Nevertheless one still needs a human to make decisions and take actions. A brief overview of the semantic Web is given in Chapter 4.

Recently there have been many developments on the semantic Web (see, for example, [THUR02b]). The World Wide Web consortium (W3C) is specifying standards for the semantic Web [WWW]. These standards include specifications for XML, RDF, and interoperability. However, it is also very important that the semantic Web be secure. That is, the components that constitute the semantic Web have to be secure. In addition, the components have to be integrated securely. The components include XML, RDF, and ontologies. In addition, we need secure information integration. We also need to examine trust issues for the semantic Web. It is therefore important that we have standards for securing the semantic Web including specifications for secure XML, secure RDF, and secure interoperability (see [THUR05]).

This chapter focuses on security for the semantic Web. In particular, XML security, RDF security, and secure information integration are discussed. We also discuss privacy for the semantic Web and then describe secure Web services. The organization of this chapter is as follows. Security for the semantic Web is discussed in Section 25.2. We detail our research on XML security further in Section 25.3. Privacy for the semantic Web is addressed in Section 25.4. Some aspects of secure Web services are discussed in Section 25.5. A note on secure grids and secure semantic grids is given in Section 25.6. Note that the differences between the Web, grid, semantic Web, and semantic grid are rather vague. We give our view of the subject. Finally we briefly discuss the work of Mehrotra et al. on security impact on the database as a service model (see [HACI04]). The idea here is to have data management as a Web service and there are several security concerns. The chapter is summarized in Section 25.7.

25.2 Security for the Semantic Web

25.2.1 Overview

We first provide an overview of security issues for the semantic Web and then discuss some details of XML security, RDF security, and secure

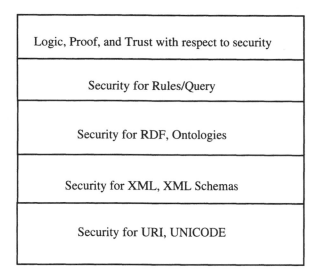

Figure 25.1 Layers for the secure semantic Web

information integration, which are components of the secure semantic Web. As more progress is made on investigating these various issues, we hope that appropriate standards will be developed for securing the semantic Web. As stated earlier, logic, proof, and trust are at the highest layers of the semantic Web. That is, how can we trust the information that the Web gives us? Closely related to trust is security. However, security cannot be considered in isolation. That is, there is no one layer that should focus on security. Security cuts across all layers and this is a challenge. We need security for each of the layers and we must also ensure secure interoperability as illustrated in Figure 25.1.

For example, consider the lowest layer. One needs secure TCP/IP, secure sockets, and secure HTTP. There are now security protocols for these various lower-layer protocols. One needs end-to-end security. That is, one cannot just have secure TCP/IP built on untrusted communication layers. We need network security. The next layer is XML and XML schemas. One needs secure XML. Access must be controlled to various portions of the document for reading, browsing, and modifications. There is research on securing XML and XML schemas. The next step is securing RDF. Now with RDF not only do we need secure XML, we also need security for the interpretations and semantics. For example, in certain contexts, portions of the document may be Unclassified whereas in certain other contexts the document may be Classified. As an example one could declassify an RDF document once a war is over. Much work has been carried out on security-constraint processing for relational databases. One needs to determine whether these results could be applied to the semantic Web (see [THUR93]).

Once XML and RDF have been secured, the next step is to examine security for ontologies and interoperation. That is, ontologies may have security levels attached to them. Certain parts of the ontologies could be Secret and certain other parts may be Unclassified. The challenge is how does one use these ontologies for secure information integration. Researchers have done some work on the secure interoperability of databases. We need to revisit this research and then determine what else needs to be done so that the information on the Web can be managed, integrated, and exchanged securely.

Closely related to security is privacy. That is, certain portions of the document may be private and certain other portions may be public or semiprivate. Privacy has received a lot of attention recently partly due to national security concerns. Privacy for the semantic Web may be a critical issue. That is, how does one take advantage of the semantic Web and still maintain privacy and sometimes anonymity?

We also need to examine the inference problem for the semantic Web. Inference is the process of posing queries and deducing new information. It becomes a problem when the deduced information is something the user is unauthorized to know. With the semantic Web, and especially with data-mining tools, one can make all kinds of inferences. Recently there has been some research on controlling unauthorized inferences on the semantic Web. We need to continue with such research (see, for example, [FARK03]).

Security should not be an afterthought. We have often heard that one needs to insert security into the system right from the beginning. Similarly security cannot be an afterthought for the semantic Web. However, we cannot also make the system inefficient if we must guarantee 100 percent security at all times. What is needed is a flexible security policy. In some situations we may need 100 percent security and in other situations, say, 30 percent security (whatever that means) may be sufficient.

25.2.2 XML Security

Various research efforts have been reported on XML security (see, for example, [BERT02]). We briefly discuss some of the key points. XML documents have graph structures. The main challenge is whether to give access to entire XML documents or parts of the documents. Bertino et al. have developed authorization models for XML. They have focused on access-control policies as well as on dissemination policies. They also considered push-and-pull architectures. They specified the policies in XML. The policy specification contains information about which users can access which portions of the documents. In [BERT02] algorithms for access control as well as computing views of the results are presented. In addition, architectures for securing XML documents are also discussed. In [BERT04] the authors go further and describe how XML documents may be published on the Web. The idea is for owners to publish documents, subjects to request access to the documents, and untrusted publishers to give the subjects the views of the documents they are authorized to see. We discuss XML security in more detail in Section 25.3.

The W3C (World Wide Web Consortium) is specifying standards for XML security. The XML security project (see [XML1]) is focusing on providing the implementation of security standards for XML. The focus is on XML-Signature Syntax and Processing, XML-Encryption Syntax and Processing, and XML Key Management. W3C also has a number of working groups including the XML signature working group (see [XML2]) and XML encryption working group (see [XML3]). Although the standards are focusing on what can be implemented in the near-term, much research is needed on securing XML documents. The work reported in [BERT02] is a good start.

25.2.3 RDF Security

RDF is the foundation of the semantic Web. XML is limited in providing machine-understandable documents, but RDF handles this limitation. As a result, RDF provides better support for interoperability as well as searching and cataloging. It also describes contents of documents as well as relationships between various entities in the document. XML provides syntax and notations and RDF supplements this by providing semantic information in a standardized way.

The basic RDF model has three types: (1) resources, (2) properties, and (3) statements. A resource is anything described by RDF expressions. It could be a Web page or a collection of pages. A property is a specific attribute used to describe a resource. RDF statements are resources together with a named property plus the value of the property. Statement components are subject, predicate, and object. So, for example, if we have a sentence of the form, "John is the creator of xxx," then xxx is the subject or resource, the property or predicate is "Creator," and the object or literal is "John." There are RDF diagrams very much like, say, ER diagrams or object diagrams to represent statements.

There are various aspects specific to RDF syntax and for more details we refer to the various documents on RDF published by the W3C. Also, it is very important that the intended interpretation be used for RDF sentences. This is accomplished by RDF schemas. A schema is sort of a dictionary and has interpretations of various terms used in sentences. RDF and XML namespaces resolve conflicts in semantics.

More advanced concepts in RDF include the container model and statements about statements. The container model has three types of container objects: (1) bag, (2) sequence, and (3) alternative. A bag is an unordered list of resources or literals. It is used to mean that a property has multiple values but the order is not important. A sequence is a list of ordered resources. Here the order is important. An alternative is a list of resources that represent alternatives for the value of a property. Various tutorials in RDF describe the syntax of containers in more detail.

RDF also provides support for making statements about other statements. For example, with this facility one can make statements of the form, "The statement A is false" where A is the statement, "John is the creator of X." Again one can use objectlike diagrams to represent containers and statements about statements. RDF also has a formal model associated with it. This formal model has a formal grammar. For further information on RDF we refer to the W3C reports (see [RDF]). As in the case of any language or model, RDF will continue to evolve.

Now to make the semantic Web secure, we need to ensure that RDF documents are secure. This would involve securing XML from a syntactic point of view. However, with RDF we also need to ensure that security is preserved at the semantic level. The issues include the security implications of the concepts resource, properties, and statements. That is, how is access control ensured? How can resources, properties, and statements be protected? How can one provide access control at a finer granularity? What are the security properties of the container model? How can bags, lists, and alternatives be protected? Can we specify security policies in RDF? How can we resolve semantic inconsistencies for the policies? How can we express security constraints in RDF? What are the security implications of statements about statements? How can we protect RDF schemas? These are difficult questions and we need to start research to provide answers. XML security is just the beginning. Securing RDF is much more challenging (see also [CARM04]).

25.2.4 Secure Information Interoperability

Information is everywhere on the Web. Information is essentially data that makes sense. The database community has been working on database integration for some decades. They encountered many challenges including interoperability of heterogeneous data sources. They used schemas to integrate the various databases. Schemas are essentially data describing the data in the databases (see [SHET90]).

Now with the Web, one needs to integrate the diverse and disparate data sources. The data may not be in databases. It could be in files both structured and unstructured. Data could be in the form of tables or in the form of text, images, audio, or video. One needs to come up with technologies to integrate the diverse information sources on the Web. Essentially one needs the semantic Web services to integrate the information on the Web.

The challenge for security researchers is how does one integrate the information securely. For example, in [THUR94] and [THUR97] the schema integration work of Sheth and Larson was extended to security policies. That is, different sites have security policies and these policies have to be integrated to provide a policy for the federated database system. One needs to examine these issues for the semantic Web. Each node on the Web may have its own policy. Is it feasible to have a common policy for a community on the Web? Do we need a tight integration of the policies or do we focus on dynamic policy integration?

Ontologies are playing a major role in information integration on the Web. How can ontologies play a role in secure information integration? How do we provide access control for ontologies? Should ontologies incorporate security policies? Do we have ontologies for specifying the security policies? How can we use some of the ideas discussed in [BERT04] to integrate information securely on the Web? That is, what sort of encryption schemes do we need? How do we minimize the trust placed in information integrators on the Web? We have posed several questions. We need a research program to address many of these challenges.

25.2.5 Secure Query and Rules Processing for the Semantic Web

The layer above the Secure RDF layer is the Secure Query and Rules processing layer. Although RDF can be used to specify security policies (see, for example, [CARM04]), the Web rules language being developed by the W3C is more powerful for specifying complex policies. Furthermore, an inference engine is also being proposed to process the rules. One could integrate ideas from the database inference controller that we have developed (see [THUR93]) with Web rules processing to develop an inference or privacy controller for the semantic Web.

The query-processing module is responsible for accessing the heterogeneous data and information sources on the semantic Web. The W3C is examining ways to integrate techniques from Web query processing with semantic Web technologies to locate, query, and integrate the heterogeneous data and information sources.

25.2.6 Trust for the Semantic Web

Recently there has been some work on trust and the semantic Web. The challenges include how do you trust the information on the Web. How do you trust the sources? How do you negotiate between different parties and develop contracts? How do you incorporate constructs for trust management and negotiation into XML and RDF? What are the semantics for trust management?

Researchers are working on protocols for trust management. Languages for specifying trust management constructs are also being developed. Also there is research on the foundations of trust management. For example, if A trusts B and B trusts C, then can A trust C? How do you share the data and information on the semantic Web and still maintain autonomy? How do you propagate trust? For example, if A trusts B, say, 50 percent of the time and B trusts C 30 percent of the time, then what value do you assign for A trusting C? How do you incorporate trust into semantic interoperability? What are the quality-of-service primitives for trust and negotiation? That is, for certain situations one may need 100 percent trust whereas for certain other situations 50 percent trust may suffice (see also [YU03]).

Other topics that are being investigated are trust propagation and propagating privileges. For example, if you grant privileges to A, what privileges can A transfer to B? How can you compose privileges? Is there an algebra and calculus for the composition of privileges? Much research still needs to be done here. One of the layers of the semantic Web is logic, proof, and trust. Essentially this layer deals with trust management and negotiation between different agents and examining the foundations and developing logics for trust management. Some interesting work has been carried out by Finin et al. (see [DENK03]).

25.3 Access Control and Dissemination of XML Documents

Bertino et al. were among the first to examine security for XML (see [BERT02] and [BERT04]). They first propose a framework for access control for XML documents and then discuss a technique for ensuring authenticity and completeness of a document for third-party publishing. We briefly discuss some of the key issues.

In the access-control framework proposed in [BERT02], security policy is specified depending on user roles and credentials (see Figure 25.2). Users must possess the credentials to access XML documents. The credentials depend on their roles. For example, a professor has access to all

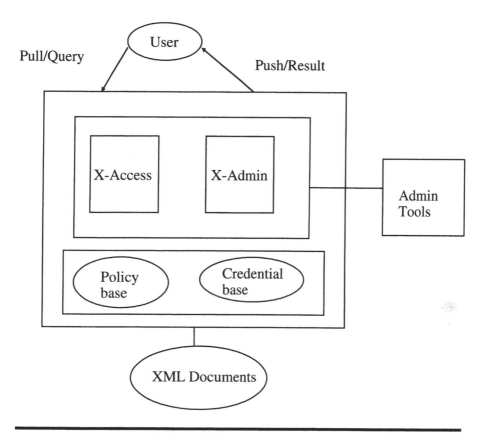

Figure 25.2 Access control for XML documents

of the details of students but a secretary only has access to administrative information. XML specifications are used to specify the security policies. Access is granted for an entire XML document or portions of the document. Under certain conditions, access control may be propagated down the XML tree. For example, if access is granted to the root, it does not necessarily mean access is granted to all the children. One may grant access to the DTDs and not to the document instances. One may grant access to certain portions of the document. For example, a professor does not have access to the medical information of students although he has access to student grade and academic information. The design of a system for enforcing access-control policies is also described in [BERT02]. Essentially the goal is to use a form of view modification so that the user is authorized to see the XML views as specified by the policies. More research needs to be done on role-based access control for XML and the semantic Web.

In [BERT04] we discuss the secure publication of XML documents (see Figure 25.3). The idea is to have untrusted third-party publishers. The

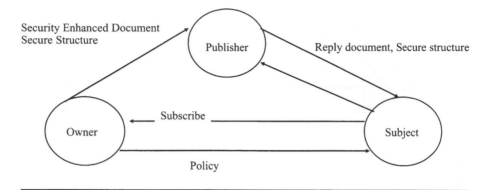

Figure 25.3 Secure XML publishing

owner of a document specifies access-control polices for the subjects. Subjects get the policies from the owner when they subscribe to a document. The owner sends the documents to the publisher. When the subject requests a document, the publisher will apply the policies relevant to the subject and give portions of the documents to the subject. Now, because the publisher is untrusted, it may give false information to the subject. Therefore, the owner will encrypt various combinations of documents and policies with his or her private key. Using Merkle signature and the encryption techniques, the subject can verify the authenticity and completeness of the document (see Figure 25.3 for secure publishing of XML documents).

There are various standards efforts regarding XML security. The challenge is for the researchers to get their ideas into the standards. There are also a number of commercial products. Therefore, researchers, standards organizations, and vendors have to work together to develop appropriate security mechanisms for XML documents. At the same time we need to start research on RDF security and security for the semantic Web.

25.4 Privacy and the Semantic Web

25.4.1 Overview

As stated in Chapter 23, privacy is about protecting information about individuals. Furthermore, an individual can specify, say, to a Web service provider the information that can be released about him or her. Privacy has been discussed a great deal in the past especially when it relates to protecting medical information about patients. Social scientists as well as technologists have been working on privacy issues. However, privacy has received enormous attention during the past year. This is mainly because of the advent of the Web, the semantic Web, counter-terrorism, and national security. For example, in order to extract information about various individuals and perhaps prevent or detect potential terrorist attacks, data-mining tools are being examined. We have heard much about national security versus privacy in the media. This is mainly due to the fact that people are now realizing that to handle terrorism, the government may need to collect data about individuals and mine the data to extract information. Data may be in relational databases or it may be text, video, or images. This is causing a major concern with various civil liberties unions (see [THUR03]).

In this section we discuss privacy threats that arise due to data mining and the semantic Web. We also discuss some solutions and provide directions for standards. Section 25.5.2 discusses issues on data mining, national security, and privacy. Some potential solutions are discussed in Section 25.5.3.

25.4.2 Data Mining, National Security, Privacy, and the Semantic Web

With the Web and the semantic Web, there is now an abundance of data information about individuals that one can obtain within seconds. The data could be structured data or could be multimedia data such as text, images, video, and audio. Information could be obtained through mining or just from information retrieval. Data mining is an important tool in making the Web more intelligent. That is, data mining may be used to mine the data on the Web so that the Web can evolve into the semantic Web. However, this also means that there may be threats to privacy. Therefore, one needs to enforce privacy controls on databases and data-mining tools on the semantic Web. This is a very difficult problem. In summary, one needs to develop techniques to prevent users from mining and extracting information from data whether they are on the Web or on networked servers. Note that data mining is a technology that is critical for, say, analysts so that they can extract patterns previously unknown. However, we do not want the information to be used in an incorrect manner. For example, based on information about a person, an insurance company could deny insurance or a loan agency could deny loans. In many cases these denials may not be legitimate. Therefore, information providers have to be very careful in what they release. Also, data-mining researchers have to ensure that privacy aspects are addressed.

Although little work has been reported on privacy issues for the semantic Web, we are moving in the right direction. As research initiatives are started in this area, we can expect some progress to be made. Note that there are also social and political aspects to consider. That is, technologists, sociologists, policy experts, counter-terrorism experts, and legal experts have to work together to develop appropriate data-mining techniques as well as ensure privacy. Privacy policies and standards are also urgently needed. That is, the technologists develop privacy solutions, but we need the policy makers to work with standards organizations so that appropriate privacy standards are developed. The W3C has made a good start with P3P (the platform for privacy preferences).

25.4.3 Solutions to the Privacy Problem

As we have mentioned in Chapter 23, the challenge is to provide solutions to enhance national security but at the same time ensure privacy. There is now research at various laboratories on privacy-enhanced/sensitive/preserving data mining (e.g., Agrawal at IBM Almaden, Gehrke at Cornell University, and Clifton at Purdue University; see, for example, [AGRA00], [CLIF02], and [GEHR02]). The idea here is to continue with mining but at the same time ensure privacy as much as possible. For example, Clifton has proposed the use of the multiparty security policy approach for carrying out privacy-sensitive data mining. Although there is some progress we still have a long way to go. Some useful references are provided in [CLIF02] (see also [EVFI02]).

We give some more details on an approach we are proposing. Note that one mines the data and extracts patterns and trends. The privacy constraints determine which patterns are private and to what extent. For example, suppose one could extract names and healthcare records. If we have a privacy constraint that states that names and healthcare records are private, then this information is not released to the general public. If the information is semiprivate, then it is released to those who have a need to know. Essentially the inference controller approach we have discussed is one solution to achieving some level of privacy. It could be regarded as a type of privacy-sensitive data mining. In our research we have found many challenges to the inference controller approach we have proposed (see [THUR93]). These challenges will have to be addressed when handling privacy constraints (see also [THUR05b]). Figure 25.4 illustrates privacy controllers for the semantic Web. As illustrated, there are data-mining tools on the Web that mine the Web databases. The privacy controller should ensure privacy-preserving data mining. Ontologies may be used by the privacy controllers. For example, there may be ontology specifications for privacy constructs. Furthermore, XML may be extended to include privacy constraints. RDF may incorporate privacy

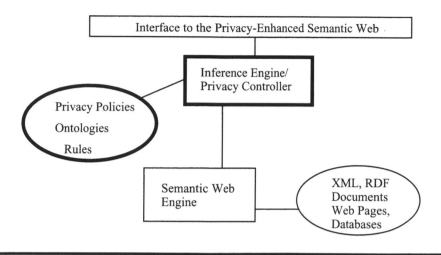

Figure 25.4 Privacy controller for the semantic Web

semantics. We need to carry out more research on the role of onotologies for privacy control.

Much of the work on privacy-preserving data mining focuses on relational data. We need to carry out research on privacy-preserving semantic Web data mining. We need to combine techniques for privacy-preserving data mining with techniques for semantic Web data mining to obtain solutions for privacy-preserving semantic Web data mining.

25.5 Secure Web Services

Web services are services such as resource management services, directory services, publishing services, subscription services, and various other services that are provided on the Web. There has to be some way to describe the communication on the Web in a structured and organized way. WSDL (Web Services Description Language) does this by defining an XML grammar for describing network services. As described in [WWW], the network services are described as a collection of communication endpoints capable of exchanging messages. A WSDL document has various elements including the following: Types, which is a container for data type definition; Message, which is the data being communicated; Operation, which is an action supported by the service; Port Type, which is a subset of operations supported by the endpoints; Binding, which is a concrete protocol and data format specification for a particular port type; Port, which is an endpoint; and Service, which is a collection of endpoints.

So WSDL is a Web services description language but what are Web services? These are services provided by the Web to its users. These could be publishing services, data management services, information management services, directory services, and so on. That is, any service that the Web provides is a Web service and WSDL provides the means to specify the service. Web services is an area that will expand a great deal in the coming years. These services will form the essence of the semantic Web.

Now these Web services have to be secure. This would mean that we need to ensure that appropriate access-control methods are enforced. We also need to ensure that malicious processes do not subvert the Web services or cause a denial of service. There has been much work these past few years or so on secure Web services (see [BHAT04]). Intrusion-detection techniques are being examined to detect and prevent malicious intrusions. Extensions to WSDL for security have been proposed. Some details can be found in [WWW].

Figure 25.5 illustrates a layered architecture that includes a secure Web services layer for the semantic Web. Although we show a hierarchy in Figure 25.6, it does not mean that all the layers have to be present. For example, the secure Web services layer may have direct communication with the secure infrastructure services layer if there is no need for the services provided by the secure data management services layer. The application services layer provides application-specific services such as carrying out banking or filing income tax papers. We also need to ensure end-to-end security. That is, not only must each service be secure, we must also ensure secure interoperability. Figure 25.7 illustrates a secure publish and subscribe service that the Web provides. This is part of the Web services layer and takes advantage of the services provided by the data management layer for getting the necessary data. Standards efforts for Web services are already under way with W3C.

25.6 Secure Agents and Related Technologies

The foundation for the semantic Web is agent technology. We described agents briefly in Chapter 4. Agents are processes that carry out specific tasks. Agents for the semantic Web have been investigated extensively by the DAML (DARPA Agent Markup Language) Program at DARPA (Defense Advanced Research Projects Agency). The goal of this program is to develop a markup language for agents. The idea is for agents to understand the Web information and process the information.

Security for agents is essential if the semantic Web is to be secure. That is, agents that carry out security-critical functions have to be trusted.

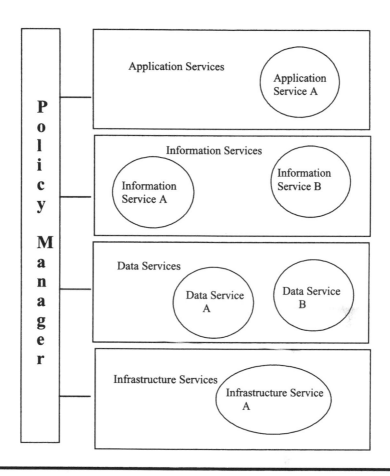

Figure 25.5 Layered architecture for secure Web services

Furthermore, agents have to communicate with each other through secure agent protocols. The main question is how many of the agents should be trusted. Because the Web has several million agents, it is impossible to trust all of them. How much of the work can be accomplished by using appropriate encryption and cryptographic techniques? For example, in [BERT04] we have shown that with appropriate encryption techniques we can ensure authenticity and completeness without having to trust the publishers when publishing XML documents. These publishers may be implemented as agents. There is also work on querying encrypted databases to ensure confidentiality (see [HACI02]). There is also a lot of work on mobile agent security. We need to examine all of this research and see how the results can be applied to secure agents for the semantic Web. Figure 25.7 illustrates secure agents for the semantic Web.

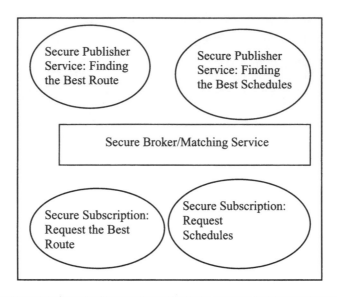

Figure 25.6   Example secure Web service

25.7 Secure Grid and Secure Semantic Grid

Sections 25.2 through 25.5 focused on the higher layers of the semantic Web, and Section 25.6 focused on the lower layers, including agents. Agents are an essential part of the semantic Web. Another concept that we believe is closely related to the semantic Web is the grid and the semantic grid. Grid computing has been around for a while, however, it is only recently that we are hearing a lot about this paradigm. Grid computing is about allocating resources in such a way that high-performance applications can be executed efficiently. We briefly discussed grid computing in Chapter 4. There is a lot of interest now on migrating from the grid to the semantic grid. The semantic grid is essentially the grid that uses ontology and intelligent information processes to reason about the resources and the allocation of the resources. One can think of the semantic grid as a layer above the grid performing intelligent functions.

If the applications are to be executed securely the grid has to be secure. This means that the nodes of the grid must have permission to execute various applications. Because applications are executed at different nodes, if there is some malicious code, then the system must ensure that the vulnerabilities are not propagated during application execution. Applications must also possess credentials to utilize various resources. There are many similarities between the grid and the Web. The semantic grid is similar to the semantic Web where knowledge and information

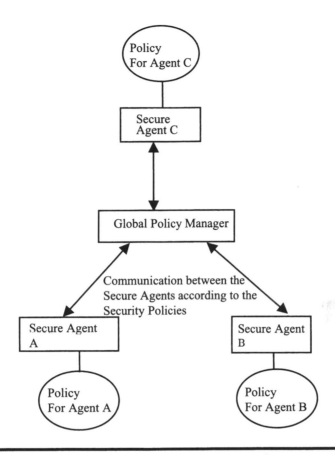

Figure 25.7   Secure agents

management play a role in allocating resources as well as in application execution. Security for the semantic grid is yet to be investigated. Closely related to the grid is what is known as the cyber infrastructure. Cyber-infrastructure essentially provides the data and computing resources for scientists and engineers to carry out tasks that are computationally inten-sive. Little work has been reported on security for the cyber infrastructure. Figure 25.8 illustrates our view of the secure grid and the secure semantic grid.

25.8 Security Impact on the Database as a Service Model

Recently Mehrotra et al. have developed an approach where the data management is provided as a service on the Web. The idea is for this

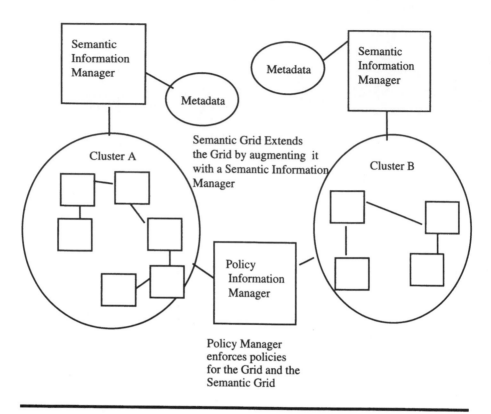

Figure 25.8   Secure grid and the semantic grid

service to eventually become part of Web services (see [HACI02] and [HACI04]). They argue due to activities such as outsourcing, an organization may have to send its data to a data provider to manage. Now, if the data provider is trusted, then there is no issue. However, in many cases the data provider is not trusted. Therefore, they have developed encryption techniques to securely query the data. Essentially the data is encrypted and the database is queried by extracting and querying the metadata. That is, extracting appropriate metadata becomes a challenge.

There have been arguments against such a model as opponents say they would not send their data to an untrusted third party. However, important data such as tax returns and other data are being sent to foreign countries for processing. These third parties are not necessarily trusted. Therefore, in the real world it is natural to have untrusted third parties. Furthermore, Bertino and others have developed techniques for publishing XML documents by untrusted third parties on the Web. Therefore, we need to integrate the techniques developed by Bertino together with those developed by Mehrotra et al. to maintain confidentiality, authenticity, and completeness of various documents. Figure 25.9 illustrates an example of

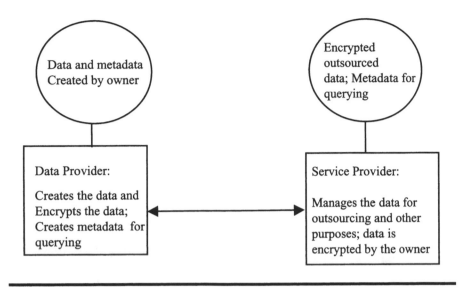

Figure 25.9 Secure database as a service model

a secure database as a service model. Mehrotra et al. believe that eventually this secure database will become part of Web services and semantic Web services.

25.9 Summary and Directions

This chapter has provided an overview of the semantic Web and discussed security standards. We first discussed security issues for the semantic Web. We argued that security must cut across all the layers. Furthermore, we need to integrate the information across the layers securely. Next we provided some more details on XML security, RDF security, secure information integration, and trust. If the semantic Web is to be secure we need all of its components to be secure. We also described some of our research on access control and dissemination of XML documents. Next we discussed privacy for the semantic Web. This was followed by a brief discussion of security for the grid and the semantic grid. Finally we provided a note on the secure database as a service model.

Much research needs to be done. We need to continue with the research on XML security. We must start examining security for RDF. This is more difficult as RDF incorporates semantics. We need to examine the work on security-constraint processing and context-dependent security constraints and see if we can apply some of the ideas for RDF security. Finally we need to examine the role of ontologies for secure information integration. We have to address some hard questions such as how do we integrate security policies on the semantic Web. How can we incorporate policies into ontologies? We also cannot forget about privacy and trust for the semantic Web. That is, we need to protect the privacy of individuals and at the same time ensure that the individuals have the information they need to carry out their functions. We also need to combine security research with privacy research. Finally we need to formalize the notions of trust and examine ways to negotiate trust on the semantic Web. We have a good start and are well on our way to building the semantic Web. We cannot forget about security and privacy. Security must be considered at the beginning and not as an afterthought.

Standards play an important role in the development of the semantic Web. The W3C has been very effective in specifying standards for XML, RDF, and the semantic Web. We need to continue with the developments and try as much as possible to transfer the research to the standards efforts. We also need to transfer the research and standards to commercial products. The next step for the semantic Web standards efforts is to examine security, privacy, quality of service, integrity, and other features such as multimedia processing and query services. As we have stressed, security and privacy are critical and must be investigated while the standards are being developed.

References

[AGRA00] Agrawal, R. and Srikant, R. Privacy-preserving data mining. In *Proceedings of the ACM SIGMOD Conference*, Dallas, TX, May 2000.

[ATKI03] Atkins, D. et al. Cyber infrastructure. NSF Report. Available at http://www.communitytechnology.org/nsf_ci_report/.

[BERT02] Bertino, E. et al. Access control for XML documents. *Data and Knowledge Engineering* 43: 3, 2002.

[BERT04] Bertino, E. et al. Secure third party publication of XML documents. *IEEE Transactions on Knowledge and Data Engineering*, 16, 2004.

[BHAT04] Batty R., Bertino, E., and Ghafoor, A. Trust-based context aware access control models in Web services. In *Proceedings of the Web Services Conference*, San Diego, July 2004.

[CARM04] Carminati, B. et al. Security for RDF. In *Proceedings of the DEXA Conference Workshop on Web Semantics*, Zaragoza, Spain, 2004.

[CLIF02] Clifton, C., Kantarcioglu, M., and Vaidya, J. Defining privacy for data mining. Technical Report, Purdue University, 2002.

[DENK03] Denker, G. et al. Security for DAML Web services: Annotation and matchmaking. In *Proceedings of the International Semantic Web Conference*, Sanibel Island, FL, 2003.

[EVFI02] Evfimievski, A., Srikant, R., Agrawal, R., and Gehrke, J. Privacy preserving mining of association rules. In *Proceedings of the Eighth ACM SIGKDD International Conference on Knowledge Discovery and Data Mining*, Edmonton, Alberta, July 2002.

[FARK03] Farkas, C. et al. Inference problem for the semantic Web. In *Proceedings of the IFIP Conference on Data and Applications Security*, Colorado, August 2003. Kluwer: Hingham, MA, 2004.

[GEHR02] Gehrke, J. Research problems in data stream processing and privacy-preserving data mining. In *Proceedings of the Next Generation Data Mining Workshop*, Baltimore, November 2002.

[HACI02] Hacigumus, H. et al. Providing database as a service. In *Proceedings of the IEEE Data Engineering Conference*, San Jose, CA, March 2002.

[HACI04] Hacigumus, H. and Mehrotra, S. Performance-conscious key management in encrypted databases. In *Proceedings of the IFIP Database Security Conference*, Sitges, Spain, Eds. C. Farkas and P. Samarati. Kluwer: Hingham, MA, July 2004.

[LEE01] Berners Lee, T. et al. The semantic Web. *Scientific American*, May 2001.

[RDF] RDF Primer. Available at http://www.w3.org/TR/rdf-primer/.

[ROUR04] Roure, D. et al. E-science. *IEEE Intelligent Systems*, 19: 1, 2004.

[SHET90] Sheth, A. and Larson, J. Federated database systems. *ACM Computing Surveys* 22: 3, 1990.

[THUR93] Thuraisingham, B. et al. Design and implementation of a database inference controller. *Data and Knowledge Engineering Journal* 11: 3, 1993.

[THUR94] Thuraisingham, B. Security issues for federated database systems. *Computers and Security* 13: 6, 1994.

[THUR97] Thuraisingham, B. *Data Management Systems Evolution and Interoperation*. CRC Press: Boca Raton, FL, 1997.

[THUR02a] Thuraisingham, B. Data and applications security: Developments and directions. In *Proceedings of IEEE COMPSAC*, Oxford, UK, 2002.

[THUR02b] Thuraisingham, B. *XML, Databases and the Semantic Web*. CRC Press: Boca Raton, FL, 2001.

[THUR03] Thuraisingham, B. Data mining, national security privacy, and civil liberties, *ACM SIGKDD,* 4: 2, 2003.

[THUR05a] Thuraisingham, B. Security standards for the semantic web. *Computer Standards and Interface Journal*, 27: 3, 2005.

[THUR05b] Thuraisingham, B. Privacy constraint processing in a privacy enhanced database system. *Data and Knowledge Engineering Journal*, 2005 (to appear).

[WWW] Available at www.w3c.org.

[XML1] Available at http://xml.apache.org/security/.

[XML2] Available at http://www.w3.org/Signature/.

[YU03] Yu, T. and Winslett, M. A unified scheme for resource protection in automated trust negotiation. In *Proceedings of the IEEE Symposium on Security and Privacy*, Oakland, CA, May 2003.

Exercises

1. Investigate security for XML and RDF.
2. How can security policies be expressed in XML and RDF?
3. Design algorithms for secure information interoperability.
4. Design a secure semantic Web.
5. Investigate privacy concerns for the semantic Web.
6. Discuss trust policies for the semantic Web.
7. Discuss security for the grid and for the semantic grid.

Chapter 26

Secure E-Commerce, Collaboration, and Knowledge Management

26.1 Overview

The previous chapters in Part IX discussed various secure Web data management technologies including secure Web databases, digital libraries, and information retrieval. We also provided an overview of security issues for the semantic Web. In particular, security for XML, RDF, and the semantic Web were discussed. In this chapter we continue with our discussion of security for various information management technologies. In Part I we provide an overview of information management including a discussion of collaboration, knowledge management, E-commerce, and other areas such as decision support, visualization, and multimedia information management. In previous chapters we examined security issues for some of the technologies including multimedia systems as well as some technologies that lie on the interface between data management and information management such as data warehousing and data mining.

In this chapter we examine security for some other key information management technologies such as collaboration, E-commerce, and knowledge management. Note that some information management technologies such as visualization have been used as tools to support security. Therefore, we do not discuss security for such technologies. Essentially all of the technologies we discussed in Part I are utilized throughout this book.

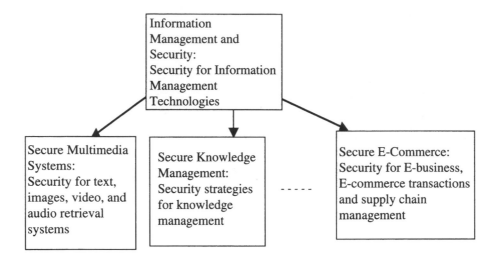

Figure 26.1 Information management and security

For example, security issues for dependable databases and sensor technologies are discussed in Part X. This chapter also includes discussions of trust and digital rights management as well as the newly emerging topic of security informatics. Note that security informatics means several things from information management for national security to information management for cyber-security.

The organization of this chapter is as follows. Secure E-commerce is discussed in Section 26.2. Secure collaboration is discussed in Section 26.3. Secure knowledge management is the subject of Section 26.4. Secure peer-to-peer data management is discussed in Section 26.5. Security for dynamic coalitions and virtual organizations is discussed in Section 26.6. Trust and rights management issues are discussed in Section 26.7. Section 26.8 is devoted to a discussion of security informatics. Finally, the chapter is summarized in Section 26.9. Figure 26.1 illustrates the relationship between information management and security. We can apply information management technologies such as data mining and visualization to security problems. On the other hand, we can incorporate security for various information management technologies such as collaboration, multimedia, and knowledge management.

26.2 Secure E-Commerce

In Chapter 3 we included a discussion of E-commerce concepts and technologies. In this section we examine the security impact. As stated earlier, E-commerce is about organizations carrying out business transactions such as sales of goods and business agreements as well as consumers purchasing items from merchants electronically. There have been numerous developments in E-commerce and some discussions on the initial progress were reported in [THUR00]. Due to the fact that E-commerce may involve millions of dollars in transactions between businesses or credit card purchases between consumers and businesses, it is important that the E-commerce systems be secure. Examples of such systems include E-payment systems and supply chain management systems.

There has been some work on secure E-commerce as well as secure supply chain management (see, for example, [GHOS98] and [ATTA03]). In the case of E-payment systems, the challenges include identification and authentication of consumers as well as businesses in addition to tracing the purchases made by consumers. For example, it would be entirely possible for someone to masquerade as a consumer, use the consumer's credit card, and make purchases electronically. Therefore, one solution proposed is for the consumer to have some credentials when he or she makes a purchase. These credentials, which may be random numbers, could vary with each purchase. This way the malicious process that masquerades as the consumer may not have the credentials and therefore may not be able to make the purchase. There will be a problem if the credentials are also stolen. Various encryption techniques are being proposed for secure E-commerce (see [HASS00]). That is, in addition to possessing credentials, the information may be encrypted, say, with the public key of the business and only the business could get the actual data. Similarly, the communication between the business and the consumer would also be encrypted. When transactions are carried out between businesses, the parties involved will have to possess certain credentials so that the transactions are carried out securely. Figure 26.2 illustrates aspects of secure E-commerce. Note that although much progress has been made on E-commerce transactions as well as secure E-commerce transactions, incorporating techniques for secure database transaction management with E-commerce is still not mature. Some work has been reported in [RAY00].

As we have stated, secure supply chain management is also a key aspect of secure E-commerce. Here the idea is for organizations to provide parts to other corporations for, say, manufacturing or other purposes. Suppose a hospital wants to order surgical equipment from a corporation; there must then be some negotiations and agreements between the hospital and the corporation. The corporation X may request some of its parts from another corporation Y and may not want to divulge the information that it is manufacturing the parts for Hospital A. Such sensitive information has to be protected. Supply chain management is useful in several areas in manufacturing for many domains including medical, defense, and

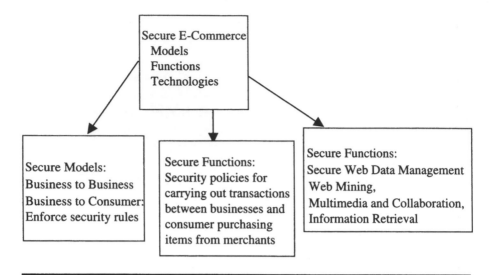

Figure 26.2   Aspects of secure E-commerce

intelligence. Some of the information exchanged between the organizations may be highly sensitive especially for military and intelligence applications. There needs to be a way to protect such sensitive information. Because the transactions are carried out on the Web, a combination of access-control rules and encryption techniques are being proposed as solutions for protecting sensitive information for supply chain management.

We have been hearing about E-commerce only since about the mid-1990s and this has been due to the explosion of the Web. Much progress has been made on developing information technologies such as databases, data mining, and multimedia information management for E-commerce, but there is still a lot to do on security. In addition, the information about various individuals will also have to be kept private. Many of the security technologies we have discussed in this book including secure Web data management and secure semantic Web will be applicable to secure E-commerce. For example, the semantic Web can be used as a vehicle to carry out E-commerce functions. By having machine-understandable Web pages, E-commerce can be automated without having a human in the loop. This means that it is critical that the semantic Web be secure. When we make progress for secure Web information management technologies, we can vastly improve the security of E-commerce transactions.

26.3   Secure Workflow and Collaboration

In Chapter 4 we provided an overview of collaborative information management and workflow technologies. Essentially this is about organizations or groups working together toward a common goal such as designing a system or solving a problem. Collaboration technologies are important for E-commerce as organizations carry out transactions with each other. Workflow is about a process that must be followed from start to finish in carrying out an operation such as making a purchase. The steps include initiating the agreement, transferring funds, and sending the goods to the consumer. Because collaboration and workflow are part of many operations such as E-commerce and knowledge management, we need secure workflow and secure collaboration. There has been a lot of work by Bertino et al. on this topic. Most notable among the developments is the BFA model (see [BERT99]) for secure workflow management systems. Some work on secure collaborative systems was initially proposed in [DEMU93]. Since then several ideas have been developed (see the *IFIP Conference Series on Database Security*). In this section we provide an overview of secure workflow and collaboration.

In the case of secure workflow management systems, the idea is for users to have the proper credentials to carry out the particular task. For example, in the case of making a purchase for a project, only a project leader can initiate the request. A secretary then types the request. Then the administrator has to use his or her credit card and make the purchase. The mailroom has the authority to make the delivery. Essentially what we have proposed is a role-based access-control model for secure workflow. There have been several developments on this topic (see *SACMAT Conference Proceedings*). Various technologies such as Petri nets have been investigated for secure workflow system (see [HUAN98]).

Closely related to secure workflow is secure collaboration. Collaboration is much broader than workflow. Workflow is about a series of operations that have to be executed serially or in parallel to carry out a task, and collaboration is about individuals working together to solve a problem. Object technologies in general and distributed object management technologies in particular are being used to develop collaboration systems. Here, the individual and the resources in the environment are modeled as objects. Communications between the individuals and resources are modeled as communication between the objects. This communication is carried out via object request brokers. Therefore, security issues discussed for object request brokers apply to secure collaboration. For example, should all parties involved be given the same access to the resources? If the access to resources is different then how can the individuals work together and share data? Figure 26.3 illustrates secure collaboration.

Trust and negotiation systems also play an important role in workflow and collaboration systems. For example, how can the parties trust each other in solving a problem? If A gives some information to B, can B share

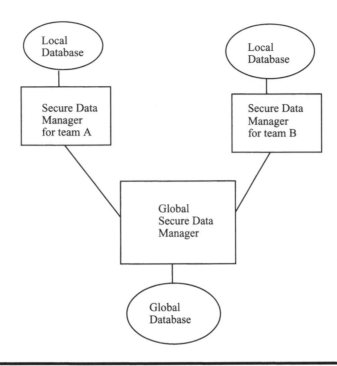

Figure 26.3 Secure data management for collaboration

the information with C even if A and C do not communicate with each other? Similar questions were asked when we discussed secure federations. Also secure data management technologies are necessary to manage the data for workflow and collaboration applications. Although much progress has been made, there is still a lot to do especially with the developments on the semantic Web and emerging technologies such as peer-to-peer data management.

26.4 Secure Knowledge Management

As mentioned in Chapter 4, knowledge management is about corporations sharing resources and expertise, as well as building intellectual capital so that they can increase their competitiveness. Knowledge management practices have been around for decades, but it is only with the advent of the Web that knowledge management has emerged as a technology area. Corporations with intranets promote knowledge management as the employees can learn about various advances in technology, get corporate information, and find the expertise in the corporation. Furthermore, when experts leave the corporation through retirement or otherwise, it is important to

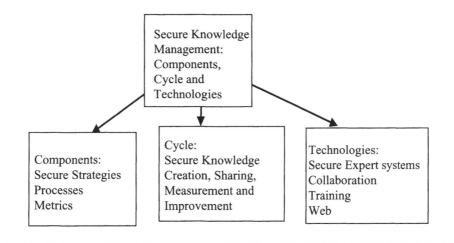

Figure 26.4   Secure knowledge management

capture their knowledge and their practices so that the corporation does not lose the valuable information acquired through many years of hard work.

One of the challenges in knowledge management is maintaining security. Now, knowledge management includes many technologies such as data mining, multimedia, collaboration, and the Web. Therefore, security for, say, Web data management, multimedia systems, and collaboration systems all contribute toward securing knowledge management practices. In addition, one needs to protect the corporation's assets such as its intellectual property. Trade secrets have to be kept highly confidential so that competitors do not have any access to them. This means one needs to enforce some form of access control such as role-based access control, credential mechanism, and encryption. Figure 26.4 illustrates the various information that must be protected to ensure secure knowledge management.

Secure knowledge management essentially extends the knowledge management categories discussed in Chapter 4 (see also [MORE01]). To have secure knowledge management, we need to have secure strategies, processes, and metrics. That is, metrics must include support for security-related information. Processes must include secure operations. Strategies must include security strategies. When knowledge is created, the creator may specify to whom the knowledge can be transferred. Additional access-control techniques may be enforced by the manager of the knowledge. Knowledge sharing and knowledge transfer operations must also enforce the access-control and security policies. A secure knowledge management architecture may be built around the corporation's intranet. This is an area that has received little attention. A workshop on secure knowledge management was held in Buffalo, New York in September 2004, and this workshop resulted in many challenging ideas and directions for secure knowledge management.

26.5 Secure Peer-to-Peer Data Management

In Chapter 17 we discussed federated data management where organizations work together and form federations. The idea is for an organization to work together with its peer organizations but at the same time have some degree of autonomy. Usually there is some manager who is in charge of the federation. However, in the case of a loose federation, the organizations manage themselves. More recently the idea of the federation has been extended to include peer-to-peer collaboration and computing. Here, the nodes work together and share data. The nodes are peers. If a node does not have the data to share with others, it will then request it from its peer. There is no notion of a node in charge or of a federation. However, many of the concepts discussed in federated data management are applicable in peer-to-peer data management. But there are also major differences. In the case of peer-to-peer data management, usually there is no notion of export schemas or global schemas. Each node manages it own data and schema and works with its peers in case it needs more resources. A node can join or leave the network when it wants to. Peer-to-peer data management also has similarities with cluster and grid data management. In summary, federated data management, peer-to-peer data management, grid data management, and collaborative data management have many similarities. They all deal with groups of nodes working together to solve a problem. A node may request from its peer data or resources to complete its task.

Many of the security concerns discussed for federated data management and grid data management apply to peer-to-peer data management. For example, when a node requests data from its peer access-control checks have to be made. The peer may negotiate with the node what data it can share and with whom when it sends data. The peer may be restricted in sending data and this restriction may be imposed by the peer who sent the data in the first place. The access-control rules may be propagated as nodes continue to share data. If peers are operating, say, at multiple security levels, then communication may have to take place through some trusted guard. When peers join and leave the network they may have to satisfy various authorization rules in addition to identification and authentication.

Security for peer-to-peer data management has received some attention recently. In addition to data sharing issues, we also need to examine the security impact on various data management functions such as query

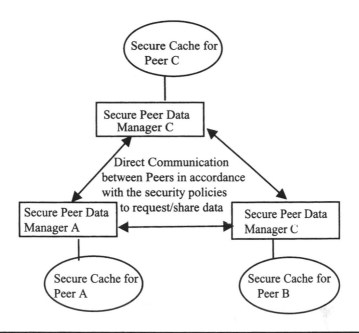

Figure 26.5 Secure peer-to-peer data management

processing, transaction management, and metadata management. For example, transactions may be executed among multiple peers and these transactions may have to satisfy integrity and security constraints. Furthermore, the query-optimization strategies may have to take into consideration the various access-control rules. In addition to security, privacy and trust issues also come into play. How much does a node trust its peer? How can trust be propagated among peers? How can privacy of a node be maintained? There are many challenging problems and we need to continue with research in this area. Figure 26.5 illustrates secure peer-to-peer data management.

26.6 Secure Dynamic Coalitions and Virtual Organizations

As stated in the previous section, federated data management, peer-to-peer data management, collaborative data management, and grid data management have many similarities. They all deal with the situation where multiple organizations or nodes work together to solve a problem. Another related concept is forming dynamic coalitions. The idea here is for organizations to form coalitions and work together and then disband after the problem is solved. That is, the coalition is dynamic in nature. The purpose of forming a coalition is perhaps to solve a short-term problem. A good example is supply chain management where organizations may have an agreement to work together and for one organization to supply the other with parts for assembling, say, a vehicle. After a while the automobile company may decide to get its supply from another organization. So it may disband the coalition with the first organization and form a coalition with another organization.

Security, privacy, and trust are important considerations for dynamic coalitions. When organizations form a coalition they must trust each other, as they may have to share some proprietary information. Then when the coalition disbands and different coalitions are formed, the organization must honor the rules and conditions agreed upon by the first coalition. The database systems managed by the organizations have to implement the rules and conditions of the coalition. There are also privacy concerns where the privacy of the individuals of the organizations may have to be maintained. Access control is also a major consideration. Do the organizations have access to the various resources they need to function in a coalition?

Closely related to dynamic coalitions is the notion of the virtual organization. Recently there has been some interest in data management for virtual organizations (DIVO) and the first workshop on this topic was held in Paris in June 2004. Some applications that need this type of technology were discussed. Two of the notable applications discussed were supply chain management and crisis management. The idea here is for organizations to come together to form coalitions, solve a problem such as crisis management, and emergency response. Security, trust, and privacy issues were also discussed at this workshop.

In summary, many new technologies have emerged since federated databases were discussed back in the late 1980s and early 1990s. Some of these technologies have emerged due to the Web and E-commerce. These include the semantic Web, peer-to-peer data management, grid data management, collaborative data management, virtual organizations, and dynamic coalitions. Security, privacy, and trust are critical for all of these technologies. We have discussed security and privacy issues throughout this book. In the next section we briefly discuss trust management and rights management.

26.7 Trust and Rights Management

Much of the discussion in this book has focused on security in general and confidentiality in particular. We have also discussed privacy and integrity. Another closely related feature is trust and rights management.

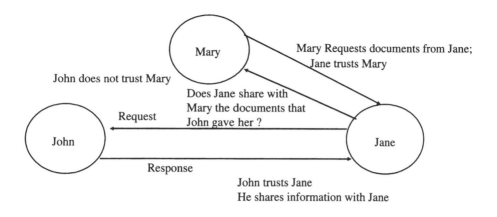

Figure 26.6   Trust negotiation

Trust management is all about managing the trust that one individual or group has for another. That is, even if a user has the access to the data, do I trust the user so that I can release the data? The user may have the clearance or possess the credentials, but he may not be trustworthy. Trust is formed by the user's behavior. The user may have betrayed one's confidence or carried out some act that is inappropriate in nature. Therefore, I may not trust that user. Now, even if I do not trust, say, John, Jane may trust John and she may share her data with John. That is, John may not be trustworthy to Jim, but he may be trustworthy to Jane.

The question is how do we implement trust. Can we trust someone partially? Can we trust, say, John 50 percent of the time and Jane 70 percent of the time? If we trust someone partially then can we share some of the information? How do we trust the data that we have received from, say, Bill? That is, if we do not trust Bill, then can we trust the data he gives us? There have been many efforts on trusted management systems as well as trust negotiation systems. Winslett et al. have carried out extensive work and developed specification languages for trust as well as designed trust negotiation systems (see [YU03]). The question is how do two parties negotiate trust. A may share data D with B if B shares data C with A. A may share data D with B only if B does not share this data with F. There are many such rules that one can enforce and the challenge is to develop a system that consistently enforces the trust rules or policies. Figure 26.6 illustrates trust management.

Closely related to trust management is managing digital rights. This whole area has come to be called DRM (Digital Rights Management). This is especially critical for entertainment applications. Who owns the copyright to a video or an audio recording? How can rights be propagated? What happens if the rights are violated? That is, can I distribute copyrighted films and music on the Web? We have heard a lot about the controversy surrounding Napster and similar organizations. Is DRM a technical issue or is it a legal issue? How can we bring technologists, lawyers, and policy makers together so that rights can be managed properly? There have been numerous articles, discussions, and debates about DRM. A useful source is [DRM].

Whether we are discussing security, integrity, privacy, trust, or rights management, there is always a cost involved. That is, at what cost do we enforce security, privacy, and trust? Is it feasible to implement the sophisticated privacy policies and trust management policies? In addition to bringing lawyers and policy makers together with the technologists, we also need to bring economists into the picture. We need to carry out economic trade-offs for enforcing security, privacy, trust, and rights management. Essentially what we need are flexible policies for security, privacy, trust, and rights management. For a discussion of the economic impact on security we refer the reader to [NSF03].

26.8 Security Informatics

Since information technology exploded in the 1990s, various types of informatics have emerged. These include medical informatics, which describes information management in medicine, engineering informatics, which describes information management for engineering, and scientific informatics, which describes information management for science. More recently we have heard of security informatics, which essentially describes information management for security. Note that security informatics is not about information management security. Information management security is about securing information management systems. Security informatics is about using information technologies for security applications. In previous chapters we gave some examples. For example, we discussed the application of data mining for national security and cyber-security. This is an aspect of security informatics. We discussed the use of ontologies for specifying security policies. This is also an aspect of security.

Information management for security applications includes federated data management for data sharing and privacy, which is needed for organizations to share information and, at the same time, maintain security and privacy. Another example is active data management where triggers and alerts are enforced when something unusual happens. Surveillance techniques are also examples of security informatics technologies. Recently there has been a series of workshops on security informatics organized by Chen et al. at the University of Arizona (see [CHEN03]). This effort

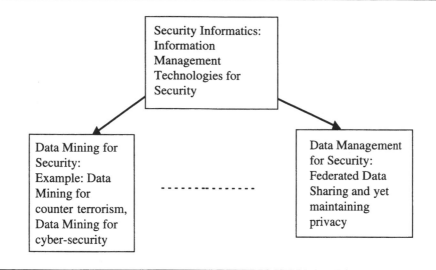

Figure 26.7 Aspects of security informatics

together with other homeland security conferences and workshops has resulted in many advances in security informatics. Figure 26.7 illustrates some aspects of security informatics.

26.9 Summary and Directions

In this chapter we have discussed security impact on various information management technologies including E-commerce, knowledge management, collaboration, and peer-to-peer computing. Essentially we extended the discussions in the previous two chapters where the focus was on secure Web databases and the secure semantic Web. Our focus is mainly on discretionary security for the emerging technologies. Although multi-level security is important and needed for military applications, we first need to understand what the discretionary security mechanisms are. Note that the terms "federated data management," "peer-to-peer computing," "semantic Web," and "dynamic coalitions" have been used to mean the same thing in many situations. We have tried to explain the differences and looked at security for each technology separately.

Much progress has been made, but many of these security mechanisms for emerging information management technologies are still in the early stages. For example, although security has been examined for E-commerce and collaboration, there is still a lot to do in secure knowledge management and secure peer-to-peer data management. We have provided some initial directions.

References

[ATTA03] Atallah, M. et al. Secure supply-chain protocols. In *Proceedings of the International Conference on Electronic Commerce*, Newport Beach, CA, 2003.

[BERT99] Bertino, E. et al. The specification and enforcement of authorization constraints in workflow management systems. *ACM Transactions on Information and Systems Security* 2: 1, 1999.

[CHEN03] *Proceedings of the First Security Informatics Symposium*, Tucson, AZ, Ed. H. Chen, June 2003.

[DEMU93] Demurjian, S. et al. Security for collaborative computer systems. *Multimedia Review: The Journal of Multimedia Computing* (Summer), 1993.

[DRM] Digital rights management architectures. Available at http://www.dlib.org/dlib/june01/iannella/06iannella.html.

[GHOS98] Ghosh, A. *E-commerce Security, Weak Links and Strong Defenses*. Wiley: New York, 1998.

[HASS00] Hassler, V. *Security Fundamentals for E-Commerce*. Artech: London, UK, 2000.

[HUAN98] Huang, W. and Atluri, V. Analyzing the safety of workflow authorization models. In *Proceedings of the IFIP Database Security Conference*, Chalidiki, Greece, July 1998. Kluwer: Hingham, MA, 1999.

[MORE98] Morey, D. Knowledge management architecture. In *Handbook of Data Management*, Ed. B. Thuraisingham, Auerbach: New York, 1998.

[MORE01] Morey, D., Maybury, M., and Thuraisingham, B. (Eds.) *Knowledge Management*. MIT Press: Cambridge, MA, 2001.

[NSF03] *Proceedings of the NSF Cyber Trust PI Meeting*, Baltimore, August 2003.

[RAY00] Ray, I. et al. A fair-exchange E-commerce protocol with automated dispute resolution. In *Proceedings of the IFIP Database Security Conference*, Amsterdam, The Netherlands, August 2000.

[THUR00] Thuraisingham, B. *Web Data Management and Electronic Commerce*. CRC Press: Boca Raton, FL, 2000.

[YU03] Yu, T. and Winslett, M. A unified scheme for resource protection in automated trust negotiation. In *Proceedings of the IEEE Symposium on Security and Privacy*, Oakland, CA, May 2003.

Exercises

1. Investigate security impact on E-commerce applications and supply chain management.
2. Develop a model for secure workflow management systems.
3. Investigate security for knowledge management systems.
4. Conduct surveys of trust and rights management technologies.

Conclusion to Part IX

Part IX has described security for Web data and information management technologies. In Chapter 24 we discussed security for Web databases and digital libraries. We discussed threats to Web databases and provided security solutions. In Chapter 25 we discussed security for the semantic Web. We discussed XML and RDF security as well as addressed privacy for the semantic Web. In Chapter 26 we discussed security for various information management technologies. In particular, security for E-commerce, collaboration, and knowledge management applications were discussed.

There is still a lot of work to be done in secure information management. Many information management technologies are still in development. These include peer-to-peer data management and knowledge management. Security has to be investigated at the beginning and not as an afterthought. Next we discuss some critical secure data management technologies including secure dependable data management as well as secure sensor data management.

EMERGING SECURE DATA MANAGEMENT TECHNOLOGIES AND APPLICATIONS

X

In Part I we discussed supporting technologies for database and applications security and in Part II we discussed discretionary security for database systems. We introduced mandatory security in Part III and in Part IV we discussed MLS/DBMSs based on the relational data model. In Part V we discussed the inference problem. In Parts VI and VII we discussed discretionary and multilevel security for object database systems as well as for distributed and heterogeneous database systems. Essentially Parts II through VII discussed database security work that was carried out until around the mid-1990s. In Part VIII we discussed security for some of the emerging technologies such as data warehousing and in Part IX we discussed security for Web data and information management technologies. Part X discusses security for some of the emerging technologies and applications.

Part X consists of three chapters. In Chapter 27 we discuss secure dependable data management. In particular we discuss developing flexible policies for dependable computing which include security, integrity, fault-tolerant computing, privacy, data quality, and real-time processing. Dependable computing has also been referred to as trustworthy computing. Chapter 28 discusses security for sensor data management as well as for wireless data management. We discuss policies and functions for secure sensor data management systems. We also address privacy concerns. Finally in Chapter 29 we briefly discuss several topics relating to secure applications including digital identity, identity theft, digital forensics, and biometrics.

Chapter 27

Secure Dependable Data Management

27.1 Overview

For many applications including command and control, intelligence, and process control, data is emanating from sensors. Timing constraints may be associated with data processing. That is, the data may have to be updated within a certain time or it may be invalid. There are trade-offs between security and real-time processing. That is, it takes time to process the access-control rules and as a result, the system may miss the deadlines. Therefore, we need flexible security policies. In certain cases real-time processing may be critical. For example, if we are to detect anomalies from the time a person checks in at the ticket counter until he boards the airplane, then this anomaly has to be detected within a certain timeframe. In this case we may have to sacrifice some degree of security. In other cases, we may have a lot of time to, say, analyze the data and in this case only authorized individuals may access the data.

Other issues include integrating fault tolerance, real-time processing, data quality, and security to design dependable and survivable systems. Much work has been carried out on fault-tolerant data management. We need to examine the fault-tolerant data processing techniques for new-generation applications such as sensor information management and mobile computing. Furthermore, the databases have to survive failures as well as malicious attacks (see [SON95]). Much of our critical infrastructure such as our telephones, power lines, and other systems have embedded sensors. The data emanating from these sensors may be corrupted maliciously or otherwise. For example, how can we ensure that the aggregate data is valid even if the components that constitute the aggregate data may be corrupted? Some directions are given in [CHAN03].

This chapter is devoted to a discussion of secure dependable data management with some emphasis on sensor applications. More details on security for sensor databases are discussed in Chapter 28. The organization of this chapter is as follows. In Section 27.2 we discuss various aspects of dependable systems. Dependable infrastructure and data managers are discussed in Section 27.3. Data quality issues are discussed in Section 27.4. Critical infrastructure protection is discussed in Section 27.5. The chapter is concluded in Section 27.6.

27.2 Dependable Systems

For a system to be dependable it must be secure, fault tolerant, meet timing deadlines, and manage high-quality data. However, integrating these features into a system means that the system has to meet conflicting requirements. For example, if the system makes all the access-control checks, then it may miss some of its deadlines. The challenge in designing dependable systems is to design systems that are flexible. For example, in some situations it may be important to meet all the timing constraints whereas in other situations it may be critical to satisfy all the security constraints.

Dependable systems have sometimes been referred to as trustworthy systems. For example, in some papers dependability includes mainly fault-tolerant systems and when one integrates fault tolerance with security then one gets trustworthy systems. Regardless of what the definitions are, for systems to be deployed in operational environments especially for command and control and other critical applications, we need end-to-end dependability as well as security. For some applications not only do we need security and confidentiality we also need to ensure that the privacy of the individuals is maintained. Therefore, privacy is also another feature of dependability. Figure 27.1 illustrates our view of dependability.

For a system to be dependable we need end-to-end dependability. Note that the components that comprise a system include the network, operating systems, middleware, infrastructure, data manager, and applications. We need all of the components to be dependable. We also need the interfaces to meet all the constraints. Figure 27.2 illustrates end-to-end dependability. In the remaining sections we discuss various aspects of dependability including dependable infrastructure and data managers. Note that a discussion of dependable networks and operating systems are beyond the scope of this chapter.

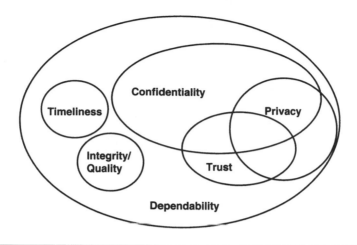

Figure 27.1   Dependable systems

27.3   Dependable Infrastructure and Data Management

27.3.1   Overview

As we have stated in Section 27.2, major components of dependable systems include dependable networks, dependable middleware including infrastructure, dependable operating systems, dependable data managers, and dependable applications. That is, we need end-to-end dependability. By dependability we mean security, integrity, fault tolerance, data quality, privacy, and real-time processing.

In this section we focus on building dependable infrastructure and data managers. We also examine security issues for dependable systems. The organization of this section is as follows. In Section 27.3.2 we discuss dependable infrastructure. Dependable data managers are discussed in Section 27.3.3. Security issues are discussed in Section 27.3.4. Note that we use sensor systems as an example to illustrate dependability features. More details on secure sensor information management are discussed in Chapter 28.

27.3.2   Dependable Infrastructure

One possibility for developing dependable infrastructure and data managers is to follow the approach we have developed for real-time command and control systems such as AWACS (Advanced Warning and Control

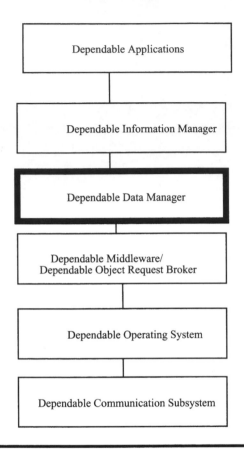

Figure 27.2   End-to-end dependability

System). Here we developed an infrastructure consisting of a real-time object request broker and services using commercial real-time operating systems. We then developed a real-time data manager and applications hosted on the infrastructure. We used object technology for integrating the various components. We also showed how such an infrastructure could be used to migrate legacy applications (see [BENS96] and [GATE97]).

We can take a similar approach to build an integrated system for dependable systems. We need appropriate operating systems and infrastructure possibly based on object request brokers. We need to host sensor data managers and applications such as multisensor data integration and fusion on the infrastructure. We need to ensure that the system is secure and survivable. We also need to ensure that the infrastructure is secure. That is, security has to be built into the system and not considered as an afterthought. Essentially we are proposing a layered architecture for sensor information management. The infrastructure consists of middleware possibly based on object request brokers for sensors. The objects that constitute the middleware include objects for interprocess communication, memory management, and support for data fusion and aggregation. On top of the infrastructure we host a sensor data manager (discussed in the next section). The data manager essentially manages sensor data, which may be in the form of streams. We also need to examine both centralized and distributed architectures for sensor data management. On the one hand we can aggregate the data and send it to a centralized data management system or we can develop a full-fledged distributed data management system. We need to conduct simulation studies and determine trade-offs between various architectures and infrastructure.

As part of our work on evolvable real-time command and control systems we examined real-time processing for object request brokers and we were instrumental in establishing a special interest group, which later became a task force within the Object Management Group (OMG). Subsequently commercial real-time object request brokers were developed. The question is, do we need special-purpose object request brokers for sensor networks. Our challenge now is to develop object request brokers for sensor networks. We need to examine special features for object request brokers for managing sensor data. We may need to start a working group or a special interest group within OMG to investigate these issues and subsequently specify standards for object request brokers for dependable data management.

Another important aspect is end-to-end dependability. This includes security, real-time processing, and fault tolerance for not only all of the components such as infrastructure, data managers, networks, applications, and operating systems, we also need to ensure the dependability of the composition of the entire system. This will be a major challenge even if we consider security, real-time processing, and fault-tolerant computing individually. Integrating all of them will be a complex task and will have to address many research issues and challenges. Figure 27.3 illustrates the components of the infrastructure for dependable systems.

27.3.3 Dependable Data Managers

Various research efforts are under way to develop dependable data management systems for a variety of applications including sensor applications. These include the efforts described in [STAN03], [DOBR02], [BROO96], and [CARN03] (see, for example, the work at Stanford University, Cornell University, MIT, the University of California at Berkeley, Brown University, and Brandeis University). Note that although dependable data management is needed for many applications, we use sensor applications as an example

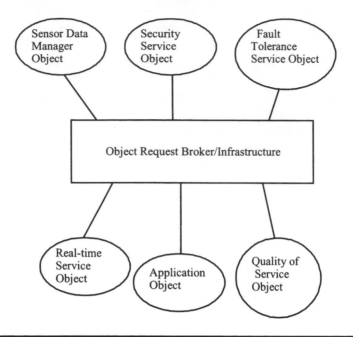

Figure 27.3 Components of the infrastructure

to illustrate the concepts. More details on secure sensor data management can be found in Chapter 28.

Sensor data may be in the form of streams. Special data management systems are needed to process stream data. For example, much of the data may be transient data. Therefore, the system has to rapidly analyze the data, discard data that is not needed, and store the necessary data. Special query-processing strategies including query-optimization techniques are needed for stream data management. Many of the queries on stream data are continuous queries. We need special query strategies for processing such continuous queries. Researchers are also examining special data models as well as extensions to the relational data model for stream data management. Query languages such as SQL (Structured Query Language) are being extended with constructs for querying stream data. Research efforts are also under way for extending XML (eXtensible Markup Language) with constructs for sensor data management. We also need to determine the types of metadata to collect as well as develop techniques to store and manage the metadata.

Although many of the efforts extend or enhance current data management systems to process sensor data, the main question is do we need a radically different kind of data model and data management system for such applications. Research is also needed on developing access methods and index strategies for stream/sensor data management systems. One also needs to examine the notion of a transaction and determine the type of transaction model suitable for stream databases. Finally we need to examine techniques for managing main-memory databases and real-time databases and see whether they are applicable to stream data management. There has been much progress during the last few years, but much research still remains to be done.

Sensors are often distributed and in many cases embedded in several devices. We need distributed data processing capabilities for managing the distributed sensors. Data, possibly in the form of streams, may be emanating from multiple sensors. Each sensor may have its own data management system and the various data management systems may be connected. The distributed data management system may process the sensor data emanating from the sensors. In some cases the data may be aggregated and sent to a central data management system. We need trade-off studies between developing distributed sensor data management systems and aggregating the data and managing at a central location.

Aggregating the sensor data and making sense out of the data is a major research challenge. The data may be incomplete or sometimes inaccurate. We need the capability to deal with uncertainty and reason with incomplete data. We also need to examine various distributed data management strategies including distributed query processing and managing metadata in a distributed environment. For example, we need to develop distributed query-optimization strategies as well as techniques for data aggregation. Each sensor may have limited memory. Therefore, we need to examine techniques for managing distributed main-memory sensor databases as well as examine distributed real-time data management and scheduling techniques for sensor data management.

Information management includes extracting information and knowledge from data as well as managing data warehouses, mining the data, and visualizing the data. Much work has been carried out on information management for the last several years. We now need to examine the applicability of various information management technologies for managing sensor/stream data.

For example, sensor data has to be visualized so that one can better understand the data. We need to develop visualization tools for the sensor data. One may also need to aggregate the sensor data and possibly build repositories and warehouses. However, much of the sensor data may be transient, and therefore we need to determine which data to store and which data to discard. Data may also have to be processed in real-time. Some of the data may be stored and possibly warehoused and analyzed for conducting analysis and predicting trends. That is, the sensor data emanating from surveillance cameras has to be processed within a certain time. The data may also be warehoused so that one can later analyze the data.

Sensor data mining is becoming an important area (see [KANN02]). We need to examine the data-mining techniques such as association-rule mining, clustering, and link analysis for sensor data. As we have stressed, we need to manage sensor data in real-time. Therefore, we may need to mine the data in real-time also. This means not only building models ahead of time so that we can analyze the data in real-time, we may also need to build models in real-time. That is, the models have to be flexible and dynamic. This is a major challenge. We also need many training examples to build models. For example, we need to mine the data emanating from sensors and detect and possibly prevent terrorist attacks. This means that we need training examples to train the neural networks, classifiers, and other tools so that they can recognize in real-time when a potential anomaly occurs. Sensor data mining is a fairly new research area and we need a research program for sensor data management and data mining.

A good starting point for designing a dependable data manager in our approach to building a real-time data manager for the command and control systems is to host it as an application object on top of the infrastructure, which is essentially an object request broker (see [BENS96]). The data manager is also based on an object model tailored for real-time applications. The data manager manages the track information. We also developed special concurrency-control algorithms for real-time data processing. These algorithms integrate the priority ceiling algorithms with semantic concurrency-control algorithms (see [DIPP01]). We need to examine this research and see if we can take a similar approach for a sensor network. Essentially, can we develop an object model for sensor information management? How do we host such a data manager on top of the infrastructure developed for sensor networks? Furthermore, how do we ensure security and dependability? As we have stated, integrating security, fault-tolerant computing, and real-time processing is a major challenge. In the next section we examine some security issues for dependable information management. Figure 27.4 illustrates the components of a dependable data manager.

27.3.4 Security Issues

As we have stated in previous sections, we need dependable infrastructure and data managers that are flexible, secure, fault tolerant, and can process data in real-time. That is, we need flexible policies that can adapt to the environment. In this section we discuss some aspects of security.

Much work has been carried out on securing data management systems (see [FERR00]). The early work was on access control and later researchers

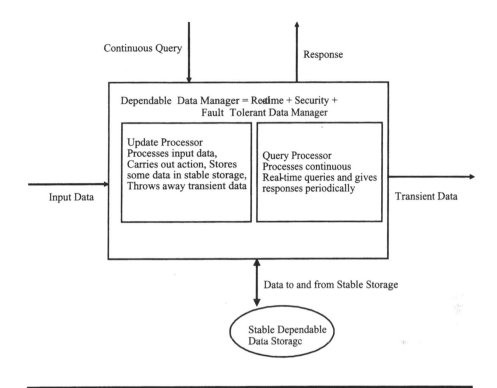

Figure 27.4   Components of the dependable data manager

focused on multilevel secure database management systems. More recently research is focusing on role-based access-control models as well as examining security for new kinds of databases as well as applications such as E-commerce and medical information systems (see, for example, [THUR02]).

We need to conduct research on security for dependable data management. For example, can we apply various access-control techniques for sensor and stream databases? That is, can we give access to the data depending on the roles of the users such as the airport security officer has access to all of the sensor data emanating from the sensors and the airport ticketing agent may have limited access to certain sensor data. Another challenge is granting access to aggregated data. Individual data may be unclassified and the aggregated data may be highly sensitive. This is in a way a form of the inference problem in database systems. Note that inference is the process of posing queries and obtaining unauthorized information from the legitimate responses received. Due to the aggregation and fusion of sensor data, the security levels of the aggregated data may be higher than those of the individual data sets. We also need to be aware of the privacy of the individuals. Much of the sensor data may be about individuals such as video streams about activities and other personal information. This data has to be protected from the general public and from those who are unauthorized to access the data. We have looked at privacy as a subset of security (see, for example, [THUR03a]). There is also research on privacy-preserving data mining and the techniques have to be examined for sensor data mining [GEHR03].

Finally we need to examine security policies for sensor data. These security policies may be dynamic and therefore we need to develop ways to enforce security constraints that vary with time. We also need techniques for integrating security policies especially in a networked and distributed environment. For example, different policies may apply to different sensor databases. These policies have to be integrated when managing distributed databases. One of the major questions here is what are the special considerations for security for sensor and stream data. Do the access-control models that have been developed for business data-processing applications work for stream data? We need to start a research program on secure sensor networks and secure sensor information management. Some preliminary directions are given in [THUR04a] and [THUR04b].

As we have stated in previous sections, we need end-to-end security. That is, the infrastructure, data managers, applications, networks, and operating systems have to be secure. OMG has developed standards for securing object request brokers. We need to take advantage of such developments. However, we need to examine security issues specific to object request brokers for sensor information management. We also need to examine composability of the various secure components. For example, are the interfaces between the various components satisfying the security properties? How can we integrate or compose the security policies of the various components? There has been little work reported on securing large-scale information systems. Now we not only have to examine security for such systems, we also need to examine security for such systems that manage and process sensor data. In addition, we need not only secure systems but also systems that are dependable and survivable. As stated earlier, developing such systems will be a major challenge.

One approach is to develop various features incrementally for data managers and middleware. However, this often means that at the end some features are left out. For example, if we build components and examine only security and later on examine real-time processing, then it may be difficult to incorporate real-time processing into the policy. This means that we need to examine all of the features simultaneously. This means security engineering has to be integrated with software engineering. Aspects of secure dependable systems are illustrated in Figure 27.5.

Aspects of Secure Dependable Systems:

Flexible policies enforcing security,
real-time processing, fault tolerance,
integrity, etc.

In time-critical situations, realtime
processing may have higher priority than security

In other situations, the system may need 100 percent security

Security is considered to be part of dependability

Figure 27.5   Secure dependable systems

27.4   Data Quality

27.4.1   Overview

There has been much research and development on data quality for the past two decades or so. Data quality is about understanding whether data is good enough for a given use. Quality parameters will include the accuracy of the data, the timelines of the data, and the precision of the data. Data quality has received increased attention after the revolution of the Web and E-commerce. This is because organizations now have to share data coming from all kinds of sources, and intended for various uses, and, therefore, it is critical that organizations have some idea as to the quality of the data. Furthermore, heterogeneous databases have to be integrated within and across organizations. This also makes data quality more important. Another reason for the increased interest in data quality is warehousing. Data warehouses are being developed by many organizations and data is brought into the warehouse from multiple sources. The sources are often inconsistent, so the data in the warehouse could appear to be useless to users.

In addition to security, integrity, fault tolerance, and real-time processing, data quality is also an important attribute for dependable systems. In this section we focus on various data quality issues for dependable systems. The organization of this section is as follows. In Section 27.4.2 we discuss some of the developments in data quality. Section 27.4.3 discusses some of the research on using annotations for data quality. We discuss some of the emerging directions in data quality in Section 27.4.4. In particular, data quality for the semantic Web is discussed. Data quality and data mining are the subjects of Section 27.4.5. Security, integrity, and data quality are discussed in Section 27.4.6.

27.4.2 Developments in Data Quality

There has been a lot of work in data quality for the last several years. Notable among the efforts is the work carried out at the Sloan School of the Massachusetts Institute of Technology (MIT) [DQ]. Some of the early work focused on incorporating data quality primitives for data models such as the entity-relationship model. Data quality primitives include information such as the timeliness of the data, the accuracy of the data, and precision of the data.

As mentioned earlier, much interest in data quality is as a result of the Web. There is now so much data on the Web that we need some measure as to the accuracy of the data. The accuracy depends on the source of the data. Furthermore, data gets propagated from one source to another and as a result the quality could very well deteriorate. Therefore, we need some way to determine the quality as data is passed from one to another.

Data quality is also an important factor when integrating heterogeneous data sources. An organization often cannot be responsible for the quality of the data belonging to another organization. Therefore, when organizations share they need to have some idea of the quality of the data.

High-quality data is critical for E-commerce transactions. These transactions may involve millions of dollars if much of the data is of poor quality; the consequences may be disastrous. Many of the businesses that have studied data quality have found that quality problems can lead directly to significant loss of revenue.

There are sites for data quality-related information (see, e.g., [DQ]). These sites have information about data quality journals and products including data cleansing tools, as well as information about the various organizations that do data quality work. These organizations include government organizations as well as commercial organizations around the world. In addition, MIT also now has a series of workshops on information quality. Figure 27.6 illustrates aspects of data quality.

27.4.3 Annotations for Data Quality

Hughes et al. (see [HUGH01]) have conducted research on using annotations for data quality. This effort spent about two years learning about

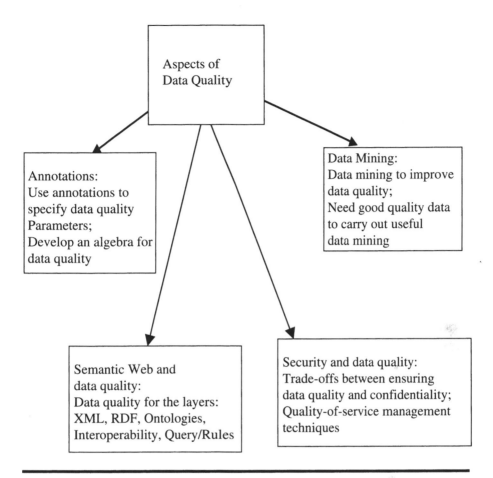

Figure 27.6   Aspects of data quality

the data quality problems and the efforts of a set of government organizations that share military intelligence information. These organizations share a database system, and connect it to many other databases and tools in a complex system of systems.

The investigators state that data quality is a significant problem, and one of the main barriers to addressing it is the need to include both technical changes to systems and managerial changes to the processes used in the organization. Many of the data quality annotations (precision, timeliness, accuracy, etc.) that have been defined for business information systems are equally relevant to government and military systems (see [HUGH01]).

The project also identified a need for data quality annotations, that is, metadata that describes the quality of individual data records, rather than only using aggregate metrics (as is the focus of several prior efforts). For example, many organizations have devised ways of estimating the average accuracy of their data sets, improving that accuracy, and benefiting from the improvement. It was felt that in addition to such aggregate measures, one also needed to understand the quality of individual data records.

One case where these per item quality annotations are important is when quality varies significantly from one record to the next. In this case, if users cannot understand the quality of presented data, they may not differentiate the good from the bad. If the data is used to make decisions (as is usually the case), then either bad data can lead to bad decisions, or data of uncertain quality can lead to less well-informed decisions. As a result, users may not trust the system as a whole, even though it contains valuable data. A methodology for adding such annotations to a system was defined, and this methodology is used to improve data quality.

27.4.4 Semantic Web and Data Quality

In the previous sections we provided an overview of the developments in data quality as well as one approach to manage data quality. In this section we discuss data quality for the semantic Web.

As stated in previous chapters, the semantic Web is essentially about machine understandable Web pages. In the article on the semantic Web by Berners Lee et al. [LEE01]), the semantic Web is described as a Web that can understand and interpret Web pages and manage activities for people. These activities could be maintaining appointments, giving advice, and essentially making human life as easy as possible.

If the semantic Web is to be effective, then we need to ensure that the data and information on the Web are timely, accurate, and precise. Note that with bad data one cannot make good decisions. Therefore, the techniques being used to understand data need to be widened to understand data quality. These technologies include XML, RDF (Resource Description Framework), and agents. There is little work reported on data quality for the semantic Web. In fact, data quality is an essential ingredient in understanding the semantics of data, and the semantic Web approaches should take advantage of the work that has been done to define data quality annotations.

27.4.5 Data Mining and Data Quality

In Chapter 21 we discussed data quality for data warehousing. As we have stated, having good data is essential for making effective decisions. Data mining is about posing queries and extracting information previously unknown from large quantities of data using pattern matching and statistical reasoning (see [THUR98]). One of the challenges in data mining is to get the data ready for mining. One has to determine where the data is, assemble the data, and clean the data. This would also include removing redundant data as well as inconsistent data. Data also has to be complete. Various tools are being developed to ensure that the data is ready for mining. However, much remains to be done.

Another relationship between data mining and data quality is to use data mining to improve the quality of the data. That is, although data quality is important for mining, we could use mining to improve the quality of the data. Data-mining techniques could be used to determine the bad data as well as data that is incomplete. That is, in the same way we use mining to detect unusual occurrences and patterns, our patterns here are bad data. We need to define what bad data means and perhaps train tools such as neural networks to detect bad data. This is an area that is getting much attention recently.

27.4.6 Security and Data Quality

There have been many discussions on the trade-offs between security and integrity. For example, if we are to enforce various access-control rules, then the transactions may miss the timing constraints due to the time it takes to make all the checks. As a result, the data may not be current. As a result, the quality of the data may be compromised. Another issue is that to enforce high levels of security, one may need to give out cover stories. This will also compromise data quality, as the data given out may not be accurate. In other words, there are trade-offs between security and data quality.

There have been various studies carried out between security and integrity as well as between security and real-time processing. We need all aspects. That is, security, integrity, and real-time processing, as well as data quality, are all important. The question is how can all of them be enforced in a system. This is where quality of service comes in. We need to develop flexible policies that can deal with security, integrity, real-time processing, and data quality essentially on a case-by-case basis. There will be cases where security will be absolutely critical and there will be cases where we cannot live with bad data. Some issues were discussed in [THUR99].

27.5 Critical Infrastructure Protection

Closely related to secure dependable data management is critical infrastructure protection. This includes protecting infrastructure such as a

Critical Infrastructure Protection:

Protecting the critical infrastructure against natural
disasters and malicious attacks

Infrastructures:
Power lines, Telephone lines, Gas lines, Food crops
and supplies, Water reservoirs, Buildings, - - - -

Figure 27.7 Critical infrastructure protection

power grid and telecommunication lines. Attacks on critical infrastructure
could cripple a nation and its economy. Infrastructure attacks include
attacking the telecommunication lines; the electronic, power, gas, reservoirs and water supplies; food supplies; and other basic entities that are
critical for the operation of a nation.

An adversary could corrupt the software that runs the telecommunications industry and close down all the telecommunications lines. Similarly
software that runs the power and gas supplies could be attacked. Attacks
could also occur through bombs and explosives. That is, the telecommunication lines could be attacked through bombs. Attacks on transportation
lines such as highways and railway tracks are also attacks on infrastructure.

Infrastructure could also be attacked by natural disasters such as
hurricanes and earthquakes. It could also be attacked through malicious
code. The challenges include determining the attack and recovering from
the attack in timely manner. Essentially what we need are dependable
data and information management. Data-mining and related data management technologies have also been examined to detect and prevent such
infrastructure attacks (see [THUR03b]). Simulation studies have also been
conducted to study the types of attacks and how a system could recover
from the attacks. Figure 27.7 illustrates critical infrastructure protection.
Note that we discussed this topic in Chapter 22. We discuss it again in
this chapter for completeness.

27.6 Summary and Directions

This chapter has provided an overview of secure dependable systems.
We started with a discussion of dependable infrastructure and data managers. We used sensor information management as an application. Because

this application requires many features such as real-time processing, security, and integrity, we also discussed developments and directions for data quality. We discussed the need for data quality and then showed an approach to manage data quality. This approach is to use annotations. That is, quality information is defined and treated as part of the data. Next we discussed some of the emerging trends such as data quality for the semantic Web and the relationship between data mining and data quality. We also briefly discussed critical infrastructure protection.

Because of the developments of the Web, the importance of technologies such as data warehousing and data mining, and emerging applications such as sensors and wireless information systems, the need to have good data cannot be overemphasized for dependable systems. Furthermore, we need to build systems that integrate security, integrity, fault tolerance, and real-time processing. Although there is some progress in the area of dependable computing, much remains to be done. We have discussed some initial directions. Secure dependable computing is now an active research area and a new journal has been established by the IEEE Computer Society called *IEEE Transactions on Dependable and Secure Computing*. We can expect to see much progress in this challenging area. We cannot stress the importance of designing flexible systems for ensuring security, integrity, real-time processing, privacy, data quality, and fault tolerance as needed.

Note that we have used sensor information management to illustrate the needs of dependable computing. There are many other challenging issues that need to be addressed for secure sensor data management. We discuss secure sensor data management including a discussion of secure wireless/mobile data management in the next chapter.

References

[BENS96] Bensley, E. et al. Object-oriented approach to developing real-time infrastructure and data manager. In *Proceedings of the IEEE Workshop on Object-Oriented Real-time Systems*, Laguna Beach, CA, February 1996.

[BROO96] Brooks, R. and Iyengar, S.S. Robust distributed computing and sensing algorithm. *IEEE Computer* 29: 6, 1996.

[CARN03] Carney, D. et al. Operator scheduling in a data stream manager. In *Proceedings of the 29th International Conference on Very Large Data Bases*, Berlin, Germany, 2003.

[CHAN03] Chan, H. and Perrig, A. Security and privacy in sensor networks. *IEEE Computer* 36: 10, 2003.

[DIPP01] DiPippo, L. et al. Scheduling and priority mapping for static real-time middleware. *Real-time Systems Journal* 20: 2, 2001.

[DOBR02] Dobra, A. et al. Processing complex aggregate queries over data streams. In *Proceedings of the 2002 ACM Sigmod International Conference on Management of Data*, Madison, WI, 2002.

[DQ] MIT Total Data Quality Management Pr ogram. Available at http://web.mit.edu/tdqm/www/index.shtml.

[FERR00] Ferrari, E. and Thuraisingham, B. Secure database systems. In *Advances in Database Management*, Ed. M. Piatini and O. Diaz. Artech: London, UK, 2000.

[GATE97] Gates, M. et al. Integration of real-time infrastructure, data manager, and tracker. In *Proceedings of the IEEE Workshop on Object-Oriented Real-time Systems (WORDS)*, Newport Beach, CA, February 1997.

[GEHR03] Gehrke, J. Special issue on data mining and privacy. *SIGKDD Explorations*, 4: 2, 2003.

[HUGH01] Hughes, E. and Thuraisingham, B. Data quality. In *Proceedings of the IFIP Integrity and Control Conference*, Brussels, Belgium, 2001. Kluwer: Hingham, MA, 2002.

[KANN02] Kannan, R. et al. Minimal sensor integrity in sensor grids. In *Proceedings of the International Conference on Parallel Processing*, 2002.

[LEE01] Lee, T. et al. The semantic Web. *Scientific American* (May) 2001.

[SON95] Son, S. et al. An adaptive policy for improved timeliness in secure database systems. In *Proceedings of the Ninth IFIP Working Conference in Database Security*, Rensselaerville, New York, August 1995. Chapman & Hall: London, 1996.

[STAN03] Stanford Sensor Data Management Group. STREAM: The Stanford stream data manager. *IEEE Data Engineering Bulletin* 26: 1, 2003.

[THUR98] Thuraisingham, B. *Data Mining: Technologies, Techniques, Tools and Trends*. CRC Press: Boca Raton, FL, 1998.

[THUR99] Thuraisingham, B. and Mauer, J. Survivability of real-time command and control systems. *IEEE Transactions on Knowledge and Data Engineering* 11: 1, 1999.

[THUR02] Thuraisingham, B. Data and applications security: Developments and directions. In *Proceedings of the IEEE COMPSAC Conference*, Oxford, UK, August 2002.

[THUR03a] Thuraisingham, B. Data mining, national security, privacy and civil liberties. *SIGKDD Explorations*, 4: 2, 2003.

[THUR03b] Thuraisingham, B. *Web Data Mining and Applications in Business Intelligence and Counter-Terrorism*. CRC Press: Boca Raton, FL, 2003.

[THUR04a] Thuraisingham, B. Secure sensor information management. *IEEE Signal Processing* (May) 2004.

[THUR04b] Thuraisingham, B. Security and privacy for sensor databases. *Sensor Letters*, 2: 1, 2004.

Exercises

1. Define a model for dependable data management and describe the design for a dependable data management system.
2. Examine standards from OMG for security and real-time processing. What are the additional features for ORBs for secure dependable data management?

Chapter 28

Secure Sensor and Wireless Information Management

28.1 Overview

Chapter 27 discussed secure dependable data management with sensor information management as an application area. This chapter discusses in more detail issues relating to secure sensor data and information management as well as issues on wireless information management. Telecommunication information management security, which encompasses wireless information management security, is also covered. In addition, a note on security for moving databases is also provided.

Sensors are everywhere and they have become part of our daily lives. We have sensors in our heating systems, air-conditioning systems, supermarkets, airports, shopping malls, and even in offices. These sensors are continually monitoring the environment, events, activities, people, vehicles, and many other objects, gathering data from these objects, aggregating the data, and then making sense out of the data and finally taking actions based on the analysis of the data. For example, we have sensors to monitor the temperature of a manufacturing plant periodically and if the temperature exceeds a certain value, then raise an alarm. At the other extreme, we now have sensors monitoring the activities of people and if these activities are considered to be suspicious, the law enforcement officials are notified. We also now have biological sensors that can perhaps detect whether an individual is carrying a biological agent such as anthrax. If so, the sensor then alerts appropriate health and law enforcement officials so that prompt actions can be taken. Sensors are also being employed to detect the spread of smallpox and other diseases. Video surveillance cameras that have embedded sensors can be found on highways to detect speeding and also in shopping malls to detect theft. Finally sensors are being used to detect insider threats both in physical as well as in computing environments. That is, sensors are everywhere.

We need sensors to be intelligent. That is, sensors must not only be able to monitor the situation, they must also be able to rapidly analyze the data gathered and make decisions. This is because there is a lot of data that is out there and the sensors cannot be expected to analyze all of the data in real-time and take action. That is, the sensors must process certain data and discard certain other data and perhaps store a third set of data for future analysis. Very often the sensors do not have the luxury of massive database management capability. They are limited in their storage capabilities. Therefore, the challenge is to develop algorithms for sensors to manage the data and information under massive resource and timing constraints. Essentially we need data and information management techniques for managing the sensor data and extracting useful information from the sensor data.

Recently database researchers have been focusing on developing data management techniques for managing sensor databases. They have examined the techniques developed for traditional database management and investigated ways of adapting them for sensor databases. Much progress has been made on sensor database management, but there is still a lot to be done. For example, very little consideration has been given to security and privacy for sensor databases. Sensors are operating in an open environment and are vulnerable. Many of the sensors are placed in enemy territory. These sensors could be attacked physically. Furthermore, the data managed by the sensors may be compromised. That is, we need security techniques to ensure that the sensor data is protected. We must also ensure that the data is not maliciously corrupted. Security cannot be an afterthought. It must be included right from the beginning in the design of the systems. That is, while the database and information management researchers are examining techniques for efficient query processing, they must also consider secure sensor data and information management. Furthermore, privacy is an added consideration. That is, the sensors are gathering information about all kinds of events and people. The people may want the information collected about them to be private or to be accessed only by certain individuals.

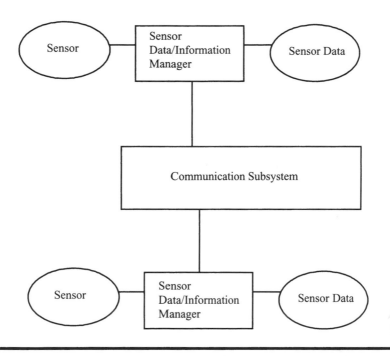

Figure 28.1   Sensor network

Closely related to sensor information management is wireless information management. Wireless and mobile devices have embedded sensors. This chapter provides a discussion of security for sensor and wireless information management systems. In particular we discuss various types of security mechanisms as well as architectures, policies, and functions of sensor database management. We provide an overview of telecommunications information management security. In a way telecommunications security encompasses wireless systems security. Finally we discuss security for moving (or mobile) databases.

The organization of this chapter is as follows. In Section 28.2 we discuss security for sensor databases. Secure sensor data management issues unique to sensor networks are discussed in Section 28.3. A note on wireless information management and security is discussed in Section 28.4. Telecommunications information management security is provided in Section 28.5. Security for moving databases is covered in Section 28.6. Directions for future research are given in Section 28.7. Our view of a sensor network is illustrated in Figure 28.1. In this network, sensor data managers are connected through some communication subsystem. The modules of a sensor data manager are illustrated in Figure 28.2. Background information on data management, sensor networks, and sensor data managers is given in [KANN03] and [CARN03].

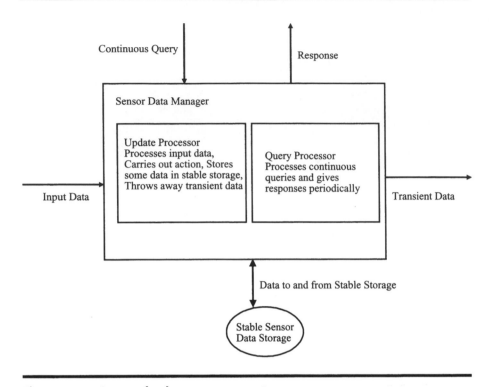

Figure 28.2 Sensor database management

28.2 Security for Sensor Databases

28.2.1 Overview

Security includes confidentiality where sensitive information about individuals is protected, secrecy where individuals are only given access to the data that they are authorized to know, and integrity where unauthorized and malicious modifications to the data are prohibited. Much work has been carried out on security for database systems (see, for example, [FERR00]). However, there is virtually little research on security for sensor databases. In this chapter we examine security issues for sensor databases. We also examine privacy where sensitive data and information about individuals gathered by the sensors have to be protected. Some initial directions are provided in [THUR04a] and [THUR04b]. Note that for an overview of security for wireless sensor networks we refer the reader to [PERR04].

In Section 28.2.2 we discuss the elements that constitute a security policy for sensor databases. We examine access-control models as well as multilevel security for sensor databases. Note that much of the information has been adapted from our work on secure multimedia databases. We also discuss security constraints. Security architectures are discussed in Section 28.2.3. We essentially examine the architectures discussed in Chapter 8 for secure sensor data management. Then in Section 28.2.4 we examine various sensor database functions and discuss the security impact on these functions. Managing sensor data in a secure distributed environment is discussed in Section 28.2.5. Note that sensor database systems may be distributed. Furthermore, each sensor database system may belong to one or more clusters. The inference problem for sensor data is discussed in Section 28.2.6. Because sensor data has to be aggregated, there is a potential for making unauthorized inferences. Privacy considerations are discussed in Section 28.2.7.

28.2.2 Security Policy

Security policy essentially specifies the application-specific security rules and application-independent security rules. Application-independent security rules would be rules such as the following.

- The combination of data from two sensors is always sensitive.
- A sensor operating at level L1 cannot read data from a sensor operating at level L2 if L2 is a more sensitive level than L1.

The second rule above is usually enforced for multilevel security. Now the main question is how does the policy for secure data management apply to sensor data. We could have sensors operating at different levels. Sensors in the Middle East may be highly classified whereas sensors in Europe may be less classified. Classified sensors will gather Classified data and Unclassified sensors will gather Unclassified data. Furthermore, sensor data may be in the form of streams. Therefore we need access-control policies for data streams. Within each level, one could enforce application-specific rules. Application-specific security rules include the following.

- Only law enforcement officials have authorization to examine data emanating from sensor A.
- Data from sensors A and B taken together are sensitive.
- All the data emanating from sensors in Washington, DC federal buildings is sensitive but the data emanating from sensors in North Dakota federal buildings is not sensitive.

Essentially application-specific rules are specified using security constraints. We discuss security-constraint processing in a later section.

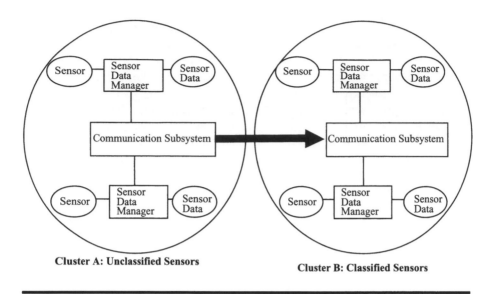

Cluster A: Unclassified Sensors

Cluster B: Classified Sensors

Figure 28.3   Security levels and clusters of sensors

Another question is do the sensors at different levels communicate with each other. Now, if the Bell and LaPadula policy is to be enforced, a Classified sensor cannot send any data to an Unclassified sensor. Data can move in the opposite direction. The sensor network must ensure such communication. We can also have clusters of sensors at different levels. For example, sensors in cluster A operate at the Unclassified level and sensors at cluster B operate at the Secret level. Communication flows from A to B. Communication in the reverse direction is not permitted. Therefore, if cluster A sensors are in Europe and cluster B sensors are in the Middle East, the sensor data from Europe is sent to the sensors in the Middle East and processed at the higher level. However, we may not want too much data to reside in, say, an enemy territory. Therefore, all of the data may be sent to the United States and processed at the Classified level. Note also that when the Unclassified data is aggregated, it may be sensitive. This is the inference problem and it is discussed in a later section. Clusters operating at different levels are illustrated in Figure 28.3.

A sensor could also be multilevel. That is, a sensor could process data at different levels. The multilevel sensor can then give data to the users at the appropriate level. For example, a multilevel sensor may give Secret sensor data to an intelligence officer, and it may give out only Unclassified data to a physician. One could also enforce role-based access control where users access data depending on their roles. A physician may have access to sensor information about the spread of diseases and he may not have access to sensor data about potential terrorists. Discretionary access-control techniques such as role-based access control as well as administration policies discussed in Chapter 5 need to be examined for sensor data management systems.

Security policy integration is a major challenge. That is, each sensor may enforce its own security policy and have its own constraints. The challenge is to integrate the different policies especially in distributed and cluster environments. For example, in the case of a cluster, each cluster of sensors may have its own policy, which is derived from the security policies of the individual sensors. The policies of the clusters will have to be combined to get an integrated policy. Security policy integration is illustrated in Figure 28.4. Many of the ideas have been obtained from our earlier work on security for federated database systems (see [THUR94]).

28.2.3 Security Architectures

Various security architectures have been proposed for secure database systems and we discussed them in Chapter 8. We also examined these architectures for multimedia systems in Chapter 20. We examine them for sensor databases in this chapter. That is, we examine four architectures discussed in Chapter 8 for secure sensor data management.

Consider architecture I which is the integrity lock architecture. In this architecture, there is a trusted agent that resides between the sensors and the sensor data manager. The trusted agent computes a cryptographic checksum for each sensor data element (or stream) depending on the security level of the sensor and the value of the data. The data, the level, and the checksum are stored in the sensor database. When the data is retrieved, the trusted agent recomputes the checksum based on the data value and the level that are retrieved. If the newly computed checksum equals the checksum that is stored, then the trusted agent assumes that the data has not been tampered with. The idea here is to make the sensor data manager untrusted. It will be very hard to trust the sensor data manager as these data managers could reside all over the world. Furthermore, there will be millions of such data managers. The main question is, can we afford to have a trusted agent for each sensor data manager or do we have a trusted agent to manage, say, each cluster of sensors. We need to carry out a trade-off study in determining how many trusted agents we need. In a resource-constrained environment, we may have to employ fewer trusted agents. Figure 28.5 illustrates the integrity lock architecture.

The next architecture we discuss is the distributed architecture. Here we partition the data depending on the level. Here again there is a trusted agent that receives sensor data and sends the data to the appropriate

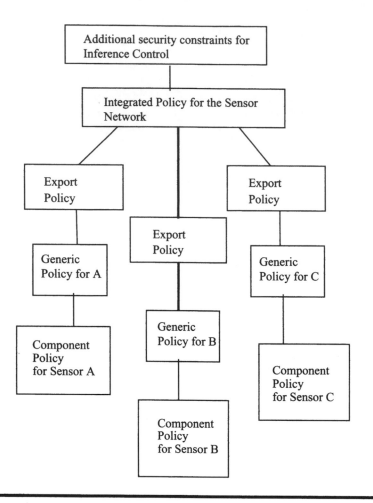

Figure 28.4 Security policy integration

sensor data manager. Classified data is sent to the Classified sensor data manager and the Unclassified data is sent to the Unclassified sensor data manager as shown in Figure 28.6. If data has to be retrieved, say, by an intelligence officer then the trusted agent retrieves the data from both the Classified and Unclassified data managers. If the data has to be retrieved by, say, a physician then the data is retrieved from only the Unclassified sensor data manager. There is, however, an issue as to whether data could be covertly leaked from a Trojan horse operating at the Classified level by inserting some values into the query. For example, the fact that there is a mission called Operation X could be Classified. However, a Trojan horse at the Classified level could send the query to the Unclassified sensor manager to monitor the situation with respect to Operation X. Now, one could enforce security constraints by the trusted agent to detect

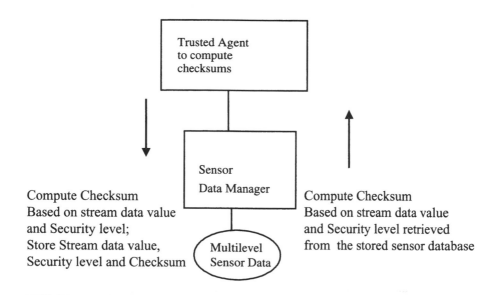

Figure 28.5   Integrity lock architecture

such violations. That is, the trusted agent could enforce the security constraint that the fact that Operation X exists is Classified and not send the query to the Unclassified sensor data manager. Another option is to replicate all the Unclassified sensor data at the Classified level. However, this goes against the assumption that we have limited resources and limited storage capabilities for sensor databases.

The third architecture is the operating system providing mandatory access-control architecture. Here, although each sensor data manager can handle multiple levels, there is an instance of a sensor data manager operating at each level. The sensor data is partitioned and access to the data is managed by the operating system. That is, the Unclassified sensor data is stored in an Unclassified file and the Secret sensor data is stored in a Secret file. Then the data is recombined during query and managed by the sensor data manager operating at the user subject's level. This architecture is illustrated in Figure 28.7. Note that with this architecture the sensor data manager is untrusted.

The fourth architecture is the kernel extensions architecture. Here the operating system provides the access control, but kernel extensions are needed to handle inference and aggregation problems. For example, in the case of sensor data management, the sensor data has to be fused. By aggregating the data, there may be some additional security issues. The kernel extensions could enforce the policy extensions. This is illustrated in Figure 28.8.

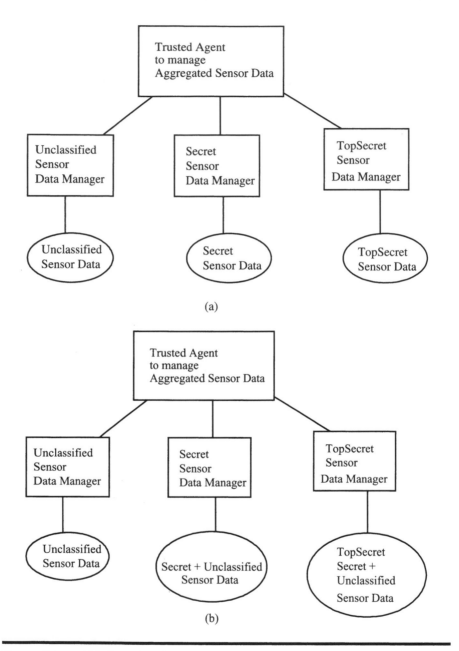

Figure 28.6   Distributed architecture

The final architecture is the trusted subject architecture. That is, whereas the first three architectures keep the sensor data manager untrusted, in this architecture we trust a portion of the sensor data manager that is controlling access to the sensor data. This is illustrated in Figure 28.9. We

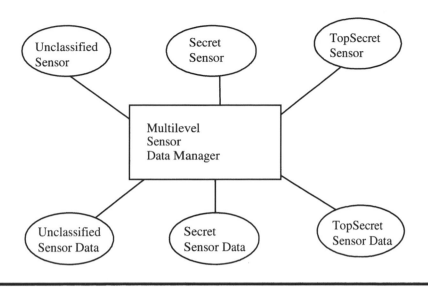

Figure 28.7 Operating system providing access-control architecture

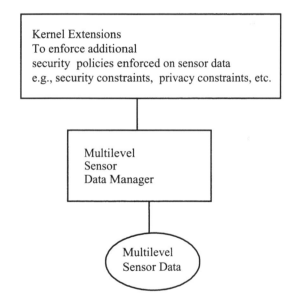

Figure 28.8 Kernel extensions architecture

need to conduct an architecture analysis study and experimentation to determine which architecture is suited for secure sensor data management. This will depend on the amount of trust that has to be placed, the number of sensors employed, and environments where the sensors will be

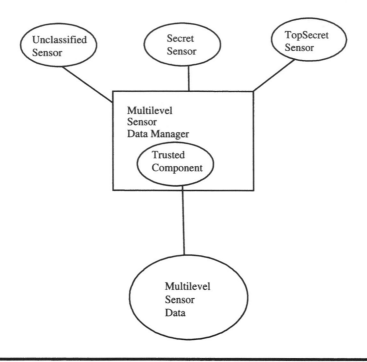

Figure 28.9   Trusted subject architecture

deployed. For example, if the environment is hostile then should we use the trusted architecture? On the other hand, if we are employing millions of sensors, then trusting each sensor data manager even though it is a small component will be quite expensive.

28.2.4 Security Impact on Sensor Database Functions

Security has an impact on all of the functions of a sensor data manager. Consider the query operation. The query processor has to examine the access-control rules and security constraints and modify the query accordingly. For example, if the existence of Operation X is Classified, then this query cannot be sent to an Unclassified sensor node to monitor the situation. Similarly the update process also examines the access-control rules to see if the data coming from a particular sensor can be inserted into the sensor database. That is, say, data coming from a sensor that manages an operation in the Middle East may not be entered into a sensor data manager in Southeast Asia.

Secure sensor transaction processing is another issue. First, what does transaction processing mean? One could imagine a sensor at site A and a sensor at site B monitoring the environments and making simultaneous updates to the sensor database. Both updates have to be carried out as a transaction. This is conceivable if both, say, temperature values depend on the final computation of some parameter. So assuming that the notion of a transaction is valid, what does it mean to process transactions securely? There has been a lot of work on secure transaction processing both for single-level and multilevel transactions. In the case of a single-level transaction it is assumed that the transaction is processed at a single security level. In the case of multilevel transactions, the transaction may operate at multiple security levels. The main challenge is to ensure that information does not flow covertly from a higher level to a lower level. Sensor transaction processing will also have similar challenges. We need to examine the techniques from secure transaction processing and real-time transaction processing to see if we can develop specific techniques for dependable sensor transaction processing.

Next consider the storage manager function. The storage manager has to ensure that access is controlled to the sensor database. The storage manager may also be responsible for partitioning the data according to the security levels. The security impact of access methods and indexing strategy for sensor data are yet to be determined. Metadata management is also another issue. For example, we need to first determine the types of metadata for sensor data. Metadata may include descriptions about the data and the source of the data, as well as the quality of the data. Metadata may also be classified. In some cases the metadata may be classified at a higher level than the data itself. For example, the location of the data may be highly sensitive but the data could be unclassified. We should also ensure that one cannot obtain unauthorized information from the metadata. Figure 28.10 illustrates the security impact on the query and update operations of sensor databases.

28.2.5 Secure Distributed Sensor Data Management

As we have stated in this chapter, there may be millions of sensors connected throughout the network. The collection of sensors functions like a distributed database management system. Therefore, ensuring security for a sensor network is in many ways like ensuring security for distributed database management systems.

The distributed architecture we have discussed in Section 28.2.3 is one such architecture that could be employed for a secure distributed sensor data manager. That is, data is partitioned according to security levels and managed by a trusted agent. We may also want to connect several sensor data managers each based on one of the architectures we have discussed in Section 28.2.3. That is, we can build a true secure distributed sensor data manager by connecting the different secure sensor data managers as

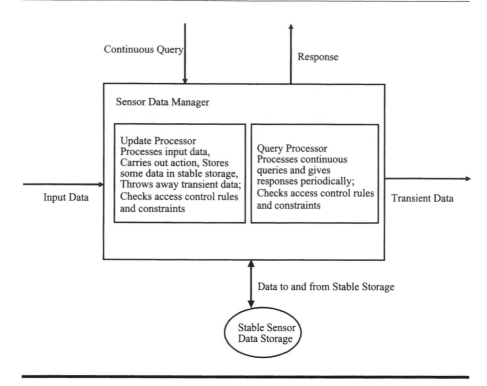

Figure 28.10   Functions of a secure sensor data manager

shown in Figure 28.11. As we have stated, we assume that the communication network that connects the sensor data managers is secure. We
have to ensure that when the different sensor data managers are connected
no higher-level information is sent to a lower-level sensor. That is, we
could assume that at each sensor site there could be an instance of a
sensor data manager operating at level L communicating with another
sensor data manager also operating at level L.

Another challenge is to enforce distributed access control. Each sensor
node would have its own security policy. We need to form an integrated
policy, possibly as shown in Figure 28.4. The integrated policy has to be
enforced across all the sensor nodes. The aggregation problem is exacerbated as the sensors process data and the processed data may have to
be aggregated across sensors. The aggregated data may be highly sensitive.
We discuss the inference problem in the next section.

28.2.6   Inference Problem

We discussed the inference problem in Part V. Chapter 12 discussed
security-constraint processing to handle the inference problem. Such an
approach could be adapted for secure sensor data management. Some

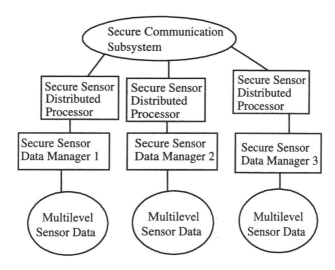

Figure 28.11   Secure distributed sensor data manager

examples of security constraints for sensor data were given in Section 28.2.2. These were application-specific constraints.

Figure 28.12 illustrates an architecture for an inference controller. In a shared sensor data-processing environment, because a lot of data has to be aggregated and fused, there could be potential for inference problems. That is, the aggregated data from sensor nodes A, B, and C could be highly sensitive. For example, one sensor could monitor the situation in the Middle East and another sensor could monitor the situation in Asia and the combined sensed information could be highly sensitive. The inference controller has to examine the constraints and prevent such sensitive information from being released to individuals who are not authorized to acquire this information.

Although much progress has been made on the inference problem for relational databases, we need to examine the techniques for sensor databases. However, new technologies such as sensor data mining exacerbate the inference problem. Furthermore, by mining surveillance data and other kinds of sensor data, privacy of individuals could be violated. We discuss the problems in Part VIII. We discuss privacy for sensor data management in the next section.

28.2.7 Privacy Considerations

In Chapter 22 we discussed the use of data mining for solving security problems such as intrusion detection and auditing. Data mining could also be used to detect intrusions in sensor networks. However, data mining

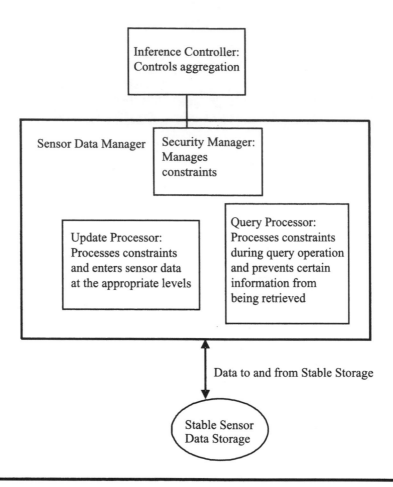

Figure 28.12 Sensor database inference controller

also causes security violations and exacerbates the inference and the privacy problems. We addressed privacy in Chapter 23. We revisit this topic for sensor databases.

Sensors are especially vulnerable to attacks as they function in an open environment. That is, sensors could be anywhere in the world and the sensor data managers could be compromised and the results aggregated. As a result the most private information could be divulged. The sensors could monitor, say, people in a shopping mall and the activities of the people may be monitored by law enforcement agencies as well as hackers who have hacked into the sensor system. Furthermore, based on the events monitored, the law enforcement agencies could arrest innocent individuals, especially if the analysis tools do not give accurate information.

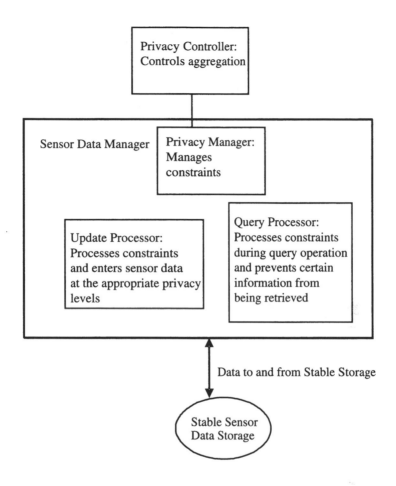

Figure 28.13   Sensor database privacy controller

For a discussion of data mining for national security we refer to [THUR03]. Our approach to privacy constraint processing is illustrated in Figure 28.13.

There has been some work recently on privacy-preserving sensor surveillance by Mehrotra et al. [MEHR04]. The idea here is for users to wear RFID tags (Radio Frequency ID); these tags are detected by sensors. If it is a tag that the sensor can recognize then the person's identity is hidden. If the sensor cannot recognize the tag then the person is displayed and privacy is not maintained about him or her. Note that as stated in a recent special issue of *IEEE Spectrum* (see [IEEE04]), RFID technology raises many interesting security and privacy questions. Furthermore, it is stated that sensor and wireless technology will revolutionize information technology.

28.3 Secure Sensor Data Management Issues Unique to Sensor Networks

28.3.1 Overview

Much of the discussion in the previous section has focused on some generic security issues that are applicable to sensor networks. That is, we need security architectures as well as secure data management functions. However, there are also secure data management issues that are unique to sensor networks. We discuss these issues in this section.

Sensors have resource constraints and therefore routing is affected. Some considerations of this aspect are discussed in Section 28.3.2. Another feature for sensor networks is that not all sensors can handle all security levels. That is, one sensor may process all the Classified data and other sensors in the network may process Unclassified data. Communication between incomparable levels is discussed in Section 28.3.3. The impact of the security architectures on sensor networks is discussed in Section 28.3.4. Finally in Section 28.3.5 we discuss some additional issues that take into consideration some unique constraints of sensor networks with respect to energy, hardware, and power systems resources.

28.3.2 Strategic Path Reliability in Information-Gathering Sensor Networks

Sensors in the network simultaneously participate in the collaborative decision making required for aggregation of data in an efficient way. As discussed by Kannan et al., path length, path reliability, and sensor energy consumption are the three major constraints affecting routing in resource-constrained, unreliable wireless sensor networks (see [KANN02]. Thus energy-constrained routing with the data aggregation in wireless sensor networks is crucial to a successful query-reporting database system. Although the energy efficiency of routes is an important parameter, maximizing network information utility and lifetime implies that the *reliability* of a data transfer path from reporting to querying sensor is also a critical metric. This is especially true given the susceptibility of sensor nodes to denial-of-service attacks and intrusion by adversaries who can destroy or steal node data. The possibility of sensor node failure due to operation in hazardous environments cannot be discounted, especially for environmental monitoring and battlefield sensor network applications. For such networks to carry out their tasks meaningfully, sensors must route strategic and time-critical information via the most reliable paths available.

Kannan et al. (see [KANN02]) describe a game-theoretic paradigm for solving the problem of finding reliable energy-optimal routing paths with bounded path length. They define two routing games in which sensors obtain benefits by linking to healthy and reliable nodes while paying a portion of path length costs. Thus sensor nodes modeled as intelligent agents cooperate to find optimal routes. This model has the following benefits.

- Each sensor will tend to link to more reliable and healthier nodes. Thus network partition will be delayed.
- Because each node shares the path length cost, path lengths will tend to be as small as possible. Thus delay is restricted in this model. Also shorter path lengths will prevent too many nodes from taking part in a route, thus reducing overall energy consumption.

Kannan et al. state that computing optimal paths in arbitrary sensor networks is a key element in designing a secure database system for complex information-gathering tasks. These interesting paradigms will further kindle considerable interest in the study of security and privacy of sensor database systems [KANN02].

28.3.3 Handling Non-overlapping and Incomparable Security Levels

In many cases sensors operate at different levels. That is, one sensor may process data at levels L1 through L4 and another sensor may process data at levels L5 through L8. This means there is no level that is common among the sensors. In such a case communication has to occur through a secure guard. There have been various secure or trusted guards that have been developed. However, these guards are not specific to sensors. We need research on designing guards that process sensor and stream data.

We illustrate some of the ideas behind the guards. When, say, data at level L2 and data at level L5 are to be combined at level L5, the guard will examine the data at level L2 and upgrade it to level L5 and send it to the sensor to process the data at level L5. In some cases there may be overlapping levels. That is, one sensor may handle levels L1 to L4 and another sensor may handle levels L4 to L7. If data at level L1 has to be sent to a sensor to process at level L4, then the data at level L1 is upgraded to L4 and the two sensors communicate at level L4.

Finally we may have sensors at incomparable levels. This is much more difficult to handle. That is, the guard cannot just upgrade the data at a particular level and send it to another level. The guard will have to check whether integrating data at incomparable levels will cause any security violations.

28.3.4 Security Architectural Impact on Sensor Networks

In Section 28.2.3 we discussed various security architectures. These included integrity lock, distributed, trusted, operating system providing access control, and kernel extension architectures. In this section we examine how the security architectures can fit in with the sensor network architecture that we have illustrated in Section 28.1.

The security architectures that we have discussed are clearly for the sensor data manager that we have illustrated in Figure 28.1. That is, each sensor data manager could be designed based on, say, either the operating system providing access control, or distributed, or integrity lock, or the trusted architecture. But in a sensor network, there are multiple layers with each layer carrying out some functions. For example, the communication layer is responsible for communication between the sensors, the middleware layer is responsible for middleware services such as interposed communication, and the application layer carries out functions such as multisensor integration and fusion.

The security architectures, the way they are designed at present, are independent of the other layers of the sensor network. Because the sensors are operating in a resource-constrained environment, we may need to design flexible security architectures that can adapt to the environment. In some cases, due to resource constraints, we may not be able to partition the sensor data according to the security level. Furthermore, it may be efficient to have some trust placed on the data manager rather than operating systems providing access. For example, if the operating system provides access, then access is at the file level. It may be time-consuming to recombine the sensor data in the files to provide a complete secure view to the user. That is, a trusted architecture may be more efficient. However, we need to examine the cost of designing a trusted architecture. In summary, we need to carry out a trade-off study of these architectures for sensor networks.

28.3.5 Handling Unique Constraints

As we have stated in Section 28.3.1, sensor networks have unique constraints with respect to energy, hardware, and power system resources. Any security solution must take into consideration these unique constraints. We discuss some of the issues in this section.

There is much research on developing energy-efficient sensors. These sensors can operate at different capacities as needed without disrupting the environment and operation. If the data manager associated with such a sensor is performing a security-critical function such as performing access-control checks, then the system must ensure that there is sufficient energy to complete the operations. Sensors are also constrained by power resources. That is, the sensor may come up and down as needed without disrupting the environment. Here again the security-critical functions must be executed and the results must be sent to the appropriate sensors or stored in some stable storage so that when the system comes up again the information is not lost. Sensors are also vulnerable to hardware failures. In the case of system failures we need to have backup sensors so that the operation is not disrupted. If the resources are limited and there are no backup sensors, then some other sensor should be able to take on the functions of the failed sensor.

Sensor databases may be attacked from various sites and prone to malicious attacks. This is because they may be in enemy territory and not have the protection that, say, computers have in a closed environment. We need to investigate data mining for detecting unauthorized intrusions. Data mining is showing a lot of promise for intrusion detection. We need to examine the techniques for sensor data. Data mining may also be used to determine whether it is likely that an attack would occur based on patterns and trends observed.

28.4 Secure Wireless and Mobile Data Management

Wireless devices include telephones, PDAs (Personal Digital Assistants), and more recently laptop computers. These devices have sensors embedded in them. Therefore all of the security issues discussed for sensor data and information management apply to wireless information management. There are also additional considerations for wireless information management.

An excellent introduction to security in wireless networks was given recently in [PERR04]. The authors state that these networks are susceptible to various attacks including denial of service, node capture, and physical tampering. These networks are used for various applications including monitoring building safety and earthquakes, as well as for military applications. Various security solutions including encryption, authentication, and privacy are discussed in [PERR04]. In addition, challenges for secure group communication as well as intrusion detection are discussed.

In the case of secure data management for wireless networks the challenges include secure query processing, transaction management, storage management, and metadata management. For example, how can queries be optimized efficiently? The users of the mobile devices may not stay in one location and therefore the query response has to be routed to the user's location. Is the user authorized to see the response? How can access control be enforced? How can the user be authenticated? How can the aggregation problem be handled? As stated in [PERR04], the sensor data has to be aggregated before it is sent to the base station so that the base station is not flooded with data. Does the user have access to the aggregated data?

In the cases of transaction management, we need to first define the notion of a transaction. Multiple users may be updating the data managers attached both to the wireless nodes as well as to the base stations. Do the transactions have to be serializable? Can we live with weak serializability? Now, can access control be enforced during transaction processing?

Storage management issues include managing the storage attached to the wireless nodes as well as the base stations. The wireless nodes may have limited storage capability. In addition, they also have limited power capability. Therefore, the challenge is what data should be maintained by the wireless node and what data should be stored at the base station. How can replicated copies be kept consistent? How can the integrity and security constraints be enforced? What is the security impact on access methods and index strategies?

Finally in the case of metadata management, we need to first define what metadata is for wireless networks. Typically metadata for wireless networks would include information about the nodes, their capacity, power consumption-related information, as well as security policies enforced. Storing and managing the metadata is a challenge. If the data storage is limited at the wireless nodes, then where is the metadata to be stored? Is it feasible to store the metadata at the base stations and retrieve it each time it is needed?

Attacks such as intrusions, denial of service, eavesdropping, and spoofing. Although we need security solutions for wireless networks, are there additional challenges for data management? Many organizations including university campuses have gone wireless. Therefore, building security solutions for wireless networks and data managers, as well as other information management technologies, is critical.

28.5 A Note on Secure Telecommunications Information Management

In the previous section we discussed security for wireless information management systems. The challenge is to provide security and privacy for wireless systems including telephones, PDAs, and wireless personal computers. Telecommunications networks and systems encompass wireless networks and systems. That is, telecommunications includes wired networks and systems as well as wireless systems. Much work has been carried out on security for telecommunications networks and systems.

Special protocols have also been developed. It is only recently that research has begun on secure data management for telecommunications systems (see, for example, [LORE01]).

Telecommunications systems may use database systems to maintain customer information and other information that requires long-term storage. In addition, there is also information about the various cables, modems, and telecommunication devices. Data managers may also be used to store information about the various connections and call centers. From an initial analysis, protecting the databases that contain information for the operation of telecommunication systems is similar to other secure data management security issues. However, the information needed for telecommunication systems may have to be maintained in real-time databases. That is, timing constraints may be associated with this information. Telecommunication lines are also prone to faults due to natural disasters such as hurricanes or terrorist attacks. Therefore, we need techniques for survivable and dependable telecommunication data managers. In other words, we need to integrate various aspects such as security, fault-tolerant computing, real-time processing, integrity, and privacy. Some of the challenges were discussed in Chapter 27.

28.6 Security for Moving Databases

Recently there have been many efforts on developing moving database systems. These systems are also called mobile databases or motion databases. Several papers have been published on mobile databases. Some research has also been carried out on security [LUBI98]. In this section we briefly discuss some of the challenges.

First of all we need to develop secure query-processing strategies. In mobile databases, users are moving continuously and data may also be migrating. Therefore, we need dynamic query-processing strategies as the size of the databases as well as communication distances may vary from time to time. We also need special techniques to handle the movement of data and users. Special transaction-processing techniques are also needed. We may have to sacrifice strict serializability of transactions, as the data is dynamic in nature. Furthermore, we need to examine security for transaction management in a mobile environment.

Many of the algorithms will depend on the security policies enforced. For example, what are the application-specific security constraints? How can we handle missing information? How can we enforce flexible security policies? How can we securely route the information to the mobile users? How do we handle data that migrates from place to place? Some directions are provided in [LUBI98]. There is much research to be done in this area.

28.7 Summary and Directions

We have discussed a number of security issues for sensor data management and also given privacy some consideration. We have also discussed secure wireless information management. Much of our focus has been on access control. We have also discussed security and privacy-constraint processing for sensor data. In a sensor network it is important that users be given access to the sensor data based on their user IDs and clearance levels. However, in many cases user IDs alone may not be sufficient. This is because we have a very open environment and anyone could masquerade as the user. Therefore, in addition we also specify credentials. That is, users must have certain credentials to access certain sensor data. Credential-based authorization policies have been investigated for Web security. We need to investigate such policies for sensor networks. We have also discussed some security issues that take into consideration the unique constraints of sensor networks. More research is needed in this area. Finally we have discussed security for wireless information management, telecommunication information management, and moving/mobile databases.

There are also several areas for future research. As stated in Section 28.3, sensor databases may be attacked from various sites. We need to investigate the use of data-mining techniques for detecting unauthorized intrusions. Technologies such as data mining do cause some security problems. That is, data mining exacerbates the inference problem as well as the privacy problem: that is, with data-mining tools users can make all kinds of inferences and violate the privacy of individuals. One area that is receiving a lot of attention is privacy-preserving data mining. We need to examine this area for sensor databases.

We cannot overemphasize the need for good encryption mechanisms. We discussed some in our descriptions of the integrity lock architecture as well as secure peer-to-peer sensor data management. Encryption is critical for communicating data across sensors as well as storing the data in sensor databases. Querying encrypted databases is getting some attention recently. We need to examine the techniques and determine their applicability for querying encrypted sensor databases.

The Web is having a major impact on many technologies including both sensors and databases. Sensors are connected via the Web and databases are accessed via the Web. Therefore, we need to examine Web security techniques as well as Web data management techniques for secure sensor data management on the Web. Other research areas include peer-to-peer sensor data management where collections of sensors act as peers and share information with each other. Trust management also needs consideration for sensor networks. In summary, the security technologies include access control based on user roles, IDs and credentials, data mining for detecting and preventing intrusions, Web security, and trust management, as well as encryption.

References

[CARN03] Carney, D. et al. Operator scheduling in a data stream manager. In *Proceedings of the 29th International Conference on Very Large Data Bases,* Berlin, Germany, 2003.

[FERR00] Ferrari, E. and Thuraisingham, B. Secure database systems. In *Advances in Databases,* Eds. Piatini, O. and Diaz, O. Artech: London, UK, 2000.

[IEEE04] *IEEE Spectrum,* 41: 7, 2004.

[KANN02] Kannan, R. et al. Minimal sensor integrity in sensor grids. In *Proceedings of the International Conference on Parallel Processing,* Vancouver, British Columbia, Canada, 2002.

[KANN03] Kannan, R. et al. Energy and rate based MAC protocol for wireless sensor networks. *ACM SIGMOD Record* 32: 4, 2003.

[LORE01] Lorenz, G. et al. Public telephone network vulnerabilities. In *Proceedings of the IFIP Data and Applications Security Conference,* Lake Niagara, Canada, July 2001. Kluwer: Hingham, MA, 2002.

[LUBI98] Lubinski, A. Security issues in mobile database access. In *Proceedings of the IFIP Database Security Conference,* Chalkidiki, Greece, July 1998. Kluwer: Hingham, MA, 1999.

[MEHR04] Mehrotra, S. et al. Privacy preserving surveillance. Demonstration, University of California, Irvine, 2004.

[PERR04] Perrig, A. et al. Security in wireless sensor networks. *Communications of the ACM,* 47: 6, 2004.

[THUR94] Thuraisingham, B. Security issues for federated database systems, *Computers and Security,* 13: 6, 1994.

[THUR03b] Thuraisingham, B. *Web Data Mining and Applications in Business Intelligence and Counter-Terrorism.* CRC Press: Boca Raton, FL, 2003.

[THUR04a] Thuraisingham, B. Secure sensor information management. *IEEE Signal Processing* (May) 2004.

[THUR04b] Thuraisingham, B. Security and privacy for sensor databases. *Sensor Letters,* 1: 2, 2004.

Exercises

1. Give a detailed discussion of security for sensor data management.
2. Give a detailed discussion of the security issues for wireless and mobile data management.
3. Discuss privacy issues for surveillance technologies.
4. Provide a survey of information management for wireless networks and telecommunications networks.
5. What are the security challenges for moving databases?

Chapter 29

Digital Identity, Forensics, and Related Topics

29.1 Overview

The previous chapters focused on security for data management as well as information management technologies. In particular we discussed security for various types of database systems, data warehouses, knowledge management, E-commerce, information retrieval, multimedia, sensors, and the semantic Web. Some of these are systems-oriented and others such as E-commerce are applications-oriented. In this chapter we discuss several topics that require attention with respect to security. These are challenges that we are faced with today due to technologies such as electronic banking and wireless devices. As we stated in Chapter 23, technologies such as data mining cause security and privacy concerns. As we make more progress with technologies such as wireless devices and E-commerce systems, there are also many security concerns such as stolen identities as well as encoding messages in images and video.

In this chapter we discuss a number of problems that need to be resolved. The organization of this chapter is as follows. In Section 29.2 we discuss digital identity. Identity management is about managing the identity of the individuals but at the same time ensuring privacy. In Section 29.3 we discuss identity theft. We hear about stolen credit cards and bank

```
┌─────────────────────────────────────────────────┐
│                                                 │
│   Some Emerging Security Concerns/Solutions:    │
│                                                 │
│   Digital Identity Management                   │
│   Identity Theft Management                     │
│   Biometrics                                    │
│   Digital Forensics                             │
│   Steganography and Digital Watermarking        │
│   Risk and Economic Analysis                    │
│                                                 │
└─────────────────────────────────────────────────┘
```

Figure 29.1 Emerging security concerns

accounts. How can we handle such threats? Section 29.4 addresses digital forensics. That is, how can we carry out essentially a postmortem on cyber-crimes? In Section 29.5 we discuss biometrics, which deals with technologies to identify a person based on, say, facial features. Section 29.6 discusses digital watermarking and steganalysis which deal with techniques for detecting encoded messages in images and video. In Section 29.7 we discuss risk management. That is, how can we analyze what the risks are and mitigate the risks? We also address economic analysis with respect to trust and security. In Section 29.7 we discuss various types of applications security such as securing e-mail. The role of database and applications security in homeland security is discussed in Section 29.8. The chapter is summarized in Section 29.9. Figure 29.1 illustrates the various topics addressed in this chapter.

29.2 Digital Identity

Digital identity is essentially the identity that a user is given to have any sort of access to an electronic resource. This could be an e-mail account, bank account, or any information we need to carry out our daily tasks. In many cases users may also want to protect their identities and as a result could have many identities for the different tasks they carry out. For example, a physician may have one identity for her work as a physician and to access medical resources, another identity to access her bank accounts, and a third identity to access her e-mail for personal use. Having multiple identities could cause problems as the identities may be stolen. An adversary could masquerade as a legitimate user and steal funds from a bank. Managing the multiple identities has become a major challenge.

Digital identity management has emerged as an important area in information security. Digital identities are managed by databases and therefore the techniques for managing database systems apply to such systems also. In addition, these databases have to be protected from unauthorized intrusions. Multiple identities of a person have to be managed by the digital identity databases. Therefore, we need techniques to make associations among the multiple identities of the same person. Research is being carried out on developing ontologies for identities (see, for example, [BERT04]). Ontology matching, conflict resolution, and handling semantic heterogeneity are some of the research challenges. Data mining is also a technology that is useful for identity management. One may need to mine the identity databases to detect any abnormal or unusual patterns.

More recently a notion called federated identity has emerged (see [DID]). In many cases organizations have to work across boundaries. Organizations such as OASIS and the Liberty Alliance Project are defining mechanisms for corporations to share identities in order to work across boundaries. However, an organization also has to maintain its own identity and have some autonomy. In a way the concepts are somewhat similar to federated data sharing across organizations. Standards are being developed to specify and manage federated identities. The benefits include reducing costs associated with password resetting as well as providing more efficient audit and secure data access functions. Essentially what is being proposed is individual identity management within an organization and federated identity management across organizations.

Many technologies have to work together to better support identity management. These include database management, data mining, ontology management, and federated computing. Research on identity management is just beginning. We need to ensure that actions of users can be traced but at the same time ensure the privacy of an individual. Figure 29.2

Aspects of Digital Identity Management

Techniques to manage the multiple identities of an individual to carry out his or her multiple roles

Managing the digital identity databases

Use of ontologies for identity representation

Figure 29.2 Aspects of identity management

illustrates various aspects of identity management that we have discussed in this section.

29.3 Identity Theft Management

Secure identity management has two purposes: one is to ease the burden of managing numerous identities for a user and the other is to ensure that a user's identity is not misused. One of the reasons for not having multiple identities is to ensure that the identities are not stolen by unauthorized users. Once the identities are stolen the owner has essentially given up all the information about him including his personal data, medical data, and financial data. The person who steals the identity can then masquerade as the owner and essentially take advantage of all the benefits that the owner has.

Secure identity management is essential for preventing identity theft. We hear a lot about individuals and corporations losing millions and even billions of dollars due to identity theft. Identity theft includes stealing physical identity such as signatures, social security numbers, and other attributes an owner may have, or it may include stealing the digital identity which are the user-IDs and password that a user has. The security techniques that we have discussed in the previous chapters can be applied to secure the identity databases. Access control together with digital signatures and encryption techniques are being used to avoid identity theft. For example, a merchant may sign the data with the public key of the user for whom the data is intended. The user can then decrypt the data with his private key. This way the critical data may not be misused. Similarly the data that a user sends to the merchant may be signed with the public key of the merchant. This way unauthorized users do not get access to the critical data intended for the merchant. Other mechanisms include obtaining certificates and credentials as well as tokens to carry out various activities. For a discussion of identity theft management we refer the reader to [IDT]. Note that various research efforts on the use of data mining for credit card fraud detection, which is a related topic, have been reported. We discussed some of them in Chapter 22 (see also [CHAN99]). Aspects of identity theft management are illustrated in Figure 29.3.

29.4 Biometrics

Biometric technologies have advanced in recent years. Early identification and authentication systems were based on passwords; now biometrics

---

Aspects of Identity Theft Management:

Access control, encryption, and digital signatures

Certificates, credentials, and token mechanisms

Data mining for fraud detection and other security threat detection

---

Figure 29.3   Aspects of identity theft management

systems are intended to use a person's physical characteristics for identi-fication and authentication. We discuss some of the concepts and chal-lenges as discussed in [BIOM]. This work is being carried out by the researchers at Michigan State University.

As stated in [BIOM], biometrics is about automatic identification of a person based on his or her physiological or behavioral properties. These properties could be his or her features such as eyes, voice, fingerprints, signatures, figure, and other features. Proponents of biometrics technolo-gies argue that passwords could be stolen but one cannot steal a person's eyes and physical features in general.

As an example, when a person wants to withdraw money from an ATM machine, her face is photographed and sent to a face recognition machine. This machine will then match her face with the photograph that it has of the person and then authenticate her. There are now techniques that can match the eyes including the lashes and the eyeballs and see if the person is authentic. Fingerprinting and voice recognition are other biometric techniques that are also being applied.

Computer graphics and vision are some of the contributing technolo-gies for biometrics. Other technologies include pattern matching, visual-ization, and networking. For example, the images and voice data have to be transferred over networks to remote sites for authentication. Therefore, real-time networking as well as pattern-matching capability is needed.

As stated in [BIOM] it is expected that biometrics technology will not only replace computer access, but it will also replace, say, entry into homes and automobiles. One does not have to carry his key with him all the time. With biometrics technologies he can be identified to enter his house or buildings. He can enter his car and drive with appropriate identification techniques. That is, biometrics supports keyless entry into automobiles and buildings.

```
Aspects of Biometrics:

Fingerprint, voice, and facial feature recognition

Human motion analysis

Patten matching and visualization

Data mining and machine-learning techniques
```

Figure 29.4 Aspects of biometrics

In a recent talk, Thuraisingham discussed the use of data mining for biometrics. She described new machine-learning techniques (e.g., neural networks) that may be used to learn about the behavior and features of a person and the trained system may be used to identify a person based on facial expression or facial features. There is a lot of work to be done on data mining for biometrics [THUR04]. Figure 29.4 illustrates the various aspects of biometrics.

29.5 Digital Forensics

Digital forensics is about investigating cyber-crime. There are many parallels between forensic medicine and digital forensics. When a person has an abnormal death, law enforcement together with forensic experts analyze various aspects of the death including taking blood samples, hair samples, and DNA information for further testing. In the same way when a computer crime is committed, law enforcement together with digital forensic experts have to gather every piece of evidence including information from the crime scene (such as the person's computer) and analyze the evidence to detect who has committed the cyber-crime. The law enforcement agencies may have gathered profiles of cyber-terrorists and other historical information and they use this information in their investigation and analysis. Digital forensics is about building and using the analysis tools to detect cyber-crimes.

Many articles have appeared on digital forensics and a useful collection can be found in [DFOR]. Intrusion detection approaches are a type of digital forensic analysis techniques. That is, with intrusion detection techniques such as data-mining techniques, one can figure out what the intrusions are and perhaps who the intruders are. That is, intrusion detection is about analyzing a cyber-crime and that is unauthorized intrusions.

Other digital forensic techniques include analyzing the log files. When a user enters the system and commits a crime such as masquerading as a legitimate user, the log files will have information showing from which terminal the user logged on. From there, the investigators could narrow down their choices as to who the criminals are. There are also criminal profiling tools one can use to build profiles of criminals. Criminal profiling uses the available information from a crime scene and builds a psychological profile of a terrorist. Tracing tools are also needed to trace back to the crime. That is, we start with what we have at the crime scene and through various analysis tools as well as interviews with people in an organization, try to form a picture of the crime. Laws and policies are key here. That is, we need to have clear legal rules and policies as to what is permitted and what is not. The law enforcement officer may also subpoena the information that he or she needs such as log files, backup disks, hard drives, and any other information that may be needed to carry out an analysis. E-mails are often useful information when conducting an analysis of a crime. Therefore, an organization's e-mail messages may also be analyzed and perhaps mined to extract previously unknown information. There are policy questions here as to whether an organization can analyze the e-mail messages. That is why it is important to set up the laws and policies ahead of time.

The *International Journal of Digital Evidence* is a useful resource for those interested in digital forensics. For example, in an article by Giordano and Maciag (see [GIOR02]) the authors discuss some of the unique military requirements and challenges in cyber-forensics. The authors give a military cyber-forensic definition and discuss various challenges. In a military environment, the military commanders and other personnel will also be involved in a forensic investigation. Furthermore, there may also be classified information involved in the forensic analysis. Can such information be released to the law enforcement and forensic experts? One may also need foreign language experts to analyze the data not specified in English.

In summary, although tremendous progress has been made in digital forensics, there is still a lot to be done. We need to develop forensic analysis techniques for different environments. We discussed some of the needs for military environments as given in [GIOR02]. We also need to examine other environments such as medical and scientific environments. We need to continue to improve the analysis tools as well as develop new tools. Finally technologies such as data mining need to be examined for digital forensics. Figure 29.5 discusses aspects of digital forensics.

Aspects of Digital Forensics:

Crime scene analysis

Analysis of log files and other computer data

Build profiles of criminal activities
and use data mining techniques for analysis

Legal and policy issues

Figure 29.5 Aspects of digital forensics

29.6 Steganography and Digital Watermarking

Steganography is about hiding information within other information. The hidden information is the message that terrorists may be sending to their peers in different parts of the world. This information may be hidden in valid texts, images, films, and various other media. The challenge for steganalysis is to develop techniques that can analyze a paper, image, or video clip and be able to detect if there are any hidden messages. A useful resource for steganography and digital watermarking is [STEG]. In addition, Johnson and Jajodia have written a good text on this subject (see [JOHN00]). They explore data-hiding techniques for images and propose a method for detecting such attacks.

Digital watermarking is closely related. It is about inserting information into the data without being noticed. It has applications in copyright protection. That is, a manufacturer of a media product may copyright it and insert the copyright into the data without it being noticed. If the data is copied then the copy is analyzed to see who the real owner of the data is. That is, copyrighted material could be protected. There is also copy protection where it is not possible to copy copyrighted material and it is usually difficult to achieve. For more information on digital water-marking we refer the reader to [DWM].

The challenge is to develop techniques that can detect hidden messages. Now, in the case of copyrighted material, detecting the hidden messages is needed for the applications. However, in the case of terrorists inserting messages, we need techniques to detect such criminal acts. Steganography makes the task of forensic experts even more difficult as they now have to analyze data that is hidden and not explicit. In a recent

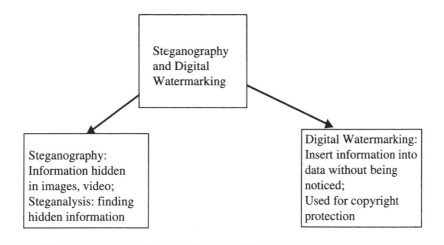

Figure 29.6   Aspects of steganography and digital watermarking

book edited by Katzenbeisser and Petitcolas, a collection of papers on steganalysis and digital watermarking is presented (see [KATZ00]). Communication protocols for steganalysis as well as techniques for detecting hidden messages are discussed. Some progress has been made on detecting information-hiding techniques, but we need to analyze the complexity of the techniques. We also need more efficient tools for steganalysis and digital watermarking. Figure 29.6 illustrates the various aspects of steganography and digital watermarking.

29.7 Risk and Economic Analysis

Before we develop and install a secure system or a network we need to conduct a risk analysis study. That is, what is the risk that a threat will occur? How damaging is the threat? How often will the threat occur? We need to model the risks and then decide whether it is feasible to incorporate all of the security features into the system. That is, if the threat is small and the impact is not great, then do we still want to install all of these security features and, say, slow down the system? Various articles have been published on risk management, assessment, and analysis. A useful resource can be found in [RISK]. In this section we discuss some of the key issues.

Various types of risk analysis methods have been studied. In the quantitative approach, events are ranked in the order of risks and decisions are made based on the risks involved. The problem with this approach is that the data may not always be reliable and therefore any analysis

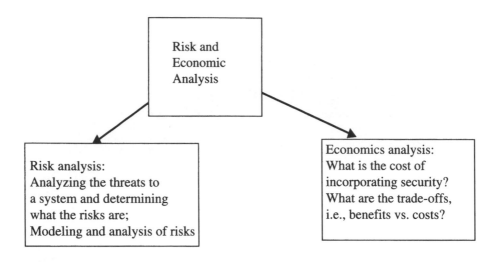

Figure 29.7   Aspects of risk and economic analysis

performed using the data may not be useful. In the qualitative method for risk analysis, only estimates are used and therefore results are more meaningful. Various threats and system vulnerabilities are also taken into consideration for risk analysis. There is also a conference series on risk assessment (see [RISK04]). Note that risks may include computer security risks as well as risks to national security.

Another closely related subject is economic analysis for security and trust management. Risk is obviously a factor in considering the economics of building a system. If the security risks are high and if the damage is significant then the organization would want to spend the funds and install a highly secure system. However, if the threats are not high and the cost is low, then a more flexible security policy may be enforced. Computer security experts are now working with economists to determine features such as trust, integrity, data quality, and confidentiality that need to be incorporated into a system and various cost–benefit studies are being carried out. A recent workshop on economics and information security held at the University of California at Berkeley provided many new directions for research and experimentation on this topic (see [ECON]). Figure 29.7 illustrates aspects of risk and economic analysis for information security.

29.8   Other Secure Systems and Applications

In the previous chapters as well as in this chapter we have provided an overview of various secure systems and applications. We discussed discretionary and mandatory security for relational systems as well as for object systems and distributed systems. We discussed the inference problem, secure data warehousing, and data mining for security, privacy, secure Web data, and information management as well as some emerging technologies such as secure sensor data management. We also briefly discussed digital identities, digital forensics, and watermarking. There are numerous areas that have not been covered in this book. We briefly list some of the topics.

- *E-Mail Security:* Secure e-mail is one of the most important application security areas. Almost all of us are inundated with spam and other miscellaneous e-mail messages. If only we had good filtering tools to eliminate such messages, our lives would be so much less complicated. We do not want to delete the useful messages together with the spam. This is a big challenge.
- *Benchmarking:* We need benchmarking tools for secure query and transaction management. The benchmarks can be used to determine the efficiency of the various systems.
- *Simulation and Performance Studies:* We need to conduct simulation as well as performance studies. What is the cost of incorporating security? What are the risks involved? Modeling and simulation would be very useful in determining such aspects.
- *Emerging Technologies:* As new technologies emerge we need to ensure that security is incorporated at the beginning. We have explored many technologies in this book. We need to continue with examining security for the emerging technologies.
- *Composition:* We are seeing systems being built from various components. Although each of the components may be secure we need to ensure that the composite system is secure. We discussed this briefly in Chapter 19.
- *Verification and Validation:* We need to continue to develop testing methods as well as formal verification tools to verify and validate the emerging systems.
- *Covert Channel Analysis:* We discussed covert channels that could occur in multilevel transaction processing (see Chapter 10). We need to continue to study this area as new types of systems such as the semantic Web and Web information systems emerge.
- *Language Translation and Text Summarization:* Multilingual translation and text summarization are important research areas in natural language processing. When languages are translated the security policies have to be maintained. Furthermore, when text is summarized, one has to ensure that security is not compromised.
- *Robotics and Security:* Robotics technologies have been applied for many applications including defense and intelligence. One has to ensure that security policies are encoded correctly when operating the robots.

Aspects of Secure Systems and Applications:

E-mail security
Benchmarking (e.g., secure query and transactions)
Composition of systems
Verification and validation
Covert channel analysis
Simulation and performance studies
Security for emerging technologies

Figure 29.8   Aspects of secure systems and applications

■ *Electronic Voting Systems:* There has been much research recently on electronic voting systems. Rubin et al. have carried out some very good research (see [KOHN04]). It is important that the electronic voting machines maintain integrity and security.

As we have stated, we have tried to give a broad but comprehensive overview of database and applications security. Each of the areas still needs further work. Because the field has expanded so rapidly over the past three decades, it is impossible for us to cover all of the developments. Figure 29.8 illustrates aspects of secure systems and applications discussed in this section.

29.9   The Role of Database and Applications Security for Homeland Security

At the IFIP Data and Applications Security Conference in Sitges, Spain in July 2004, there was a panel on the role of data and applications security for homeland security. Note that in Chapter 22 we discussed data-mining applications in national security. Various other data management technologies such as active database management and data warehousing are being applied to national security applications (see [CHEN03]). In this section we focus on how data and applications security technologies may be used for homeland security.

We have discussed several data and applications security technologies in this book. These include secure relational databases, secure object databases, and secure distributed da6abases. Note that many of the secure database and distributed system technologies may be used to build critical infrastructure for homeland security. Other data and applications security technologies that may help homeland security include digital identity management, federated data sharing, and biometrics. For example, biometrics technologies are being explored not only for access into computers but also access into buildings and vehicles. Federated data sharing technologies enable organizations to share data and yet maintain security and privacy. Identity management enables one to manage the identities of the individuals and detect the identities of suspicious individuals. Other technologies that may help homeland security include secure surveillance technologies where user activities are monitored and suspicious behavior flagged. In summary, although data management technologies have many applications in homeland security, we need to investigate further the use of data and applications security technologies for homeland security.

29.10 Summary and Directions

In this chapter we have provided an overview of various topics in database and applications security. In particular, we discussed digital identities, identity theft, biometrics, digital forensics, steganography, and risk/economic assessments. We also briefly mentioned some other topics such as secure e-mail, performance analysis, and verification and validation.

This brings us to the end of Part X and essentially the end of the technical aspects of the book. We have addressed a variety of topics in database and applications security. We started with a discussion of supporting technologies and then discussed discretionary and mandatory security for databases. Then we discussed multilevel security for relational databases. Next we focused on secure distributed and heterogeneous databases as well as secure object databases. Next we discussed security for some of the emerging technologies such as data warehousing and data mining. Then we provided an overview of security for Web data and information management technologies. Finally we provided an overview of emerging secure data management technologies such as secure sensors and dependable data management as well as some emerging directions in digital identity management and biometrics. As we have stated, there are so many developments that it is impossible for us to list all of them. We have tried to give a broad but fairly comprehensive overview of the field.

References

[BERT04] Bertino, E. et al. Managing digital identity. In *Proceedings of the CERIAS Conference,* Lafayette, IN, March 2004.
[BIOM] Biometrics. Available at http://biometrics.cse.msu.edu/info.html.

[CHAN99] Chan, P. et al. Distributed data mining in credit card fraud detection. *IEEE Intelligent Systems* 14: 6, 1999.

[CHEN03] *Proceedings of the First Security Informatics Symposium*, Tucson, AZ, June 2003, Ed. H. Chen.

[DFOR] Digital forensics. Available at http://www.forensics.nl/links/.

[DID] Digital identity. Available at http://www.pingidentity.com/index.php?cid= whyfederate.

[DWM] Digital watermarking. Available at http://www.watermarkingworld.org/.

[ECON] Available at http://www.sims.berkeley.edu/resources/affiliates/work-shops/econsecurity/.

[GIOR02] Giordano, J. and Maciag, C. Cyber forensics: A military perspective. *International Journal of Digital Evidence* 1: 2 (Summer) 2002.

[IDT] Identity theft. Available at http://www.identitytheft911.com/index.jsp.

[IFIP04] The role of data and applications security for homeland security: Panel discussion. Addendum to the *Proceedings of the IFIP Data and Applications Security Conference*, Sitges, Spain, 2004.

[JOHN00] Johnson, N. and Jajodia, S. *Information Hiding, Steganography and Watermarking: Attacks and Countermeasures.* Kluwer: Hingham, MA, 2000.

[KATZ00] Katzenbeissser, S. and Peticolas, F. (eds.) *Information Hiding Techniques for Steganography and Digital Watermarking*, Artech: London, UK, 2000.

[KOHN04] Kohnr, T. Analysis of electronic voting systems. In *Proceedings of the IEEE Symposium on Security and Privacy*, Oakland, CA, April 2004.

[RISK] Available at http://www.security-risk-analysis.com/.

[RISK04] *Risk Analysis 04, Fourth International Conference on Computer Simulation in Risk Analysis and Hazard Mitigation*, Rhodes, Greece, 2004.

[STEG] Steganography. Available at http://www.jjtc.com/Steganography/.

[THUR04] Thuraisingham, B. Data mining for biometric applications. In *Proceedings of the Women in Software Engineering Conference*, Baltimore, March 2004.

Exercises

1. Select three topics discussed in this book (e.g., digital identity, identity theft, biometrics, digital forensics, digital watermarking, and steganography) and conduct a detailed survey of each of them.
2. Conduct a survey of risk modeling and analysis techniques.
3. How can economics analysis be used in the design of secure systems?

Conclusion to Part X

Part X described security for emerging technologies and applications. In Chapter 26 we discussed secure dependable data management In particular, we discussed developing flexible policies for dependable computing which include security, integrity, fault-tolerant computing, privacy, data quality, and real-time processing. Dependable computing has also been referred to as trustworthy computing. Chapter 28 discussed security for sensor data management as well as for wireless data management. We discussed policies and functions for secure sensor data management systems. We also addressed privacy concerns. Finally in Chapter 29 we briefly discussed several topics relating to secure applications including digital identity, identity theft, digital forensics, and biometrics.

This brings us to the end of Part X and essentially to the end of the technical aspects of the book. We have addressed a variety of topics in database and applications security. We started with a discussion of supporting technologies and then discussed discretionary and mandatory security for databases. Then we discussed multilevel security for relational databases. Next we focused on secure distributed and heterogeneous databases as well as secure object databases. Next we discussed security for some of the emerging technologies such as data warehousing and data mining. Then we provided an overview of security for data and information management technologies. Finally we provided an overview of emerging secure data management technologies such as secure sensor and dependable data management.

The database and applications security field has advanced a great deal over the past three decades. We have tried to discuss many of the essential points. Chapter 30 concludes the book.

Chapter 30

Summary and Directions

30.1 About This Chapter

This chapter brings us to a close of *Database and Applications Security: Integrating Information Security and Data Management*. We discussed several aspects including supporting technologies for database and applications security, discretionary and mandatory security in relational databases, design principles for multilevel secure database systems, and secure object databases as well as secure distributed and heterogeneous databases, secure data warehousing, data mining for security, privacy, secure Web data management, secure information management, secure semantic Web, secure dependable data management, secure sensor data management, and various topics such as digital identity management and biometrics. This chapter provides a summary of the book as well as gives directions for database and applications security.

The organization of this chapter is as follows. In Section 30.2 we give a summary of this book where we have taken the summaries from each chapter to form the summary. In Section 30.3 we discuss directions for database and applications security. In Section 30.4 we give suggestions as to where to go from here.

30.2 Summary of This Book

We summarize the contents of each chapter essentially taken from the summary and directions section of each chapter. Chapter 1 provided an

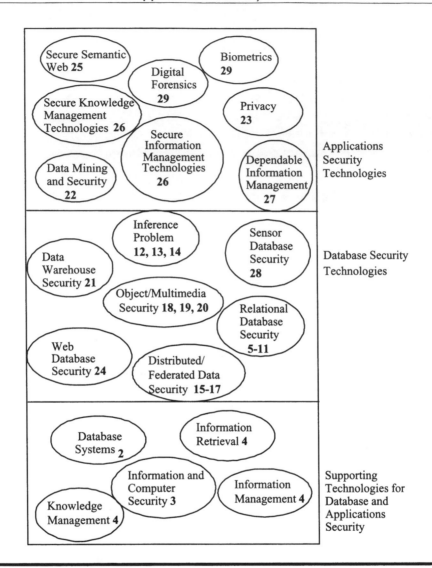

Figure 30.1 Components addressed in this book

introduction to the book. We first provided a brief overview of the supporting technologies for database security. Then we discussed various topics addressed in this book including multilevel secure databases and secure object systems. Parts I through X of this book elaborated on the sections of Chapter 1. We also discussed a framework for organization purposes. Our framework is a three-layer framework and each layer was addressed in one or more parts of this book. This framework was illustrated in Figure 1.17. We replicate this framework in Figure 30.1.

The book is divided into ten parts. Part I, which described the supporting technologies for database and applications security, consisted of three chapters: 2, 3, and 4. Chapter 2 discussed various aspects of database systems and provided some background information to understand the various chapters in this book. We began with a discussion of various data models. We chose relational and entity-relationship models, as they are more relevant to what we have addressed in this book. Then we provided an overview of various types of architectures for database systems. These include functional and schema architectures. Next we discussed database design aspects and database administration issues. We also provided an overview of the various functions of database systems. These included query processing, transaction management, storage management, metadata management, security, integrity, and fault tolerance. Finally we briefly discussed distributed databases and interoperability. This was followed by a discussion of data warehousing, data mining, and the impact of the Web. We also provided a brief overview of object technology.

Chapter 3 provided a brief overview of the developments in secure systems. We first discussed basic concepts in access control as well as discretionary and mandatory policies. Then we provided an overview of secure systems. In particular, secure operating systems, secure databases, secure networks, and emerging technologies were discussed. Next we discussed the impact of the Web. Finally we discussed the steps to building secure systems.

Chapter 4 provided an overview of a number of information management technologies. These included information retrieval, multimedia, collaboration, and knowledge management, as well as technologies such as sensor information management and E-commerce.

Part II, which described discretionary security for database systems, consisted of two chapters: 5 and 6. Chapter 5 provided an overview of discretionary security policies in database systems. We started with a discussion of access-control policies including authorization policies and role-based access control. Then we discussed administration policies. We briefly discussed identification and authentication. Finally we discussed auditing issues as well as views for security.

Chapter 6 discussed policy enforcement issues with respect to the various policies we discussed in Chapter 5. The major issues in policy enforcement are policy specification, policy implementation, and policy visualization. We discussed SQL extensions for specifying policies as well as provided an overview of query modification. We also briefly discussed how policy visualization might be used to integrate multiple policies. Finally we discussed some prototypes and products that implement discretionary security. We focused mainly on relational databases systems.

Part III, which described mandatory security for database systems, consisted of two chapters: 7 and 8. Chapter 7 provided a broad overview of the historical developments of MLD/DBMSs. We defined MLS/DBMSs and discussed the early efforts. Then we focused on the developments with the Air Force Summer Study as well as provided a summary of the major efforts in the 1980s. Then we provided an overview of the TDI and discussed several types of MLS/DBMSs. Finally we discussed some hard problems as well as issues on examining multilevel security for emerging systems.

Chapter 8 provided an overview of mandatory access control and policies for MLS/DBMSs as well as described a taxonomy for the designs of MLS/DBMSs. We first described the differences between access control in operating systems and access control in DBMSs. Then we provided an overview of the Bell and LaPadula security policy and its adaptation for MLS/DBMSs. Finally we provided a detailed overview of various security architectures for MLDS/DBMSs. These included integrity lock, operating system providing access control, kernel extensions, trusted subject, and distributed architectures. We discussed the advantages and disadvantages of each architecture.

Part IV, which described multilevel secure relational database systems, consisted of three chapters: 9, 10, and 11. Chapter 9 discussed multilevel relational data models. We started with a discussion of granularity of classification and provided an overview of classifying various entities such as relations, tuples, and attributes. Then we discussed the concept of polyinstantiation and also provided an overview of standards for multilevel relational data models.

Chapter 10 examined the functions of a DBMS and discussed the security impact. In particular, we discussed secure query processing, transaction management, storage management, metadata management, and integrity management for an MLS/DBMS.

Chapter 11 provided an overview of some of the prominent MLS/DBMS prototypes and products. Many of the developments began after the Air Force Summer Study in 1982 and were funded by federal agencies such as the Air Force Research Laboratory in Rome, New York, and the National Security Agency. Our purpose was to discuss the technical concepts and not promote any particular prototype or product.

Part V, which described the inference problem, consisted of three chapters: 12, 13, and 14. Chapter 12 defined the inference problem and examined the approaches to handle the problem. In particular, we discussed statistical database inference, security constraint processing, and the use of conceptual structures. We also briefly discussed deductive MLS/DBMSs for inference as well as the complexity of the inference problem.

Chapter 13 first defined various types of security constraints. Security constraints are rules that assign security levels to the data. Then we described an integrated approach to constraint processing. That is, some constraints are handled during query processing, some during database updates, and some during database design. We then described the design of a system, which processes constraints during query and update operations. We also described the design of a database design tool. We also briefly discussed an alternative approach to security-constraint processing during release processing.

Chapter 14 extended semantic data models to multilevel semantic data models in order to capture the semantics of multilevel applications. In particular, we defined the notion of a multilevel semantic net and discussed reasoning strategies to detect security violations via inference during application design time.

Part VI, which described secure distributed databases, consisted of three chapters: 15, 16, and 17. Chapter 15 provided an overview of the significant developments in secure distributed database systems. We focused mainly on discretionary security. In particular, we discussed security policies, access control, and query modification. Various issues on integrating security policies as well as enforcing access-control rules were discussed. Finally we discussed the security impact on some of the emerging technologies such as data warehousing, data mining, collaboration, distributed objects, and the Web.

Chapter 16 provided an overview of the developments in multilevel secure distributed database systems. We started with a discussion of both the partitioned approach and the replication approach proposed by the Air Force Summer Study in 1982 and then discussed security for architectures based on distributed control and distributed data. Next we provided an overview of data modeling and secure distributed database functions. Finally we discussed the inference problem in distributed databases.

Chapter 17 discussed security for heterogeneous and federated databases. We started by providing some background and related work and then discussed architectures, schema integration, and security policy integration. We also discussed the security impact on the functions of a secure federated system and provided an overview of the inference problem in a federated environment. Finally we provided a brief overview of the migration of databases and applications.

Part VII, which described secure object systems, consisted of three chapters: 18, 19, and 20. Chapter 18 provided an overview of discretionary security and mandatory security for object database systems. We started with a discussion of discretionary security policies and also provided an overview of prototypes and products including a discussion of the ORION and GEMSTONE systems. Then we discussed mandatory security policy as well as system design issues. This was followed by a discussion of the various efforts regarding developing multilevel secure object database systems.

Chapter 19 discussed the various aspects of objects and security. We noted that security could be incorporated into object databases, object languages such as Java, and object-based middleware such as object request brokers. We also noted that object models could be used to represent and reason about secure applications. We first discussed security for object request brokers and described various standards being developed by OMG. Then we discussed the use of object models for designing secure applications and described in particular the use of OMT and UML.

Chapter 20 provided some of the developments and directions in secure multimedia database management. We started with a discussion of security policy issues and then discussed secure multimedia data management functions. We also discussed some special multimedia systems such as geospatial information systems.

Part VIII, which described data warehousing, data mining, security, and privacy, consisted of three chapters: 21, 22, and 23. Chapter 21 discussed secure data warehousing. We started with a discussion of a definition for a secure data warehouse, the technologies for a secure data warehouse, functions of a secure data warehouse, and issues in developing a secure data warehouse. Key concepts in secure data warehousing include developing a secure data model, security architecture, and access methods and index strategies. We also discussed data quality and multilevel security issues.

Chapter 22 discussed data mining for security applications. We first started with a discussion of data mining for national security and then provided an overview of data mining for cyber-security. In both cases we discussed the various threats and showed how data-mining techniques could help detect abnormal behavior patterns. Although information security is the main focus of our book, we also addressed national security concerns as the methods used to detect both physical attacks and cyber-attacks are somewhat similar.

Chapter 23 was devoted to the important area of privacy related to Web and data mining. Although there have been efforts toward applying data mining for handling national security and information security problems such as intrusion detection, in this chapter we focused on the negative effects of data mining. In particular, we discussed the inference problem that can result due to mining as well as ways of compromising privacy especially due to Web data access.

Part IX, which described secure Web information management technologies, consisted of three chapters: 24, 25, and 26. Chapter 24 discussed various cyber-threats in general and threats to Web databases in particular.

The threats include access-control violations, sabotage, infrastructure attacks, and insider threat analysis. Next we proposed various solutions including data-mining techniques and role-based access control. As we have stated, the cyber-threats are very real and we need to do everything we can to detect, prevent, and manage the threats. The damages have to be contained. We also provided an overview of secure digital libraries including secure Web databases and secure information retrieval systems.

Chapter 25 provided an overview of the semantic Web and discussed security standards. We first discussed security issues for the semantic Web. We argued that security must cut across all the layers. Furthermore, we need to integrate the information across the layers securely. Next we provided some more details on XML security, RDF security, secure information integration, and trust. If the semantic Web is to be secure we need all of its components to be secure. We also described some of our research on access control and dissemination of XML documents. Next we discussed privacy for the semantic Web. We also briefly discussed security for the grid and the semantic grid.

Chapter 26 discussed security impact on various information management technologies including E-commerce, knowledge management, collaboration, grid databases, and peer-to-peer computing. Our focus was mainly on discretionary security for the emerging technologies. Multilevel security is important and needed for military applications, however, we first need to understand what the discretionary security mechanisms are. Note that the terms federated data management, peer-to-peer computing, semantic Web, and dynamic coalitions have been used to mean the same thing in many situations. We have tried to explain the differences and looked at security for each technology separately.

Part X, which described emerging secure data management technologies, consisted of three chapters: 27, 28, and 29. Chapter 27 provided an overview of secure dependable systems. We started with a discussion of dependable infrastructure and data managers. We used sensor information management as an application because this application requires many features such as real-time processing, security, and integrity. We also discussed developments and directions for data quality. We discussed the need for data quality and then showed an approach to manage data quality. This approach is to use annotations. Next we discussed some of the emerging trends such as data quality for the semantic Web and the relationship between data mining and data quality. We also briefly discussed critical infrastructure protection.

Chapter 28 discussed a number of security issues for sensor data management and also gave privacy some consideration. Much of our focus was on access control. We also discussed security and privacy-constraint processing for sensor data. Finally we discussed some security issues that take into consideration the unique constraints of sensor networks as well as security for wireless and mobile data management.

Chapter 29 provided an overview of various topics in database and applications security. In particular, we discussed digital identities, identity theft, biometrics, digital forensics, steganography, and risk/economic assessments. We also briefly mentioned some other topics such as secure e-mail, performance analysis, and verification and validation.

As we have stressed, there are many developments in the field and it is impossible for us to list all of them. We have provided a broad but fairly comprehensive overview of the field. The book is intended for technical managers as well as technologists who want to get a broad understanding of the field. It is also intended for students who wish to pursue research in database and applications security. To our knowledge this is the first book that provides a fairly comprehensive survey of the field that spans over thirty years.

30.3 Directions for Database and Applications Security

There are many directions for database and applications security. We discuss some of them for each topic addressed in this book. Figure 30.2 illustrates the challenges.

- *Supporting Technologies:* We need to continue to make advances in database management, information security, and information management. Although relational databases are a mature technology, there is a lot to be done in XML databases, RDF databases, and other emerging database technologies. In the area of information security, with the explosion of wireless devices, wireless network security is becoming a major area on which to focus. In the area of information management, there is a lot to be done in almost all the areas including knowledge management, search engines, and information retrieval.
- *Discretionary Security:* Discretionary security for relational databases is a mature technology, but there is a lot to do on discretionary security for XML and RDF databases. For example, how can we specify policies in XML? How can XML be secured? What sorts of temporal authorization models are appropriate for the emerging database systems? These are all interesting challenges.
- *Mandatory Security:* We have focused on multilevel security for various types of databases. Although research in this area is not as active as it used to be, we have learned a lot in conducting research in MLS/DBMSs. Furthermore, such systems are still needed

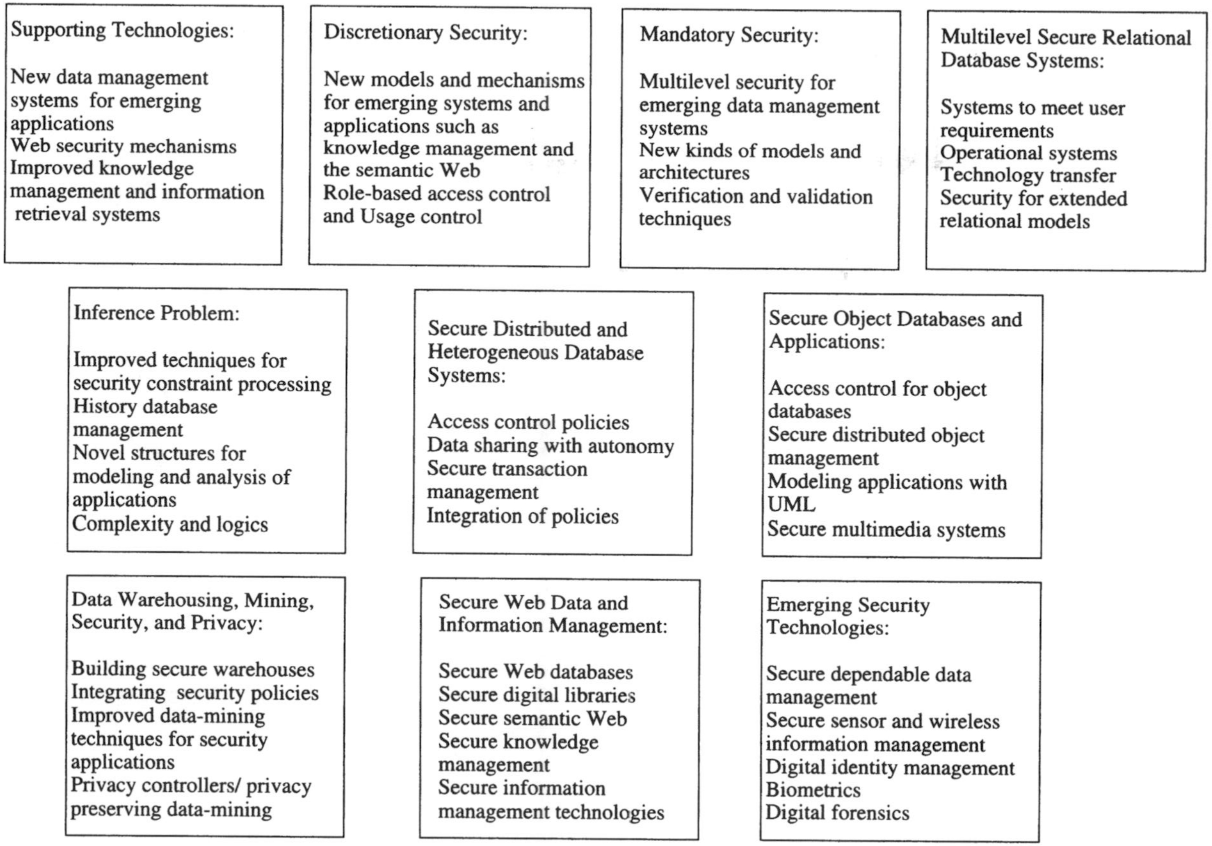

Supporting Technologies:

New data management systems for emerging applications
Web security mechanisms
Improved knowledge management and information retrieval systems

Discretionary Security:

New models and mechanisms for emerging systems and applications such as knowledge management and the semantic Web
Role-based access control and Usage control

Mandatory Security:

Multilevel security for emerging data management systems
New kinds of models and architectures
Verification and validation techniques

Multilevel Secure Relational Database Systems:

Systems to meet user requirements
Operational systems
Technology transfer
Security for extended relational models

Inference Problem:

Improved techniques for security constraint processing
History database management
Novel structures for modeling and analysis of applications
Complexity and logics

Secure Distributed and Heterogeneous Database Systems:

Access control policies
Data sharing with autonomy
Secure transaction management
Integration of policies

Secure Object Databases and Applications:

Access control for object databases
Secure distributed object management
Modeling applications with UML
Secure multimedia systems

Emerging Security Technologies:

Secure dependable data management
Secure sensor and wireless information management
Digital identity management
Biometrics
Digital forensics

Data Warehousing, Mining, Security, and Privacy:

Building secure warehouses
Integrating security policies
Improved data-mining techniques for security applications
Privacy controllers/ privacy preserving data-mining

Secure Web Data and Information Management:

Secure Web databases
Secure digital libraries
Secure semantic Web management
Secure information management technologies

Figure 30.2   Directions and challenges in database and applications security

for military and intelligence applications. The challenges here include developing new kinds of models and architectures for MLS/DBMSs as well as building high-assurance systems.

■ *Multilevel Secure Relational Database Systems:* Much research has been carried out on this topic. Our challenge is to use such systems in operational environments. Furthermore, how can we develop systems that meet user requirements and at the same time meet performance requirements? Should we develop customized MLS/DBMSs?

■ *Inference Problem:* This is a very difficult problem, and it continues to fascinate researchers. We need to build constraint processors that are more efficient and manage prior knowledge. We also need to examine the complexity of the problem. There is a lot of interesting theoretical work to do in this area.

■ *Secure Distributed and Heterogeneous Databases:* Although some progress has been made, we need an extensive investigation of security for distributed, heterogeneous, and federated databases. What sorts of access-control models are appropriate for such systems? How can we share data and still have security and autonomy? How can security policies be integrated across organizations? How can distributed transactions be executed securely?

■ *Secure Object Databases and Applications:* There has been work on both discretionary and mandatory security for object databases. How can we apply the principles for object-relational systems inasmuch as such systems are dominating the marketplace? Are the security mechanisms for distributed object management systems sufficient? How can we provide fine-grained access control? How can UML be used to design secure applications?

■ *Secure Data Warehousing, Mining, Security, and Privacy:* There are many challenges here. How can we build a secure warehouse from the data sources? How can we develop an integrated security policy? What is the security impact on the functions of a warehouse? What are the data-mining techniques appropriate for national security and cyber-security? How can we solve the privacy problem? How can we build effective privacy controllers? What is the complexity of the privacy problem?

■ *Secure Web Data and Information Management:* There is a lot of work to be done on secure Web data and information management. For example, how can we build secure Web database systems? What are the security issues for digital libraries? How do we secure the semantic Web? How can we maintain trust on the semantic Web? How can we secure emerging applications such as knowledge management, multimedia, collaboration, E-commerce, and peer-to-peer data management?

- *Emerging Security Technologies:* Little work has been reported on secure dependable data management. For example, how can we build systems with flexible policies that can handle security, real-time processing, fault tolerance, and integrity? How can we secure sensor database systems? What are the security issues for wireless information management? Finally how can we further the developments in digital identity management, digital forensics, and biometrics?

30.4 Where Do We Go from Here?

This book has discussed a great deal about database and applications security. We have stated many challenges in database and applications security in Section 30.3. We need to continue with research and development efforts if we are to make progress in this very important area.

The question is where do we go from here. First of all those who wish to work in this area must have a good knowledge of the supporting technologies including database management, information security, and information management. For example, it is important to understand network security issues in order to solve problems in database and applications security. Furthermore, one also needs to understand the various query-processing strategies as well as knowledge management techniques. Next, because the field is expanding rapidly and there are many developments in the field, the reader has to keep up with the developments including reading about the commercial products. We also encourage the reader to work on the exercises we have given in this book. Finally we encourage the reader to experiment with the products and also develop security tools. This is the best way to get familiar with a particular field. That is, work on hands-on problems and provide solutions to get a better understanding. Although we have not given any implementation exercises in this book, our design problems could be extended to include implementation. The Web will continue to have a major impact on database and applications security. Many of the databases and applications will have to be accessed via the Web. Therefore, one cannot overemphasize the importance of Web security.

We need research and development support from the federal and local government funding agencies. Agencies such as the National Security Agency, the United States Army, Navy, Air Force, and the Defense Advanced Research Projects Agency have funded a great deal of research in information security in the past. The Cyber Trust Theme at the National

Science Foundation is an excellent initiative to support some fundamental research. We also need commercial corporations to invest research and development dollars so that progress can be made in industrial research as well as transfer the research to commercial products. We also need to collaborate with the international research community to solve problems that are not only of national interest but of international interest as well.

Appendix A

Data Management Systems: Developments and Trends

A.1 Overview

In this appendix we provide an overview of the developments and trends in data management as discussed in our previous book *Data Management Systems Evolution and Interoperation* [THUR97]. Because database systems are an aspect of data management, and database security is an aspect of database systems, we need a good understanding of data management issues for data and applications security.

As stated in Chapter 1, recent developments in information systems technologies have resulted in computerizing many applications in various business areas. Data has become a critical resource in many organizations and therefore efficient access to data, sharing the data, extracting information from the data, and making use of the information have become urgent needs. As a result, there have been several efforts on integrating the various data sources scattered across several sites. These data sources may be databases managed by database management systems or they could simply be files. To provide the interoperability between the multiple data sources and systems, various tools are being developed. These tools enable users of one system to access other systems in an efficient and transparent manner.

We define data management systems as systems that manage the data, extract meaningful information from the data, and make use of the information extracted. Therefore, data management systems include database systems, data warehouses, and data-mining systems. Data could be structured data such as that found in relational databases or it could be unstructured such as text, voice, imagery, and video. There have been numerous discussions in the past to distinguish among data, information, and knowledge. We do not attempt to clarify these terms. For our purposes, data could be just bits and bytes or it could convey some meaningful information to the user. We do, however, distinguish between database systems and database management systems. A database management system is that component which manages the database containing persistent data. A database system consists of both the database and the database management system.

A key component of the evolution and interoperation of data management systems is the interoperability of heterogeneous database systems. Efforts on the interoperability between database systems have been reported since the late 1970s. However, it is only recently that we are seeing commercial developments in heterogeneous database systems. Major database system vendors are now providing interoperability between their products and other systems. Furthermore, many of the database system vendors are migrating toward an architecture called the client/server architecture, which facilitates distributed data management capabilities. In addition to efforts on the interoperability between different database systems and client/server environments, work is also directed toward handling autonomous and federated environments.

The organization of this appendix is as follows. Inasmuch as database systems are a key component of data management systems, we first provide an overview of the developments in database systems. These developments are discussed in Section A.2. Then we provide a vision for data management systems in Section A.3. Our framework for data management systems is discussed in Section A.4. Note that data mining and warehousing, as well as Web data management, are components of this framework. Building information systems from our framework with special instantiations is discussed in Section A.5. The relationship between the various texts that we have written (or are writing) for CRC Press is discussed in Section A.6. This appendix is summarized in Section A.7. References are given at the end of this appendix.

A.2 Developments in Database Systems

Figure A.1 provides an overview of the developments in database systems technology. Early work in the 1960s focused on developing products based on the network and hierarchical data models, but many of the

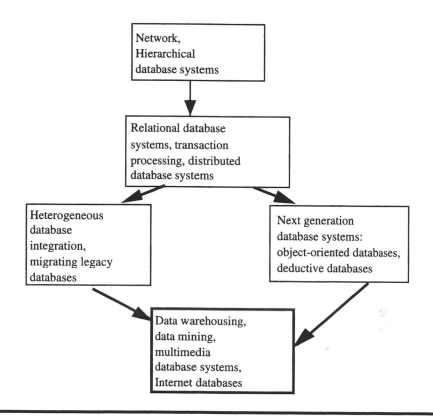

Figure A.1   Developments in database systems technology

developments in database systems took place after the seminal paper by Codd describing the relational model [CODD70] (see also [DATE90]). Research and development work on relational database systems was carried out during the early 1970s and several prototypes were developed throughout the 1970s. Notable efforts include IBM's (International Business Machine Corporation's) System R and the University of California at Berkeley's INGRES. During the 1980s, many relational database system products were being marketed (notable among these products are those of Oracle Corporation, Sybase Inc., Informix Corporation, INGRES Corporation, IBM, Digital Equipment Corporation, and Hewlett Packard Company). During the 1990s, products from other vendors have emerged (e.g., Microsoft Corporation). In fact, to date, numerous relational database system products have been marketed. However, Codd has stated that many of the systems that are being marketed as relational systems are not really relational (see, for example, the discussion in [DATE90]). He then discussed various criteria that a system must satisfy to be qualified as a relational database system. Although the early work focused on issues such as data models, normalization theory, query-processing and optimization strategies, query languages, and access strategies and indexes, later the focus shifted toward supporting a multiuser environment. In particular, concurrency control and recovery techniques were developed. Support for transaction processing was also provided.

Research on relational database systems as well as on transaction management was followed by research on distributed database systems around the mid-1970s. Several distributed database system prototype development efforts also began around the late 1970s. Notable among these efforts include IBM's System R*, DDTS (Distributed Database Testbed System) by Honeywell Inc., SDD-I and Multibase by CCA (Computer Corporation of America), and Mermaid by SDC (System Development Corporation). Furthermore, many of these systems (e.g., DDTS, Multibase, Mermaid) function in a heterogeneous environment. During the early 1990s several database system vendors (such as Oracle Corporation, Sybase Inc., Informix Corporation) provided data distribution capabilities for their systems. Most of the distributed relational database system products are based on client/server architectures. The idea is to have the client of vendor A communicate with the server database system of vendor B. In other words, the client/server computing paradigm facilitates a heterogeneous computing environment. Interoperability between relational and nonrelational commercial database systems is also possible. The database systems community is also involved in standardization efforts. Notable among the standardization efforts are the ANSI/SPARC three-level schema architecture, the IRDS (Information Resource Dictionary System) standard for data dictionary systems, the relational query language SQL (Structured Query Language), and the RDA (Remote Database Access) protocol for remote database access.

Another significant development in database technology is the advent of object-oriented database management systems. Active work on developing such systems began in the mid-1980s and they are now commercially available (notable among them include the products of Object Design Inc., Ontos Inc., Gemstone Systems Inc., and Versant Object Technology). It was felt that new-generation applications such as multimedia, office information systems, CAD/CAM, process control, and software engineering have different requirements. Such applications utilize complex data structures. Tighter integration between the programming language and the data model is also desired. Object-oriented database systems satisfy most of the requirements of these new-generation applications [CATT91].

According to the Lagunita report published as a result of a National Science Foundation (NSF) workshop in 1990 (see [NSF90] and [SIGM90]), relational database systems, transaction processing, and distributed (relational) database systems are stated as mature technologies. Furthermore, vendors are marketing object-oriented database systems and demonstrating the interoperability between different database systems. The report goes on to state that as applications are getting increasingly complex, more sophisticated database systems are needed. In addition, because many organizations now use database systems, in many cases of different types, the database systems need to be integrated. Although work has begun to address these issues and commercial products are available, several issues still need to be resolved. Therefore, challenges faced by the database systems researchers in the early 1990s were in two areas. One was next-generation database systems and the other was heterogeneous database systems.

Next-generation database systems include object-oriented database systems, functional database systems, special parallel architectures to enhance the performance of database system functions, high-performance database systems, real-time database systems, scientific database systems, temporal database systems, database systems that handle incomplete and uncertain information, and intelligent database systems (also sometimes called logic or deductive database systems). Ideally, a database system should provide the support for high-performance transaction processing, model complex applications, represent new kinds of data, and make intelligent deductions. Although significant progress has been made during the late 1980s and early 1990s, there is much to be done before such a database system can be developed.

Heterogeneous database systems have been receiving considerable attention during the past decade [ACM90]. The major issues include handling different data models, different query-processing strategies, different transaction-processing algorithms, and different query languages. Should a uniform view be provided to the entire system or should the users of the individual systems maintain their own views of the entire system? These are questions that have yet to be answered satisfactorily. It is also envisioned that a complete solution to heterogeneous database management systems is a generation away. Research should be directed toward finding such a solution, but work should also be carried out to handle limited forms of heterogeneity to satisfy customer needs. Another type of database system that has received some attention lately is the federated database system. Note that some have used the terms heterogeneous database system and federated database system interchangeably. Although heterogeneous database systems can be part of a federation, a federation can also include homogeneous database systems.

The explosion of users on the Web as well as developments in interface technologies has resulted in even more challenges for data management researchers. A second workshop was sponsored by NSF in 1995, and several emerging technologies have been identified as important as we

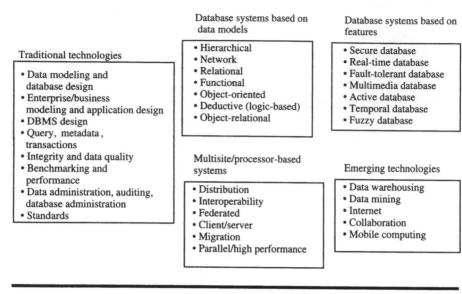

Figure A.2 Comprehensive view of data management systems

go into the twenty-first century [NSF95]. These include digital libraries, managing very large databases, data administration issues, multimedia databases, data warehousing, data mining, data management for collaborative computing environments, and security and privacy. Another significant development in the 1990s was the development of object-relational systems. Such systems combine the advantages of both object-oriented database systems and relational database systems. Also, many corporations are now focusing on integrating their data management products with Web technologies. Finally, for many organizations there is an increasing need to migrate some of the legacy databases and applications to newer architectures and systems such as client/server architectures and relational database systems. We believe there is no end to data management systems. As new technologies are developed, there are new opportunities for data management research and development.

A comprehensive view of all data management technologies is illustrated in Figure A.2. As shown, traditional technologies include database design, transaction processing, and benchmarking. Then there are database systems based on data models such as relational and object-oriented. Database systems may depend on features they provide such as security and real-time. These database systems may be relational or object-oriented. There are also database systems based on multiple sites or processors such as distributed and heterogeneous database systems, parallel systems, and systems being migrated. Finally, there are the emerging technologies such as data warehousing and mining, collaboration, and the Web. Any

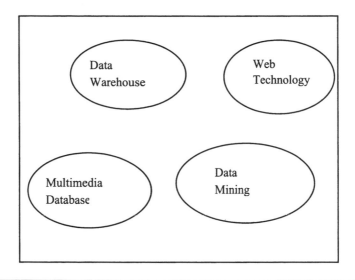

Figure A.3   Stand-alone systems

comprehensive text on data management systems should address all of these technologies. We have selected some of the relevant technologies and put them in a framework. This framework is described in Section A.5.

A.3   Status, Vision, and Issues

Significant progress has been made on data management systems. However, many of the technologies are still stand-alone technologies as illustrated in Figure A.3. For example, multimedia systems are yet to be successfully integrated with warehousing and mining technologies. The ultimate goal is to integrate multiple technologies so that accurate data, as well as information, are produced at the right time and distributed to the user in a timely manner. Our vision for data and information management is illustrated in Figure A.4.

The work discussed in [THUR97] addressed many of the challenges necessary to accomplish this vision. In particular, integration of heterogeneous databases, as well as the use of distributed object technology for interoperability, was discussed. Although much progress has been made on the system aspects of interoperability, semantic issues still remain a challenge. Different databases have different representations. Furthermore, the same data entity may be interpreted differently at different sites. Addressing these semantic differences and extracting useful information from the heterogeneous and possibly multimedia data sources are major challenges. This book has attempted to address some of the challenges through the use of data mining.

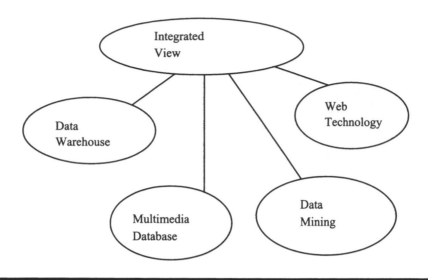

Figure A.4   Vision

A.4   Data Management Systems Framework

For the successful development of evolvable interoperable data management systems, heterogeneous database systems integration is a major component. However, there are other technologies that have to be successfully integrated with each other to develop techniques for efficient access and sharing of data as well as for the extraction of information from the data. To facilitate the development of data management systems to meet the requirements of various applications in fields such as medical, financial, manufacturing, and military, we have proposed a framework (which can be regarded as a reference model) for data management systems. Various components of this framework have to be integrated to develop data management systems to support the various applications.

Figure A.5 illustrates our framework, or model, for data management systems. This framework consists of three layers. One can think of the component technologies, which we also refer to as components, as belonging to a particular layer to be more or less built upon the technologies provided by the lower layer. Layer I is the Database Technology and Distribution Layer. This layer consists of database systems and distributed database systems technologies. Layer II is the Interoperability and Migration Layer. This layer consists of technologies such as heterogeneous database integration, client/server databases, and multimedia database systems to handle heterogeneous data types, and migrating legacy databases. Layer III is the Information Extraction and Sharing Layer. This layer

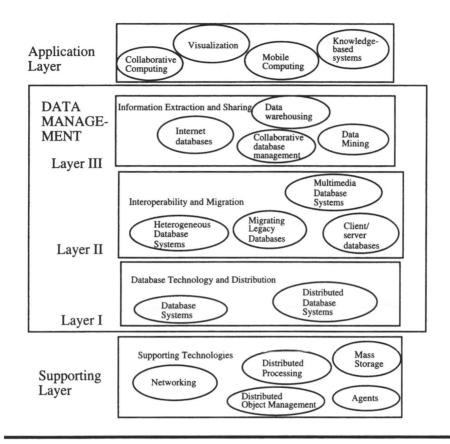

Figure A.5 Data management systems framework

essentially consists of technologies for some of the newer services supported by data management systems. These include data warehousing, data mining [THUR98], Web databases, and database support for collaborative applications. Data management systems may utilize lower-level technologies such as networking, distributed processing, and mass storage. We have grouped these technologies into a layer called the Supporting Technologies Layer. This supporting layer does not belong to the data management systems framework. This supporting layer also consists of some higher-level technologies such as distributed object management and agents. Also shown in Figure A.5 is the Application Technologies Layer. Systems such as collaborative computing systems and knowledge-based systems which belong to the Application Technologies Layer may utilize data management systems. Note that the Application Technologies Layer is also outside the data management systems framework.

The technologies that constitute the data management systems framework can be regarded as some of the core technologies in data management.

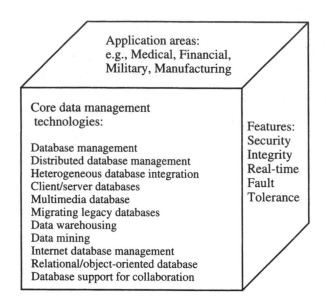

Figure A.6   A three-dimensional view of data management

However, features such as security, integrity, real-time processing, fault tolerance, and high-performance computing are needed for many applications utilizing data management technologies. Applications utilizing data management technologies may be medical, financial, or military, among others. We illustrate this in Figure A.6, where a three-dimensional view relating data management technologies with features and applications is given. For example, one could develop a secure distributed database management system for medical applications or a fault-tolerant multimedia database management system for financial applications.

Integrating the components belonging to the various layers is important in developing efficient data management systems. In addition, data management technologies have to be integrated with the application technologies to develop successful information systems. However, at present, there is limited integration between these various components. Our previous book *Data Management Systems Evolution and Interoperation* focused mainly on the concepts, developments, and trends belonging to each of the components shown in the framework. Furthermore, our current book on Web data management focuses on the Web database component of Layer 3 of the framework of Figure A.5.

Note that security cuts across all the layers. Security is needed for the supporting layers such as agents and distributed systems. Security is needed for all of the layers in the framework including database security, distributed database security, warehousing security, Web database security, and collaborative data management security. This is the topic of this book. That is, we have covered all aspects of data and applications security including database security and information management security.

A.5 Building Information Systems from the Framework

Figure A.5 illustrated a framework for data management systems. As shown in that figure, the technologies for data management include database systems, distributed database systems, heterogeneous database systems, migrating legacy databases, multimedia database systems, data warehousing, data mining, Web databases, and database support for collaboration. Furthermore, data management systems take advantage of supporting technologies such as distributed processing and agents. Similarly, application technologies such as collaborative computing, visualization, expert systems, and mobile computing take advantage of data management systems.

Many of us have heard the term "information systems" on numerous occasions. These systems have sometimes been used interchangeably with data management systems. In our terminology, information systems are much broader than data management systems, but they do include data management systems. In fact, a framework for information systems will include not only the data management system layers, but also the supporting technologies layer as well as the application technologies layer. That is, information systems encompass all kinds of computing systems. It can be regarded as the finished product that can be used for various applications. That is, although hardware is at the lowest end of the spectrum, applications are at the highest end.

We can combine the technologies of Figure A.5 to put together information systems. For example, at the application technology level, one may need collaboration and visualization technologies so that analysts can collaboratively carry out some tasks. At the data management level, one may need both multimedia and distributed database technologies. At the supporting level, one may need mass storage as well as some distributed processing capability. This special framework is illustrated in Figure A.7. Another example is a special framework for interoperability. One may need some visualization technology to display the integrated information from the heterogeneous databases. At the data management level, we have heterogeneous database systems technology. At the supporting technology level, one may use distributed object management technology to encapsulate the heterogeneous databases. This special framework is illustrated in Figure A.8.

```
┌─────────────────────────┐
│                         │
│    Collaboration,       │
│    Visualization        │
│                         │
└─────────────────────────┘

┌─────────────────────────┐
│                         │
│   Multimedia database,  │
│   Distributed database  │
│   systems               │
│                         │
└─────────────────────────┘

┌─────────────────────────┐
│                         │
│     Mass storage,       │
│     Distributed         │
│     processing          │
│                         │
└─────────────────────────┘
```

Figure A.7   Framework for multimedia data management for collaboration

```
┌─────────────────────────┐
│                         │
│     Visualization       │
│                         │
└─────────────────────────┘

┌─────────────────────────┐
│                         │
│    Heterogeneous        │
│    database             │
│    integration          │
│                         │
└─────────────────────────┘

┌─────────────────────────┐
│    Distributed Object   │
│    Management           │
└─────────────────────────┘
```

Figure A.8   Framework for heterogeneous database interoperability

Finally, let us illustrate the concepts that we have described above by using a specific example. Suppose a group of physicians/surgeons wants a system where they can collaborate and make decisions about various patients. This could be a medical video teleconferencing application. That is, at the highest level, the application is a medical application and, more specifically, a medical video teleconferencing application. At the application technology level, one needs a variety of technologies including

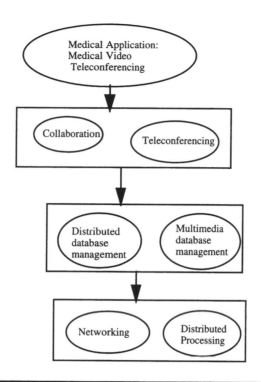

Figure A.9   Specific example

collaboration and teleconferencing. These application technologies will make use of data management technologies such as distributed database systems and multimedia database systems. That is, one may need to support multimedia data such as audio and video. The data management technologies in turn draw upon lower-level technologies such as distributed processing and networking. We illustrate this in Figure A.9.

In summary, information systems include data management systems as well as application-layer systems such as collaborative computing systems and supporting-layer systems such as distributed object management systems.

Although application technologies make use of data management technologies and data management technologies make use of supporting technologies, the ultimate user of the information system is the application itself. Today numerous applications make use of information systems. These applications are from multiple domains such as medical, financial, manufacturing, telecommunications, and defense. Specific applications include signal processing, electronic commerce, patient monitoring, and situation assessment. Figure A.10 illustrates the relationship between the application and the information system.

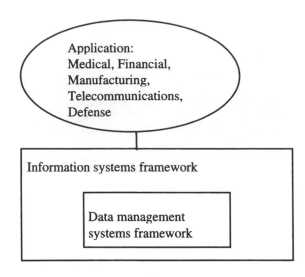

Figure A.10 Application-framework relationship

A.6 Relationship between the Texts

We have published six books on data management and mining and currently are writing one more. These books are *Data Management Systems Evolution and Interoperation* [THUR97], *Data Mining Technologies, Techniques, Tools and Trends* [THUR98], *Web Data Management and Electronic Commerce* [THUR00], *Managing and Mining Multimedia Databases for the Electronic Enterprise* [THUR01], *XML, Databases and The Semantic Web* [THUR02], *Web Data Mining, Business Intelligence and Counter-Terrorism* [THUR03], and *Database and Applications Security: Integrating Databases and Information Security* [THUR04] (which is this book). All of these books have evolved from the framework that we illustrated in this appendix and address different parts of the framework. The connection between these texts is illustrated in Figure A.11.

Note that security was addressed in all of our previous books. For example, we discussed security for multimedia systems in [THUR01]. Security and data mining were discussed in [THUR98]. Secure data interoperability was discussed in [THUR97]. Essentially this book integrates all of the concepts in security discussed in our previous books. In addition, we have also addressed many more topics in database and applications security.

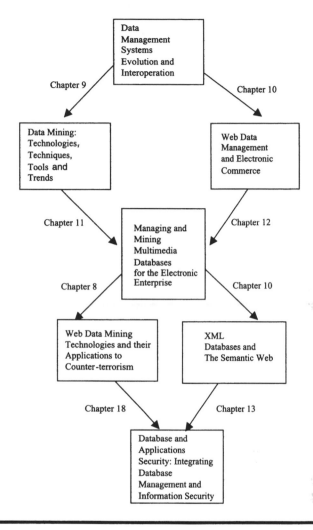

Figure A.11   Relationship between texts

A.7   Summary

In this appendix we have provided an overview of data management. We first discussed the developments in data management and then provided a vision for data management. Then we illustrated a framework for data management. This framework consists of three layers: database systems layer, interoperability layer, and information extraction layer. Web data management belongs to Layer 3. Finally, we showed how information systems could be built from the technologies of the framework.

Let us repeat what we mentioned in Chapter 1 now that we have described the data management framework we introduced in [THUR97]. The chapters in this book discuss security which cuts across all the layers. Many of the technologies discussed in the framework of Figure A.5 need security. These include database systems, distributed database systems, data warehousing, and data mining.

We believe that data management is essential to many information technologies including data mining, multimedia information processing, interoperability, and collaboration and knowledge management. This appendix stresses data management. Security is critical for all data management technologies.

References

[ACM90] Special issue on heterogeneous database systems. *ACM Computing Surveys,* 22: 3, 1990.

[CATT91] Cattell, R. *Object Data Management Systems.* Addison-Wesley: Reading, MA, 1991.

[CODD70] Codd, E.F. A relational model of data for large shared data banks. *Communications of the ACM* 13: 6 (June) 1970.

[DATE90] Date, C.J. *An Introduction to Database Management Systems.* Addison-Wesley: Reading, MA, 1990 (6th edition published in 1995 by Addison-Wesley).

[NSF90] *Proceedings of the Database Systems Workshop.* National Science Foundation, Lagunita, CA, March, 1990.

[NSF95] *Proceedings of the Database Systems Workshop.* National Science Foundation, Lagunita, CA, March, 1995.

[SIGM90] Next generation database systems. *ACM SIGMOD Record,* 19: 4, 1990.

[THUR97] Thuraisingham, B. *Data Management Systems Evolution and Interoperation.* CRC Press: Boca Raton, FL, 1997.

[THUR98] Thuraisingham, B. *Data Mining: Technologies, Techniques, Tools and Trends.* CRC Press: Boca Raton, FL, 1998.

[THUR00] Thuraisingham, B. *Web Data Management and Electronic Commerce.* CRC Press: Boca Raton, FL, 2000.

[THUR01] Thuraisingham, B. *Managing and Mining Multimedia Databases for the Electronic Enterprise.* CRC Press: Boca Raton, FL, 2001.

[THUR02] Thuraisingham, B. *XML, Databases and The Semantic Web.* CRC Press: Boca Raton, FL, 2002.

[THUR03] Thuraisingham, B. *Web Data Mining Technologies and Their Applications in Business Intelligence and Counter-Terrorism.* CRC Press: Boca Raton, FL, 2003.

[THUR04] Thuraisingham, B. *Database and Applications Security: Integrating Data Management and Information Security.* CRC Press: Boca Raton, FL, 2004.

Appendix B

Suggested Reading: Books in Database Systems and Information Security

Database Systems

C.J. Date, *Introduction to Database Systems*. 5th ed. Addison-Wesley: Reading, MA, 1990.

R. Elmasri and S. Navathe, *Fundamentals of Database Systems*. 4th ed. Addison Wesley: Reading, MA, 2003.

H. Garcia-Molina, J. Ullman, and J. Widom, *Database Systems: The Complete Book*. Prentice-Hall: Upper Saddle River, NJ, 2001.

B. Thuraisingham, *Data Management Systems Evolution and Interoperation*. CRC Press: Boca Raton, FL, 1997.

J. Ullman, *Principles of Database and Knowledge Base Systems*. Computer Science Press: Rockville, MD, 1988.

Information and Database Security

R. Anderson, *Security Engineering: A Guide to Building Dependable Distributed Systems*. Wiley: New York, 2001.

M. Bishop, *Computer Security: Art and Science*. Addison-Wesley: Reading, MA, 2002.

S. Castano, M. Fugini, and G. Martella, *Database Security*, Addison-Wesley: Reading, MA, 1995.

D. Denning, *Cryptography and Data Security*. Addison-Wesley: Reading, MA, 1982.

E. Fernandez, R. Summers, and E. Wood, *Database Security and Integrity*. Addison-Wesley: Reading, MA, 1981.

M. Gasser, *Building a Secure Computer System*. Van Nostrand Reinhold: New York, 1988.

A. Ghosh, *E-Commerce Security: Weakest Links, Best Defenses*. Wiley: New York, 1998.

V. Hassler, *Security Fundamentals for E-Commerce*. Artech: London, UK, 2000.

Distributed Database Systems

D. Bell and J. Grimson, *Distributed Database Systems*. Addison-Wesley: Reading MA, 1992.

S. Ceri and G. Pelagetti, *Principles of Distributed Database Management Systems*. McGraw-Hill: New York, 1984.

M. Ozsu and P. Valduriez, *Principles of Distributed Database Systems*. Prentice-Hall, Upper Saddle River, NJ, 1990.

Object Databases, Distributed Objects, and Object Modeling

E. Bertino and L. Marttino, *Object-Oriented Database Systems: Concepts and Architectures*. Addison-Wesley: Reading, MA, 1993.

R. Cattell, *Object Data Management: Object-Oriented and Extended Relational Database Management Systems*. Addison-Wesley: Reading, MA, 1991.

M. Fowler, *UML Distilled: A Brief Guide to the Standard Object Modeling Language*. 3d ed. Addison-Wesley: Reading, MA, 2003.

T. Mowbray and R. Zahavi, *The Essential CORBA: Systems Integration Using Distributed Objects*. Addison-Wesley: Reading, MA, 1995.

Multimedia Databases

B. Prabhakaran, *Multimedia Database Management Systems*. Kluwer: Hingham, MA, 1997.

B. Thuraisingham, *Management and Mining Multimedia Databases*. CRC Press: Boca Raton, FL, 2001.

Intelligent and Deductive Database Systems

E. Bertino, G. Zarri, and B. Catania, *Intelligent Database Systems*. Addison-Wesley: Reading, MA, 2001.

R. Colomb, *Deductive Databases and Their Applications*. CRC Press: Boca Raton, FL, 1998.

Data Warehousing and Mining

M. Berry and G. Linoff, *Data Mining Techniques*. Wiley: New York, 1997.
J. Han and M. Kamber, *Data Mining: Concepts and Techniques*. Morgan-Kaufmann: San Francisco, 2000.
W. Inmon, *Building the Data Warehouse*. Wiley: New York, 1993.
M. Kantardzic, *Data Mining*. Wiley Interscience: New York, 2003.
B. Thuraisingham, *Data Mining: Technologies, Techniques, Tools and Trends*, CRC Press: Boca Raton, FL, 1998.

Digital Libraries, Web Database Management, and the Semantic Web

G. Antoniou and F. vanHarmelen, *A Semantic Web Primer*, MIT Press: Cambridge, MA, 2004.
T. Berners-Lee, *Weaving the Web: The Original Design and Ultimate Destiny of the World Wide Web*. Harper Business: New York, 2000.
M. Daconta, L. Orbst, and K. Smith, *The Semantic Web: A Guide to the Future of XML, Web Services, and Knowledge Management*. Wiley: New York, 2003.
M. Lesk, *Practical Digital Libraries: Books, Bytes, and Bucks*. Morgan-Kaufmann, San Francisco, 1997.
B. Thuraisingham, *Web Data Management and E-Commerce*. CRC Press: Boca Raton, FL, 2000.
B. Thuraisingham, *XML, Databases and the Semantic Web*. CRC Press: Boca Raton, FL, 2002.
B. Thuraisingham, *Web Data Mining and Applications in Business Intelligence and Counter-Terrorism*. CRC Press: Boca Raton, FL, 2003.

Knowledge Management

T. Groff and T. Jones, *Introduction to Knowledge Management: KM in Business*. Butterworth-Heinemann: Stoneham, MA, 2004.
K. Mertins, P. Heisig, and J. Vorbeck, *Knowledge Management: Concepts and Best Practices*. Springer-Verlag: Heidelberg, 2003.

Sensor Networks and Sensor Information Management

E. Callway, Jr. and E. Callway, *Wireless Sensor Networks: Architectures and Protocols*. Auerbach: Boca Raton, FL, 2003.
F. Zhao and L. Guibas, *Wireless Sensor Networks: An Information Processing Approach*. Morgan-Kaufmann: San Francisco, 2004.

Index

Index

Printed and bound by CPI Group (UK) Ltd, Croydon, CR0 4YY

17/10/2024

01775692-0006